Electricity
Purchasing
Handbook

Electricity
Purchasing
Handbook

by
John M. Studebaker

PennWell Books
PennWell Publishing Company
Tulsa, Oklahoma

Copyright © 1997 by Studebaker, John M.
Published by PennWell Publishing Company
1421 South Sheridan/P.O. Box 1260
Tulsa, Oklahoma 74101

Library of Congress
Cataloging-in-Publication Data

Printed in the United States of America
1 2 3 4 5 01 00 99 98 97

Dedication

This book is dedicated to Cory Ellenhorn and Barry Mountain, my business partners and friends.

Contents

Figures

Tables

Acknowledgments

The author wishes to express his thanks to the many electric utilities, regulatory agencies, students, and clients whose information, insight, and questions have made this publication possible.

Every effort has been made to provide dependable and accurate information. However, changes occur almost on a daily basis due to the very activity that encompasses the electric utility industry.

The issues that cause these changes such as competition, customer requirements, etc. are very important for the electricity purchaser to be aware of on a continuing basis.

This publication addresses these issues as they currently exist as well as provides strategies for the future so that the electricity purchaser can remain informed on an ongoing basis.

Introduction

In the 1970's, most electric utilities had insufficient generating capacities to meet their customer's growing demands. As a result of this lack of capacity, the electric utility industry began massive capital construction programs to build what they and their customers considered "reasonable generating capacity" to meet their expected future needs.

In general, the industries felt that growth would continue at an ever-expanding rate for an indefinite period of time. Lending credibility to this viewpoint was the natural gas shortages which at the time appeared to greatly broaden the potential for the use of electricity.

Also, the electric utility industries projected an ever-increasing demand for energy together with an ever-increasing cost of oil.

On top of this, federal and state regulatory agencies in agreement with the "ever-increasing demand" philosophy, caused the electric utilities to spend and commit to future spending enormous sums of money on generating facilities.

As is so often the case, the scenario that was envisioned never materialized. Customer's demands did not continue increasing at an unabatedrate; and, most importantly, oil prices did not continue to escalate. Since these things did not happen as anticipated, the obvious results occurred—overcapacity in generation became more and more widespread. In addition, the commitments requiring long-term capital investments became less attractive and in some cases unaffordable. Change had to take place!

As a result of the overexpectations in the 1970's concerning electrical requirements, today's electrical prices on a cost per million Btu basis are often more expensive than other forms of energy.

Many electric utilities are now finding themselves in the position of having large base load excess capacity availability. The decline in oil and gas prices, the deregulation of natural gas and imbalances on their system will be worsened by continuing deregulation in the electricity industry.

Electricity generation and distribution pricing in the United States is changing in a way that has never before taken place in this industry. True competition for customer's electricity usage is taking place at a pace that would not have even been imagined five years ago.

The electricity environment is changing so rapidly that by the time you read this publication there will be new things occurring that were not available at the time of its writing.

The purpose of this publication is to sort out all of the potential opportunities and pitfalls that both in the present as well as in the future may increase or reduce electricity costs. To accurately assess electricity costs, a purchaser must have at least a minimal understanding of how electricity flows from where it originates to where the purchaser is located, and how costs are accumulated in the process.

There are other publications that currently address electricity in one manner or another. There are also many seminars held annually in the United States that address various aspects of electricity. If this is true, why add one more publication to what appears to be an already cluttered field?

Many of the publications as well as the seminars address specific areas of the process but do not tie all of the loose ends together. Also, it seems that an assumption exists that everyone knows all of the basics so the publications and seminars can concentrate on one or two specific areas of information.

This publication is intended to be of value to electricity purchasers that need to know the best and least costly method of obtaining electricity at their facility based upon their usage characteristics. The philosophy I use is quite simple—"How can I get what I need as inexpensively as possible when I need it!" If this appeals to you, then this publication can help you realize your goals of least cost and best reliability in purchasing electricity.

Chapter 1

Electricity-An Overview

The Background of Electricity

For commercial and industrial users, buying electricity in the past was so simple that little or no attention was given to the matter. The local electric utility delivered the electricity and it was paid for on a monthly basis—it was that simple!

What has happened? Why is it important to know the current status of electricity? Because of the radical change in the way electric utilities operate (interstate and intrastate regulation) a comprehensive knowledge of options which are available is a must if the savings potential available in today's environment is to be realized.

The Picture Prior to the 1990s

Under the traditional system, the typical commercial/industrial buyer purchased for electricity from its local electric utility. The electric utility generated its electricity and delivered it to the retail customer.

Today and the Future

Today the electric utility industry is at the same place the natural gas industry was several years ago. They generally discourage cogeneration and retail wheeling (transportation of power purchased by customers from third party electric suppliers). The time it will take before the same forces which successfully convinced regulators to allow the transportation of third party supplied natural gas, can not be estimated accurately. However, if the natural gas scenario is any indicator, it probably will not be long in coming.

The electric utility industry must recognize that change is inevitable and that to resist is counter productive and detrimental to its own well being. Ultimately, electric consumers will have the right to choose the least expensive, best suited source of power. In many instances, unfortunately, electric utilities do not accept or suggest the innovative measures required to assist the consumer in the quest for reduced costs. When this occurs, the regulators will devise the means for the utilities to reduce the consumer's cost for electrical power. But for the utilities, many traditional cost recovery and operational procedures currently enjoyed will be forfeited.

Electric utilities must become market responsive if they want to remain viable in their industries. Failure to do so will subject them to a process of fierce competition from third party suppliers and regulatory imposition of mandatory retail wheeling of power. The long-term outlook for electrical power alternatives is good and for many companies the savings realized through these various alternatives will be even more cost reducing than has been possible in the natural gas area.

The electric utility industry is at the threshold of change and the prospects of cost reduction are great. However, as changes occur, an awareness on a continuing basis must be maintained. To be able to understand how changes occur in electric utilities, a knowledge of what they are and how they are regulated must be available.

Probably one of the most discussed and least understood areas in electricity today is retail wheeling. This is the process whereby customers purchase electricity (kVA/kW and kWh) from a utility other than their own serving utility. This procedure, from the customer's viewpoint, is very similar to customer transportation of natural gas where the customer purchases the actual natural gas themselves and utilizes the serving utility only to transport the natural gas to the point of use. While this process works well in natural gas and causes most natural gas utilities no real supply or cost problems, the same is not true for electric utilities where retail wheeling of electricity takes place. The reason for this is that most natural gas utilities do not actually have the natural gas they sell, but purchase their system supplies on the open market.

In electricity, the serving utility normally generates all or at least a portion of the electricity they sell the customer. When a customer elects not to use the serving utility's electricity, the utility's generation utilization is reduced, causing increased costs to occur for the utility. Many electric utilities are now finding themselves in the position of having large base load excess capacity availability. These excess capacity problems will be worsened by customer wheeling of electricity.

The utilities also maintain that electric generating facility costs that have been incurred must be recovered from their customers, and that any reduction in the customer base through the use of wheeled power would, of necessity, increase costs to the remaining retail sales customers.

In electricity utility service, the commodity being sold is produced by the utility that serves the customer. In this case, if the customer obtains electricity from a source other than the local electric company (retail wheeling), the electric utility suffers a real loss—not having a sale for the electricity they produce. Retail wheeling can have a very real impact on the very existence of an electric utility. How the origination points of the commodity (electricity/natural gas) vary are shown on Figure 1.1 following.

Figure 1.1

Commodity Origination Points
Electricity versus Natural Gas

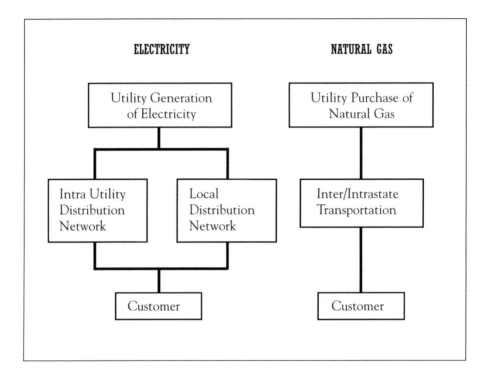

Figure 1.1 shows that an electric utility generates its commodity (electricity) where a natural gas utility generally purchases its commodity (natural gas). While this difference may seem to be of no particular concern to the customer, it is of great importance to an electric utility. Since the electric utility generates its commodity, it relies upon its customers to purchase the electricity it generates. If customers have the choice not to purchase the generated electricity,the utility has to find other customers or reduce its generation output which affects its overall system efficiency.

Another electric utility worry is customer cogeneration of electricity. In this scenario, the customer installs a generation system that utilizes both electrical as well as thermal (heat) outputs to supplement and reduce their dependence upon utility supplied electricity. Although cogeneration is not a new process, its use has become more widespread as utility supplied electricity has become more costly. As is evident, many electricity customers currently, or in the near future, will have options to typical utility supplied electricity.

The question an electricity user will have to answer will be—which method of electricity purchasing is most cost effective? To answer this question, it is important to know what is available and how to most effectively utilize the best options. This publication will provide information needed by a customer to utilize the least expensive electricity available while assuring that supply integrity is maintained.

Figure 1.2
Potential Options for the Electricity User

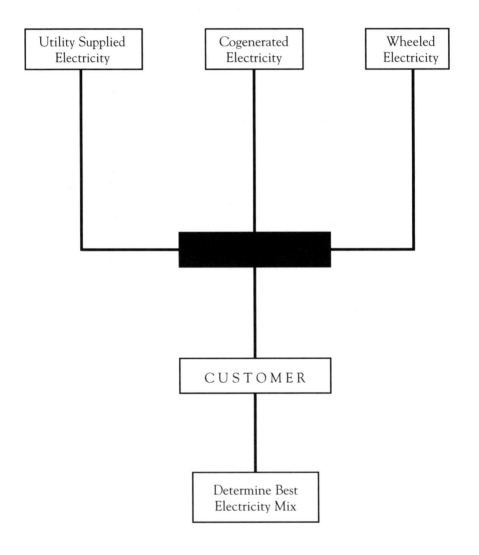

Chapter 2

Regulation of Electric Utilities

Regulation in General

Utilities, generally speaking, are considered to be regulated monopolies. A regulated monopoly is an entity that has no competition since no other provider of the same commodity can compete for the monopoly holder's customer. Since a position of no competition can lead to abuse in both cost and service, a check and balance system is in place that requires utilities to be held accountable for costs, services, etc. Utilities are regulated in at least two areas, "interstate" (between states) and "intrastate" (within states).

Interstate Regulation

Interstate regulation in electricity is the responsibility of the Federal Energy Regulatory Commission (FERC). This agency was created in 1977 and has the responsibility for oversight and regulation of interstate transportation policies and rates concerning electricity. Since this agency has these responsibilities, it would be well to understand its impact on rates and transportation conditions.

Since electricity distribution from one state to and for use in another state is always interstate (between states), FERC has jurisdiction over the rules and regulations applying to it.

Figure 2.1

Regulation of Electric Utilities

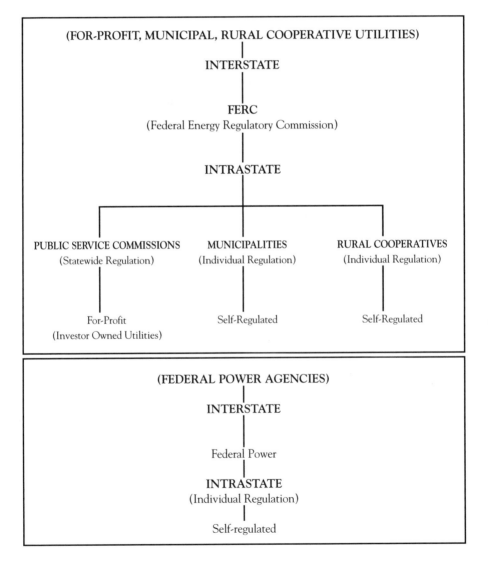

Members of FERC are appointed by the President of the United States with (five) commission positions being available. More and more the rulings of FERC meet with something less than enthusiasm on the part of the electric utilities it regulates, due primarily to its increasingly open access policies with relation to electricity.

Know what is happening at the Federal regulatory level so that as changes in electricity occur, utilities will have a strategy in mind. The following is the current address and telephone numbers of FERC:

Federal Energy Regulatory Commission
825 North Capitol Street, N.E.
Washington, D.C. 20426
Telephone (202) 208-0055
FAX (202) 208-2106
Bulletin Board (202) 208-8997

Areas Regulated by FERC

- Establishes and enforces rates and charges for electric energy transmission and sales for resale.
- Establishes and enforces conditions, rates and charges for electric energy interconnections.
- Certifies small power production and cogeneration facilities.
- Issues and enforces licenses for non-Federal hydroelectric power facilities.
- Issues and enforces certificates for construction and abandonment of interstate electricity transmission facilities.
- Establishes and enforces rates and charges for distribution and sale of natural gas.
- Establishes and enforces oil pipeline rates, charges and valuation.
- Establishes and enforces oil pipeline common carrier duties.

- Hears appeals from Department of Energy remedial orders and denials of adjustments.

Energy Policy Act of 1992

House Rule 776, Report 102-1018
Dated October 5, 1992

The Energy Policy Act of 1992 includes many energy related provisions pertaining to many kinds of energy sources including electricity, natural gas, alternative fuels, electric motor vehicles, renewable energy, and coal to name a few. For any utility user, a copy of this Energy Policy Act is probably a wise investment. It can be obtained as follows:

Ordering Information -
  Energy Policy Act of 1992
  House Report 776
  Report 102-1018
  Date - October 5, 1992
  Cost $20.00
  Phone: (202) 782-3238
  Address:
    United States Government Printing Office
    Superintendent of Documents
    Washington, DC 20402

Of particular interest in this Act is the section on "Energy Efficiency By Electric Utilities" (Subtitle B-Utilities, Sec. 111, pp. 21-32).

This section outlines the steps all electric utilities must take to conserve electric energy usage (kWh) and demand usage (kVA/kW). Because of its application/impact on electric energy users, part of this section is quoted following:

Subtitle B—Utilities

Sec. 111. ENCOURAGEMENT OF INVESTMENT IN CONSERVATION AND ENERGY EFFICIENCY BY ELECTRIC UTILITIES.

(a) AMENDMENT TO THE PUBLIC UTILITY REGULATORY POLICIES ACT—The Public Utility Regulatory Policies Act of 1978 (P.L. 95-617; 92 Stat. 3117; 16 U.S.C. 2601and following) is amended by adding the following at the end of Section 111(d):

"(7) INTEGRATED RESOURCE PLANNING.—Each electric utility shall employ integrated resource planning. All plans or filings before a State regulatory authority to meet the requirements of this paragraph must be updated on a regular basis, must provide the opportunity for public participation and comment, and contain a requirement that the plan be implemented.

"(8) INVESTMENTS IN CONSERVATION AND DEMAND MANAGEMENT.—The rates allowed to be charged by a State regulated electric utility shall be such that the utility's investment in and expenditures for energy conservation, energy efficiency resources, and other demand-side management measures are at least as profitable, giving appropriate consideration to income lost from reduced sales due to investments in and expenditures for conservation and efficiency, as its investments in and expenditures for the construction of new generation, transmission, and distribution equipment. Such energy conservation, energy efficiency resources and other demand-side management measures shall be appropriately monitored and evaluated.

"(9) ENERGY EFFICIENCY INVESTMENTS IN POWER GENERATION AND SUPPLY.—The rates charged by any electric utility shall be such that the utility is encouraged to make investments in, and expenditures for, all cost-effective improvements in the energy efficiency of power generation, transmission and distribution. In considering regulatory changes to achieve the objectives of this paragraph, State regulatory authorities and non-regulated electric utilities shall consider the disincentives caused by existing rate making policies, and practices, and consider incentives that would encourage better maintenance, and investment in more efficient power generation, transmission and distribution equipment."

(b)   PROTECTION FOR SMALL BUSINESS.—The Public Utility Regulatory Policies Act of 1978 (P.L. 95-617; 92 Stat. 3117; 16 U.S.C. 2601 and following) is amended by inserting the following new paragraph at the end of subsection 111(c):

"(3) If a State regulatory authority implements a standard established by subsection (d) (7) or (8), such authority shall—

"(A) consider the impact that implementation of such standard would have on small businesses engaged in the design, sale,supply, installation or servicing of energy conservation, energy efficiency or other demand-side management measures, and

"(B) implement such standard so as to assure that utility actions would not provide such utilities with unfair competitive advantages over such small businesses."

(c)   EFFECTIVE DATE.—Section 112(b) of such Act is amended by inserting "(or after the enactment of the Comprehensive National Energy Policy Act in the case of standards under paragraphs (7), (8), and (9) of Section111(d)" after "Act" in both places such word appears in paragraphs (1) and (2).

(d) DEFINITIONS.—Section 3 of such Act is amended by adding the following new paragraphs at the end thereof:

"(19) The term 'integrated resource planning' means, in the case of an electric utility, a planning and selection process for new energy resources that evaluates the full range of alternatives, including new generating capacity, power purchases, energy conservation and efficiency cogeneration and district heating cooling application, and renewable energy resources, in order to provide adequate and reliable service to its electric customers at the lowest system cost. The process shall take into account necessary features for system operation, such as diversity, reliability, dispatch ability, and other factors of risk; shall take into account the ability to verify energy savings achieved through energy conservation and efficiency and the projected durability of such savings measured over time; and shall treat demand and supply resources on a consistent and integrated basis.

"(20) The term 'system cost' means all direct and quantifiable net costs for an energy resource over its available life, including the cost of production, distribution, transportation, utilization, waste management, and environmental compliance.

"(21) The term 'demand side management' includes load management techniques."

(e) REPORT.—Not later than 2 years after the date of the enactment of the Act, the Secretary shall transmit a report to the President and to the Congress containing —

(1) a survey of all State laws, regulations, practices, and policies under which State regulatory authorities implement the provisions of paragraphs (7), (8), and (9) of Section 111(d) of the Public Utility Regulatory Policies Act of 1978;

(2) an evaluation by the Secretary of whether and to what extent, integrated resource planning is likely to result in —

(A) higher or lower electricity costs to an electric utility's ultimate consumers or to classes or groups of such consumers;

(B) enhanced or reduced reliability of electric service; and

(C) increased or decreased dependence on particular energy resources; and

(3) a survey of practices and policies under which electric cooperatives prepare integrated resource plans, submit such plans to the Rural Electrification Administration and the extent to which such integrated resource planning is reflected in rates charged to customers.

The report shall include an analysis prepared in conjunction with the Federal Trade Commission, of the competitive impact of implementation of energy conservation, energy efficiency, and other demand side management programs by utilities on small businesses engaged in the design, sale, supply, installation, or servicing of similar energy conservation, energy efficiency, or other demand side management measures and whether any unfair, deceptive, or predatory acts exist, or are likely to exist, from implementation of such programs.

SEC. 112. ENERGY EFFICIENCY GRANTS TO STATE REGULATORY AUTHORITIES.

(a) ENERGY EFFICIENCY GRANTS.—The Secretary is authorized in accordance with the provisions of this section to provide grants to State regulatory authorities in an amount not to exceed $250,000 per authority, for purposes of encouraging demand side management including energy conservation, energy efficiency and load management techniques and for meeting the requirements of paragraphs (7), (8), and (9) of Section 111(d) of the Public Utility Regulatory Policies Act of 1978 and as a means of meeting gas supply needs and to meet the requirements of paragraphs(3) and (4) of Section 303(b) of the Public Utility Regulatory Policies Act of 1978. Such grants may be utilized by a State regulatory authority to provide financial assistance to nonprofit subgrantees of the Department of Energy's Weatherization Assistance Program in order to facilitate participation by such subgrantees in proceedings of such regulatory authority to examine energy conservation, energy efficiency, or other demand side management programs.

(b) PLAN.—A State regulatory authority wishing to receive a grant under this section shall submit a plan to the Secretary that specifies the actions such authority proposes to take that would achieve the purposes of this section.

(c) SECRETARIAL ACTION.—(1) In determining whether, and in what amount, to provide a grant to a State regulatory authority under this section the Secretary shall consider, in addition to other appropriate factors, the actions proposed by the State regulatory authority to achieve the purposes of this section and to consider implementation of the rate making standards established in—

(A) paragraphs (7), (8), and (9) of Section 111(d) of the Public Utility Regulatory Policies Act of 1978; or

(B) paragraphs (3) and (4) of Section303(b) of the Public Utility Regulatory Policies Act of 1978.

(2) Such actions—

(A) shall include procedures to facilitate the participation of grantees and non-profit subgrantees of the Department of Energy's Weatherization Assistance Program in proceedings of such regulatory authorities examining demand side management programs; and

(B) shall provide for coverage of the cost of such grantee and subgrantees' participation in such proceedings.

(d) RECORDKEEPING.—Each State regulatory authority that receives a grant under this section shall keep such records as the Secretary shall require.

(e) DEFINITION.—For purposes of this section, the term "State regulatory authority" shall have the same meaning as provided by Section 3 of the Public Utility Regulatory Policies Act of 1978 in the case of electric utilities, and such term shall have the same meaning as provided by Section 302 of the Public Utility Regulatory Policies Act of 1978 in the case of gas utilities, except that in the case of any State without a statewide rate making authority, such term shall mean the State energy office.

(g) AUTHORIZATION.—There is authorized to be appropriated $5,000,000 for each of the fiscal years 1994, 1995, and 1996 to carry out the purposes of this section.

Of particular interest in this extracted data on Subtitle B—Utilities, are the following items:

1. Paragraph (7) Integrated Resource Planning —This paragraph and following, through the end of Section 111, covers conservation which electric utilities must implement. Of interest to electricity users is the fact that electric utilities will be required to offer demand-side management programs to customers to encourage them to reduce their demand usage, at least, during utility peak demand periods.

Read this information carefully to determine whether a particular utility is offering such programs. Also, note that in subsection (e) REPORT—not later than (2) years after the date of this Act (October 5, 1994) a report to the President and Congress is due which describes the local electric utility service representative to determine their implementation plans/actions to comply with the requirements outlined in this Act.

2. Sec. 112—Energy Efficiency Grants—This section of the Act provides for the granting of not more than $250,000 per authority (state) for the purpose of encouraging demand-side management including energy efficiency and load management techniques. This money is available for any state for uses as outlined in the Act. Check with your local utility regulatory agency to determine whether they have applied for available funds and if they have, how they are being utilized.

It is always a good idea to have a copy of the Energy Policy Act or, at least, a copy of this extracted information to describe the program to the local regulatory agency representative since they may not be familiar with the Act or its provisions.

Now is the time to know how the interstate regulation of electricity process works since the rulings of FERC will increasingly affect the viability of retail wheeling of electricity.

Intrastate Regulation

Intrastate regulation occurs within the borders of a state and is the responsibility of one of at least three types of regulatory bodies. Who regulates what is determined by the type of electric utility that serves a customer. For-profit electric utilities are regulated on a statewide basis by a commission or group of individuals appointed or elected at the state level.

All for-profit electric utilities, regardless of their geographic location within a given state, are regulated by this commission or group of individuals. Municipal electric utilities (utilities owned/operated by a city or county) are self-regulated. They are autonomous and structure their rates as they see necessary with minimal or no state supervision or legislation. Cooperative electric utilities are similar to municipal electric utilities in that they are self-regulated with little state oversight.

Cooperative utilities often come into being when a for-profit utility does not provide service to a given area, generally because of a lack of a sufficient profit making opportunity. A cooperative utility is usually created when a group of potential users form their own utility to provide a commodity (electricity, natural gas or water/sewer) for themselves that otherwise would not be available.

Both municipal and cooperative utilities are completely self-governing with little state intervention except with relation to rate case procedures and public notification guidelines. Ordinarily the state will require that normal rate case protocol is followed with relation to due process and input by affected customers (intervenor groups).

It is very important to know what is happening at the state regulatory level because of the impact of rate case decisions on customer costs. As a rule, at the federal (FERC) (interstate) level, electricity is more deregulated than at the state (intrastate) level. Since regulation at the intrastate level is generally more restrictive and in many instances results in tariff provisions that cause customer rates to be more costly than they could be, remain aware of pending rate cases in your intrastate electric utility so that you can develop a strategy based upon fact not hope.

Areas Regulated By Intrastate Agencies—Intrastate terms and conditions relating to tariff structures and pricing criteria.

In the case of electricity, the following areas are very important to the customer:

1. **Types of service that should be available—**
   A. **Firm**
   B. **Interruptible**
   C. **Negotiable Rate**—Rates that compete with alternate sources of electricity.
   D. **Firm Transportation**—Transportation of the retail customer's electricity through the serving utility's distribution system.
   E. **Interruptible Transportation**—Transportation of the retail customer's electricity through the serving utility's distribution system.
   F. **Market Service**—Acts as customer's agent for wheeled electricity.

A "full service" electric utility would offer all of the options shown above but the sad truth is none do. At the time of this publication, most electric utilities offer only options A and B. It does no good to have deregulation at the interstate level (FERC) if at the intrastate level the advantages cannot be utilized because of restrictive tariff schedule provisions. There remains much to be done at the intrastate level before the true value of interstate deregulation will be recognized by many customers.

Three Types of Utilities Regulated on an Intrastate Basis

I. **For-Profit (Investor-Owned Companies) Regulation**—All for-profit investor-owned utilities that operate within state boundaries.

Regulation is on a statewide basis since intrastate regulation of utilities concerns the intrastate activities of a utility. State agencies regulate the intrastate transportation and operation of electric utilities. Since electricity may be distributed from a location outside of the boundaries of the state in which the customer is situated, there are both federal and state regulations which apply.

The state agencies usually take the form of Public Service Commission (PSC) or Public Utility Commissions (PUC). The functions of these entities are to regulate the intrastate distribution and operation of utilities. These agencies also determine and approve individual utility rates of return, grant franchises to utilities for specific areas of operation, and in general, regulate the operation of utilities which are within a given state.

Although PSC or PUC structures are the most common forms of state regulation, other methods are used. In some states,these commissions regulate utilities only outside the incorporation limits of a municipality or city such as in Georgia, Texas, etc. There are rather strange situations which occur in a few states. For instance in the State of Texas, the Public Utility Commission regulates electricity outside of municipalities; however, outside of these same municipalities an entity called the "Railroad Commission of Texas" regulates natural gas.

Generally, a retail customer will have more contact with the state regulatory agency than with the federal agencies. Since state agencies determine rate of return and approve or disapprove rate increase requests of utilities, the likelihood of involvement with these agencies will be greater.

To remain informed on utility matters, a knowledge of the operation and function of the state agencies is required. To follow state regulatory matters can be very time-consuming and costly if done on an individual basis. One alternative to this is to become a member of a state energy users group commonly called a State Intervenor Group. These groups are comprised of numerous individuals which have common concerns, typically electricity and natural gas costs and regulations. Collectively these groups can accomplish much at the state regulatory level. Currently, at least the following states have intervenor groups as shown in Figure 2.2.

Figure 2.2

States with Intervenor Groups

Alabama	Kentucky	Oklahoma
Arkansas	Louisiana	Oregon
California	Maryland	Pennsylvania
Colorado	Michigan	South Carolina
Connecticut	Missouri	Tennessee
Delaware	Montana	Texas
Florida	New Hampshire	Utah
Georgia	New Jersey	Virginia
Illinois	New Mexico	West Virginia
Indiana	New York	Wisconsin
Iowa	North Carolina	Wyoming
Kansas	Ohio	

Any user or intervenor group is required to be registered with the appropriate State Regulatory Agency. Therefore, to determine whether a state has intervenor groups, contact the appropriate Regulatory Agency.

Listed in Figure 2.3 are all know intervenor groups by state. Since the telephone numbers of contact persons in these groups change frequently, the State Regulatory Agency telephone number is shown. By contacting the appropriate Regulatory Agency, the current telephone number for a particular intervenor group can be obtained.

Figure 2.3

State Intervenor Groups

ALABAMA
Alabama Industrial Group
Regulatory Agency (205) 242-5209

ARKANSAS
Arkansas Electric Energy Consumers
Regulatory Agency (501) 682-2051

CALIFORNIA
California Manufacturers Association
California Industrial Users
Regulatory Agency (415) 557-0647

COLORADO
Colorado Multiple Intervenor Group
Regulatory Agency (303) 894-2000

CONNECTICUT
Connecticut Industrial Energy Consumers
Regulatory Agency (203) 827-1553

DELAWARE
Delaware Energy Users Group
Regulatory Agency (302) 739-4247

FLORIDA
Florida Industrial Power Users Group
Regulatory Agency (904) 488-3464

GEORGIA
Georgia Industrial Group
Regulatory Agency (404) 656-4501

ILLINOIS
Illinois Industrial Energy Consumers
Illinois Industrial Utility Consumers
Regulatory Agency (217) 782-5793

INDIANA
Indiana Industrial Energy Consumers, Inc.
Indiana Industrial Intervenors
Regulatory Agency (317) 232-2801

IOWA
Iowa Industrial Intervenors
Iowa Energy Group
Iowa Mid-Size Industrials
Regulatory Agency (515) 281-5979

KANSAS
Kansas Industrial Intervenor Group
Regulatory Agency (913) 281-5979

KENTUCKY
Kentucky Industrial Utility Customers
Regulatory Agency (502) 564-3940

LOUISIANA
Louisiana Energy Users Group
Regulatory Agency (504) 342-4427

MARYLAND
Maryland Industrial Group
Regulatory Agency (301) 333-6000

MICHIGAN
Association of Businesses Advocating
Tariff Equity
Regulatory Agency (517) 334-6445

MISSOURI
Missouri Industrial Energy Consumers
Wolf Creek Industrial Intervenors
Regulatory Agency (314) 751-3234

MONTANA
Montana Industrial Intervenor Group
Regulatory Agency (406) 444-6199

NEW HAMPSHIRE
Business and Industry Association
of New Hampshire
Regulatory Agency (603) 271-2431

NEW JERSEY
New Jersey Industrial Energy Users
Association
Regulatory Agency (201) 648-2026

NEW MEXICO
New Mexico Industrial Energy Consumers
Regulatory Agency (505) 827-6940

NEW YORK
Multiple Intervenors
Industrial Power Consumers Conference
Regulatory Agency (518) 474-7080

Figure 2.3

State Intervenor Groups (Continued)

NORTH CAROLINA
Carolina Industrial Group for Fair Utility Rates
Carolina Utility Customers Association
North Carolina Industrial Energy Consumers
Regulatory Agency (919) 733-4249

OHIO
Ohio Power Industrial Energy Consumers
Ohio Industrial Electricity Consumers
Ohio Manufacturers Association
Ohio Retail Merchants Council
Regulatory Agency (614) 644-8927

OKLAHOMA
Oklahoma Industrial Energy Users Group
Regulatory Agency (405) 521-2261

OREGON
Industrial Customers of Northwest Utilities
Regulatory Agency (503) 378-6611

PENNSYLVANIA
Industrial Energy Consumers of Pennsylvania
The PENELEC Intervenor Group
Regulatory Agency   (717) 783-1740

SOUTH CAROLINA
South Carolina Energy Users Committee
Regulatory Agency (803) 737-5100

TENNESSEE
Tennessee Associated Valley Industries
Tennessee Valley Industrial Committee
Regulatory Agency (615) 741-5100

TEXAS
Texas Industrial Energy Consumers
Regulatory Agency (512) 458-0100

UTAH
Utah Industrial Energy Consumers Group
Regulatory Agency (801) 530-6716

VIRGINIA
Old Dominion Committee for Fair Utility Rates
Virginia Committee for Fair Utility Rates
Regulatory Agency (804) 786-3603

WEST VIRGINIA
West Virginia Energy Users Group
Regulatory Agency (304) 430-0300

WISCONSIN
Wisconsin Industrial Electricity
Consumers Group
Regulatory Agency (608) 266-2001

WYOMING
Wyoming Intervenor Group
Regulatory Agency (307) 777-7427

Public Utility Commission Periodic Reports

Periodically, all public utility commissions that regulate for-profit utilities are required to issue status reports. These reports are generally issued on a weekly basis and provide data on all currently pending rate cases within their jurisdictions. Copies of these reports are available to anyone who requests them. In most states there is no cost but even in those states where costs are incurred, they generally do not exceed $100 per year. If a customer's utility is regulated by a public utility commission, it is important to keep updated on what is going on at the commission level. Typically the following information is detailed in these reports:

1. Docket or case number of the proceeding being discussed.
2. Brief report concerning the status of the proceeding.
3. Identification of parties in the proceeding.
4. Timetable and place of next commission meeting concerning the proceeding.

For further information on how to receive commission reports, contact the commission involved.

For-Profit Utility Regulation Synopsis
(Investor-Owned Utilities)

1. **Intrastate regulatory body**—State regulatory agency.
2. **Utilities in this classification**—Any utility that is in business for the stated purpose of making a profit and is owned by investors through the purchase shares of stock.
3. **Regulation process**—Any rate changes must include at least the following items:
   A. Public notification of intent to change a rate.
   B. Adequate notification period prior to actual rate case

presentation (this period defined by state law) to allow interested parties to study the merits of the change request.

C. Presentation of rate request at a hearing open to the public before the appropriate regulatory agency.

D. Allow input from interested customer groups (intervenors) relating to rate change requests. The state regulatory body, based upon testimony presented at rate case hearings, approves actual rates that will be put into effect.

II. Municipalities

When municipalities regulate utilities, they are self-governing, that is, they are not subject to state regulatory rulings. Generally, when municipalities undertake the providing and regulation of utilities, they are purchasing the commodities at wholesale rates from a for-profit or federally regulated utility, and then retail these utilities to the public. This is especially true with electricity and natural gas. In the case of water and sewage, the municipality generally has control or jurisdiction over the entire process.

Municipal utilities are self-regulated and generally are presided over by a utility commission or board of appointed or elected members. As in the case of all utility regulatory agencies, "due process" must occur before changes can be made with respect to rates and conditions under which utilities are provided. This means that public notice must be given and adequate time allowed for public input prior to a change being instituted.

Typically, municipal utilities do not have as many rate classes or options as will for-profit investor-owned utilities since they generally do not have as diverse a class of customers. There are over 1,900 municipal utilities in the United States, but in terms of total energy supplied (electricity and natural gas), they constitute a minority when compared to the for-profit investor owned utilities. However, one area that is almost 100% municipal utility supplied is water and sewage services.

MUNICIPAL UTILITY REGULATION SYNOPSIS

1. **Regulatory body**—Self-regulated by the body or agency selected by the municipality to oversee utility matters. Can be separate for each utility regulated.
2. **Utilities in this classification**—Any utility controlled and regulated by a municipality on a not-for-profit basis.
3. **Regulation process**— Similar to for-profit investor-owned utilities.
    A.   Public notification.
    B.   Adequate notification period.
    C.   Presentation of rate request.
    D.   Allow input from interested customer groups.

III. Rural Electric Cooperative Utilities

Cooperative utilities are formed generally when a for- profit investor-owned utility elects not to serve a geographic area or customer base. Cooperative utilities generally serve rural areas where there is not a large customer load base. Generally, power is purchased at wholesale from a for-profit utility and distributed by the cooperatives' lines and/or pipes to the individual customers' locations. These utilities are like municipal utilities in that they are self-regulated but also are required to provide "due process" before instituting changes in the utility rate base. They are also very different from any other type of utility since they are classified as a "cooperative" entity.

The term "cooperative," as far as utilities are concerned, literally means that each customer is a part owner of the utility and as such, at least in theory, has their proportionate say in how the utility is operated. They are similar to all other types of utilities in rate change cases. They propose rate changes, hear customer input and allow all other "due process" practices before actually instituting rate changes. Cooperative utilities are smaller in terms of total energy supplied, than are municipal utilities and in general are located in rural types of service areas.

Cooperative Utility Regulation Synopsis

1. **Intrastate regulatory body**—Self-regulated. All customers are part owners of the utility and as such have their proportionate say or vote based upon their usage in relation to other customers. In practice many times, a board of overseers is appointed to represent customer interests with respect to the utility operation.
2. **Utilities in this classification**— Any utility defined as cooperative and is owned and operated by the customers served.
3. **Regulation process**—Similar to other types of utilities and includes:
    A.   Public notification
    B.   Adequate notification
    C.   Presentation of rate request
    D.   Allow input from customers

Federal Power Agencies

These types of utilities are of Federal origin and regulation. Generally, intrastate regulation is not applicable since these types of utilities are operated on an interstate basis. The Federal Government has the overall responsibility of regulation and operating procedures. Generally, these utilities wholesale the majority of their power to for-profit investor owned companies, municipalities and cooperatives who in turn are regulated by their respective regulatory bodies. When direct sales are made to customers, regulation parameters are by Federal guidelines. Federal entities in this classification are shown in Figure 2.4.

Figure 2.4
Federal Power Agencies

1. Alaska Power Administration
   Juneau, AK - (907) 586-7405

2. Bonneville Power Administration
   Portland, OR - (503) 230-3000

3. International Boundary & Water Commission
   United States and Mexico
   El Paso, TX - (915) 534-6700

4. Southeastern Power Administration
   Elberton, GA - (706) 283-9911

5. Southwestern Power Administration
   Tulsa, OK - (918) 581-7474

6. Tennessee Valley Authority
   Knoxville, TN - (615) 632-2101

7. U.S. Army Corps of Engineers
   Washington, DC - (202) 272-0001

8. U.S. Bureau of Indian Affairs
   Mission Valley Power
   Polson, MT - (406) 883-5461

9. U.S. Bureau of Indian Affairs
   San Carlos Irrigation Project
   Coolidge, AZ - (602) 723-5439

10. U.S. Bureau of Reclamation
    Washington, DC - (202) 208-4662

11. Western Area Power Administration
    Golden, CO - (303) 231-1513

The Influence Intrastate
Regulation Has on Utility Costs

State agencies regulate the intrastate distribution of electricity. And electricity utilizes a combination of "inter" (between states) and "intra" (within a state) components, and therefore both federal and state regulation occurs.

Since state agencies provide the predominate day-to-day regulatory functions concerning electricity, it is important to know that they function in a manner that benefits the customer. One of the most discouraging factors in intrastate regulation is the number of regulatory agencies that allow the utilities they regulate to not offer truly "Cost Of Service" tariff schedule rates.

It does a customer no good to have interstate access to less expensive electricity if the intrastate utility does not allow wheeling of that electricity through their transmission system. To be better able to visualize the flow of electricity through electric utilities, see Figure 2.5.

Figure 2.5

Flow of Electricity

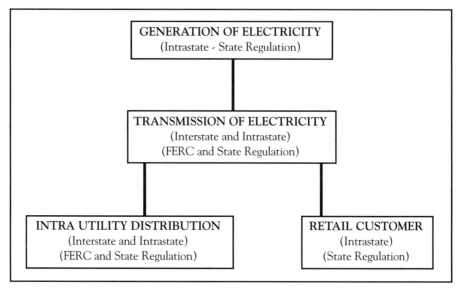

The various types and numbers of utilities are listed in Figure 2.6 on a state-by-state basis—(for-profit, municipal and/or rural electric/cooperatives, and their individual state totals).

Figure 2.6

Types and Numbers of Utilities on a State-by-State Basis

STATE	FOR-PROFIT UTILITIES	MUNICIPAL UTILITIES	RURAL ELECTRIC UTILITIES (COOPERATIVES)	STATE UTILITY Totals
Alabama	1	36	24	61
Alaska	0	25	17	42
Arizona	2	31	15	48
Arkansas	4	15	20	39
California	5	42	5	52
Colorado	1	29	32	62
Connecticut	2	7	1	10
Delaware	1	9	1	11
Dist. of Columbia	1	0	5	6
Florida	4	33	19	56
Georgia	2	52	47	101
Hawaii	3	0	0	3
Idaho	4	11	14	29
Illinois	7	41	29	77
Indiana	6	72	45	123
Iowa	7	138	50	195
Kansas	5	122	37	164
Kentucky	4	20	30	63
Louisiana	5	21	15	41
Maine	2	6	4	12
Maryland	5	5	2	12
Massachusetts	7	40	2	49
Michigan	8	41	15	64
Minnesota	4	124	50	178
Mississippi	2	23	28	53
Missouri	6	88	51	145
Montana	4	2	28	34
Nebraska	0	147	0	157
Nevada	3	8	35	46
New Hampshire	4	5	2	11
New Jersey	4	9	1	14
New Mexico	3	7	19	29
New York	7	48	5	60
North Carolina	3	76	29	108
North Dakota	3	11	27	41
Ohio	9	83	30	122
Oklahoma	4	62	31	97
Oregon	3	17	23	43
Pennsylvania	8	35	15	58
Rhode Island	3	1	0	4
South Carolina	3	22	25	50
South Dakota	6	34	37	77
Tennessee	1	63	26	90
Texas	8	79	85	172
Utah	1	40	8	49
Vermont	2	15	5	22
Virginia	5	16	17	38
Washington	3	43	21	67
West Virginia	4	2	1	7
Wisconsin	6	82	31	119
Wyoming	5	13	14	32
Totals	200	1,972	1,073	3,245

Chapter 3

Electricity Cost Reduction Strategies

Developing a Strategy For Reducing Electricity Costs

The first step in understanding anything is the obtaining of accurate information relating to the subject being investigated. In the case of electricity, the first step in understanding begins with the obtaining of data that relates to the pricing on a unit basis of the commodity (electricity) being purchased. Since all utilities are regulated in one way or another, written records of usage and pricing data as it relates to customers must be available to any interested party that requires it.

Items Needed from the Utility and State

Listed following are the mandatory basic informational items that must be obtained before any understanding of electricity rates will be realized. All of these items are a matter of public record and must be made available to any one who requests them. They are typically available from at least three sources—(1) the utility itself, (2) regulatory agencies, and (3) university libraries. Generally, the most logical place to obtain this information is from the utility or the utility regulatory agency themselves.

If a request is received by a utility from one of its customers,there generally is no problem or cost involved. However, if a request is received from a non-customer, some problems may arise both with respect to availability as well as the potential for a cost being assessed for the material.

Remember, all utility rate information that is approved by a regulatory body for use in determining rates and conditions to which a customer is subject, must be a matter of public record and, as such, available for public inspection. Typically, the utility service representative responsible for the customer involved is contacted and a request is made for the information needed.

Generally, a telephone or face-to-face request is most productive from the requester's point of view. Normally, a utility will not charge one of its own customers for this information but may assess a "copy" charge to a non-customer. This charge should be reasonable and reflect the time and material required to furnish the information. The importance of obtaining the following information cannot be overstated since these items are basic to understanding utility costs.

With relation to information that is required from the state, the best way to proceed is to contact the state agency involved directly.Generally,there will be no problems in obtaining either sales tax or economic development/enterprise zone information from the state. It is always best to contact the proper state agency directly by telephone since letters seem to get lost or misplaced rather frequently.

In Figures 3.1 - 3.6 are shown the various items needed prior to analyzing any electricity billing. Figure 3.1 lists the items that are normally obtained from the service representative of the utility involved. Figure 3.6 lists the items that are obtained from the state where the customer is located. If all of the items described in these two figures are obtained, a thorough comprehensive analysis of the specific utility involved can be done.

Figure 3.1

Basic Electric Utility Data Needed

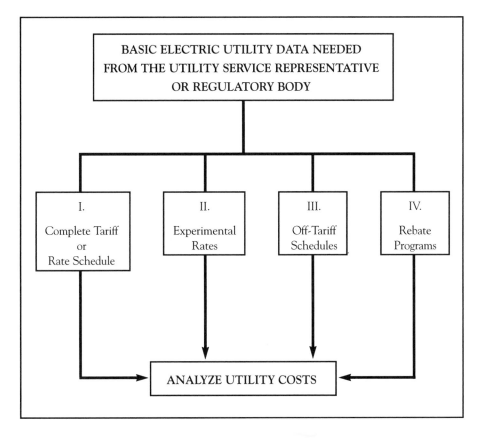

Basic Electric Utility Data Needed—Recap of Figure 3.1

I. Complete Tariff or Rate Schedule

A complete tariff or rate schedule covers all rates, terms, and conditions that were approved in a rate case. All classes of customers are addressed—residential, commercial, and industrial. These tariffs or schedules can range from several sheets to several hundred sheets in length. Contained in this information will be all data relating to customer rates, costs, terms for service, etc.

The importance of this source document cannot be overemphasized since it is absolutely mandatory for an understanding of utility costs. Make certain that the request is made for a "complete" tariff or rate schedule since utilities tend to provide only a particular schedule that currently applies to the customer making the request. It is important that the "complete" schedule be available since only then can comparisons between different rates and options be made. A typical complete tariff or rate schedule will contain the following items:

1. Complete list and explanation of all customer rates available.

2. Complete list of all items or riders that modify or change rate costs.

3. Alternative rates that may be available on a "customer request" basis for certain customer classes.

4. Information on "special" rates that may be available in certain geographic areas.

5. **Complete explanation as to how all cost components of utility usage are measured and applied.**

Complete tariff or rate schedules remain in effect until a new rate case is filed and approved by the appropriate regulatory agency. Only one complete schedule is required for a given utility since all customer classes are addressed therein.

II. Experimental Rates

Experimental rates are not normally contained in complete tariff or rate schedules since they are developed on an experimental basis by utilities and are not mandated for any customer class. These types of rates are not available in all utilities, but if they are, they can be a source of cost reduction potential. These types of rates are developed by the utility and approved on an experimental basis initially. The experimental category allows the utility to evaluate the potential for a different type of rate structure.

Experimental rates are never mandated and are used only on a customer voluntary basis. Also, if a customer chooses an experimental rate and it results in an increased cost, typically the utility will not assess any cost more expensive than what would have resulted from the regular schedule of rates.

If an experimental rate proves successful, the typical next step is to include it as an optional rate in the base tariff/rate schedule and not mandatory for any customer class. The final step is to change the optional classification to "mandatory" for a certain customer class in the base tariff/rate schedule.

Types of Rates

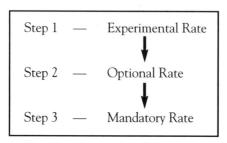

An example of what an experimental real time pricing electric rates could look like is shown in Figure 3.2. Keep up-to-date on experimental rates since long term they have a way of becoming mandatory for some customer classes.

The most common experimental rate structure currently being used in electricity seems to be the "real time pricing" structure. Ask your utility service representative if experimental rates are available and, if they are, obtain a copy and determine the immediate applicability as well as the long term implications if they are later included in the base tariff/rate schedules as mandatory for your customer class.

Figure 3.2

Example of an Experimental (Real Time) Tariff Schedule

1. SCHEDULE—EX-RPT-3 (Experimental Real Time Pricing)

2. APPLICABILITY -

   Applicable to any general service customer with service delivered at a voltage level of 4,160 to 69,000 volts. To qualify for this rate, the customer must have maintained a monthly billing demand level of at least 200 kW for the last 12-month period.

   This rate is available on a experimental basis and the minimum term is for a one-year period.

3. BASE MONTHLY RATES -

   A. Customer Charge $250.00

   B. Demand Charge - per kW   (None)

   C. Energy Charge:
      (1) Base Energy Charge - per kWh (Fuel Cost) $ .0023
      (2) Energy Charge - per kWh   (Variable) ($.0216 - $.2371)

4. COST DATA -

   Cost data shall be calculated on a hourly basic every day. No later than 8:00 A.M.every day the next day's hourly rates beginning at12:01 A.M.will be provided to the customer via a telecommunication link with the customer mandatory dedicated telephone line. This data will provide the (24) hourly variable energy charge components for the next billing period.This data will be provided every day of the year. The energy charge components will reflect the utility's actual costs as detailed in the Public Utility Commission approved rate filing 427-AF dated 07-06, pages 476-A through 493-C.

5. VARIABLE ENERGY CHARGES -

   Variable energy charges will range from a minimum of $.0216/kWh to a maximum of $.2371/kWh per hourly measurement period.

6. MINIMUM BILLING -

   The minimum monthly billing shall consist of the following item:

   A. Customer Charge $250.00

7. MISCELLANEOUS PROVISIONS -

   A. There shall be no demand (kW) charges applied to this rate.
   B. The utility will provide and maintain the appropriate metering and related equipment to accurately measure the kWh consumption on an hourly basis, at no cost to the customer.
   C. The utility retains the right to limit the number of customers on this rate.
   D. The utility retains the right to withdraw this rate upon one month's notice.

Analysis of Figure 3.2

This experimental rate allows a customer to purchase electricity on an hour-by-hour basis paying only for usage (kWh). The problem with a rate of this type is that usage (kWh) charges will probably be more expensive at times when the customer's usage will be the greatest.

For example, in the experimental rate shown in Figure 3.3, it is likely that the $.2371/kWh charge will occur from about 11:00 A.M. through 3:00 P.M. on normal work days (Monday-Friday). If this is true, very costly electricity will be consumed during most customers' largest usage period.

Generally, this type of rate will be of benefit only to the customer that can shift the electrical usage to the utility's normal off-peak periods which would generally be during the evening, night, early morning, weekends, and holidays.

Most electricity users do not have the flexibility to shift usages to the extent needed to benefit from this type of rate. However, if the customer can adjust the usage patterns on a daily/hourly basis, a rate of this type can be very cost effective. An item-by-item analysis of this rate follows:

1. **Schedule—EX-RPT-3 (Experimental Real Time Pricing)**
   This schedule number (EX-RPT-3) designates the rate case tariff schedule identification number assigned to this rate by the utility/regulatory agency as a result of the utility's rate case concerning this rate.

   If a customer wanted to examine all pertinent data presented in this rate case filing, this could be accomplished by requesting the data from either the utility or the regulatory agency by schedule number (EX-RPT-3).

2. **Applicability**—This section addresses the type of customer that can be served on this rate. In this particular rate, the customer must be

served at a primary voltage level of from 4,160 to 69,000 volts. Also, the customer must have maintained a minimum billing demand level of 200 kW monthly for the last 12 months.

Generally, applicability provisions are instituted because the utility has determined that this minimum voltage/demand threshold would be required by a customer to benefit from the rate. Also sometimes, especially on a rate of this type (experimental), the utility may want to test the rate's validity or applicability only to a certain type or class of customers.

3. **Base Monthly Rates—**

   A. **Customer Charge—($250.00)** This is the minimum monthly charge, in the absence of other rate imposed minimums, that an individual customer would have to pay to be served on this rate. This charge covers the utility's cost of maintaining and reading the meter and miscellaneous other monthly billing cost items.

   B. **Demand Charge—(None/kW)** This particular type of rate has no demand charge as such. Nevertheless, demand costs are calculated and included in the energy charges associated with this rate.

   Although a rate with no demand (kW) charge may seem to be a very "cost-effective" type of rate, the truth of the matter is that demand costs are calculated and included in the energy charge portion of this rate. In fact, a rate of this type actually would probably be more expensive for most customers that could not shift usage patterns on a daily/hourly basis, which is very difficult to do.

   Just because demand is not included as a specific billing item does not mean that its impact on the utility's costs has not been considered. It has, and in this particular type of rate, is included in the variable energy charge portion of the billing.

C. Energy Charge:

(1) **Base Energy Charge—Per kWh (fuel cost) — $.0023** This energy charge of $.0023/kWh represents the utility's fuel cost to operate their generation equipment. This charge is sometimes called fuel cost adjustment and it is always applied to the energy (usage, kWh) portion of the billing. All customers of a utility are assessed the same charge on each kWh used. All of these charges are approved by the appropriate regulatory agency.

(2) **Energy Charge—Per kWh (Variable) ($.0216—$.2371)** This charge represents the variable usage (kWh) charges by the utility on a daily/hourly basis. The extremely wide range of variability, over $.2100 per kWh ($.2371 - $.0216 = $.2155) is due to the cost of electricity that is experienced by the utility based upon its generation load/utilization at various times of the day.

Since this type of rate has no specific demand charge, it is part of and included in the energy charge shown here. Since this rate is variable and is priced by the day and hour, it actually can change on a daily basis. To see what a daily usage cost printout from the utility might look like, see Figure 3.3.

Illustrated in this hourly kWh cost data is the cost of electricity during the hours of normal operation for most customers. The kWh cost from 7:01 A.M. through 6:00 P.M. ranges from $.0810 to $.2371.

Figure 3.3

Example of a Daily Usage Cost Printout

RATE — EX-RPT-3 DATA FOR — Tuesday, 09-17			
Time of Day	Hourly kWh Cost	Time of Day	Hourly kWh Cost
2:01 AM- 1:00 AM - $.0216		12:01 PM- 1:00 PM - $.1743	
1:01 AM- 2:00 AM - .0216		1:01 PM- 2:00 PM - .2371	
2:01 AM- 3:00 AM - .0297		2:01 PM- 3:00 PM - .1420	
3:01 AM- 4:00 AM - .0297		3:01 PM- 4:00 PM - .1420	
4:01 AM- 5:00 AM - .0321		4:01 PM- 5:00 PM - .1376	
5:01 AM- 6:00 AM - .0321		5:01 PM- 6:00 PM - .1011	
6:01 AM- 7:00 AM - .0796		6:01 PM- 7:00 PM - .0710	
7:01 AM- 8:00 AM - .0810		7:01 PM- 8:00 PM - .0600	
8:01 AM- 9:00 AM - .0910		8:01 PM- 9:00 PM - .0327	
9:01 AM-10:00 AM - .0910		9:01 PM-10:00 PM - .0251	
10:01 AM-11:00 AM - .1176		10:01 PM-11:00 PM - .0216	
11:01 AM-12:00 PM - .1312		11:01 PM-12:00 AM - .0216	

If a customer uses the majority of the electricity during these hours, then the cost for the electricity will be very high. If, however, a customer has the majority of the usage between the hours of 12:01 A.M./7:00 A.M. and 6:01 P.M./12:00 A.M., then the cost per kWh would range from $.0216 to $.0796 which could result in savings when compared to a typical tariff schedule rate for this same type of usage pattern.

Basically a real time pricing rate is generally only cost effective if customers can vary the electrical loads on a daily time-related basis, or if typically operate during periods of low utility load demand intervals of time—typically evening, night, early morning and weekends. If a customer was served on this rate, they would receive a daily printout of data similar to the one shown here for every day of the month including weekends and holidays.

4. **Cost Data**—This section explains how the hourly kWh charges will be calculated.

5. **Variable Energy Charges**—This section simply restates the information shown in Item 3.C.(2) previously.

6. **Minimum Billing**—This section details what will constitute a minimum monthly customer bill. Basically the minimum charge will consist of the customer charge ($250).

7. **Miscellaneous Provisions**—This section enumerates miscellaneous provisions associated with this tariff schedule rate.

As can be seen from analyzing the provisions of this example of a real time pricing rate, it is not a rate for all customers. Generally, a rate of this type will not be cost effective for customers who operate on a one shift basis during normal daytime hours between 7:00 A.M. and 6:00 P.M.

However, if a customer operates hours other than these, or can shift his/her usage on a daily and hourly basis, or can work many hours on weekends (typically Saturday and Sunday), then a rate of this type may prove to be very cost effective. Before changing to a rate of this type, always have the utility do an analysis of the past year for the facility/operation in questions to determine the cost effectiveness of a change.

III. Off-Tariff Schedules

Off-tariff schedules differ from both base tariff as well as experimental rates in the way they are developed and applied. Off-tariff schedules are rates that are negotiated generally between a utility and a specific customer. They, at least initially, are generally discriminatory in nature and typically apply to larger customers.

Rates of this type are negotiated between a utility and a specific customer and must be approved by the appropriate regulatory agency. Generally, off-tariff rates are developed for large user customers that have either extremely large loads or unusual use characteristics that are not addressed adequately in base tariff structures.

Most off-tariff schedules occur in larger utilities with diverse customer bases. To establish an off-tariff schedule is at best a drawn out procedure. First, the utility as well as the regulatory agency has to be convinced of the need for a rate of this type—no easy tasking itself. Second, other utility customers may protest a discriminatory rate since it could impact their utility costs unfavorably—someone could have to pay for the lost revenue that generally results from an off-tariff schedule.

Off-tariff schedules in the past have not been widely used or applicable to a large user base, but this is changing with the potential of electricity retail wheeling becoming a reality. Evaluate the base tariff schedule in terms of usage characteristics and if large differences appear between actual usage patterns and those specified in the base schedule, the potential for an off-tariff schedule may exist.

To determine whether off-tariff schedules are available, contact the utility service representative and request a copy of any off-tariff schedules that are currently available. An example of what an off-tariff schedule might look like is shown in Figure 3.4.

Figure 3.4

Example of an Off-Tariff Schedule Developed to Encourage a Customer to Greatly Expand Their Usage of Electricity

1. **SCHEDULE** - A OTS-B (Extra Large Power Service Rider)

2. **APPLICABILITY** -

   Applicable to any large power service (Schedule LPS-1) customer who establishes a minimum demand of 5,000 kVA in at least 6 consecutive billing months out of the previous 12 billing months. Also, available to any large power service customer (Schedule LPS-1) who adds a minimum demand of 4,000 kVA and who can document to the utility's satisfaction that this demand will continue to exist for at least 6 consecutive billing months out of the next 12 billing months. This rate rider is available at the utility's discretion as approved by the P.U.C. in rate case Docket No. E07/GR-94-067.

3. **CHARACTER OF SERVICE** - AC; 60 hertz 3 phase at 128,000 volts or higher.

4. **RATE** -

   A. Customer Charge - Schedule LPS-1 charge plus $750.00
   B. Demand Charge - 1,500 kVA - As provided for in Schedule LPS-1
      All over 1,500 kVA - $3.50 per kVA demand
   C. Energy Charge -
      All kWh up to 1,000,000 kWh as provided for in Schedule LPS-1
      All kWh over 1,000,000 kWh - $.013 per kWh

5. **MINIMUM BILL** - Total charges applicable in Schedule LPS-1 plus $750.00 customer charge for this rate rider.

6. **FUEL COST ADJUSTMENT** - Same as provided for in Schedule LPS-1.

7. **TAXES** - Same as applicable to Schedule LPS-1.

8. **BILLING DEMAND** -

   The billing demand shall be the greatest of the following and be in addition to any demand charges established in Schedule LPS-1 for the billing month.

   A. The highest measured 15-minute demand established during the billing month;
   B. 95% of the highest demand established during the immediately preceding 11 months;
      OR
   C. 4,000 kVA.

9. **MISCELLANEOUS PROVISIONS** -

   A. This utility in a general rate case is allowed to seek recovery of the difference between the Standard Tariff Schedule Rate (LPS-1) and this Rider (A OTS-B), times usage level of the customer's utilizing this rider during a test year period if it is found that rate (A OTS-B) yields less revenue than rate (LPS-1) would have yielded for the last year if rate (A OTS-B) was not available.
   B. The maximum possible kVA demand available for this rider shall be no more than 100,000 kVA.
   C. The term of service of this rider will be no less than one year and no longer than 5 years.

Analysis of Figure 3.4

This example of an off-tariff schedule is typical of the types of rates/riders established on an off-tariff basis for the benefit initially of probably only one specific customer. In this example, the rider rate established is to supplement a regular tariff schedule currently in effect (LPS-1).

Its purpose is to retain current extra large (LPS-1) customers as well as to encourage the addition of electrical usage by these customers. This rider rate basically supplements the current (LPS-1) rate through the institution of a full-blown rate case application rather than developing this off-tariff rate rider. However, a complete rate case is a very expensive and lengthy process, so the off-tariff schedule route is probably the most cost effective means of fulfilling this particular need.

Probably the need for a rate rider of this type was necessitated because the (LPS-1) rate structure did not address the need for extra large electrical usage rates. Possibly because at the time the (LPS-1) rate was designed, industrial growth was not anticipated to the extent that it has actually occurred, or to the extent that the utility would like for it to grow.

1. **Schedule—A OTS-B** This schedule number (A OTS-B) designates the rate case tariff schedule identification number assigned to this rate by the utility/regulatory agency as a result of the utility's rate case requesting this rate. If a customer wanted to examine all pertinent data presented in this rate case filing, he/she could do so by requesting the data from either the utility or the regulatory agency by schedule number (A OTS-B).

2. **Applicability**—This section addresses the types of customers that can apply/qualify for this rate rider. In this particular case, a customer must currently be served by the (LPS-1) tariff schedule rate and have either a current demand of at least 5,000 kVA or add at least 4,000 kVA to the existing load. The reason for the institution of this rate was probably

because of a very large customer(s) threats to leave this utility's service territory if their electricity costs were not reduced. Also, a very large customer(s) could have requested rate concessions to add new load at their facilities. The utility in either of these scenarios evidently determined that they had the required additional capacity to fulfill the customer's needs, at least up to a total system level of 100,000 kVA (See 9. B.). Generally, a rate concession of this type is good for both the utility as well as the customers since it allows the utility to sell more of its electricity; and, if the additional capacity is available, the incremental cost to the utility per unit of electricity generated should be less, which should benefit all utility customers.

3. **Character of Services**—This section addresses the type of electricity service, voltage/hertz (cycles), at which a customer receives their electricity from the utility. This character of service designation is probably the same as required in the LPS-1 rate since the A OTR-B rate is a rider to the regular LPS-1 rate.

4. **Rate**—
   A. **Customer Charge**—**($750.00)** This is the additional customer charge applicable to this rate rider. The total customer charge would be the LPS-1 rate customer charge plus this customer charge. Customer charges cover the utility's cost of maintaining and reading the meter and miscellaneous other monthly billing costs.

   B. **Demand Charge**—**($3.50 per kVA over 1,500 kVA)** This section details the demand charge per kVA. Notice that this charge occurs only over 1,500 kVA. This is an unusual demand requirement but it is structured in this manner because this rate is a rider to the regular LPS-1 rate.

C. **Energy Charge—($.013 per kWh over 1,000,000 kWh)** This electricity usage or energy charge is structured in much the same way as the demand charge is. It is applicable only over 1,000,000 kWh. This charge pays for usage during the billing month.

5. **Minimum Bill—(LPS-1 Charges Plus $750.00 Customer Charge)** This section details the minimum customer cost to utilize this rider on a monthly basis.

6. **Fuel Cost Adjustment—(Same as for LPS-1)** The applicable fuel cost for any electricity used in this rider will have a fuel cost adjustment applied in the same manner as does the LPS-1 rate.

7. **Taxes—(Same as for LPS-1)** Whatever taxes (Federal, State, Municipal, etc.) that are applicable to the customer in rate LPS-1 will be equally applicable to this rider.

8. **Billing Demand—(Ratchet Method)** The billing demand on this rider is calculated in one of three methods with the method that is utilized resulting in the highest billing demand. This method is call "Ratcheting."

   Either (A) the actual highest 15-minute demand, (B) 95% of the highest demand established in the immediately preceding 11 months, or (C) 4,000 kVA, whichever results in the highest demand figure will be utilized as the customer billing demand. Also, notice that the demand billed for in this rider is in addition to that billed for in the LPS-1 rate.

9. **Miscellaneous Provisions—**
   A. This utility has filed for and had approved a rate case that allows them to recover any lost revenue that might result through the utilization of this rate rider. It would be unlikely that this rider would

ever result in lost revenue to the utility since it would, by definition, only be applicable to extra large usages which might not occur if this rider was not available.

A rider like this generally will result in more revenue than would occur in a normal tariff schedule rate. The reason for this is that, if the utility has the excess energy available and does not have to construct or enlarge current generation and/or distribution equipment, the more electricity sold results in lower incremental (kVA/kWh) costs for the utility.

At this time, most electric utilities have excess base load (kWh) available all during the year and most have excess demand (kVA) at least during part of the year. Any of this excess (kVA/kWh) that can be sold for at least a small profit to the utility over its actual cost will result in additional revenue that helps to spread various utility cost factors over more units sold. This then reduces the utility's incremental cost per unit and, at least in theory, results in a more profitable bottom line for the utility.

B. The utility is limiting its overall exposure by stating that total kVA available in this rider is limited to no more than 100,000 kVA. Probably this limit represents the utility's available excess power without additional expenditures for generation and/or distribution facilities.

C. A customer that wants to utilize this rider must agree to remain on this rider for at least (one) year and no longer than (five) years. This is a normal provision for a rate of this type and any customer that would want to utilize this rider should be certain that the usage requirements will remain such that this rider will be of benefit for the committed time.

IV. Rebate Programs

Demand-side Management. These three little words promise to change the electric energy use profile of American's big buildings.[1]

At the heart of DMS is a paradox: Electric utilities find it more economical to give money away to building owners in the form of rebates and incentives for energy conservation measures, than to build new generating facilities to meet increased demand.

Does your building need a new chiller or boiler? An upgraded temperature control system? State-of-the-art lighting? Do you want to retrofit your mechanical equipment with high-efficiency motors? DMS programs, which now total near $2 billion annually, will subsidize the cost.

Throw a dart at a map and you'll find a utility that promotes DMS for the commercial-industrial building sector. A recent analysis by the Electric Power Research Institute (EPRI) counted 1,150 programs aimed at commercial buildings, and another 706 for industrial structures. Here is a sampling.

Des Moines, IA: Iowa Power pays sliding scale rebates from $9/hp to $783/hp for efficient motor and motor drive programs.

Augusta, ME: Central Maine Power pays rebates for up to 90% (this is not a typographical error) of energy- efficiency costs. It's no wonder that 335 big building owners already have signed on.

Sacramento, CA: Sacramento Municipal Utility District offers builder incentives up to $4,200 for thermal storage systems.

Kennewick, WA: Benton County Public Utility District reimburses up to 70% of the differential cost for efficient equipment like low-E glass, occupancy sensors, and other measures.

Reno, NV: Sierra Pacific Power pays $15 per occupancy control device, $50/ton for coil cleaning, and up to $5/hp for motors.

Free Lighting. If this weren't attractive enough, the New England Electric System in Westboro, MA, already has given free installed lighting equipment to more than 5,300 nonresidential customers in its service territory.

Many state public utility commissions have had DSM programs for at least 10 years. For states that haven't yet promoted it, the Energy Policy Act of 1992 gives them a not-so-gentle nudge in that direction. Today, virtually every state has entered the demand-side management circle.

A 1993 report from Oak Ridge National Laboratory (ORNL) portrays the scope of DSM programs. At last count in 1991, just under 9900 utilities (of about 3,520) had DSM programs,Their investment in DSM accounted for 1% of total utility revenues in that year.

The payoff was significant:a cut of potential peak demand of 26,700 MW (4.8% of the national total) and a reduction in annual energy use by 23,300 GWh (0.9% of the national total).

So far, the big rebate dollars (for 1991, the last year analyzed by Oak Ridge) have come from utilities in California ($332 million), Florida ($130 million), New York ($128 million), North Carolina ($101 million), and Massachusetts ($90 million).

Some utilities are paying significant rebates as a percentage of their annual sales. The City of Seattle leads the list with a 6.6% outlay, followed by the City of Tacoma at 6.3%. Nationally, the figure is just below 1%.

Varieties of Rebates. Rebates to building owners come in nine varieties. EPRI's analysis shows this pattern of rebates and incentives.

Audit and building envelope: These programs focus on energy-oriented assessments of commercial buildings recommended measures to improve efficiency. The average annual energy savings for audit participants is 62.3 MWH per participant; for weatherization, the savings are 233.6 MWH per participant.

HVAC: Rebates for chillers range from $7 to $156 per ton, or from $75 to $700 per kW reduced. The average rebate for chillers is $33 per ton, and $276 per kW reduced.

Lighting-lighting controls: Some utilities sell or lease equipment at reduced prices, with discounts ranging from 50% to 70%. At least 18 utilities off the "ultimate" lighting incentive, free equipment and free installation. Incentives are based on demand reduction and range from $10 to $400 per kW, with the average pegged at $137.52

Energy-efficient equipment: Frequent participants are smaller non-residential buildings like supermarkets, retail outlets, and the like. Incentives are paid for efficient water-heating equipment, refrigeration systems, materials handling, glass display doors, strip curtains, and ventilation systems.

Thermal storage: EPRI counted 169 thermal storage programs, an estimated 33,000 participants served by 143 utilities. Although most participants are residential, commercial owners qualify for 71% of the programs. These include rebates on ice, chilled water, or eutectic sales storage.

Load control: Nearly 500 utilities have such programs, with more to come. The 6.4 million cases include nearly 2.8 million air conditioners, 2.7 million water heaters, and 750,000 controlled space-heating programs. Within this are 55,000 commercial and 1,400 industrial applications.

Special rates: More than 83,000 commercial accounts participate in a variety of interruptible, time-of-use, and other rate structures. Some utilities sweeten the offer for thermal storage customers.

Motors-motor drives: About 24,000 industrial customers and 10,000 commercial accounts participate in programs for motors that start at 1 hp. The "ubiquitous" presence of motor-driven loads makes them a "logical" target, says EPRI.

Standby generation: Utilities pay for customers' on-site generation equipment, for use during peak demand or in case of utility system emergencies. A total of 34 such programs are now on stream. The payoff is in the form of monthly credit, which ranges from as low as $5 to $100 per kWh per year. The average is $36 per kW per year.

Future of Rebates. How long will the utilities continue to pay out DSM dollars? The outlays will more than double, growing by 120% from 1991 to 2001. But within that 10-year increase, from $1.7 billion to $3.8 billion, there is some variability. Some regions will grow big.

The New York-New Jersey region will more than treble incentives, from $268 million to $628 million. Next door in New England, the outlays will contract slightly, from $282 million to $266 million.

If your building is sited in the Northwest, the news is even rosier. Future DSM funds will flow freely from utilities connected to the Bonneville Power Administration. During the next decade, Bonneville will spend about $2.8 billion on conservation—which is less than the cost of adding large new power plants.

ORNL reports that utilities are expected to continue DSM programs into the next century. However, beyond that, the crystal ball is murky. Utility executives have begun to ask themselves if the dollars- for-load-reduction programs can be justified by a cost benefit analysis.

In some markets, the utilities' DSM budgets are depleted by the second quarter; in others, state regulators ask if too much of the burden of the rebates is being borne by ratepayers who do not benefit directly. Others question the measurements and verifications of energy savings.

The building owner who ignores DSM does so at his peril. Although the dollars continue to flow, it is well to heed the advice of Will Rogers about the importance of investing in land: "They aren't making any more of it."

Some electric utilities currently have peak power demand (kVA/kWh) deficits. This means that even though a utility may not have a base load (kWh) problem, they may experience a generation capacity shortfall during some periods of a 24-hour day.

To compensate for this generation capacity shortfall, the utility can do several things. They can construct new generation plants (**supply-side planning**) that are very expensive or they can offer their customers financial incentives to reduce demand during the utility's generation shortfall periods (demand-side planning).

Many utilities offer rebate programs that encourage customers to reduce their demand needs by paying for or providing rebates for those items that favorably impact the utility's demand shortfall problems. Rebate programs range from, "not worth much" to "extremely beneficial." These programs change frequently and sometimes a specific amount of money is allocated for a program which means that when the money is gone, the program ends.

If a utility has a rebate program, they will also generally have an in-house rebate specialist that can be utilized for an on site evaluation of a facility to determine the applicability of the utility program to a particular situation. The utility service representative can provide rebate program information as well as arrange for an on site evaluation by the utility rebate specialist.

These programs typically include the following items/processes although not all items are included in all rebate programs:

1. Utility audits for rebate applicability
2. Fluorescent lighting
3. High Intensity Discharge lamping
4. Electronic ballasts
5. Efficient magnetic hybrid ballasts
6. Reflectors
7. Occupancy sensors
8. Miscellaneous lighting controls
9. Rooftop air conditioning
10. Window air conditioning
11. Electric chillers
12. Gas-fired air conditioning
13. Heat pumps
14. Boiler/water heaters
15. Cool storage—thermal storage
16. Energy management systems (EMS)

17. Energy efficient motor drives
18. Power factor correction capacitors
19. Thermal insulation and window film
20. Custom rebate programs structured to individual customer requirements. These programs are individually negotiated on a customer/utility basis

Figure 3.6 shows a sample of a utility data request form. This sample, if utilized, may assist in the obtaining of utility data that will be needed to analyze utility costs. This form is presented only as a sample but it does contain the basic elements that should be present in any request. The request should be submitted by the customer of the utility company to the customer's own utility service representative.

Figure 3.5

Sample Letter for Requesting Information from the Utility Company

Dear (Service Representative of Utility Company):

As part of an ongoing program in our company to reduce operating costs, we are evaluating areas for investigation. One of these areas is (insert commodity name—electricity,natural gas, water or sewer).Please provide the following information as soon as possible:

1. Complete tariff schedule including riders, attachments, etc.

2. Experimental rates, if applicable

3. Off-tariff schedules, if applicable

4. Rebate programs, if applicable

We appreciate your attention to this matter and thank you for your help.

Sincerely,

(Utility Customer)

Figure 3.6

Basic State Data Needed

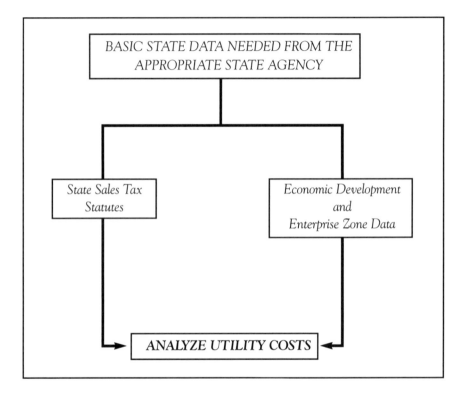

Basic State Data Needed—Recap of Figure 3.6

State Sales Tax Statutes

Generally, most people would not consider sales tax to be a utility cost but many state tax utilities (electricity, natural gas, water/sewer, propane, fuel oil, etc.) at whatever the state's regular rate of taxation is, normally 3- 6%. This is especially true for commercial and industrial customers, Also, the majority (32) of the states offer some type of credit or offset for certain classes of customers.

In most cases, this credit or offset is related to whether a customer is manufacturing a product. What is considered to be classified as manufacturing is subject to wide and varying interpretation by the various states but generally the two following items have to be present or take place in a process:

1. A change in form of the product or process has to occur.
2. A furthering or adding to a product or process has to occur.

Although these two items have to be present, there is considerable latitude in interpretation as to when they are present. For example, it has been accepted that the inputting of information on a computer floppy disc constitutes manufacturing even though there is no physical or perceptible change in the disc.

It is also widely accepted that a restaurant can be considered to be manufacturing if it processes its food on the premises. But if the restaurant purchases its food in the prepared frozen state and only heats or cooks it, no manufacturing occurs. Also, within a given state different interpretations concerning a given situation can be obtained simply by consulting different state taxation department employees.

The best strategy to follow is—if you think that you have a sales tax exemption situation, contact the State Department of Sales Tax and obtain a copy of the applicable sales tax statute. When you read the statute, you may find considerable latitude in the interpretation of what can be exempted and what cannot be exempted from sales tax.

If at this point you feel that your situation qualifies for a sales tax exemption, process an application. The worst that can happen is that the application will be rejected—but a rejection can be appealed and won. The best that can happen is that your application will be approved and you will have reduced your overall utility costs.

In general, if your company or organization is paying state sales tax and is a manufacturing, not-for-profit, municipal, state, or federal organization, and is sited in one of the (32) states that allow exemptions (See Figure 3.7, Item 1), process a sales tax exemption.

If your company or organization is approved for sales tax exemption, you can also recover sales tax paid in the past up to the state statute of limitations time period—generally three to five years in the past. A sample sales tax refund request is shown in Figure 3.8. This sample will cover both electricity as well as natural gas.

Information to Obtain From the State

To determine if exemptions are available, it will be necessary to contact the state directly so that copies of regulations, laws, or statutes concerning exemptions can be obtained. Generally, one of the following state agencies can provide the information needed:

1. State Department of Taxation
2. State Department of Revenue

When contact has been made with the proper authority, ask for the following items:

1. Copies of taxation exemption regulations, laws, or statutes.
2. Copies of taxation exemption forms to be completed to qualify for exemption.

3.   Copies of retroactive refund regulations, laws or statutes.

4.   Copies of retroactive refund forms to be completed to qualify for retroactive refunds.

Once this information is available, the difficult part starts. Unless there is familiarity with the way in which legal documents are written or worded, the process of determining eligibility for exemption can be confusing, to say the least. Do not hesitate to call a state taxation or revenue officer for assistance.

Once the exemption forms are submitted to the state, you can normally expect to have a waiting period of six to nine months before the petition for exemption will be ruled on. This process may seem complicated, but if the state guidelines are followed and the exemption forms are completed as instructed, exemption approval will be received if eligibility is approved.

To assist you in becoming familiar with what various states allow with regard to exemption, Figure 3.7 lists all 50 states and their current state sales tax regulations relating to utility exemptions.

Figure 3.7

Listing of All 50 States, the District of Columbia and Their Current State Sales Tax Regulations Relating To Utility Exemptions

1.

The (32) states that, in general,
allow sales tax exemptions on utility purchases.

(Specific exemption conditions vary widely by state.)

Alabama . . . . .limited exemption
California . . . . .general exemption
Colorado . . . . .exemption by application only
Connecticut . . . . .exemption by application only
Dist. of Columbia . . . . .exemption by application only
Florida . . . . .limited exemption
Idaho . . . . .general exemption
Indiana . . . . .exemption by application only
Iowa . . . . .exemption by application only
Kentucky . . . . .exemption by application only
Maine . . . . .limited exemption
Maryland . . . . .exemption by application only
Massachusetts . . . . .exemption by application only
Michigan . . . . .exemption by application only
Minnesota . . . . .exemption by application only
Mississippi . . . . .exemption by application only
Nevada . . . . .general exemption
New Jersey . . . . .general exemption
New York . . . . .exemption by application only
North Carolina . . . . .lower rate
Ohio . . . . .general exemption
Oklahoma . . . . .exemption by application only
Pennsylvania . . . . .exemption by application only
Rhode Island . . . . .exemption by application only
South Carolina . . . . .exemption by application only
Tennessee . . . . .lower rate
Texas . . . . .exemption by application only
Virginia . . . . .exemption by application only
Washington . . . . .general exemption
West Virginia . . . . .exemption by application only
Wisconsin . . . . .offset on other state fees
Wyoming . . . . .exemption by application only

Figure 3.7 (Continued)

2.

The (14) states that, in general allow no exemption on utility purchases.

Arizona	Missouri
Arkansas	Nebraska
Georgia	New Mexico
Hawaii	North Dakota
Illinois	South Dakota
Kansas	Utah
Louisiana	Vermont

3.

The (5) states that do not have sales tax.

Alaska	New Hampshire
Delaware	Oregon
Montana	

Figure 3.7 (Continued)

4.

State General Sales Tax Rates

(effective at the time of this publication)

State	Percent Rate	State	Percent Rate
* Alabama	4	Montana	0
Alaska	0	Nebraska	5
Arizona	5	* Nevada	6.5
Arkansas	4.5	New Hampshire	0
California	6	* New Jersey	6
* Colorado	3	New Mexico	5
* Connecticut	6	* New York	4
* Dist.of Columbia	6	* North Carolina	4
Delaware	0	North Dakota	5
* Florida	6	* Ohio	5
Georgia	4	* Oklahoma	4.5
Hawaii	4	Oregon	0
* Idaho	5	* Pennsylvania	6
Illinois	6.25	* Rhode Island	7
* Indiana	5	* South Carolina	5
* Iowa	5	South Dakota	4
Kansas	4.9	* Tennessee	6
* Kentucky	6	* Texas	6.25
Louisiana	4	Utah	5
* Maine	5	Vermont	5
* Maryland	5	* Virginia	3.5
* Massachusetts	5	* Washington	6.5
* Michigan	4	* West Virginia	6
* Minnesota	6.5	* Wisconsin	5
* Mississippi	7	* Wyoming	4
Missouri	4.225		

* States that allow sales tax exemptions

Processing of an Exemption/Refund Application

Since the processing of an exemption/refund application varies greatly by state, from a simple declaration of eligibility to a complex itemization of all manufacturing costs, broad generalizations are not practical or accurate. Since a generalized set of instructions is not possible, the next best approach is to provide an example of a difficult state application.

We will discuss a hypothetical state procedure, that requires complex detailed analysis of various types to comply with the various regulations involved. This example will provide an approach to an exemption/refund situation that requires an in-depth analysis of utility usage as related to manufacturing costs.

The example we will use will assume that if the utilities are predominantly (over 50% by this state's definition) used in the manufacturing process, then all utilities are exempt from state taxation.

The process of complying with this requirement is not really difficult but does require time and accuracy in accumulating the relevant data. Before discounting the exemption process as being too complicated or time consuming to be worthwhile, consider this fact.

In states that assess sales tax, the rate of taxation is between 3% and 6.5% of the gross utility bill. If a total natural gas and electric yearly billing were $100,000, then $3,000 to $6,500 could be wasted each year, plus the fact that this excess cost would continue year after year.

Also, since all states that allow exemptions have retroactivity provisions, a refund can be filed for previously paid state taxes up to the statute of limitations, normally three to five years in the past; and furthermore, sometimes interest may be available on these amounts. With the amount of money that can be involved, if an operation is in a state that grants exemptions, be sure to utilize the opportunity that is possible to reduce costs.

Figure 3.9 is a sample filled-out application for tax exemption and/or refund from the state sales tax. Included in this sample for natural gas and electricity are the following procedures:

1. Completed Sales Tax Exemption Request.
2. Completed Sales Tax Refund Request.

Figure 3.8

Completed Sales Tax Exemption/Refund Request

State Department of Revenue
Sales Tax Division

SUBJECT: SALES TAX EXEMPTION/REFUND REQUEST

UTILITY SALES TAX EXEMPTION/REFUND APPLICATION INFORMATION
(Natural Gas and Electricity)

I. OVERVIEW OF OPERATION AND ENERGY USAGE AT THE _____ PLANT OF THE _____ CORPORATION.

This facility consists of a manufacturing operation housed in a 300,000 sq.ft. metal structure. The manufacturing processes that occur at this location include the following:

1. Making steel stampings.
2. Fabrication operations.

The steel that is stamped and fabricated at this facility is used in the manufacturing of automobiles exclusively. The natural gas and electricity usage at this facility is predominantly used in the manufacturing process.

II. SPECIFIC NATURAL GAS USAGE INFORMATION.

The following information is calculated using the standard values for natural gas equivalents as follows:

1. 1 Mcf = 1,000 cu.ft. of natural gas
2. 1 Mcf = 1,000,000 Btu heat value

Total natural gas usage for the 12-month period being analyzed was 436,000 Mcf. Following is the specific equipment information requested by you.

Sincerely,

Figure 3.8 (Continued)

SECTION - A
PRODUCTION RELATED EQUIPMENT

1. (1) Heat treating furnace to anneal steel stampings. Natural gas usage of this furnace is 8 Mcf/hr. Approximate energy usage for 12-month period is as follows:

(8 Mcf X 12 hour X 6 day X 40 week = 23,040 Mcf)

2. (1) Heat treating furnace to anneal steel stampings. Natural gas usage of this furnace is 5 Mcf/hr. Approximate energy usage for 12-month period is as follows:

(5 Mcf X 8 hour X 5 day X 40 week = 8,000 Mcf)

3. (1) Heat treating furnace to anneal steel stampings. Natural gas usage of this furnace is 2 Mcf/hr. Approximate energy usage for 12-month period is as follows:

(2 Mcf X 12 hour X 5 day X 32 week = 3,840 Mcf)

4. (2) Shielding atmosphere generator utilizing natural gas as the base feed stock. Natural gas usage is 5 Mcf/hr. Approximate energy usage for 12-month period is as follows:

(5 Mcf X 24 hour X 7 day X 40 week X 2 = 67,200 Mcf)

TOTAL PRODUCTION RELATED NATURAL GAS USAGE:

Item 1.	23,040 Mcf
Item 2.	8,000 Mcf
Item 3.	3,840 Mcf
Item 4.	67,200 Mcf
TOTAL	**102,080 Mcf**

Figure 3.8 (Continued)

SECTION - B
NON-PRODUCTION RELATED EQUIPMENT

1. Heating for production areas.

   Natural gas usage of this equipment is 13 Mcf/hr. Approximate energy usage for 12-month period is as follows:

   (13 Mcf X 16 hour X 6 day X 30 week = 37,440 Mcf)

2. Miscellaneous unaccounted for energy usage = 880 Mcf

TOTAL NON-PRODUCTION RELATED NATURAL GAS USAGE:

Item 1.	37,440 Mcf
Item 2.	880 Mcf
TOTAL	**38,320 Mcf**

III. SPECIFIC ELECTRICAL USAGE INFORMATION.

The following information is calculated using the standard values for electrical equivalents as follows:

1. 1 hp (horse power)   =   .74570 kW
2. 1 Btu (British thermal unit) =   .000393 kW

Total electrical usage for the 12-month period being analyzed was 117,383,520 kWh. Following is the specific equipment information requested.

Figure 3.8 (Continued)

SECTION - C
PRODUCTION RELATED EQUIPMENT

1. (2)   1,000 ton stamping presses. Electrical usage of each of these presses is 1,000 kW Approximate energy usage for 12-month period is as follows:

    (1,000 kW X 12 hour X 6 day X 26 week X 2 presses = 3,744,000 kWh)

2. (1)   750 ton stamping press. Electrical usage of this press is 750 kW. Approximate energy usage for 12-month period is as follows:

    (750 kWX 16 hour X 6 day X 40 week = 2,880,000 kWh)

3. (1)   500 ton stamping press. Electrical usage of this press is 500 kW. Approximate energy usage for 12-month period is an follows:

    (500 kWX 16 hour X 6 day X 40 week = 1,920,000 kWh)

4. (1)   500 ton stamping press. Electrical usage of this press is 600 kW. Approximate energy usage for 12-month period is as follows:

    (600 kWX 12 hour X 6 day X 40 week = 1,728,000 kWh)

5. (3)   500 hp air compressors used to provide process air. Approximate energy usage for 12-month period is as follows:

    (500 hp X .74570 X 12 hour X 6 day X 50 week X 3 units = 4,026,780 kWh)

6. (3)   200 hp air driers used to dry process air produced by air compressors in Item #5. Approximate energy usage for 12-month period is as follows:

    (200 hp X .74570 X 12 hour X 7 day X 50 week X 3 units = 1,879,164 kWh)

7. (50)   Miscellaneous stamping and fabrication processing equipment as follows:

a.	(21)	Stamping presses	- 21 kW total
b.	(16)	Fabrication machines	- 8 kW total
c.	(10)	Drilling machines	- 10 kW total
d.	(3)	Assembly machines	- 2 kW total
		TOTAL	- **41 kW**

Approximate energy usage for 12-month period is as follows:

(41 kW X 12 hour X 7 day X 50 week = 172,200 kWh)

Figure 3.8 (Continued)

SECTION - C (Continued)
PRODUCTION RELATED EQUIPMENT

8. Miscellaneous equipment.

| a. | (4) | Heat treating furnaces | - | 5 kW total |
| b. | (2) | Atmosphere generators | - | 2 kW total |

TOTAL   -   7 kW

Approximate energy usage for 12-month period is as follows:

(7 kW X 24 hour X 7 day X 40 week = 47,040 kWh)

TOTAL PRODUCTION RELATED ELECTRICAL USAGE:

Item 1	3,744,000 kWh
Item 2	2,880,000 kWh
Item 3	1,920,000 kWh
Item 4	1,728,000 kWh
Item 5	4,026,780 kWh
Item 6	1,879,164 kWh
Item 7	172,200 kWh
Item 8	47,040 kWh

TOTAL   16,397,184 kWh

Figure 3.8 (Continued)

SECTION - D
NON-PRODUCTION RELATED EQUIPMENT

1. 3,000,000 Btu of office air conditioning equipment. Approximate energy usage for 12-month period is as follows:

   (3,000,000 Btu X .000393 X 6 hour X 6 day X 40 week = 1,697,760 kWh)

2. 1,050 kW of office and factory lighting. Approximate energy usage for 12-month period is as follows:

   (1,050 kW X 12 hour X 6 day X 52 week = 3,931,200 kWh)

3. 1,000 kW of miscellaneous outside lighting, hot water heating and office equipment energy needs. Approximate energy usage for 12-month period is as follows:

   (1,000 kW X 8 hour X 6 day X 52 week = 2,496,000 kWh)

4. Miscellaneous unaccounted for energy usage = 12,488 kWh

TOTAL NON-PRODUCTION RELATED ELECTRICAL USAGE:

Item 1	7,724,808 kWh
Item 2	7,644,000 kWh
Item 3	7,280,000 kWh
Item 4	12,488 kWh
TOTAL	**8,137,448 kWh**

Figure 3.8 (Continued)

IV. RECAP OF PRODUCTION/NON-PRODUCTION USAGES

	NATURAL GAS (Mcf)	ELECTRICITY (kWh)
PRODUCTION RELATED	102,080	16,397,184
(%)	72.7%	51%
NON-PRODUCTION RELATED	38,320	8,137,448
(%)	27.3%	49%
TOTAL	**140,400**	**24,534,632**
(%)	**100 %**	**100 %**

Based upon the information presented herein, the _____ Plant of the
_____ Corporation does qualify for State Tax exemption, since this plant
complies with the "predominantly used" definition as stated in the Department of
Revenue Sales Tax Information Bulletin. Based upon the following utility costs for
(Year)_____, we request the refund as indicated below.

(Year)_____	-	Natural gas cost	@	$3.25/Mcf	$ 456,300
(Year)_____	-	Electricity cost	@	$0.06/kWh	$ 1,472,078
				TOTAL	**$ 1,928,378**

REFUND REQUESTED

Total Natural Gas and Electricity Cost	$ 1,928,378	
State Sales Tax Percentage	X 5%	(.05)
TOTAL REFUND REQUESTED	**$ 96,419**	

Sincerely,

(Mr/Ms)_____

Figure 3.8 (Continued)

Department of State Revenue
State Office Building

SUBJECT: SALES TAX REFUND

Based upon the information in the "SALES TAX DIVISION INFORMATION
BULLETIN", in the paragraphs entitled —

1. "Used In Manufacturing"
2. "Separately Metered Or Predominantly Used"

the following data is submitted:

Having submitted the necessary form which confirms our exemption status, we
are requesting a refund for the following previously paid State Sales Tax

YEAR	AMOUNT
_____	$ 91,641
_____	$ 93,040
_____	$ 95,620
_____	$ 96,419
Refund	$ 376,720
Interest (5%)	$ 18,836
TOTAL REFUND REQUESTED	**$ 395,556**

To the $395,556 total refund detailed above, the total month's taxes plus interest
paid will have to be added until the applied-for State Sales Tax exemption becomes
effective.

Sincerely,

(Mr/Ms)_____

As can be seen in this example of exemption and refund application, the total savings can be quite large depending upon utility usage. This example shows that a considerable amount of money can be saved in those states that allow exemptions if you are willing to process the required paperwork.

If the required information and production data requested is properly documented and explained, both exemption status and retroactive refunds will be obtained without undue delay and/or state regulatory "red tape." A typical processing time by a state from the date of requesting an exemption and retroactive refunds will be from six to nine months.

Utility Holdback Provisions (Processing Fee)

If state sales tax is shown on a utility billing (electricity, natural gas, water, or sewage) the utility is acting as the collection agent for the state. When the utility acts as agent for the state, it is usual for the state to allow payment for the service the utility provides.

This payment takes the form of what is called a "holdback" or "processing fee", and is generally a percentage of the tax revenue collected by the utility on behalf of the state. Typically, this amount is about 1/2 of 1%. For example, if the sales tax rate is 5% and the utility holdback rate is 1/2%, only the funds that represent 4 1/2% would be sent to the state with the utility retaining the other 1/2% as a handling charge.

Example—
1. Total Utility Billing Amount
    Subject to State Sales Tax $1,675.00

2. Sales Tax Rate of 5% $83.75

3. Utility Fee 1/2%
    (Amount sent to state 5%-1/2% = 4 1/2%) $75.38

4.   Amount Utility Retains as a Fee $9.90

The utility fee, as a percent of total revenue collected, works out approximately to 8%–10% depending upon the sales tax rate and the amount of dollars involved.

If a sales tax exemption/refund claim is filed and approved, the utility fee is also eligible to a refund subject to the same terms as the sales tax refund. Where a utility retains a fee percent, any refunds from the state will reflect only the amounts actually forwarded to them by the utility less any utility fees.

To obtain the fee amounts, direct application to the utility must be made. There are no specific forms or procedures to follow and unfortunately most utility employees are not even aware of these fee provisions. Expect probably more problems in receiving the utility refund than the state refund since there are no specific procedures to follow.

To determine utility fee status in a given state, contact the state department of revenue or taxation and hopefully the state representative will be able to provide sufficient information on the subject. Eligibility for the utility fee refund is evidenced by the sales tax exemption number that will be assigned by the state and must be submitted to the utility involved for exemption status to begin.

Potential Hidden Sales Tax Charges

If you have a facility in a state where sales tax exemptions exist on your type of business and there is no sales tax charges on any of your utility bills, it is still possible that full sales tax is being charged. Many companies that have multiple facility locations opt for what is called "direct payment" of sales tax.

This process occurs when a company notifies a state that they wish to pay any sales tax charges directly to the state on a periodic basis, generally a three month (quarterly) basis. This procedure is generally chosen by companies with many facility locations to allow them to exercise closer controls on costs at the various facilities. In cases where "direct payment" has been chosen, no sales tax charges will be shown on any utility billing—e.g. electricity, natural gas, water/sewer, propane, or fuel oils. It is wise to consider the following questions if there is any doubt as to whether sales tax is being paid.

1.   Is the facility in question located in a sales tax exemption state?

2.   Is the facility in the category that would be exempt from sales tax according to state sales tax statutes?

3.   Do any utility bills show any state sales tax charges?

4.   Does the company that owns the facility in question have multiple facility locations in this and/or other states?

5.   Does the company that owns the facility in question generally perform other financial accounting procedures on a corporate rather than an individual facility basis?

Figure 3.9
The Sales Tax Worksheet

The Sales Tax Worksheet		
Itemized Savings Potential	Electricity	Natural Gas
1. Current Total Cost Monthly		
2. Current State Tax Monthly		
3. Cost if State Tax Eliminated		
4. Savings Potential Monthly		
5. TOTAL POTENTIAL SAVINGS MONTHLY		
6. TOTAL POTENTIAL SAVINGS YEARLY ($_____ x 12 months = $_____)		

State Economic Development/Enterprise Zones

Information on State Economic Development and Enterprise Zones Programs is included in this publication even though it has nothing to do directly with electricity but can indirectly affect its cost.

All 50 states and the District of Columbia have economic development programs that are designed to assist both commercial and industrial companies to reduce their operating costs. Items that are typically available in these programs include the following:

1. Revenue bond financing for land, buildings and equipment
2. Foreign trade zones
3. Reduced or eliminated personal franchise, inventory, and sales and use taxes
4. Tax credits for job creation and capital investments
5. Low or no interest loans for working capital and fixed asset financing
6. Industrial revenue bonds at low or no interest
7. Incentive utility rates (electricity, natural gas and water/sewer)
8. Business development funds at low or no interest
9. Work force development incentive programs
10. Infrastructure improvement incentives for water/sewer lines, utility lines/pipes and rail sidings
11. Property tax exemptions and abatements
12. Research tax credits
13. Child care tax credits
14. Custom designed incentive programs based upon a particular commercial or industrial company's needs

Not all states have all provisions listed in their economic development programs. However, many states are flexible in their guidelines and are willing to consider innovative assistance programs if needed by a commercial or industrial company.

At least 35 of the 50 states/District of Columbia currently have enterprise zone designations within their jurisdictions. In addition, two states have pending legislation to create such zones and two other states have incentive job credit programs. Incentive zones are created to stimulate the economy in a given geographic area of a state.

These zones have nothing to do with utilities specifically, but in their effort to stimulate the economy, they generally allow credits for new or increased usage of utilities in the enterprise zone areas. Typically the utility incentives take the form of credits or concessions on new or increased utility usages with the credit or concession gradually disappearing over a period of time, generally five years. An example would be as follows:

1st year	80% credit or concession
2nd year	60% credit or concession
3rd year	40% credit or concession
4th year	20% credit or concession
5th year	0% credit or concession

These credits or concessions are directly deducted from the monthly billing for the utility involved. All utilities are generally included—electricity, natural gas, water/sewer, fuel oils, propane, etc. These credits or concessions do not cost the utilities since they are allowed a corresponding offset on their state tax liability. To determine what economic development programs or enterprise zones exist in a particular state, consult Figure 3.11. Also, shown in this figure are the appropriate telephone numbers to call for each of the 50 states and the District of Columbia.

Figure 3.11

State Enterprise Zones

States	Zones		Telephone Numbers
Alabama	27		205-263-0400
Alaska	None		907-465-2017 (Economic Dev.)
Arizona	11		602-280-1307
Arkansas	456		501-682-2555
California	10		916-322-5665
Colorado	16		303-450-5106
Connecticut	11		203-258-4203
Delaware	30	Targeted areas	302-739-4271
District of Columbia	3	Development zones	202-727-6600
Florida	30		904-488-5507
Georgia	2	Enterprise & Industrial zones	404-656-3556
Hawaii	24		808-586-2355
Idaho	None		800-842-5858 (Economic Dev.)
Illinois	88		312-814-2354
Indiana	15	Urban zones	317-232-8800
Iowa	None		515-242-4725 (Economic Dev.)
Kansas	255		913-296-3483
Kentucky	10		502-564-7140
Louisiana	1,000		504-342-5402
Maine	4		207-289-3153
Maryland	17		410-333-6985
Massachusetts	Pending legislation to create zones		617-727-3206
Michigan	1	Benton Harbor	517-373-7230
Minnesota	16		612-297-1291
Mississippi	No zones. Incentives offered under Economic Development Reform Act,1989		601-359-3449
Missouri	40		314-751-4241
Montana	None		406-444-3797 (Economic Dev.)
Nebraska	None		402-471-3111 (Economic Dev.)
Nevada	2		702-687-4325
New Hampshire	None		603-271-2591 (Economic Dev.)
New Jersey	10		609-292-7751
New Mexico	None		505-827-0300 (Economic Dev.)
New York	19		518-474-4100
North Carolina	None		919-733-4977 (Economic Dev.)
North Dakota	None		701-223-8583 (Economic Dev.)
Ohio	263		614-466-2317
Oklahoma	89		405-843-9770
Oregon	30		530-373-1200
Pennsylvania	43		717-787-6500
Rhode Island	Pending Legislation		401-277-2601
South Carolina	Job credit program, no specific zones		803-737-0400
South Dakota	None		605-773-5032 (Economic Dev.)
Tennessee	1	North Memphis area	615-741-3282
Texas	101		512-472-5059
Utah	15		801-538-8708/801-538-8804
Vermont	3		802-828-3221
Virginia	18		804-371-8100
Washington	None		206-753-5630 (Economic Dev.)
West Virginia	None		304-348-0400 (Economic Dev.)
Wisconsin	12		608-256-4567
Wyoming	None		307-777-7284 (Economic Dev.)

Who is Ultimately Responsible for Utility Costs?

The Federal Regulatory Commission together with all state regulatory agencies agree that the customer is ultimately responsible for being on the most cost effective rate. There are no state statutes that require a utility to ensure that a customer is served under the most economical or least costly rate available. Neither are there any requirements that a utility refund any excess monies paid by a customer if they are on a correct rate even if it is not the most cost effective. It is the customer's responsibility to select the least costly rate schedule.

The customer cannot rely upon or accuse the utility of not being fair and equitable if the customer allows the utility to make the decision concerning the rate on which they should be served.

Due to the vast number of customers most utilities serve, and the changes and revisions their customers are constantly experiencing, it would be impossible to assure that any customer is at all times on the most economical rate available. Each customer is responsible for the cost effectiveness of the rate under which they are served. Unfortunately, most utility customers know very little about the rate that forms the basis of their utility billing. Through information provided in this publication, the correct approach to reducing electricity costs can be understood. With this knowledge, customers can determine the steps needed to be assured their electricity costs are what they should be.

References

1. Mahoney, Thomas; "Will the Rebate Deluge Ever Run Dry." *Engineered Systems*, November, 1995.

Chapter 4

Electricity Retail Wheeling

Retail Wheeling of Electricity

Retail wheeling of electricity is simply the purchasing of electricity by a retail customer from a source other than their own serving utility. The process is very similar to retail customer purchase of natural gas; however, the effect on the electric utility is very different from that on the natural gas provider.

In the purchase of electricity from a utility, the commodity (electricity) being purchased is generally originated or generated by the electric utility. In the purchase of natural gas, in the majority of instances, the commodity (natural gas) being purchased does not originate within the provider but is simply purchased by the provider and resold to the retail customer.

Although these differences between electric and natural gas may seem to be of little importance to a retail electricity customer, they actually are critical to the utilities/providers and their differing attitudes towards the customer's direct purchase of the commodities they sell. Since most natural gas providers purchase the commodity they sell from someone else, it does not disrupt their operation or profitability to any great extent whether their customers purchase "provider" natural gas or arrange for their own natural gas and simply utilize provider pipes, meters, and services. If the provider charges are based upon true cost of service principles,most natural gas providers would probably rather retail customers obtain their own natural gas since it would result in less headaches for the provider.

An electric utility, however, takes a very different view of direct purchase of electricity by its retail customers since generally the serving electric utility generates the electricity it sells to retail customers. When a retail electricity customer purchases electricity from some source other than the serving utility, the lost electricity sales for the serving utility result in lost revenue.

The lost revenue, in theory at least, may not be capable of being replaced by the serving utility. If this is true, as retail customers choose to purchase their electricity from sources other than the serving utility, the utility will be required to increase electricity incremental rates to offset the reduced electricity sales. As this happens, more and more retail customers might opt to obtain their electricity from other than the serving utility. This scenario has a name which electric utilities call the "Death Spiral." This means that as less and less electricity is purchased by retail customers from their serving utilities, the incremental electricity cost will continue to rise. Ultimately, the serving electric utility's incremental rates will become prohibitively expensive,resulting in financial disaster for the utility involved. Is this scenario realistic and will wholesale electric utility bankruptcies
result if retail wheeling becomes widespread? Probably, as has happened in many industries when competition has presented itself, the affected entities find ways to compete.

The question at this point might be—what happens if my electric utility declares bankruptcy?If a utility bankruptcy occurs, an interim administrator would be appointed by the courts until a purchaser for the utility assets could be located. Utility bankruptcies, while not a common occurrence, have happened recently with the results being that the utilities declaring bankruptcy have been purchased and have continued to operate.

Retail wheeling of electricity is inherently neither good nor bad, but depending upon your perspective, a valid case can be made both for and against the process. From a customer's viewpoint, due to the large variation in electric utility rates caused by a lack of true competition and inefficiencies, retail wheeling of electricity would seem to be a welcomed option. From an electric utility viewpoint, someone has to pay for its investment in materials and generation capacity; and, if customers can purchase their electricity anywhere on the distribution grid, the utility has no way to recoup its costs. Both of these views have some validity, but what will ultimately determine the reality of the process will be the retail customers causing it to happen.

If retail electricity customers take a "wait and see" attitude, then retail wheeling will probably never be widely available since most electric utilities are not going to push for a process that will ultimately force them to compete for their customer base. Retail wheeling of electricity is not something that is technologically impossible to do since almost all electric utilities currently "wholesale" wheel electricity between themselves on a daily basis.

The real problem electric utilities have with retail or customer wheeling of electricity is that it will require them to obtain and keep their retail customer base through competition, not through regulatory commission mandated service territory boundaries. It is best to keep the lines of communication open between the retail customer and the electric utility, seeking the utility's opinion regarding retail wheeling of electricity and asking your electric utility's service representative such questions as—

1. Does your utility recognize that retail wheeling will have a dramatic effect on how utilities operate?

2. When and how does your utility think retail wheeling of electricity will affect them and the way they market electricity?

3. Does your utility feel that retail wheeling will increase or reduce their customer base?

4. What customer retention strategies has your utility developed to cope with or to utilize retail wheeling of electricity?

5. Does your utility currently have any experimental or off-tariff schedules that have been developed to address retail wheeling?If

any of these types of rates are currently available, ask the service representative for copies of them.

Retail wheeling will affect each electric customer whether they ever wheel electricity themselves or not. Know what is going on in this area of electricity retail sales. What you don't know can cost you!

How Retail Wheeling Will Evolve

One of the real questions concerning retail wheeling of electricity is how will the wheeled electricity get from the point of generation to the point of use over various transmission grids. The stated problem is one of logistics - how to get the electricity from the point of generation to an individual specific retail customer that is perhaps located on a distribution grid different from the one on which the electricity is generated.

A good overview of some of the potential problems relating to retail wheeled electricity is found in the publication "Overview of Issues Relating to the Retail Wheeling of Electricity," published by The National Regulatory Research Institute, May, 1994. Material found on pages 59-67 and 69 follows. (Note: Information on how to receive a copy of this publication can be found in the Appendix.)

Overview of Issues
Relating to the Retail Wheeling of Electricity

Parallel Path and Loop Flow Problems

The actual path taken by electric power wheeled across transmission systems is difficult to predict and impossible to measure. Electric current moves according to Kirchoff's Laws and essentially flows on the path of least electrical resistance. As a result of these physical laws, power moves across many parallel lines in often circuitous routes.

For example, assume that four utilities (A,B,C, and D) are interconnected to each other through a tie-line between each of them. If utility A plans to wheel power to utility D, one might assume that the power will flow over transmission line AD which connects utility A to utility D. Realistically, the current may flow from utility A over line AB to utility B and then line BD to utility D.

Alternatively, the current may also flow from utility A over line AB to utility B, then down to line BC to utility C and then over CD to utility D. In actuality, the current has numerous possible paths it can take depending on the loads on the individual transmission lines at the time. Most likely though, a portion of the wheeled current traveling over each transmission line would hinge upon transmission loads on those lines at the time.

In sum, the actual flow of power may, and typically does, diverge widely from the contract path. As a result, the supposed economics of the contract path frequently have little to do with the actual costs of the power transfer. Furthermore, these loop flows can affect third parties distant from the intended power flows, and these third parties may, and often do, incur costs without compensation. Most utilities, however, consider the parallel path problem as a cost of interconnection and generally prevent other utilities from wheeling only if the additional transmission system loads cause capacity overload problems on portions of their transmission grid.

Network Congestion and Line Capacity

If the transmission network is heavily loaded,bottlenecks may lead to congestion that will prevent full use of the cheapest plants. Often referred to as"out-of-merit" dispatch, the constrained use of the plants frequently can create a significant opportunity cost that can be assigned to consumers causing the congestion.

The congestion limitations arise in two principal forms. The first is the limit on the flow of power on an individual line. The thermal capacity of a transmission line sets an upper limit on the flow of power on that line.

Through the interactions of Kirchoff's laws, a line limitation affects every other flow in the network. A change in generation or load at any buss will have some effect on the flow on the constrained line; hence, the constraint can affect the loading profile at each buss.

A second major source of congestion in a power network arises from voltage magnitude constraints at busses. In normal operations or as an approximation of the more complicated worst-contingency analysis, voltage constraints define operating bounds that can limit the amount of power flowing on transmission lines.

Even when power flows do not approach the thermal limits of the system and the transmission lines appear to have excess capacity, voltage limits can constrain the transfer capacity.

Voltage constraints inevitably require attention to both the real and reactive power loads and transfers in the alternative current (AC) transmission system. Recall that real power (the power that lights our lamps) is measured in watts or megawatts (MWs) and reactive power is measured in voltage-reactive or VARS and megaVARS (MVARS).

Power generation, load, and flow in an AC system are divided into both real and reactive power components. Without voltage constraints, the only matter of concern is the real power flow; it is common practice to ignore the associated reactive power analysis. But voltage can be affected by both real and reactive power loads, and the interaction between the two is critical in determining the induced limits on real power flows.

In reality, voltage limitations and the associated reactive-power compensation are prevalent. For example, the power shortages in New England and New York in 1988 were largely attributed to voltage and reactive power problems. Consequently, accounting for the congestion limits created by thermal limitations on transmission lines may not by itself prevent losses of real power flows.

Any new regime for transmission access must address the congestion problem created by reactive power and voltage constraints. The most direct method is to account for both real and reactive power when designing wheeling prices.

Existing transmission and distribution lines are capable of providing electrical service to all electric customers currently within a utility's service territory. Today's transmission and distribution system was primarily designed and constructed to transmit electricity from a utility's on-system generators at specific locations to its customers within its territory, and secondarily to transmit electricity from interconnection points for reliability and economy power transactions.

This same transmission system may therefore be incapable of transmitting large quantities of power from outside sources to its retail customers or to other utilities. Additionally, every transmission line is designed to carry a certain maximum amount of electric current. If this maximum current is exceeded, then the transmission line will be damaged. Consequently, a wheeling transaction may overload and damage the line.

Line Losses

Even if a wheeling transaction does not cause transmission line damage, it can increase transmission line power losses. Transmission line power loss can be defined as the loss of power, in the form of wasted heat, associated with transmitting electrical current over a transmission line.

Line loss is generally unavoidable and is directly proportional to the mathematical square of the current. Therefore, doubling the current on a transmission line would cause quadrupled line losses. Line losses also are directly proportional to transmission distance—the greater the distance of electrical transmission over the same size transmission line, the greater the line losses associated with the flow of power. Wheeling transactions can increase transmission line losses substantially.

Metering Problems

The electricity requirements of a system constantly fluctuate. The actual power supplied to the system is dependent upon its load requirements at any given time. Thus, the party selling power must be sensitive to these load fluctuations. Two different methods are commonly used to handle this problem.

The first and most efficient method focuses on the use of meters at the purchaser's delivery point(s). The amount of power delivered to the delivery points is instantaneously summed and telemetered to the generation dispatch center of the utility selling the power. In this way, the seller is constantly aware of the purchaser's instantaneous power requirements.

In the second method, the seller of power provides scheduled allocations of power to the purchaser on a day-to-day basis. The party wheeling the power is responsible for providing the actual power requirements to the purchaser and for load fluctuations on the purchaser's system.

Since metered delivery points are a requirement of any party purchasing off-system power, the exact amount of power supplied to the purchaser is known. The meters are read on a periodic basis (usually monthly) and the actual power supplied to the party purchasing off-system power is determined.

The amount of actual power supplied is compared to the amount of scheduled power provided and the difference is calculated. If more power was actually supplied during the period than was scheduled, the seller would reimburse the party wheeling the off-system power for the previous month's deficiency in its following month's schedule power.

The metering problems associated with retail wheeling could be complex and cumbersome. In order to accurately track customer's loads, a network of meters and telemetering would have to be installed from retail customers to the parties generating and supplying their power. Since the system load is adjusted automatically, the computer would instantaneously sum the demands of the retail customers and automatically adjust for the increase or decrease in load.

Distribution System Concerns

Certain technical problems associated with wheeling of electricity are intertwined with legal issues. If a consumer decided to purchase off-system power, he would have to purchase the distribution services from his host's utility grid or construct his own distribution grid. If he purchases the service, the wheeled power would in most cases be distributed to him easily as long as it is within the distribution system limits. If he opts to construct his own grid, a whole host of legal issues would likely arise.

Generation and Transmission Planning

If a customer in a utility's service area contracts for off-system power and wheeling, does that utility still have the responsibility to plan for generation and transmission capacity to serve that customer? Must the utility stand ready to service a former customer during system emergencies experienced by this customer's current supplier? Must the utility resume service to a former customer who wishes to again become that utility's customer at some future time? These are questions that will require answers before capacity planning can be done efficiently.

Retail wheeling could certainly harm a utility's ability to forecast future generating capacity requirements. A utility's load would now depend, among other things, upon the difference between the utility's own retail rates and the market price of electricity.

Retail wheeling would also create transmission planning problems for utilities. Utilities wishing to provide service to off-system retail customers could require costly transmission line and system improvements. As a utility added and lost different off-system retail customers, changes in that utility's transmission system could be required.

Construction of New Lines

Although a utility's transmission and distribution systems are capable of serving customers within its service area, existing transmission systems were not built with wheeling in mind. In particular, the points of interconnection between utilities were not designed for retail wheeling. Thus, in order to make retail wheeling possible, in some instances improvements to the current transmission systems may be necessary. Construction of new transmission lines presents a large obstacle for retail wheeling.

Utilities face many barriers in constructing new transmission lines. Construction of a transmission line is a lengthy and expensive project. Before construction of the transmission line begins, the required land must be purchased.

Transmission lines are restricted to certain areas. Consequently, the proposed transmission-line construction must meet the requirements and obtain the approval of different federal and state agencies. The next section briefly illustrates how to improve the capabilities of the transmission and distribution network.

Technical Measures To Correct For Wheeling Impediments

To make wheeling and competition possible, the previously discussed technical impediments have to be carefully handled. Legal, administrative, and pricing policies could correct for loop flow, metering, planning, and distribution problems. Line limitations and losses represent physical problems that could be solved only by either expanding or improving the networks physical capabilities.

Because of environmental concerns and regulatory delays, electric utilities are now seeking practical alternatives to constructing high-voltage and ultra-high-voltage transmission lines. A recent utility trend is to more effectively use existing transmission lines and rights-of-way. For example, the power transfer capability of lines not operating at their thermal limits can be increased by the addition of series, shunt compensation, or the use of phase shifting transformers.

Rights-of-way also can be made to carry more power by (1) raising the voltage on existing lower voltage lines, (2) converting AC lines to DC (direct current), (3) using hybrid lines where AC and DC lines occupy the same tower or the same right-of-way, or (4) by compacting the lines where more circuits are permitted in a given space. High-phase order transmission is one promising form of compaction that has been investigated.

High-voltage DC (HVDC) transmission is an area of particular importance. Thyristor converters rated 500kV, 2,000 A have been developed using both air and liquid cooling. Several areas of development have made HVDC systems more cost effective over time and have greatly improved their performance.

They include direct light firing of thyristors,the development of higher voltage cells that lead to lower losses, greater control flexibility through the use of microprocessors and sophisticated new control functions, (for example,multiterminal operation, real and reactive power control, and damping of subsynchronous oscillations),the reduction of convertor transformer losses, and better protection of equipment against over voltages with the development of zinc oxide arresters.

HVDC should play an increasingly important role in enhancing the capability of the transmission network to accommodate increased wheeling and competitive activities.

An economical way to increase the power transfer capability of an AC line is to install capacitors in series with the line to reduce its electrical impedance. Using zinc oxide discs with high-energy handling capability, series capacitors can be reliably protected against overvoltage by connecting series-parallel arrays of discs directly across the capacitors.

The protection of turbine generators against subsynchronousoscillations, which may arise when series capacitors are used, has been accomplished using either passive filters or active thyristor dampers.

Another means of increasing the power transfer capability of existing transmission lines is the addition of shunt compensation of the form of switched capacitor banks or static VAR controls. Static VAR controls were initially applied to control the voltage flicker produced by electric arc furnaces.

More recently, static VAR controls were applied to control rapid voltage fluctuations on power transmission systems and to improve the stability of large networks. Static VAR controls consist of thyristor switches, sometimes in conjunction with mechanical switches, to regulate the amount of inductance or capacitance connected to the transmission line for purposes of voltage regulation and increased power transfer.

These measures should significantly enhance the over all reliability and capability of electric power systems to comply with the new competitive regime. They have limitations and costs, however. In a recent study, the enhancement potential and installation costs of five options of different technical measures were compared.

These options, proposed to enhance the network transfer capabilities, are (1) fixed series capacitors and static VAR compensators (SVCs); (2) adjustable series and SVCs, and uncontrolled parallel paths; (3) the first option plus, and parallel paths controlled; and (5) the fourth option plus rapid response generation.

The study concludes that power transfer could be increased by 35percent, 50 percent, 60 percent, 70 percent, and 90 percent with the adoption of options 1 through 5,respectively. Assuming option 1 is the bench mark, the study found that the installation of option 2,3,4, and 5 are approximately 100 percent, 150 percent, 500 percent, and 800 percent more expensive than the installation cost of option 1.

The savings that would result from the transfer of cheap and remove power by the enhanced network should be accounted for when conducting a cost/benefit analysis. The questions remains whether utilities would be willing to invest in such measures if the economic benefits and rewards accrue mainly to customers.

Final Comments

Society has limited tolerance for actions which may disrupt electric service over a wide area. If numerous players are encouraged to engage in any sort of competition in the electric network, some workable enforcement procedures should be established to ensure that variances from the rigorous and unforgiving nature of operations on the grid are not compromised because of competitive pressure.

Unlike natural gas transmission,electric wheeling can affect the reliability and stability of service over a wide area. Because electric utilities are interconnected and operate in parallel,the actions of one utility affect other utilities.

Economic/Policy Considerations

General Effects of Retail Wheeling

Retail wheeling would undoubtedly advance the competition that is evolving in the electric power industry. Along with EPAct and emerging market pressures, retail wheeling would move the future path of the industry toward a more balanced mix of market factors and regulation in determining performance and structure.

Allowing retail customers the right to purchase power from competing generators would affect the electric power industry in five major ways. First, by weakening a utility's monopoly power, it would directly enhance competition in retail markets. Second, it would eventually cause a change in the rate-making practices of state regulators. Third, it would stimulate vertical disintegration of the industry where some utilities may decide to exit the generation business. Fourth, it would reshape the "regulatory compact" by changing the service obligations of utilities and their status as the sole supplier of power within their franchise areas.

Fifth, it would cause the industry to become more cost-conscious and accommodating to the needs of individual customers.

Another good evaluation of retail wheeling of electricity is found in the publication "Retail Competition In The United States Electricity Industry," published by the Electricity Consumers Resource Council (ELCON), June 1994. This publication outlines eight principles for achieving competitive, efficient and equitable retail electricity markets. The eight principles as listed are as follows: (Note: Information on how to receive a copy of this publication can be found in the Appendix.)

- PRINCIPLE NO. 1
  Market forces can do a better job than any government or regulatory agency in determining prices for a commodity such as electricity.

- PRINCIPLE NO. 2
  Laws and regulations that restrict the development of competitive electricity markets should be rescinded or amended. The need for burdensome regulation will be reduced where competitive electricity markets are allowed to flourish.

- PRINCIPLE NO. 3
  The benefits from completion will never fully materialize unless and until there is competition in both wholesale and retail electricity markets. But not all retail electric services are natural monopolies and therefore they should not be regulated as such.

- PRINCIPLE NO. 4
  The owners and operators of transmission and distribution facilities, and

the providers of coordination and system control services, should be required to provide access to those facilities and services to any buyer or seller on a nondiscriminatory, common-carrier basis.

- **PRINCIPLE NO. 5**
  Rates for the use of transmission and distribution facilities should reflect the actual cost of providing the service. If the facility is a natural monopoly, those rates should be based on actual costs and these services provided on a nondiscriminatory and comparable basis to all users.

- **PRINCIPLE NO. 6**
  Resource planning is not a natural monopoly. The types and market shares of generation and end-user technologies that will be supplied in wholesale and retail markets should be decided in the marketplace.

- **PRINCIPLE NO. 7**
  Legitimate and verifiable transition costs that develop as a result of competition should be recovered by an equitable split amount ratepayers, shareholders and taxpayers. The costs of assets that were uneconomical in the existing regulatory regime are not transition costs.

- **PRINCIPLE NO. 8**
  The potential for transition costs should not be used as an excuse to prevent or delay the onset of a competitive electricity market.

As can be seen, there are both obstacles to and advantages in retail wheeling of electricity. When and whether retail wheeling occurs to any great extent will depend upon how involved potential retail wheeling customers become in the process. Although there are many questions on how the process will work, I feel that in all practicality the process will or should evolve as follows:

1. Retail wheeling of electricity will, at least initially, occur internally on each of the nine North American Electric Reliability Council Regions (NERC) in the contiguous United States. Currently there are nine regions in the contiguous United States. Following are the geographic areas served by each of these regions together with each region's name.

Figure 4.1

Nine NERC Regions

Region Name	Geographic Area Served
1. WESTERN SYSTEMS COORDINATING COUNCIL (WSCC)	Arizona California Colorado Idaho Montana (partial) Nevada New Mexico (partial) Oregon Utah Washington Wyoming
2. MID CONTINENT AREA POWER POOL (MAPP)	Iowa Minnesota Montana (partial) Nebraska North Dakota South Dakota
3. SOUTHWEST POWER POOL (SPP)	Arkansas Kansas Louisiana Mississippi (partial) Missouri (partial) New Mexico (partial) Oklahoma Texas (partial)
4. ELECTRIC RELIABILITY COUNCIL OF TEXAS (ERCOT)	Texas (partial)
5. MID AMERICAN INTERPOOL NETWORK (MAIN)	Illinois Missouri (partial) Wisconsin

Figure 4.1 (Continued)

Region Name	Geographic Area Served
6. EAST CENTRAL AREA RELIABILITY COORDINATION AGREEMENT (ECAR)	Indiana Kentucky (partial) Maryland (partial) Michigan (partial) Ohio Pennsylvania (partial) Virginia (partial) West Virginia
7. SOUTHEASTERN ELECTRIC RELIABILITY COUNCIL (SERC)	Alabama Delaware District of Columbia Florida Georgia Kentucky (partial) Missouri (partial) North Carolina South Carolina Tennessee Virginia (partial)
8. NORTHEAST POWER COORDINATING COUNCIL (NPCC)	Connecticut Maine Massachusetts New Hampshire New York Rhode Island Vermont
9. MID ATLANTIC AREA COUNCIL (MAAC)	Maryland (partial) Michigan (partial) New Jersey Pennsylvania (partial)

Figure 4.2

Chart Showing Typical Generation (GWH), Production Costs (¢/kWh), and Retail Rates (¢/kWh) for Each of the Nine NERC Regions

NERC Region	Electric Generation (GWH)	* Production Costs (¢/kWh)	Retail Rates (¢/kWh)
WSCC	39,800	1.7	7.9
MAPP	11,500	1.5	5.3
SPP	21,500	1.9	6.0
ERCOT	16,400	1.9	6.5
MAIN	17,900	1.9	6.5
ECAR	38,700	2.0	5.7
SERC	51,700	1.8	6.2
NPCC	14,800	2.2	10.7
MAAC	15,400	2.2	8.3
Total Generation	227,700 GWH		
Average Costs		1.9¢/kWh	7.1¢/kWh

Note: *Electric generation/production costs/and retail rates for each of the NERC regions varies each hour, day, week, and month. The figures shown are typical and are not intended to represent any actual month. This data is presented only to provide insight into differences between the regions in actual generation amounts, production costs and retail rates.*

* *Production Costs include fuel prices and non-fuel O & M costs.*

In my opinion logically intra NERC region retail wheeling competition would be the first step in overall retail wheeling of electricity. This would make sense both with respect to transmission distribution (intra region only) and variations in specific utility production costs and retail rates.

This type of competition, to a limited extent, is already taking place in various parts of the United States. Although there is very little retail wheeling competition currently, there is very real concern within individual utilities about their costs/rates in comparison to an adjoining utility's costs/rates.

2. A large portion of retail customers that could retail wheel electricity will never do so because their serving utility will negotiate a concessionary rate with the customer to retain their base load. Remember that in a utility that generates the electricity, their good retail base load customers are critical to the profitability of that utility.

I have personally been involved in negotiations with electric utilities in a client's behalf where the utility was willing to negotiate rates, project cost concessions and various other cost reductions with the client even where there was no opportunity for the client to leave the serving utility. Why do these types of negotiations occur? Because the serving utility really does want to keep their retail customers satisfied, if possible.

The Electricity Retail Wheeling Process

This section concerning retail wheeling addresses the basis of true electricity costs based upon cost per Btu. This data is needed if a factual relationship between electricity and other energy forms are to be evaluated. Retail wheeling will impact electricity costs and whether this impact is positive or negative, will to a large degree depend upon the purchaser's knowledge of the process.

The learning of the basics contained in this section will assist the electricity purchaser to determine whether their electricity costs are what they should be. Also, contained in this section is information concerning the probable categories of retail wheeled electricity, and information on the probable retail wheeling process from the purchaser's viewpoint.

I. Electricity Costs on a True Energy Cost Basis

Frequently, electricity competes with other energy sources for various uses—heating, cooling, processing, etc. Both electricity and other energy equipment providers tend to favor their own particular equipment to the exclusion of other types or processes that result in the same process or product.

As a user of either electricity or other energy sources, it is important to evaluate different sources of the energy that might be available for use. When evaluating electricity versus other energy sources for a process, one of the most important cost considerations is the energy cost. The only accurate way electricity can be compared with other energy sources is on a uniform cost basis.

Since electrical (kWh) and the measurements used in other energy sources are not comparable, another unit of measure must be used. This unit is the British Thermal Unit (Btu). If the true (Btu) value of both electricity and other energy sources are known, then an accurate comparison between the cost differences of the two processes can be determined. Shown here are the various factors that need to be known to accurately evaluate electricity versus other energy source costs.

Figure 4.3

Energy Btu Comparisons

Energy Source	Unit of Measure	Total Btu
Electricity	(1) Kilowatthour (kWh)	3,412
Natural Gas	(1) Dekatherm (Dth)	1,000,000
Fuel Oil #2	(1) Gallon (Gal)	140,000
Fuel Oil #6	(1) Gallon (Gal)	150,000
Propane	(1) Gallon (Gal)	91,500
Coal	(1) Ton (2,000 lb)	24,000,000

Using the information shown in Figure 4.3, the true cost of electricity per the Btu standard of measure of (1,000,000 Btu) is as follows:

(1) kWh = 3,412 Btu

Number of kWh in 1,000,000 Btu —
(1,000,000 Btu ÷ 3,412 Btu) = 293.08 kWh

There are 293.08 kWh per 1,000,000 Btu

True electricity costs, when stated in cost per 1,000,000 Btu, are as follows:

Figure 4.4
True Electricity Costs

Cost of Electricity (Cost per kWh)	Cost Per 1,000,000 Btu
$ .01	$ 2.93 (293 kWh X $.01)
.02	5.86
.03	8.79
.04	11.72
.05	14.65
.06	17.58
.07	20.51
.08	23.44
.09	26.37
.10	29.30
.11	32.23
.12	35.16
.13	38.09 (293 kWh X $.13)

Examples of Electricity Costs to Other Forms of Energy

Figure 4.5
Electricity vs Natural Gas

Electricity Cost-	$0.07/kWh
Natural Gas Cost-	$3.50/1,000,000 Btu
Electricity Cost-	$20.51 (1,000,000 Btu)
Natural Gas Cost-	$ 3.50 (1,000,000 Btu)

True cost comparisons can be calculated for any energy source if the true Btu value of the source can be obtained. When doing cost comparisons, always consider efficiency of the energy source being considered. All natural gas, fossil fuel, and/or petroleum distillates are less than 100% efficient. In the extracting of energy from these sources typically, combustion must occur which releases a waste stream of products of combustion that contain heat value or Btu's. Usually, efficiencies for these energy sources are between 60%-90%. Also, electricity can be more than 100% efficient in some applications. For example, an electric heat pump application can be 200% to 400% efficient since heat or (Btu) value can be extracted from the air, ground, water, etc. Always consider true efficiency when doing cost comparisons between energy sources.

An example of a comparison between an electric heat pump application that is 200% efficient with a natural gas fired application that is 75% efficient follows:

ELECTRIC COST (kWh) $.06 = $17.58 /1,000,000 Btu
True Energy Cost at 200% Process Efficiency—
$17.58 ÷ 2 = $8.79 /1,000,000 Btu

NATURAL GAS COST (1,000,000 Btu) = $3.75
True Energy Cost at 70% Process Efficiency—
$3.75 ÷ .75=$5.00 /1,000,000 Btu

As can be seen in this example, the initial cost difference between electricity and natural gas true energy cost appears to be very large. However, when the two processes are calculated utilizing their true efficiencies, the cost differential becomes much less.

Figure 4.6

Natural Gas/Electricity Cost Differential

Apparent Cost Differences:

Electricity Cost -	$17.58 /1,000,000 Btu
Natural Gas Cost -	$ 3.75 /1,000,000 Btu
Apparent Difference -	**$13.83 /1,000,000 Btu**

True Cost Difference:

Electricity Cost - (200% efficient) $17.58 ÷ 2 = $8.79 /1,000,000 Btu

Natural Gas Cost - (75% efficient)$ 3.75 ÷ .75 = $5.00 /1,000,000 Btu

Actual Difference   **$3.79 /1,000,000 Btu**

Figure 4.7

Electricity vs Fuel Oil #2

Electricity Cost-	$0.06 /kWh
Fuel Oil #2 Cost-	$0.48 /gallon

Electricity Cost-	$17.58 (1,000,000 Btu)
Fuel Oil #2 Cost-	$ 3.43 (1,000,000 Btu)

(Fuel Oil = 140,000 Btu/gal)

1,000,000 Btu ÷ 140,000 Btu/gal = 7.143 gal

7.143 X $0.48 = $3.43 /1,000,000 Btu

II. Categories of Retail Wheeled Electricity

This section addresses the two classes of retail wheeled electricity that will probably be available. An understanding of these classes of wheeled electricity is necessary to be able to cost effectively retail wheel electricity from other than the serving utility sources.

Firm Service. Electricity that is purchased under this category is the type that is typically purchased from the serving utility and has the highest priority of delivery. If any electricity is available, it will flow to firm service customers.

Generally firm service customers have no back-up generation capability and as a result, pay the highest tariff rate applicable. Depending upon the serving utility's tariff schedules, firm category customers may or may not be eligible for other than firm service electricity.

Probably a retail wheeling customer, if he/she requires an uninterrupted flow of electricity, will purchase firm distribution capacity from the serving utility or back themselves up with on-site generation capacity.

Interruptible Service. This category of service is the type that probably will be most widely available to retail wheeling customers. Those retail wheeling customers who can accommodate interruption of electric service on short notice, generally in peak load seasons or situations, will benefit from this class of service.

This category of service is less expensive than firm service. A customer who chooses this type of service will probably either have a type of business that can withstand interruption or will have a back-up generation source to supplement a disruption of electricity service.

Most electricity retail wheeled through other than the normal serving utility transmission grids will be interruptible. Many times the cost differential is such that a back-up generation supply can be obtained with the savings realized. And, if this can be done, the end result is increased customer flexibility with respect to electricity supply sources.

This type of service is becoming widely available from serving electric utilities even without the advent of retail wheeling. Investigate your serving utility's tariff schedules to determine the availability and applicability of interruptible electric service to a particular situation.

III. The Retail Wheeling Process

Who will most probably utilize the retail wheeling process? Will there be other options available? The most probable "first" customers for retail wheeling will be large electricity users where electricity costs have considerable impact on their product/processes. Since true retail wheeling of electricity will or could negatively affect the serving utility's profitability, there will probably be much pressure on the customer to not wheel or at least to consider other options that cause them to remain with the serving electric utility.

As has happened in natural gas, electric utilities will probably be inclined to be responsive to customers' needs to keep them as satisfied users of the serving utility electricity. These utility efforts will probably take many forms to help their customers reduce their electricity costs—e.g., negotiated incremental rates and/or financial assistance to customers.

Serving electric utilities will begin to operate more on a competitive rather protected monopolistic basis. This change will not come easily since competition is not something any company likes to have to contend with. Many negative things are said about retail wheeling with relation to overall electricity system reliability and utility "stranded" investment costs if currently captive customers leave their serving utility. But the fact is that competition in the electricity industry is here to stay and grow. Electric utilities will either adopt and grow or resist and fail—there will be no middle ground. Change is not easy but resistance is fatal.

Not all potential retail customers will choose to or find it financially prudent to wheel their own electricity. However, these customers will find, in many cases, that they will be able to negotiate less costly electricity rates with their serving utility. As with any situation that involves competition, even those not directly affected will in many cases find that they too can benefit from the process.

One thing that electric utilities say will happen if retail wheeling becomes widely available, is that some customer's rates will have to increase as a result of lost utility revenue. This would be true if the utilities were to continue to operate in the same method that they currently do.

What will happen in all likelihood is that electric utilities will take either one of two possible positions—view retail wheeling as a new opportunity for growth or resist and fight the process and see their market share continue to erode. Those that see it as an opportunity will grow and all of their customers will benefit from the process. Those that resist will ultimately fail, go bankrupt or be purchased by a company that through vision sees opportunities rather than disaster.

Retail wheeling will come regardless of what electric utilities want, there will be problems and failures but once the transitional period is over, electricity will become a commodity rather than a protected monopolistic service regardless of individual feelings about the process.

Figure 4.8, in flow chart form, shows the various steps that probably will be present in the retail wheeled electricity process. Remember that the process shown here is the one envisioned by the author and may not be completely accurate with what actually may come to pass when retail wheeling becomes commonplace. Utilize this data only as a guide to the probable incremental steps that will be required in a retail wheeling transaction.

Figure 4.8
Wheeled Electricity Flow Chart

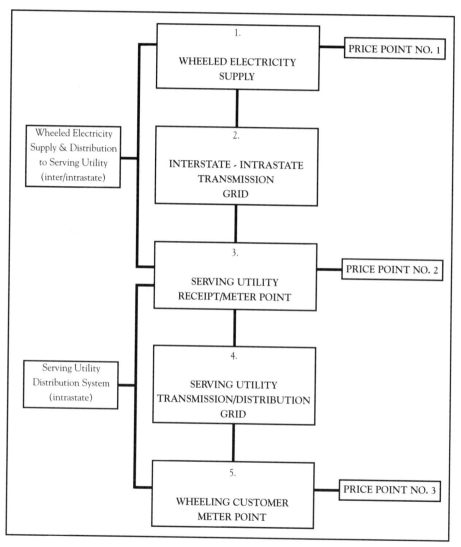

Explanation of Figure 4.8—
Wheeled Electricity Flow Chart

1. **Wheeled Electricity Supply—(Price Point No.1)**

   This will be the utility that is supplying the retail customer wheeled electricity. This utility will have to be physically connected to the electricity transmission/distribution grid that the customer's serving utility utilizes.

   The wheeling utility may be adjacent to the customer's serving utility or it may be in a different state as long as both the wheeling and wheeled-to parties have access to a common transmission grid.

   The costs accumulated at this point include the actual wheeling utility charges for the electricity. These costs will probably include both demand (kW) and usage (kWh) charges. Also, the customer being wheeled to will probably have a choice of either firm or interruptible service (kW and kWh).

2. **Interstate-Intrastate Transmission Grid**

   This is the transmission grid that links the wheeling utility to the wheeled customer's utility. This transmission grid may be interstate or intrastate depending upon where the wheeling utility is physically located in relation to the wheeled customer's utility. Generally, the grid will be governed by the Federal Energy Regulatory Commission. It is likely that the wheeled customer will have a choice of firm or interruptible transmission service.

3. **Serving Utility Receipt/Meter Point—(Price Point No.2)**
    This point will be where the wheeled customer's utility receives, meters, and takes title to the wheeled electricity. The costs at this point will include the wheeled electricity costs as accumulated in Price Point No. 1, plus the transmission grid costs to deliver the wheeled electricity to the wheeling customer's utility.

    Included in the transmission costs will be line loss factors due to the resistance of flow of electrons through the transmission grid. Generally, it will be advantageous for the wheeling customer to utilize as high a transmission voltage as is possible since there is less line loss at higher voltages.

4. **Serving Utility Transmission/Distribution Grid**
    This portion of the transmission/distribution system is intrastate and is part of the customer's serving utility grid. It is regulated on an intrastate basis by the appropriate regulatory agency. As retail wheeling of electricity evolves, it is the intrastate portion of the wheeling transaction that will be subject to the most regulatory change or (deregulation).

    Both the utilities as well as the regulatory agencies will have to perceive a real customer desire for retail wheeling before any major deregulation will occur. It is likely that line loss factors will affect this portion of the transaction much the same as occurred in the transmission/distribution grid between the wheeled electricity supply and the serving utility receipt point.

5. **Wheeling Customer Meter Point—(Price Point No. 3)**

This is the point at which the wheeled electricity passes through the retail customer's on-site electricity meter. Remember, the electricity the retail customer actually receives probably will never include any of the actual wheeled electrons that were transported to the serving utility. The reason for this is that the retail customer's wheeled electricity is co-mingled with all other electricity that is present in the transmission/distribution grid, both between the wheeled electricity supply and the serving utility receipt point, as well as between the serving utility receipt point and the retail customer's meter point. There is no problem with this since actual electrons of electricity are all the same.

The actual electrons of electricity that the customer will receive in the retail wheeling transaction will in all likelihood be the same as prior to the wheeling arrangement, much like the natural gas transportation process. The wheeled electricity received and metered at the serving utility receipt point will be recorded and credited to the retail wheeling customer much like a deposit in a bank savings account. During the billing month, the retail wheeling customer will have these deposits available to utilize as determined by the retail wheeling agreement.

The exact electrons deposited in the wheeling customer's account will probably not be the same electrons that are utilized by the wheeling customer, but as long as there are not more withdrawals than deposits, the overall system will remain in equilibrium. This may sound inordinately complicated, but basically this same process goes on daily where utilities wheel among themselves on a wholesale basis.

It would be very difficult to trace a given electron from generation point to use point, but the system works and remains in balance as long as the same quantity of deposits of electricity are available as there are withdrawals made. Since electricity cannot be practically stored, this electricity generation, transmission/distribution, use system must be essentially balanced all of the time—no small feat given the complexities of electricity generation/distribution in the United States.

Physically, retail wheeling will work. The problem will be all of the metering and related billing calculations concerning—line losses (under or over), usage of electricity by the customer, and many other cost items that will need to be addressed by all of the entities involved.

The total retail wheeled electricity cost to the using customer will be the sum of the costs accumulated in Price Points Nos. 1 and 2 and totaled in Price Point No. 3.

In most scenarios, the retail wheeling customer will probably utilize interruptible electricity and transmission up to the serving utility receipt point because of the probable differentials between firm and interruptible electricity costs to these points.

If a retail wheeling customer requires firm or non-interrupible electricity, there will probably be a back-up arrangement negotiated with the serving utility for supplemental electricity in the event of interruption of the customer's wheeled electricity.

Although retail wheeling of electricity is nothing like customer transportation of natural gas in technical and operational characteristics, it will appear similar in the process to the natural gas transportation transaction.

Figure 4.9
Retail Wheeled Electricity Cost Flow Chart

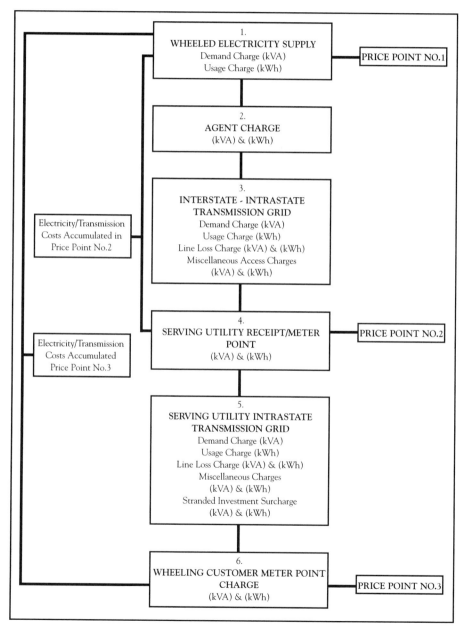

Explanation of Figure 4.9—
Retail Wheeled Electricity Cost Flow Chart

1. **Wheeled Electricity Supply-(Price Point No. 1)**

    Costs that are incurred in this area include the charges that the wheeling utility assesses for the electricity that is being wheeled to the retail wheeling customer.

    These charges will include both demand (kVA) costs as well as usage (kWh) costs. Additionally, there may be other charges based upon various factors which may affect either or both demand and usage costs. These wheeling customer charges could include items as follows:

    A. **Demand Measurement-(kVA)** Demand is utilized on a daily basis and is normally measured in intervals (15 or 30 minute periods, 24 hours a day); and, if the wheeling customer requires their demand during the wheeling utility's high demand periods, more expensive demand charges may occur.

    Alternately interruption of wheeled demand over a certain "base" threshold may occur as contractually agreed upon by both the wheeling and wheeled parties.

    B. **Available Rate Options-**There may be various options available to the wheeling customer similar to typical electricity tariff schedule rates that will require evaluation to determine the most advantageous rate structure to utilize.

    C. **Usage Penalties-**There may be power factor penalties when the wheeling utility measures demand in kW if the wheeling customer's efficiency falls below a certain level (80-90%). This type of penalty will not be present if the wheeling utility measures their demand in (kVA) since (kVA) does not require power factor correction factors.

D. Miscellaneous Charges-There may be various wheeled utility cost factors such as fuel cost adjustments, regulatory fees and taxes that could be passed through to the wheeling customer.

2. **Agent Charges—**Probably most wheeling customers will utilize the services of a third party to initiate and follow-up on the wheeling process much as is generally done in customer transportation of natural gas.

These third parties, whether brokers, marketers or producers, are technically known as agents since they act in the customer's behalf. These entities will probably perform at least the following functions for the retail wheeling customer:

A. Select an appropriate wheeled electricity supply source.

B. Select an appropriate interstate/intrastate transmission grid to move the customer's wheeled electricity from its origination point to the customer's serving utility meter/receipt point.

C. Negotiate the least expensive wheeled electricity and transmission rates for the customer.

D. Assist the wheeling customer in the contractual agreements that will be required. Probably there will be at least (three) different contracts required. One contract will be between the wheeled electricity supplier and the wheeling customer. A second contract will be between the transmission grid utilized between the wheeled electricity supply and the serving utility meter/receipt point, and the wheeling customer. And, a third contract will be required between the customer's serving electric utility for the transmission and other services that they provide to the wheeling customer. These contracts in a flow chart form will look as follows:

Figure 4.10

Contract Flow Chart

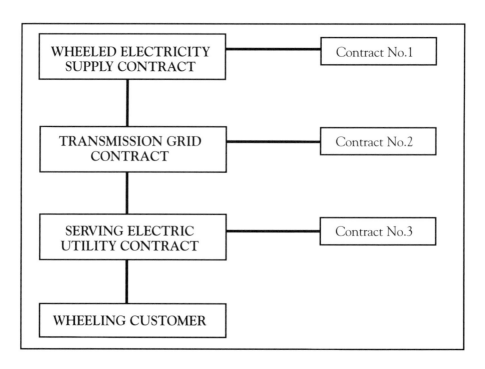

3. **Interstate/Intrastate Transmission Charges-**These charges will include the cost to move the customer's wheeled electricity from the generation point of the wheeling utility to the meter/receipt point of the wheeling customer's serving utility.

   Charges in this area will probably include both demand (kVA) as well as usage (kWh) charges. Also, transmission line loss costs will be calculated in this transaction. Other charges may occur such as transmission and access fees, FERC and/or state regulatory fees, and demand variability penalties or fees.

4./5. **Serving Utility Charges-**The serving utility charges will include probably both demand (kVA) as well as usage (kWh) costs. Also, line loss costs may be calculated in this area for the serving utility's transmission grid losses.

   Miscellaneous other charges that will probably be present may include state regulatory fees, state and/or local taxes, and rental/lease fees on meters and/or equipment that the wheeling customer requires to utilize their electricity and that is provided by the serving utility. Also, included in this section will probably be a charge for the serving utility's stranded investment costs.

   These stranded investment charges will be what the serving utility considers to be its investment in generation/distribution facilities for the wheeling customer. These facilities are not being utilized when the customer elects to purchase electricity from a source other than the serving utility.

   Whether these charges are justified or not is open to debate but at least initially expect to see these types of charges present on any retail wheeling transaction you initiate.

6. **Wheeling Customer Meter Point-**The total wheeled electricity charges will include all costs listed in items 1-5. The total of these costs will be compared to non-wheeled electricity costs to determine the viability of utilizing retail wheeling.

Figure 4.11 shows the probable incremental steps in retail wheeled electricity. This outline is the author's best estimate as to the various incremental costs that will be present in a typical retail wheeling transaction. Do not necessarily expect all retail wheeling transactions to contain the exact incremental steps as shown here.

This outline is provided only as a tool to provide insight into what probably will happen on an incremental basis in retail wheeling transactions. When retail wheeling actually becomes available on a widespread basis, the various utilities involved will have their own individual incremental cost steps much the same as they now have different types of tariff schedules.

Figure 4.11

The Probable Incremental
Steps in Retail Wheeled Electricity

Total peak demand required per month _____

Total usage required per month _____

Incremental Pricing of Wheeled Electricity	Cost Per kVA	Cost Per kWh	Monthly Charge
1. Wheeled electricity generation point.(PRICE POINT #1)	$ _____	$ _____	$ _____
2. Fuel cost adjustment.	$ _____	$ _____	$ _____
3. Agent charges.	$ _____	$ _____	$ _____
4. Interstate transmission grid charges:			
A. Firm.	$ _____	$ _____	$ _____
B. Interruptible.	$ _____	$ _____	$ _____
5. Interstate transmission losses.	$ _____	$ _____	$ _____
6. FERC mandated charges.	$ _____	$ _____	$ _____
7. Miscellaneous charges:			
_____	$ _____	$ _____	$ _____
_____	$ _____	$ _____	$ _____
8. Intrastate receipt point. (PRICE POINT #2)			
(Total of Items #1 through #7)	$ _____	$ _____	$ _____
9. Intrastate transmission grid charges:			
A. Firm.	$ _____	$ _____	$ _____
B. Interruptible.	$ _____	$ _____	$ _____
10. Intrastate transmission losses.	$ _____	$ _____	$ _____
11. State Regulatory Agency mandated fees	$ _____	$ _____	$ _____
12. Intrastate utility charges including.			
(Transformation, Switchgear, Meter, etc. charges)	$ _____	$ _____	$ _____
13. Miscellaneous charges:			
_____	$ _____	$ _____	$ _____
_____	$ _____	$ _____	$ _____
14. Customer meter point. (PRICE POINT #3)			
(Total of Items #1 through #7 and Items #9 through #13)	$ _____	$ _____	$ _____

To better understand how costs might look in an actual retail wheeling transaction, Figure 4.12 is provided. The actual incremental costs shown in this figure are my best estimate as to how these costs will be structured.

I have no hard facts to serve as a basis for the costs shown other than my insight into the way electric utility costs occur in general. This cost data should be utilized only as an example of what will be involved in a typical retail wheeling transaction. For the purpose of this figure, the following assumptions will be made:

1. Peak demand required on a monthly basis - 1,250 kVA
2. Usage on a monthly basis - 850,000 kWh.
3. Customer will utilize interruptible demand and usage for the wheeled electricity and transmission to the serving utility's meter/receipt point (#8).
4. Customer will utilize serving utility (intrastate) firm transportation so that back-up demand and usage is available if there is an interruption of wheeled power.
5. The rate structure will be a standard rate type with no (on, shoulder, or off-peak) demand designations. Also, the usage will be a standard single cost non-ratcheted structure.
6. The wheeling customers power factor will be 95%+ so that no power factor penalty will occur on the serving utility's system where demand will be measured in kW, not kVA.

Figure 4.12

The Probable Incremental Steps in
Retail Wheeled Electricity - (Filled Out Form)

Total peak demand required per month _____1,250 kVA_____

Total usage required per month _____850,000 kWh_____

Incremental Pricing of Wheeled Electricity	Cost Per kVA	Cost Per kWh	Monthly Charge
1. Wheeled electricity generation point.(PRICE POINT #1)	$ 4.5000	$ .0111	$ _____
2. Fuel cost adjustment.	$ _____	$ .0100	$ _____
3. Agent charges.	$ _____	$ .0010	$ _____
4. Interstate transmission grid charges:			
A. Firm.	$ _____	$ _____	$ _____
B. Interruptible.	$ _____	$ .0030	$ _____
5. Interstate transmission losses. (1%)	$ .0450	$ .0002	$ _____
6. FERC mandated charges.	$ _____	$ .0001	$ _____
7. Miscellaneous charges:			
(Grid access charges)	$ _____	$ .0001	$ _____
_____	$ _____	$ _____	$ _____
8. Intrastate receipt point. (PRICE POINT #2)			
(Total of Items #1 through #7)	$ 4.5450	$ .0255	$ _____
9. Intrastate transmission grid charges:			
A. Firm.	$ .2500	$ .0030	$ _____
B. Interruptible.	$ _____	$ _____	$ _____
10. Intrastate transmission losses. (1%)	$ .0480	$ .0003	$ _____
11. State Regulatory Agency mandated fees	$ _____	$ .0001	$ _____
12. Intrastate utility charges including.			
(Transformation, Switchgear, Meter, etc. charges)	$ _____	$ _____	$ 200.00
13. Miscellaneous charges:			
(Customer charge)	$ _____	$ _____	$ 100.00
(Stranded investment cost adjustment)	$ _____	$ .0010	$ _____
14. Customer meter point. (PRICE POINT #3)			
(Total of Items #1 through #7 and Items #9 through #13)	$ 4.8430	$ .0299	$ 300.00

Explanation of Data in Figure 4.12

The information shown in Figure 4.13 provides an illustration of how a cost comparison could be done between retail wheeled and serving utility provided electricity.

Figure 4.13
Wheeled Electricity Cost Per Month

1,250 kVA	X	$ 4.843/kVA	=	$ 6,053.75
850,000 kWh	X	$.0299/kWh	=	$ 25,415.00
Customer/equipment Charge ($300.00)			=	$ 300.00
		TOTAL	**=**	**$ 31,768.75**

COST PER kWh $ .0374

SERVING UTILITY PROVIDED ELECTRICITY COST PER MONTH

1,250 kVA	X	$ 6.00/kVA	=	$7,500.00
850,000 kWh	X	$.0420/kWh	=	$ 35,700.00
Customer/equipment Charge ($200.00)			=	$ 200.00
		TOTAL	**=**	**$ 43,400.00**

COST PER kWh $ .0510

SAVINGS   = $ 11,631.25

% SAVINGS   =   27%

1. **Wheeled Electricity Generation Point—(Price Point #1)**
    Cost per kVA - $4.5000
    Cost per kWh - $0.0111

Shown here is the cost of the generated electricity for both demand (kVA) and usage (kWh). These are the costs for the wheeled electricity at the point of generation. These costs do not include any distribution of the electricity.

These costs will be negotiated between the seller (wheeling utility) and the purchaser (wheeling customer). These costs probably will be negotiated monthly or fixed for a certain period such as 6 to 12 months.

A spot market pricing index will probably be established to be utilized as a guide to wheeled electricity costs at point of generation. This spot market pricing index probably will be similar to what is now used in the natural gas industry.

In all probability, these electricity costs will be based upon an interruptible basis. The wheeling customer will "firm up" the transaction on either the serving utility's distribution grid or by the installations of on-site back-up generation capacity.

2. **Fuel Cost Adjustment—**
    Cost per kWh - $0.0100

The fuel cost adjustment allows the wheeling utility to recover the actual cost of fuel to operate their generation facilities. These costs apply to all utility customers equally without regard to usage size.

The cost shown here would apply to retail customers of this utility the same as it would to those wheeling electricity. The fuel cost adjustment always occurs where the electricity is generated. Also, this cost only applies to usage (kWh), not to demand (kVA).

3. **Agent Charges—**
   Cost per kWh   - $0.0010

This charge is to compensate the wheeling customer's agent for his/her services. These services would generally include the following items:

A. Evaluate and obtain the lowest cost electricity for the wheeling customer.

B. Arrange for and initiate required contracts in behalf of wheeling customer.

C. Evaluate and obtain the best, least costly distribution path for the wheeling customer's electricity.

D. Provide special services for the wheeling customer such as firm pricing for a fixed period of time, providing assurance that the wheeled electricity will be distributed to the customer's serving utility receipt point (see item #8).

   Assure that the customer will be held harmless (legally not liable) for any wheeling customer serving utility penalties or other charges relating to non-delivered electricity to serving utility receipt point.

E.   Negotiate discounted interstate transmission rates because of the volume of wheeled electricity they send through the grid on the behalf of multiple individual retail wheeling customers. These discounts should always be passed through to the individual retail wheeling customers represented by the agent.

The actual fee that is paid to the agent will be negotiable based both upon the volume of electricity the wheeling customer utilizes, as well as negotiation abilities the wheeling customer possesses. Although it will probably be possible for a wheeling customer to perform the entire wheeling transaction without agent assistance, it probably will not be cost effective to do so.

4.   Interstate Transmission Grid Charges—
Interruptible Cost per kWh   - $0.0030

This is the charge the wheeling customer pays to the interstate transmission grid owner to transport the wheeled electricity across this grid. Normally, these transmission grids will be interstate in nature—between or outside of individual states.

The terms and conditions for transportation of wheeled electricity will be determined by the Federal Energy Regulatory Commission (FERC). Even though these transmission grids cross many individual states, they are considered to be interstate (between states) in nature.

It is likely that these transmission grids will be required to transport wheeled electricity on a nondiscriminatory basis and generally offer at least two categories of service—firm and interruptible. Where possible, a wheeling customer should utilize all transmission grids available for transportation of the wheeled electricity.

Doing this will provide increased flexibility in transmission grid capacity as well as the potential for lower transportation rates due to competition. If the wheeling customer utilizes an agent, the agent should provide this service without charge. Both firm (non-interrupible) and interruptible transportation will probably be offered to retail wheeling customers.

It will probably be normally less expensive to utilize interruptible interstate transportation of wheeled electricity and, if required, opt for firm serving utility transportation. It would be of no value to utilize firm wheeled electricity and firm interstate transmission grid transportation only to have the electricity interrupted on the serving utility's distribution grid. If firm wheeled electricity is required, only "firm up" the transaction in the serving utility's territory.

5. **Interstate Transmission Losses (1%)—**
    Cost per kVA   -   **$0.0450**
    Cost per kWh   -   **$0.0002**

These charges are for electricity losses on the transmission grid due to the resistance of flow of electrons across the grid. These losses are real and appear as generation capacity loss to the generating utility.

The losses shown in this section will have been approved by the appropriate regulatory agency, in this case FERC. The losses indicated in this section will apply to all transmission grid users whether retail wheeling or not. These losses will probably be applicable to both demand (kVA) as well as usage (kWh).

6. **FERC Mandated Charges—**
    Cost per kWh   - $0.0001

Since FERC will probably be in charge of the retail wheeling transaction across the interstate transmission grid, they may assess some retail wheeling customer charges. These charges will be structured to return the costs FERC incurs in their oversight of the retail wheeling transaction.

These charges, if they exist, will probably be assessed on the usage portion of the transaction (kWh). Whatever form these fees take, they will be uniformly assessed across all retail wheeling customers.

7. **Miscellaneous Charges—(Grid Access Charges)**
    Cost per kWh   - $0.0001

As this item indicates, any charges/costs that occur on a random or inconsistent basis are itemized/accumulated in this miscellaneous section. In this particular example, grid access charges are being assessed.

Many utilities contend that when a retail wheeling customer wants to utilize their transmission grid, there should be a charge for doing so. Part of this reasoning is that when a retail wheeling customer utilizes the normally wholesale transmission grid, there are special metering, switching, and other retail wheeling specific costs that occur.

Whether this rationale is valid is open to conjecture. If retail wheeling across a transmission's grid is priced based upon true "cost of service" principles, there is no rationale for access charges.

However, do not be surprised if these types of charges are present at least initially in the retail wheeling transaction, if for no other reason than "revenue enhancement."

8. **Intrastate Receipt Point—(Price Point #2)**
    (Total of Items #1 through #7)
    Cost per kVA   - $4.5450
    Cost per kWh   - $0.0255

This receipt point cost includes all costs accumulated from the point of the electricity generation through its transmission to the wheeling customer's serving utility receipt or meter point. At this point, the costs incurred are primarily interstate and as such will probably be regulated by FERC.

9. **Intrastate Transmission Grid Charges—**
    Firm Cost per kVA   - $0.2500
    Firm Cost per kWh   - $0.0030

This transmission cost reflects the wheeling customer's serving utility's charge to transport the wheeled electricity across this grid. The terms and conditions for this wheeling transportation charge will be regulated on an intrastate regulatory agency basis.

If a retail wheeling customer cannot be interrupted, or if he/she has no on-site back-up generation capacity, this will be the point to opt for firm transportation. Firm transportation of wheeled electricity across this grid simply means one of two things will occur based upon the serving utility's tariff schedule provisions relating to firm transportation as follows:

A.   The serving utility may consider firm transportation as being that the serving utility will assure the wheeled electricity will arrive at the customer's meter point if the serving utility receives it at the receipt point.

In effect, this arrangement only assures delivery of the wheeled electricity if it is delivered to the serving utility's receipt point. The serving utility does not assure that any wheeled electricity will be delivered to the customer if the utility does not receive any of the customer's wheeled electricity from the interstate transmission grid. This type of firm transportation is not as desirable as the second type.

B.   The serving utility may consider firm transportation as providing the wheeling customer assurance that electricity will be delivered to the customer's meter point even though the customer's wheeled electricity does not arrive at the utility's receipt point.

In this arrangement, the serving utility will provide the wheeling customer with "system supply" electricity if the wheeled electricity is interrupted. Of the two types of firm transportation, this is the preferred interpretation.

If the serving utility only assures delivery of the customer's wheeled electricity across the transmission grid, the customer may still have to provide on-site back-up generation if interruptability cannot be tolerated.

Also, remember firm transportation, even in its best form, is actually like term insurance—it accrues no value and ceases to exist if the required fee is not paid on a monthly basis.

When evaluating firm transportation, always consider whether it would be more advantageous to utilize the firm transportation surcharges to construct an on-site back-up generation facility which would have real value.

10. **Intrastate Transmission Losses (1%)—**
    Cost per kVA   - $0.0480
    Cost per kWh   - $0.0003

This item is similar to item #5 and compensates the serving utility for any transmission losses due to the resistance of flow of electrons across the intrastate transmission grid.

11. **State Regulatory Agency Mandated Fees—**
    Cost per kWh   - $0.0001

These fees are similar to those in item #6. Many states, because of difficult financial conditions, are requiring all state agencies that directly regulate or serve a specific public sector to obtain their revenue from that sector.

In the past, many of these agencies received their funds from general state revenues. These fees are normally assessed on a unit basis, (kWh) in electricity and (Dth) in natural gas.

12. **Intrastate Utility Charges Including—**
    (Transformation, Switchgear, Meter, Etc. Charges)
    Monthly Charge   - $200
    These charges would not normally appear as line-item entries on an

electric utility billing since they would be included in other areas of the "bundled" charges.

Since a retail wheeling customer will only be utilizing the serving utility's transmission grid and not normally be consuming serving utility generated electricity, these "equipment" charges must be itemized as separate entries.

13. Miscellaneous Charges—
    Monthly Customer Charge   - $100
    Stranded Investment Cost Adjustment   - $0.0010/kWh

These charges as indicated in the headings are miscellaneous in nature. This is a "catch-all" classification and may include many items not addressed in other areas of the transaction. In this particular example, two items are included—customer and stranded investment charges as follows:

A.   **Customer Charges**—These are charges that the utility assesses a customer just to be a customer. These charges generally are to compensate the utility for its cost to service the customer's account—meter reading, billing, etc.

     Customer charges range from nothing to many thousands of dollars per month. Customer charges, if present, are approved by the appropriate regulatory agency before they are implemented.

B.   **Stranded Investment Cost Adjustment**—$0.0010/kWh These charges, at least in theory, are to compensate the serving utility for its investment in various tangible assets for the retail customer's use. If the retail customer only utilizes the serving utility's transmission grid to retail wheel the customer's electricity, then the utility's generation investment for the retail customer is stranded.

When this happens, the serving utility reasons that it should be compensated for at least the unrecovered portion of such investment. In a regulated monopolistic environment, this reasoning can probably be rationalized. But if true open market pressures occur, serving utilities will find it difficult to win surcharges like this. Do not be surprised if, at least initially, these types of charges are assessed to retail wheeling customers.

14. **Customer Meter Point—(Price Point #3)**
    Total Cost Per kVA   - $ 4.8430
    Total Cost Per kWh   - $ 0.0299
    Total Monthly Charges   - $ 300

This entry totals all of the various costs that have occurred in Items #1 through #13. These costs represent the retail wheeling customer's total cost to retail wheel electricity to the meter point.

As was outlined at the beginning of this billing analysis, don't expect a particular retail wheeling transaction to look exactly like this example. Use the information provided to obtain an overview of how the retail wheeling transaction might appear as well as an outline of the components that will be required in the procedure.

Roadblocks to Retail Wheeling of Electricity

Thus far, it might appear that there are few hindrances to the retail wheeling process; however, this is far from the truth of the matter. Technically, the process is possible but the problem is within the utility structure itself and its resistance to change. In defense of the utilities, it is and will be very difficult to make the transition. No one eagerly embraces competition—I certainly do not.

To move from a highly regulated and vertically integrated structure with a virtual lack of true competition is no easy task. It will happen, however, due to retail customer and general
market pressures—some utilities will grow and become stronger and some will cease to exist. The reasons for these difficult transitions are many but some of the more prominent are described.

The majority of the electric power market in the United States historically has been the responsibility of for-profit investor-owned utilities operating as a monopoly with regulation at both the federal and state levels. These "regulated monopolies", at least in theory, have the necessary checks and balances in place that preclude the problems normally associated with monopolistic entities.

The problem is that potentially, from a cost point of view, the current system leaves something to be desired. True "cost of service" electricity rates, even when present, tend to be inflated due to operating cost pass-throughs that probably would not be tolerated in a deregulated environment.

The simple fact is that with no direct competition, electric utilities, even with the current regulatory safeguards, tend to be cost plus operations, which from a purchaser's viewpoint may not result in the least costly electricity that could be provided. A monopolistic industry may provide many things, but generally efficiency and competitive costs are not included in the list of benefits.

Currently, there are approximately 200 for-profit, 1,972 municipal, and

1,073 cooperative electric utilities in the United States that are all separately regulated. Each of these approximately 3,200+ utilities are separately regulated through federal, state, and local regulatory bodies whose rate making policies sometimes defy logic.

These are instances where electric utilities that are side-by-side have very different types of rates as well as substantial cost differences. These utilities may be on the same transmission grid, in the same state, and serve the same types of customers, yet have very different incremental cost structures.

One of the first roadblocks that must be removed before electric utilities will be truly competitive is the overly complex and highly structured state regulatory process. Although dismantling or, at the very least, reducing the control state regulators have over the electric utilities would seem to be a logical step to take—there is much resistance to this. Both the regulators themselves, as well as the electric utilities they regulate, are for the most part very opposed to any such tinkering with their systems. Each of these groups has a vested interest in preserving its power, resources, and prestige and, each may attempt to camouflage their real concern (competition) with well written rhetoric.

Politically active, well organized and well financed, they could cause electricity users to pay more for electricity than could probably result in a less regulated, more competitive environment. Another roadblock to some extent is self-interest. State Regulatory Commissioners who serve in utility regulatory capacities could be at least indirectly affected if electricity should become more deregulated—they could find themselves out of a job.

Another voiced concern is that of the degradation of service to small consumers who cannot take direct advantage of the competitive environment. Will utilities leave the marginally or less profitable market segment without dependable service? What about safety or integrity of the electricity generation system—will competition force utilities to lower costs by keeping older marginal equipment in service?

Will they be forced to reduce system maintenance which could result in massive power outages?What will happen if some electric utilities cannot compete—will they go out of business; and, if they do, what will happen to their customers?What about the transmission grid capacity—will it fail because of all of the retail customers that will choose to wheel their electricity if given the opportunity?

What about an electric utility's stranded investment in capital equipment that would not be utilized if retail customers elected to wheel their electricity. Who would pay for this investment—the customers that are captive to the utility, or the utility stockholders?

I do not pretend to be able to answer all of these questions, but the same types of questions could be asked in any industry that is faced with competition. No one that is in business (myself included) likes competition because it is more difficult to be profitable if someone else can offer the same product or service to a customer I now have. I personally do not feel that electric utilities are the "bad guys." Change is difficult, especially as dramatic a change as is currently being thrust upon electric utilities. Probably there has never been a more radical change taking place in the electric utility industry than there now is.

Electricity is going to be more a commodity than a service in the future and when any product or service is reduced to this status, it becomes more difficult to make or provide it at a profit. Customer retail wheeling of electricity will occur whether the arguments for or against it are valid or not because the electricity customer wants it.

It will be neither all bad nor all good, but it will change forever the way in which electric utilities operate. As a retail electricity customer, if you want to keep your costs as low as they can be, you need to understand the impact this change will have on you in particular and the industry in general.

A good pro and con argument about retail wheeling of electricity can be had from the following sources:

PRO Retail Wheeling -

Retail Wheeling - Expanding Competition in the Electric Utility Industry, April 1991, by: Jay B. Kennedy and Richard A. Baudino. (202) 383-0151

CON Retail Wheeling -

The Case Against Retail Wheeling, July 1992, by: Staff of Edison Electric Institute with assistance of Joe D. Pace and William W. Lindsay of Putnam, Hayes & Bartlett, Inc. (202) 508-5425

The Agents That Will Be Used for Other Than Serving Utility-Supplied Electricity

This section details the various agents for retail wheeled electricity. This information will provide the background necessary to be able to intelligently determine which method should be used to provide the electricity you will need at the reliability required. The information given herein provides the foundation for doing retail wheeling transactions.

Retail Wheeling Information

Generally, retail wheeling (direct purchase) will be provided by at least three different entities—(1) brokers, (2) marketers, and (3) producers. The three entities are explained:

1. **Brokers**—Most retail wheeled electricity that will be available to customers will not be obtained from the serving utility. Other parties like brokers will actively market electricity to retail customers. The main and most important distinction between

brokers and producers will be the fact that brokers will not take or assume title to the electricity they will market.

These brokers will act only as third party facilitators. They, in effect, will sell for someone else. Brokers will act as agents, but will not actually take title to the electricity they will sell. Brokers will be paid a fee for their services by either the buyer or seller.

This is not to say broker retail wheeled electricity will be unreliable or in anyway different from purchasing from a titled source. The thing to remember is that since title will not pass to the brokers, their warranty as to availability will be no better than their source will provide.

In general, the fewer steps required to arrive at the actual electricity generation source, the more reliable the supply. Do not disregard broker supplied electricity but remember they will be able to provide no better title to the electricity they will market than what they will have—which is none.

If a broker will be used, make sure(1) their source will be identified, (2) the supply will be assured for the duration of the contract, and (3) their source will have title to the electricity that they will provide to you. In general, it will probably be better, both on long-term cost and availability, if you contract with either a marketer or an electricity producer.

2.   **Marketers**—Marketers will differ from brokers in that they will take title to the electricity they will sell the wheeling customer. A marketer will take title to the electricity but probably will not have or own the generation facilities.

Marketers, or marketing affiliates, will also probably be known in the electric industry as "traders."While all of this may seem confusing, remember the difference between this category and the broker category will be that title to the electricity will pass with the marketer where it will not with the broker.

The difference between marketers and producers, will be that producers will own electricity generation facilities and marketers will not.

The marketer category probably will be the largest supplier of retail wheeled electricity. As with any group of individual entities, there will be good and bad available, so be certain that any contracts to be negotiated will conform in general to the one that will be described in this section.

3. **Producers**—Producers will have title to and will also own electricity generation facilities. They will be the original owners of the electricity and will be responsible for its generation and distribution to an interstate transmission grid.

Some producers will probably market their own electricity directly to the retail wheeling customers. And, most likely, several generators will join together to form a cooperative that will in turn market the electricity to retail wheeling customers.

Producers, as such, probably will not be a dominant force in the retail wheeling market. They, in general, will sell their product to either a transmission grid, serving utility, or marketer, who in turn will supply the retail wheeling customer.

Basic Differences Between Brokers, Marketers and Producers

1.   Brokers- Will not take title to or will not own generation facilities.
2.   Marketers- Will take title to but probably will not own generation facilities.
3.   Producers- Will have title to and will own generation facilities.

Synopsis

Generally, there will be no reason to limit the choice of your supplier strictly on the basis of the category (broker, marketer, or producer). The criteria for selecting a supplier will be based upon data such as-

1.   Reliability of supply
2.   Price
3.   Transmission distribution routing
4.   Contract language
5.   Retail wheeling customer service
6.   Congeniality between buyer and seller

Making these evaluations will be no simple matter. Sometimes reliance upon the broker, marketer, or producer for help will be possible; however, they will be motivated primarily by a desire to sell their service, not necessarily to satisfy the needs of the customer. The surest method to follow will be to have a set of guidelines like the ones described in this publication, and evaluate any potential supplier in terms of these guidelines.

Chapter 5

Understanding Electric Utility Billing

Understanding the Electric Billing

To be able to analyze the electric bill, an understanding of the items on the bill is a must. The following items are common to practically all electric bills and each needs to be analyzed individually to assure that the billing is as low as possible.

Items Common to Electric Billings

1. **Meter Readings**—Meters are normally read on a monthly basis with kWh registers progressing numerically depending upon the usage. Generally, kW registers are reset to "0" each month since demand is calculated on a timer basis, ordinarily the 15 or 30 minute highest kW period of the month.

2. **Meter Multiplier**—Meter correction factor.

3. **Usage**—Measurement of combined electrical usage of all equipment during the billing period.

4. **Demand**—Measurement of peak pressure or utility generation capacity utilized during the billing period.

5. **Customer Rate Classification**—Indicates tariff schedule rate applicability.

6. **Voltage Levels**—Secondary, primary, etc.

7. **Power Factor**—Efficiency at which electricity is used.

8. **Contract Demand**—This can apply to an actual contract established between the customer and the utility; or, it can apply to a tariff clause that establishes a floor for costs regardless of usage.

9. **Customer Charge**—Monthly charge for the meter, reading of the meter, and other billing related items.

10. **Ratchet Clauses**—Can apply both to demand and usage components in the billing process. This clause establishes a floor below which costs will not fall regardless of usage.

11. **Fuel Cost Adjustment Clause**—This clause allows for fuel cost variations to be passed through to the customer base of the utility.

12. **Facility Charges**—When this charge is present, it represents some physical piece of equipment that is required or requested by the customer for their usage. This charge represents a lease cost by the customer.

13. **Special Public Utility Commission (PUC) Charge**—This charge is for the operation of the State Regulatory Commission.

14. **Non-fuel Energy Charge and Miscellaneous Energy Cost Adjustments**—These and other miscellaneous charges may be present in various utility service districts and can only be addressed when and where they occur.

15. **Taxes**—Taxes can be many—state sales tax, state utility tax, municipal tax, school tax, etc.

16. **Total Current Bill**—This is the accumulative total of charges for the billing month shown.

17. **Previous Amount Due, Payment Received, Total Amount Due**—These figures record the last month's payment data and shows the customer's total charges due for the billing month.

To better understand what all of the 17 items might look like on an actual electricity billing, a sample has been given in Figure 5.1. This sample is a composite of several different actual billings and will serve to illustrate what these 17 items could look like on a real electricity billing. On most billings not all of the 17 items will be present, but it is important to recognize any of these items if they are listed.

Always remember that electric billings, both as to form and content, vary greatly from utility to utility. It sometimes seems that the only uniformity in utility billing is that there is no uniformity in procedures or data provided. If a utility billing cannot be understood, contact the local utility service representative for an explanation of the terms contained on the billing.

Figure 5.1

Sample—Composite Electric Utility Billing

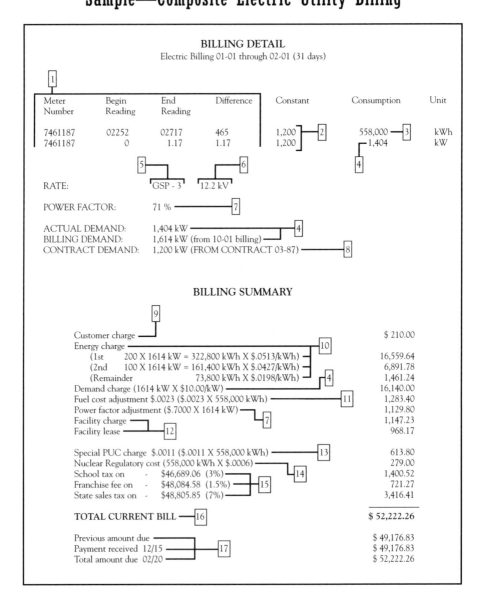

BILLING DETAIL
Electric Billing 01-01 through 02-01 (31 days)

1

Meter Number	Begin Reading	End Reading	Difference	Constant	Consumption	Unit
7461187	02252	02717	465	1,200 ⎤2	558,000 —3	kWh
7461187	0	1.17	1.17	1,200 ⎦	⌐1,404	kW

5⎤   ⌐6   4

RATE: GSP - 3   12.2 kV

POWER FACTOR: 71 % ——————7

ACTUAL DEMAND: 1,404 kW ——————————4
BILLING DEMAND: 1,614 kW (from 10-01 billing) ⎦
CONTRACT DEMAND: 1,200 kW (FROM CONTRACT 03-87) ——————8

BILLING SUMMARY

9

Customer charge ⎤9	$ 210.00
Energy charge ——————————————10	
(1st 200 X 1614 kW = 322,800 kWh X $.0513/kWh) ⎤	16,559.64
(2nd 100 X 1614 kW = 161,400 kWh X $.0427/kWh) ⎦	6,891.78
(Remainder 73,800 kWh X $.0198/kWh) ⌐4	1,461.24
Demand charge (1614 kW X $10.00/kW) ———————	16,140.00
Fuel cost adjustment $.0023 ($.0023 X 558,000 kWh) ——————11	1,283.40
Power factor adjustment ($.7000 X 1614 kW) ⎤	1,129.80
Facility charge ⎤ 7	1,147.23
Facility lease ——⎦12	968.17
Special PUC charge $.0011 ($.0011 X 558,000 kWh) ——————13	613.80
Nuclear Regulatory cost (558,000 kWh X $.0006) ———————	279.00
School tax on - $46,689.06 (3%) ⎤	1,400.52
Franchise fee on - $48,084.58 (1.5%) ⎤14	721.27
State sales tax on - $48,805.85 (7%) ⎦15	3,416.41
TOTAL CURRENT BILL ⎤16	**$ 52,222.26**
Previous amount due ———————	$ 49,176.83
Payment received 12/15 ——————17	$ 49,176.83
Total amount due 02/20 ———————	$ 52,222.26

Explanation of Composite Electric Billing in Figure 5.1

1. Meter Readings—

    Usage difference 465 units

    Demand difference 1.17 units

    Meter readings are normally read on a monthly basis with kWh registers progressing numerically based upon the actual kWh usage during the month. Generally, kW demand level readings are reset to "0" at the beginning of each month. KW demand level is calculated differently from kWh readings since kW demand level is measured on an incremental time basis, generally 15 or 30 minute intervals.

    KW demand is not a recording of electricity usage but rather is an indication of utility reserve capacity utilized by the customer during the billing month. The actual usage of electricity during this billing month as recorded by this meter was 465 kWh units.

    The actual reserve capacity required from the utility by the customer in this billing month as recorded on this meter was 1.17 kW units. Since electricity meters measure electricity flow at some fractional percentage of actual electricity flow, a multiplying constant is applied to the raw meter readings to determine the actual quantities used in the billing month.

    In this particular meter, the multiplying constant is 1,200. This means that all actual meter readings must be multiplied by 1,200 to determine true electricity usage levels. (See Item 2 following— "Meter Multiplier".) Meter multipliers are utilized to allow meter construction to be less costly.

If meters were installed directly across the total electricity load, they would be prohibitively expensive to build. To circumvent this problem, meters sample at some fraction of true total electricity flow and utilize a multiplying factor to connect actual meter readings to true electricity usage data.

2. Meter Multiplier—

Figure 5.2
Meter Multiplier Example

Meter Number	7461187	7461187
Begin Reading	02252	
End Reading	02717	1.17
Difference	465	1.17
Constant	1,200	1,200
Consumption	558,000	1,404
Unit	kWh	kW

The meter multiplier is utilized to correlate actual meter readings with actual usages. Meters generally do not measure the entire electrical load being utilized by the customer, but rather sample or measure a portion of the total load. To correlate the meter sample reading with the actual electrical load, it is necessary to determine a "constant" by which the meter reading can be multiplied to arrive at true usage figures.

The meter on the billing has a "constant" of 1,200, which means that the "raw" meter figures must be multiplied by 1,200 to arrive at a true usage number for both usage (kWh) and demand (kW). On the usage (kWh) portion of the meter, the beginning meter reading was 02252 and the ending reading was 02717. The total meter indicated usage was (02252 - 02717) = 465 . This number, 465, must be multiplied by 1,200 to arrive at the total usage (465 X 1,200) = 558,000 kWh.

On the demand (kW) portion of the meter, the indicated demand was the highest 15 minute interval in the month. Since the demand cycle starts over each month, the meter is reset to "0" each month and records the highest peak generated during the month. The monthly peak demand data is stored within the meter and extracted at the month's end by the meter reader.

It will be noted that the demand meter reading numbers are much smaller than are those for the usage portion of the meter since the total demand unit (1.17) is much smaller than the usage (465) number. As with the usage number, the demand number is multiplied by 1,200 to arrive at the actual total.

$$(1.17 \ X \ 1,200 \ = \ 1,404 \ kW)$$

3. Usage—
558,000 kWh
Total Energy Charge: $24,912.66

Usage, as it appears on an electricity utility billing, represents the total number of kilowatt hours (kWh) used during the billing period. In this particular billing, a total of 558,000 kWh were used. For Rate Code GSP-3 in the tariff schedule, the cost per kWh of electricity is established based upon the relationship of usage (kWh) to ratcheted demand (kW) as follows:

- The first 200 kWh of usage X billing demand for current month (1,614 kW) at $0.0513/kWh.
  200 X 1,614 = 322,800 kWh X $0.0513/kWh = $16,559.64

- The second 100 kWh of usage X billing demand for the current month (1,614 kW) at $0.0427/kWh.
  100 X 1,614 = 161,400 kWh X $0.0427/kWh = $6,891.78

- All kWh over the amount consumed in the first two steps (322,800 kWh + 161,400 kWh = 484,200 kWh) will be billed at $0.0198/kWh.
  Total kWh usage 558,000/kWh - 484,200 kWh = 73,800 kWh 73,800 kWh X $0.0198/kWh = $1,461.24

Total KWH Charge For Current Billing Month = $24,912.66

When kWh are billed in this manner, the utility is in reality telling the customer to reduce the demand (kW) in relation to their usage (kWh) since this will not only reduce overall demand cost, but will also reduce usage cost since fewer (kWh) units will be calculated at the higher first increments.

Example:

If the billing demand for this month were 1,000 kW, the following (kWh) usage charges would result:

- 1st 200 kWh of usage -
  200 X 1,000 = 200,000 kWh X $0.0513/kWh = $10,260.00

- 2nd 100 kWh of usage -
  100 X 1,000 = 100,000 kWh X $0.0427/kWh = $4,270.00

- All other kWh -
  258,000 kWh X $0.0198/kWh = $5,108.40

  Total KWH Cost for Current Billing Month = $19,638.40
  The savings in (kWh) cost alone would be—
  $24,912.66 - $19,638.40 = $5,274.26
  (or over 10% of the total billing amount)

Corrective Measures: Try to reduce demand (kW) in relation to (kWh) usage.

4. **Demand—**
   Actual demand: 1,440 kW
   The actual demand for this month was 1,440 kW. This particular utility, as defined in the tariff schedule, measures the demand on a 15 minute integrated average. To determine the monthly demand level, the highest 15 minute integrated average peak is utilized.

Unfortunately, the actual demand for this particular month had no impact on demand cost since the billing demand was determined by the demand (1,614 kW) established in October of the previous year due to a demand ratchet clause in the tariff schedule.

5.   **Customer Rate Classification—**
     Rate: GSP-3
     The rate classification for this billing is GSP-3. This rate when identified in the tariff schedule is described as a "General Service, Primary Voltage Rate." Once the rate classification is located in the tariff schedule, a detailed description of the terms and conditions of the rate are available.

6.   **Voltage Level—**
     12.2 kV
     The voltage level is shown to be primary voltage in the Rate Code GSP-3. The specific voltage is shown here as 12.2 kV (12,200 volts). Many times the specific voltage is not shown on the utility billing but can always be determined from the tariff schedule description for the rate code being utilized.

7.   **Power Factor—**
     Power factor: 71%
     Power factor adjustment: $1,129.80
     The power factor or relative efficiency of the customer's electrical system is shown to be 71%. Checking the tariff schedule, listed under "Power Factor Penalties," it is found that the following conditions apply:

     > *"For any power factor less than 85%, a penalty of $.05 per kW of billing demand for every 1% under 85% will be imposed."*

On this particular billing, this penalty is calculated as follows:
85% - 71% = 14%
14 X $.05 = $.70
$.70 X 1,614 kW billing demand = $1,129.80 total penalty

In this particular case, since the penalty is on the billing demand (1,614 kW) and not the actual demand (1,440 kW), the cost becomes even greater than if the actual demand was used in the calculation.

8.   **Contract Demand—**
Contract demand: 1,200 kW (from contract 03-87)
Contract demand is described as the minimum demand load that the customer is obligated to pay for regardless of actual demand load usage in any particular month. The utility's rationale for a tariff schedule provision like this is that they have invested capital in transformation and related equipment based upon the customer's needs, and that they should realize some minimum monthly income based upon that investment.

It does not appear that the 1,200 kW provision in this case is causing a hardship for the customer since actual demand loads are considerably above the contract level.

Typically contracts are signed initially for a five-year period with a year-to-year automatic renewal thereafter. There generally is a 90-day window each year in which either party can request a change in the contract. If it appears that the contract demand is beginning to be the determining factor for monthly billing demand, it would probably be wise to consider renegotiation of the contract demand level downward.

9. **Customer Charge—**
Customer charge: $210.00
The customer charge, when used, is the basic charge that the utility assesses to the customer for being on a particular rate. It is a general charge that compensates the utility for the meter cost and related equipment. Customer charges can range from nothing to several thousands of dollars per month. Customer charges are detailed in the tariff schedule for a particular rate code or classification. In some utilities, there are no customer charges spelled out since these items are included in the various usage category costs under demand (kW) and usage (kWh) components.

10. **Ratchet Clauses—**
Billing demand: 1,614 kW (from 10-01 billing)
Demand charge - $12,912.00
Ratchet charges are those tariff schedule provisions that allow a utility to base demand (kW) charges on maximum demand loads in some period of time not necessarily the current billing month.

The rationale for this type of billing procedure is that the utility must have available to the customer some maximum demand capacity even if the customer does not utilize that capacity in any given month. The ratchet clause on this particular billing states that monthly billing demand will be determined as follows:
Billing demand will be higher of the following -
1. *Actual monthly demand,*
2. *Highest monthly demand in the last 11 months,*
3. *Contract demand.*

On this billing, the actual demand was 1,440 kW, the ratchet demand from the 10-01 billing was 1,614 kW and the contract demand was 1,200 kW. For this month the 1,614 kW was the higher of the three options so it was utilized to determine kW cost (1,614 kW X $8.00) = $12,912.00.

The cost per kW ($8.00) is detailed in the appropriate tariff schedule. For this particular month a penalty in the demand cost resulted since the actual demand was less than a demand that occurred in the last 11 months.

Demand from 10-01 billing	1,614 kW
Current monthly demand	1,440 kW
Excess demand	174 kW

174 kW X $8.00 = $1,392.00 penalty

Since the ratchet period extends back 11 months, the 1,614 kW base will be utilized for several more months unless actual demand exceeds 1,614 kW.

In a situation like this, it is necessary to determine what caused the 1,614 kW demand to occur and try to stabilize demand loads so that excessive peaks do not occur. The $1,392 penalty buys nothing for the customer; so if possible, all reasonable means should be utilized to reduce the demand variability on a month to month basis.

Corrective Measures: Have the utility provide demand profiles for several months to determine when peaks occur. Then utilize this demand profile information to analyze and reduce demand levels by shifting loads, limiting loads by utilization of energy management systems, or through utilization of an onsite generation capacity.

11. Fuel Cost Adjustment Clause—
    Fuel cost recovery $.0023 / $1,283.40

The fuel adjustment clause allows the utility to adjust the cost they pay for fuel to operate their generation stations on a periodic basis. This clause assigns a cost for fuel on a usage basis (kWh). This charge can range from a negative number or a credit per kWh to a penalty cost or positive adder per (kWh).

The utility generally does not have to institute a rate case proceeding to change the adjustment charge but must on an on-going basis justify to the appropriate regulatory agency the rationale for any changes. On this particular billing, the adjustment charge was a positive adder ($.0023/kWh) to the base kWh used -

$$\$.0023 \times 558,000 \text{ kWh} = \$1,283.40$$

12. **Facility Charges—**
Facility charge - $1,147.23
Facility lease - $968.17
Facility charged leases represent those charges that occur when the utility, in agreement with and sometimes at the request of the customer, installs special or nonstandard equipment for the customer's special needs or use.

These charges will always be supported by a written agreement between the utility and the customer that defines all aspects of the special or nonstandard equipment and related charges. In this particular situation, special switchgear and metering was installed by the utility for the customer's special needs and at the request of the customer.

Things to Check: Read the contract to find out exactly what is covered and then determine if the special or nonstandard condition creating these facility charges still exists. If they do not, cancel the contract, if

possible. If the special or nonstandard need still exists, check with the utility to see if the equipment can be purchased at its current depreciated value.

In this particular example, it was found that the equipment could be purchased by the customer for $26,515 which would represent a payback of 12.6 months or 1.05 years. ($26,515 − $2,115.40/month cost = 15.2 months) In this situation, if the equipment was not highly specialized requiring specific utility maintenance, it probably would be wise to purchase the equipment so that the monthly facility charge would be eliminated.

13. Non-fuel Energy Charge and Miscellaneous Energy Cost—
    Special PUC charges - $.0011 - $613.80

    These charges generally are the result of some action of a regulatory body with relation to some special costs that would not be covered in normal fuel cost recovery charges. This particular charge was the result of the public utility commission being mandated by the state to pay for its own existence through assessment of a fee or charge to the entities it served.

    In this case, all customers of all electric utilities under the jurisdiction of this regulatory body are equally assessed the fee or cost of $.0011 per kWh. Other areas regulated by this body— natural gas, telephone, railroads, etc. are assessed similar fees based upon uniform units of measure common to the particular entity involved.

14. Non-fuel Energy Charge and Miscellaneous Energy Cost
    Adjustments—
    Nuclear Regulatory cost - $0.0006 - $279.00

Charges like this will vary with utility and state jurisdictional areas. This particular energy cost adjustments is to compensate the regulatory agency for some particular nuclear regulatory oversight not included in the special PUC charge (Item #13).

15. Taxes—

School tax on - $46,689.06 (3%) $ 1,400.52
Franchise fee on - $48,084.58 (1.5%) $ 721.27
State sales tax on - $48,805.85 (7%) $ 3,416.41

There are many taxes that can be levied on utility billings. On this particular billing, there are three distinct taxes, although only two are stated as taxes, as follows:

1. **School tax**—This tax is for the support of local schools and is levied on a municipality-by-municipality basis depending upon whether a school tax is in effect. The tax rate of 3% is assessed on the total utility bill of-
   ($46,689.06 X 3% = $1,400.52)

2. **Franchise fee**—This is in reality a tax since a fee of this type represents a charge that a municipality assesses on a utility to conduct business in the municipality's jurisdiction.
   This fee or tax is passed on to the utility customers in that municipality's jurisdiction. The fee or tax rate of 1.5% is assessed on both the total utility billing and the school tax assessed in (#1.)-
   ($48,084.58 X $.015 = $721.27)

3. **State sales tax**—This is the sales tax assessed by the state on utility services and if it applies to electricity, it probably also applies to natural gas and water/sewer charges. This tax rate is 7% and is assessed on not only the total utility billing, but

also the school tax and the franchise fee -

($48,805.85 X $.07 = $3,416.41)

Things to Check: Check the applicable state sales tax statute to determine whether any sales tax exemptions are available to commercial or industrial users of utility services. If exemptions are available, utilize them to the extent possible. Also, apply for a refund of all sales tax paid in the past up to statute of limitation provisions, generally 3 to 4 years.

16. Total Current Bill—
    $52,222.26
    This figure indicates the total amount due from the customer for all Items #1-16 in this particular billing month.

17. Previous Amount Due, Payment Received, Total Amount Due—
    Previous amount due - $49,176.83
    Payment received - $49,176.83
    Total amount due - $52,222.26
    These figures indicate that the previous amount due ($49,176.83) has been paid and that the total amount due is this month's current billing amount ($52,222.26).

What was found as a result of analyzing and understanding the items contained on this billing-

1. Power factor (Item #7)-Potential to reduce or eliminate the penalty charge of $1,129.80 by installing power factor correction capacitors.

2. Demand (Items #4, #8 & #10)—Potential to reduce variability of monthly demand levels which for the month analyzed caused a penalty charge of $1,392.

3. **Facility charge (Item #12)-**By determining the value of the equipment from the utility ($26,515), it was found that probably the prudent course of action would be to purchase the special equipment from the utility and save the monthly charge ($2,115.40). Based upon the monthly charge, the equipment would be paid for in 12.6 months.

4. **Taxes (Item #15)-**After consulting the state sales tax statutes, determine the applicability of state sales tax exemptions and the associated potential for refund of state sales tax paid in the past.

A thorough understanding of utility billing data will greatly assist in determining ways to reduce utility costs.

Chapter 6

The Basic Cost
Components of Electricity Billing

There are at least four basic cost components in the electricity billing process. These components are-

I.   The Customer's Voltage Level
II. The Power Factor or Relative Efficiency of the Customer's Distribution System
III. The Demand Peak Level of the Customer's System
IV. Usage or the Quantity of (kWh) the Customer Utilizes on a Monthly Basis

Each of these items can have a large impact on the customer's monthly billing costs, and they need to be understood in order to be evaluated for potential cost reduction opportunities. It is important to understand the terminology that will be utilized before discussing the first of these four components—voltage level.

To assist in this, following are two illustrations—Figure 6.1 which shows how electricity is distributed from the point of generation to the point of customer usage and Figure 6.2 which shows the difference between primary and secondary metering. It is important that these basics be understood since they are fundamental to the electricity usage environment.

Figure 6.1

The Incremental Steps in Electricity Distribution

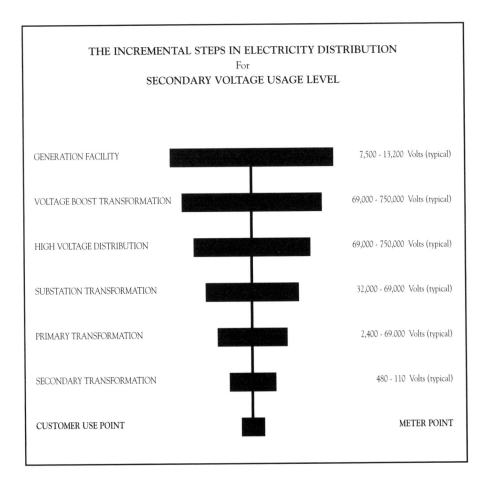

THE INCREMENTAL STEPS IN ELECTRICITY DISTRIBUTION
For
SECONDARY VOLTAGE USAGE LEVEL

GENERATION FACILITY	7,500 - 13,200 Volts (typical)
VOLTAGE BOOST TRANSFORMATION	69,000 - 750,000 Volts (typical)
HIGH VOLTAGE DISTRIBUTION	69,000 - 750,000 Volts (typical)
SUBSTATION TRANSFORMATION	32,000 - 69,000 Volts (typical)
PRIMARY TRANSFORMATION	2,400 - 69.000 Volts (typical)
SECONDARY TRANSFORMATION	480 - 110 Volts (typical)
CUSTOMER USE POINT	METER POINT

Figure 6.2
Primary/Secondary Metering and Transformer Ownership

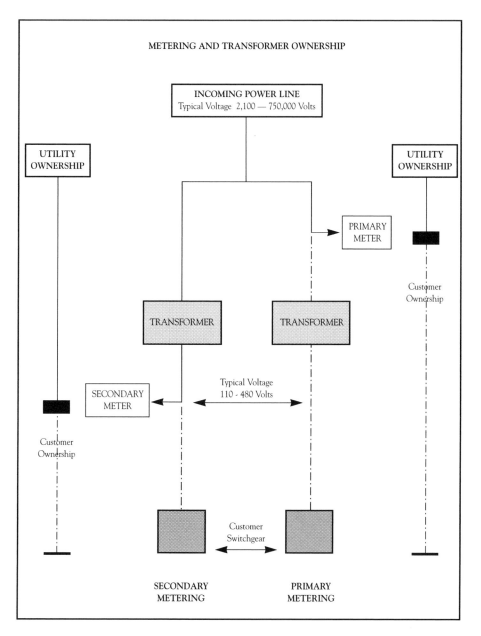

I. Voltage Level

Many small and medium size industries are taking over a service once provided solely by the electric utility. That service is converting the high voltage power which runs through a utility's transmission lines (128,000, 69,000, 4,100 volts, etc.) to the low voltage (440, 220, 110 volts) used by most end-users. They are doing this by purchasing or leasing transformer installations themselves. When a customer switches to a so-called primary or high voltage rate from a secondary or low voltage rate, electric costs are reduced.

Although large industrial users such as steel mills, aluminum processors, large assembly plants, etc. have been purchasing electricity at high voltage rates for many years; smaller industries are just now investigating the procedure because of its cost reduction potential.

Also, for the most part, utilities are willing to assist a customer in this effort since it helps them to attract and keep current business. The savings potential is not only for industrial users, but also has as much application for municipalities, universities, shopping centers, and hospitals to name a few. Can there be significant savings?

Typical savings range from 3%–10% of total electrical costs when comparing primary versus secondary voltage levels of electricity. The cost to convert to primary from secondary service varies greatly but the cost can be minimized when utility owned transformers are purchased at the depreciated value.

Successful conversions to primary voltage have been possible in instances where the total electric cost was as low as $20,000 per year. This is an area that could help reduce electrical costs greatly and the process is simple to start. The utility is your source of information and they probably will be cooperative in helping you to determine your potential for savings. To assist you in a logical step-by- step analysis of the potential for primary voltage in a particular situation, the following guide is given.

A. If a facility is served at secondary voltage level and if the tariff schedule provides for primary voltage, perform the following investigation:

    1.   Have the utility company calculate the annual savings of switching from secondary to primary voltage levels (see Figure 6.6).

          There should be no charge by the utility for doing this analysis.

    2.   Have the utility company provide the depreciated value of the transformation equipment necessary to convert to primary voltage. Utilities generally depreciate straight line method from 30 to 40 years.

    3.   Determine the most economical method to convert to primary voltage as follows:

        (a) Purchase transformation equipment at depreciated value. See Figure 6.3 following for examples of how utilities calculate equipment depreciation.

        (b) Lease transformation equipment from the utility, if applicable by tariff schedule. See Figure 6.5 for an example of a utility equipment lease agreement.

        (c) Lease transformation equipment from a third party if utility lease is not available. A third party lease is accomplished by purchasing the transformation equipment at its depreciated value from the utility and selling it to the third party who takes title to the equipment.

The third party then leases the equipment to the customer the same as the utility would do in a utility lease. A typical third party would be the manufacturer of the equipment itself or a company that specializes in leasing of industrial equipment.

The example in Figure 6.3 is a composite of the actual utility calculation methods that are utilized to determine "current net value" of equipment they own. The same calculation methods are utilized for any equipment that a customer may be considering for purchase from a utility.

Figure 6.3

Example of Utility Depreciation Calculation Processes

Recap of installation of (1) 2000 kVA 12470/7200 volts-480/277 volts pad mount transformer. This installation includes 1100 ft. of 4-2 ACSR primary and neutral overhead conductor, and 120 ft. of 3-2 AL. 15 kV concentric neutral primary underground cable from an overhead pole to a 2000 kVA pad mounted transformer. Installation completed (date).

Items	Cost	Totals
1-50' Pole	$ 211	
3-45' Pole	432	
14-8' XA	364	
1-PTP	5	
7-1WR	28	
1-NB	3	
6-8" PA	66	
12 Down Guy and Guard	300	
4400' - 2 ACSR		
Overhead Conductor (502#)	604	
11-Pin Ins	22	
18-Epoxylator Ins	234	
1-Ground Rod	7	
1-Driven Ground	16	
4-Butt Ground	48	
3-LA	63	
3-Co (Riser)	165	
3-UGDF LA	450	
120'-2Al. UG Cable (3/C)	264	
6-200A Terminators	150	
		$ 3,432
Miscellaneous	168	
Company Labor	2,050	
SF & H (22%)	792	
Labor Overheads (57%)	1,169	
Sub Total		$ 7,611
Construction Overheads (24%)	1,827	
1-2999 kVA 12470/7200-480/277		$ 9,438
Volt Pad Mount Transformer	19,500	
TOTAL COST		$28,938

Total installed cost—**$28,938**
Depreciation method—**30 years, straight line**
Years since installation—**17 years**
Current net value-[($28,938 ÷ 30) X (30 - 17)] = ($965 X 13) = **$12,545**

The current depreciated value of the equipment in this example is $12,545. At this point, there are two methods that utilities use to determine customer buy out value of equipment as follows:

1. **Use of current depreciated value-**This method is very straight forward since it is the actual current depreciated value of the equipment the customer wants to purchase. In this example it would be $12,545.

2. **Use of current depreciation factor applied to new equipment cost-**This method is used by some utilities to rationalize that if the customer had to purchase other than utility equipment, he/she would have to pay for new equipment. Since new equipment would be probably prohibitively expensive for a customer who wants to change from secondary to primary voltage levels, the utility will allow the depreciation factor of the existing equipment to be applied to the cost of the new equipment.

    I have never completely understood this logic but the net result for the customer is that the buy out cost of the equipment will increase as opposed to that shown in Figure 6.4. An example of how the customer's buy out cost could be affected follows:

Figure 6.4

Example of Customer's Buy Out Cost

Items	Original Cost	Current Cost
1-50' Pole	$ 211	$ 376
3-45' Poles	432	612
14-8' XA	364	670
1-PTP	5	10
7-1WR	28	37
1-NB	3	12
6-8" PA	66	72
12-Down Guy and Guard	300	476
4400'-2ACSR		
Overhead Conductor (502#)	604	762
11-Pin Ins	22	36
18-Epoxylator Ins	234	476
1-Ground Rod	7	12
1-Driven Ground	16	18
4-Butt Ground	48	72
3-LA	63	96
3-Co (Riser)	165	276
3-UGDF LA	450	513
120'-2Al. UG Cable (3/C)	264	673
6-200A Terminators	150	312
	$ 3,432	$ 5,511
Miscellaneous	168	476
Company Labor	2,050	5,600
SF & H (22%)	792	1,317
Labor Overheads (57%)	1,169	3,192
Sub Total	$ 7,611	$ 16,096
Construction Overheads (24%)	1,827	3,863
	$ 9,438	$ 19,932
1-2000 kVA 12470/7200-480/277V		
Pad Mount Transformer	$ 19,500	$ 42,176
TOTAL COST	$ 28,938	$ 62,108

Current net value using the original depreciation factor applied to the current installation cost would be -

    [($62,108 ÷ 30) X (30 - 17)] = $2,070 X 13 = $26,910

The customer buy out would be $26,910 as opposed to $12,545 that was established utilizing the original cost method. This method more than doubles the cost ($26,910 − $12,545 = $14,365) over the original cost method. When considering a buy out of any utility equipment whether the utility uses the original cost or current cost, always remember the two following items:

1. Generally the buy out of utility equipment is subject to negotiation if it is in the utility's best interest to assist a specific customer.
2. Generally customer buy out of utility equipment is not specifically addressed in any rate tariff schedules and consequently does not require regulatory approval for the transaction to take place.

The primary thing to remember in the purchase of any utility owned equipment is that within limits, there are opportunities for negotiation on costs if it makes sense for both the utility and the customer. If an atmosphere of teamwork rather than adversity can be established, both parties can benefit.

Figure 6.5

Example of a Typical Utility Equipment Lease Agreement

(For the purposes of this example, the equipment cost data from Figure 6.4 will be utilized.)

LEASED FACILITIES SUPPLEMENT
TO ELECTRIC SERVICE CONTRACT

WHEREAS,_____ of _____(Customer), has need for electric service on its property for use in operating a facility and could build its own distribution system to take service at one location, and

WHEREAS,_____(Utility) is willing to provide the necessary transformers and facilities as shown on Exhibit "A" and Customer is willing to pay to the Company a facility charge to cover its costs which include expenses of operation, maintenance, depreciation, taxes, insurance and a return on this investment.

NOW, THEREFORE, in consideration of the premises and the mutual benefits herein contained, it is agreed as follows:

1. Company will construct, own, operate and maintain the above mentioned facilities required by Customer necessary to provide one-point delivery and metering by Company.

2. Customer agrees to pay the Company, during the term of this contract, a monthly facility charge based on 28.0 percent per year of the Company's total investment as shown by the following tabulations:

Total investment	=	$28,938
Monthly facility charge	=	(Investment x 28.0%)/12
Monthly facility charge	=	$ 675.22

Said facility charge is subject to change by _____ (Utility) upon thirty days written notice. Such change will be either an upward or downward adjustment, when conditions arise which materially affect the investment in the facilities covered by this Supplemental Agreement, or a change in the Company's fixed costs as previously set out, or a change in the State or Federal Tax provisions to the extent the provisions affect the Facility Lease Charge.

Figure 6.5 (Continued)

Exhibit "A"

Items	Original Cost	Current Cost
1-50' Pole	$ 211	
3-45' Pole	432	
14-8' XA	364	
1-PTP	5	
7-1WR	28	
1-NB	3	
6-8" PA	66	
12 Down Guy and Guard	300	
4400' - 2 ACSR		
Overhead Conductor (502#)	604	
11-Pin Ins	22	
18-Epoxylator Ins	234	
1-Ground Rod	7	
1-Driven Ground	16	
4-Butt Ground	48	
3-LA	63	
3-Co (Riser)	165	
3-UGDF LA	450	
120'-2Al. UG Cable (3/C)	264	
6-200A Terminators	150	
		$ 3,432
Miscellaneous	168	
Company Labor	2,050	
SF & H (22%)	792	
Labor Overheads (57%)	1,169	
Sub Total		$ 7,611
Construction Overheads (24%)	1,827	
		$ 9,438
1-2999 kVA 12470/7200-480/277		
Volt Pad Mount Transformer	19,500	
TOTAL COST		**$28,938**

This example details how most utility equipment lease agreements are structured. The equipment detailed here would cost $675.22 monthly for as long as the customer leased it. If, through leasing this equipment, the customer could change from secondary to primary voltage levels and save more than the $675.22 monthly lease payment, it would probably be the right choice to make.

When evaluating whether to purchase or lease utility owned equipment, it is well to remember that even if savings generally are greater with purchase of equipment, responsibility for equipment has to be considered. When equipment is leased, the lessor (utility in this case) is responsible for any and all equipment-related problems. When equipment is purchased, the purchaser is responsible for all equipment-related problems.

When trying to objectively determine whether utility equipment should be leased or purchased, consider the following items:

1. Will utility lease equipment to a customer?
2. Will utility lease cost be less than savings that result from switching from secondary to primary voltage levels?
3. Could equipment be leased for less from a third party?
4. If equipment is purchased by the customer, does the customer have the expertise to maintain and repair the equipment?
5. Has the fact been taken into consideration that any purchased equipment that fails is the responsibility of the purchaser?
6. Can or will the customer who purchases the equipment perform the required periodic preventative maintenance that is required?
7. Can a better deal be negotiated with the utility?

Leasing or purchasing of utility-owned equipment can be very advantageous for the customer but, as with any decision, all aspects must be considered before a final decision is made.

Transformer Maintenance

The following information will provide an outline of what should be performed in the maintenance of transformers. Before purchasing transformers, be certain that the skills required are present in your organization. If in-house expertise is not available, consider outside contracting to assure that transformers are properly maintained. Remember transformers typically provide no advance notice of failure. Frequently this failure, when it occurs, is catastrophic and requires major repair or replacement at sometimes major cost. Leasing of transformers is generally the best method to utilize when savings due to secondary/primary conversion are desired.

Transformer Maintenance Data

I.   Transformers: Dry Type[1]

   1.   Small Transformers: Dry Type, Air Cooled (600Volt and Below) (less than 100 kVA single-phase or 300 kVA three-phase)

      A.   Inspect for physical damage, broken insulation, tightness of connections,defective wiring, and general condition.

      B.   Thoroughly clean unit prior to making any tests.

      C.   Perform insulation-resistance test.

         Calculate polarization index. Measurements shall be made from winding-to-winding and windings-to-ground. Test voltages and minimum resistance shall be in accordance with Table 6.3. Results to be temperature corrected in accordance with Table 6.1.

D. Verify that the transformer is set at the specified tap.

II. Transformers: Dry Type, Other than Small

1. Visual and Mechanical Inspection

A. Inspect for physical damage, cracked insulators, tightness of connections,defective wiring, and general mechanical and electrical conditions.

B. Verify proper auxiliary device operation such as fans and indicators.

C. Check tightness of bolted connections and/or cable connections by calibrated torque-wrench method in accordance with manufacturer's published data or Table 6.4. In lieu of torquing, perform thermographic survey in accordance with Section V.

D. Perform specific inspections and mechanical tests as recommended by manufacturer.

E. Make a close examination for shipping brackets or fixtures that may not have been removed during original installation. Insure resilient mounts are free.

F. Verify proper core grounding.

G. Verify proper equipment grounding.

H. Thoroughly clean unit prior to testing unless as-found and as-left tests are required.

I. Verify that the tap-changer is set at specified ratio.

2. Electrical Tests

A. Perform insulation-resistance tests,winding-to-winding and windings-to-ground, utilizing a megohmmeter with test voltage output as shown in Table 6.3. Test duration shall be for 10 minutes with resistance tabulated at 30 seconds, 1 minute, and 10 minutes. Calculate polarization index.

B. Perform power-factor or dissipation-factor in accordance with the manufacturer's instructions.

C. Perform a turns-ratio test between windings at as-found tap setting.

D. Perform winding-resistance tests for each winding at as-found tap position.

E. Perform individual excitation current tests on each phase.

F. Perform tests and adjustments for fans,controls, and alarm functions.

G. Verify proper secondary voltage phase-to-phase and phase-to-neutral after energization and prior to loading.

3. Test Values

A. Insulation-resistance test values should be less than values recommended in Table 6.3. Results shall be temperature corrected in accordance with Table 6.6.

B. The polarization index should be above 1.2 unless an extremely high value is obtained initially, which when doubled will not yield a meaningful value.

C. Turns-ratio test results should not deviate more than one-half percent from either the adjacent coils or the calculated ratio.

D. C_H and C_L dissipation factor/power factor values will vary due to support insulators and bus work utilized on dru transformers. The following should be expected on CHL power factors:

Power Transformers: three percent or less
Distribution Transformers: five percent or less

E. Winding-resistance test results should compare within one percent of adjacent windings.

F. Typical excitation current test data pattern for three-legged core transformer: two similar current readings and one lower current reading.

III. Transformers: Liquid-Filled

1. Visual and Mechanical Inspection

A. Inspect for physical damage, cracked bushings, leaks, tightness of connections, and general mechanical and electrical conditions.

B. Verify proper auxiliary device operation such as fans and indicators.

C. Check tightness of bolted connections and/or cable connections by calibrated torque-wrench method in accordance with manufacturer's published data or Table 6.4. In lieu of torquing, perform thermographic surveys in accordance with Section V.

D. Verify proper liquid level in all tanks and bushings.

E. Perform specific inspections and mechanical tests as recommended by manufacturer.

F. Verify proper equipment grounding.

2. Electrical Tests

A. Perform insulation-resistance tests, winding-to-winding and windings-to-ground, utilizing a megohmmeter with test voltage output as shown in Table 6.3. Test duration shall be for 10 minutes with resistances tabulated at 30 seconds, 1 minute, and 10 minutes. Calculate polarization index.

B.   Perform a turns-ratio test between windings at designated tap position. The tap setting is to be determined by the owner/user's electrical engineer and set by the testing firm.

C.   Perform insulation power-factor tests or dissipation-factor tests on all windings and bushings. Overall dielectric-loss and power factor (C_H, C_L, C_{HL}) shall be determined. Test voltages should be limited to the line-to-ground voltage rating of the transformer winding.

D.   Perform individual excitation current tests on each phase.

E.   Perform winding-resistance tests on each winding in final tap position.

F.   Perform tests and adjustments on fan and pump controls and alarm functions.

G.   Verify proper core grounding if accessible.

H.   Perform percent oxygen test on the nitrogen gas blanket.

I.   Sample insulating liquid in accordance with ASTM D-923. Sample shall be laboratory tested for—

(1)   Dielectric breakdown voltage:
ASTM D-877 OR ASTM D-1816.

(2)   Acid neutralization number:ASTM D-974.

(3)   Specific gravity: ASTM D-1298.

(4)   Interfacial tension:
ASTM D-971 OR ASTM D-2285.

(5)   Color: ASTM D-1500.

(6)   Visual condition: ASTM D-1524.

(7)   Perform dissolved gas analysis (DGA) in accordance with ANSI/IEEE C57.104 (IEEE Guide for the Interpretation of Gasses Generated in Oil-Immersed Transformers) or ASTM D-3612.

(8)   Parts per million water: ASTM D-1533. Required on 25 kV or higher voltages and on all silicone-filled units.

(9)   Measure total combustible gas (TCG) content in accordance with ANSI/IEEE C57.104 (IEEE Guide for the Interpretation of Gasses Generated in Oil-Immersed Transformers) or ASTM D-3284.

(10)   Measure dissipation factor or power factor in accordance with ASTM D-924.

IV.   Transformer Test Values

1.   Bolt-torque levels shall be in accordance with Table 6.4 unless otherwise specified by manufacturer.

2. Insulation-resistance and absorption test. Test voltages to be in accordance with Table 6.3. Resistance values to be temperature corrected in accordance with Table 6.6.

3. The polarization index should be above 1.2unless an extremely high value is obtained initially, which when doubled will not yield a meaningful value.

4. Turns-ratio test results shall not deviate more than one-half percent from either the adjacent or the calculated ratio.

5. Maximum dissipation factor/power factor of liquid-filled transformers corrected to 20°C shall be in accordance with Table 6.1.

6. Bushing power factors and capacitances that vary from nameplate values by more than ten percent should be investigated.

7. Typical excitation current test data pattern for three-legged core transformer:two similar current readings and one lower current reading.

8. Dielectric fluid should comply with Table 6.2.

9. Winding-resistance test results should compare within one percent of adjacent windings.

10. Investigate presence of oxygen in nitrogen gas blanket.

V. Transformer Thermographic Survey Data

1. Visual and Mechanical Inspection

   A. Inspect for physical, electrical, and mechanical condition.

   B. Remove all necessary covers prior to thermographic inspection.

   C. Equipment to be inspected shall include all current-carrying devices.

   D. Provide report including the following:

      (1) Discrepancies.

      (2) Temperature difference between the area of concern and the reference area.

      (3) Cause of temperature difference.

      (4) Areas inspected. Identify in accessible and/or unobservable areas and/or equipment.

      (5) Identify load conditions at time of inspection.

      (6) Provide photographs and/or thermograms of the deficient area.

   E. Test parameters

      (1) Inspect distribution systems with imaging equipment capable of detecting a minimum

temperature difference of 1°C at 30°C.

(2) Equipment shall detect emitted radiation and convert detected radiation to visual signal.

(3) Thermographic surveys should be performed during periods of maximum possible loading but not less than forty percent of rated load of the electrical equipment being inspected. (NFPA 70B-1990, paragraph 18-16.5)

F. Test results
(1) Temperature differences of 1°C to 3°C indicate possible deficiency and warrant investigation.

(2) Temperature differences of 4°C to 15°C indicate deficiency; repair as time permits.

(3) Temperature differences of 16°C and above indicate major deficiency; repair immediately.

VI. Capacitor Maintenance Data

1. Visual and Mechanical inspection

A. Inspect capacitors for physical damage, proper mounting, and required clearances.

B. Verify that capacitors are electrically connected in the proper configuration.

C. Check tightness of bolted connections by calibrated

torque-wrench method in accordance with manufacturer's published data or Table 6.4 for proper torque levels.

2. Electrical tests

A. Perform insulation-resistance tests from terminal(s) to case for one minute. Test voltage and minimum resistance shall be in accordance with manufacturer's instructions or Table 6.5.

B. Measure the capacitance of all terminal combinations and compare with manufacturer's published data.

C. Verify that internal discharge resistors are operating properly.

3. Test values

A. Bolt-torque levels shall be in accordance with Table 6.4 unless otherwise specified by manufacturer.

B. Insulation resistance values less than Table 6.5 shall be investigated.

C. Investigate capacitance values differing from manufacturer's published data.

D. Residual voltage of a capacitor shall be reduced to 50 volts in the following time intervals after being disconnected from the source of supply:

Rated Voltage	Discharge Time
≤ 600V	1 minute
> 600V	5 minutes

Table 6.1

Recommended Dissipation Factor/Power Factor of Liquid-Filled Transformers

	Oil Maximum	Silicone Maximum	Tetrachloroethylene Maximum	High Fire Point Hydrocarbon Maximum
Power Transformers	2.0%	0.5%	3.0%	2.0%
Distribution Transformers	3.0%	0.5%	3.0%	3.0%

Table 6.2

Suggested Limits for Service-Aged Insulating Fluids

Test	ASTM Method	Silicone * *	Less Flammable Hydrocarbon * * *
Dielectric Breakdown, kV minimum	D877	25	24
Visual	D2129	Colorless, clear, free of particles	N/A
Water Content, ppm maximum	D1533	100	45
Dissipation factor, % max. @ 25°C	D924	0.2	1.0
Viscosity, cSt @ 25°C	D445	47.5 - 52.5	N/A
Fire Point, °C, minimum	D92	340	300
Neutralization number, mg KOH/g max	D974	0.2	N/A
Neutralization number, mg KOH/g max.	D664	N/A	0.25
Interfacial Tension, mN/m minimum @ 25°C	D971	N/A	22

MINERAL OIL *			
Test	ASTM Method	69 kV and Below	Above 69 kV through 288 kV	345 kV and Above
Dielectric breakdown, kV minimum	D877	26	26	26
Dielectric breakdown, kV minimum @ 0.04 gap	D1816	23	26	26
Dielectric breakdown, kV minimum @ 0.08 gap	D1816	34	45	45
Interfacial Tension, mN/m minimum	D971	24	26	30
Neutralization number, mg KOH/g maximum	D974	0.2	0.2	0.1
Water Content, ppm maximum	D1533	35	25	20
Power factor at 25°C, %	D924	1.0 * * * *	1.0 * * * *	1.0 * * * *
Power factor at 100°C, %	D924	1.0 * * * *	1.0 * * * *	1.0 * * * *

*   IEEE C57.106-1991 (Guide for Acceptance and Maintenance of Insulating Oil in Equipment), Table 5.
* *   IEEE C57.111-1989 (Guide for Acceptance of Silicone Insulating Fluid and Its Maintenance in Transformers), Table 3.
* * *   IEEE C57.121-1988 (Guide for Acceptance and Maintenance of Less Flammable Hydrocarbon Fluid in Transformers), Table 3.
* * * * IEEE Std. 637-1985 (IEEE Guide for the Reclamation of Insulating Oil and Criteria for Its Use).

Table 6.3

Transformer Insulation-Resistance Test Voltage

Transformer Coil Rating Type	Minimum DC Test Voltage	Recommended Minimum Insulation Resistance in Megohms	
		Liquid Filled	Dry
0 - 600 Volts	1000 Volts	100	500
601 - 5000 Volts	2500 Volts	1000	5000
5001 - 15000 Volts	5000 Volts	5000	25000

Table 6.4

U.S. Standard Bolt Torques for Bus Connections, Heat-Treated Steel-Cadmium or Zinc Plated

GRADE	SAE 1 & 2	SAE 5	SAE 7	SAE 8
MINIMUM TENSILE (P.S.I.)	64 K	105 K	133 K	150 K
BOLT DIAMETER IN INCHES	TORQUE (FOOT POUNDS)			
1/4	4.0	5.6	8.0	8.4
5/16	7.2	11.2	15.2	17.6
3/8	12.0	20.0	27.2	29.6
7/16	19.2	32.0	44.0	48.0
1/2	29.6	48.0	68.0	73.6
9/16	42.4	70.4	96.0	105.6
5/8	59.2	96.0	133.6	144.0
3/4	96.0	160.0	224.0	236.8
7/8	152.0	241.6	352.0	378.4
1.0	225.6	372.8	528.0	571.2

Table 6.5

Insulation Resistance Tests on Electrical Apparatus and Systems

Maximum Voltage Rating of Equipment	Minimum Test Voltage, DC	Recommended Minimum Insulation Resistance in Megohms
250 Volts	500 Volts	25
600 Volts	1,000 Volts	100
5,000 Volts	2,500 Volts	1,000
8,000 Volts	2,500 Volts	2,000
15,000 Volts	2,500 Volts	5,000
25,000 Volts	5,000 Volts	20,000
35,000 Volts	15,000 Volts	100,000
46,000 Volts	15,000 Volts	100,000
69,000 Volts	15,000 Volts	100,000

NOTE: This table has recommended minimum insulation values identical to those in the NETA Acceptance Testing Specification for new equipment. Well maintained insulation in favorable ambient conditions should continue to provide these values.

(See Table 6.6 for temperature correction factors.)

Table 6.6

Insulation Resistance Conversion Factors for Conversion of Test Temperature to 20°C

Temperature		Multiplier	
°C	°F	Apparatus Containing Immersed Oil Insulations	Apparatus Containing Solid Insulations
0	32	0.25	0.40
5	41	0.36	0.45
10	50	0.50	0.50
15	59	0.75	0.75
20	68	1.00	1.00
25	77	1.40	1.30
30	86	1.98	1.60
35	95	2.80	2.05
40	104	3.95	2.50
45	113	5.60	3.25
50	122	7.85	4.00
55	131	11.20	5.20
60	140	15.85	6.40
65	149	22.40	8.70
70	158	31.75	10.00
75	167	44.70	13.00
80	176	63.50	16.00

Figure 6.6

Example Secondary vs Primary Voltage Level Analysis

RATE SCHEDULE LC - 8   (Secondary Voltage)

12-Month Analysis   (Current Customer Rate)

Secondary Distribution	Total Units	Cost Per Unit	Total Cost/Year
Customer Charge		$ 17.20/mo	$ 206
Demand Charge:			
Secondary Basic Demand	44,112 kW	$ 3.60/kW	$ 158,803
Summer Peak Demand	12,164 kW	$ 6.66/kW	$ 81,012
Winter Peak Demand	30,154 kW	$ 3.54/kW	$ 106,745
Total Demand Charge			$ 346,766
Energy Charge	10,693,200 kWh	$ 0.03103/kW	$ 331,810
Fuel Adjustment Factor	10,693,200 kWh	$ 0.00000/kW	$ 00
			$ 678,576

Potential Savings

$ 678,576

RATE SCHEDULE LC - 8   (Primary Voltage)

12-Month Analysis   (Proposed Customer Rate)

Primary Distribution	Total Units	Cost Per Unit	Total Cost/Year
Customer Charge		$ 17.20/mo	$ 206
* Demand Charge:			
Primary Basic Demand	45,435 kW	$ 1.93/kW	$ 87,690
Summer Peak Demand	12,529 kW	$ 6.47/kW	$ 81,063
Winter Peak Demand	31,059 kW	$ 3.44/kW	$ 106,843
Total Demand Charge			$ 275,802
Energy Charge	11,013,996 kWh	$ 0.0301/kWh	$ 331,511
Fuel Adjustment Factor	11,013,996 kWh	$ 0.0000/kWh	$ 00
			$ 607,313

$ 607,313

* Includes 3% Transformer Loss Factor

$ 71,263

Figure 6.6 shows a sample analysis comparing a customer currently served on a Secondary Voltage Rate schedule with a proposed Primary Voltage Rate schedule. This analysis, which generally is provided by the utility at no cost, has a potential savings of $71,263. The detailed results are as follows:

1. Potential savings—$ 71,263

2. Cost to purchase transformation equipment using current depreciated value of transformers—$ 150,000

3. Payback on investment to purchase transformers—
   ($150,000 ÷ $71,263) = 2.11 Years

4. Cost of lease transformers from a third party leasing agent yearly, on a 10-year lease, including maintenance & transformer replacement, if required—$ 35,000

5. Payback, if transformers leased—($71,263 – $35,000) = $ 36,263

Although the purchase of the transformers involved would seem to be the most cost beneficial method to utilize, the lease method also provides some attractive savings as well as other benefits. If the transformers are purchased, the owner is responsible for all maintenance and has the burden of transformer replacement, if required. With the lease option, maintenance and transformer replacement are the responsibility of the lessor not the lessee.

Figure 6.7

Examples of Tariff Schedule Provisions Concerning Credit Given for Primary vs Secondary Voltage Levels

1. **TRANSFORMER DISCOUNT:** $.055 per month per kW billing demand to any customer meeting primary service qualifications. Customer must supply his own transformers, substation equipment, etc., and be served at 4,160 volts or higher.

2. If customer furnishes utility-approved primary voltage transformers, the demand charge will be reduced by $0.70 per kW.

3. **DISCOUNT:** For service at primary voltage, $0.40 per kW demand and $0.07 per kWh.

4. **DISCOUNTS:** 6% of the kWh when energy is metered at primary voltage. When customer furnishes and maintains the required substation for service at primary or transmission line voltage, the following discounts will be allowed on each monthly bill:

Monthly Delivery Voltage	Credit per kW of Billing Demand
2,300 - 12,000	$0.20
13,200 and over	$0.35

5. **DEMAND CHARGE:**

   $13.00 per kW on-peak billing demand, plus
   $ 4.75 per kW maximum demand, (less than 24 kV) primary service
   $ 3.00 per kW maximum demand, (24 to 41.6 kV) subtransmission voltage level
   $ 1.90 per kW maximum demand, (120 kV and above) transmission voltage level

6. **DEMAND CHARGE:**

   $ 6.00 per kW - secondary distribution
   $ 4.10 per kW - primary distribution
   $ 3.00 per kW - transmission line

7. **DISCOUNT:** 5% of energy charge when customer owns and maintains or, at utility's option, leases all transformers and other facilities necessary to take service at the primary or transmission voltage delivered.

Questions to Ask
in the Leasing of Transformers

1. What is the current voltage level — primary or secondary?

2. Who currently owns the power transformer?

3. If the transformer is utility-owned, what is the depreciated value?

4. Is there a PCB (polychlorinated biphenyl) contamination problem with the transformer that is being considered for lease or purchase?

5. Has an infrared scan been performed on the transformer to locate any hot spots or high temperature differentials that could ultimately result in premature failure?

6. If the transformer is utility-owned, what would be the monthly rent or lease cost?

7. What would be the monthly cost of a third party lease?

8. What is the current monthly electrical cost?

9. What would be the monthly cost if voltage were at primary level?

10. What would be the payback?

II. Power Factor

Power factor, technically stated, is "the ratio of real power-kilowatts (kW), to apparent power-kilovoltamperes (kVA) for any given load and time."Generally, it is expressed as a percentage ratio. Simply stated, it is "the efficiency at which electricity is consumed."

Since utilities provide electrical energy in units of kilovoltamps (kVA) and a customer's usage is generally measured in kilowatts (kW), power factor or relative efficiency of the customer's usage may be calculated as follows:

Utility-provided peak kVA
for a given billing period   376 kVA

Customer utilized peak demand in
kW for a given billing period   268 kW

The power factor in this example would be-[(268 kW ÷ 376 kVA) = 71.3%]. Since the utility had to provide 28.7% [(100.00% – 71.3%) = 28.7%] more kVA than was represented in the customer's kW peak demand (376 kVA vs 268 kW), there would probably be a power factor correction penalty which would be detailed in the applicable tariff schedule.

Most utilities measure power factor since the inefficient use of electricity requires more power reserves than would be needed if the power were used efficiently. Also, most utility tariff schedules provide for the institution of penalty charges if power factor percentages are under minimum figure, normally 85%.

If the power ratio falls below the minimum penalty point, it can normally be raised to a non-penalty level by the installation of capacitors which will store the electrical power required during inefficient power usage periods.

These capacitors can be in the form of capacitor banks or groups installed at the main electrical distribution point, or they can be installed individually at specific areas of inefficient electrical usage. Power factor correction can be a source of considerable savings and generally is rather straight forward in being corrected.

The steps to take in investigation of power factor correction are as follows:

1.   Determine if the utility imposes power factor surcharges. This can generally be determined from the monthly billing.

2.   If low power factor surcharges are imposed,determine how much they are. Discussion with the utility service representatives can help to determine what these charges are if they are not apparent from the monthly utility billing.

3.   In conjunction with the utility, determine the amount of capacitance correction that is required for the system. Generally, the utility will install the required capacitors for you if they can be installed at the main electrical distribution point.

Naturally, there is a charge for this but it may be best to have the utility to do the installation since they are most familiar with the system. Also, capacitors can be purchased or leased from third party suppliers.

4.   Calculate the payback by comparing the monthly low power factor surcharge with the cost of installing the required capacitors. In many cases, the payback will be less than one year.

Figure 6.8

Power Factor Correction-No. 1

The following is a sample of a power factor correction utilizing a capacitor bank to correct a power factor problem.

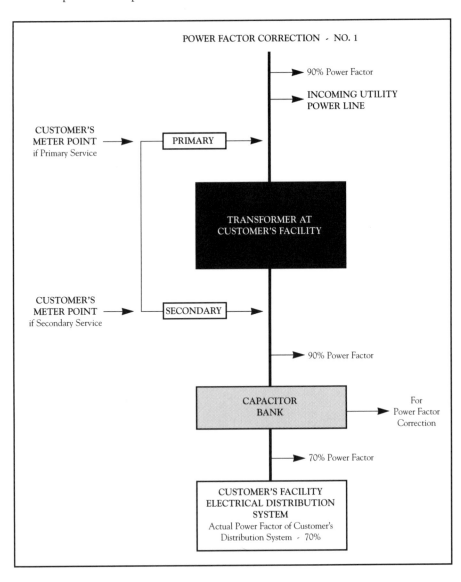

POWER FACTOR CORRECTION - NO. 1

90% Power Factor

INCOMING UTILITY POWER LINE

CUSTOMER'S
METER POINT
if Primary Service

PRIMARY

TRANSFORMER AT CUSTOMER'S FACILITY

CUSTOMER'S
METER POINT
if Secondary Service

SECONDARY

90% Power Factor

CAPACITOR BANK

For Power Factor Correction

70% Power Factor

CUSTOMER'S FACILITY
ELECTRICAL DISTRIBUTION
SYSTEM
Actual Power Factor of Customer's
Distribution System - 70%

The type of power factor correction as shown in Figure 6.8 addresses only utility-imposed power factor penalty charges. Electrical inefficiencies continue to exist within the customer's electrical distribution system. These inefficiencies manifest themselves through reduced electrical distribution capacity within the customer's system.

Poor power factor on an electrical distribution system is similar to the condition that arises when the arteries and veins of a person become clogged with plaque which results in reduced blood flow. The result in an electrical system is reduced electrical carrying or distribution capacity.

One indication of insufficient electrical carrying capacity in an electrical distribution system is the presence of excessive heat within the system. The method of power factor correction to reduce or eliminate utility surcharges as shown in this example represents the procedure most frequently utilized due to the ease and cost of the installation.

Remember, this method only masks the real problem, it does not address the cause of the problem. Power factor penalties are generally easy to determine since they appear on the monthly utility billing, and thus, payback periods can be quickly calculated.

Figure 6.9

Power Factor Correction-No. 2

The following is a sample of a power factor correction utilizing individual power factor correction capacitors at individual points of low or poor power factor points throughout the customer's facility electrical distribution system.

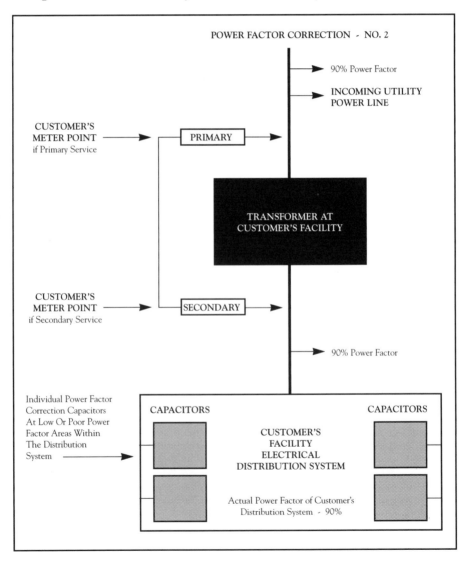

The type of correction, as shown in Figure 6.9, is the method to utilize to actually address electrical line efficiencies that result in poor power factor problems. Unfortunately, this method is not often used when analyzing existing electrical distribution problems because of the cost and time that might be required to find all areas of poor power factor on an electrical distribution system. Some of the correct methods in keeping an electrical distribution system efficient are as follows-

1. Design new electrical systems to some predetermined power factor threshold, 85–90% as an example.

2. As changes occur on an existing electrical system, correct for potential poor power factor areas as required.

3. Survey the existing electrical system to determine whether any of the following conditions exist so that measures to correct problems can be undertaken:

   A. Intermittent operation of an electric motor. Contributing to poor power factor is the period of idling time of an electric motor.

   B. Oversized electric motors. Example—using a 50 hp motor where a 30 hp motor would be sufficient.

   C. Fluorescent lighting using transformer-type ballasts. Correct this through solid state/energy efficient design ballasts. NOTE: Many times utility rebate programs assist with the cost related to changing over to energy efficient fluorescent lighting.

These items certainly are not all inclusive of the things that contribute to poor power factor, but represent some of the more common problem areas. Probably a good place to start in analyzing any electrical system would be to contact the electric utility service representative to determine what assistance the utility company could provide in determining low power factor problems.

Sometimes utilities have in-house personnel that can assist a customer through an on-site evaluation at no cost. Other times the utility company can suggest reputable outside sources that can provide an evaluation of specific needs at reasonable costs. Basic facts about power factor implications in electrical systems follow.

Facts About Electrical Systems

Electrical systems are installed for one purpose only—to do work. Through the purchase and installation of transformers, motors, contractors, cables, etc., a business operates and makes money. Very simply, the electrical system is capital investment to yield output and consequent dollar revenue.[2]

As with any equipment, an electrical system handles its job to some degree of efficiency ranging from poor to excellent. The measure of electrical is known as Power Factor.

Doing work electrically requires voltage and current working together. And, the closer they work together the greater the amount of work that can be realized from the installed parts—more dollar revenue to the owner from a more efficient system.

In most electrical circuits a considerable amount of the amperes of current flow does not work with voltage - does not produce output. This is due to the type of load which may be applied to the system. Many electrical devices, such as transformers, motors, reactors, etc. require magnetizing current for their cores. This is called reactive current and it flows in the electrical system parts but doesn't contribute directly to output dollar revenue. Therefore, system efficiency is reduced—we have low Power Factor.

WORKING LOAD of an electrical system is the voltage times the work amperes of current flow. It is measured by a wattmeter.

$$\text{Working load} = \text{watts, or W}$$

NON-WORKING LOAD of an electrical system is the voltage times the reactive amperes of current flow. It may be measured by a varmeter: Non-working load = volt amperes reactive, or VAr TOTAL LOAD of an electrical system is the voltage time the total amperes of current flow. It includes both working and non-working parts. Total load is measured by multiplying the voltmeter reading times the ammeter reading:

$$\text{Total load} = \text{volt amperes, or VA}$$

Often you will see the preceding references as the familiar kW, kVAr and kVA. The "k" is for the word "kilo", which means "1000". Thus:

1000 watts = 1 kilowatt = 1kW

1000 volt amperes reactive = 1 kilovolt ampere reactive = 1kVAr

1000 volt amperes = 1 kilovolt ampere = 1 kVA

$$\text{POWER FACTOR} = \frac{\text{volts x work amperes}}{\text{volts x total amperes}} = \frac{\text{watts}}{\text{Volt amperes}} = \frac{W}{VA} = \frac{W}{kVA}$$

Example:

(1) If kW = 800 and kVA = 1000   (2) If kW = 300 and kVA = 300

$$PF = \frac{800}{1000} = .80 \text{ or } 80\% \qquad PF = \frac{300}{300} = 1.00 \text{ or } 100\%$$

The 80% power factor example would be considered low power factor—only 80% of the system producing work output. The second example shows the best realizable condition of 100% power factor—none of the system capability being wasted (Discounting small heating losses).

DETERMINE THE POWER FACTOR
- By asking the system manager
- By asking the local Utility
- By calculating it yourself

To calculate power factor you need VOLTS, AMPERES, and WATTS or KILOVOLTS,

AMPERES and KILOWATTS. In the following examples we will arbitrarily reference V, A and W values:

Using line to line volts and load amperes -
OBTAIN watts from kW demand (watts = kW x 1000) or, if kW is not metered

OBTAIN watts from the watthour meter as follows:

$$\text{Watts} = \frac{3600 \text{ x REV x P x Kh}}{t}$$

where REV = revolutions of the meter disk
$\quad$ P = PT ratio X CT ratio
$\quad$ Kh = meter disk constant as stamped on the disk or nameplate
$\quad$ t = time in seconds

Then, Power Factor = $\dfrac{W}{VA}$ = for single-phase system

$\quad$ Power Factor = $\dfrac{W}{1.73 \text{ VA}}$ for three-phase system

EXAMPLE No. 1:

240 V, Single-phase Service drawing 45 Amps
Nameplate Kh is 7.2
In 48 seconds the meter disk makes 16 revolutions
No PT or CT used

$$W = \frac{3600 \text{ x } 16 \text{ x } 7.2}{48} = 8640 \text{ watts}$$

$$VA = 240 \text{ x } 45 = 10800$$

$$PF = \frac{8640}{10800} = .80 \text{ or } 80\%$$

EXAMPLE No. 2:

4160 V, Three-phase 4 Wire Service drawing 87 Amps

2400: 120 PT (20: 1 ratio)

75.5 CT (15: 1 ratio)

Nameplate Kh is 1.8

In 36 seconds the meter disk makes 10 revolutions

$$W \quad = \quad \frac{3600 \ \times \ 10 \ \times \ 1.8 \ \times \ 20 \ \times \ 15}{36} \quad = \quad 540,000 \ \text{watts}$$

$$PF \quad = \quad \frac{540,000}{1.73 \ \times \ 4160 \ \times \ 87} \quad = \quad \frac{540,000}{626,000} \quad = \quad 863 \ \text{or} \ 86.3\%$$

The Power Capacitor. Power capacitors improve electrical system efficiency - improve POWER FACTOR. They are designed to remove the effects of that non-working current flow and make each business more profitable, at a fraction of the per unit cost of the installed system. Most often it is economically feasible to capacitor-improve electrical systems into the 95 to 100% PF range.

Inefficient electrical systems—systems with low power factor—are hurting all ways.

- Ability to handle work load is not what it should be - the system is being clogged up with non-working load or kVArs.
- The non-working current flow is causing higher than normal losses in conductors.
- The non-working current flow is causing greater than normal voltage drop.

In addition to above, the power bill is higher for inefficient systems—in areas where the supplying utility enforces power factor penalty, much higher.

Power Capacitors Clean up Electrical Systems Completely and reduce power bills. The supply the non-working kVAr load requirements, relieving the much more expensive system transformers, lines, etc. from this zero revenue load and its effects on loadability, losses, voltage and Power Bill.

Since power capacitors apply directly to the system they are designed to help, and function to

supply the system's non-working kVAr load, they are rated, both single and three-phase, in terms of:
- VOLTAGE
- kVAr

Standard units are available as catalog items for either low voltage or high voltage applications:

2.5 through 50 kVAr; 240 V, 480 V, 600 V

25 through 400 kVAr; 2400 V through 21,600 V

Standard equipments are available for unlimited kVAr needs, using combinations of standard units and racks

Summary. Here are described the basic characteristics of electrical circuits including the elements of system measurements; volts, amps, watts and vars. From this introduction system power factor can now be calculated.

Capacitor KVAR & Load Capacity. How many capacitors do you need to improve power factor from its present level to any desired value?

Using the Power Factor Improvement Table shown, locate original power factor on the vertical scale; trace horizontally across the table to directly below the desired power factor point; multiply the number found by the load kilowatts—result is directly in capacitor kVAr.

Example: 400 kW at 77% PF

Desired improvement is to 95% PF

From the Table reference, trace horizontally, at the 77% "Original PF" level, to directly below 95%

"Desired PF in Percent" - read .500. Then, multiply .500 x 400 = 200 kVAr of capacitors needed.

Table 6.7

Power Capacitor Improvement Table

DESIRED POWER FACTOR IN PER CENT

Original PF	100	99	98	97	96	95	94	93	92	91	90	89	88	87	86	85	84	83	82	81	80
50	1.732	1.590	1.529	1.481	1.442	1.403	1.369	1.337	1.306	1.276	1.248	1.220	1.192	1.165	1.139	1.112	1.086	1.060	1.034	1.008	.982
51	1.687	1.544	1.484	1.436	1.397	1.358	1.324	1.292	1.261	1.231	1.203	1.175	1.147	1.120	1.094	1.067	1.041	1.015	.989	.962	.937
52	1.643	1.500	1.440	1.392	1.351	1.314	1.280	1.248	1.217	1.187	1.159	1.131	1.103	1.076	1.050	1.023	.997	.971	.945	.919	.893
53	1.600	1.457	1.397	1.349	1.314	1.271	1.237	1.205	1.174	1.144	1.116	1.088	1.060	1.033	1.007	.980	.954	.928	.902	.876	.850
54	1.559	1.416	1.356	1.308	1.267	1.230	1.196	1.164	1.133	1.103	1.075	1.047	1.019	.992	.966	.939	.913	.887	.861	.835	.809
55	1.519	1.377	1.316	1.268	1.228	1.190	1.156	1.124	1.090	1.063	1.035	1.007	.979	.952	.926	.899	.873	.847	.821	.795	.769
56	1.480	1.338	1.277	1.229	1.189	1.151	1.117	1.085	1.051	1.024	.996	.968	.940	.913	.887	.860	.834	.808	.782	.756	.730
57	1.442	1.300	1.239	1.191	1.151	1.113	1.079	1.047	1.013	.986	.958	.930	.902	.875	.849	.822	.796	.770	.744	.718	.692
58	1.405	1.263	1.202	1.154	1.114	1.076	1.042	1.010	.976	.949	.921	.893	.865	.838	.812	.785	.759	.733	.707	.681	.655
59	1.368	1.226	1.165	1.117	1.077	1.039	1.005	.973	.939	.912	.884	.856	.828	.801	.775	.748	.722	.696	.670	.644	.618
60	1.334	1.192	1.131	1.083	1.043	1.005	.971	.939	.905	.878	.850	.822	.794	.767	.741	.714	.688	.662	.636	.610	.584
61	1.299	1.157	1.096	1.048	1.008	.970	.936	.904	.870	.843	.815	.787	.759	.732	.706	.679	.653	.627	.601	.575	.549
62	1.265	1.123	1.062	1.014	.974	.936	.902	.870	.839	.809	.781	.753	.725	.698	.672	.645	.619	.593	.567	.541	.515
63	1.233	1.091	1.030	.982	.942	.904	.870	.838	.804	.777	.749	.721	.693	.666	.640	.613	.587	.561	.535	.509	.483
64	1.200	1.058	.997	.949	.909	.871	.837	.805	.771	.744	.716	.688	.660	.633	.607	.580	.554	.528	.502	.476	.450
65	1.169	1.027	.966	.918	.878	.840	.806	.774	.740	.713	.685	.657	.629	.602	.576	.549	.523	.497	.471	.445	.419
66	1.138	.996	.935	.887	.847	.809	.775	.743	.709	.682	.654	.626	.598	.571	.545	.518	.492	.466	.440	.414	.388
67	1.108	.966	.905	.857	.817	.779	.745	.713	.679	.652	.624	.596	.568	.541	.515	.488	.462	.436	.410	.384	.358
68	1.079	.937	.876	.828	.788	.750	.716	.684	.650	.623	.595	.567	.539	.512	.486	.459	.433	.407	.381	.355	.329
69	1.049	.907	.840	.798	.758	.720	.686	.654	.620	.593	.565	.537	.509	.482	.456	.429	.403	.377	.351	.325	.298
70	1.020	.878	.811	.769	.729	.691	.657	.625	.591	.564	.536	.508	.480	.453	.427	.400	.374	.348	.322	.296	.270
71	.992	.850	.783	.741	.701	.663	.629	.597	.563	.536	.508	.480	.452	.425	.399	.372	.346	.320	.294	.268	.242
72	.963	.821	.754	.712	.672	.634	.600	.568	.534	.507	.479	.451	.423	.396	.370	.343	.317	.291	.265	.239	.213
73	.936	.794	.727	.685	.645	.607	.573	.541	.507	.480	.452	.424	.396	.369	.343	.316	.290	.264	.238	.212	.186
74	.909	.767	.700	.658	.618	.580	.546	.514	.480	.453	.425	.397	.369	.342	.316	.289	.263	.237	.211	.185	.159
75	.882	.740	.673	.631	.591	.553	.519	.487	.453	.426	.398	.370	.342	.315	.289	.262	.236	.210	.184	.158	.132
76	.855	.713	.652	.604	.564	.526	.492	.460	.426	.399	.371	.343	.315	.288	.262	.235	.209	.183	.157	.131	.105
77	.829	.687	.620	.578	.538	.500	.466	.434	.400	.373	.345	.317	.289	.262	.236	.209	.183	.157	.131	.105	.079
78	.803	.661	.594	.552	.512	.474	.440	.408	.374	.347	.319	.291	.263	.236	.210	.183	.157	.131	.105	.079	.053
79	.776	.634	.567	.525	.485	.447	.413	.381	.347	.320	.292	.264	.236	.209	.183	.156	.130	.104	.078	.052	.026
80	.750	.608	.541	.499	.459	.421	.387	.355	.321	.294	.266	.238	.210	.183	.157	.130	.104	.078	.052	.026	.000
81	.724	.582	.515	.473	.433	.395	.361	.329	.295	.268	.240	.212	.184	.157	.131	.104	.078	.052	.026	.000	—
82	.698	.556	.489	.447	.407	.369	.335	.303	.269	.242	.214	.186	.158	.131	.105	.078	.052	.026	.000	—	—
83	.672	.530	.463	.421	.381	.343	.309	.277	.243	.216	.188	.160	.132	.105	.079	.052	.026	.000	—	—	—
84	.645	.504	.437	.395	.355	.317	.283	.251	.217	.190	.162	.134	.106	.079	.053	.026	.000	—	—	—	—
85	.620	.478	.417	.369	.329	.291	.257	.225	.191	.164	.136	.108	.080	.053	.027	.000	—	—	—	—	—
86	.593	.451	.390	.343	.301	.265	.230	.198	.167	.137	.109	.081	.053	.026	—	—	—	—	—	—	—
87	.567	.425	.364	.317	.275	.238	.204	.172	.141	.111	.082	.055	.027	—	—	—	—	—	—	—	—
88	.540	.398	.337	.290	.248	.211	.177	.145	.114	.084	.056	.028	—	—	—	—	—	—	—	—	—
89	.512	.370	.309	.262	.220	.183	.149	.117	.086	.056	.028	—	—	—	—	—	—	—	—	—	—
90	.484	.342	.281	.234	.192	.155	.121	.089	.058	.028	—	—	—	—	—	—	—	—	—	—	—
91	.456	.314	.253	.206	.164	.127	.093	.061	.030	—	—	—	—	—	—	—	—	—	—	—	—
92	.426	.284	.223	.176	.134	.097	.063	.031	—	—	—	—	—	—	—	—	—	—	—	—	—
93	.395	.253	.192	.145	.103	.066	.032	—	—	—	—	—	—	—	—	—	—	—	—	—	—
94	.363	.221	.160	.113	.071	.034	—	—	—	—	—	—	—	—	—	—	—	—	—	—	—
95	.328	.187	.126	.079	.037	—	—	—	—	—	—	—	—	—	—	—	—	—	—	—	—
96	.292	.150	.089	.042	—	—	—	—	—	—	—	—	—	—	—	—	—	—	—	—	—
97	.251	.108	.047	—	—	—	—	—	—	—	—	—	—	—	—	—	—	—	—	—	—
98	.203	.061	—	—	—	—	—	—	—	—	—	—	—	—	—	—	—	—	—	—	—
99	.142	—	—	—	—	—	—	—	—	—	—	—	—	—	—	—	—	—	—	—	—

ORIGINAL POWER FACTOR IN PER CENT

System Load Capacity

An electrical system is installed for its load ability. Each part—transformers, cables, switches, etc.—are rated to carry a predesigned amount of electrical current. When the system operates at low power factor these expensive parts are not being used to good efficiency. Part of the load ability is being used to carry non-working current.

Let's look at a simple example of loading. Suppose we have an industrial plant with several induction motors, each drawing 10 amperes of line current at 80% power factor. At 80% power factor, only 8 amperes are used to produce horsepower. The remaining 2 amperes result from motor magnetizing current. This current does no useful work but is necessary to magnetize the motor.

Loading Examples

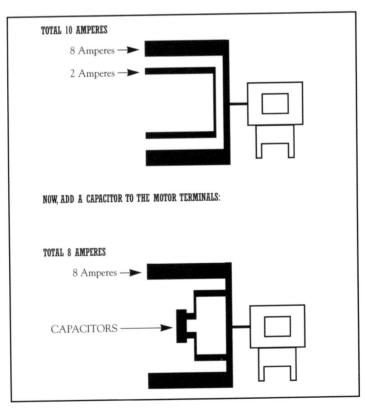

Addition of the capacitor has improved line power factor and subtracted the 2 amperes of non-working current from the lines—it is now supplied by the capacitor. For every set of four similar work stations this customer could now add one more motor with no increase in total current demand.

Capacitors Improve System Capacity

It's easy to figure how much system capacity may be gained by installing power capacitors where they are needed. Assuming that . . .

1. 20% MORE LOAD is expected in a typical plant, operating 480-volt, three-phase. How many capacitors are needed to carry this new load?
2. MONTHLY POWER BILLS show the load to be 400-kW demand at a power factor of 77 per cent.
3. HOW HIGH MUST THE POWER FACTOR be raised to gain 20% additional capacity? Using the graph below, you can see that to obtain a gain of 20% in kW capacity will require the power factor to be raised from 77 to 95%.
4. HOW MUCH WOULD THE CAPACITORS COST? Table 6.8 shows that increasing the power factor from 77 to 95% for 1 400-kW load requires 200 kVAr of capacitors. Assuming $10 per kVAr as the complete installed cost of capacitors, the 200 kVAr would cost about $2000.

This additional 20% capacity is immediately available for new motor and lighting loads without installing any new transformers or power lines. It is accomplished simply by installing 200 kVAr of capacitors.

Savings in power costs are in addition to this increased load capacity. With a power factor clause enforced by the local utility bonus savings are realized every year, in addition to the permanent increase in capacity of 20%.

Table 6.8

Corrected Power Factor of Present Load
(required to release additional capacity desired)

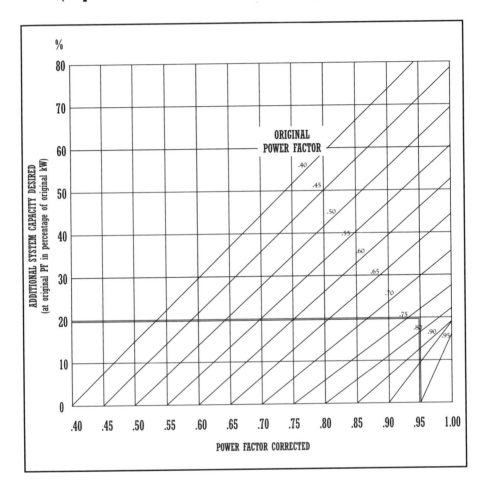

System Benefits From Improved Power Factor.
* BETTER VOLTAGE
* LOWER LOSSES
* LOWER POWER BILL
* POWER CAPACITORS improve electrical systems completely, whether applied to low voltage Industrial Plant loads or high voltage Utility distribution lines—voltage, losses, power bill.

The basic difference in estimating actual rewards from these improvements:

* Utility distribution lines have long wire runs, usually in miles of distance. We estimate system gains by referencing LOAD power factor and SYSTEM line characteristics.
* Industrial plant cables are relatively short in length. Therefore, we may reasonably neglect cable runs and estimate plant system improvements by referencing LOAD power factor and SUPPLY TRANSFORMER characteristics.

To show how electrical system benefits may be estimated we will work examples for both low voltage industrial and high voltage utility applications. Study either, or both, depending upon your sales responsibilities.

Keep in mind:

* Excessive voltage drops make motors overheat, cause poor lighting, interfere with motor controls and instruments.
* Extra losses result in extra power bill charges and shorter equipment life.
* Power Factor penalty clauses, enforced by many utilities, result in added dollars to each power bill.

Lower Voltage Industrial
* BETTER VOLTAGE

Percent voltage rise = $\dfrac{\text{kVAr of capacitors} \times \text{percent impedance of transformer}}{\text{kVA of transformer}}$

Example:

200 kVAr of capacitors installed

1000 kVA transformer with nameplate impedance of 5%

% voltage rise = $\dfrac{200 \times 5\%}{1000 \text{ kVA}}$ = 1.0% 1000

• LOWER LOSSES

$$\text{Percent reduction in losses} = 100 - 100 \left[\frac{\text{Original power factor}}{\text{Improved power factor}} \right]^2$$

Example: System with 5% losses, 100,000 kWh/month, 70% power factor
Power factor is improved to 95%

$$\% \text{ reduction in losses} = 100 - 100 \left[\frac{70}{95} \right]^2 = 100 - 100 \, (.54)$$

$$= 100 - 54 = 46\%$$

Therefore, the original losses of 5% are reduced by .46 x 5 = 2.3% and this reduction applies directly to the 100,000 kWh monthly billing

$$
\begin{aligned}
100,000 \times .023 &= 2300 \text{ kWh savings} \\
\text{A 4¢ per kWh rate this is } \$.04 \times 2300 &= \$92 \text{ per month} \\
&= \$1104 \text{ per year saving}
\end{aligned}
$$

This savings is bonus reward! Since low voltage capacitors are installed primarily to improve system load capacity, the savings in losses are extra contribution.

High Voltage Utility. Based on a 12470/7200 volt system with usual wire size and wire spacing —

• BETTER VOLTAGE

$$\text{Percent voltage rise} = \frac{\text{kVAr of capacitors x miles of line}}{1940}$$

EXAMPLE: 300 kVAr of capacitors installed 10 miles from substation

$$\% \text{ voltage rise} = \frac{300 \times 10}{1940} = 1.55\%$$

Lower Losses Percent system losses vs. power factor are shown in the abbreviated reference below.

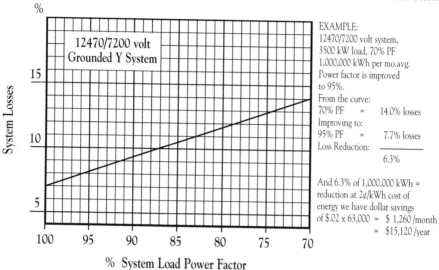

EXAMPLE:
12470/7200 volt system,
3500 kW load, 70% PF
1,000,000 kWh per mo.avg.
Power factor is improved
to 95%.
From the curve:
70% PF   =   14.0% losses
Improving to:
95% PF   =   7.7% losses
Loss Reduction: ____
                                6.3%

And 6.3% of 1,000,000 kWh =
reduction at 2¢/kWh cost of
energy we have dollar savings
of $.02 x 63,000 = $ 1,260 /month
                               = $15,120 /year

Utility line losses are of appreciable magnitude, especially at low power factors. Therefore, it is frequently practical to install high voltage capacitors for this dollar return. See how this works in our example:

From the Power Capacitor Improvement Table, the capacitor kVAr necessary to raise 70% PF to 95% PF is—

.691 x 3500 kW = 2400 kVAr, approximately

Estimating about $5/kVAr installed cost—

$5 x 2400 = $12,000

Reduction in losses will pay for capacitors in

$$\frac{\$12,000}{\$15,120} = 0.79 \text{ years}$$

Power Factor Penalty Clauses.

Many utilities penalize their customers for operating at low power factor levels. An abbreviated example of an actual penalty clause, with its effects on power bill charges, is given below: Since energy charges are not involved in this particular example they are not shown.

Example:

Small Industrial Plant	Utility Rate Schedule
480 v, 3 phase service	Demand Charge:
400 kW demand	$2.75 per kW first 100 kW demand
520 kVA demand	Power Factor: When the power factor
77% power factor	is less than 85%, the demand may be taken at
	85% of the measured kVA.

From the Rate Schedule Power Factor Clause: Extra billing from the low, 77% power factor —

Billing Demand will become $(442 - 400) \times \$2.00 = \$84$ per month

.85 X 520 = 442 kW   or = $1008 per year

Improving the power factor 85% by adding capacitors will save $1008 per year in billing demand alone.

From the Power Capacitor Improvement Table, the capacitor kVAr to improve 77% power factor to 85% power factor is —

.209 x 400 kW = 83.6 kVAr

Estimating the cost of 460 volt capacitors at $10/kVAr and rounding the 83.6 kVAr to a practical value of 85 kVAr —

$10 X 85 kVAr = $850

Therefore, eliminating the penalty charge will allow payment of capacitors in —

$$\frac{\$850}{\$1008} = 0.84 \text{ years}$$

Locating and Switching Pole-Type Capacitors on Utility Distribution Lines.

It is usually not necessary to make detailed location analysis of each feeder capacitor bank application. Little additional loss reduction or voltage benefits can be obtained. The power factor should be improved to nearly 100% during peak load conditions. To meet light load as well as seasonal load variations it may be necessary to install the total capacitor kVArs to each feeder in 3 or 4 banks, with some of the equipments switched. The banks can be located on convenient poles from 50–75 percent of the distance along the three-phase primary main. On feeders with long laterals extending beyond the primary main it may be desirable to install some capacitor kVArs on these laterals. This will provide additional voltage improvement to consumers in the more remote areas.

Table 6.9

Oil Switch

Max. 3-phase, 60 cycle capacitor kVAr that may be switched

Volts	kVAr
2400	600
4160	1080
4800	1215
7200	1845
7960	2070
12470	3240
13200	3420
13800	3555

Switched Pole-Type Equipments

use an oil switch. Three of these single-phase devices plus a junction box are mounted directly on the equipment. External 120 volt power is needed to actuate the switch mechanism. Maximum capacitor kVAr that may be handled by this switch at the distribution voltages are shown in the table.

Fusing Pole-Type Capacitors. Capacitors installed in pole-type equipments may be connected in Delta, Floating Wye or Ground Wye, depending upon system practice and voltage. Note, however, that capacitor banks are never grounded when applied to an ungrounded system.

Standard distribution system installation practice is to group fuse capacitors that are mounted in pole-type equipments, using standard cutouts. The cutout selected must be able to carry the 1.35 times rated bank current and be fused according to applicable electrical engineering standards.

Rated capacitor bank current is calculated as follows:

Single-phase equipments

$$\text{Current} = \frac{\text{Capacitor Bank kVAr}}{\text{Line kV}}$$

Three-phase equipments

$$\text{Current} = \frac{\text{Capacitor Bank kVAr}}{1.73 \text{ x line-to-line kV}}$$

Example:

600 kVAr three-phase, capacitor bank connected floating wye on a 12470 volt system. Bank is made up with (3) 200 kVAr units.

$$\text{Bank current} = \frac{600}{1.73 \text{ x } 12.47} = 27.8 \text{ Amperes}$$

Select a cutout with load rating at least equal to the — 27.8 x 1.35 = 37.5 Amperes

APPENDIX

C = Capacitance in microfarads
V = Voltage
A = Current
K = 1000

$$C = \frac{10^6}{(2\pi f) X_C} \qquad KVAR = \frac{(2\pi f) C(KV)^2}{10^3} \qquad X_C = \frac{10^6}{(2\pi f) C}$$

$$C = \frac{KVAR \text{ X } 10^3}{(2\pi f) (KV)^2} \qquad\qquad KVAR = \frac{(KV)^2 \text{ X } 10^3}{X_C}$$

Capacitor Current: $\dfrac{KVAR \text{ X } 10^3}{V \sqrt{3}}$, for three phase—

$\dfrac{KVAR \text{ X } 10^3}{V}$, for single phase

Load Factor: The average load divided by the peak load for a given period of time. Reading from a watt-varmeter serves as a source of determining load factor for both components of current.

Loss Factor: The average losses divided by the peak load losses. The System loss factor is a value somewhere between (load factor)^2 and (Load Factor) to the first power. Usually (Load Factor)$^{1.6}$ is assumed as the lost factor.

$\dfrac{X}{R}$ Ratio: The ratio of the system reactance and resistance in ohms.

Power Factor $= \text{COS}\, \emptyset = \dfrac{KW}{KVA}$

Since the installation of capacitors can cause electric system harmonics problems, the following discussion of harmonics is included in this publication.

Fundamentals of Harmonics

Invariably, any discussion of power quality must include the subject of harmonics. Virtually any repetitive disturbance, such as the cyclical firing of an SCR in a rectifier, can be expressed in terms of the harmonics that it injects into the system. Because of this, the effect of such disturbances can be minimized by reducing the magnitude of the harmonics and/or by increasing equipment's ability to withstand harmonics.[3]

Most customers seem to believe that harmonics are somewhat of a mystery. Since this is the case, this section is provided to explain what harmonics are, where they come from, how they affect system wave forms, how they affect system equipment, and how they can be controlled or reduced.

What are harmonics? A harmonic is a sinusoidal wave form that is a multiple of some fundamental frequency. For example, the second harmonic of 60 hertz is 2 x 60 = 120 hertz. Figure 6-10 shows two cycles of a 120 volt, 60 hertz wave form accompanied by its third harmonic (180 hertz).

Notice that in the same time that the fundamental completes two full cycles, the third harmonic completes six full cycles. Notice also that both wave forms are sine waves. Table 6-10 lists some of the key harmonics which may be encountered in a power system along with their frequency.

Table 6.10

Time in Seconds

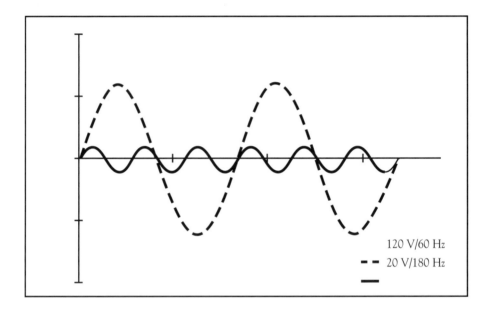

120 V/60 Hz
--- 20 V/180 Hz
———

Where do harmonics come from? An alternating voltage or current is produced by a repetitive action. The 60 hertz alternating voltage created by a generator is caused by the repetitive cutting of lines of flux as it rotates. Because the rotation of a generator is smooth, continuous action, it creates a smooth, continuous voltage wave form called a sine wave. Both of the wave forms shown in Figure 1 are sine waves. Other system events can also inject alternating currents or voltages into a power system. For example:

- A voltage transformer which is saturating at the peak of every current wave form will produce an output voltage with a flattened top. Since this flattening occurs repetitively and since it is nonsinusoidal it amounts to injecting harmonics into the system.

- Rectifiers which used silicon-controlled rectifiers will create a variety of alternating voltages which will distort the 60 hertz wave form.

- Fluorescent lighting fixtures will produce alternating voltages which will also distort the 60 hertz wave form.

Table 6.11
Harmonics and Their Frequencies (60 Hz Base)

Harmonic Number	Frequency
1	60
2	120
3	180
5	300
7	420
9	540
11	660
13	780
15	900
21	1260
25	1500

How do harmonics affect system voltage and current wave forms?

Figure 6-11 shows an output wave form which might appear at the secondary of a transformer that is saturating at the voltage or current peaks. Figure 6-12 is a diagram of the type of distortion that might appear at the input to a fluorescent lighting fixture. Figure 6-13 is the distortion introduced by a typical six-pulse recitifer.

Table 6.12

120 Volt, 60 Hz Plus 16.7% 3rd

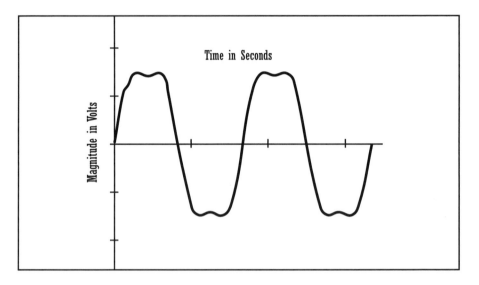

Table 6.13

Fluorescent Light Voltage

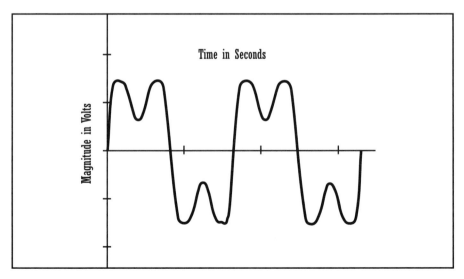

Each of these figures is a worst-case diagram. That is, the amount of distortion is shown as though the transformer, light, or rectifier were the only load in the system. Since any given piece of equipment will be only a small part of the overall load the actual distortion will usually be less than what is shown. At the same time, if there are many such pieces of equipment, they will all add up.

This is a very important point. Figures 6-12, 6-13, and 6-14 were created using a program called MathCad[+1]. They were created by adding the sum of several harmonics. For example, Figure 6-12 was created from the following formula:

$$f(t) = 120\sin(60) + 20\sin(180)$$

f(t) was then graphed on the vertical axis versus t on the horizontal axis. In other words, Figure 2 is the result of adding 16.7 percent third harmonic to a 120 volt fundamental sine wave. Therefore, repetitive, distorted voltages or currents can be evaluated by expressing them as the sum of their harmonics. Figures 6-13 and 6-14 were created in a similar manner although their formulas are quite a bit more complex. This shows that various pieces of equipment distort the system voltage and/or current. The distorted wave forms can be corrected by subtracting or removing the harmonics that are present. Consequently, the distortion can be treated as though the devices created harmonics and added them into the power system.

How do harmonics affect the power system equipment? The answer to this questions depends on the equipment. For example:

- The presence of a high level of second harmonic (120 hertz) in a generator circuit can cause the rotor to overheat even when total current is not higher than full load. Second harmonic is often the result of unbalanced phase currents which can cause reverse rotating magnetic fields in the air gap of the generator. This reverse field can severely overheat the rotor.

- Many of the harmonics in a power system are negative sequence. That is, the A-phase fifth harmonic leads the C-phase component by 120 degrees and lags the B-phase component by 120, the exact opposite of the 60 hertz component. These negative sequence currents reverse rotating magnetic fields which will cause heating in virtually all three-phase magnetic circuits.

- Odd third order harmonics (3rd, 9th, 15th, etc.) are in phase in the three-phase wires. This means that they add up in the neutral. Under severe circumstances, the neutral can actually be carrying more current than any of the three-phase wires. This is why the neutral wire may have to be over-sized in some circuits.

Table 6.14

Pulse Rectifier Distortion

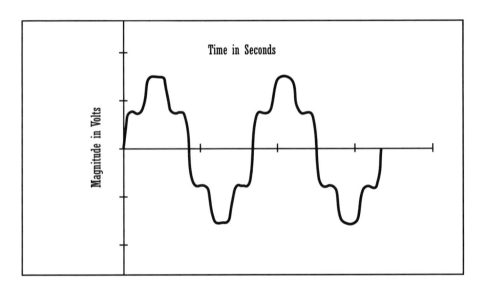

- The magnetic fields created by alternating currents tend to force them to flow toward the outside of a conductor. The higher the frequency the greater the concentration. This condition is called the "skin effect." Since the current is being forced into a smaller cross-sectional area, it will encounter more resistance. This causes more heating.

- The magnetic circuits of motors, transformers, generators, relays, and other such devices are designed to operate at 60 hertz. At frequencies other than 60, efficiency falls off and heating goes up.

- Sensitive electronic equipment may pick up the higher frequency harmonics of a distorted wave form. This can often cause the computer to misoperate.

- Power system capacitors have a lower reactance at the harmonic frequencies. Therefore, they will tend to draw more current at these frequencies. Such a condition can cause the capacitors to fail even though system voltages seem to be normal.

Clearly, harmonics can cause significant problems in a power system and should be mitigated before they cause such damage.

How can harmonics be reduced and controlled in a power system? Like most power quality problems, harmonic mitigation is best handled using a logical, step-by-step approach.

1. Model a power system using a computerized harmonic load flow program. There are many such programs available in the market. There are also many engineering consulting firms that will perform such services. Note that this step is a relatively small addition to the overall engineering studies such as short-circuit analysis, coordination, and load flow.

2. Using a model of the system developed in step one, perform a harmonic load flow and identify potential trouble areas in your system where high harmonic voltages and/or currents exist. IEEE Standard 519 is the industry standard for maximum allowable harmonic percentage levels.

3. Using recording equipment, monitor the locations in the system which have been identified as trouble areas. If in-house expertise is not available, testing companies and some consulting engineers will perform this service.

4. In those locations where harmonic content is higher than desired, filters may be applied. Harmonic filters are shunt devices which are tuned to pass the harmonic values while blocking the 60 hertz component. Thus, undesired harmonics are shunted and the desired 60 hertz voltage is passed on to the load. Techniques other than filtering are also available; however, because of the relative sophistication of such procedures, it is recommended that, for assistance sake, an outside consultant be retained.

5. Keep the system model up to date so that you can play "what if" games when you plan to put in new equipment.

6. Install synchronous condensers. (See next section addressing the utilization of these condensers)

Conclusion. Harmonics have become an increasing problem in the modern era. Interestingly, many of the devices that are sensitive to them are also contributors of them. Rectifiers, computers, and many other types of equipment are all very sensitive to and a source of harmonic distortion in power systems.

For further reading, obtain a copy of IEEE Standard 519. Also, Chapter 9 of the IEEE Red Book has an excellent coverage of the subject. And, finally, no power quality library is complete without a copy of The Dranetz Field Handbook for Power Quality Analysis. While not specifically aimed at harmonics, the Dranetz Handbook covers most of the power quality issues in excellent detail.

Synchronous Condensers

Utilization of synchronous condensers to improve power factor and not add to existing harmonics in large electrical systems.[4]

CORRECTING POWER FACTOR

A low power factor can be offset by the addition of reactive power using capacitors or condensers.

Table 6.15
Capacitors

Adding Reactive Power Without Power Source

Table 6.16
Condensers

Adding Reactive Power With Power Source

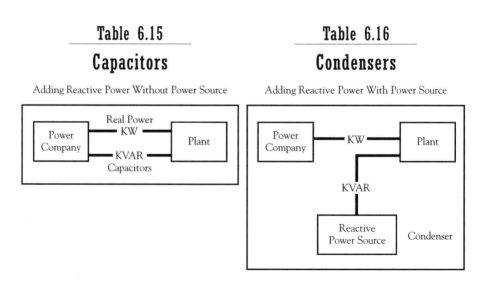

CONDENSER ADVANTAGES

Condenser Feature	Benefit
1. Reactive Power Source	Stiffens bus voltage, assists in motor starting.
2. No voltage spikes such as those caused downtime due to electronic	Safe for electronic equipment, reduces by switching capacitors equipment failure caused by voltage spikes.
3. Absorbs low level harmonic, does not add to existing harmonics.	Safe for electronic equipment, reduces downtime, resulting in cleaner power.
4. Automatic power factor monitoring and control.	Higher reliability than other methods of power factor control. (See section under condenser Starting and Control.)
5. Installed at a single location.	Convenience.
6. If purchased with an extended shaft can act as spare motor.	Dual purpose.
7. Typical payback under two years.	Cost effective.

The synchronous condenser is a specific application-designed motor utilized for power factor correction. They typically range in correction capacity from 1500 KVAR up to more than 15,000 KVAR.

Synchronous Condensers. As loads increase, synchronous condensers become the equipment of choice for many plants.

A synchronous condenser is a custom designed unit used for power factor correction. It operates at no load and at constant speed. The condenser monitors the system and adjusts the power factor to a set point when necessary.

The major components of a synchronous condenser are as follows:
- Stator
- Rotor
- Brushless exciter
- Controls

Stator Construction. The stator laminations are made of thin sheets of low loss, high grade silicon steel. Vent spacers are integral to the stator core. Made of high strength steel, they create core vents for cooling air to remove generated heat. The laminations and vent spacers are stacked between two heavy steel end plates, compressed under high pressure and then secured. This stacking procedure serves to reduce electrically generated noise and vibration.

The electrical conductors of the stators are rectangular copper wire strands. Each copper strand is coated with a heavy polyester film and then covered with a double layer of fused polyester and dacron-glass wrap. These materials serve as the turn-to-turn insulating materials. A coil consists of several turns of copper wire, which is formed to the desired shape for insertion into the stator core.

Each coil is wrapped with multiple layers of glass-backed resin-bonded MICA tape which serves as the ground wall insulation. An additional layer of glass tape is applied over the entire coil to serve as an abrasion resistant covering. For high voltage designs, a layer of conductive tape is applied to the slot portion of each coil to protect against insulation damage due to corona. A set of coils is then carefully inserted into a stator core. End coils are braced and supported to assure mechanical strength.

Vacuum Pressure Impregnation (VPI) is the process used to encapsulate each coil in the wound stator and complete the insulation system. The completely wound and connected stator is heated to drive off any moisture and then placed in a pressure vessel. A vacuum is drawn to remove the air within the coils and slots. While still under vacuum, the vessel is flooded with a 100% solid synthetic resin.

Pressure is then applied to the vessel which forces the resin into the slots and into the layers of tape. When baked, the stator coils and slots become completely filled and no detrimental movement of coils can take place. Also, since the slots and coils no longer have any coils, there is a built-in resistance to corona.

The VPI process is important from the standpoint of making the stator a homogeneous structure for support of the coils, but it also serves to effectively seal the stator from such contaminants as oil, chemicals, conductive dusts and moisture.

Rotor Construction. Synchronous condensers utilize shaft designs that are computer matched to give optimum configuration for bearing spans, rotor weights and operating speed. Shafts with large cross-sections eliminate potential shaft stiffness and critical speed problems, thus maximizing rotor stability.

Rotor spiders are constructed of either individually punched heavy steel laminations, ductile castings, or stress-relieved steel fabrications, depending on the requirements of the application. The individual poles are held to the spider either with dovetails or by bolting, again depending upon the anticipated rotational forces. The shaft-spider is designed to handle the stresses imposed by the centrifugal forces caused by the rotating elements. It also allows ample cooling air to flow into the rotor, thereby eliminating hot spots and maximizing performance.

Poles are fabricated using low loss sheet steel laminations. This steel selection affords lower operating cost due to higher efficiencies. Individual laminations are then stacked, compressed under high pressure, and welded.

The amortisseur or damper winding of large diameter high conductive copper bars are inserted, the bar ends connected and welded to form a closed or short circuit loop. Insulated copper coils are wound directly onto the individual poles, insulated, and braced. The poles are sealed utilizing a 100% solid, high bond strength, epoxy insulation and cured with heat to provide a strong mechanical structure to withstand the high rotational forces . . . even those of high overspeed conditions. This pole construction also provides superior protection against the effects of abrasion, moisture and chemical attack.

Bearings. Self Aligning Split Sleeve Bearings are standard on almost all synchronous condensers. The bearing chambers utilize large oil reservoirs to assure adequate lubrication and heat dissipation for cooler running bearings. Sleeve bearings are typically self-cooled. They are designed for optimum length-to-diameter ratios making possible low bearing loading for longer operating life. An inboard seal and close running fits are used to maintain a positive pressure so no oil vapors can pass to the inside of the machine. Venting chambers equalize the pressure in the bearings keeping the oil in the chamber.

Excitation. The best excitation for a synchronous condenser is of the brushless type.

The brushless rotating exciter with rotating rectifier unit is used for providing excitation current to the rotating field of the condenser. The superior design of the brushless unit simplifies maintenance of the equipment by eliminating parts subject to wear, thereby assuring prolonged periods of dependable, trouble-free operation.

The complete excitation unit consists of two basic component assemblies; a three-phase, rotating alternating current generator; and a three-phase, full-wave rectifier composed of six semiconductor diodes mounted on a heat sink fixed to an insulating hub. Surge supressors are provided to protect the diodes against over-voltage.

The exciter armature and the rectifier assembly are mounted on the main rotor shaft, and are electrically interconnected with each other and the main field winding. The field current for the exciter is provided by a stationary source in the Field Application Panel that houses all the condenser controls.

Condenser Starting and Control—Methods of Synchronous Condenser Starting and Control Across the Line Starting.
The easiest and most cost effective method is to start the condenser across-the-line as a synchronous motor. The advantages to this are the low cost motor starter and uncomplicated synchronization equipment. The main disadvantage is that when the line has a very limited capacity, the voltage drop experienced at machine start-up may be objectionable.

Reduced Voltage Starting. The second method of starting synchronous condensers is the use of reduced voltage starting techniques. There is no load torque on the shaft, and no starting torque required, except for the breakaway torque of the bearings. The machine may be started with any number of reduced voltage methods; series parallel or autotransformer starters being preferred. Reduced voltage starting techniques have the advantage of reducing the inrush required of the plant service, minimizing the voltage drop experienced on the line. Across-the-line starting and reduced voltage starting use the same power factor control equipment. The disadvantage of reduced voltage starting is that the motor starter is slightly more expensive and complicated.

Pony Motor Starting. The third starting method is the use of a small induction motor to accelerate the condenser to near synchronous speed. The condenser is then connected to the line. The advantage of this method is that the induction motor draws a smaller current from the line eliminating most of the voltage drop. This motor starting technique is less complicated than that used with a reduced voltage starter. The same type of power factor control is used with either method. One disadvantage of this method is that the starting motor or pony motor is connected to the shaft and must rotate with the condenser at all times. Therefore it cannot be used for other purposes.

Pony Motor Starting with Bus Synchronization. The fourth starting method is the use of a pony motor as described previously, but instead of closing in the unexcited condenser to the line, one must synchronize to the line as though paralleling a generator. The advantages of this system are a low inrush during acceleration and a smooth transition as the condenser is placed on line. The disadvantage of this method is that the voltage regulator must change operating parameters when the condenser is connected to the line. Before the condenser is connected, the controller regulates the voltage output of the condenser. After this transition, the controller regulates the voltage output of the condenser. After this transition, the controller regulates the power factor by using different circuitry. Additional circuitry is needed to achieve a smooth transition from one mode of operation to the other.

Automatic Power Factor Control. Synchronous condensers are designed to maintain power factor at a preset level. This is accomplished automatically by the use of a power factor controller. The power factor controller continually senses voltage and current and the phase angle between the two. If the phase angle between voltage and current extends beyond the allowed preset band, it signals the voltage regulator to change the excitation of the field to bring the phase angle within the preset band. Power factor control is accomplished smoothly and automatically. The engineering approach to the viability of utilizing synchronous condensers in a specific application would include the following items:

A.   Preliminary Engineering Support Including:
1.   Evaluate power system, demand and load types to size the proper condenser(s).
2.   Evaluate power supply and recommend proper condenser starting and control equipment.

B.   Provide Condenser and Controls Including:
1.   Bearing temperature detectors
2.   Stator temperature detectors
3.   Space heaters
4.   Lighting arrestors
5.   Surge capacitors
6.   Starting and control panels

C. Certified Routine Test Reports Including:
    1. Running current
    2. Saturation curves
    3. High potential test
    4. Winding resistance
    5. Vibration check

D. Certified Performance Tests Including:
    1. Temperature rise
    2. Starting current
    3. KW losses at 1/2, 3/4 and full KVAR output
    4. KVAR output at synchronous speed

E. Start-up Service and Maintenance Support Including:
    1. Check electrical installation
    2. Examine overall installation
    3. Verify proper functioning of the controls
    4. Annual maintenance check

F. Turnkey Installation:
    This would include all Items A through E being provided by the manufacturer/installer.

Figure 6.10

Examples of Tariff Schedules Concerning Power Factor

Power Factor Adjustments

1. Power Factor Adjustment: The rate is based upon the operation of the customer's equipment at an average monthly power factor of 85%. When the average power factor is above or below 85%, the sum of the demand and energy charges will be multiplied by the following constants:

AVERAGE MONTHLY POWER FACTOR	CONSTANT
100%	0.9510
95%	0.9650
90%	0.9810
85%	1.0000
80%	1.0230
75%	1.0500
70%	1.0835
65%	1.1255
60%	1.1785
55%	1.2455
50%	1.3335

2. Power Factor Adjustment: When the customer's power factor is less than 85% lagging, the utility may adjust the kW measured to determine the demand by multiplying the measured kW by 85% and dividing by the actual power factor.

3. Excess kVA Charge: $0.58 for each kVA of demand in excess of the maximum demand in kW created during the on-peak and off-peak hours. Such kVA shall be determined by dividing the maximum demand by the average power factor for the month.

4. Reactive Demand Charge: $0.59 per kVAr over one-third of kW demand.

To better understand how low power factor can affect the monthly billing, see Figure 6.11. This billing is typical of how many utilities penalize for low power factor. Many times on the face of a billing it is never actually spelled out that there is a penalty; or furthermore, if there happens to be a penalty—how much is it? This billing contains many of the 17 basic elements previously described in Chapter 5, Figure 5.1-"Items Common to Electric Billings." In Figure 6.11 there are 13 of the 17 items present on this billing. Can you identify them?

Figure 6.11

Electric Billing Detail Example of Power Factor Penalty

SERVICE PERIOD			TYPE OF METER READING		
Jan 04 to Feb 07			Actual		

METER NUMBER	Present	METER READING Previous	METER CONSTANT	kWh USAGE	ACTUAL DEMAND
A7132168	(On-peak) 1406	1299	1400	149800	
B7132168	(Off-peak) 1340	1228	1400	156800	
C7132168	.96	0	1400		1344.0 kVA
D7132168	.69	0	1400	_____	966.0 kW
				306600	

RATE: (G4P) Time-of-Use Large Power

PREVIOUS BALANCE 12/09			$ 27,786.14
PAYMENT			- 27,786.14
BALANCE FORWARD			.00

CUSTOMER CHARGE:				$ 65.58
DEMAND CHARGE:		1209.6 kVA X $8.750	=	$ 10,584.00
USAGE CHARGE:	(On-peak)	149800 kWh X $ .03658	=	$ 5,479.20
	(Off-peak)	156800 kWh X $ .02447	=	$ 3,836.39
FUEL CHARGE:		306600 kWh X $ .02516	=	$ 7,714.06
HIGH VOLTAGE DISCOUNT:		(12.4 kV) 1209.6 X $.5300	=	$ (614.08)
SALES TAX		(Exempt)		
TOTAL CURRENT AMOUNT:				$ 27,038.15
TOTAL ACCOUNT BALANCE:				$ 27,038.15

Explanation of Electric Billing in Figure 6.11

The item being investigated on this billing is *power factor*. Is it present? And if it is, what is its impact? The three items on this billing that must be examined are as follows:

1. The actual peak kVA that the utility provided—1344 kVA
2. The actual peak kW that the customer used—966 kW
3. The demand amount billed—1209.6 kVA

There are three different quantities shown on this billing which may seem to have little relationship to each other but actually make sense when analyzed.

1. The actual peak energy that was provided by the utility was 1344 kVA.
2. The actual peak demand load that the customer incurred was 966 kW.
3. The monthly demand billed by the utility was 1209.6 kVA.

The two key items to understand are the differences between what the utility had to provide (1344 kVA) and what was actually recorded in kW through the customer's usage (966 kW). The relationship of 1344 kVA to 966 kW is 72%, or the utility provided 28% more kVA than appeared on the customer's demand usage (966 kW ÷ 1344 kVA) = 72%. This 28% difference results in 378 kVA (1344 kVA – 966 kW) that could represent lost revenue for the utility if actual kW was used as the billing figure.

To eliminate this situation the utility, in the tariff schedule for this particular rate code (G4P),details the method to be utilized to determine billing demand as follows:

"**Monthly Billing Demand will be the greatest of the following—**

1. The maximum 15 minute measured kW demand in the billing month.
2. 90% of the maximum 15 minute measured kVA demand in the billing month."

Since the relationship of actual kVA to actual kW for the month being billed was 72% (966 kW ÷ 1344 kVA), actual kW cannot be utilized to determine billing demand. The method used to determine billing demand was to multiply the kVA by 90% (1344 x 90%) = 1209.6 kVA billing demand.

Although there is no indication on the billing with relation to power factor penalty, in actuality, a penalty of 243.6 kW occurred (1209.6 kVA − 966 kW). This 243.6 kW cost $2131.50 (243.6 x $8.75). Since this billing represents an actual case, the resolution to this low power factor problem was to install power factor correction capacitors as shown in Figure 6.8. The payback was less than one year, and the utility did the installation and billed on a monthly basis until the installation was completely paid, which eliminated the requirement for any up-front costs to the customer.

Any time a monthly billing shows a billing demand figure different than the actual monthly demand, check for extra costs due to either power factor or ratchet provisions in the tariff schedule. Do not expect the monthly billing necessarily to explain or even show if an actual penalty occurred or even how much it may be. It is the customer's responsibility to manage their own usage costs.

The 13 items present on this billing from the 17 items listed in Chapter 5, Figure 5.1—"Items Common to Electric Billings" are as follows:

#1	Meter number/reading	
#2	Meter multiplier (constant)	(1400)
#3 (& #10)	Usage	(306600 kWh)

#4 (& #11)	Demand	(966 kW)
#5	Customer rate classification	(G4P)
#6	Voltage level	(12.4 kV)
#7	Power factor	(1344 kVA vs 966 kW)
#9	Customer charge	($65.58)
#10 (& #3)	Usage	(306600 kWh)
#11 (& #4)	Fuel cost adjustment clause	
#15	Taxes	
#16	Total current bill	
#17	Previous payments	

III. Demand

Demand as it applies to an electrical system is defined as, "the rate at which electric energy is delivered to or by a system, part of a system, or a piece of equipment expressed in kilowatts (kW), kilovoltamperes (kVA), or other suitable units at a given instant or average over a designated period of time." The primary source of demand is the power consuming equipment of a customer.

Peak or maximum demand charges are applied to the maximum demand for energy required by a system in a given period of time. All utilities charge a monthly fee based upon the maximum quantity of power (generally expressed as kilowatts) averaged in a given period of time, generally either a 15 or 30-minute interval.

The peak or maximum demand charge can vary from less than $2.00 to over $18.00 per kilowatt per month. The reduction of these peaks can result in sizeable savings. Many times a revision in how and when equipment is turned on or off can be all that is needed to reduce the monthly demand charges. In other instances, a computer controlled energy management system can be installed which will sense and adjust changing energy requirements to reduce peak demands.

The following steps can assist in determining and correcting peak demands.

1. Determine current peak demand and the monthly charges related to it. (This information can generally be obtained from the monthly utility bill.) Make certain that power factor or ratchet provisions are understood and taken into consideration when analyzing demand data.

2. Contact the utility and request that a strip chart recorder be installed in the system for at least a one-month period. The purpose of this recorder is to document, in strip chart form by day and time-of-day, the variations in the electrical demand of the operation.

    When the recorder chart strip is received, it will look very similar to an electrocardiogram in that it will show the peaks and valleys caused by changing demands. When the chart strip is analyzed, try to determine if there are any repetitive peak patterns, from hour-to-hour, day-to-day, or week-to-week.

    If there are repetitive patterns, determine what is happening at those times that cause the peaks to occur: e.g., start of a work shift, employee break or lunch times, equipment testing, etc.

    Once the information is received on the peak periods, a determination can be made as to the corrective action to take. Do not try to level demand to a perfectly uniform usage at all times since in most cases this will not be possible, but try to reduce perhaps the top 25% or 30% of the peak periods.

    This is not only the least costly approach but in most cases can be done by either procedural changes in equipment usage or personnel schedules. Work with the utility company on this since they can provide much technical insight into how to lower specific peak demand periods.

Demand is billed in at least two different ways—Non-time Differentiated and Time-of-Use/Time-of-Day. Non-time Differentiated demand billing means that the maximum peak demand period will be billed at a fixed rate without regard to when the demand occurred.

Time-of-Use/Time-of-Day demand billing means that the maximum peak demand period will be billed at a variable rate depending upon what time of the day or in some instances what time of the year the demand occurred. In Figure 6.12, the same demand peak period is shown in both Non-time Differentiated and Time-of-Use/Time-of-Day billing methods.

Figure 6.12

Analyzing Non-time Differentiated Profiles
Compared to Time-of-Use/Time-of-Day Demand Profiles

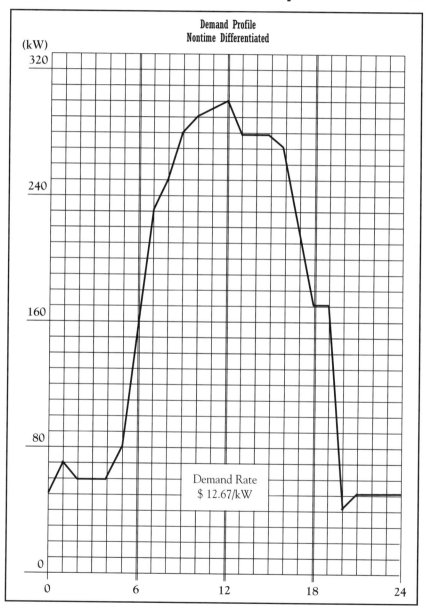

Figure 6.12 (Continued)

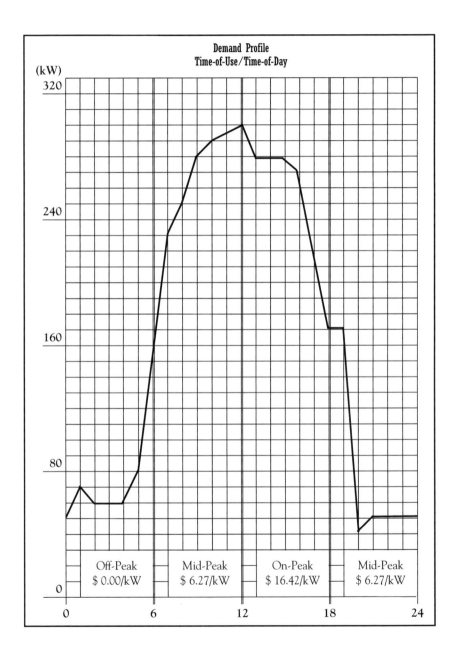

Explanation of Information in Figure 6.12

The two demand profiles represent only a one-day period but each represents the same demand characteristics. The only difference between the two profiles is in the determination of how the peak demand cost is calculated. In both profiles, the peak demand occurred at 12 noon and was 300 kW. The differences are summarized as follows:

1. **Demand profile Non-time Differentiated—**
   The demand cost per kW in this example is $12.67/kW. This cost per kW is the same regardless of where the peak kW occurs. If the peak occurred at 1 AM, 6 AM, 12 noon, 6 PM or at any other time, the cost per kW would remain at $12.67/kW.

   When peak demand is billed in this manner, the only way to reduce demand cost is to reduce the demand peak. Shifting or moving the demand peak will not result in any savings as far as cost per peak kW is concerned.

   When a situation such as this is present, the use of a demand profile analysis as shown in Figure 6.14 will assist in determining how to reduce the demand peaks.

2. **Demand profile Time-of-Use/Time-of-Day—**
   The demand cost in this example ranges from $16.42/kW to $0.00/kW depending upon when the demand peak occurs. Since the on-peak or expensive demand cost period is from 12 noon to 8 PM (20th hour) and the demand peak on this example occurred at 12 noon, the cost would be $16.42/kW.

   If the demand peak could be shifted to 11:55 AM or some other period prior to 12 noon, the cost would be reduced to $6.27/kW, or a savings of $10.15/kW. In this example, the total savings would be (300 kW X $10.15/kW) = $3,045. As can be seen, the savings potential to shift this peak demand to a less expensive period would probably be well worth the effort involved.

The use of a demand profile analysis as shown in Figure 6.14 will assist in both analyzing the magnitude of the demand peaks as well as when they are occurring so that both reduction as well as shifting of the peak periods can be investigated. The first step in analyzing demand cost is the creation of a demand profile so that variability in magnitude as well as time of occurrence can be observed.

Demand Data Recovery

To record demand peaks, a utility generally utilizes either totalizing or electronic pulse type of metering. In a totalizing meter, the maximum demand peak is recorded on the meter but the time the peak occurred or demand levels at other than the peak period are not recorded. On this type of meter, the demand register is generally reset monthly to zero. When this type of meter is utilized, a demand profile cannot be obtained since demand data is not accumulated.

When an electronic pulse type of meter is utilized, all individual demand peaks are recorded and stored within the meter. This type of meter is utilized when Time-of-Use/Time- of-Day Rates are utilized. Since individual demand peak data is available, a demand profile can be charted that provides complete demand peak data.

If a totalizing meter is currently being utilized to record demand and usage data, it will be necessary to have the utility install a pulse type of meter so that complete demand data can be evaluated. Typically, utilities will provide this service at little or no cost ($50-$500). The data that will result from a pulse meter will be in a form similar to the sample shown in Figure 6.13. Since data in this form is difficult to analyze, always have the utility translate the digital data to analog or chart form as shown in Figure 6.14. There should be no charge for providing the data in both digital as well as analog or chart forms.

Figure 6.13

Digital Data Chart

Digital data as retrieved from a digital pulse recording in 15-minute recording intervals.

DATE: 10/04/

					DIGITAL DATA						
TIME	DEMAND	TIME	DEMAND	TIME	DEMAND	TIME	DEMAND	TIME	DEMAND	TIME	DEMAND
0:15	522	0:30	515	0:45	520	1:00	520	1:15	518	1:30	515
1:45	520	2:00	515	2:15	511	2:30	515	2:45	515	3:00	518
3:15	524	3:30	518	3:45	518	5:00	524	4:15	522	4:30	520
4:45	515	5:00	522	5:15	515	5:30	503	5:45	511	6:00	566
6:15	868	6:30	895	6:45	914	7:00	1075	7:15	2310 Max	7:30	1966
7:45	1703	8:00	1569	8:15	1599	8:30	1703	8:45	1703	9:00	1709
9:15	1768	9:30	1807	9:45	1761	10:00	1832	10:15	1895	10:30	1826
10:45	1845	11:00	1908	11:15	1866	11:30	1870	11:45	1926	12:00	1878
12:15	1874	12:30	1926	12:45	1905	13:00	1880	13:15	1920	13:30	1943
13:45	1891	14:00	1872	14:15	1949	14:30	1932	14:45	1872	15:00	1935
15:15	1955	15:30	1910	15:45	1918	16:00	2003	16:15	1964	16:30	1991
16:45	2047	17:00	2012	17:15	1914	17:30	1926	17:45	2014	18:00	1611
18:15	1569	18:30	1713	18:45	1642	19:00	1601	19:15	1611	19:30	1425
19:45	1382	20:00	1432	20:15	1386	20:30	1430	20:45	841	21:00	839
21:15	829	21:30	778	21:45	649	22:00	618	22:15	601	22:30	540
22:45	520	23:00	503	23:15	499	23:30	499	23:45	493 Min	24:00	505

Explanation of Figure 6.13

This sample of digital data as extracted from an electronic pulse meter shows the data that would be available for a one-day period. The measurement interval is 15 minutes with the data being plotted from left to right. For example, the first reading is 0:15 which is at 12:15 AM on the date shown and the demand peak for this period is 522 kW. The next reading 0:30 is at 12:30 AM with the demand peak of 515 kW. There are 96 individual readings per 24-hour day or 2976 readings in a 31-day month. On the particular day this sample represents, the minimum peak demand occurred at 24:00 (12:00 midnight) and was 493 kW.

The maximum peak demand occurred at 7:15 (7:15 AM) and was 2310 kW. To completely analyze the demand peaks for an entire 31-day month would require the evaluation of 2976 individual pieces of data which in and of itself is a major undertaking.

Since the analyzation of data in this form is difficult and time- consuming, the translation to chart form is shown in Figure 6.14. The data as detailed in Figure 6.20 for a one-day period was accumulated for an entire 31-day month and translated to the chart shown in Figure 6.14.

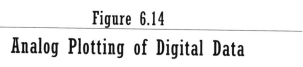

Figure 6.14
Analog Plotting of Digital Data

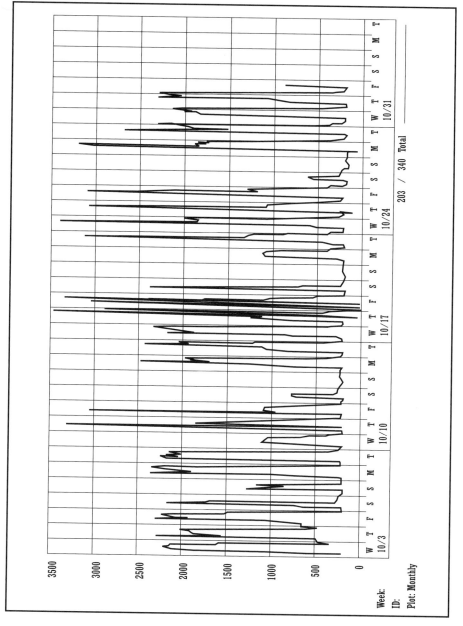

Explanation of Figure 6.14

The data plotted on this chart originated in digital form as shown in Figure 6.13. As can be seen from this chart, large variations in peak demand levels occurred from less than 500 kW to a high of 3490 kW. When evaluating data as shown on a chart like this, the upper demand peaks are the ones to investigate since the highest peak demand, 3490 kW in this case, determines the demand cost for the month.

The question to ask is—how much can the peak demand be reduced?One of the things to look at is how many times peak demand exceeded some threshold. In this example, demand peaks exceeded 3000 kW only 16 times in a 31-day period.

Since there are 2976 15-minute intervals in a 31-day period, on a percentage basis the 3000 kW level was exceeded only one-half of one percent of the time $(16 \div 2976) = .005$. Since demand reduction is not an exact science, it would seem that a maximum level of 3000 kW might be attainable based upon the data for this month.

The next step is to evaluate when all demand peaks over 3000 kW occurred and, if possible, why they occurred. The digital data as shown in Figure 6.13 would be evaluated for each of the demand peaks over 3000 kW to determine exact times of occurrence. Once exact times are known, facility personnel can be used to determine reasons for the high demand peaks.

Hopefully some event can be traced to the time of the high peaks. If an event can be identified, then the process of determining whether that event can be eliminated or shifted to some other period can begin. In the particular situation profiled here, demand was reduced to a maximum level of no more than 3100 kW by shifting certain operations to other time periods. There was no capital cost to do this and the on-going monthly reduction amounted to about 300 kW at a savings of $8.75/kW or over $2,600 per month.

When analyzing a demand profile, try to determine ways to reduce the highest demand peaks. If the demand peak billing method is Time-of-

Use/Time-of-Day, try to shift demand peaks to less expensive billing periods—from on-peak to mid- or off-peak periods (see Figure 6.12).

Sometimes the utilization of an EMS (Energy Management System) can assist in reducing demand peaks by shifting or cycling operating loads to reduce or shift peaks so that demand costs will be lowered. The first step in demand peak control is to have a demand profile available to analyze. A thorough analysis of profile data together with consultation with the persons involved at the facility level can lead to reduced electrical costs with little or no capital expenditure.

Figure 6.15
Controlled vs. Uncontrolled Demand

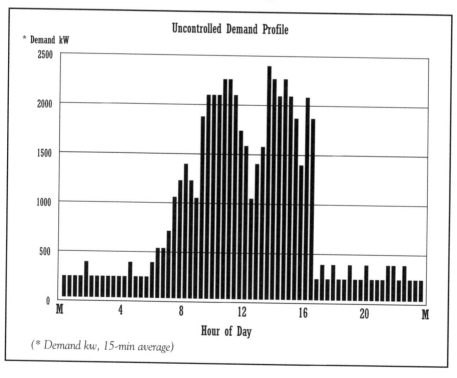

Uncontrolled demand profile reveals poorly distributed loading during the work portion (6:00 AM/5:00 PM) of the 24-hour day assuming the profile shown is the high day for the month. The total demand cost for the month would be calculated as follows —cost/kW - $10, a high demand of 2250 kW occurred at 2:00/2:15 PM, 2250 kWx$10 = $22,500.

Figure 6.16
Controlled vs. Uncontrolled Demand

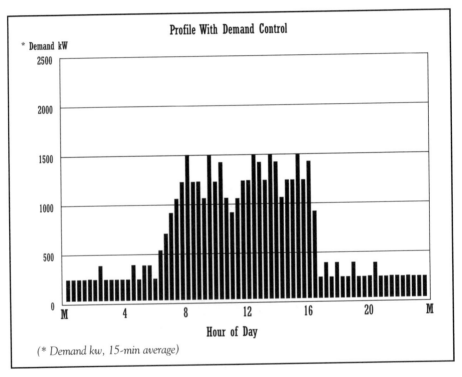

Profile With Demand Control

(* Demand kw, 15-min average)

Controlled demand profile reveals a maximum demand of 1500kW. At $10/kW the demand cost would be 1500 kWx$10 =$15,000. The savings achieved through demand control is—($22,500 – $15,000)=$7,500, or 33%. Control in this example was accomplished by the installation of an energy management System (EMS).

Figure 6.17
Load Rescheduling Impact

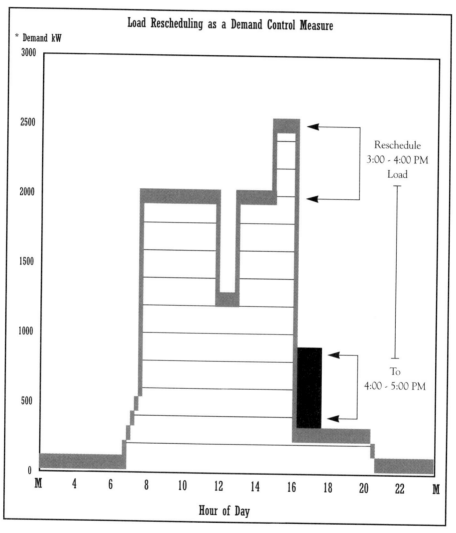

This demand profile illustrates a facility that in general has a demand level of 2000 kW except for the period from15:00/16:00 hours (3:00/4:00 PM). During this one hour interval the demand rises 500 kW. If demand costs

$10/kW, this one hour incurs a penalty of 500 kW x $10 = $5,000. What was performed once the demand profile information was analyzed, was to shift the 500 kW demand to the 16:00/17:00 hour (4:00/5:00 PM) period.

This reduced the demand impact by 500 kW or saved $5,000 in demand charges for the period involved. In this instance a batch process that could be moved by a one-hour period was rescheduled to operate one hour later than had been the normal practice.

Without the benefit of the demand profile, the impact of this process on total demand cost would not have been likely since there would have been no visualization of its impact. There will be many times when reducing demand levels will require more rescheduling or coordinating than this figure represents, but demand profile characteristics will have tobe visualized to reduce overall demand levels.

Electricity Submetering

Electricity submetering can be utilized to identify/reduce both demand (kW/kVA) as well as usage (kWh). Submetering allows the visualization of small subsections of electricity usage characteristics within the total usage framework of a facility. Submeters measure energy and power use and present information in a format where it can be manipulated and analyzed.[5]

The Typical Electric Bill. Electric utility rate structures can be complex documents, and few are alike from one utility to the next. Although the basic unit price of energy is perceived to be the kilowatthour (kWh), this figure is actually an average cost often combining many costs including an energy use charge, demand charge, power factor charge, fuel adjustment factor charge and other charges. It is also important to note that many utility Demand Side Management (DSM) Programs base rebates on the number of kWh removed from use (energy consumption) or kW removed from load (demand for power).

Energy Use Charge. Utilities charge by the kilowatthour (kWh) consumed by the facility's electrical systems over the course of the billing period. In few cases, there is a flat charge per kWh regardless of time of usage or volume of usage. For example, a sliding block rate structure may be used where the unit price declines based on increasing volume of consumption. This unit price may change depending on season or whether the energy is consumed during peak or off-peak hours. Often, summer rates are higher than winter rates, sometimes as much as 50 percent higher.

Demand Charge. While the energy use charge presents a cost for consumption of electricity, the demand charge is based on the cost to the utility necessary to build and maintain the production, transmission and distribution equipment required to service the building's peak load. The amount of power required of the utility at any instant, regardless of whether equipment is operational (and consuming energy) or not, is expressed in kilowatts of demand. Even if the maximum amount of power is only used a small portion of the month, the utility charges for its capability to have this power available.

To maintain fairness, a utility will use a special demand-meter to measure actual demand and charge the facility accordingly. This meter measures average demand in kW in increments of time called the demand interval (which is typically 15-30 minutes). The utility then charges per kW for the interval when demand peaked for that month.

For example, if the demand charge per kW is $8 and a facility's peak use is 1500 kW for 15 minutes, there will be a $12,000 charge on the electric bill.

The Ratchet Clause. The utility may include a "ratchet clause" in its revenue structure. When a ratchet clause is included, the demand charge reflects maximum demand recorded in the recent past. Demand charges are generally highest in the summer peak period due to air conditioning. A given ratchet clause may require that any demand charge imposed during the winter months cannot dip lower than a percentage of the maximum demand charge levied during the previous summer.

For example, suppose a given utility uses 70% as its percentage (which is fairly typical) and levies, as in the previous example, $12,000 as the maximum demand charge during the summer peak period. During a winter month in the early part of the next calendar year, the demand charge is $7,100. The utility charges the facility $8,400 instead of $7,100 for that month.

The Value of Energy Use and Demand Monitoring. Because the primary charges on an electric bill are for energy and demand use, monitoring to discern usage is essential for effective energy management to reduce operating costs (especially through the elimination of waste). This information is simply not available from a standard utility meter, but it can be gained via submetering. Submeters monitor and record energy and demand usage for an entire building, space, or process down to a piece of equipment required to produce specific goods or services. For example, various plots, curves and breakdowns can be produced profiling the heating and cooling system alone, or for an occupancy-related process.

The information provided allows more strategic energy management and more intelligent decisions regarding energy use. It can be simply read and logged manually as an indicating device or it can feed information into a recording center such as a computer equipped with software that stores the data and allows its manipulation for analysis.

Basic examples of using submeter-generated information include—(1) identifying high energy-using areas to take corrective action, (2) identifying energy use prior to and after a test installation of retrofit equipment or a complete retrofit, and (3) monitoring the performance of equipment.

Energy and Demand Monitoring and Corrective Action. A submeter can be used to identify the most energy-consuming areas and equipment. By gathering information about where and how energy is used, energy-saving measures can be taken most intelligently. Often, limited resources are available for investment in retrofits such as new lighting systems, adjustable frequency drives, and high-efficiency electric motors. Submeters allow identification of areas which will produce the highest energy savings.

Submeters can also identify high-demand areas and expensive periods of peak demand. This allows facility management to conduct a manual load shedding program, shifting load and eliminating peaks by turning off machinery or sequencing start-up of equipment that requires a high in-rush current, such as electric motors.

It is important to record energy use data for later, not simply immediate or near future, evaluation. By developing a history of energy use data, forecasts on load can be established which assists with developing operating budgets.

Monitoring Retrofit Performance. Whether in a test installation or complete retrofit, submeters can measure the actual savings generated by, for example, a new lighting system, or an economizer in the HVAC system. This allows energy savings to be more accurately determined rather than relying on projections which cannot reliably predict all operating conditions that would affect savings.

This benefit is especially important should the facility management be in a rebate situation with the local utility where the utility pays for installation of energy-efficient equipment based on kWh and kW saved. It is equally important should facility management be in a performance contract situation with an Energy Service Company (ESCO) where energy savings are split between the owner and the ESCO.

Monitor the Performance of Equipment. Submeters can assist with preventative maintenance and provide other benefits generated by monitoring equipment performance. New equipment can be submetered to ensure that the equipment meets specifications and to provide other valuable performance data. To gain the most reliable data, meter only when equipment has reached normal operating conditions. Submeters can also indicate whether the equipment is operational, is experiencing abnormal operation or is in a breakdown mode. An example of this latter case is an installation of metal halide lamps in a sports stadium, where numerous banks of fixtures are monitored. When a drop in energy use occurs, it signals the maintenance personnel that a lamp has failed.

Electronic Versus Electromechanical Submeters. Electronic submeters offer several distinct advantages over electromechanical submeters. While the first submeters were electromechanical, they have largely been surpassed by the more sophisticated features in electronic submeters. These advantages are:

- **Compact design:** Electronic submeters are compact. They can stand as small as six inches high, four inches wide and three inches deep — approximately one-tenth the size of a standard electromechanical submeter. Electronic submeters can also be ganged — grouped with up to 25 submeters—within a cabinet as small as 30 inches high, 24 inches wide and six inches deep. Electromechanical submeters are encased in glass, are heavier, and tend to be more bulky.

- **Clear readouts:** The electronic submeter provides simple digital readouts. Electromechanical submeters, which commonly use multiple concentric rotating dials, sometimes create confusion to those recording energy use. Certain electronic submeters may also provide a convenient reset button to further eliminate confusion from reading month-to-month energy use. Upgrading such features on an electromechanical submeter requires buying a new meter, because the read-out features are built into the meter itself. For electronic submeters it is as simple as plugging a special enhancements.

- **Convenient installation:** A key point in considering the advantages of certain electronic submeters is that they avoid the time and money incurred by powering down. Electromechanical submeters require the installer to cut into power lines in order to pass them through the mounted unit for the submeter. Rather than powering down to install an electronic submeter, the installer can attach unique split-core current sensors (if available for the given submeter model) which fasten around conductor lines without cutting in. Installation time falls to approximately one half-hour as compared to around four hours for a typical electro- mechanical submeter.

- **Lower Cost:** There are tremendous cost differences between the two submeter types. The electromechanical submeter, installed, costs about double that of the electronic submeter which starts at approximately $600.

Available Enhancements. Monitoring enhancements are easily added to an electronic submeter. With traditional electro-mechanical submeters, the only way to enhance the component is to purchase an upgraded model. Enhancements available include computer interface, high resolution, digital-to-analog outputs and panel-mounted demand display/control modules. Available computer software allows engineers to select individual submeters or groups and view energy consumption and the demand rate in several different profiles. It can also automatically read the submeter, which also simplifies maintenance. When used with a telephone modem, the software allows remote access to the submeter energy data virtually anywhere there is phone service.

Use Submetering to Gain Information. Accurate and affordable information on energy and demand usage is vital for effective energy management. Submetering is the key to this information. Electronic submeters as the engineer will use this information to modify energy use and monitor equipment performance. One would not purchase a car without looking under the hood—submeters offer an in-depth study of energy use so that both energy and power are used most efficiently and intelligently.

Figure 6.18

Examples of Tariff Schedule Provisions Concerning Demand Billing Procedures

RATCHET BILLING

1. Billing Demand: The greatest of the following —

   a) The maximum 15-minute measured kW demand in the month;
   b) 80% of the maximum 15-minute measured kVA demand in the month; (power factor clause)
   c) The maximum demand as so determined above during the preceding 11 months; (ratchet clause)
   d) 50 kW.

PEAK BILLING

2. Billing Demand: The maximum 15-minute measured demand during the on-peak hours of 8 AM–8 PM, Monday-Friday. The off-peak demand shall be the maximum demand created during the remaining hours. (Time-of-Use/Time-of-Day)

STANDARD KW BILLING PLUS BASE THRESHOLD

3. Demand Charge:

   $90.00 for first 20 kW demand or less,
   $3.10 per kW all additional kW demand.

STANDARD KW BILLING

4. Demand Charge:

   $5.00 per kW demand.

BASE BILLING PLUS VOLTAGE ADDER

5. Demand Charge: (Base charge plus adder based upon voltage levels):

   $12.73 per kW, plus;
   $3.75 per kW maximum demand (less than 24 kV) primary service;
   $2.75 per kW maximum demand (24 to 41.6 kV) subtransmission voltage level;
   $1.50 per kW maximum demand (120 kV and above) transmission voltage level.

SEASONAL BILLING

6. Demand Charge:

   $15.02 per kW demand (July-October),
   $6.43 per kW demand (November-June).

Figure 6.19

Examples of Tariff Schedule Provisions Concerning On-Peak, Intermediate, and Off-Peak Demand Billing Hours

STANDARD ON-PEAK/OFF-PEAK BILLING

1. On-Peak Hours: 12 noon–8 PM, Monday–Friday. Intermediate Hours: 8 AM–12 noon and 8 PM–12 midnight Monday–Friday. All Other Hours: including the holidays of New Year's Day, Rev. Martin Luther King's Birthday, Washington's Birthday, Memorial Day, Independence Day, Labor Day, Columbus Day, Veteran's Day, Thanksgiving Day, and Christmas Day as designated by the Federal Government, shall be consider off-peak.

STANDARD ON-PEAK/OFF-PEAK BILLING WITH CUSTOMER OPTION FOR ON-PEAK PERIODS

2. At customer's option, the On-Peak Hours are 7 AM–3 PM, 8 AM–4 PM, or 9 AM–5 PM, Monday–Friday, inclusive, New Year's Day, Memorial Day, Independence Day, Labor Day, Thanksgiving Day, and Christmas Day.

STANDARD ON-PEAK/OFF PEAK BILLING WITH OPTION FOR UTILITY TO CHARGE PEAK PERIODS

3. On-Peak Hours: 8 AM–8 PM, Monday–Friday. All Other Hours: will be considered off-peak. Utility reserves the right to change the on-peak hours from time-to-time. The off-peak hours will not be less than 12 hours daily.

NOTE: Item #3 could be the most costly tariff provision on this sheet from the customer's point of view since the utility has the right to shift on-peak hours any time period of the day so long as off-peak hours are not less than 12hours daily. How does a customer shift their hours of operation to match a revised on-peak period?

IV. Usage (kWh)

Usage (kWh) is a function of connected load times hours of usage. One kWh = 1000 watts sustained for a one hour period of time. For example, (10) 100 watt incandescent lamp bulbs operated for one hour would result in the use of one kWh of electrical energy; or, one 10,000 watt piece of equipment operated for a one hour period would result in the use of one kWh of electrical energy usage.

Reduction of kWh

Reducing usage (kWh) of electricity requires the utilization of more energy-efficient equipment or a reduction of the quantity and/or time of operation of individual pieces of electricity-utilizing equipment. Each individual analysis for usage (kWh) reduction will be different based upon the peculiarities of a given situation. But in general, there are common items of investigation that will be utilized in all such analysis.

The following is a list of 50 items of the most frequently utilized evaluation considerations for reducing electricity usage (kWh) and in some instances demand (kW/kVA). These 50 items are categorized into five specific areas—mechanical systems, lighting and power distribution, architectural issues, user issues, and commissioning. These 50 items are especially important when building or revising an existing facility. Naturally, there are more things that could be listed, especially if considered on a specific entity basis, but for a good general overview basis these 50 items are a good starting point.

50 Ways to Reduce Energy Costs

Mechanical Systems[6]

1. **General HVAC system evaluation.** Energy use is a variable to be quantified in this process and economics should be carefully considered. This step should no sidestep additional enhancements.

2. **Indoor air quality and energy efficiency.** Every design should make indoor air quality a cornerstone and energy efficiency then should be considered in light of this factor. Engineers can take advantage of system enhancements such as heat pipes and run-around hydronic heat recovery loops to minimize the impact on energy use due to current ventilation standards.

3. **Project design criteria.** Building use should be understood and design criteria tailored to specific needs. Operating data from similar buildings would be of value in this process, but it is not generally available. When determining final criteria the engineer should consider the flexibility to accept future increases in design factors so that the current design will not be burdened with overly conservative design criteria guidelines. Have the client review and understand this criteria.

4. **Advanced design methods.** Use the best design tools available to accurately size and select system components. Specify equipment that meets these calculations and don't oversize unless future load increases are part of the design criteria.

5. **Part-load efficiency.** Select equipment that remains efficient over a wide range of load conditions. Equipment will operate at part load a great percentage of the time.

6. **Duct system pressure losses.** Fan energy is significant. Sizing ductwork is often based on rules of thumb and doesn't consider the distribution system as a whole. Computer-based duct sizing programs are becoming widespread and, with the integration into CAD systems, will become more important. Optimized balancing damper locations to reduce losses during the design.

7. **Duct losses.** Reduce leakage and thermal losses by specifying low-leakage sealing methods and better duct insulation.

8. **Diffuser selection.** Proper air distribution to deliver conditioned air to the occupied space must

be considered. Selection and location of diffuser will both save energy and improve HVAC system control. Select diffusers with high induction ratios, low pressure drop, and good partial-flow performance.

9. **Low-face-velocity coils and filters.** Reducing velocity across coils and filter will reduce energy directly lost through each component, allow more efficient fan selection, and reduce acoustical attenuation needs (which affect energy loss).

10. **Underfloor air distribution.** Once the solution only for computer rooms, displacement ventilation is gaining acceptance in other building types. This solution involves coordination with architectural and structural design, and any analysis should consider the integrated benefits (architectural, power, and telecommunication wiring systems) as decision factors. Underfloor systems can operate at higher supply air temperatures, with a greater number of outdoor-air free cooling hours available and chillers operating at higher efficiency when they are needed. Systems also have lower fan energy requirements. Indoor air quality also should benefit because greater quantities of outdoor air can be used, and room air distribution can be more uniform.

11. **Chiller selection.** Improved-performance equipment is on the market, and even better equipment is under development, for all product sizes. Integrated controls are available to increase operating flexibility and the ability to work with other HVAC components. Refrigerant conversion of outdated chillers containing environmentally harmful refrigerant needs to be considered for its energy impact.

12. **System efficiency vs. component efficiency.** Cooling system components should be optimized together, including chiller, pumping, cooling tower, and distribution. This approach may be somewhat contrary to utility rebate structures that often focus on individual components, but should be considered as perhaps the best solution. Analyze the benefits of increased chilled water and decreased condenser water temperatures.

13. **Multiple chiller system sizing.** Most installations having a chiller plant should have multiple, unequal size chillers. This allows for the most efficient chiller for a given load to operate.

14. **Desiccant dehumidification.** Such systems can prove effective where latent loads are significant, such as humid climates or low-humidity spaces. Adsorbent enthalpy wheels, which use exhaust air to dehumidify or cool supply air, or heat-regenerated enthalpy wheels can both significantly

reduce electrical power needs for refrigerant-based dehumidification.

15. **Gas and absorption cooling.** While not likely saving energy, this approach can reduce energy costs and be cost effective. A heat source, typically from natural gas, is used for driving the absorption refrigeration process. Direct-fired gas equipment can be selected to provide hot water for building heating needs in addition to chilled water, which improves efficiency and economics.

16. **Thermal energy storage.** More of a load-management tool, TES systems shift energy needs from expensive energy cost periods to cheaper time periods. Depending on the approach this can save energy as well, and from a utility perspective, will use energy at a time when more efficient generation and transmission is possible.

17. **Hydronic pumping systems.** Primary/secondary pumping systems with variable speed drives should be considered for their part-load energy improvements. Design should optimize head loss with a minimum of flow-balancing controls. Hydronic system additives may soon be on the market to reduce friction loss and thus pumping energy.

18. **Heat exchangers.** Select heat exchangers with low approach temperatures and reduced pressure drops.

19. **Heating system options.** Consider condensing boilers, match output temperatures to load, use temperature reset strategies and select equipment with good part-load ability. Specify multiple, stages operation wherever possible.

20. **Heat recovery.** Where simultaneous heating and cooling loads occur, evaluate the use of heat-recovery chillers. High ventilation loads would benefit with air-to-air heat recovery systems for both sensible and latent recovery.

21. **High-efficiency motors.** Premium-efficient motors are suggested for all applications because of energy savings, longer life times, and reduced maintenance. Motors should be properly sized to reduce part-load losses.

22. **Variable-speed drives.** These systems have significantly advanced over recent years and offer a proven means of substantially reducing fan and pump energy at part-load losses.

23. **Mechanical drive efficiency.** Losses in the power transmitted from motor to driven equipment can be surprising. Consider direct-drive equipment and review actual loss factors on other belt- or gear-driven equipment.

24. **Direct digital controls.** Now nearly considered the norm, DDC systems offer greater accuracy, flexibility, and operator interface than pneumatic systems. On this latter factor, one can argue that greater operator abilities will reduce maintenance labor that will more than offset initial cost premiums. Use sensors having the greatest accuracy to improve energy efficiency.

25. **Advanced control strategies.** Greater operating efficiencies result from use of a DDC system. System optimization, dynamic control, integrated lighting/HVAC control, and variable-air-volume-box airflow tracking are available strategies.

26. **Domestic hot water options.** Efficient equipment with water temperature matched to load should be specified. Heat pumps, heat recovery, tankless water heaters, and combination space heating/water heating systems should be considered.

27. **Low-flow plumbing fixtures.** While this might seem like only a water-conservation issue, energy also will be saved because of reduced pumping energy and water heating use. Standard products are available for a wide range of applications and are expected to become standard practice in many areas.

28. **Hot water system standby losses.** Losses from both distribution piping and storage tanks can be more than 30% of input heating energy. Tank insulation, anti-convection valves/heat traps, optimized tank location and smaller heaters with higher recovery rates can reduce loss factors.

Lighting and Power Distribution

29. **Design criteria.** Often attention paid to illumination criteria is minimal, without consideration of Illumination Engineering Society guidelines. IES target illumination levels for various visual tasks should be considered for specific guidance.

30. **Lamp selection.** Over the past two years, the lighting industry has developed a significant number of high-efficiency lamps. The Federal government has mandated future use of these lamps with the Energy Policy Act of 1992. Be aware of these changes and specify the more efficient source.

Additionally, match lamp sources to intended uses. Selecting incandescent lamps for accent lighting or in situations where dimming is preferred is no longer warranted with today's new compact high-intensity discharge and dimmable fluorescent lamps.

31. **Electronic ballasts.** One of the largest improvements for lighting efficiency over the past few years has been the introduction of a reliable electronic ballast, which is 10% to 20% more efficient than the most efficient magnetic-coil ballast. These devices have a higher frequency of lamp excitation and a higher power factor, resulting in lower energy use. The latest ballasts have substantially reduced induced harmonics, one of their previous drawbacks.

32. **Fixture optics.** Opportunities for energy efficiency are available for both new construction and retrofit to take advantage of better optical control (getting more light on visual task and reducing glare or spilled light). Reflectors can be computer designed and optimized for efficiency and control. Louver finish options also are available for visual comfort and integration into areas where VDTs are used. Specifying fluorescent fixtures with heat extraction over the lamp cavity also will improve fixture efficiency, with cooler lamps producing more light output.

33. **Occupancy sensors.** Now being recognized as an alternative to local light switching in energy codes, this technique should see greater use in all types of commercial construction. Studies have shown savings potential greater than 60% depending on type of occupancy. Recent project experience shows this to be less costly than programmable control or dual-level manual switching.

34. **Efficient exit signs.** Today's efficient products need only one to six watts, compared to 40 watts in older models. These fixtures operate 24 hours a day. Given the number of exit signs in a typical project, savings can be sizable.

35. **Daylighting integration.** Often poorly understood by today's architect, the use of daylighting was a standard design goal in the early 1900s. Building form and orientation play key roles in effective daylighting integration and the consultant should consider it early in the design to assist the architect. Computerized modeling tools aid in quantitative and qualitative evaluation.

36. **Daylighting control strategies.** Every building should properly address lighting control in response to natural light from all envelope sources, a practice required by many energy codes. Be aware of basic options and effective daylighting performance. Dimmable and stepped daylighting controls take advantage of latest technology. Continuously dimmed control systems have the highest level

of energy savings and user acceptance and offer additional energy-saving operational strategies, but have greater initial cost.

37. **Advanced task-lighting products.** Inefficient incandescent and under-counter strip fluorescent fixtures may no longer match occupant needs and are outdated when compared to advanced products now available. Issues such as luminance ratios (critical in VDT environments), veiling reflectance glare and asymmetrical light distribution are factors to consider. High performance task lights with occupancy sensors, compact fluorescent sources, asymmetric reflectors and electronic ballasts are available that reduce energy use by more than 50% compared to past options.

38. **Lumen maintenance control.** Luminaire light output decreased through its operating lifetime, due to factors such as inherent lumen depreciation, dirt accumulation, and other factors. Energy savings can be achieved by controlling light output in accordance with these factors by specifying continuously dimmed ballasts in combination with photocells.

39. **Light-level tuning.** Light fixture layouts often are developed by the architect to standard spacing and fixture sizes for visual appeal. They do not necessarily correspond to the layout of work stations or illumination criteria. In response to such a situation lighting levels can be dimmed or "tuned" to desired levels and energy use reduced.

40. **Improved cavity optics.** As much as 30% of light in offices comes from reflected light off walls, ceilings, tables, and furniture. Use of bright colors and reflective surfaces play a big role in energy savings. The consultant plays an important role in coordinating these issues.

41. **Advanced design methods.** Accurate computer design tools are available to eliminate past practices of over lighting to compensate for conservative standards engineers accept due to the complexity of formal analysis methods. Such tools are best suited for non-typical applications and may not be needed on standard applications after the engineer has completed a number of runs and has better experience factors to draw on.

42. **Specific visual tasks.** With the VDT becoming standard in all building types, considerations for lower ambient lighting levels are gaining acceptance. Such task/ambient systems reduce overhead light levels and provide supplemental task illumination only in required areas. Substantial energy saving of 20% to 40% are achieved by providing higher light levels only at the task.

43. **Higher building utilization voltages.** Less energy is lost in distribution systems with higher system voltages.

44. **Power factor improvement.** Poor power factor results in increased distribution and motor losses that require additional energy to offset. Motor selection, motor sizing, and correction equipment should be used as appropriate.

Architectural Issues. While the engineer should not attempt to supplant the architect in the consideration of the following issues, he or she should have an appreciation for the architectural design process and provide an assessment of their impact on energy use.

45. Siting, form, orientation and landscaping.

46. Solar control, shading and glazing optimization.

47. Thermal mass.

48. Infiltration control and insulation.

User Issues

49. **Office equipment.** Electricity use by office equipment is growing faster than any other category of electricity use in U.S. commercial buildings. Worse, after all of the efficiency gains are made in mechanical, electrical, and architectural design, buildings will have a majority of their remaining energy used by office equipment. Purchasing and operating factors are outside of the engineer's realm, but still can be influenced. The engineer should advise building users of the impact of such energy use and also act as an information source on new office equipment now coming on the market. Reductions of more than 75% are possible with these latest machines, and future products may further economize.

Commissioning

50. **Operation issues.** Last, but certainly not least, the building needs to be operated in accordance with the engineer's design intent. The best system will not perform unless the design is understood by building operators and proper operating procedures are followed. Commissioning of building

systems is receiving greater attention by sophisticated building owners and by utility companies, who want to improve demand-side management programs. Engineers play a key role in this process in providing technical direction.

Figure 6.20

Examples of Tariff Schedule Provisions Concerning Energy (kWh) Charges

STANDARD BILLING

1. Energy Charge:

   $0.04276 per kWh.

RATCHET BILLING

2. Energy Charge: Ratchet of usage (kWh) to demand (kW) —

   $0.07342 per kWh first 250 kWh per kW demand,
   $0.06913 per kWh next 100 kWh per kW demand,
   $0.06685 per kWh all additional kWh.

TIME-OF-USE BILLING

3. Energy Charge: Time-of-Use/Time-of-Day —

   $0.0450 per kWh (Off-Peak),
   $0.0668 per kWh (On-Peak).

TIME-OF-USE/TIME-OF-YEAR BILLING

4. Energy Charge: Time-of-Use/Time-of-Day, as well as Time-of-Year —

	(JUN-OCT)	(NOV-MAY)
On-Peak	$0.14606 per kWh	$0.06875 per kWh
Intermediate	$0.07632 per kWh	$0.06458 per kWh
Off-Peak	$0.05947 per kWh	$0.05589 per kWh

References

1. International Electrical Testing Association; "Maintenance Testing Specifications for Electric Power Distribution Equipment and Systems." Copyright, 1993.

2. General Electric Corporation Publication; "Power Capacitor Primer," PCPS-1010.

3. Cadick, John, P.E.; Cadick Corporation; "Training for the 21st Century - Fundamentals of Harmonics." *NETA Publication*, Winter, 1995/96.

4. Louis Allis/Magnetek, Corporation; "Synchronous Condensers for Power Factor Correction."

5. Bovankovich, David; "Submetering - Information That Can Reduce Power." *Cogeneration and Competitive Power Journal*, Vol. 9, No.3, Fairmont Press, Publisher.

6. Bisel, Clark, P.E.; "50 Ways to Save a Watt." *Consulting-Specifying Engineer*, March, 1994.

Chapter 7

An Introduction to Cogeneration

Cogeneration of Electricity

The cogeneration process is, in broad terms, roughly similar to having an on-site back-up energy source. Cogeneration is not a new technology, but until recently it was not a practical option for most end-users. Knowing how cogeneration operates can be very profitable if properly implemented.

Cogeneration is technically defined as, "the sequential production of electrical or mechanical power and useful heat from the same primary energy source of fuel." In general terms, it is self-generation of electricity with the resulting heat from the generation process being utilized to make steam or hot water.

The process of cogeneration can turn almost any industrial or commercial concern into its own power generation company. The types of companies that are using cogeneration are very diverse and include paper, chemical, pharmaceutical, general manufacturing, shopping centers, apartment buildings, hotels, motels, and fast food outlets.

Also many utilities which just a few years ago vehemently opposed the end-user cogeneration process because they viewed it as a source of competition and a means to erode their monopoly status, now view it with approval.

This change has been brought about because of the realization on the part of utilities that end-user cogeneration can be a way to meet future capacity needs without having to make risky and costly new plant investments. The process of cogeneration is an old concept having been available for many years but has only recently been seriously considered as an alternative to tariff electricity because of recent Federal Energy Regulation.

Cogeneration is encouraged by Federal law, principally the Public Utility Regulatory Policies Act (PURPA), which requires Federal rules to stimulate cogeneration arrangements. Under PURPA, a cogenerator is allowed to sell the entire output of electricity from the cogeneration source to a utility at a price which equals the cost avoided by the utility by not having to generate the purchased electricity.

The utility's avoided cost is comprised of two segments, avoided capacity and avoided energy. Depending upon the utility, avoided costs can be very low and in the majority of cases will not equal the cost of the cogenerated electricity. In most instances, the use of cogeneration to sell energy to a utility will not be a cost-effective process. The majority of the time, the predominate savings in cogeneration will be in the area of use of the process to supply customer electrical power or self-generation. Figure 7.1 shows a typical cogeneration process.

Figure 7.1

Cogeneration Process

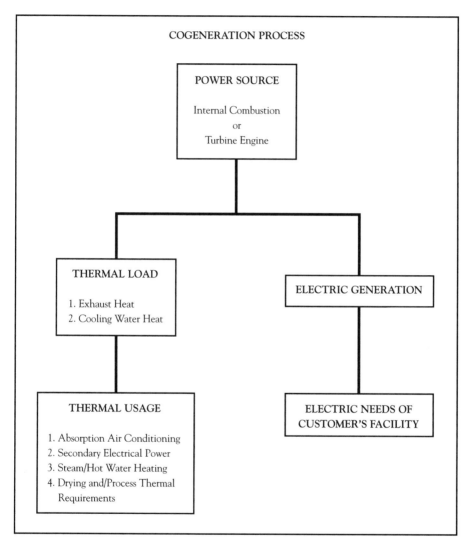

Types of Cogeneration

There are many types of cogeneration processes insofar as the fuel source and method of generating the electrical power is concerned. Several types of processes are described below.

1. **Internal Combustion Engine Driven Generator.** This type of unit utilizes an internal combustion engine which can be fueled by natural gas, propane, fuel oil, or gasoline.

2. **Turbine Engine Drive Generator.** This process utilizes a turbine engine similar to those used on aircraft to power the generator. It can be fueled by natural gas, propane, or fuel oil.

3. **Steam Boiler Turbine Powered Generator.** This process utilizes a fuel-fired boiler to generate steam, to power a turbine, to generate electricity. The boiler fuel can be natural gas, propane, fuel oil, or coal.

Since cogeneration reliability or availability time is of great importance to any potential user, the following information relating to this matter is presented:

Reliability of Natural Gas Cogeneration Systems

Cogeneration systems fueled by natural gas exceed the reliability of most central station power generating units, according to a study conducted by ARINC Corporation for Gas Research Institute (GRI).[1]

In the study, researchers obtained operating data from 122 natural gas cogeneration units nationwide representing 2,200 megawatts (MW) of capacity and nearly 2 million hours of operating time at 37 facilities. Units were grouped into categories reflecting size (from 60 kilowatts to 100 MW), type of system (gas engine or gas turbine technology), use of emission controls, and type of thermal application. Various types and sizes of gas systems reported average availability factors ranging from 90.0 to 95.8% versus a weighted average of 85.9 percent for fossil-fuel steam, nuclear, and gas-turbine-based central station power generating units. Comparisons are based on study data and data reported by the North American Electric Reliability Council for utility power plants.

Gas cogeneration can improve utility operations because as a group the relatively small, dispersed cogeneration units are more reliable than one or more large central station units of similar capacity.

Cogeneration developers favor natural gas cogeneration systems by a wide margin because of their high efficiency, environmental compliance benefits, low costs, and short construction lead times (Figure 7-1). Such systems can be sized from a few kilowatts to hundreds of megawatts depending on electrical and thermal energy requirements.

The reliability of gas cogeneration systems is a concern to electric utilities, which must maintain adequate generating capacity to serve all customers, including cogeneration users who occasionally require back-up power supply. Reliability is also very important to the cogeneration system's owner or operator. Systems that operate reliably provide maximum economic benefits to the user. Conversely, unexpected system failures have a strong negative impact on economic viability because of the high cost of emergency repairs and premium rates for back-up power.

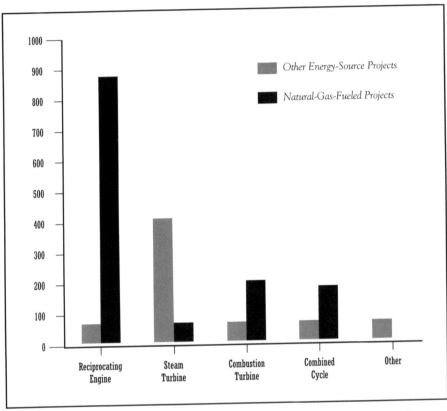

Number of Cogeneration Projects by Type of Technology

To quantify the operational reliability of various gas-fueled cogeneration systems, GRI initiated the development of a comprehensive data base on gas cogeneration reliability. The results provide greater detail and more accuracy than any previous studies. Useful in evaluating both existing and planned cogeneration projects, the results should also help cogeneration operators, manufacturers, system packagers, engineering consultants, and others to identify cost-effective improvements that further enhance operational reliability and economic performance.

In the study, researchers obtained and screened operating and maintenance data from 122 gas cogeneration units representing 2,200 MW of capacity and nearly 2 million hours of service time at 37 host facilities. The evaluation focused on systems driven by gas reciprocating engines and turbines, which represent the majority of all operating and planned cogeneration installations. Systems were grouped in six categories by size. Reciprocating engine systems ranged from 60 kW autoderivative engine systems to 6.5 MW dual-fuel systems; gas turbine systems ranged in size from 1.1 MW to 104 MW. Sixteen technology subcategories were also defined to detail prime mover characteristics and ancillary equipment.

When compared with operational data reported by the North American Electric Reliability Council for large central-station power plants, each group of gas cogenerators demonstrated better averages for key reliability measures (Table 7.1).

Table 7.1 Reliability of Natural-Gas-Fueled Cogeneration Systems

Operational Reliability Measure [b]	Reciprocating Engine			Gas Turbine Engine			Electric Utility [a]
	Group 1 60 kW	Group 2 80-800 kW	Group 3 >800 kW	Group 4 1-5 MW	Group 5 5-25 MW	Group 6 >25 MW	1986-1990
Availability Factor, %	95.8	94.5	91.2	92.7	90.0	93.3	85.9
Forced Outage Rate, %	5.9	4.7	6.1	4.8	6.5	2.1	24.7
Scheduled Outage Factor, %	0.2	2.0	3.5	3.0	4.1	4.8	9.9
Service Factor, %	63.0	68.8	80.0	85.3	85.2	92.5	40.0

[a] Average values are weighted by unit-years for fossil-boiler, nuclear, jet engine, gas turbine, and combined-cycle units from data reported in Generating Unit Statistics, 1986-1990, North American Electric Reliability Council/Generating Availability Data System.

[b] All figures are averaged. Operational reliability measures are consistent with American National Standards Institute/Institute of Electrical and Electronics Engineers' Standard 762

One important reliability measure is the availability factor, which reflects the total time the system is available for operation. Reported data for gas-fueled cogenerators show average availability factors in the range of 90.0 percent to 95.8 percent, compared with a weighted average of 85.9 percent for central-station plants. Another key measure is the forced outage rate, which indicates the time that the system is not available for operation as expected.

The study found a forced outage rate of only 2.1 percent to 6.1 percent across the six categories examined, compared with 24.7 percent for utility plants. These results indicate that gas cogeneration systems are much more reliable than commonly thought. Moreover, gas cogeneration can improve utility operations because as a group the relatively small, dispersed cogeneration units are more reliable than one or more large central-station units of similar capacity.

For each of 9,500 recorded failure and outage events, researchers assigned standard cause codes consistent with the Institute of Electrical and Electronics Engineers' Standard 762. A specially created data base structure was developed to calculate statistics for several important operational reliability measures including the availability factor and forced outage rate. Because cogeneration units may operate in cyclic patterns, such measures provide a meaningful indication of a unit's ability to produce energy during its demand periods.

Detailed data on the performance of cogeneration subsystems identified component and subsystem improvements that could further enhance the reliability of gas systems. For example, in Group 1 (autoderivative reciprocating engines from 60 to 75 kW), the engine and plant services subsystems together accounted for 49 percent of total unit forced outage hours. In particular, many failures involved high engine-coolant temperature resulting from inadequate system design and installation practices.

In gas turbine Groups 4 (1 to 5 MW) and 5 (5 to 25 MW), electronic control failures were the greatest contributor to forced outage events. Follow-on research is planned to expand the statistical basis of these findings and to address the need for subsystem and component improvements.

References

1.   Caterpillar; "The Intelligent Way to Cut Energy Costs." Brochure LED X 8291; September, 1988.

Chapter 8

The Detailed Cogeneration Process

As with any process, proper understanding and implementation are required for a successful outcome to result. The following are areas that will help to determine whether cogeneration or self-generation can be of benefit. If these areas are carefully investigated, a successful cogeneration or self-generation process can be implemented.

- Cogeneration—Is It For You?
- Feasibility Analysis for Cogeneration
- Methods of Paying for the Cogeneration Installation
- Selection of a Cogeneration Equipment Supplier
- The Cogeneration Equipment Supplier Contract
- Utility Involvement in Cogeneration
- Basic Cogeneration and Project Data Analysis Reports

Cogeneration—Is It For You?

Cogeneration is a valuable alternative to tariff electricity if it is properly used. Usually to be less costly than tariff electricity, both components of the cogeneration process need to be utilized. These components are electricity and heat. The ideal situation for the efficient use of cogeneration occurs where both electricity and process heat are required.

The process heat requirement generally needs to be in the form of hot water and/or steam. If these requirements are present, then potentially cogeneration can be utilized to reduce electrical costs. If a need for process heat does not exist, it does not necessarily preclude the use of cogeneration but it does raise the cost of the process.

In general, the cost of electricity obtained in the cogeneration process is from $0.035 to $0.060 per kWh if process heat is utilized. If process heat is not utilized, the electricity cost is from $0.065 to $0.090 per kWh.

Some locations where tariff electric costs might exceed cogeneration costs even where process heat is not utilized are as follows:

CALIFORNIA
Long Beach
San Diego
San Francisco

CONNECTICUT
Bridgeport

ILLINOIS
Chicago
Napierville

INDIANA
Gary

KANSAS
Wichita

NEW JERSEY
Newark

NEW YORK
Buffalo
New York
Rochester

OHIO
Cleveland
Toledo
Youngstown

PENNSYLVANIA
Philadelphia
Pittsburgh
Scranton

MICHIGAN	VERMONT
Detroit	Burlington
Flint	

If facilities are located in these areas, there is a possibility that cogeneration can be on a profitable basis even if a need for process heat is nonexistent. Also, these areas may not be representative of the only high electrical cost locations—there are no doubt many other areas where costs may be even higher. Be sure to check electric utility billings to determine cost. If it is above $0.080 per kWh, it might be beneficial to consider cogeneration even without utilization of process heat.

The place to begin in determining whether cogeneration will be of benefit in a given circumstance is to ask the following questions. If the answer is "yes" to either question, then proceed to the next step, "The Feasibility Study."

A. Are electrical costs more than $0.050 per kWh, and can process heat be utilized?

B. Are electrical costs more than $0.080 per kWh, but process heat cannot be utilized?

Feasibility Analysis for Cogeneration

The installation of a cogeneration system begins with the feasibility analysis. Careful consideration at this stage helps to insure the installation of the most cost- effective and reliable system applicable. The steps in the feasibility analysis should include the following items:

A. **Determination of heat and electrical demand relationships. The following needs to be determined:** (1)The thermal energy demand, (2)The coincidence of thermal and electrical energy demand,

(3)The points of use and transmission of the cogeneration energy.

In this step it will be determined if the heat can be utilized and its needs in relationship to the electrical needs. Also analyzed is where the heat and electrical needs are in physical relationship to each other.

B. **Determination of current electrical costs versus cogeneration costs.** The current electrical costs in relationship to the cogeneration costs in terms of operation, upkeep, and initial investment, need to be quantified so that savings information can be developed.

C. **Determination of energy cost savings.** Actual energy cost savings are determined by analyzing cost comparisons relating to cogeneration costs and the payback from the investment in the cogeneration equipment.

This step determines how long it will take a cogeneration system to pay for itself based upon current electrical costs. A typical cogeneration system installed will cost from $900 to $1,300 per kW depending upon the size of the unit. If a unit that is capable of generating 100 kW is needed, the cost will be about $100,000–$130,000 installed and ready to operate.

D. **Determination of equipment size and cost.** Thermal demand and the proximity of the locations where energy will be needed have to be analyzed to properly size and determine the number of units required. This step will determine the initial equipment costs.

E. **Coordination of project with the local utility.** Coordination of the cogeneration project with the local utility must be done so that interface problems do not occur between the utility and cogeneration equipment.

F. **Determination of physical equipment installation consideration.** Structural, soundproofing, vibration isolation, and environmental code considerations need to be analyzed in order for the installation to be a long-term satisfactory project. This step considers the physical aspects of the installation and is one of the most commonly overlooked areas since it is not directly related to cogeneration as such. Any project involving the installation of mechanical equipment needs to be subjected to the same investigation procedures.

When these areas have been analyzed and the findings utilized, it will be apparent that the cogeneration system that is specified, based upon the information generated, is the most appropriate and economical one available for a particular circumstance. Do not shortcut the feasibility section of the cogeneration process since it will pay many dividends in the future satisfaction with the system selected.

Remember, no two cogeneration systems are alike, so carefully analyze how the system will impact operations, capital budget, and the current energy system. Utilize someone experienced with cogeneration systems who will be able to identify the best alternatives for a facility and provide confidence about future operation of the selected system.

The person utilized also needs to understand the system financing alternatives, technical specifications of the equipment, and how to integrate a cogeneration installation into a facility. If these items are developed, the cogeneration system will be successful.

Typically an initial engineering study will be required to determine, on a factual basis, the viability of a cogeneration project. This study will be very comprehensive and typically will cost between $12,000–$16,000. Normally the serving natural gas utility will provide these funds since a cogeneration installation will provide a very uniform natural gas monthly base load for the natural gas utility.

If the potential cogeneration customer utilizes the cogeneration engineering data to negotiate a concessionary electricity rate with the electric utility, the potential cogeneration customer will probably have to reimburse the natural gas utility for the engineering fee.

The Turnkey Approach to Cogeneration

Today the meaning of cogeneration and what advantages that it offers is not unknown to the facility manager, plant manager, or operations engineer. However, installed cost, cost overruns, performance guarantees, electric intertie cost, maintenance cost, and construction schedules very often are unknown and therefore create an attitude of uncertainty and indecision on the part of the energy managers and decision makers.[1]

The Turnkey approach has been developed to overcome cogeneration project uncertainties that often occur. By placing the responsibility upon the developer to design, construct and place in operation for a fixed amount, a facility that performs according to its design criteria reduces or eliminates the uncertainties.

The Turnkey approach is basically a contractual agreement between two parties (developer and owner). Its purpose is to insure that each party identify his/her area of responsibility and commitment to a comprehensive project, as well as protecting the design integrity of the project.

The merit of this arrangement can be realized by reviewing the roles of the owner and the developer.

(A) The responsibility of the developer is to design, construct, and demonstrate the system performance before final acceptance of the system by the owner.

(B) The developer is obligated to contain the installed cost to the agreed Turnkey contract amount.

(C) The owner is obligated to hold in reserve a contingency amount apart from the contract amount of about 8% to 10% of the contract price.

(D) The contract allows the owner to hold retainage until performance is demonstrated.

(E) The developer has the authority to hold retainage on all subcontractors and vendors as an incentive on their part to meet scheduled requirements.

(F) The developer is obligated to construct and place in operation the facility as expeditiously as is possible.

The Turnkey approach to cogeneration systems has proven to be effective for small systems (1 MW to 10 MW) and there is no reason to doubt its effectiveness in larger systems.

Areas of Development.
There are seven recommended areas of development in the Turnkey arrangement. The first one is the "feasibility study."

Area 1—The Feasibility Study

The cogeneration project's conception generally begins with a study of facts relating to a facility's energy purchases (electricity, natural gas, oil, etc.) and how they are utilized (process, heating, cooling, manufacturing); also any by-product of process that can be reused as an energy form (high temperature water, air, combustible gas, combustible solids, etc.). The feasibility study information is generally retrieved from gas and electric utility bills, electric utility supplied-demand printouts, boiler records, production records, energy management systems (E.M.S.) records and data.

The funding of this initial study can be through a local utility company or by a state energy conservation program. However, many times this information is readily available and has been compiled by the plant energy manager. In general, the feasibility study is at no cost to the Owner. The purpose of the feasibility study is to gather information of energy purchases and use of energy, then to develop a thermal and electric profile to determine the method or cycle recommended, system size, preliminarily installed cost, projected avoided cost and the operating expenses of the cogeneration facility.

Study Format

The format is generally about five pages with each page containing the following.

Page 1: General overview and description of the existing facility and its energy purchases. The thermal and electric unit cost (per kilowatt hour, kilowatt, MM/Btu, 1000LB/HR#, therm). The thermal and electric consistent base load and peaks. The recommended system size and output in M.W. and MMBtu/HR.

Page 2: One year projected avoided cost of electric purchases based on present rate structure and recommended size, then correlated to the previous 12 months actual electricity used.

Page 3: One year projected avoided cost of thermal energy based on the facilities, then correlated to the previous 12 months actual energy used.

Page 4: Yearly fuel cost to operate the cogeneration facility. Maintenance and operational cost. The unit amount it will cost to produce a kilowatt hour from the facility.

Page 5: Projected installed cost of the recommended system. A summary of the various avoided cost. A summary of the yearly operating expenses. The net savings per year and a simple payback calculation as well as a projected rate of return based on system life cycle.

A separate letter is also presented with the feasibility study provided the study indicates a good project. The letter requests that funds be made available for Phase I Engineering.

Area 2—Phase I Engineering

The cost of Phase I Engineering should be kept to a minimum ($12,000 to $16,000 depending on the size and system type). The purpose of Phase I Engineering is to develop a comprehensive design specification, equipment selection, construction schedule, establish utility intertie cost, as well as a cost breakdown of the project and a proposal containing the Turnkey installed price with performance guarantee. The funding of Phase I Engineering should be made by the owner as an expression of good will on his part.

Phase I Format

The Phase I design document and proposal should contain approximately nine sections.

Section 1—Project Overview: This section provides a concise description of the facility, size in MW, cogeneration cycle method, the thermal output, and yearly avoided cost.

Section 2—Development Activities: Phase I Engineering method of development and purpose are identified. The results of the development activities of Phase I are basis for the development of Phase II Engineering.

Section 3—Facility Design and Layout: This section contains a description of the system and component parts as well as their location in the facility. The layout drawings of the cogeneration building and equipment are part of this section.

Section 4—Engineering Design (Mechanical and Electrical): A description of the thermal flow and volume calculations, electrical one-line drawings for power and instrumentation, mechanical schematics and equipment drawings, system efficiency calculations for qualified certification. Thermal and electrical guaranteed outputs.

Section 5—Project Participants: A description and information of the experience, qualifications and financial stability of the developers.

Section 6—Construction: This section projects a construction specification by discipline and includes relative cash flow. Specifications for foundations, cogeneration building, mechanical and electrical equipment, control systems, codes, permits, etc.

Section 7—Start Up Assistance: Identifies the procedures for an organized construction phase and start up of the system. Describes the contract management team responsibilities.

Section 8—Project Schedule: Projected schedule for construction and commissioning based on verified equipment deliveries and subcontractor specifications.

Section 9—Economics and Budget: This section lists the proposed Turnkey price of the project, a breakdown of project cost by discipline, projected yearly operational expenses of the system including fuel purchases, maintenance and labor. Avoided yearly cost of thermal and electric energy. A simple payback calculation and a projected rate of return based on the system life cycle. After Section 9, a formal letter of proposal by the Developer is presented to the owner with the Turnkey price and performance guarantees listed.

Area 3—Formal Contract

The format of this document is a legal agreement between the developer (to provide a cogeneration facility as described and specified according to performance) and the owner (to pay the Turnkey price upon its demonstrated performance and certification of the system).

Financing of the project must be available at the signing of the contract. However, if this is to be by others, then this may be a separate development area. Construction cost and construction cash flow may also be part of the formal contract.

Area 4—Phase II Engineering

Phase II Engineering should start immediately after the contract signing and construction of the building within 30 to 60 days since subcontractor cost was part of Phase I. However, final vendor selection may now be based on previous demonstrated performance and the Owner may participate in this selection.

Phase II will provide construction drawings and individual specification according to discipline, submittals of equipment and start up procedure.

Area 5—Contract Management

The Contract Management is critical for system integrity and schedule compliance. The management team must be clearly defined by job description and chain of command to the subcontractors and the Owner. The Contract Management will develop schedules for all subcontractors and vendors. A scheduled weekly performance meeting shall be arranged by the Contract Manager for all subcontractors and necessary vendors. Minutes shall be published each week for the previous week and distributed to the subcontractors and the Owner's representative prior to the weekly meeting.

Area 6—Commission and Start Up

The Contract Management team (as described in Phase I Engineering and Area 5) shall oversee and organize the commissioning of the facility.

Load testing separately and jointly of the thermal and electrical output and corresponding fuel input. Utility interconnect coordination, testing and certification, licensing, and training, operational procedures, and customer acceptance.

Area 7—Maintenance and Contract Development

This area is dedicated to developing a preventative maintenance schedule and identifying procedures for consistent operation of the facility. The development of a maintenance agreement between the owner and the developer based on the projected maintenance cost listed in Phase I may also be part of this section.

Summary. The Turnkey approach may not be unique in developing a cogeneration system, but it offers some stability for installed cost and integrity to design, by guaranteed performance.

It provides opportunity (in a major emerging industry) for the developer through his demonstrated ability, to design and install more systems.

The Impact of Operation and Maintenance Costs of Cogeneration

Many of the determinations that impact the Operation and Maintenance (O&M) costs of Cogen plants are made months and years before these plants are in actual routine operation. These early decisions are made during the five phases of a Cogen project preceding Routine Operation — (1) Project Development, (2) Engineering and Design, (3) Procurement, (4) Construction, and (5) Start up and all affect the long term O&M costs of a plant. The impact on O&M costs of these early determinations and suggests that an established Company experienced in all of these phases will produce the lowest O&M costs in Cogen or IPP plants.[2]

Project Development Phase. This is the project phase that determines the economic feasibility of a project and tailors the Cogen plant to the general needs of a customer. After it has been determined that the proposed plant location is friendly with regard to environmental permitting, zoning, fuel/water/labor/site availabilities, and power and/or steam needs the general energy cycle and sizing of the major equipment such as gas turbines, boilers, steam turbine generator, cooling tower, is accomplished. A few of the Project Development criteria are listed below and relayed to routine operation O&M costs:

1) **Revenue And Return Upon Investment**—Certainly the project must produce an acceptable revenue during the life of the project based not only on the usual financial considerations but also on the anticipated economical, legal, and fuel-use attitudes and regulations. A change in an environmental regulation can affect O&M costs in the form of additional treatment facilities requiring chemicals, maintenance, and supervision.

2) **Required Reliability**—What are the reliability needs of the power and/or steam customer? Is the Cogen plant supplying steam to a petrochemical plant where utilities reliability is extremely important to prevent such hazards as vapor releases, or to a batch process where the loss of utilities is of little consequence? Reliability in the form of redundant control systems, conservative designs, or extra operators can affect both initial capital and long-term O&M costs.

3) **Dispatching**— Will frequent dispatching of major equipment be required? Which of the available major equipment in the market place handles cycling with the least amount of deterioration and maintenance requirements?

4) **Historical O&M Costs**—What is the industrial record of O&M costs of the available major equipment that will fit the desired energy cycle and operating mode? What are the several year costs of the major spare parts that deteriorate and must be replaced on a periodic basis?

5) **General Plot Plan**—Is there sufficient space available for equipment removal and laydown? Is contractor parking available for major equipment inspections?

6) **Effluent**—Effluent disposal plans. Will a permit be required? Will long term effluent transportation be required?

Design/Engineering Phase. In this phase, specifications are developed, equipment selections made, operation and control philosophies determined, redundancies identified, major and expendable spares identified, materials of construction selected, O&M manuals prepared and most importantly the primary boiler feedwater water treating method and equipment is selected and sized based on historical quality records of the raw water supply. How do the preceding affect routine O&M costs?

1) **Specifications**—If specifications are inadequate, expensive field corrections could be required one time or continue for several months or years after plant start up. (Example: Trouble alarms not specified would have to be added in the field but possibly not before equipment damage occurs that causes circumferential stresses that translate into later troubles.)

2) **Vendor Proposals**—Proposals should be requested only from vendors who have demonstrated a favorable track record in the areas of quality control, accepting responsibility for defects, and generally being customer-oriented. It is not improbable for the O&M costs of a 100 MW plant to vary by $50,000/year due to a single unresponsive major equipment vendor.

3) **Equipment Selection**—The equipment quality and reliability from the various vendors is cyclical depending upon the vendor's profit picture, experience level, and quality control. Equipment selections should be made from manufacturers that tend to be on the "high side" of the quality cycle. It would be embarrassing to purchase a troublesome and costly boiler feedwater pump to find that industry-wide the pumps had been in disfavor for several years.

4) **Control Philosophies**—Will this be a plant with: (a) a proven central distributive control system (DCS), or (b) a plant with the various equipment systems such as the gas compressor, demineralization equipment, and chemical fee systems having individual instrumentation packages located at the equipment site? If the DCS system is truly an effective total plant control, a 100-150 MW plant would probably require no more than two operators per shift or possibly one and one-half operators if sharing with a nearby plant is possible. Individual system control packages for the same plant would require a minimum of three operators to obtain the equivalent level of reliability as the DCS controlled plant.

5) **Redundancies**—Redundant pumps, uninterruptible power supplies, electrical feeders, and back-up gas turbine fuels all increase the reliability of a plant but also increase the preventive and corrective maintenance load. These redundancies have an upkeep cost. (Industry is beginning to think that in some cases the extra maintenance load and cost for redundancy is more than offset by the decreased stress and equipment costs caused by unnecessary full-load emergency trips.)

6) **Spare Parts**—The availability of on-site spares for quickly changing out defective components

eliminates the maintenance time and cost for "improvising," repairing when repairing is not economical and searching for available spares from other owners. Major spare parts should be included in the request for vendor proposals when the discount leverage is the greatest. No doing this could result in paying list price one, two, or three years later.

7) **Materials of Construction**—If the proper materials of construction are not selected, especially involving corrosion and high temperature, the O&M costs can be drastically affected. (Example: The materials of construction for a boiler feedwater pump handling 150 mmho water is not adequate for handling a 10 mmho water. Selecting the improper material can create the need for periodic epoxy coating and weld overlaying causing higher maintenance costs for the life of the plant. Another_example: A waste heat boiler duct liner should be selected based upon the gas turbine peak, exhaust temperature, not the average, or lingering maintenance costs will occur.)

8) **Water Treating Method**—Worldwide, this is probably the most neglected facet of power plant design and when poorly done can cause the overall plant O&M costs to increase by as much as 5% over a proper design. In the area of water treating, (a) reliability should somewhat outweigh capital costs, (b) pioneering vendors should not be considered, and (c) equipment should be sized based upon a year or so of raw water analysis and a few per cent resin degradation. The controls and programming should be proven and blended with the plant DCS.

9) **Design Subtleties**—Are all of the personnel involved, design, project, and operation in agreement with the methods for handling:
   a) Waste effluent (remember, some of the effluent could be oily)
   b) Cleanliness and pressure of the available fuel
   c) Noise control
   d) Obtaining building/construction/environmental permits
   e) Adjacent environment (chemical plants, dusty activities, ambient corrosivity).
   f) Community makeup (Bedroom or industrial?)

If agreements are not obtained during design, costly O&M "fixes" will occur during the normal operating years.

Procurement. This is the phase of the project that encompasses purchasing, expediting, and receiving the equipment as defined in the design phase. What are some of the purchasing functions which, if performed improperly, could impact O&M costs?

1) **Purchase Order Preparation**—If a purchase order (PO) does not cover all of the terms in the selected proposal or those negotiated at requisition meetings, the omissions could increase O&M costs. It is not uncommon for an equipment vendor to "throw in" a multiplying factor (discount) for future spare parts to seal a deal. It is also not uncommon for a vendor to provide the start-up or first year parts in order to obtain an order. If the preceding are not precisely included in the PO, they are legally negated.

2) **PO Design Specifications**—A copy of the latest version of the design, specification should be included with the PO. There is a known case where the second level technician training provisions on a DCS had been omitted on early draft specifications but inserted in the final. However, the final version was not attached to the PO, and as a result, the second level training increased the O&M costs in year two and three of operations by about $15,000/year.

3) **PO Approval**—The POs should not be blindly signed by a project manager thinking, "surely everything is all right because so many have already reviewed the wording." Not so. Some POs have many pages but still should have a final review and comparison to the latest proposal, design specifications, and requisition meeting minutes.

4) **Expediting**—Expediting, which includes scheduling, phone contacts, on-site inspections, witnessing shop performance tests, comparing shop fabrication to design specifications and collecting the final testing paperwork is the most important function of the procurement phase of a project. It is not difficult to imagine the annual O&M cost increase that could arise in one to five years if deficiencies existed in the following areas:

    a) Pump clearances
    b) Transformer testing
    c) Alloy heat treating
    d) Turbine oil piping cleanliness
    e) Pressure testing
    f) Motor testing
    g) Materials of construction
    h) Mill tests

An experienced expediter with formal check sheets is absolutely required in the seller's market of today to properly control the materials of construction, fabrication, and assembly of key equipment.

5) **Receiving**—Receiving, checking, and especially properly storing purchased equipment to be constructed and the major spares for routine operation all too often receive little attention because it seems so simple, "Hire a clerk and check the stuff in." This causes trouble not only during construction but in later years of operation. A dry storage area arranged and cataloged for expensive valves, motors, hydraulic operators, instruments, and transformers is required. Some electronic equipment may require air conditioned storage. A case is reported by a manufacturer where $50,000 of spare electronic control boards were received by a customer during construction and stored in a windowless construction shack. Six months after the completion of construction, one of the boards was required for a turbine repair. After several hours of searching, the corroded mass was located and had to be sent to the junk pile. The replacement required for the repair had to be air freighted, further increasing the O&M cost that had already been increased by purchasing another set of boards.

Construction Phase. The construction and start-up phases are concurrent and deeply intertwined especially for the two months preceding plant start-up. However, the phases will be handled separately since they impact routine O&M costs in different ways.

It is obvious that long term problems will develop and migrate to the routine operations phase as extra expense if a plant is poorly constructed due to such factors as unqualified constructors, inexperienced managers and inspectors, informal testing and acceptance procedures, not adhering to the construction prints, taking shortcuts, and thinly staffing the front-line supervision.

During construction, the operating representative who is usually a start-up specialist or the future plant superintendent who has been involved in all of the previous project phases, now becomes an extra set of eyes for the construction manager to aid in solving and preventing problems during construction rather than later and more expensively in the routine operation phase. Also as the O&M technicians are hired, usually three to five months before start-up, they also become subordinate to the construction manager via the plant manager as inspectors, safety watches, and control checkers. A few of the specifics during construction that will prevent later O&M expense are:

1) **Field Changes**—Must be approved by the construction, design, and operating representatives.

2) **Construction Contingency Allowance**—This phase converts the final single dimension plant design into a three-dimensional real life process. An allowance should exist in the construction budget for necessary field changes as the three-dimensional shape develops and uncovers:

  a) Head knockers
  b) Inaccessible valves
  c) Shortage of drains
  d) Missing blind and disconnect facilities
  e) Missing ladders
  f) Maintenance obstructions
  g) Missing walkways
  h) Awkward manhole covers

If the preceding are not corrected during construction, they become a routine operation revision expense.

3) **Spare Parts Storage**—This was covered under the receiving section of PROCUREMENT, but again, the equipment and spares received during the construction period for routine operation must be cataloged, prepared, and stored in the proper atmosphere to prevent later increased O&M cost. Construction must provide the manpower and the storage to handle these requirements because many of the routine operation personnel have probably not yet been hired nor has a permanent warehouse been constructed.

Start-Up Phase. This is the project phase that begins one or two months before the performance test where commissioning, training (manufacturers and in-house), final control check-outs, development of start-up checksheets, final safety preparations, and "steam blowing" occurs. In this phase a start-up specialist or the plant manager assumes the role of start-up coordinator and the construction manager's role subsides in support of the start-up coordinator. The final modifications are made to the operating and maintenance manuals that were begun during the DESIGN PHASE. Three examples are listed below of how an effective START-UP PHASE can affect favorably O&M costs.

1) **Training**—It is obvious that if maintenance technicians are not trained properly, poor workmanship, "redoes," and overtime to perform a high pressure pump overhaul, could easily increase an $8,000 job to $12,000. Also, poorly trained operators will make errors that cause damage to equipment not covered by manufacturer's warranties. A formal, several week, classroom

and field training program is mandatory.

2) **Commissioning**—Each piece of electrical control and rotating equipment should have a commissioning checksheet that is completed and signed as satisfactory by the constructor, operator, and sometimes the manufacturer. An example of the checks to be performed on 500 HP boiler feedwater pump might be:

    a) Coupling aligned and documented
    b) Correct rotation
    c) No bare wires, motor megged
    d) Conduit covers secured
    e) Pump filters in service
    f) Lubrication okay (oil and pumps)
    g) Local and remote start/stop function
    h) Automatic shutdown and start functions
    i) Recirculation valve free and working
    j) Proper drains installed
    k) Seals checked
    l) No unusual noise or overheating
    m) Operate pumps with a mechanical technician present for 30-40 minutes

It is obvious if the preceding checks are not performed, damage could occur such as a scarred bearing caused by a momentary oil starvation, that does not fail until one or two years following start-up. Also, an untested malfunctioning low oil pressure automatic shutdown could cause pump damage two or three years after start-up.

3) **Final Safety Precautions**—If the transformer sprinkler systems are not checked during start-up, a fire could cause considerable O&M damage at a later date. Fire extinguishers not strategically located could result in an insignificant small fire becoming a damaging fire. Inoperative safety showers could result in a lost time accident and resulting overtime, also, possibly a legal suit. Safety procedures and manuals should all be in place to prevent these and similar occurrences that can increase O&M costs.

4) **In-Service Checks**—There are a series of activities that should take place as the equipment is actually place in service.

a) Infrared scan of electrical busses, boiler ducts, and isophase ducts.
b) Steam, boiler feedwater, or fuel leak inspections.
c) Check for strange noises or odors from rotating or electrical gear.
d) Start and stop the gas and steam turbines. Do the auxiliary oil pumps operate as designed?
e) Major rotating equipment should have continual attendance at the site for one or two shifts following initial start-up.

Expanding on 4a, it is easy to visualize what an insecure buss connection could cause in maintenance costs after start-up if arcing and ionizing began.

Normal Operation Phase. This is the normal phase of operation that follows the start-up phase and covers the day-to-day management, operation, and maintenance of the Cogen facility.

1) **Management**—This activity covers proper staffing, communication, continued training, proactive safety, morale, salary administration, planning, leading, and controlling. It is obvious that deficiencies in any of these areas would cause an increase in O&M costs due to work "redoes," employee turnover, overtime, operating mistakes, and accidents. Proper management of a plant assures that the operation and maintenance is carried out with well-informed, trained, innovative, secure, and loyal O&M technicians.

2) **Operation**—To prevent operational mistakes, the following are the minimum of the programs that should be in place:

a) Each new operator should be provided formal classroom and on-the-job training.
b) Graded examinations follow the training.
c) Each operator has a personalized training matrix on file so they know at the beginning of their employment what is expected.
d) The scheduled outages of major equipment is communicated well in advance so the operators have an opportunity to refresh themselves on shutdown procedures.
e) Start-up checksheets exist for each piece of major equipment.
f) "What If" drills are practiced monthly.
g) Complete operating manuals and emergency procedures exist.

h) Safety procedures and isolation sketches exist for preparing equipment for entry and maintenance. i) A formal risk vs. reward analysis is performed on any equipment or procedural revision.

j) Plant performance parameters are identified and continually monitored.

Again, it is obvious that the preceding decrease the chance for errors, oversights, and accidents that would increase O&M costs.

3) Maintenance—To minimize the O&M costs of a Cogen plant the following maintenance programs should be in place:

a) Formal preventive maintenance (PM) schedules should be developed blending past experience and the manufacturer's recommendations. PM should be performed on overtime within a predetermined period if not completed by the due date.

b) Major equipment inspections should be performed per manufacturer's recommendations.

c) A predictive maintenance program exists consisting of at least visual, vibration, and boroscope inspections.

d) Handle minor corrective maintenance before it becomes major corrective maintenance.

e) Formal maintenance records are kept on each piece of major equipment.

f) An adequate stock of spare parts and consumables are kept on hand.

g) On very technically specific problems, manufacturer's representatives are utilized.

h) A computerized maintenance program should be implemented which consists of:
   (1) Preventive Maintenance
   (2) Corrective Maintenance
   (3) Stores (Inventory Control)
   (4) Stores (Purchasing)
   (5) Equipment History

In conclusion, a full-service, established, and experienced company that can handle Cogen project development, design, procurement, construction, start-up, and routine operation is the company that will provide the lowest long-term O&M costs.

Small Cogeneration Systems—Are They Practical?

For a small cogeneration system to be cost-effective, it must be sized to provide the host business with needed thermal heat in the form of hot water and then produce the electricity as a by-product or bonus. The owner/user of these systems may already be using natural gas or propane as a fuel to make their hot water.[3]

The cogenerator will consume nearly the same amount of this fuel in the engine to produce the needed hot water and if the system is sized correctly, it will also produce a good share of its needed electricity.

Another advantage to the 10, 20 and 30 kW cogeneration system configuration is that these fall below the maximum 50 HP engine permit requirements of the Los Angeles air quality district and other districts.

Therefore there are no special and expensive air quality permits required as on larger cogeneration systems.

Induction cogeneration systems are usually specified as the most cost-effective type to avoid the extra cost of expensive switchgear required by the electric utility when synchronous systems are used.

Figures 8.1 and 8.2 visualize economic and energy advantages of packaged cogeneration; Figures 8.3 and 8.4 show simplified schematics.

Users of the 10, 20 and 30 kW package cogeneration systems are mostly commercial businesses such as motels, hotels, restaurants, coin laundries, health clubs, apartments with common area electric metering, condos, small hospitals and nursing and residential health care centers, wineries, greenhouse growers, YMCAs, and fish farms.

Table 8.1

Packaged Cogeneration Cash Flow

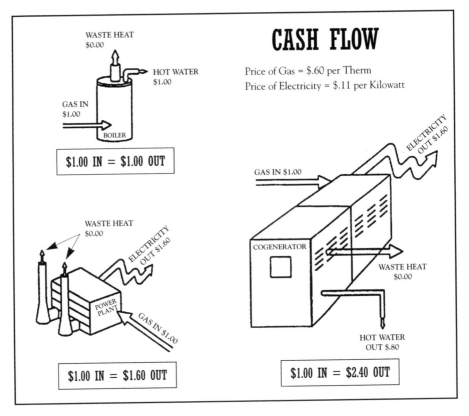

These users all have three important things in common:

1. 5,000 to 8,000 hours per year operation.
2. Hot water demands on a nearly continuous basis.
3. Electrical requirements fairly evenly distributed over the day for seven days a week.

The addition of the correct amount of thermal storage will even out the "rush hour" or peak periods usage. These operations also lend themselves to the use of induction cogeneration.

Reliability of small cogeneration systems is the key to success. The engineering design philosophies reviewed in this article are based on over 1,000,000 operating hours with over 90% operating uptime.

Utilities encounter operational difficulties with large cogeneration plants when they go off line; they must have back-up capacity ready to supply the system shortage. With thousands of small packaged cogenerators being placed in many locations over the utility grid if one goes off line the kW loss is small since the rest of the units will still be running. The probability of all micro units being off line at once is very small unless the utility has an outage.

When a utility puts out a request for thousands of megawatts this means that they are interested in someone constructing some kind of plant that will most likely produce heat for the production of electricity at a thermal efficiency of 30 to 40%.

Table 8.2

Packaged Cogeneration Energy Flow

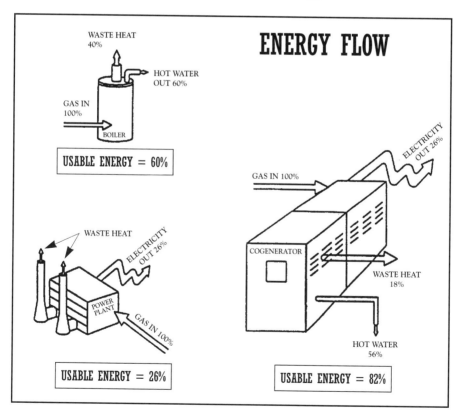

Modern design packaged units give you combined electric and thermal efficiency of 80 to 90%. This excellent efficiency means that the consumption of fuel is one-third of that used by the utility for the same power which means the reduction of fossil fuels usage saving fuel for future generations.

Table 8.3

Packaged Cogeneration Plumbing Schematic

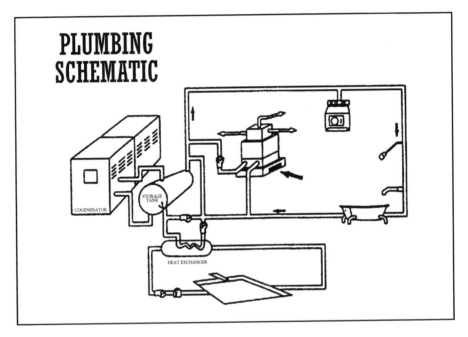

Table 8.4

Packaged Cogeneration Electrical Schematic

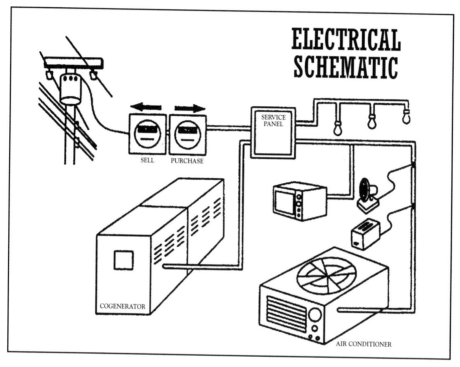

Easy Repairs. Electronics makes it simple for the service personnel to make quick and easy repairs. Computer boards have been tried by system manufacturers. Service records show that boards fail because of small vibrations that are caused by the prime mover and the generator.

Easy Installations. The problem of space limitations in commercial businesses has been overcome by offering both a low profile style for roof top installations and a vertical style for cramped inside installations.

System Design

1- The cogeneration system must include adequate hot water storage to handle the peak hours and maximum usage days of the week. Five hundred, 1000, and 2000 gallon storage tanks are used to balance the hot water load and to provide adequate storage to keep the cogeneration system running maximum hours. The number of units and their capacity will also influence the size of the storage tank.

2- Successful designs are built around the thermal load of the host. It is a loss to all when a blow- off radiator is used.

Some cogeneration companies use load balance radiators so they can put in a larger kW system and earn larger sales commissions. The problems that come later are that the utility will force owners with radiators to monitor the operation and submit the results to them and if thermal efficiency is not 42.5%, loss of low cost cogeneration fuel will happen. Also the cost of monitoring will add to the cost of the system.

Cogeneration equipment typical operating time as compared to the hours of the business is 90+%. For example, nine motel or hotel cogenerators have averaged better than 21 hours per day per cogenerator for the last 42 months. This includes preventative maintenance downtime as well as those hours in the middle of the night when no hot water is required and the cogenerator shuts down on high temperature setting of the storage tank.

3- Multiple units of 10, 20 and 30 kW are better suited to maximize savings for the owners rather than one large unit. The redundancy factor provides greater assurance of uptime. During downtime of one unit the others will continue operating/producing electricity and therefore minimizing demand charges to the client by the electric utility.

4- Many engineers argue that the cost to install and operate four units would be much greater than with a single large unit. Normally however, the cost advantages are many and tend to offset the additional cost of pipe, conduit, valves, and fittings used in the installation. Consider that the cost of a brass 2-inch valve is approximately one-fourth of the cost of a 4-inch valve.

    A- No air quality permitting delays, cost and/or devices are required since small cogenerators are powered with less than 50 hp engines. As much as six months and thousands of dollars can be saved.

    B- Small units provide flexibility in retrofit installations such as the ability to use roof tops above the existing hot water heating equipment/storage tanks and/or in the case of very close quarters such as next to or in the place of existing pool heating equipment or hot water heaters or boilers.

C- Minimizing field construction time to get building permits and inspection by the city (usually less than 30 days) saves thousands of dollars per month in interest and lost utility savings.

The Emerging Package Cogeneration Industry

Gone are most of the original small cogeneration packagers. Only quality manufacturers remain in the business; these have found their market niche and their equipment dealer's sales programs are alive and doing very well.

Quality system manufacturers will invest in product testing with a certified laboratory. The cogeneration salesperson of today is technically trained and educated, presently selling their knowledge through energy audits coupled with low energy lighting products, energy management systems, occupancy sensors, motor controllers, or HVAC equipment that is energy efficient.

More and more corporations are hiring in-house energy experts to help reduce their costs of utilities. The corporate motel and restaurant chains are the most notable on the list.

Public utility commissions are promoting rebates to induce the purchase of the above equipment nationwide so rising electrical demands can be lowered thus putting off construction of additional power plants. Some states also have their energy commissions providing low interest loans to help defray equipment installation costs. These are just some of the reasons for the new market growth. As with any cogeneration system, if they are properly sized and operated, small units can be very effective in reducing electricity costs.

Methods of Paying
for the Cogeneration Installation

Cogeneration systems installed, cost in the area of $900 to $1,300 per kW of capacity depending primarily upon the size. Whether cogeneration would be a good investment depends upon electrical usage and current electrical costs. If the cogeneration process appears to be viable financially with, for example, a two-year payback, how is the easiest way to convince a company that the money required should be spent?

Obviously the system can be paid for in several conventional ways: cash, internal company financing, third party financing, and leasing or lease buy-back arrangements. However, there is a rather novel method which is often utilized in the purchase of cogeneration installations.

This method is where the supplier of the cogeneration equipment installs and maintains the unit for a specified period of time in return for a percentage of the monthly savings realized by the customer. These savings are determined by the differential between the cost of the utility-supplied electricity and the cogeneration electricity cost.

This method does not require the utilization of up-front monies and provides the customer with ownership of the unit at the expiration of the savings sharing period, usually in four to seven years after initial installation. This method of paying for a cogeneration installation is becoming very popular since no initial investment of money is required by the customer. Whether or not this method of paying for a cogeneration/self-generation unit is best depends upon a company's fiscal policies.

Selection of a Cogeneration Equipment Supplier

As is true of most purchases, the provider of the service or the supplier of the equipment is the key to a satisfactory experience with either the service or equipment.

This is especially true in the case of cogeneration since the process and equipment are very specialized in operation and design. When selecting an equipment supplier, consider the following things before making a decision.

1. Determine how much experience the supplier has in building and installing systems of the type and size needed.

2. Obtain a list of current customers, preferably ones who have similar installations, and check out the supplier's performance with these customers.

3. Visit an installation similar in design and operation to the one being installed so that there will be an understanding of the mechanics of the cogeneration process.

4. Determine whether the supplier is trustworthy and honest.

5. Determine whether the supplier will perform the feasibility analysis and if it conforms in general with the outline presented in this section. A qualified supplier should be willing to do such a study at no cost.

6. Since interface with the local utility is involved, make certain the supplier chosen has experience in the utility's service territory.

7. Determine if the contract offered by the supplier conforms in general to the one outlined in this section, especially if the project is to be a shared savings arrangement.

If these areas are suitably addressed and answered then chances of the project being successful are great.

One of the best ways to obtain a list of qualified suppliers, is to contact the utility company and ask which suppliers have installed facilities of the type required for a given application on their system. They will assist in determining specific needs for a given application and generally will provide supplier names with which they have worked in the past in similar installations.

The Cogeneration Equipment Supplier Contract

This section will outline a typical shared savings cogeneration contract (Figure 8.1) which is fair to both parties. This outline only is to be used as a guide in any cogeneration installation where the shared savings arrangement is desired. In instances where either the installation is paid for at completion or typical financing or leasing arrangements are made; normal contracts covering these types of situations will be used.

Figure 8.1

Cogeneration Equipment Supplier Contract

Page 1

COGENERATION PROJECT DEVELOPMENT

AND

OPERATING AGREEMENT

Between

____

And

____

INDEX

Page 3

1

Parties to The Agreement

THIS AGREEMENT, made and entered into this

_____(day) of_____(month),_____(year).

By and Between:_____

With principal offices at: _____

_____

(Hereinafter referred to as "SUPPLIER"), and

By:_____

With principal offices at: _____

_____

(Hereinafter referred to as "USER")

2.

Supplier's and User's Declarations

WITNESSETH THAT:

WHEREAS, USER desires to take advantage of long-term economic savings through the use of cogeneration
at its facility; and

WHEREAS, SUPPLIER understands the types and degrees of skills required to develop, own, and operate such systems, and represents that it has the necessary personnel, experience, competence and legal right to perform such services; and

WHEREAS, USER desires to engage supplier to perform the work and supplier desires to undertake such performance under the terms, conditions and provisions here in after set forth.

NOW, THEREFORE, in consideration of the respective undertakings of the parties, and of the terms and conditions hereinafter set forth, the parties here to have agreed and do hereby agree as follows.

3.

Supplier's Responsibilities

SUPPLIER will:

3.1   Feasibility study.

Conduct site-specific energy analysis at USER'S facility to determine feasibility, annual savings, capital cost, and operating and maintenance costs of an optimal cogeneration system.

3.2   Savings model.

Construct a cogeneration savings model for the facility for use in quantifying monthly savings achieved. Savings model will be structured to reflect actual not average savings.

3.3   Engineering design.

Provide detailed engineering system design,equipment installation, debugging, electric utility interface, and long-term operation and maintenance of the cogeneration system.

3.4   Communication with USER.

Communicate regularly with USER'S plant personnel, especially during system construction, to plan access to electric and thermal interconnections, and to minimize disruptions to normal plant operations.

3.5   Correction of malfunctions.

Promptly remedy malfunctions upon notification from USER.

3.6   Right to discontinue.

Retain the right to discontinue project development at any time if, at SUPPLIER'S sole discretion, the project ceases to demonstrate adequate economic value.

3.7   Purchase option.

Offer USER the option of purchasing the cogeneration system at annual intervals according to a price schedule to be determined before system construction begins.

3.8   Insurance responsibilities.

Maintain adequate liability and workmen's compensation insurance coverage while performing work at USER'S job site.

3.9   Maintenance responsibilities.

Provide proper ongoing maintenance for all equipment in the cogeneration system, including replacement of worn parts, change of lubricants and lubricant filters, and periodic adjustments, as required.

4.

User's Responsibilities

USER will:

4.1   Facility accessibility.

Allow SUPPLIER, and its associates, subcontractors, vendors, consultants, partners, and other interested parties, access to USER'S facilities for purposes of facility analysis, system construction, operations, and trouble-shooting.

4.2   USER representative.

Appoint a Facilities Engineer to work with SUPPLIER and its associates to analyze facility energy needs, arrive at the cogeneration savings model, coordinate construction activities and act generally as USER'S technical interface throughout the project.

4.3   Access to USER data.

Provide access to all available previous utility bills (both gas and electric) as well as all information available about plant energy consumption.

4.4   Responsibility for utility bills.

Continue to be responsible for payment of all utility bills.

4.5   Shared savings agreement.

Pay SUPPLIER a monthly fee which will amount to ()% of real savings attributed to the use of cogeneration in lieu of conventional steam and hot water production and electricity procurement from local utility. The SUPPLIER will pay any penalty or fees imposed by the utility in the event the cogeneration unit is nonoperable and the customer reverts to utility supplied electricity.

The method of calculating real savings will be mutually agreed upon by both parties and will include such items as ongoing utility standby charges, taxes on utility bills, actual electric rates in effect at the time of each calculation, actual natural gas prices in effect, and all other items of this type that can be identified as affecting actual savings.

4.6   Natural gas supply.

Use its best efforts to continue to procurenatural gas (through marketing arrangements or other-wise) at minimum pricing without risking adequate supply.

4.7   Assurance of operating load.

Assure that minimum heat and electric loads remain available at the facility to operate the cogeneration system on a continuous basis, less vacation shutdown periods and maintenance outages. In the event that USER cannot provide the energy loads for any reason except an act of God, strike, lockout, civil disturbance, explosion, breakage, accident to machinery, failure of cogeneration fuel supply, prevention by Federal, state, or local law, binding order of a Court or Governmental agency during the term of this Agreement, USER will purchase system from SUPPLIER according to the price schedule denoted in Section 3.7, or will agree to pay a monthly fee to SUPPLIER for the duration of the load outage equal to the average of the previous 12 month's fee as calculated in accordance with Section 4.5.

4.8   Confidentiality

Maintain confidentiality with regard to this project, and agree not to conduct negotiations with other cogeneration project developers, equipment vendors, energy service companies or other entities until notified in writing by SUPPLIER that SUPPLIER is discontinuing project development due to causes cited in Section 3.6 above.

4.9   Payment of SUPPLIER expenses.

Agree to pay SUPPLIER for all out-of-pocket development expenses (including salaries, travel expenses, fringe benefits, etc.) plus a mutually agreed-to cancellation fee of (normally 10–30%) if USER decides to terminate project development work prior to equipment procurement and installation. If USER terminates project development after equipment procurement and/or installation, all associated costs for these functions will be borne by USER also (in addition to project development expenses noted above). In lieu of the mutually agreed-to cancellation fee of(normally 10–30%), if USER decides to terminate project due to an electric rate reduction from its electric utility, USER will pay SUPPLIER an additional fee equal to 10% of the savings realized by this rate reduction for one full year after the reduced rate goes into effect.

4.10   Water supply and treatment.

Provide adequate water supply and water treatment for steam generator makeup.

5.

Supplier Indemnification Responsibility

SUPPLIER shall indemnify, protect, and hold USER, its directors, officers and employees harmless from and against all loss, costs, damage, injury or expense (including court costs and reasonable attorneys' fees) by reason of any accident, personal injuries, deaths, or damage to property of whatever kind or nature brought by any person, association, or corporation, which loss, damage, or expense is caused by the negligence of SUPPLIER in performing work pursuant to this Agreement.

6.

User Indemnification Responsibility

USER shall indemnify, protect, and hold SUPPLIER, its directors, officers and employees harmless from and against all loss, cost, damage, injury or expense(including court costs and reasonable attorneys' fees) by reason of any accident, personal injuries, deaths, or damage to property of whatever kind of nature brought by any person, association, or corporation, which loss, damage, or expense is caused by the negligence of USER.

Page 9

7.

Indirect or Consequential Damages

USER shall not be liable to SUPPLIER and SUPPLIER shall not be liable to USER for any special, indirect, or consequential damages, including, without limitation, loss of profit, loss of product, and loss of use, arising out of the performance of this Agreement irrespective of either party's fault or negligence.

8.

Delays

Any delays in or failure of performance by either party hereto of its duties hereunder (other than the payment of money), shall not constitute default or give rise to any claims for damages if and to the extent such delays or failure of performance are caused by occurrences beyond the control of the party involved, including but not limited to, acts of God or public enemy; expropriation of facilities; compliance with any law, or proclamation, regulation, ordinance or instruction of any government or unit thereof, including Indian nations, having or asserting jurisdiction; acts of war; rebellion or sabotage or damage resulting therefrom fires, floods, explosions, accidents, riots or strikes, delay by vendors and delivery of materials and equipment, delay of construction contractors in performing construction work, or any causes, whether or not of the same class or kind as those specifically named above, which are not within the reasonable control of the party involved and which, by the exercise of reasonable diligence, the party involved is unable to prevent, provided, however, that such party shall give notice together with full particulars of such causes or occurrences in writing or by telegraph to the other party as soon as practicable after the occurrences and the causes or occurrences shall as far as possible be remedied with all reasonable diligent dispatch by the party claiming such in order to put itself in the position to carry out its obligation under this Agreement.

9.

Notice Method

All notices pertaining to this Agreement shall be in writing, and if to USER, shall be sufficient if sent via first class mail to USER at the following address:

Name:_____

Address: _____

Attention: _____

Title:_____

and if to SUPPLIER shall be sufficient if sent first class mail to SUPPLIER at the following address:

Name:_____

Address: _____

Attention: _____

Title:_____

10.

Binding of Parties to Agreement

This Agreement, shall be binding upon and inure to the benefit of the successors and assigns of each of the parties hereto.

11.

Confidentiality

Any drawings, documentation, specifications, prints, designs, ideas or other information provided by SUPPLIER to USER pertaining to the work to be performed hereunder are strictly confidential and proprietary to SUPPLIER. USER shall not, without the prior written consent of SUPPLIER, disclose any such information to a third party or use any such information for its own benefit other than in connection with the operation of this cogeneration facility.

12.

Unenforceability

SUPPLIER and USER agree that if any term or pro-vision of this Agreement is held by any court to be illegal or unenforceable, the remaining terms, provisions, rights and obligations shall not be affected and shall remain in full force and effect.

13.

Entirety of Agreement

This Agreement sets forth the entire understanding of the parties and supersedes all prior agreements, communications, representations or warranties,whether oral or written, by any officer, employee or representative of either party. Any change in the terms and conditions of this Agreement must be in writing and signed by both parties.

14.

Execution of Agreement

IN WITNESS WHEREOF, the parties have caused this Agreement to be executed by their duly authorized officers as of the day and year first above written.

USER   SUPPLIER

By_____   By _____

Title _____   Title _____

WITNESS/ATTEST   WITNESS/ATTEST

By_____   By _____

Title _____   Title _____

The Equipment Supplier Contract

Supplier Agreement. Explanation of Agreement Terms

1. **PARTIES TO THE AGREEMENT**

    This section details the parties to the agreement, the effective date and the address of both supplier and user.

2. **SUPPLIER'S AND USER'S DECLARATIONS**

    This section outlines the reasons for the agreement from both the supplier's as well as the user's prospective.

3. **SUPPLIER'S RESPONSIBILITIES**

    This section details the responsibilities and rights of the supplier.

    3.1 **Feasibility study**

    This paragraph details the responsibility for and specifics of the feasibility study. This should always be a part of supplier's responsibility.

    3.2 **Savings model**

    This paragraph outlines the model that will be developed to allow the user to justify the installation based upon measurable data. Make certain that the savings model is based upon actual data not upon average operational conditions.

3.4   Communication with user

This paragraph details the supplier's responsibility to keep the user informed of the project status. It also notes that the supplier is obligated to minimize user plant disruptions. This paragraph is general in nature, but it should be in any agreement to at least recognize the need for communication and minimum disruptions.

3.6   Right to discontinue

This section outlines the supplier's right to stop the project if it ceases to be cost effective. Since this is a shared savings agreement, the supplier has to determine if there is adequate potential for profit based upon the shared savings process.

3.7   Purchase option

This section gives the user the option, at predetermined intervals, to purchase the system outright. Some users may wish to start the project as a shared savings agreement because of their lack of knowledge concerning a system such as this.

However, once the system is in operation and performing as intended, they may want to change to an outright purchase prior to the expiration of the shared savings period. This section provides for this option.

3.8   Insurance responsibility

This paragraph assures that adequate insurance is provided by the supplier. If specific insurance coverage is required by your company, the details concerning that insurance would be inserted in this section.

3.9   Maintenance responsibility

This paragraph is important especially since this is a shared cost agreement. Make certain that all aspects of the installation are covered in this section.

4.   USER'S RESPONSIBILITIES

This section details the responsibilities and rights of the user.

4.1   Facility accessibility

Outlined here is the user's agreement to allow the supplier and various other interested parties to have access to the premises during the installation process. Although this may seem to not be required in detailed form, since it is obvious that the supplier would have to enter the user's facilities to install the unit, it is well to detail who will be involved in the installation. Sometimes limitations are imposed by the user because of union contract stipulations or company policy.

4.2   User representative

This paragraph is important since it is essential to the timely completion of the project to have a user representative available to coordinate and provide assistance in various portions of the project. This provision can be one of the most important in terms of the user obtaining a satisfactory installation. Do not skimp in this area. Provide a qualified representative and allocate enough of this time to the project to provide the interface necessary.

4.3   Access to user data

This provision is necessary to allow the supplier to calculate the financial and usage data necessary in determining the viability of the project. Also, this data is required to do the feasibility study.

4.4   Responsibility for utility bills

This provision details the user's continued responsibility for payment of utility bills.

4.5   Shared Savings Agreement

This portion of the agreement is the heart of the shared savings arrangement. Contained in it is the monthly fee or supplier's portion of the shared savings. The percentage figure will vary depending upon the details surrounding the installation. The percentage share of each party will be predicated primarily upon data obtained during the feasibility phase of the project analysis.

Also, outlined here are the various components that will be considered when making the calculation.

The percentage share ratio between supplier and user will include consideration of all items detailed in this portion of the agreement together with supplier internal calculations including their cost of the unit, their return on investment requirements, and other cost return data. Make certain that provisions covering nonoperable cogeneration conditions do not create penalties that offset savings.

4.6   Natural gas supply

Outlined here is the requirement to utilize the least costly source of energy possible without undue risk to supply considerations. Again, it is important to the shared savings arrangement that cogeneration costs be minimized insofar as is possible so that payback criteria remains valid and the project viable. If this were a typical purchase or lease agreement, then this section would probably not be included since it would affect only the user if a less cost effective fuel were used.

4.7   Assurance of operational load

This provision assures the supplier that the user will not cease or reduce usage levels to a point that the cogeneration equipment cannot be utilized. If the user were allowed to not utilize the equipment, then the supplier's share of the savings would be diminished. If this were not a shared savings agreement, this provision would not be included.

4.8 Confidentiality

Most suppliers want this type of clause in the agreement to assure them that they are not being used simply as a comparison to another supplier. The user always has the right to cancel the agreement subject to the provisions following in 4.9.

4.9 Payment of supplier expenses

This provision outlines three different conditions of cancellation by the user as follows:

1. Cancellation prior to equipment purchase and installation.

2. Cancellation after equipment purchase and/or installation.

3. Cancellation because of utility rate reduction.

These provisions protect the supplier if the user abandons the project through no fault to the supplier. Some of the provisions that are listed under the user's responsibilities may seem overly protective of the supplier, but remember the supplier is taking all of the up-front risks with equipment and installation costs, which can run into the hundreds of thousands of dollars. Therefore, there needs to be some assurance that a capricious act of the user does not cause the supplier financial harm.

4.10 Water supply and treatment

This provision simply states that the water quantity and quality necessary for heat load utilization will be available.

5. SUPPLIER INDEMNIFICATION RESPONSIBILITY

This section details the supplier's responsibility to protect the user from any loss, damages, etc. caused by the negligence of the supplier while performing work pursuant to the agreement.

6. USER INDEMNIFICATION RESPONSIBILITY

This section details the user's responsibility to protect the supplier from any loss, damages, etc. caused by negligence of the user while performing work pursuant to the agreement.

7. INDIRECT OR CONSEQUENTIAL DAMAGES

This section details the limits of liability of both the supplier and user with respect to indirect or consequential damages which might arise as a result of the performance of this agreement. The damages included in this section relate only to monetary considerations.

8. DELAYS

This section details those delays that, should they occur, will not constitute default irrespective of the party involved. They include those items over which neither the supplier nor user can be reasonably expected to be able to control or foresee so long as due care is exercised.

9. NOTICE METHOD

Outlined here is the method to be used by either party when providing notice to the other party.

10. BINDING OF PARTIES TO AGREEMENT

This section protects both supplier and user in the event their company is sold or absorbed by another company. If this happens, then the successor company is obligated by the terms of the agreement to the same extent as was the original party.

11. CONFIDENTIALITY

This section protects any proprietary data provided by the supplier to the user in connection with this agreement.

12. UNENFORCEABILITY

If any section of the agreement is or becomes legally invalid or unenforceable, it does not negate the remainder of the agreement. This clause protects both parties against unenforceable stipulations.

13. ENTIRETY OF AGREEMENT

This section states that the agreement as signed by the supplier and user is complete as written with no unattached side clause or conditions.

14. EXECUTIVE OF AGREEMENT

This section identifies both parties by company and name. The signatures of the responsible parties are notarized in the supplier's and user's individual locations. When this page is properly signed by both parties and notarized, by agreement becomes binding.

Utility Involvement in Cogeneration

Utility involvement in a cogeneration project is mandatory and close coordination with the local electric utility is required. When the point is reached where a cogeneration contract with the supplier is pending, it is then time to contact the utility and coordinate the various interface connections necessary between the equipment of the customer and the utility.

Although some utilities encourage cogeneration, it is likely that they will try to dissuade any installation of the system. The reasons given for not doing the project will vary with the utility but in general will revolve around the potential for interface problems between each set of equipment.

It is true that an improperly installed system could potentially cause problems but if the supplier selected is competent, this will not be a cause for concern. The basic reason for a utility's reluctance to have its customers cogenerate is simple—lost revenue. If the utility cannot convince the customer to cancel a project, the utility may offer a lower electric rate in order for the cogeneration system not to be installed.

Depending upon the utility and the negotiation skills of the customer, this lower rate can match the cogeneration cost; or, it can be somewhere between the current rate and the cogeneration cost. Also, be aware of some stipulations that might be connected with the lower rates suggested by the utility.

Some utilities require that a sum of money equal to the cost of the cogeneration system be deposited with them, at interest, for a specified number of years. This procedure assures the utility that the rate reduction received by the customer, required financial investment equal to the cost of the cogeneration system.

If the method of payment for the system were the "shared savings" arrangement, then obviously the depositing of funds with the utility equal to the system cost is not going to be appealing. Also, there needs to be an awareness on the part of the customer that the rate reduction that will be offered will probably have a time limit attached to it and, at some point, in the future the reduced rate will revert to the then current tariff rate structure.

A sample of an actual electric utility cogeneration purchase rate schedule (Figure 6.2) together with a cogeneration standby and supplemental service rate schedule (Figure 8.3) follows.

Figure 8.2

Electric Utility Cogeneration Purchase Rate Schedule

COGENERATION POWER PRODUCTION PURCHASES RATE SCHEDULE "CG - 2A"

AVAILABILITY

Available on any distribution line of the utility company.

APPLICABILITY

Applicable for any customer who has installed an electric generating facility of at least 100 kW capacity for the customer's own use, and desires a permanent electrical connection with the utility company's system in order to sell electrical energy to the utility company, and to secure supplementary service from the utility company. The electric generating facility must be a qualified facility (QF) under provisions of Sections 201 and 210 of the Public Utility Regulatory Policies Act of 1978.

RATE FOR PURCHASE OF ENERGY FROM
COGENERATORS AND SMALL POWER PRODUCERS

The monthly customer charge shall be paid by the customer to the utility company to cover the cost of metering equipment, meter reading, data processing, and miscellaneous expenses necessary for the proper accounting of electrical energy sold to the utility company by the customer. The payment of energy is the per kWh payment by the utility company to the customer for energy purchased by the utility company from the QF.

STANDARD RATE

Monthly Customer Charge:

Single Phase Service -	$12.00	per Customer
Three Phase Service -	$25.00	per Customer

Payment for Energy:

Billing Months of April through October -	$0.02036 per kWh for all kWh
Billing Months of November through March -	$0.01867 per kWh for all kWh

Figure 8.3

Cogeneration Standby and Supplemental Service Rate Schedule

COGENERATION STANDBY AND SUPPLEMENTAL SERVICE RATE

RATE SCHEDULE "CG-2B"

APPLICABILITY

This rate is applicable for supplementary, back-up, and maintenance power to any customer having onsite generation and requesting standby service. A customer is required to take service under this schedule if the customer's backup or maintenance capacity requirement is greater than 100 kW and less than 5,001 kW.

This rate schedule applies to electric service used by one customer in a single establishment on one premise. All service under this rate schedule shall be received at one voltage level and is for exclusive use of the customer and shall not be resold or shared with others.

AVAILABILITY AND KIND OF SERVICE

Service under this rate schedule is available on a uniform basis throughout the service territory of the utility company. The kind of service under this schedule shall be three-phase, unregulated, at the customer's nominal operating voltage level, or at a primary voltage level designated as available by the utility company.

MONTHLY RATE FOR SECONDARY SERVICE

Customer Charge -	$900 per month
Reservation Charge -	$1.25 per kW of contracted capacity
Local Facilities Charge -	$1.20 per kW of contracted capacity
Billing Demand -	$8.00 per kW
Energy Charge -	$0.02751 per kWh

DETERMINATION OF CONTRACTED CAPACITY

The contracted capacity for monthly billing purposes shall be the larger of—(1) the capacity required to be maintained as agreed to in the Contract For Service, or (2) the maximum capacity required from the utility company during the current or preceding 23 billing months.

DETERMINATION OF MONTHLY BILLING DEMAND

The customer's kW billing demand each month shall be the average kW required from the utility company during the fifteen-minute period of the customer's greatest use in the month as measured by a suitable meter and rounded to the nearest whole kW.

Explanation of Figure 8.2—
Cogeneration Power Production Purchases

This rate schedule outlines the electric utility company's purchase of customer-cogenerated energy. As is evident, the purchase price of $0.02036 per kWh that the electric utility company is willing to pay would be, in most instances, less than the cogeneration cost to generate the electricity. In practically all electric utility cogeneration purchase rate schedules, the purchase price will be less than the cost to cogenerate the electricity. Never size a cogeneration system to generate excess electricity for the express purpose of selling the over-capacity to the electric utility company.

Explanation of Figure 8.3—Cogeneration
Standby and Supplemental Service Rate

This rate schedule outlines the charges the electricutility company assesses to provide backup or standby electricity to the cogeneration customer in the event of failure of the cogeneration equipment. Almost always the cogeneration customer will opt for this type of service since cogeneration equipment failure can occur. If this type of service is not utilized and a cogeneration equipment failure does occur, the electric utility company will not provide electricity during the outage period. The cogeneration customer would have to curtail electricity usage proportionate to the cogeneration capacity.

If a cogeneration customer has not contracted for backup capacity with the electric utility company, excessive penalties will be imposed by the electric utility during any cogeneration downtime. Very often these penalties in addition to being very expensive ($20 - $100/kW) also ratchet for periods of up to one year in the future. These penalties many times more than offset any savings that result from the cogeneration process.

Two good rules to always observe when considering cogeneration are as follows—

1. Never size a cogeneration unit to provide excess electricity over what is needed by the facility,with the intent to sell the excess to the electricutility. You will almost always lose money in selling cogenerated electricity to the electricutility company.
2. Always utilize an electric utility standby/supplemental rate schedule to provide affordable electricity in the event the cogeneration equipment fails.

Basic Cogeneration and Project Data Analysis Reports

Figure 8.4 is a chart that needs to be completed in order to obtain the basic cogeneration data to establish a true cost/payback relationship.

Figure 8.4

Basic Cogeneration Data Chart

FACILITY DATA
1. Total kWh used per year _____
2. Average demand in kW per hour _____
3. Btu per hour required _____
4. Therms per year required _____

COGENERATION DATA
1. Operating hours _____
2. Total kWh generated per year _____
3. Average load in kW _____
4. Fuel cost:
    a. Diesel fuel $ _____
    b. Natural gas $ _____
    c. Other fuel $ _____
5. Heat load available in Btu/hr _____

COGENERATION UNIT DATA
1. Unit capacity in kW _____
2. Engine heat output in Btu/hr _____
3. Cost/lease amount $ _____
4. Interest rate _____
5. Term (financing period in years) _____

OPERATING EXPENSES PER YEAR
1. Debt service cost $ _____
2. Miscellaneous utility interconnect costs,
   if applicable $ _____
3. Insurance $ _____
4. Fuel cost $ _____
5. Operation/maintenance expenses $ _____

PLANT REVENUES
1. Actual value of electricity_____
2. Actual value of thermal energy _____

GROSS OPERATING PROFIT
1. Customer's percentage of share of savings_____%
2. Installer's percentage share of savings _____%

CALCULATED DATA
1. Return on investment_____
2. Simple payback _____
3. Cost per kWh _____
4. Cost per MMBtu of steam/water _____

Figure 8.5
Cogeneration Project Analysis Report

COGENERATION PROJECT — No. A-34

for

The Facility_____

of

_____Company

Page 1

Figure 8.5 (Continued)

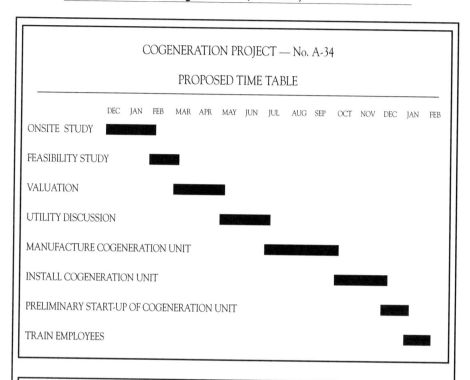

COGENERATION PROJECT — No. A-34

PROPOSED TIME TABLE

1. COGENERATION PROJECT		No. A-34
2. ESTIMATED PROJECT COST (No Up-front Capital Required)		$ 500,000
3. ESTIMATED PAYBACK PERIOD (Shared Savings Agreement)		5 Years
4. ESTIMATED PROJECT TIME PERIOD		14 Months
5. ESTIMATED PROJECT COMPLETION DATE		February

Page 2

Figure 8.5 (Continued)

COGENERATION PROJECT—No. A-34

RATIONALE FOR PROJECT

To provide a means of having electricity and hot water/steam generated onsite at the manufacturing facility to supplement utility-purchased electrical energy.

DESCRIPTION OF PROJECT

This project involves the purchase and installation of a natural gas-fueled internal combustion engine-driven generator capable of providing approximately 500 kW of electrical power. The waste heat generated by the combustion process will be utilized to supplement hot water/steam requirements in the amount of approximately 3,100 pounds per hour. The purpose of this is to provide self-generated electrical energy as well as utilization of generated-process heat to supplement the hot water/steam needs.

The payback on any system like this is in the difference between self-generated and purchased electricity costs. In this particular application it appears that sufficient differentials exist to provide a viable installation.

The method of payment for the proposed system is the shared savings plan, whereby the provider shares the electrical cost savings with the purchaser to the extent that the system is paid in an agreed-to period of time after which the system becomes the property of the purchaser. Also there is the possibility of negotiating an electrical rate reduction with the electric utility in lieu of purchasing the self-generation system; however, utility stipulations on such negotiated rates sometimes preclude this from being a viable option.

Page 3

Figure 8.5 (Continued)

COGENERATION PROJECT — No. A-34

COST ESTIMATE DETAILS

The following information may be revised pending the finalized utilization figures for the Generated Process Heat.

1.	Purchase, Installation and Start-up of a 500 kW Cogeneration Unit. Amount paid in a 5-Year Shared Savings Agreement (No up-front cost involved)	$ 500,000
2.	Training of Employees in Routine Maintenance Procedures. (The only pre-installation cost)	$ 1,000
	TOTAL COST	$ 501,000

PAYBACK ESTIMATES

1.	Yearly reduction in utility-purchased electricity and hot water/steam costs	$ 200,000
2.	Yearly share of savings to manufacturing plant during shared savings period (20%).	$ 40,000
3.	Shared savings period — 5 years. Total manufacturing plant share in this period. (5 years X $40,000)	$ 200,000
4.	Shared savings period — 5 years. Total supplier share in this period. (5 years X $180,000)	$ 800,000
5.	Yearly savings after shared savings period ends assuming usage characteristics and utility costs	$ 200,000

Page 4

335

Figure 8.5 (Continued)

COGENERATION PROJECT — No. A-34			
PROJECT COMPLETION TIMETABLE ESTIMATES			
STUDY	PURPOSE OF COGENERATION UNIT	STARTING MONTH	COMPLETION MONTH
1. ONSITE STUDY	DETERMINE (a) Steam usage. (b) Location of cogeneration unit in plant.	December	February
2. PROVIDER DETAILED FEASIBILITY STUDY Provider - Cogeneration Manufacturer	PROVIDE — (a) Potential energy savings. (b) Equipment & installation costs. (c) Shared Savings Contract. (d) Diagram of cogeneration unit, piping and wiring in plant. (e) Other supporting data necessary to make decision on project.	February	March
3. EVALUATION OF FEASIBILITY STUDY	DETERMINE VIABILITY OF PROJECT BASED UPON THE FACTORS — (a) Cost of proposed cogeneration unit. (b) Payback period of project. (c) Acceptability of Shared Savings Contract. (d) Fit of cogeneration concept in plant environment.	March	May
4. DISCUSS PROJECT WITH LOCAL UTILITY	COORDINATE PROJECT WITH UTILITY — (a) Determine if system electrical switchgear acceptable to utility (b) Document rationale for cogeneration. (c) Evaluate potential electrical rate reduction proposal submitted by utility company as incentive not to cogenerate. (d) Sign required cogeneration/utility contracts including Back-up Power Agreement if proceeding with project.	May	July
5. INSTALL COGENERATION UNIT	COMPLETE INSTALLATION — (a) Manufacturer cogeneration unit - 3 months. (b) Install cogeneration unit - 2 months. (c) Preliminary start-up of equipment - 1 month. (d) Employee training - 1 month.	July	January

Page 5

Figure 8.5 (Continued)

COGENERATION PROJECT — No. A-34

PROJECT RESPONSIBILITY

1. FACILITY (CLIENT) REPRESENTATIVE

   Engineer In Charge

2. COGENERATION MANUFACTURER

   Engineer In Charge

Page 6

Miscellaneous Electricity Cost Reduction Strategies

To thoroughly evaluate the potential for reducing electricity costs, a defined sequential plan of attack is required. In the following figures are sample electricity evaluation sheets.

Figure 8.6   GENERAL USAGE DATA

Figure 8.7   TARIFF SCHEDULE CONSIDERATIONS

Figure 8.8   TARIFF AND METER DATA

Figure 8.9   TRANSFORMER DATA

Figure 8.10   LIGHTING DATA

Figure 8.11   ELECTRICITY WORK SHEET

Figure 8.12   FILLED OUT ELECTRICITY WORK SHEET

Not all sections of all categories will be utilized on every evaluation but utilization of those sections that are applicable will assist in determining where excessive electricity costs may be reduced.

Figure 8.6
General Usage Data

GENERAL USAGE DATA

1. What is the current average cost per kilowatt hour (kWh) of electricity in this facility? (To obtain this figure, divide the total dollar amount on the monthly utility billing by the total kilowatt hours shown on the billing.)

2. What are the usages of electricity in this facility? (Office lighting, heating, air conditioning, manufacturing, warehousing, etc.) Explain uses in detail and estimate each usage category as a percent of the total uses.

3. If electricity is used in heating and/or manufacturing, are there any places where electricity is currently used that could be changed to a different energy source, e.g., natural gas, etc. Process uses such as heating, air conditioning, manufacturing/processing could be potential areas to investigate.

4. Does the electrical demand (kW/kVA) component vary greatly hour-to-hour, day-to-day, month-to-month, etc.; and, if it does, what are the reasons for the variations?

5. Has the facility every had a Demand (kW/kVA) Profile Analysis performed; and if so, what did it show?

6. Is power factor a potential problem for this facility in terms of utility penalties or internal electrical distribution capacity?

7. Does this facility utilize hot water or steam on a continuing basis in their current usage pattern; and, if so, how many hours per day is it available?

8. Are there any areas in the facility that could be temporarily curtailed if an interruptible electricity rate could be utilized to reduce costs?

9. Does the facility have an emergency or back-up generation facility onsite? If so, what is its size (kW output capacity)? And, for what purpose is it utilized?

10. If the facility has an emergency or back-up generation facility, is it wired in parallel with the normal electrical system?

11. From general observations of the facility's usage patterns, hours of operation and types of operations performed, are there any general comments that would be helpful in identifying areas of potential cost reduction opportunities not specifically outlined in other areas of this data collection form?

Figure 8.7

Tariff Schedule Considerations

TARIFF SCHEDULE CONSIDERATIONS

1. Name and address of the serving utility _____

2. Name of the utility service representative _____

3. Telephone number of the utility service representative_____

4. Utility classification —

    A. For-profit_____
    B. Municipal _____
    C. Cooperative _____
    D. Federal _____

5. Are there any pending rate cases relating to this utility? If so, what is the status of each? In general, what is the utility requesting?_____

6. Has contact been made with the utility service representative? _____

7. Are there any planned rate cases by this utility? If so, when will these be filed? In general, what will the utility be requesting?_____

8. What was the date of the last rate case requested by this utility? _____

9. Are copies of the following items available —

    A. All utility rate tariff schedules _____
    B. All experimental rate tariff schedules _____
    C. All off-tariff rate schedules_____
    D. All rebate program schedules_____
    E. All pending or current rate case filings _____
    F. All miscellaneous utility data that could assist in the evaluation
       of this facility's electricity costs _____

Figure 8.8
Tariff and Meter Data

TARIFF AND METER DATA

1. Under what tariff schedule is the facility currently served? _____

2. Are any tariff schedule riders utilized? If so, what are they? _____

3. Are any experimental rates, off-tariff rates or rebate programs utilized?
   If so, what are they? _____

4. Are there any miscellaneous, contract demand or ratchet clause charges on the facility's electricity billing? If so, explain what they are _____

5. How many electric meter points are utilized? _____

6. Do all meter identification numbers match those shown on the utility billings? _____

7. Do all meter multiplying constants match those shown on the utility billings? _____

8. Is the metering on the primary or the secondary side of the transformation point? _____

9. If more than one point of metering is utilized, what is the reason for doing so? _____

10. If a single point of metering would result in reduced electricity charges, would the facility be willing to change if a cost benefit could be shown? _____

11. What type of metering is utilized — _____

    A. Kilowatt hour register only (mechanical) _____
    B. Kilowatt demand and kilowatt hour registers (mechanical accumulation type) _____
    C. Kilowatt demand and kilowatt hour registers (electronic digital pulse) _____

12. Have any meters been recently changed? If so, identify each meter by the date the change occurred. What was the reason for the change? _____

13. On what schedule are meters read (monthly, every 30 days, every 2 months, estimated, etc.) _____

14. Has the facility ever had a problem with meters that resulted in reading errors? If so, what was the result after the errors were discovered? _____

Figure 8.9

Transformer Data

TRANSFORMER DATA

1. What are the incoming supply voltages to the transformers? _____

2. What are the outgoing stepped-down voltages leaving the transformers?_____

3. How many transformers are utilized at incoming meter points? _____

4. What are the transformer sizes (kVA or kW name plate ratings)? _____

5. Who are the manufacturers of the transformers? _____

6. Do any of the transformers contain PCB (polychlorinated biphenyl)?_____

7. What are the ages of the transformers?_____

8. If possible, from the utility, determine the current depreciated value of any transformer that is utility-owned and provided for the facility's use? _____

9. Do transformers have overhead or underground feed lines? _____

10. What type of transformer is utilized —

    A.   Dry type _____

    B.   Liquid dielectric convection cooled type _____

11. With relation to the facility, where are the transformers located?_____

12. Has the facility ever experienced any problems with the transformers? (failures, under capacity, overheating, etc.) _____

13. Does the facility have any future plans that could impact transformer capacity or physical locations? _____

Figure 8.10
Lighting Data

LIGHTING DATA

1. What types of lighting are utilized in the facility? Indicate (1) where each is used, (2) approximate number of units and, (3) approximate percent of total lighting each source represents —

    A.   Incandescent _____
    B.   Tungsten_____
    C.   Compact fluorescent _____
    D.   Mercury vapor _____
    E.   Fluorescent -
          1)   Electronic (solid state) _____
          2)   Transformer type ballast _____
    F.   Metal halide_____
    G.   High pressure sodium_____
    H.   Low pressure sodium _____

2. Does the facility rent any lighting fixtures from the utility? If so, indicate the quantity, types and locations of these units _____

3. For what purpose is the lighting used? (Office environment, industrial processing, warehousing, outside, parking lots, security, etc.)
List the uses and lighting types for each. _____

4. Has the facility ever had a Lighting Analysis performed? If so, when and by whom?_____

5. Does the facility's electric utility company offer any rebate incentive programs with relation to the installation of more efficient lighting fixtures? If so, how would the rebate program interface with the facility's uses? _____

6. Has the electric utility been contacted concerning the possibility of performing (at no cost) a Walk-through Analysis of the facility's lighting situation?
If so, what was the result? _____

7. Does the facility have any future plans that could impact lighting needs? _____

An electricity worksheet to assist in analyzing electricity billings is shown in Figure 8.11. If the information requested on this sheet is analyzed and evaluated, a good start to reducing electricity costs will result. Use of this information in conjunction with the data provided in this chapter will provide the electricity user a means of knowing what their costs should be and how to reduce them.

Figure 8.11

Electricity Worksheet

ELECTRICITY WORKSHEET

1. Today's date _____ 2. Month being analyzed _____

3. Total cost of electricity used $ _____

4. Amount of electricity used _____kWh

5. Cost of electricity per kWh. (Divide amount in #3 by amount in #4)
   ($_____ ÷ _____kWh) = $ _____

6. Current demand charge per kW $ _____

7. Current actual demand _____kVA/kW

8. Current billing demand _____kVA/kW

9. Current demand penalty. (Amount in #8, minus amount in #7, times amount in #6)
   (_____kVA/kW – _____kVA/kW) X ($_____) = $ _____

10. Total demand cost. (Amount in #6 times amount in #8)
    ($ _____ X _____kVA/kW) = $ _____

11. Current power factor charge $ _____

12. Current power factor percentage_____%

13. Amount paid in state taxes $ _____

14. Transformer rental or lease charge $_____

15. Who owns primary transformers. Company _____ Utility _____

16. Miscellaneous charges $ _____

17. Does the operation utilize hot water or steam in any processes? Yes _____ No _____

Explanation of the Electricity Worksheet

1. **Today's date**—This entry designates the date that the work sheet is being analyzed.

2. **Month being analyzed**—This indicates the month of the electrical billing being analyzed.

3. **Total cost of electricity used**—The total charges for the month being analyzed are entered on this line.

4. **Amount of electricity used**—The total kilowatt hours (kWh) used for the entire month being analyzed are entered on this line.

5. **Cost of electricity per kWh**—This entry shows the cost per kilowatt hour (kWh) for the entire month being analyzed. To calculate this amount, divide the cost of electricity used on line #3 by the total kWh used in the month on line #4. This resultant will be the cost per kWh.

6. **Current demand charge per kW**—This is the current charge per kW of demand as shown on the monthly billing.

7. **Current actual demand**—This is the amount of demand in (kW) actually used in the month being analyzed. Sometimes this demand usage is listed as "actual demand" on the electric bill.

8. **Current billing demand—(kVA)** This is the amount of demand in (kW) actually being billed in the month being analyzed. Actual and billing demand quantities may be different if the utility has ratchet provisions in its tariff schedule.

9. **Current demand penalty**—This entry determines the demand penalty by taking the amount on line #8 and subtracting it from the amount on line #7. The amount shown on this line indicates the amount of demand that was paid for but not actually used (Demand Ratchet Penalty).

10. **Total demand cost**—This entry determines the total cost of demand by multiplying the current demand charge per kW on line #6 by the billing demand in kW on line #8.

11. **Current power factor charge**—This is the amount that is charged monthly by the utility as a penalty to the user for the inefficient use of electricity. This penalty charge normally begins at an 85% efficiency or power factor level. Even if your utility does not charge now for low power factor (under 85%), check to determine whether the tariff schedule under which they operate allows them to do so if they so choose.

12. **Current power factor percentage**—This is the "efficiency" percentage of electrical usage and is the ratio of real power in kW to apparent power in kVA.

13. **Amount paid in state taxes**—This is the amount paid to the state in the form of taxes usually as a percentage of the total electrical billing amount. In addition to state taxes, there may also be city, county, and school taxes and/or local franchise fees.

14. **Transformer rental or lease charge**—If your primary transformers (the transformers that convert utility transmission voltage into normally used plant or facility voltages—440, 200, 110 volts) are owned by the utility, then a monthly rental or lease charge may be assessed. This charge is to compensate the utility for maintenance and/or upkeep on these transformers.

15. **Ownership of primary transformers**—To find out if the facility or the utility owns the primary transformers, it may be necessary to contact your local utility since a rental or lease charge for a utility-owned transformer may be buried in with other charges and not be readily apparent on the monthly billing.

16. **Miscellaneous charges**—Items listed in this entry may include any charges not accounted for in any other entry on this work sheet. They may include, but not be limited to, special facility charges or late payment fees.

17. **Does your operation utilize hot water or steam in any processes?** Although this may not appear to be related to electrical usage or

cost, it is important in considering whether cogeneration or self-generation would be a viable option.

Figure 8.12
Sample of a Filled Out Electricity Worksheet

ELECTRICITY WORKSHEET

1. Today's date _____ March 17 _____   2. Month being analyzed _____ February _____

3. Total cost of electricity used $ _____ 9,651.17 _____

4. Amount of electricity used _____ 212,643 _____ kWh

5. Cost of electricity per kWh. (Divide amount in #3 by amount in #4)
   ($ ___ 9,651.17 ___ ÷ ___ 212,643 ___ kWh) = $ _____ .0454/kWh _____

6. Current demand charge per kW $ _____ 9.25 _____

7. Current actual demand _____ 450 kW _____ kVA/kW

8. Current billing demand _____ 473 kW _____ kVA/kW

9. Current demand penalty. (Amount in #8, minus amount in #7, times amount in #6)
   (___ 473 ___ kVA – ___ 450 ___ kVA) X ($ ___ 9.25 ___) = $ ___ 212.75 ___

10. Total demand cost. (Amount in #6 times amount in #8)
    ($ ___ 9.25 ___ X ___ 473 ___ kVA) = $ _____ 4,375.25 _____

11. Current power factor charge $ _____ 94.60 _____

12. Current power factor percentage _____ 81 _____ %

13. Amount paid in state taxes $ _____ 579.07 _____

14. Transformer rental or lease charge $ _____ No _____

15. Who owns primary transformers. Company _____ Utility ___ X ___

16. Miscellaneous charges $ _____ 176.12 _____

17. Does the operation utilize hot water or steam in any processes? Yes ___ X ___ No _____

Miscellaneous Information

The following is an outline of three categories which could possibly affect your electricity costs. Some of these items are currently available so that any effort on the part of the customer to reduce electricity costs might be immediate. Others may be on the horizon as new rulings are established by the State Public Service Commissions and as utility companies become more open to the needs of their customers. Whatever the case, always be aware that many possibilities are available to reduce electricity costs.

I.   POTENTIAL CIRCUMSTANCES THAT WILL AFFECT ELECTRICITY COSTS IN THE FUTURE

II.   POINTS TO CONSIDER IN REDUCING ELECTRICITY COSTS

III.   VARIOUS LIGHTING SOURCES IN LUMENS PER WATT(EFFICIENCY)

I.   Potential Circumstances That Will Affect Electricity Costs in the Future

1. More mandatory Time-of-Use (TOU)/Time-of-Day (TOD) Rates.

Rates that assign different costs for different times of the day.

2. Longer On-Peak Rate periods.

Rates that assign a higher cost for a longer period of the day.

3. **More Interruptible Power Rate usage.**

   Rates that are less costly if power can be interrupted.

4. **Real Time Pricing Rates with no demand charges.**

   Rates that change energy (kWh) costs as frequently as every minute of every hour of everyday.

5. **More Demand Rate ratchets.**

   Rates that assess demand (kW) charges based upon a past demand level rather than the amount actually used in the current month.

6. **More Demand/Usage Rate combinations.**

   Rates that assess usage (kWh) costs based upon the amount of demand (kW) used.

7. **More Off-Tariff Rate schedules.**

   Special rates that are customer specific.

8. **More Combined Metering Procedures.**

   Rates that combine rather than totalize demand (kW) usages in multiple meter installations.

9. **Unbundled rate structures.**

   Rates that allow a customer to pick and choose different billing components in order to arrive at an overall cost.

10. **Wheeling of electricity on a customer basis.**

    The purchasing of electricity from a source other than the local electric utility company.

11. **Equipment credit/negotiation processes.**
Utility-negotiation processes whereby the utility will assist with up-front equipment costs in return for new or increased customer usage.

II. Points to Consider in Reducing Electricity Costs

1. **Negotiation on equipment costs**
   a. Transformation costs—primary vs. secondary.
   b. Equipment costs—increase of electrical usage.
   c. Equipment costs—new construction/new service territory.

2. **Municipal and Cooperative Utilities**—Request pass-through of rates offered by utilities who wholesale to these entities that might reduce a customer's electricity costs.

3. **Add demand (kW) load to the system**—If the customer has a current demand (kW) close to a minimum threshold of a less expensive tariff schedule, add (kW) demand load to reach the required minimum threshold. Example:
   Current load—490 kW
      Average cost—$0.045/kWh
   Threshold—500 kW
      Average cost—$0.039/kWh
   Add demand load of 10 kW to reach a less expensive tariff schedule threshold. Also check to see if the utility would allow the customer to pay for a minimum demand load (500 kW) without actually using (500 kW).

4. **Combination of meters**

    a.   Reduction of total demand (kW). When separate meters are used, demand is totalized. This causes demand (kW) usages to be higher than the utility actually experiences since the separate demand (kW) peaks practically never occur during the same measurement period.

    b.   Reduction of customer basic charge.

5. **Separation or addition of meters**—Many utilities require a Time-of-Use (TOU) or Time-of-Day Rate (TOD) when demand (kW) exceeds a predetermined level (100,150,200 kW). If a customer works an 8- or 12-hour day, a time differentiated rate can be much more expensive to use.

The separation of demand (kW) into two meter points can reduce the demand (kW) to below the threshold level mandated for TOU or TOD Rates. Many times savings occur even though separate customer base charges are levied on each meter point and demand levels are totalized.

6. **Zeroing of meters**—When a customer's name changes on a billing (meter) location, the meter should be zeroed (not physically, necessarily). This is especially true if demand (kW) ratchets are used, since a minimum ratchet demand may be charged whether any usage occurs at all. This is especially important in shopping centers or other places where the names of the meter point customers change frequently.

7. **Power interruptions**—When power interruptions occur because of utility distribution or weather problems that

result in electrical outages from switchgear trip protection devices, remember to do the following things—

(1) Record the day the outage occurred,

(2) Record time-of-day the outage occurred,

(3) Notify the utility of outage details as soon as possible,

(4) Analyze the utility bill for the month that the electrical outage occurred and if it appears that the electrical outage caused an increase in the electrical cost, request that the utility adjust the bill and deduct the penalty caused by the electrical outage.

Many times the electric utility companies are unaware of all interruptions that occur on their distribution systems. They generally are willing to work with a customer to deduct the cost penalty the interruption caused if they are notified of the interruption promptly. By law they generally are not required to adjust billings because of these types of interruptions, but will generally work with a customer in a situation of this type.

8. **Utilize onsite emergency generation capacity to peak shave demand kW/kVA.**

Although this process requires parallel wiring of the emergency generation equipment to the customer's general electrical distribution system, in many instances it is a cost-effective measure to consider. Since peak shaving has great potential to reduce electricity costs, an explanation of peak shaving/load shedding follows.

Peak Shaving/Load Shedding

Peak shaving involves the reduction of expensive utility-supplied electrical power during periods of peak demand. There are several ways to accomplish this, among them:[4]

Load Shedding. This method involves simply shutting down certain machines, lighting or other energy-consuming equipment during peak demand periods. It can be effective in reducing your electrical peak, but it may not be efficient in terms of your operation's productivity.

Base or Block Loading. This method involves replacing utility-supplied electrical power with a base supply of generator- supplied power. The generator is loaded and produces a constant output. The generator is turned on and off at fixed times or demand levels during the day. This mode of operation may generate much more power than is required to reduce the peak demand, thus significantly reducing or even eliminating any potential cost savings.

Modulated Output Peak Shaving. This peak shaving method uses switchgear and a generator set which automatically comes on line at a fixed kW demand to supply the demand above that fixed setpoint. The disadvantage is difficulty in determining how much peak to shave and where to place the setpoint. A properly designed system maximizes the amount of peak reduction while minimizing generator run time. This reduces operating costs plus a system of this type reduces your peak energy usage by varying the output of the generator. The system's intelligent switchgear control is programmed to automatically reduce your peak most economically. This reduction is determined through an in-depth engineering and economic analysis.

The result is a system which operates in parallel with your utility company, reduces the expensive demand portion of your energy bill and operates the generator the fewest kilowatt hours for the maximum savings.

Net savings is defined as: Avoided Demand and Consumption Charges – Generator Operating Costs = Net Savings

How Can I Determine if Peak Shaving is Feasible For Me? Peak shaving with onsite generators is not always the answer. Several specific factors much be taken into account to determine potential savings.

RULES OF THUMB

For a new system —

Demand Charge greater than $8/kW (kVA)
Peak Demand greater than 2000 kW/(kVA)

For retrofit or existing generator —

Demand Charge greater than $6/kW (kVA)

If these basic parameters are met, a feasibility analysis is conducted. Computerized tools quickly analyze electrical power usage and determine if peak shaving is a viable, cost-saving alternative for a facility.

The first analysis is a Probability of Onsite Power-Economic Test (PROSPECT). It uses information from utility bills, including monthly peak demand, monthly energy consumption, and demand and energy charges, plus estimated equipment and installation costs, and fuel and maintenance costs. PROSPECT will determine if potential savings merits further analysis.

The second analysis is a Simulated Technical and Economic Performance Study (STEPS). This study is more in-depth and requires more information than the PROSPECT analysis. Utility rate structure, electrical usage profile, generator operating costs and economic parameters such as the rate of inflation, discount rate, depreciation schedule and tax rates are taken into account.

Results are presented in a report which estimates the amount of monthly peak reduction, monthly profile plots, computer simulation results, as well as economic summary information such as estimated investment and payback period for up to five different system sizes.

How Does The System Use This Data? The computerized generator control system is capable of starting, paralleling, variably loading and stopping multiple generators. The control system senses your plant demand and operates the generators as needed to maintain the predetermined setpoint. As utility-supplied peak demand increases and nears the setpoint, the control system will start and parallel the generator set with the utility. As plant demand increases above the setpoint, generator output increases. The control system continues to monitor the plant demand and adjust generator output as needed to achieve optimum savings.

The microprocessor not only controls and monitors the generator during peak shaving operations, but also gathers system performance data to verify actual energy dollar savings. Both utility and generator demand are reported as well as the generator's fuel usage. The result is a summary of overall net energy savings.

Figure 8.13

Peak Shaving Feasibility Analysis Form

PEAK SHAVING FEASIBILITY ANALYSIS

Your Name _____

Title _____

Company Name _____

Phone No. (_____)_____

Utility Company Name _____

Utility Rate Name/Designation _____

Utility Electrical Demand Charge (Summer/Winter): _____ $/kW (kVA)

Utility Electrical Consumption Rate (Summer/Winter): _____ $/kW (kVA)

Annual Purchased Power Cost: _____ ($/Last Year)

Annual Energy Consumption: _____ (kWh/Last Year)

PEAK DEMAND kW (kVA)	ENERGY CONSUMPTION kW (kVA)
JAN	
FEB	
MAR	
APR	
MAY	
JUN	
JUL	
AUG	
SEP	
OCT	
NOV	
DEC	

Type of Fuel Available: _____ (Diesel, Natural Gas, Both)

Fuel Cost: _____ ($/Gal, $/Mcf)

By filling out this form and submitting it to a qualified peak shaving equipment manufacturer, a determination can be made with relation to the viability of peak shaving for a given situation.

III. VARIOUS LIGHTING SOURCES IN LUMENS PER WATT(EFFICIENCY)

	LIGHT TYPE	LUMENS PER WATT
1.	Incandescent	10 - 25
2.	Tungsten Halogen Incandescent	12 - 37
3.	Compact Fluorescent	35 - 70
4.	Mercury Vapor	30 - 85
5.	Fluorescent	37 - 85
6.	Metal Halide	80 - 112
7.	High Pressure Sodium	65 - 135
8.	Low Pressure Sodium	100 - 185

References

1. Kimball, James A.; "Reliability of Natural Gas Cogeneration systems." Gas Research Institute.

2. Sinclair, Joseph; "The Turnkey Approach to Cogeneration." *The Cogeneration Journal*, Vol.3, No.1, Fairmont Press, Publisher.

3. Theisen, Rudy, P.E.; "Operation and Maintenance Costs of Cogeneration and IPP Plants." *The Cogeneration Journal*, Vol.7, No. 2, Fairmont Press, Publisher.

4. Evans, Dr. R. Michael; "Making the Most of Small Scale Cogeneration." *The Cogeneration Journal*, Vol.7, No. 4, Fairmont Press, Publisher.

Appendices

Please take time to examine these Appendices since they contain much basic information relating to many aspects of electricity. If the material in these Appendices is understood, it will be much easier to reduce/control electricity cost.

Appendix A

Listing of For-Profit Utility Regulatory Agencies

This listing includes United States Federal and State Regulatory agencies as well as other non-United States agencies. This information is courtesy of the National Association of Regulatory Utility Commissioners, 1102 Interstate Commerce Commission Building, P.O. Box 684, Washington, DC 20044-0684; Tel. (202) 898-2200.

REGULATORY AGENCIES

(Year of agency's or predecessor's establishment shown after name)

US FEDERAL REGULATORY AGENCIES

FEDERAL ENERGY REGULATORY COMMISSION (FERC) (1930)
825 North Capitol Street, NE, Washington DC 20426
Tel. (202) 208-1088, Fax 208-2106, Bulletin Board 208-8997

NUCLEAR REGULATORY COMMISSION (NRC) (1946)
Washington, DC 20555, Tel. (301) 492-7000, Fax 504-1672

**RURAL ELECTRIFICATION ADMINISTRATION (REA) (1935),
UNITED STATES DEPARTMENT OF AGRICULTURE**
Independence Avenue & 14th Street, SW, Washington, DC 20250
Tel. (202) 720-1255, Fax 720-1725

UNITED STATES DEPARTMENT OF ENERGY (DOE) (1977)
1000 Independence Avenue, SW, Washington, DC 20585
Tel. (202) 586-5000, Fax 586-8134, 586-4403

US STATE REGULATORY AGENCIES

ALABAMA PUBLIC SERVICE COMMISSION (PSC) (1881)
P.O. Box 991, Montgomery, AL 36101-0991
Tel. (205) 242-5209, Fax 240-3079

US STATE REGULATORY AGENCIES (Continued)

ALASKA PUBLIC UTILITIES COMMISSION (PUC) (1959)
1016 West Sixth Avenue, Suite 400, Anchorage, AK 99501
Tel. (907) 276-6222, Fax 276-0160

ARIZONA CORPORATION COMMISSION (PUC) (1959)
1200 West Washington Street, Phoenix, AZ 85007
Tel. (602) 542-2931, Fax 542-5560

ARKANSAS PUBLIC SERVICE COMMISSION (PSC) (1935)
1000 Center Building, Little Rock, AR 72201
Tel. (501) 682-2051, Fax 682-5731

CALIFORNIA PUBLIC UTILITIES COMMISSION (PUC) (1911)
California State Building, 205 Van Ness Avenue,
San Francisco, CA 94102-3298
Tel. (415) 703-1282, Fax 703-1758

COLORADO PUBLIC UTILITIES COMMISSION (PUC) (1885)
Logan Tower, Office Level 2, 1580 Logan Street,
Denver, CO 80203
Tel. (303) 894-2000, Fax 894-2065

CONNECTICUT DEPT. OF PUBLIC UTILITY CONTROL (DPUC) (1911)
1 Central Park Plaza, New Britain, CT 06051
Tel. (203) 827-1553, Fax 827-2613

DELAWARE PUBLIC SERVICE COMMISSION (PSC) (1949)
1560 South DuPont Highway, P.O. Box 457,
Dover, DE 19903-0457
Tel. (302) 739-4247, Fax 729-4849

DISTRICT OF COLUMBIA PUBLIC SERVICE COMMISSION (PSC) (1913)
450 Fifth Street, NW, Washington, DC 20001
Tel. (202) 626-5100, Fax 638-1785

US STATE REGULATORY AGENCIES (Continued)

FLORIDA PUBLIC SERVICE COMMISSION (PSC) (1887)
101 East Gaines Street, Fletcher Building,
Tallahassee, FL 32399-0850
Tel. (904) 488-3464, Fax 487-0509

GEORGIA PUBLIC SERVICE COMMISSION (PSC) (1879)
244 Washington Street, SW, Atlanta, GA 30334-5701
Tel. (404) 656-4501, Fax 656-2341

HAWAII PUBLIC UTILITIES COMMISSION (PUC) (1913)
465 South King Street, Kekuanao's Building, #103
Honolulu, HI 96813
Tel. (808) 586-2020, Fax 586-2066

IDAHO PUBLIC UTILITIES COMMISSION
P.O. Box 83720, Boise, ID 83720-0074
Tel. (208) 334-0300, Fax 334-3762

ILLINOIS COMMERCE COMMISSION (CC) (1871)
Leland Building, 527 East Capitol Avenue,
P.O. Box 19280, Springfield, IL 62794-9280
Tel. (217) 782-7295, Fax 782-1042

INDIANA UTILITY REGULATORY COMMISSION (URC) (1913)
Suite E306, Indiana Government Center South,
302 West Washington Street, Indianapolis, IN 46204
Tel. (317) 232-2701, Fax 232-6758

IOWA UTILITIES BOARD (UB) (1878)
Lucas State Office Building, Des Moines, IA 50319
Tel. (515) 281-5979, Fax 281-8821

KANSAS STATE CORPORATION COMMISSION (SCC) (1883)
1500 SW Arrowhead Road, Topeka, KS 66604-4027
Tel. (502) 564-3940, Fax 271-3354

US STATE REGULATORY AGENCIES (Continued)

KENTUCKY PUBLIC SERVICE COMMISSION (PSC) (1934)
730 Schenkel Lane, P.O. Box 615, Frankfort, KY 40602
Tel. (502) 564-3940, Fax 564-7279

LOUISIANA PUBLIC SERVICE COMMISSION (PSC) (1899)
P.O. Box 91154, Baton, Rouge, LA 70821-9154
Tel. (504) 342-4427, Fax 342-4087

MAINE PUBLIC UTILITIES COMMISSION (PUC) (1914)
242 State Street, State House Station 18,
Augusta, ME 04333
Tel. (207) 287-3831, Fax 287-1039

MASSACHUSETTS DEPARTMENT OF PUBLIC UTILITIES (DPU) (1919)
100 Cambridge Street, Boston, MA 02202
Tel. (617) 727-3500, Fax 723-8812

MICHIGAN PUBLIC SERVICE COMMISSION (PSC) (1873)
Mercantile Building, 6545 Mercantile Way,
P.O. Box 30221, Lansing, MI 48909-7721
Tel. (517) 334-6445, Fax 882-5170

MINNESOTA PUBLIC UTILITIES COMMISSION (PUC) (1871)
121 East 7th Place, Suite 350, St. Paul, MN 55101-2147
Tel. (612) 296-7124, Fax 297-7073

MISSISSIPPI PUBLIC SERVICE COMMISSION (PSC) (1884)
19th Floor, Walter Sillers State Office Building,
P.O. Box 1174, Jackson, MS 39215-1174
Tel. (601) 961-5400, Fax 961-5469

MISSOURI PUBLIC SERVICE COMMISSION (PSC) (1913)
P.O. Box 360, Truman State Office Building,
Jefferson City, MO 65102
Tel. (314) 751-3234, Fax 751-1847

US STATE REGULATORY AGENCIES (Continued)

MONTANA PUBLIC SERVICE COMMISSION (PSC) (1907)
1701 Prospect Avenue, P.O. Box 202601,
Helena, MT 59620-2601
Tel. (406) 444-6199, Fax 444-7618

NEBRASKA PUBLIC SERVICE COMMISSION (PSC) (1906)
300 The Atrium, 1200 N Street, P.O. Box 94927,
Lincoln, NE 68509-4927
Tel. (402) 471-3101, Fax 471-0254

NEVADA PUBLIC SERVICE COMMISSION (PSC) (1911)
727 Fairview Drive., Carson City, NV 89710
Tel. (702) 687-6001, Fax 687-6110

NEW HAMPSHIRE PUBLIC UTILITIES COMMISSION (PUC) (1911)
8 Old Suncook Road, Building No 1,
Concord, NH 03301-5185
Tel. (603) 271-2431, Fax 271-3878

NEW JERSEY BOARD OF PUBLIC UTILITIES (BPU) (1907)
44 South Clinton Avenue, CN-350, Trenton, NJ 08625-0350
Tel. (609) 777-3300, Fax 777-3330

NEW MEXICO PUBLIC UTILITY COMMISSION (PUC) (1941)
Marian Hall, 224 East Palace Avenue,
Santa Fe, NM 87501-2013
Tel. (505) 827-6940, Fax 827-6973

NEW YORK PUBLIC SERVICE COMMISSION (PSC) (1855)
Three Empire State Plaza, Albany, NY 12223
Tel. (518) 474-7080, Fax 290-4435

NORTH CAROLINA UTILITIES COMMISSION (UC) (1891)
430 North Salisbury Street, Dobbs Building,
Raleigh, NC 27611
Tel. (919) 733-4249, Fax 733-7300

US STATE REGULATORY AGENCIES (Continued)

NORTH DAKOTA PUBLIC SERVICE COMMISSION (PSC) (1889)
State Capitol, Bismarck, ND 58505
Tel. (701) 224-2400, Fax 224-2410

OHIO PUBLIC UTILITIES COMMISSION (PUC) (1867)
180 East Broad Street, Columbus, OH 43215-3793
Tel. (614) 466-3016, Fax 466-7366

OKLAHOMA CORPORATION COMMISSION (CC) (1907)
Jim Thorpe Office Building, P.O. Box 52000-2000,
Oklahoma City, OK 73152-2000
Tel. (401) 521-2211, Fax 521-6045

OREGON PUBLIC UTILITY COMMISSION (PUC) (1887)
550 Capitol NE, Salem, OR 97310-1380
Tel. (503) 378-6611, Fax 378-5505

PENNSYLVANIA PUBLIC UTILITIES COMMISSION (PUC) (1908)
P.O. Box 3265, Harrisburg, PA 17105-3265
Tel. (717) 783-1840, Fax 787-4193

RHODE ISLAND PUBLIC UTILITIES COMMISSION (PUC) (1839)
100 Orange Street, Providence, RI 02903
Tel. (401) 277-3500, Fax 277-6805

SOUTH CAROLINA PUBLIC SERVICE COMMISSION (PSC) (1879)
P.O. Drawer 11649, Columbia, SC 292211
Tel. (803) 737-5100, Fax 737-5199

SOUTH DAKOTA PUBLIC UTILITIES COMMISSION (PUC) (1885)
State Capitol, Pierre, SD 57501-5070
Tel. (605) 773-3201, Fax 773-3809

TENNESSEE PUBLIC SERVICE COMMISSION (PSC) (1897)
460 James Robertson Parkway, Nashville, TN 37243-0505
Tel. (615) 741-2904, Fax 741-2336

US STATE REGULATORY AGENCIES (Continued)

TEXAS PUBLIC UTILITY COMMISSION (PUC) (1975)
7800 Shoal Creek Boulevard, Austin, TX 78757
Tel. (512) 458-0100, Fax 458-8340

TEXAS RAILROAD COMMISSION (RC)
1701 North Congress Avenue, Room 12-100,
P.O. Box 12967, Austin, TX 78711-2967
Tel. (512) 463-7288, Fax 463-7161

UTAH PUBLIC SERVICE COMMISSION (PSC) (1917)
160 East 300 South, P.O. Box 45585
Salt Lake City, UT 84145
Tel. (801) 538-3011

VERMONT PUBLIC SERVICE BOARD (PSB) (1886)
City Center Building, 89 Main Street, Drawer 20,
Montpelier, VT 05602-2701
Tel. (802) 828-2358, Fax 828-3351

VIRGINIA STATE CORPORATION COMMISSION (SCC) (1902)
Tyler Building, P.O. Box 1197, Richmond, VA 23209
Tel. (804) 371-9608, Fax 371-9376

WASHINGTON UTILITIES AND TRANSPORTATION COMMISSION (UTC) (1905)
Chandler Plaza Building, P.O. Box 47250,
Olympia, WA 98504-7250
Tel. (206) 753-6423, Fax 586-1150

WEST VIRGINIA PUBLIC SERVICE COMMISSION (PSC) (1913)
201 Brooks Street, P.O. Box 812,, Charleston, WV 25323
Tel. (304) 340-0300, Fax 340-0325

WISCONSIN PUBLIC SERVICE COMMISSION (PSC) (1874)
4802 Sheboygan Avenue, Madison, WI 53705
Tel. (608) 266-5481, Fax 266-3957

WYOMING PUBLIC SERVICE COMMISSION (PSC) (1915)
700 West 21st Street, Cheyenne, WY 82002
Tel. (307) 777-7427, Fax 777-5700

CANADIAN PROVINCIAL REGULATORY AGENCIES

ALBERTA PUBLIC UTILITIES BOARD (PUB) (1915)
10055 - 106th Street, 11th Floor,
Edmonton, Alberta, T5J 2Y2
Tel. (403) 427-4901, Fax 427-6970

BRITISH COLUMBIA UTILITIES COMMISSION (UC) (1939)
Sixth Floor, 900 Howe Street, Vancouver,
British Columbia, V6Z 2N3
Tel. (604) 660-4700, Fax 660-1102

**NEW BRUNSWICK BOARD OF COMMISSIONERS OF PUBLIC
    UTILITIES (BCPU)**
110 Charlotte Street, P.O. Box 5001,
Saint John, New Brunswick, E2L 4Y9
Tel. (506) 658-2504, Fax 633-0163

**NEWFOUNDLAND AND LABRADOR BOARD OF COMMISSIONERS OF
    PUBLIC UTILITIES (BCPU)**
P.O. Box 21040, St. John's, Newfoundland A1A 5B1
Tel. (709) 726-6432, Fax 726-9604

NOVA SCOTIA UTILITY AND REVIEW BOARD (UARB) (1909)
Suite 300, 1601 Lower Water Street, Postal Unit M.,
P.O. Box 1692, Halifax, Nova Scotia B3J 3S3
Tel. (902) 424-4448, Fax 424-3919

ONTARIO ENERGY BOARD (EB)
P.O. Box 2319, 2300 Yonge Street, 26th Floor,
Toronto, Ontario, M4P 1E4
Tel. (416) 481-1967, Fax 440-7656

CANADIAN PROVINCIAL REGULATORY AGENCIES (Continued)

ONTARIO HYDRO
700 University Avenue, Toronto, Ontario, M5G 1X6
Tel. (416) 592-9621

PRINCE EDWARD ISLAND REGULATORY & APPEALS COMMISSION (RAC) (1946)
P.O. Box 577, Suite 501, 134 Kent Street,
Charlottetown, Prince Edward Island, C1A 7L1
Tel. (902) 892-3501, Fax 566-4076

QUEBEC NATURAL GAS BOARD
Case postale 001, Tour de la Bourse, 800 Place Victoria,
2eme etage, bureau 255, Montreal, Quebec, H4Z 1A2
Tel. (514) 873-2452, Fax 873-2070

OTHER REGULATORY AGENCIES

ARGENTINA ENTE NACIONAL REGULADOR DEL GAS
Av. Julio A. Roca 541, 2" Piso, (1322),
Buenos Aires, Republica Argentina
Tel. (541) 349-5333, Fax 334-5138

GUAM PUBLIC UTILITIES COMMISSION
Suite 400, GCIC Building, P.O. Box 862,
Agana, Guam 96910
Tel. (671) 477-9708, Fax 477-0783

ISRAEL MINISTER OF ENERGY AND INFRASTRUCTURE
Minister of Energy and Infrastructure, Government
of Israel, 234 Jafa Street, Jerusalem, Israel

NEW ORLEANS CITY COUNCIL UTILITIES REGULATORY OFFICE (1954)
Room 1E04A, City Hall, 1300 Perdido Street,
New Orleans, LA 70112
Tel. (504) 565-6355, Fax 565-6361

OTHER REGULATORY AGENCIES (Continued)

NEW ORLEANS DEPARTMENT OF UTILITIES (1912)
1300 Perdido Street, Room 2W14, City Hall,
New Orleans, LA 70112
Tel. (504) 565-6260, Fax 565-6449

NEW YORK POWER AUTHORITY
1633 Broadway, New York, NY 19919
Tel. (212) 468-6000, Fax 468-6478

PUERTO RICO PUBLIC SERVICE COMMISSION (1952)
P.O. Box 870, Hato Rey Station, San Juan 00919-0870
Tel. (809) 756-1919, Fax 758-0630

UNITED KINGDOM OFFICE OF WATER SERVICES
Centre City Tower, 7 Hill Street,
Birmingham B5 4UA, UK
Tel. 021-625-1300, Fax 021-625-1400

VIRGIN ISLANDS PUBLIC SERVICES COMMISSION (1940)
P.O. Box 40, Charlotte Amalie, St. Thomas 00804-0040
Tel. (809) 776-1291, Fax 774-4971

Appendix B

Listing of For-Profit Utilities

ALABAMA
Alabama Power Co.   (205) 250-1000

ALASKA
Alaska Electric Light & Power Co.   (907) 586-2222
Alaska Power & Telephone Co.   (206) 385-1733
Bethel Utilities Corp., Inc.   (907) 562-2500
Haines Light & Power Co., Inc.   (907) 766-2331
McGrath Light & Power   (907) 524-3009
Pelican Utility Co.   (907) 735-2204

ARIZONA
Arizona Public Service Co.   (602) 250-1000
Citizens Utilities Co.   (203) 329-8800
Tucson Electric Power Co.   (602) 622-6661

ARKANSAS
Arkansas Power & Light Co.   (501) 377-4000
Energy Power, Inc.   (504) 529-5262
Southwestern Electric Power Co.   (318) 222-2141

CALIFORNIA
Pacific Gas & Electric Co.   (415) 972-7000
Pacific Power & Light Co.   (503) 464-5000
San Diego Gas & Electric Co.   (619) 696-2000
Sierra Pacific Power Co.   (702) 689-4011
Southern California Edison Co.   (818) 302-1212

COLORADO
Public Service Colorado   (303) 571-7511

CONNECTICUT
Bozrah Light & Power Co.   (203) 889-7388
Citizens Utilities Co.   (203) 329-8800
Connecticut Light & Power   (203) 249-5711
Fletcher Electric Light Co.   (413) 569-6158
Unites Illuminating Co.   (203) 787-7200

DELAWARE
Delmarva Power & Light Co.   (302) 429-3011

DISTRICT OF COLUMBIA
Potomac Electric Power Co.   (202) 872-2000

FLORIDA
Florida Power & Light Co.   (305) 552-3552
Florida Power Corp.   (813) 866-5151
Florida Public Utilities Co.   (407) 832-2461
Gulf Power Co.   (904) 444-6111

GEORGIA
Georgia Power Co.   (404) 525-6526
Savannah Electric & Power Co.   (912) 232-7171

HAWAII
Hawaiian Electric Co.   (808) 543-7771
Maui Electric Co.   (808) 871-8961

IDAHO
Idaho Power Co.   (208) 383-2200

ILLINOIS
Central Illinois Public Service   (217) 523-3600
Central Illinois Light Co.   (304) 672-5271
Commonwealth Edison Co.   (312) 294-4321
Illinois Power Co.   (217) 424-6600
Interstate Power Co.   (319) 582-5421
Iowa Illinois Gas & Electric Co.   (319) 326-7111
Mt. Carmel Public Utility Co.   (618) 262-5151
Union Electric Co.   (314) 621-3222

INDIANA
Indiana Michigan Power Co.   (219) 425-2111
Indianapolis Power & Light   (317) 261-8261
Northern Indiana Public Service   (219) 853-5200
PSI Energy, Inc.   (317) 839-9611

Southern Indiana Gas & Electric   (812) 424-6411

IOWA
IES Utilities, Inc.   (319) 398-4411
Interstate Power Co.   (319) 582-5421
Iowa Illinois Gas & Electric   (319) 326-7111
Iowa Power, Inc.   (515) 281-2900
Iowa Public Service, Co.   (712) 277-7500
Midwest Power Systems   (712) 277-7500

KANSAS
Centel Corp.   (312) 399-2500
Empire District Electric Co.   (417) 623-4700
Kansas City Power & Light co.   (816) 556-2200
Kansas Gas & Electric Co.   (316) 261-6611
Southwestern Public Service Co.   (806) 378-2121
Western Resources - KP&L   (913) 296-6300

KENTUCKY
Kentucky Power Co.   (606) 327-1111
Kentucky Utilities Co.   (606) 255-2100
Louisville Gas & Electric Co.   (502) 672-2000
Union Light, Heat & Power   (513) 381-2000

LOUISIANA
Central Louisiana Electric Co.   (318) 484-7400
Gulf States Utilities Co.   (409) 838-6631
Louisiana Power & Light   (504) 366-2345
New Orleans Public Service   (504) 595-3100
Southwestern Electric Power Co.   (318) 222-2141

MAINE
Bangor Hydro Electric Co.   (207) 945-5621
Central Maine Power Co.   (207) 623-3521
Maine Public Service Co.   (207) 768-5811
Maine Yankee Atomic Power   (207) 622-4868

MARYLAND

Baltimore Gas & Electric Co.	(301) 234-5000
Conowingo Power Co.	(301) 398-1400
Delmarva Power & Light Co.	(301) 429-3011
Potomac Edison Co.	(301) 790-3400

MASSACHUSETTS

Boston Edison Co.	(617) 424-2000
Cambridge Electric Light Co.	(617) 225-4000
Canal Electric Co.	(617) 291-0950
Commonwealth Electric Co.	(617) 291-0950
Eastern Edison Co.	(617) 580-1213
Fitchburg Gas & Electric Co.	(508) 343-6931
Great Bay Power Corp.	(617) 357-9590
Holyoke Water Power Co.	(413) 536-5520
Massachusetts Electric Co.	(508) 366-9011
Montaup Electric Co.	(617) 678-5283
Nantucket Electric Co.	(617) 228-1870
New England Power Co.	(508) 366-9011
Western Massachusetts Electric Co.	(413) 285-5871
Yankee Atomic Electric Co.	(508) 779-6711

MICHIGAN

Consumers Power Co.	(517) 788-0550
Detroit Edison Co.	(313) 237-8000
Edison Sault Electric Co.	(906) 632-2221
Indiana Michigan Power Co.	(219) 425-2111
Upper Peninsula Power Co.	(906) 487-5000
Wisconsin Public Service Co.	(414) 433-1234

MINNESOTA

Interstate Power Co.	(319) 582-5421
Minnesota Power & Light	(218) 722-2641
Northern States Power, Minnesota	(612) 330-5500
Otter Tail Power Co.	(218) 739-8200

MISSISSIPPI

Mississippi Power & Light	(601) 864-1211

| Mississippi Power Co. | (601) 969-2311 |
| System Energy Resources | (601) 984-9000 |

MISSOURI

Empire District Electric Co.	(417) 623-4700
Kansas City Power & Light	(816) 556-2200
St. Joseph Light & Power	(816) 233-8888
Union Electric Co.	(314) 621-3222
Utilicorp United, Inc.	(816) 421-6000

MONTANA

Black Hills Power & Light Co.	(605) 348-1700
Montana-Dakota Utilities Co.	(701) 722-7900
Montana Power Co.	(406) 723-5421

NEBRASKA

None

NEVADA

| Nevada Power Co. | (702) 367-5000 |
| Sierra Pacific Power Co. | (701) 689-4011 |

NEW HAMPSHIRE

Connecticut Valley Electric	(603) 543-3188
Exeter Hampton Electric Co.	(603) 772-5916
Granite State Electric Co.	(603) 448-1290
North Atlantic Energy	(603) 474-9521
Public Service New Hampshire	(603) 669-4000
Rockland Electric Co.	(201) 327-6900

NEW JERSEY

Atlantic City Electric Co.	(609) 645-4100
Jersey Central Power & Light	(201) 455-8200
Public Service Electric & Gas	(201) 430-7000
Rockland Electric Co.	(201) 327-6900

NEW MEXICO

| Public Service New Mexico | (505) 848-2700 |

Southwestern Public Service Co.   (806) 378-2121

NEW YORK

Allegheny Generating Co.	(212) 752-2121
Central Hudson Gas & Electric	(914) 452-2000
Consolidated Edison Co.	(212) 460-4600
Long Island Lighting Co.	(516) 933-4590
New York State Electric & Gas	(607) 729-2551
Niagara Mohawk Power Corp.	(315) 474-1511
Orange & Rockland Utility	(914) 352-6000
Pennsylvania Electric Co.	(817) 533-8111
Pike County Light & Power	(914) 856-4422
Rochester Gas & Electric Corp.	(716) 546-2700

NORTH CAROLINA

Carolina Power & Light Co.	(919) 546-6111
Duke Power Co.	(704) 373-4011
Nantahala Power & Light Co.	(704) 524-2121
Virginia Electric & Power Co.	(807) 771-3000

NORTH DAKOTA

Montana-Dakota Utilities	(701) 222-7900
Northern States Power Co.	(612) 330-5500
Otter Tail Power Co.	(218) 739-8200

OHIO

Cincinnati Gas & Electric Co.	(513) 381-2000
Cleveland Electric Illuminating Co.	(216) 622-9800
Columbus Southern Power	(614) 464-7700
Dayton Power & Light Co.	(513) 224-6000
Indiana Kentucky Electric Corp.	(614) 289-2376
Monongahela Power Co.	(304) 366-3000
Ohio Edison Co.	(216) 384-5100
Ohio Power Co.	(216) 456-8173
Ohio Valley Electric Corp.	(614) 289-2376
Toledo Edison Co.	(419) 249-5000

OKLAHOMA

Oklahoma Gas & Electric Co.	(405) 272-3000
Public Service Oklahoma	(918) 599-2000
Southwestern Public Service Co.	(806) 378-2121

OREGON

Pacificorp	(503) 464-5000
Portland General Electric Co.	(503) 464-8000

PENNSYLVANIA

Duquesne Light Co.	(412) 393-6000
Metropolitan Edison Co.	(215) 929-3601
Peco Energy Co.	(215) 841-4000
Pennsylvania Electric Co.	(814) 533-8111
Pennsylvania Power & Light	(215) 774-5151
Philadelphia Power Co.	(412) 652-5531
Philadelphia Electric Co.	(215) 841-4000
Pike County Light & Power Co.	(717) 296-7323
UGI Utilities, Inc.	(717) 283-0611
Wellsboro Electric Co.	(717) 724-3516
West Penn Power Co.	(412) 837-3000
York Haven Power Co.	(717) 266-3654

RHODE ISLAND

Blackstone Valley Electric	(401) 333-1400
Block Island Power Co.	(401) 466-5851
Narragansett Electric Co.	(401) 941-1400
Newport Electric Corp.	(401) 849-4455

SOUTH CAROLINA

Carolina Power & Light Co.	(919) 456-6111
Duke Power Co.	(704) 373-4011
Lockhart Power Co.	(803) 545-2211
South Carolina Electric & Gas	(803) 748-3000

SOUTH DAKOTA

Black Hills Power & Light	(605) 348-1700
Montana Dakota Utility Co.	(701) 222-7900

Northern States Power Co.   (612) 330-5500
Northwestern Public Service   (605) 352-8411
Otter Tail Power Co.   (218) 739-8200

TENNESSEE
Arkansas Power & Light   (501) 337-4000
Kingsport Power Co.   (615) 378-5000

TEXAS
Central Power & Light Co.   (512) 881-5300
El Paso Electric Co.   (915) 543-5711
Gulf States Utilities   (409) 838-6631
Houston Lighting & Power   (713) 228-9211
Southwestern Electric Service Co.   (214) 741-3125
Southwestern Public Service Co.   (806) 378-2121
Texas Utilities Electric Co.   (214) 812-4600
Texas-New Mexico Power Co.   (817) 731-0099
West Texas Utility Co.   (915) 674-7000

UTAH
Utah Power & Light Co.   (503) 464-5000

VERMONT
Central Vermont Public Service   (802) 773-2711
Citizens Utilities Co.   (203) 329-8800
Franklin Electric Light Co.   (802) 285-2912
Green Mountain Power Corp.   (802) 864-5731
Rochester Electric Light & Power   (802) 773-9161
Vermont Electric Co.   (802) 773-9161
Vermont Yankee NUC Power   (802) 257-5271

VIRGINIA
Appalachian Power Co.   (203) 329-8800
Delmarva Power & Light Co.   (302) 429-3011
Old Dominion Power Co.   (606) 255-2100
Potomac Edison Co.   (302) 790-3400
Virginia Electric & Power Co.   (804) 771-3000

WASHINGTON
Pacific Power & Light Co.	(503) 464-5000
Puget Sound Power & Light	(205) 454-6363
Washington Water Power Co.	(509) 489-0500

WEST VIRGINIA
Appalachian Power Co.	(703) 985-2300
Black Diamond Power Co.	(304) 342-2721
Elk Power Co.	(304) 342-2721
Elkhorn Public Service Co.	(304) 342-2721
Kimball Light & Water Co.	(304) 342-2721
Monongahela Power Co.	(304) 366-3000
Potomac Edison Co.	(301) 790-3400
Union Power Co.	(304) 342-2721
United Light & Power Co.	(304) 342-2721
War Light & Power Co.	(304) 342-2721
Whaling Power Co.	(304) 234-3000

WISCONSIN
Consolidated Water Power	(715) 422-3111
Madison Gas & Electric Co.	(608) 252-7000
Northern States Power Co.	(612) 330-5508
Superior Water, Light & Power	(714) 394-5511
Wisconsin Electric Power Co.	(414) 221-2345
Wisconsin Power & Light	(608) 252-3311
Wisconsin Public Service	(414) 433-1598

WYOMING
Black Hills Power & Light Co.	(605) 348-1700
Cheyenne Light Fuel & Power Co.	(307) 638-3361
Pacific Corp.	(503) 464-5000

Appendix C

Listing of Municipal Utility Regulatory Agencies

This listing includes all Municipal Utility Agencies in the United States. This information is courtesy of the American Public power Association, 2301 M Street, N.W., Washington, DC 20037-1484; (202) 467-2948.

ALABAMA

Alabama Municipal Electric Authority
804 S. Perry St., Suite 200, Drawer 5220
Montgomery, AL 36103
(205) 2626-1126

Albertville, City of
Box 130
Albertville, AL 35950
(205) 878-3761

Alexander City, City of
Russell Road, Box 637
Alexander, AL 35010
(205) 329-8426

Andalusia Utilities Department
Box 790
Andalusia, AL 36420
(205) 222-1332

City of Athens Utilities
Box 1089
Athens, AL 35611
(205) 232-1440

Bessemer, City of
1600 First Avenue
Bessemer, AL 35020
(205) 481-4333

Brundidge, City of
Box 338
Brundidge, AL 36010
(205) 735-2321

Courtland, City of
Box 160
Courtland,, AL 35618
(205) 637-2707

Cullman Power Board
204 Second Avenue, Drawer 927
Cullman, AL 35056
(205) 734-2343

Decatur Utilities
1002 Central Parkway, S.W., Box 2232
Decatur, AL 35609
(205) 552-1440

Dothan, City of
3100 South Park Avenue
Dothan, AL 36301
(205) 712-2500

Elba, City of
200 Buford Street
Elba, AL 36323
(205) 897-2261

Evergreen, City of
Box 229
Evergreen, AL 36401
(205) 578-1574

Fairhope, City of
161 North Section Street, Drawer 429
Fairhope, AL 36533
(205) 928-2136

Florence, City of
110 West College Street, Box 877
Florence, AL 35631
(205) 760-6440

Fort Payne Improvement Authority
118 Godfrey Avenue, S.E.
Fort Payne, AL 35967
(205) 845-0671

Guntersville Electric Board
325 Gunter Avenue
Guntersville, AL 35976
(205) 582-5691

Hartford, City of
203 West Main Street
Hartford, AL 36344
(205) 588-2245

City of Hartselle Utilities
113 Sparkman Street, N.W., Box 968
Hartselle, AL 35640
(205) 773-2533

Huntsville Utilities
112 Spragins Street, Box 2048
Huntsville, AL 35804
(205) 535-1200

Lafayette, City of
Box 87
Lafayette, AL 36862
(205) 864-9581

Lanett, City of
401 North Lanier Avenue
Lanett, AL 36863
(205) 644-2141

Luverne, City of
106 East Fifth Street
Luverne, AL 36049
(205) 335-3741

Muscle Shoals Electric Board
1015 Avalon Avenue, Box 2547
Muscle Shoals, AL 35660
(205) 386-9290

Opelika, City of
1010 Avenue C, Box 390
Opelika, AL 36801
(205) 705-5570

Opp, City of
106 North Main Street
Opp, AL 36467
(205) 493-4571

Piedmont, City of
109 North Center Avenue, Box 112
Piedmont, AL 36272
(205) 447-9007

Riviera Utilities
413 East Laurel Avenue, Drawer 550
Foley, AL 36536
(205) 943-5001

Robertsdale, City of
Box 429
Robertsdale, AL 36567
(205) 947-2144

Russellville, City of
400 North Jackson Avenue, Box 1148
Russellville, AL 35653
(205) 332-3850

Scottsboro Electric Power Board
Box 550
Scottsboro, AL 35768
(205) 576-2680

Sheffield Utilities
300 North Nashville Avenue, Box 580
Sheffield, AL 35660
(205) 389-2000

Sylacauga Utilities Board
225 North Norton Avenue, Box 207
Sylacauga, AL 35150
(205) 249-8501

City of Tarrant
1604 Pinson Valley Parkway, Box 170220
Tarrant, AL 35217
(205) 841-1721

Troy, City of
Box 459
Troy, AL 36081
(205) 383-0321

Tuscumbia, City of
202 East Sixth, Street, Box 269
Tuscumbia, AL 35674
(205) 383-0321

Tuskegee, City of
101 Fonville Street
Tuskegee, AL 36083
(205) 724-2133

ALASKA

Akutan Electric Utility
General Delivery
Akutan, AK 99553
(907) 698-2228

Anchorage, Municipality of Municipal
Light & Power Dept.
1200 East First Avenue
Anchorage, AK 99501
(907) 279-7671

Atmautluak, City of
Atmautluak, AK 99559

Birch Creek Electric Utility
Box 61593
Fairbanks, AK 99706
(907) 479-5527

Chefornak, City of
Box 11
Chefonak, AK 99561
(907) 867-8528

Chignik, City of
Box 110
Chignik, AK 99564
(907) 749-2300

Coffman Cove Utilities
Coffman Cove, AK 99918
Haines, AK 99827 (907) 767-5505

Division of Energy (formerly Alaska Energy Authority)
701 East Tudor Road, Box 190869
Anchorage, AK 99519
(907) 561-7877

Eagle Village Energy Systems
Box 19
Eagle, Alaska 99738
(907) 547-2270

Effin Cove Utility Commission
Box 2
Effin, AK 99825
(907) 239-2218

Fairbanks Municipal Utilities System
645 Fifth Avenue, Box 2215
Fairbanks, AK 99707
(907) 239-2218

Galena, City of
Box 149
Galena, AK 99741
(907) 656-1301

Igiugig Electric Company
Box 4027
Igiugig, AK 99613
(907) 533-3211

Ipnatchiaq Electric Company
Deering, AK 99736
(907) 363-2157

Ketchikan Public Utilities
2930 Tongass Avenue
Ketchikan, AK 99901
(907) 225-1000

King Cove, City of
Box 37
King Cove, AK 99612
(907) 497-2340

Klukwan Electric Utilities
Box 210 (907) 329-2225

Kokhanok Electric
Box 1007
Kokhanok, AK 99606
(907) 282-2202

Kotlik, City of
Box 92543
Kotlik, AK 99620
(907) 899-4111

Kwig Power Company
Box 30
Kwigillingok, AK 99622
(907) 588-8626

Larsen Bay, City of
Utility Box 126
Larsen Bay, AK 99624
(907) 847-2211

Manokotak, City of
Box 65
Manokotak, AK 99628
(907) 289-1062

Metlakatla Power & Light
Box 359
Metlakatla, AK 99926
(907) 886-6661

Nightmute Power Plant
Box NME
Nightmute, AK 99690
(907) 344-2631

Nome Joint Utility System
Fifth Avenue W & K Street, Box 70
Nome, AK 99762
(907) 443-5288

North Slope Borough Department of
Municipal Services
Box 69
Barrow, AK 99723
(907) 852-2611

City of Quzinkie
Quzinkie, AK 99644
(907) 680-2209

Pedro Bay Village Council Electric
Box 47020
Pedro Bay, AK 99647
(907) 850-2225

Perryville Electric
Native Village of Perryville, Box 101
Perryville, AK 99648
(907) 853-2203

Petersburg, City of
11 South Nordic Drive, Box 329
Petersburg, AK 99833
(907) 772-4203

St. Paul Municipal Electric
Mail Pouch #1
St. Paul, AK 99660
(907) 546-2331

Seward, City of
Box 167
Seward, AK 99664
(907) 224-3331

City & Borough of Sitka Electric Department
1306 Halibut Point Road
Sitka, AK 99835
(907) 747-6633

Tatitlek Electric Utility
Box 171
Tatitlek, AK 99677
(907) 325-2311

City of Tenakee Springs
Box 52
Tenakee Springs, AK 99841
(907) 736-2207

Thorne Bay, City of
Box 110
Thorne Bay, AK 99919
(907) 828-3380

Tlingit Haida Regional Electrical Authority
Box 210149
Auke Bay, AK 99821
(907) 789-3196

Unalaska, City of
Box 89
Unalaska, AK 99685
(907) 581-2160

City of White Mountain
Box 84130
White Mountain, AK 99784
(907) 638-3411

Wrangell, City of
Box 531
Wrangell, AK 99929
(907) 874-2381

AMERICAN SAMOA

American Samoa Power Authority
Wickenburg, AZ 85358
Pago Pago, American Samoa 96799
(684) 644-5251

ARIZONA

Aquila Irrigation District
Box 263
Aquila, AZ 85320
(602) 685-2233

Arizona Power Authority
1810 West Adams Street
Phoenix, AZ 85007-2697
(602) 542-4263

Colorado River Indian Irrigation Project
Box 9-C, Route 1
Parker, AZ 85344
(602) 669-6121

Fredonia, Town of
Box 217
Fredonia, AZ 86022
(602) 643-7241

Harquahala Valley Power District
Star Route 2, Box 397
Buckeye, AZ 85326
(602) 372-4791

Maricopa County, Electrical District No.7 of
14629 West Peoria Avenue
Waddell, AZ 85355
(602) 935-6253

Maricopa County, Electrical District No.8 of
1001 North Central Avenue, #601
Phoenix, AZ 85004
(602) 258-8401

Maricopa Water District
Box 900
Waddell, AZ 85355
(602) 546-8266

McMullen Valley Water Conservation &
Drainage District
Box 21539 Box PPB

(602) 684-5247
Mesa, City of
730 North Mesa Drive, Box 1466
Mesa, AZ 85211
(602) 644-2265

Navajo Tribal Utility Authority
Box 170
Fort Defiance, AZ 86504
(602) 729-5721

Page Electric Utility
Box 1955
Page, AZ 86040
(602) 645-2419

Pinal County, Electrical District No. 2 of
Box 548
Coolidge, AZ 85228
(602) 723-7741

Pinal County, Electrical District No. 3 of
Box 870
Stanfield, AZ 85272
(602) 424-3337

Pinal County, Electrical District No. 4 of
Box 1008
Red Rock, AZ 85245
(602) 682-3442

Pinal County, Electrical District No. 6 of
4444 North 32nd Street, Suite 200
Phoenix, AZ 85001
(602) 956-8878

Roosevelt Irrigation District
Box 95
Buckeye, AZ 85326
(602) 935-4271

Safford Municipal Utilities
717 Main Street, Box 272
Safford, AZ 85548
(602) 428-2762

Salt River Project
Box 52025
Phoenix, AZ 85072
(602) 236-5900

Thatcher, Town of
1130 College Avenue
Thatcher, AZ 85552
(602) 428-2290

Tohono O'odham Utility Authority
Box 816
Sells, AZ 85634
(602) 383-2236

Wellton-Mohawk Irrigation and Drainage District
30570 Wellton-Mohawk Drive
Wellton, AZ 85356
(602) 785-3351

Wickenburg, Town of
120 East Apache Street, Box 1269
Wickenburg, AZ 85358
(602) 684-5451

ARKANSAS

Augusta, City of
South Fourth Street
Augusta, AR 72206
(501) 347-2041

Benton Power & Light
1314 Venturi Drive
Benton, AR 72015
(501) 776-5940

Bentonville, City of
115 West Central Avenue
Bentonville, AR 72712
(501) 271-3135

Clarksville Light & Water Company
Box 99
Clarksville, AR 72830
(501) 754-3148

Conway Corporation
1319 Prairie Street, Box 99
Conway, AR 72032
(501) 450-6020

Hope Water & Light Commission
105 North Elm Street, Box 2020
Hope, AR 71801
(501) 777-3000

Jonesboro City Water & Light
400 East Monroe Street, Box 1289
Jonesboro, AR 72403
(501) 935-5581

North Little Rock, City of
Eighth & Main Streets, Box 159
North Little Rock, AR 72115
(501) 372-0100

Osceola, City of
316 West Hale Street
Osceola, AR 72370
(501) 563-5245

Paragould Light & Water Commission
303 West Court Street, Box 9
Paragould, AR 72451
(501) 239-7700 100

Paris, City of
100 North Express, Box 271
Paris, AR 72855
(501) 963-2450

Piggott Municipal Light, Water & Sewer
411 North Thornton
Piggott, AR 72454
(501) 598-2997

Prescott, City of
118 West Elm Street
Prescott, AR 71857
(501) 887-2210

Siloam Springs, City of
410 North Broadway Street, Box 80
Siloam Springs, AR 72761
(501) 524-5136

West Memphis, City of
604 East Cooper Street
West Memphis, AR 72301
(501) 735-3355

CALIFORNIA

Alameda Bureau of Electricity
Box H
Alameda, CA 94501
(510) 748-3901

Anaheim, City of
South Anaheim Blvd., Box 3222
Anaheim, CA 92803
(714) 254-5173

Azusa, City of
Box 9500
Azusa, CA 91702
(818) 334-0215

Banning, City of
176 East Lincoln, Box 998
Banning, CA 92220
(909) 922-1245

Biggs, City of
464 B Street
Biggs, CA 95917
(916) 868-5493

Burbank Public Service Department
164 West Magnolia Blvd., Box 631
Burbank, CA 91503
(818) 953-9640

California Department of Water Resources
Box 942836
Sacramento, CA 94236-0001
(916) 653-7007

Colton, City of
650 North LaCadena Drive
Colton, CA 92324
(909) 370-5104

East Bay Municipal Utility District
375-11th Street, Box 24055
Oakland, CA 94623
(415) 835-3000

Escondido, City of
Civic Center Plaza, 201 North Broadway
Escondido, CA 92025
(619) 741-4657

Glendale, City of
119 North Glendale Avenue
Glendale,, CA 91206
(818) 548-2107 201

Gridley, City of
685 Kentucky Street
Gridley, CA 95948
(916) 846-5695

Hayfork Valley Public Utility District
Highway 3, Box 356
Hayfork, CA 96041
(916) 628-4454

Healdsburg, City of
Box 578
Healdsburg, CA 95448
(707) 431-3346

Imperial Irrigation District
333 East Barioni Blvd., Box 937
Imperial, CA 92251
(619) 339-9477

Kings River Conservation District
4886 East Jensen Avenue
Fresno, CA 93725
(209) 237-5567

Lassen Municipal Utility District
Box 361
Susanville, CA 96130
(916) 257-4175

Lodi, City of
221 West Pine Street, Box 3006
Lodi, CA 95241
(209) 333-6762

Lompoc, City of
100 Civic Center Plaza
Lompoc, CA 93438
(805) 736-1261

Los Angeles Department of Water & Power
Box 111
Los Angeles, CA 90051
(213) 367-4211

Merced Irrigation District
2423 Canal Street, Box 2288
Merced, CA 95344
(209) 722-5761

Metropolitan Water District of Southern California
350 South Grand Avenue
Los Angeles, CA 90071
(213) 217-6211

Modesto Irrigation District
1231 11th Street, Box 4060
Modesto, CA 95352
(209) 526-7373

M-S-R Public Power Agency
Box 4060
Modesto, CA 95352
(209) 526-7450

City of Needles Department of Public Utilities
817 Third Street, Box 190
Needles, CA 92363
(619) 326-5700

Northern California Power Agency
180 Cirby Way
Roseville, CA 95678
(916) 781-3636

Oroville-Wyandotte Irrigation District
2310 Quincy Road, Box 581
Oroville, CA 95965
(916) 534-1221

City of Palo Alto
250 Hamilton Avenue
Palo Alto, CA 94301
(415) 329-2273

Pasadena Water & Power Department
150 South Los Robles, Suite 200
Pasadena, CA 91101
(818) 405-4409

Placer County Water Agency Room 1550,
24625 Harrison Street, Box 667
Foresthill, CA 95631
(916) 367-2291

Redding, City of
760 Parkview Avenue
Redding, CA 96001
(916) 224-4300

Riverside, City of
3900 Main Street
Riverside, CA 92522
(909) 782-5781

Roseville Electric Department
2090 Hilltop Circle
Roseville, CA 95747
(916) 774-5601

Sacramento Municipal Utility District
6201 S Street, Box 15830
Sacramento, CA 95817
(916) 452-3211

Hetch Hetchy Water & Power, City of San Francisco
1155 Market Street
San Francisco, CA 94103
(415) 554-0725

Santa Clara, City of
1500 Warburton Avenue
Santa Clara, CA 95050
(408) 984-5190

Shasta Dam Area Public Utility District
1650 Stanton Drive
Central Valley, CA 96019
(916) 276-8827

Southern California Public Power Authority
200 South Los Robles, Suite 155
Pasadena, CA 91101
(818) 793-9364

Tri-Dam Power Authority
Box 1158
Piecrest, CA 95364
(209) 965-3996

Trinity County Public Utilities District
Box 1216
Weaverville, CA 96093
(916) 623-5536

Truckee-Donner Public Utility District
Box 309
Truckee, CA 96160
(916) 587-3896

Tuolumne County Public Power Agency
Two South Green Street
Sonora, CA 95370
(209) 533-5518

Turlock Irrigation District
333 East Canal Drive, Box 949
Turlock, CA 95381
(209) 883-8300

Ukiah, City of
300 Seminary Avenue
Ukiah, CA 95482
(707) 463-6200

Vernon, City of
4305 Santa Fe Avenue
Vernon, CA 90058
(213) 583-8811

Yuba County Water Agency
1402 D Street, Box 1569
Marysville, CA 95901
(916) 741-6278

COLORADO

Arkansas River Power Authority
South Main Street, Box 70
Lamar, CO 81952
(719) 336-3496

Aspen, City of
130 South Galena Street
Aspen, CO 81611
(303) 920-5083

Burlington, City of
415 15th Street
Burlington, CO 80807
(719) 346-8585

Center, City of
400 South Worth, Box 400
Center, CO 81125
(719) 754-3497

Colorado Springs Utilities
30 South Nevada Avenue, Box 1103
Colorado Springs, CO 80947
(719) 636-5580

Delta, City of
360 Main Street, Box 19
Delta, CO 81416
(303) 874-8400

Denver, City & County of
1600 West 12th Avenue
Denver, CO 80204
(303) 628-6550

Estes Park, Town of
Box 1200
Estes Park, CO 80517
(303) 586-5331

Fleming, City of
Box 466
Fleming, CO 80728
(303) 265-2692

Fort Collins Light & Power Utility
700 Wood Street, Box 580
Fort Collins, CO 80522
(303) 221-6700 3409

Fort Morgan, City of
710 East Railroad Avenue
Fort Morgan, CO 80701

Fountain, City of
116 South Main Street
Fountain, CO 80817
(719) 382-5604

Frederick, Town of
Box 435
Frederick, CO 80530
(303) 833-2388

Glenwood Springs, City of
806 Cooper Avenue
Glenwood Springs, CO 81601
(303) 945-2575

Granada, Town of
109 East Goff Street, Box 258
Granada, CO 81041
(719) 734-5411

Gunnison, City of
201 West Virginia Avenue
Gunnison, CO 81230
(303) 641-8020

Haxtun, Town of
145 South Colorado Avenue, Box 205
Haxtun, CO 80731
(303) 774-6104

Holly, City of
Box 458
Holly, CO 81047
(719) 537-6622

Holyoke, City of
207 West Denver Street
Holyoke, CO 80734
(303) 854-2266

Julesburg, City of
122 West First Street
Julesburg, CO 80737
(303) 474-3344

La Junta, City of
601 Colorado Avenue, Box 630
La Junta, CO 81050
(719) 384-8454

Lamar Utilities Board
100 North Second Street
Lamar, CO 81052
(719) 336-7456

Las Animas, City of
532 Carson Avenue
Las Animas, CO 81054
(719) 456-1621

Longmont, City of
1100 South Sherman Street
Longmont, CO 80501
(303) 651-8386

Loveland Light and Power
200 North Wilson
Loveland, CO 80537
(303) 962-3559

Lyons, Town of
Box 49
Lyons, CO 80540
(303) 823-6622

Oak Creek, Town of
Box 128
Oak Creek, CO 80467
(303) 736-8231

Platte River Power Authority
2000 East Horsetooth Road
Fort Collins, CO 80525
(303) 226-4000

Springfield, City of
Box 4
Springfield, CO 81073
(719) 523-4528

Trinidad, City of
Box 880
Trinidad, CO 81082
(719) 846-9843

Wray, City of
245 West Fourth Street, Box 35
Wray, CO 80758
(303) 332-4431

Yuma, City of
221 South Main Street, Box 265
Yuma, CO 80759
(303) 848-3878

CONNECTICUT

Connecticut Municipal Electric
Energy Cooperative
30 Stott Avenue
Norwich, CT 06360
(203) 889-4088

Groton Department of Utilities
295 Meridian Street, Box 820
Groton, CT 06340
(203) 446-4000

Jewett City Electric Light Plant
19709 9 East Main Street
Jewett City, CT 06351
(203) 376-2955

Norwalk, City of, Third Taxing
District
2 Second Street, Box 451
Norwalk, CT 08856
(203) 866-9271

Norwich, City of
34 Courthouse Square
Norwich, CT 06360
(203) 887-2555

South Norwalk Electric Works
State Street, Box 400
South Norwalk, CT 06856
(203) 866-3366

Wallingford, Town of
100 John Street
Wallingford, CT 06492
(203) 265-1593

DELAWARE

Clayton, Town of
314 Main Street
Clayton, DE 19938
(302) 653-8419

Dover, City of
860 Buttner Place
Dover, DE 19901
(302) 736-7070

Lewes Board of Public Works
East Third Street, Box 518
Lewes, DE 19958
(302) 645-6228

Middletown, Town of
216 North Broad Street
Middletown, DE
(302) 378-2711

Milford, City of
201 South Walnut Street, Box 159
Milford, DE 19963
(302) 422-6616

New Castle Board of Water & Light
Commissioners
216 Chestnut Street, Box 208
New Castle, DE 19720-0208

Newark, City of
220 Elkton Road, Box 390
Newark, DE 19715
(302) 366-7080

Seaford, City of
302 East King Street
Seaford, DE 19973
(302) 629-9173

Smyrna, Town of
27 South Market Street, Box 307
Smyrna, DE 19977
(302) 653-3483

FLORIDA

Alachua, City of
US 441 & SR 235, Box 9
Alachua, FL 32615
(904) 462-1231

Bartow, City of
450 North Wilson Avenue, Box 1069
Bartow, FL 33830
(813) 533-0911

Blountstown, City of
125 West Central Avenue
Blountstown, FL 32424
(904) 674-5488

Bushnell, City of
Box 115
Bushnell, FL 33513
(904) 793-2591

Chattahoochee, City of
22 Jefferson Street, Box 188
Chattahoochee, FL 32324
(904) 663-4046

Clewiston, City of
141 Central Avenue
Clewiston, FL 33440
(813) 983-2171

Florida Municipal Power Agency
7201 Lake Ellenor Drive, Suite 100
Orlando, FL 32809
(407) 859-7310

Fort Meade, City of
Box 856
Fort Meade, FL 33841
(813) 285-8191

For Pierce Utilities Authority
Box 3191
Fort Pierce, FL 34948
(407) 466-1600

Gainesville, City of
Box 147117
Gainesville, FL 32614
(904) 334-3400

Green Cove Springs, City of
City Hall, 229 Walnut Street
Green Cove Springs, FL 32043
(904) 284-5621

Havana Power & Light Company
711 North Main Street, Box 1068
Havana, FL 32333
(904) 539-6494

Homestead, City of
675 North Flagler Avenue
Homestead, FL 33030
(305) 247-1801

Jacksonville Electric Authority
21 West Church Street
Jacksonville, FL 32202
(904) 623-6000

Jacksonville Beach, City of
11 North Third Street
Jacksonville Beach, FL 32250
(904) 247-6281

City Electric System
1001 James Street, Drawer 6100
Key West, FL 33041
(305) 294-5272

Kissimmee Utility Authority
Box 423219
Kissimmee, FL 34742
(407) 933-7777

Lake Worth, City of
1776 Lake Worth Road
Lake Worth, FL 33460
(407) 586-1665

Lakeland, City of
501 East Lemon Street
Lakeland, FL 33801
(813) 499-6300

Leesburg, City of
2010 West Griffin Road
Leesburg, FL 34748
(904) 728-9834

Moore Haven, City of
Box 399
Moore Haven, FL 33471
(813) 946-0711

Mount Dora, City of
1250 North Highland Street
Mount Dora, FL 32757
(904) 735-7155

New Smyrna Beach Utilities
Commission
120 Sams Avenue
New Smyrna Beach, FL 32168
(904) 427-1361

Newberry, City of
Box 369
Newberry, FL 32669
(904) 472-2161

Ocala, City of
Box 1270
Ocala, FL 32679
(904) 351-6600

Orlando Utilities Commission
Box 3193
Orlando, FL 32802
(407) 423-9100

Quincy, City of
404 West Jefferson Street, Box 1619
Quincy, FL 32351
(904) 627-7681

Reedy Creek Improvement District
Box 10170
Lake Buena Vista, FL 32830
(407) 828-2241

St. Cloud, City of
2901 17th Street
St. Cloud, FL 34769
(407) 957-7297

Sebring Utilities Commission
321 Mango Street, Box 971
Sebring, FL 33871
(813) 385-0191

Starke, City of 99 Riverside Drive,
209 North Thompson Street, Drawer C
Starke, FL 32091
(904) 964-5027

Tallahassee, City of
300 South Adams Street
Tallahassee, FL 32301
(904) 891-8511

Vero Beach, City of
1053 20th Place, Box 1389
Vero Beach, FL 32961
(407) 567-5151

Wauchula, City of
Box 818
Wauchula, FL 33873
(813) 773-3131

Williston, City of
Box 160
Williston, FL 32696
(904) 528-3060

GEORGIA

Acworth, City of
4375 Senator Russell Square
Acworth, GA 30101
(494) 974-5233

Adel, City of
Box 658
Adel, GA 31620
(912) 896-4504

Albany Water, Gas & Light
Commission
Box 1788
Albany, GA 31703
(912) 883-8330

Barnesville, City of
109 Forsythe Street
Barnesville, GA 30204
(404) 358-0181

Blakely, City of
Box 350
Blakeley, GA 31723
(912) 723-3677

Brinson, Town of
Box 728
Brinson, GA 31725
(912) 246-4062

Buford, City of
95 Scott Street
Buford, GA 30518
(404) 945-6761

Cario, City of
Box 29
Cairo, GA 31728
(912) 377-1954

Calhoun, City of
Box 248
Calhoun, GA 30701
(706) 629-0151

Camilla, City of
30 East Broad Street, Box 328
Camilla, GA 31730
(912) 336-5636

Cartersville, City of
320 South Erwin Street, Box 1390
Cartersville, GA 30120
(404) 387-5688

Chickamauga, City of
Box 69
Chickamauga, GA 30707
(404) 375-3177

College Park Power
1886 West Harvard Avenue
College Park, GA 30337
(404) 669-3772

Commerce, City of
Box 348
Commerce, GA 30529
(706) 335-3164

Covington, City of
2111 East Conyers Street
Covington, GA 30209
(404) 786-5324

Crisp County Power Commission
201 South Seventh Street
Cordele, GA 31015
(912) 273-3811

Dalton Water, Light and Sinking
Fund Commission
1200 Harris Street
Dalton, GA 30722-0869

Doerum, City of
Box 37
Doerun, GA 31744
(912) 782-5444

Douglas, City of North Wall Street,
220 East Bryan Street, City Hall
Douglas, GA 31533
(912) 284-3302

East Point, City of
2777 East Point Street
East Point, GA 30344
(404) 765-1027

Elberton, City of
234 North McIntosh Street
Elberton, GA 30635
(404) 786-1129

Ellaville, City of
Wilson Street, Box 829
Ellaville, GA 31806
(912) 937-2207

City of Fairburn
56 Malone Street, Box 145
Fairburn, GA 30213
(404) 964-2244

Fitzgerald Water, Light and Bond
Commission
200 North Hooker Street, Drawer F
Fitzgerald, GA 31750

Forsyth, City of
Box 1447
Forsyth, GA 31029
(912) 994-2444

Fort Valley Utility Commission
Box 1529
Fort Valley, GA 31030
(912) 825-7701

Grantville, City of
Box 126
Grantville, GA 30220
(404) 583-2289

Griffin Electric Department
120 North Sixth Street, Drawer T
Griffin, GA 30224
(404) 229-6406

Hampton, City of
Box 225
Hampton, GA 02338
(404) 946-4306

Hogansville, City of
400 East Main Street
Hogansville, GA 30230
(706) 637-8629

Jackson, City of
135 South Mulberry Street.
Jackson, GA 30233
(404) 775-7535

LaFayette, City of
Box 89
LaFayette, GA 30728
(706) 638-1082

LaGrange, City of
200 Ridley Avenue, Box 430
LaGrange, GA 32040
(706) 883-2065

Lawrenceville, City of
Box 1017
Lawrenceville, GA 30246
(404) 963-2414

Mansfield, City of
21 West First Avenue
Mansfield, GA 30255
(404) 786-7235

Marietta Power
205 Lawrence Street, Box 609
Marietta, GA 30061
(404) 528-0525

Monroe, City of
Box 725
Monroe, GA 30655
(404) 267-5756

Monticello, City of
115 East Green Street
Monticello, GA 31064
(706) 468-6062

Moultrie, City of
Box 580
Moultrie, GA 31776
(912) 985-1974

Municipal Electricity Authority of Georgia
1470 Riveredge Parkway, N.W.
Atlanta, GA 30328
(404) 952-5445

Newnan Water, Sewerage and Light
Commission
70 Sewell Road
Newnan, GA 30263
(404) 253-5516

Norcross, City of
65 Lawrenceville Street
Norcross, GA 30071
(404) 448-2122

Oxford, City of
810 Whatcoat Street, Box 207
Oxford, GA 30267
(404) 786-7004

Palmetto, City of
549 Main Street, Drawer 190
Palmetto, GA 30268
(404) 463-3388

Quitman, City of
Box 208
Quitman, GA 31643
(912) 263-4166

Sandersville, City of
Box 71
Sandersville, GA 31082
(912) 552-3475

Sylvania, City of
Box 555
Sylvania, GA 30467
(912) 564-7411

Sylvester, City of
105 East King Street
Sylvester, GA 31791
(912) 776-8508

Thomaston, City of
613 North Church Street
Thomaston, GA 30286
(706) 647-6633

Thomasville Water & Light Department
411 West Jackson Street, Box 1397
Thomasville, GA 31799
(912) 226-3518

Washington, City of
Box 9
Washington, GA 30673
(706) 678-3277

West Point, City of
Box 487
West Point, GA 31833
(706) 645-2226

Whigham, City of
Box 71
Whigham, GA 31797
(912) 762-4114

IDAHO

Albion Light and Water Plant
Box 163
Albion, ID 83311
(208) 673-5351

Bonners Ferry, City of
104 Main Street, Box 149
Bonners Ferry, ID 83805
(208) 267-3105

Burley, City of
2020 Parke Avenue, Box 1090
Burley, ID 83318
(208) 678-2538

Decio, City of
Box 159
Decio, ID 83323
(208) 654-2124

Heyburn, City of
Box 147
Heyburn, ID 83336
(208) 678-8158

Idaho Falls, City of
140 South Capital, Box 50220
Idaho Falls, ID 83405
(208) 529-1430

Minidoka, City of
Box 85
Minidoka, ID 83343
(208) 532-4575

Plummer, City of
Box B
Plummer, ID 83851
(208) 686-1386

Rupert, City of
Box 426
Rupert, ID 83350
(208) 436-9608

Soda Springs, City of
9 West Second Street, South
Soda Springs, ID 83276
(208) 547-2600

Weiser, City of
55 West Idaho Street
Weiser, ID 83672
(208) 549-1965

ILLINOIS

Albany, City of
101 North Lime Street, Box 356
Albany, IL 61230
(309) 887-4064

Allendale, Village of
Allendale, IL 62410
(618) 299-3181

Altamont, City of
202 North 2nd Street, Box 305
Altamont, IL 62411
(618) 483-5212

Batavia, City of
100 North Island Avenue
Batavia, IL 60510
(708) 879-1424

Bethany, Village of
201 West Main Street, Box 352
Bethany, IL 61914
(217) 665-3351

Breese, City of
800 North 1st Street
Breese, IL 62230
(618) 526-7151

Bushnell, City of
148 East Hail Street
Bushnell, IL 61422
(309) 772-2029

Cairo Public Utility Commission
1100 Commercial Avenue
Cairo, IL 62914
(618) 734-3200

Carlyle Municipal Electric
850 Franklin Street
Carlyle, IL 62231
(618) 594-3221

Carmi Light and Water
225 East Main Street
Carmi, IL 62821
(618) 382-5555

Casey, City of
108 East Main Street, Box 425
Casey, IL 62420
(217) 932-4885 Box 85

Chatham, Village of
116 East Mulberry Street
Chatham, IL 62629
(217) 483-2451

Fairfield, City of
109 Northeast 2nd Street
Fairfield, IL 62837
(618) 842-4821

City of Farmer City Light and Power
105 South Main Street, Box 49
Farmer City, IL 61842
(309) 928-3421

Flora, City of
122 North Main Street
Flora, IL 62839
(618) 662-8313

Freeburg Municipal Light and Power
412 West High
Freeburg, IL 62243
(618) 539-3112

Geneseo, City of
101 South State
Geneseo, IL 61254
(309) 944-5899

Geneva, City of
1800 South Street
Geneva, IL 60134
(708) 232-1503

Greenup, Village of
115 Cumberland Street
Greenup, IL 62428
(217) 923-3490

Highland, City of
1115 Broadway Street
Highland, IL 62249
(618) 654-7511

Illinois Municipal Electric Agency
919 South Spring
Springfield, IL 62704
(217) 789-4632

Ladd, Village of
121 North Main Street, Box 305
Ladd, IL 61329
(815) 894-2351

Marshall Utilities
708 Archer Avenue, Box 298
Marshall, IL 62441
(217) 826-8087

Mascoutah, City of
40 West Union Street
Mascoutah, IL 62258
(618) 566-2965

McLeansboro, City of
102 West Main Street
McLeansboro, IL 62859
(618) 643-2224

Metropolis, City of
106 West Fifth Street
Metropolis, IL 62960
(618) 524-2711

City of Naperville Department of
Public Utilities
400 South Eagle Street, Box 3020
Naperville, IL 60566
(708) 420-6131

Newton, City of
108 North Van Buren Street, Box 165
Newton, IL 62448
(618) 783-8452

Oglesby, City of
128 West Walnut Street, Box 10
Oglesby, IL 61348
(815) 883-9380

Peru, City of
1415 Water Street, Box 299
Peru, IL 61354
(815) 223-0044

Princeton, City of
2 South Main Street
Princeton, IL 61356
(815) 872-5551

Rantoul, Village of
100 West Grove Street
Rantoul, IL 61866
(217) 897-2178

Red Bud, City of
200 East Market Street
Red Bud, IL 62278
(618) 282-3339

Riverton, Village of
313 East Jefferson Street
Riverton, IL 63561
(217) 629-9122

Rochelle, City of
333 Lincoln Highway
Rochelle, IL 61068
(815) 562-4155

City of Rock Falls
205 East Third Street
Rock Falls, IL 61071
(815) 622-1145

Roodhouse, City of
City Hall
Roodhouse, IL 62082
(217) 589-4635

St. Charles, City of
2 East Main Street
St. Charles, IL 60174
(708) 377-4407

Springfield City Water, Light & Power
7th and Monroe Streets
Room 207
Springfield, IL 62757
(217) 789-2060

Sullivan, City of
2 West Harrison Street
Sullivan, IL 61951
(217) 728-4383

Waterloo, City of
104 West Fourth Street
Waterloo, IL 62298
(618) 939-6413

Winnetka, Village of
510 Green Bay Road
Winnetka, IL 60093
(708) 501-6000

INDIANA

Advance Municipal Light and Power
Town of Advance, 112 North Main Street
Advance, IN 46102
(317) 676-6611

Anderson Municipal Light and Power
550 Baxter Road
Anderson, IN 46011
(317) 646-5741

Argos, Town of
101 South First Street
Argos, IN 46501
(219) 892-5717

Auburn, City of
Cedar and Ninth Streets
Auburn, IN 46706
(219) 925-8251

Avilla, City of
117 South Main Street, Box 49
Avilla, IN 46710
(219) 897-2781

Bainbridge, Town of Municipal Building,
Box 343
Bainbridge, IN 46105
(317) 522-6238

Bargersville Power and Light
Box 420
Bargersville, IN 46106
(317) 422-5115

Bluffton, City of
128 East Market Street
Bluffton, IN 46714
(219) 824-2500

Boonville, City of
Box 508
Boonville, IN 47601
(812) 897-0140

Bremen Electric Light and Power Co.
104 West Plymouth Street
Bremen, IN 46506
(219) 546-4324

Brooklyn, Town of
10 North Main Street
Brooklyn, IN 46111
(311) 831-3343

Brookston, Town of
215 East Third Street, Box 238
Brookston, IN 47923
(317) 563-3171

Cannelton, City of
610 Washington Street
Cannelton, IN 47520
(812) 547-7919

Centerville, Town of
204 East Main Street
Centerville, IN 47330
(317) 855-5515

Chalmers, Town of
Box 827
Chalmers, IN 47929
(219) 984-5494

Coatesville, Town of
Box 143
Coatesville, IN 46121
(317) 386-7205

Columbia city, City of
316 South Towerview Drive
Columbia City, IN 46725
(219) 248-5115

Covington, City of
413 Washington Street
Covington, IN 47932
(317) 793-2331

Crawfordsville Electric, Light and Power
808 Lafayette Road, Box 428
Crawfordsville, IN 47933
(317) 362-1900

Darlington Light & Power Company
104 South Franklin Street
Darlington, IN 47940
(317) 794-4496

Dublin, Town of
Cumberland Street
Dublin, IN 47335
(317) 478-4878

Dunreith, City of
Box 219, 115 Washington Street
Dunreith, IN 47337
(317) 987-7957

Edinburgh Municipal Utility
107 South Holland Street, Box 65
Edinburgh, IN 46124
(812) 526-3512

Etna Green, Town of
Box 183
Etna Green, IN 46524
(219) 858-9321

Ferdinand, Town of
123 West Fifth Street, Box 7
Ferdinand, IN 47532
(812) 367-2280

Flora, Town of
27 West Main Street
Flora, IN 46929
(219) 967-4844

Frankfort, City of
1000 Washington Avenue, Box 458
Frankfort, IN 46041
(317) 654-44224

Frankton Municipal Light & Water Company
105 Church Street, Box 286
Frankton, IN 46044
(317) 754-7285

Garrett, City of
South Randolph Street, Box 120
Garrett, IN 46738
(219) 357-4400

Gas City, City of
200 East North A Street
Gas City, IN 46933
(317) 674-6995

Greendale, Town of
510 Ridge Avenue
Lawrenceburg, IN 47025
(812) 537-2125

Greenfield, City of
333 South Franklin Street
Greenfield, IN 56140
(317) 462-8522

Hagerstown, Town of
Town Hall, 49 East College Street
Hagerstown, IN 47346
(317) 489-5132

Huntingburg, City of
511 Fourth Street
Huntingburg, IN 47542
(812) 683-2327

Indiana Municipal Power Agency
11610 North College Avenue
Carmel, IN 46032
(317) 573-9955

Jamestown, Town of
Box 165
Jamestown, IN 46147
(317) 676-6331

Jasper, City of
610 Main Street, Box 750
Jasper, IN 47547
(812) 482-6881

Kingsford Heights, Town of
504 Grayton Road
Kingsford Heights, IN 46346
(219) 939-3309

Knightstown, Town of
26 South Washington Street
Knightstown, IN 46148
(317) 345-5977

Ladoga Light & Power
121 East Main Street, Box 187
Ladoga, IN 47954
(317) 942-2531

Lawrenceburg, City of
405 Main Street, Box 112
Lawrenceburg, IN 47025
(812) 537-2420

Lebanon, City of
201 East Main Street, Box 479
Lebanon, IN 46052
(317) 482-5100

Lewisville, City of
Box 288
Lewisville, IN 47352
(317) 987-7979

Linton, City of
49 N.W. A Street
Linton, IN 47441
(812) 847-4971

Logansport, City of
601 East Broadway, #101
Logansport, IN 46947
(219) 753-6231

Middletown, Town of
102 North Fifth Street
Middletown, IN 47356
(317) 354-2911

Mishawaka Utilities
126 North Church Street
Mishawaka, IN 46544
(219) 258-1630

Montezuma, Town of
1235 North Jackson Street
Montezuma, IN 47862
(317) 245-2749

New Carlisle, Town of
113 South Arch Street
New Carlisle, IN 46552
(219) 654-7554

New Ross, City of
Box 156
New Ross, IN 47968
(317) 723-1154

Paoli Water and Light Department
Municipal Building
Paoli, IN 47454
(712) 723-2739

Pendleton, Town of
119 West State Street
Pendleton, IN 46064
(317) 778-2173

Peru Utilities
335 East Canal Street, Box 67
Peru, IN 46970
(317) 473-6681

Pittsboro, Town of
Box 185
Pittsboro, IN 46167
(317) 892-3326

City of Rensselaer
425 North Van Rensselaer Street
Rensselaer, IN 47978
(219) 866-8475

Richmond Power and Light
2000 U.S. 27 South, Box 908
Richmond, IN 47375
(317) 973-7200

Rising Sun Municipal Utility
301 South Poplar Street, Box 38
Rising Sun, IN 47040
(812) 438-3616

Rockville, Town of
103 West High Street, Box 143
Rockville, IN 47872
(317) 569-3569

Scottsburg, City of
2 East McClain Avenue
Scottsburg, IN 47170
(812) 752-4343

South Whitley, Town of
118 East Front Street
South Whitley, IN 46787
(219) 723-5312

Spiceland, City of
130 East Main Street, Box 368
Spiceland, IN 47385
(317) 987-1211

Straughn, Town of
Box 427
Straughn, IN 47387
(317) 332-2828

Tell City, City of
700 Main Street, Box 9
Tell City, IN 47586
(812) 547-3411

Thorntown, City of
109 West Main Street
Thorntown, IN 46071
(317) 436-2627

Tipton Municipal Electricity Utility
113 Court Street, Box 288
Tipton, IN 46072
(317) 675-7629

Troy, City of
Box 57
Troy, IN 47588
(812) 547-7501

Veedersburg, Town of
118 Railroad Avenue
Veedersburg, IN 47987
(317) 294-2728

Walkerton, City of
510 Roosevelt Road
Walkerton, IN 46574
(219) 586-3711

Warren Municipal Electric Utility
132 Wayne Street
Warren, IN 46792
(219) 375-2656

Washington, City of
City Utility Building, Box 800
Washington, IN 47501
(812) 254-5171

Waynetown, City of
Washington Street
Waynetown, IN 47990
(317) 234-2154

Williamsport, City of
29 North Monroe Street
Williamsport, IN 47993
(317) 762-2154

Winamac, Town of
120 West Main Street
Winamac, IN 46996
(219) 946-3451

IOWA

Afton, City of
101 West Kansas Street
Afton, IA 50830
(515) 347-5578

Akron, City of
Box 85
Akron, IA 51001
(712) 568-2041

Algona Municipal Utilities
104 West Call Street, Box 10
Algona, IA 50511
(515) 295-3584

Alta, City of
223 Main Street
Alta, IA 51002
(712) 284-1122

Alton Municipal Light and Power
905 Third Avenue, Box J
Alton, IA 51003
(712) 756-4314

Ames, City of
502 Carroll Avenue
Ames, IA 50010
(515) 239-5171

Anita Municipal Utilities
828 Main Street, Box 426
Anita, IA 50020
(712) 762-3845

Anthon, City of
301 East Main
Anthon, IA 51004
(712) 373-5218

Aplington, City of
927 Parrot Street
Aplington, IA 50604
(319) 347-2425

Atlantic Municipal Utilities
15 West Third Street, Box 517
Atlantic, IA 50022
(712) 243-1395

Auburn, City of
Box 238
Auburn, IA 51433
(712) 434-2025

Aurelia, City of
235 Main Street
Aurelia, IA 51005
(712) 434-2025

Bancroft Municipal Utility
108 North Portland
Bancroft, IA 50517
(515) 885-2382

Bellevue, City of
900 North Riverview
Bellevue, IA 52031
(319) 872-3357

Bloomfield, City of
111 West Franklin Street
Bloomfield, IA 52537
(515) 664-2260

Breda Municipal Utilities
118 Main Street
Breda, IA 51436
(712) 673-4221

Brooklyn, City of
207 Front Street
Brooklyn, IA 52211
(515) 522-9292

Buffalo, City of
409 Third Street
Buffalo, IA 52728
(319) 381-2226

Burt, City of
110 Walnut Street, Box 197
Burt, IA 50522
(515) 924-3618

Callender, City of
730 Thomas Street
Callender, IA 51523
(515) 548-3859

Carlisle, City of
115 School Street
Carlisle, IA 50047
(515) 989-0840

Cascade Municipal Utilities
201 Pierce Street S.W., Box 410
Cascade, IA 52033
(319) 852-3614

Cedar Falls Utilities
612 East 12th Street, Box 769
Cedar Falls, IA 50613
(319) 266-1761

Coggon Municipal Light Plant
131 West Main
Coggon, IA 52218
(319) 435-2436

Coon Rapids Municipal Utilities
123 Third Avenue, Box 207
Coon Rapids, IA 50058
(712) 684-2225

Corning, City of
501 Benton Avenue
Corning, IA 50841
(515) 322-3920

Corwith, City of
404 Main Street
Corwith, IA 50430
(515) 583-2342

Danville, City of
105 West Shepherd Street, Box 265
Danville, IA 52623
(319) 392-4685

Dayton Light & Power
101 South Main Street, Box 45
Dayton, IA 50530
(515) 547-2711

Denison Municipal Utilities
West Broadway & 7th Streets, Box 518
Denison, IA 51442
(712) 263-4154

Denver, City of
107 North State Street
Denver, IA 50622
(319) 984-5642

Dike, City of
540 Main Street
Dike, IA 50624
(310) 989-2291

Durant Municipal Electric Plant
601 4th Street
Durant, IA 52747
(319) 785-6213

Dysart, City of
436 Main Street
Dysart, IA 52224
(319) 476-5690

Earlville Light and Water System
Box 67
Earlville, IA 52041
(310) 923-3365

Eldridge, city of
305 North Third Street
Eldridge, IA 52748
(319) 285-4841

Ellsworth, City of
1551 Dewitt Street
Ellsworth, IA 50075
(525) 836-4751

Estherville, City of
2 North Seventh Street
Estherville, IA 51334
(712) 362-7771

Fairbank, City of
116 East Main Street, Box 447
Fairbank, IA 50629
(319) 635-2869

Farnhamville, City of
Box 97
Farnhamville, IA 50538
(515) 544-3361

Fonda, City of
Box 367
Fonda, IA 50540
(712) 288-6618

Fontanelle, City of
313 Washington Street
Fontanelle, IA 50846
(515) 745-3961

Forest City, City of
Box 346
Forest City, IA 50436
(515) 582-2362

Fredericksburg, City of
151 West Main Street
Fredericksburg, IA 50630
(319) 237-5725

Glidden, City of
108 Idaho Street, Box 349
Glidden, IA 51443
(712) 659-3010

Gowrie Municipal Utilities
1102 Main Street
Gowrie, IA 50543
(515) 352-3065

Graettinger, City of
Box 178
Graettinger, IA 51342
(712) 8589-3844

Grafton, City of
Box 263
Grafton, IA 50440
(515) 748-2735

Grand Junction, City of
305 11th Street
Grand Junction, IA 50107
(515) 736-2285

Greenfield Municipal Utilities
Box 95
Greenfield, IA 50849
(515) 743-2914

Grundy Center, City of
506 Seventh Street, Box 307
Grundy Center, IA 50638
(319) 824-5207

Guttenberg Municipal Electric
502 South First Street, Box 580
Guttenberg, IA 52052
(319) 252-1161

Harlan, City of
Box 71
Harlan, IA 51537
(712) 755-5182

Hartley, City of
11 South Central Avenue
Hartley, IA 51346
(712) 728-2240

Hawarden Municipal Utilities
700 Seventh Street
Hawarden, IA 51023
(712) 552-2565

Hinton, City of
205 West Main Street
Hinton, IA 51024
(712) 947-4229

Hopkinton, City of
Box 129
Hopkinton, IA 52237
(319) 926-2480

Hudson, City of
329 Fifth Street
Hudson, IA 50643
(319) 252-1161

Independence Light and Power
Seventh Avenue N.E., Box 754
Independence, IA 50644
(319) 334-3880

Indianola Municipal Electric and Water Utility
111 South Buxton, Box 445
Indianola, IA 50125
(515) 961-9444

Keosauqua, City of
Box 216
Keosauqua, IA 52565
(319) 293-3406

Kimballton, City of
Kimballton, IA 51543
(712) 773-3451

La Porte Utilities
200 Main Street
La Porte, IA 50651
(319) 342-3139

Lake Mills, City of
201 South Mill
Lake Mills, IA 50450
(515) 592-2441

Lake Park, City of
217 Market Street
Lake Park, IA 51347
(712) 832-3667

Lake View, City of
305 Main Street
Lake View, IA 51450
(712) 657-2122

Lamoni Municipal Utilities
111 South Chestnut Street
Lamoni, IA 50140
(515) 784-6911

Larchwood, City of
Box 216
Larchwood, IA 51241
(712) 477-2366

Laurens, City of
272 North Third
Laurens, IA 50554
(712) 845-4610

Lawler, City of
Box 215
Lawler, IA 52154
(319) 238-3614

Lehigh, City of
241 Elm Street, Box 317
Lehigh, IA 50557
(515) 359-2311

Lenox, City of
Box 96
Lenox, IA 50851
(515) 333-2550

Livermore, City of
501 4th Street, Box 16
Livermore, IA 50558
(515) 379-1074

Long Grove Electric Company
Box 210
Long Grove, IA 52756
(319) 285-7201

Manilla, City of
443 Main Street, Box 398
Manilla, IA 51554
(712) 654-3952

Manning, City of
719 Third Street
Manning, IA 51455
(712) 653-3214

Mapleton, City of
513 Main Street
Mapleton, IA 51034
(712) 882-1351

Maquoketa Municipal Electric Utility
201 East Pleasant
Maquoketa, IA 52060
(319) 652-6891

Marathon, City of
Box 189
Marathon, IA 50565
(712) 289-2261

McGregor, City of
126 First Street
McGregor, IA 52157
(319) 873-2258

Milford Municipal Utilities
907 11th Street
Milford, IA 51351
(712) 338-2401

Montezuma Municipal Light and Power
501 East Main, Box 340
Montezuma, IA 50171
(515) 623-5102

Mount Pleasant, City of
509 North Adams Street, Box 637
Mount Pleasant, IA 52641
(319) 385-2121

Muscatine Power and Water
3205 Cedar Street, Box 899
Muscatine, IA 52761
(319) 263-2631

Neola, City of
103 Third Street, Box 67
Neola, IA 51559
(712) 485-2307

New Hampton Municipal Light Plant
921 Canty Avenue
New Hampton, IA 50659
(515) 394-3002

New London Municipal Utilities
601 East Main Street
New London, IA 52645
(319) 367-7703

Ogden Municipal Utilities
N.W. Third and West Locust, Box 70
Ogden, IA 50212
(515) 275-2437

Onawa, City of
914 Diamond
Onawa, IA 51040
(712) 723-1511

Orange City, City of
125 Central Avenue, S.E.
Orange City, IA 51041
(712) 737-4885

Orient Municipal Utilities
106 West Second, Box 116
Orient, IA 50858
(515) 337-5711

Osage Municipal Utilities
720 Chestnut Street, Box 207
Osage, IA 50461
(515) 732-3731

Ottumwa, City of
Ottumwa, IA 52501
(515) 684-4606

Panora, City of
102 N.W. Second Street
Panora, IA 50216
(515) 755-2164

Paton, City of
Paton, IA 50217
(515) 968-4133

Paulina Municipal Electric Utility
127 South Main Street, Box 239
Paulina, IA 51046
(712) 448-3428

Pella Electric Department
717 Main Street, Box 345
Pella, IA 50219
(515) 628-4173

Pocahontas, City of
23 West Elm
Pocahontas, IA 50574
(712) 335-4841

Preston, City of
12 West Gillet Street, Box 37
Preston, IA 52069
(319) 689-3081

Primghar, City of
1551 First Street, S.W., Box 39
Primghar, IA 51245
(712) 757-2435

Readlyn, City of
Box 70
Readlyn, IA 50668
(319) 279-3411

Remsen, City of
125 East First Street
Remsen, IA 51050
(712) 786-2136

Renwick, City of
Box 174
Renwick, IA 50577
(515) 824-3511

Rock Rapids Municipal Utilities
310 South Third Avenue
Rock Rapids, IA 51246
(712) 472-2511

Rockford Municipal Light Plant
18 First Street South
Rockford, IA 50468
(515) 756-2215

Sabula, City of
411 Broad Street
Sabula, IA 52070
(319) 687-2420

Sanborn Municipal Light Plant
102 Main Street, Box 548
Sanborn, IA 51248
(712) 729-3974

Sergeant Bluff, City of
Box 703
Sergeant Bluff, IA 51054
(712) 943-4244

Shelby Municipal Utilities
419 East Street
Shelby, IA 51570
(712) 544-2404

Sibley, City of
1108 Third Avenue
Sibley, IA 51249
(712) 754-3454

Sioux Center Municipal Utilities
335 First Avenue, N.W.
Sioux Center, IA 51250
(712) 722-0761

Spencer Municipal Utilities
Box 5046
Spencer, IA 51301
(712) 262-3027

Stanhope Municipal Electric Utility
665 Iowa Street
Stanhope, IA 50246
(515) 826-3290

Stanton, City of
Box H
Stanton, IA 51573
(712) 829-2613

State Center, City of
Box 668
State Center, IA 50247
(515) 483-2590

Story City, City of
504 Broad Street
Story City, IA 50248
(515) 733-4691

Stratford, City of
Shakespeare Avenue
Stratford, IA 50249
(515) 838-2311

Strawberry Point, City of
111 Commercial Street, Box 297
Strawberry Point, IA 52076
(319) 933-4482

Stuart, City of
1211 Front Street
Stuart, IA 50250
(515) 523-2915

Sumner, City of
105 Wapsie Street, Box 267
Sumner, IA 50674
(319) 578-5611

Tennant, City of
Tennant, IA 51572
(712) 744-3449

Tipton, City of
407 Lynn Street
Tipton, IA 52772
(319) 886-6187

Traer Municipal Utilities
649 Second Street
Traer, IA 50675
(319) 478-8760

Villisca Municipal Power Plant
City Hall, South Third Avenue
Villisca, IA 50864
(712) 826-3192

Vinton Municipal Electric Utility
501 First Avenue
Vinton, IA 52349
(319) 472-3663

Wall Lake, City of
Box 27
Wall Lake, IA 51466
(712) 664-2216

Waverly Light and Power
1002 Adams Parkway, Box 329
Waverly, IA 50677
(319) 352-6251

Webster City, City of
Box 217
Webster City, IA 50594
(515) 832-5701

West Bend, City of
City Hall, Box 37
West Bend, IA 50597
(515) 887-5585

West Point, City of
313 Fifth Street
West Point, IA 52656
(319) 837-6313

Westfield, Town of
Box 5
Westfield, IA 51062
(712) 568-2631

Whittemore, City of
Box 127
Whittemore, IA 50598
(515) 884-2265

Wilton, City of
104 East Fourth Street
Wilton, IA 52778
(319) 732-2929

Winterset, City of
321 North First Street
Winterset, IA 50273
(515) 462-2152

Woodbine, City of
517 Walker Street
Woodbine, IA 51579
(712) 647-2340

Woolstock, City of
Box 57
Woolstock, IA 50599
(515) 839-5531

KANSAS

Alma, City of
326 Missouri City Hall,
Alma, KS 66401
(913) 765-3922

Altamont, City of
407 South Houston, Box 305
Altamont, KS 67330
(316) 784-5612

Anthony, City of
124 South Bluff Avenue
Anthony, KS 67003
(316) 842-5960

Arcadia, City of
Box 126
Arcadia, KS 66711
(316) 638-4310

Arma, City of
701 East Washington, Box 829
Arma, KS 66712
(316) 376-4125

Ashland, City of
703 Main Street, Box 547
Ashland, KS 67831
(316) 635-2512

Attica, City of
Box 421
Attica, KS 67009
(316) 254-7228

Augusta, City of
Sixth and School Streets, Box 489
Augusta, KS 67010
(316) 775-7051

Axtell, City of
401 Maple Street, Box A
Axtell, KS 66403
(913) 736-2834

Baldwin City, City of
Box 86
Baldwin City, KS 66006
(913) 594-3261

Belleville, City of
1819 L Street, Box 280
Belleville, KS 66935
(913) 527-2288

Beloit, City of
119 North Hersey, Box 567
Beloit, KS 67420
(913) 638-3551

Blue Mount, City of
Blue Mount, KS 66010
(913) 756-2281

Bronson, City of
505 Clay Street, Box 54
Bronson, KS 66716
(316) 939-4578

Burlingame, City of
101 East Santa Fe
Burlingame, KS 66413
(913) 654-2414

Burlington, City of
301 Neosho Street, Box 207
Burlington, KS 66839
(316) 364-5334

Cawker City, City of
804 Locust Street
Cawker City, KS 67430-0002
(913) 781-4713

Centralia, City of
517 Fourth Street
Centralia, KS 66415
(913) 857-3764

Chanute, City of
101 South Lincoln
Chanute, KS 66720
(316) 431-5200

Chapman, City of
402 Marshall Street, Box 321
Chapman, KS 67431
(913) 922-6582

Chetopa, City of
332 Maple Street, Box 203
Chetopa, KS 67336
(316) 236-7511

Cimarron, City of
119 South Main Street, Box 467
Cimarron, KS 67835
(316) 855-2322

Clay Center Public Utilities
427 Court Street
Clay Center, KS 67432
(913) 632-2137

Coffeyville, City of
Box 1629
Coffeyville, KS 67337
(316) 252-6180

Colby, City of
585 North Franklin Street
Colby, KS 67701
(913) 462-4400

DeSota City of
33150 West 83rd Street, Box C
DeSota, KS 66018
(913) 585-1182

Dighton, City of
Box 848
Dighton, KS 67839
(316) 397-5541

Ellinwood, City of
Box 278
Ellinwood, KS 67526
(316) 564-2211

Elsmore, City of
Elsmore, KS 66732
(316) 754-3875

Elwood, City of
Box 357
Elwood, KS 66024
(913) 365-6871

Enterprise, City of
206 South Factory, Box 245
Enterprise, KS 67441
(913) 934-2323

Erie Municipal Light and Power
224 South Main Street
Erie, KS 66733
(316) 244-3488

Eudora, City of
Seventh and Main Streets
Eudora, KS 66025
(913) 542-3100

Fredonia Municipal Power Plant
314 North 7th Street
Fredonia, KS 66736
(316) 378-2231

Galva, City of
208 South Main Street
Galva, KS 67443
(316) 654-3561

Garden City, City of
301 North Eight Street, Box 499
Garden City, KS 67846
(316) 276-1234

Gardner, City of
112 South Elm
Gardner, KS 66030
(913) 884-7029

Garnett, City of
131 West Fifth Street, Box H
Garnett, KS 66032
(913) 448-5496

Girard, City of
100 South Ozark Street
Girard, KS 66743
(316) 724-8918

Glasco, City of
Box 356
Glasco, KS 67445
(913) 568-2705

Glen Elder, City of
101 South Market Street, Box 55
Glen Elder, KS 67445
(913) 545-3322

Goodland, City of
17th and Cherry Streets
Goodland, KS 67735
(913) 899-4530

Greensburg, City of
239 South Main Street
Greensburg, KS 67054
(316) 723-2691

Haven, City of
118 South Kansas Avenue
Haven, KS 67543
(316) 465-3618

Herington, City of
19 North Broadway, Box 31
Herington, KS 67449
(913) 258-2271

Herndon, City of
Box 98
Herndon, KS 67739
(913) 322-5341

Hill City, City of
205 North Pomeroy
Hill City, KS 67642
(913) 674-5613

Hillsboro, City of
116 East Grand Street
Hillsboro, KS 67063
(316) 947-3162

Hoisington, City of
164 South Elm Street, Box 418
Hoisington, KS 67544
(316) 653-4125

Holton, City of
1000 New Jersey
Holton, KS 66436
(913) 364-2721

Holyrood, City of
110 South Main Street, Box 67
Holyrood, KS 67450
(913) 252-3652

Horton, City of
205 East Eighth Street, Box 30
Horton, KS 66439
(913) 486-2681

Hugoton, City of
114 East Fifth Street, Box 788
Hugoton, KS 67951
(316) 544-8531

Iola, City of
2 West Jackson Street
Iola, KS 66749
(316) 365-2771

Isabel, City of
Box 97
Isabel, KS 67065
(316) 739-4347

Iuka, City of
Box 127
Iuka, KS 67066
(316) 546-2565

Jetmore, City of
501 South Main Street
Jetmore, KS 67854
(316) 357-8344

Johnson, City of
206 South Main Street
Johnson, KS 67855
(316) 492-2322

Kansas City Board of Public Utilities
700 Minnesota Avenue
Kansas City, KS 66101
(913) 573-9000

Kansas Municipal Energy Agency
6950 Sqibb Road, Suite 414,, Box 2179
Mission, KS 66201
(913) 677-2885

Kingman, City of
332 North Main Street
Kingman, KS 67068
(316) 532-3111

Kiowa, City of
618 Main Street, Box 206
Kiowa, KS 67070
(316) 825-4128

La Crosse, City of
Box 339
La Crosse, KS 67548
(913) 222-2511

La Harpe, City of
Box 121
La Harpe, KS 66751
(316) 496-2241

Lakin, City of
121 North Main Street, Box 148
Lakin, KS 67860
(316) 355-6252

Larned, City of
Third and Main Streets
Larned, KS 67550
(316) 285-3544

Lincoln Center, City of
153 West Lincoln Avenue, Box 126
Lincoln Center, KS 67455
(913) 524-4280

Lindsborg, City of
101 South Main Street, Box 70
Lindsborg, KS 67456
(913) 227-3355

Lucas, City of
Box 308
Lucas, KS 67648
(913) 525-6353

Luray, City of
Luray, KS 67649
(913) 698-2302

Mankato, City of
202 East Jefferson
Mankato, KS 66956
(913) 378-3141

Marion, City of
203 North Third
Marion, KS 66861
(316) 382-3703

McPherson, City of
400 East Kansas Avenue
McPherson, KS 67460
(316) 245-2525

Meade, City of
132 South Fowler Avenue
Meade, KS 67864
(316) 873-2091

Minneapolis, City of
218 North Rock Street
Minneapolis, KS 67467
(913) 392-2176

Montezuma, City of
Box 37
Montezuma, KS 67876
(316) 846-2264

Moran, City of
Box 236
Moran, KS 66755
(316) 237-4301

Morrill, City of
Box 146
Morrill, KS 66515
(913) 459-2231

Moundridge, City of
Box 636
Moundridge, KS 67107
(316) 345-8456

Mount Hope, City of
112 West Main, Box 56
Mount Hope, KS 67108
(316) 667-2211

Mulberry Municipal Light Plant
Box 206
Mulberry, KS 66756
(316) 764-3815

Mulvane, City of
North Second Street, Box 211
Mulvane, KS 67110
(316) 777-1143

City of Muscotah
Muscotah, KS 66058
(913) 872-3585

Neodesha, City of
102 South Fourth Street
Neodesha, KS 66757
(316) 325-2925

Norton, City of
301 East Washington Street
Norton, KS 67654
(913) 877-2255

Oakley, City of
209 Hudson Avenue
Oakley, KS 67748
(913) 672-3135

Oberlin, City of
107 West Commercial Street
Oberlin, KS 67749
(913) 475-2217

Osage City, City of
Fifth and Main Streets
Osage City, KS 66523
(913) 528-3851

Osawatomie, City of
Main at Fifth, Box 37
Osawatomie, KS 66064
(913) 755-4138

Osborne, City of
133 West Main Street
Osborne, KS 67473
(913) 346-2722

Ottawa, City of
Fourth and Walnut Streets
Ottawa, KS 66067
(913) 242-2190

Oxford, City of
121 South Sumner Street
Oxford, KS 67119
(316) 455-2223

Pomona, City of
Box 67
Pomona, KS 66076
(913) 566-3522

Pratt, City of
321 West Tenth Street, Box 807
Pratt, KS 67124
(316) 672-2022

Prescott, City of
Main Street
Prescott, KS 66767
(913) 471-4521

Radium, City of
Box 162, Route 2
Radium, KS 67571
(316) 982-4695

Robinson, City of
Box 36
Robinson, KS 66532
(913) 544-6737

Russell, City of
Eighth and Maple Streets, Box 112
Russell, KS 67665
(913) 483-7112

Sabetha Municipal Light Department
Box 187
Sabetha, KS 66534
(913) 284-2158

St. Francis, City of
Box 517
St. Francis, KS 67756
(913) 332-3031

St. John, City of
Box 367
St. John, KS 67576
(316) 549-3800

St. Marys, City of
Box 146
St. Marys, KS 66536
(913) 437-2311

Savonburg, City of
Savonburg, KS 66772
(316) 754-3278

Scranton, City of
Box 218
Scranton, KS 66537
(913) 793-2814

Seneca, City of
531 Main Street
Seneca, KS 66538
(913) 336-2747

Severance, City of
RR 1, Box 102
Severance, KS 66081
(913) 359-6696

Seward, City of
Box 256
Seward, KS 67577
(316) 458-5931

Sharon Springs, City of
Box 490
Sharon Springs, KS 67758
(913) 852-4232

Stafford, City of
112 West Broadway
Stafford, KS 67578
(316) 234-5561

Sterling, City of
114 North Broadway Street
Sterling, KS 67579
(316) 278-3411

Stockton, City of
Box 512
Stockton, KS 67669
(913) 425-6625

Summerfield, Town of
Summerfield, KS 66541
(913) 244-6227

Toronto, City of
Box 235
Toronto, KS 66777
(316) 637-2605

Troy, City of
137 West Walnut
Troy, KS 66087
(913) 985-2265

Udall, City of
110 South Main Street
Udall, KS 67146
(316) 782-3512

Vermillion, City of
Second and Main Streets, Box 127
Vermillion, KS 66544
(913) 382-6224

Wamego, City of
430 Lincoln Street, Box 86
Wamego, KS 66547
(913) 456-9119

Washington Municipal Power Plant
Park Road, Box 296
Washington, KS 66968
(913) 325-2231

Waterville, City of
204 East Front
Waterville, KS 66548
(913) 785-2367

Wathena, City of
206 St. Joseph Street, Box 27
Wathena, KS 66090
(913) 989-4711

Webber, City of
Webber, KS 66970
(913) 753-4401

Wellington Municipal Utilities
317 South Washington Street
Wellington, KS 67152
(316) 326-3871

Winfield, City of
200 East Ninth Street, Box 646
Winfield, KS 67156
(316) 221-5500

KENTUCKY

Barbourville, City of
Daniel Boone Drive, Box 1600
Barbourville, KY 40906
(606) 546-3187

Bardstown, City of
220 North Fifth Street, Box 368
Bardstown, KY 40004
(502) 348-5947

Bardwell, City of
Box 277
Bardwell, KY 42023
(502) 628-3833

Benham, City of
Box E
Benham, KY 40807
(606) 848-5506

Benton Electric System
Box 196
Benton, KY 42025
(502) 527-3651

Bowling Green Municipal Utilities
801 Center Street, Box 10300
Bowling Green, KY 42102
(502) 782-1200

Corbin Utilities Commission
901 South Main Street
Corbin, KY 40701
(606) 528-4026

Falmouth, City of
212 Main Street
Falmouth, KY 41040
(606) 654-6937

Frankfort Electric and Water Plant Board
315 West Second Street
Frankfort, KY 40601
(502) 223-3401

Franklin Electric Plant Board
309 North High Street, Box 349
Franklin, KY 42135
(502) 586-4441

Fulton Electric Systems
501 Walnut Street, Box 130
Fulton, KY 42041
(502) 472-1362

Glasgow, City of
100 Mallory Drive, Box 1809
Glasgow, KY 42142
(502) 651-8341

Henderson City Utility Commission
419 Water Street, Box 8
Henderson, KY 42420
(502) 826-2726

Hickman, City of
Box 228
Hickman, KY 42050
(502) 236-3951

Hopkinsville Electric System
1820 East Ninth Street, Box 544
Hopkinsville, KY 42241
(502) 887-4210

Madisonville, City of
37 East Center Street, Box 705
Madisonville, KY 42131
(502) 824-2105

Mayfield Electric and Water System
301 East Broadway Street
Mayfield, KY 42066
(502) 247-4661

Monticello, City of
615 Columbia Avenue, Box 657
Monticello, KY 42633
(606) 347-8102

Murray Electric
401 Olive Street, Box 1095
Murray, KY 42071
(502) 753-5312

Nicholasville, City of
517 North Main Street
Nicholasville, KY 40356
(606) 885-9473

Olive Hill, City of
Box 460
Olive Hill, KY 41164
(606) 286-2192

Owensboro Municipal Utilities
115 East Fourth Street, Box 806
Owensboro, KY 42303
(502) 926-3200

Paducah Power System
1400 Broadway Street, Box 180
Paducah, KY 42001
(502) 575-4000

Paris, City of
800 Pleasant Street
Paris, KY 40361
(606) 987-2110

Princeton, City of
Box 608
Princeton, KY 42445
(502) 365-2031

Providence, City of
North Willow Street, Box 128
Providence, KY 42450
(502) 667-5463

Russellville Electric Plant Board
Box 418
Russellville, KY 42276
(502) 726-2466

Vanceburg, City of
611 Front Street, Box 489
Vanceburg, KY 41179
(606) 796-2641

Williamstown Utility Commission
Main Street
Williamstown, KY 41097
(606) 824-3352

LOUISIANA

Abbeville, City of
101 North State Street
Abbeville, LA 70510
(318) 893-8550

Alexandria, City of
Box 71
Alexandria, LA 71309
(318) 449-5008

Boyce, Town of
Box 146
Boyce, LA 71409
(318) 793-2175

Town of Elizabeth
Elizabeth, LA 70638
(Telephone number not available)

Erath, Town of
115 West Edwards
Erath, LA 70533
(318) 937-8401

Gueydan, Town of
600 Main Street
Gueydan, LA 70542
(318) 536-9415

Jonesville, City of
Box 428
Jonesville, LA 71343
(318) 339-8596

Kaplan, City of
511 North Cushing Avenue
Kaplan, LA 70548
(318) 643-8602

Lafayette, City of
Walker Road, Box 4017-C
Lafayette, LA 70502
(318) 268-5800

Lafayette Public Power Authority
1314 Walker Road
Lafeyette, LA 70502
(318) 268-5855

Louisiana Energy and Power Authority
315 Johnston Street
Lafayette, LA 70501
(318) 269-4046

Minden Light and Water Department
Box 580
Minden, LA 71058
(318) 377-2144

Morgan City, City of
Avoca Road, Box 1218
Morgan City, LA 70381
(504) 385-1770

Natchitoches, City of
314 Amulet Street, Box 37
Natchitoches, LA 71457
(318) 352-2901

New Roads, City of
211 West Main Street, Box 280
New Roads, LA 70760
(504) 638-5360

Plaquemine City Light and Water
Box 777
Plaquemine, LA 70764
(504) 687-2461

Rayne, City of
201 Third Avenue, Box 69
Rayne, LA 70578
(318) 334-5870

Ruston, City of
Box 280
Ruston, LA 71273
(318) 255-0800

St. Martinville, City of
120 New Market Street, Box 379
St. Martinville, LA 70582
(318) 394-5591

Terrebonne Parish Utilities Department
Box 6097
Houma, LA 70361
(504) 873-6755

Vidalia, Town of
409 Texas Street
Vidalia, LA 71373
(318) 336-5206

Vinton, City of
1200 Horridge Street
Vinton, LA 70668
(318) 589-7453

Welsh, City of
Box 786
Welsh, LA 70591
(318) 734-2231

Winnfield, City of
Box 509
Winnfield, LA 71483
(318) 628-2744

MAINE

Houlton Water Company
21 Bangor Street, Box 726
Houlton, ME 04730
(207) 532-2250

Kennebunk Light and Power
4 Factory Pasture Lane
Kennebunk, ME 04043
(207) 985-3311

Madison, Town of
26 Weston Avenue
Madison, ME 04950
(207) 696-4401

Matinicus Plantation Electric Company
Matinicus, ME 04851
(207) 366-3970

Van Buren Light and Power District
Box 128
Van Buren, ME 04785
(207) 868-3321

MARYLAND

Berlin, Town of
10 William Street
Berlin, MD 21811
(410) 641-4313

Easton Utilities Commission
142 North Harrison Street
Easton, MD 21601
(410) 822-6110

Hagerstown Light Department
425 East Baltimore Street
Hagerstown, MD 21740
(301) 790-2600

Thurmont Municipal Light Company
10 Frederick Road, Box 385
Thurmont, MD 21788
(301) 271-7872

Williamsport, Town of
Town Hall
Williamsport, MD 21795
(301) 223-7711

MASSACHUSETTS

Ashburnham, Town of
86 Central Street
Ashburnham, MA 01430
(508) 827-4423

Belmont, Town of
450 Concord Avenue
Belmont, MA 02178
(617) 484-2780

Boylston, Town of
Sanatorium Road
Boylston, MA 01505
(508) 869-2626

Braintree, Town of
44 Allen Street
Braintree, MA 02184
(617) 848-1130

Chester Municipal Electric Light Department
Middlefield Street
Chester, MA 01011
(413) 354-7811

Chicopee Municipal Lighting Plant
725 Front Street, Box 405
Chicopee, MA 01021
(413) 598-8311

Concord Municipal Light Plant
135 Keyes Road
Concord, MA 01742
(508) 371-6320

Danvers, Town of
2 Burroughs Street
Danvers, MA 01923
(508) 774-0005

Georgetown Municipal Light Department
Corner - Moulton and West Main Streets
Georgetown, MA 01833
(508) 352-5730

Groton Electric Light Department
Station Avenue, Box 679
Groton, MA 01450
(508) 448-6655

Massachusetts Water Resources Authority
100 First Avenue, Charlestown Navy Yard
Boston, MA 02129
(617) 241-4636

Merrimac Municipal Light Department
32 South Main Street
Middleborough, MA 02346
(508) 346-8311

Middleborough Gas and Electric Department
32 South Main Street
Middleborough, MA 02346
(508) 947-1371

Middleton, Town of
1997 North Main Street
Middleton, MA 01949
(508) 774-4313

North Attleboro, Town of
43 South Washington Street
North Attleboro, MA 02760
(508) 699-7542

Norwood, Town of
206 Central Street
Norwood, MA 02062
(617) 762-3203

Paxton, Town of
578 Pleasant Street
Paxton, MA 01612
(508) 756-9508

Peabody Municipal Light Plant
Box 3209
Peabody, MA 01961
(508) 531-5975

Princeton Municipal Light Department
4 Town Hall Drive, Box 247
Princeton, MA 01541
(508) 464-2815

Reading Municipal Light Department
25 Haven Street, Box 150
Reading, MA 01867
(617) 944-1340

Rowley, Town of
47 Summer Street
Rowley, MA 01969
(508) 948-3992

Russell Municipal Light Department
200 Main Street
Russell, MA 01071
(413) 862-4400

Shrewsbury's Electric Light Plant
100 Maple Avenue
Shrewsbury, MA 01545
(508) 845-4881

South Hadley, Town of
85 Main Street
South Hadley, MA 01075
(413) 536-1050

Sterling Municipal Light Department
50 Main Street, Box 430
Sterling, MA 01564
(508) 422-8267

Taunton Municipal Lighting Plant
Box 870
Taunton, MA 02781
(508) 824-5844

Templeton Municipal Light Plant
2 School Street
Baldwinville, MA 01436
(508) 939-5323

Wakefield Municipal Light Department
9 Albion Street, Box 190
Wakefield, MA 01880
(617) 246-6363

Wellesley, Town of
455 Worcester Street, Box 364
Wellesley, MA 02181
(617) 235-7600

West Boylston Municipal Lighting Plant
4 Crescent Street
West Boylston, MA 01583
(508) 835-3681

Westfield Gas and Electric Light Department
100 Elm Street, Box 990
Westfield, MA 01086
(413) 572-0100

MICHIGAN

Baraga, Village of
801 US-41 South, Box 290
Baraga, MI 49908
(906) 353-6237

Bay City, City of
900 South Water Street
Bay City, MI 48708
(517) 894-8344

Charlevoix, City of
210 State Street
Charlevoix, MI 49720
(616) 547-3270

Chelsea Department of Electric and Water
104 East Middle Street
Chelsea, MI 48118
(313) 475-1771

Clinton, Village of
Box E
Clinton, MI 49236
(517) 456-4507

Coldwater Board of Public Utilities
28 West Chicago Street, Box 469
Coldwater, MI 49036
(517) 279-9531

Croswell, City of
100 North Howard Avenue
Croswell, MI 48422
(313) 679-2120

Crystal Falls, City of
401 Superior Avenue
Crystal Falls, MI 49920
(906) 875-6647

Daggett Electric Department
Daggett, MI 49821
(906) 753-4085

Detroit Public Light Department
9449 Grinnell Avenue
Detroit, MI 48213
(313) 267-7258

Dowagiac, City of
203 Chestnut Street
Dowagiac, MI 49047
(616) 782-8200

Eaton Rapids, City of
200 South Main Street
Eaton Rapids, MI 48827
(517) 663-8118

Escanaba, City of
1711 Sheridan Road
Escanaba, MI 49829
(906) 786-0061

Gladstone, City of
1100 Delta Avenue, Box 32
Gladstone, MI 49837
(906) 428-3737

Grand Haven, City of
1700 Eaton Drive
Grand Haven, MI 49417
(616) 846-6250

Harbor Springs, City of
349 East Main Street
Harbor Springs, MI 49740
(616) 526-2122

Hart Hydro, City of
407 State Street
Hart, MI 49420
(616) 873-2488

Hillsdale Board of Public Utilities
45 Monroe Street
Hillsdale, MI 49242
(517) 437-3387

Holland Board of Public Works
625 Hastings Avenue
Holland, MI 49423
(616) 394-1320

L'Anse, Village of
101 North Main Street
L'Anse, MI 49946
(906) 524-7393

Lansing Board of Water and Light
123 West Ottawa Street
Lansing, MI 48901
(517) 371-6000

Lowell Light and Power
127 North Broadway Street
Lowell, MI 49331
(616) 897-8402

Marquette Board of Light and Power
2200 West Wright Street
Marquette, MI 49855
(906) 228-0320

Marshall, City of
323 West Michigan
Marshall, MI 49068
(616) 781-3967

Michigan Public Power Agency
809 Centennial Way
Lansing, MI 48917
(517) 323-8919

Michigan South Central Power Agency
720 Herring Road, Box 62
Litchfield, MI 49252
(517) 542-2346

Negaunee Electric Department
600 Cherry Street
Negaunee, MI 49866
(906) 476-9993

Newberry Water and Light Board
307 East McMillian Avenue
Newberry, MI 49868
(906) 293-8531

Niles Utilities Department
322 East Main Street, Box 217
Niles, MI 49120
(616) 683-4700

Norway, City of
915 Brown Street
Norway, MI 49870
(906) 563-8015

Village of Paw Paw Department of Public Works
110 Harry L. Bush Blvd.
Paw Paw, MI 49079
(616) 657-3169

Petoskey, City of
100 West Lake Street
Petoskey, MI 49770
(616) 347-2500

Portland, City of
259 Kent Street
Portland, MI 48875
(517) 647-6912

St. Louis, City of
412 North Hill Street
St. Louis, MI 48880
(517) 681-3351

Sebewaing, City of
110 West Main Street
Sebewaing, MI 48759
(517) 883-2700

South Haven, City of
539 Phoenix Street
South Haven, MI 49090
(616) 637-0750

Stephenson, City of
Stephenson, MI 49887
(906) 753-4769

Sturgis, City of
130 North Nottawa, Box 280
Sturgis, MI 49091
(616) 651-2321

Traverse City Light and Power Department
400 Boardman Avenue
Traverse City, MI 49684
(616) 922-4470

Union City Electric Department
208 Broadway
Union City, MI 49094
(517) 741-8591

Wakefield, City of
311 Sunday Lake Street
Wakefield, MI 49968
(906) 229-5131

Wyandotte Municipal Service Commission
3005 Biddle Avenue, Box 658
Wyandotte, MI 48192
(313) 282-7100

Zeeland Board of Public Works
350 East Washington Avenue
Zeeland, MI 49464
(616) 772-6212

MINNESOTA

Ada Water and Light Department
Drawer 32
Ada, MN 56510
(218) 784-4467

Adrain Public Utilities Commission
Box 187
Adrain, MN 56110
(507) 483-2680

Aitkin Public Utilities Commission
120 First Street N.W.
Aitkin, MN 56431
(218) 927-3222

Alexandria Board of Public Works
316 Fillmore Street
Alexandria, MN 56308
(612) 763-6501

Alpha, City of
Box 97
Alpha, MN 56111
(507) 847-3557

Alvarado, City of
Box 935
Alvarado, MN 56710
(218) 965-4911

Anoka, City of
2015 First Avenue, North
Anoka, MN 55303
(612) 421-6630

Arlington, City of
312 Alden Street
Arlington, MN 55307
(612) 964-2378

Austin, City of
Box 368
Austin, MN 55912
(507) 433-8886

Bagley Public Utilities Commission
18 Main Avenue, South; Box M
Bagley, MN 56621
(218) 694-2300

Barnesville Electric Department
Box 550
Barnesville, MN 56514
(218) 354-2292

Baudette, City of
106 West Main Street
Baudette, MN 56623
(218) 634-2432

Benson, City of
1410 Kansas Avenue
Benson, MN 56215
(612) 843-3707

Bigelow, City of
1710 Broadway, Box 67
Bigelow, MN 56117
(507) 683-2682

Biwabik Public Utilities
Box A
Biwabik, MN 55708
(218) 865-4183

Blooming Prairie Public Utilities
Box 55
Blooming Prairie, MN 55917
(507) 583-6683

Blue Earth Light and Water Department
118 East Sixth Street
Blue Earth, MN 56013
(507) 526-2191

Brainerd, City of
101 Laurel Street, Box 373
Brainerd, MN 56401
(218) 829-2193

Breckenridge, City of
420 Nebraska Avenue, Box 410
Breckenridge, MN 56520
(218) 643-4681

Brewster, City of
906 Third Avenue
Brewster, MN 56119
(507) 842-5936

Brownton, City of
528 Second Street, North
Brownton, MN 55312
(612) 328-5318

Buffalo Municipal Utility
212 Central Avenue
Buffalo, MN 55313
(612) 682-1181

Buhl, City of
Box 704
Buhl, MN 55713
(218) 258-3226

Caledonia, City of
231 East Main Street, Box 232
Caledonia, MN 55921
(507) 724-3450

Ceylon, City of
Office of the Clerk
Ceylon, MN 56121
(507) 632-4653

Chaska, City of, Utility Department
660 Victoria Drive
Chaska, MN 55318
(612) 448-2851

Darwin, City of
Box 67
Darwin, MN 55324
(612) 693-7632

Delano Municipal Utilities
11 West Bridge Avenue
Delano, MN 55328
(612) 972-3211

Detroit Lakes, City of
Box 647
Detroit Lakes, MN 56501
(218) 847-7609

Dundee, City of
Box 65
Dundee, MN 56126
(507) 468-2731

Dunnell, Village of
Box 94
Dunnell, MN 56127
(507) 695-2942

East Grand Forks Water, Light, Power and
Building Commission
303 Fourth Street, N.W., Box 322
East Grand Forks, MN 56721
(218) 773-1163

Eitzen, City of
Box 110
Eitzen, MN 55931
(507) 495-3259

Elbow Lake, City of
Box 1079
Elbow Lake, MN 56531
(218) 685-4483

Elk River Municipal Utilities
322 King Avenue
Elk River, MN 55330
(612) 441-2020

Ely, City of
209 East Chapman Street
Ely, MN 55731
(218) 365-3225

Fairfax, City of
112 S.E. First Street
Fairfax, MN 55332
(507) 426-7255

Fairmont Public Utilities Commission
100 Downtown Plaza
Fairmont, MN 56031
(507) 238-9461

Fosston, City of
220 East First Street
Fosston, MN 56542
(218) 435-1737

Gilbert Water and Light
Box 368
Gilbert, MN 55741
(218) 741-9617

Glencoe Light and Power Commission
305 11th Street, E.
Glencoe, MN 55336
(612) 864-5184

Grand Marais, City of
15 North Broadway
Grand Marais, MN 55604
(218) 387-1848

Grand Rapids Public Utilities Commission
420 North Pokegama Avenue, Box 658
Grand Rapids, MN 55744
(218) 326-6704

Granite Falls, Town of
885 Prentice Street
Granite Falls, MN 56241
(612) 564-3011

Grove City Public Utilities
Box 98
Grove City, MN 56243
(612) 857-2322

Halstad Municipal Utilities
RR.2, Box 1
Halstad, MN 56548
(218) 456-2128

Harmony, City of
15 2nd Street, N.W., Box 488
Harmony, MN 55939
(507) 886-8122

Hawley Public Utilities Commission
319 Sixth Street
Hawley, MN 56549
(218) 483-3331

Henning, City of
Box 55
Henning, MN 56551
(218) 583-2402

Hibbing Public Utilities Commission
Sixth Avenue East and 19th Street
Hibbing, MN 55746
(218) 263-7515

Hutchinson Utilities Commission
225 Michigan Street
Hutchinson, MN 55350
(612) 587-4746

Jackson, City of
80 West Ashley Street
Jackson, MN 56143
(507) 847-4410

Janesville, City of
219 North Main Street
Janesville, MN 56048
(507) 234-5112

Kandiyohi, City of
Box 276
Kandiyohi, MN 56251
(612) 382-6110

Kasota, City of
201 Webster Street
Kasota, MN 56050
(507) 931-3290

Kasson, City of
122 West Main Street
Kasson, MN 55944
(507) 634-7302

Keewatin Public Utilities Commission
City Hall, Box 190
Keewatin, MN 55753
(218) 778-6544

Kenyon Municipal Utilities
713 Second Street
Kenyon, MN 55946
(507) 789-6573

Lake City, City of
205 West Center Street
Lake City, MN 55041
(612) 345-5383

Lake Crystal Municipal Power Plant
100 East Robinson Street
Lake Crystal, MN 56055
(507) 726-2260

Lake Park Public Utilities
Second Street
Lake Park, MN 56554
(218) 238-5337

Lakefield Public Utilities
Box 1023
Lakefield, MN 56150
(507) 662-6363

Lanesboro Public Utility Commission
202 Parkway Street
Lanesboro, MN 55949
(507) 467-3722

Le Sueur, City of
228 North Main Street
Le Sueur, MN 56058
(612) 665-3338

Litchfield Public Utility Commission
421 East Third Street, Box 521
Litchfield, MN 55355
(612) 693-3277

Luverne, City of
203 East Main, Box 348
Luverne, MN 56156
(507) 283-2388

Mabel, City of
Box 425
Mabel, MN 55954
(507) 493-5299

Madelia Municipal Light and Power
24 Abbott Avenue
Madelia, MN 56062
(507) 642-8803

Madison, City of
109 Seventh Avenue
Madison, MN 56256
(612) 598-3239

Marshall Municipal Utilities
113 South Fourth Street
Marshall, MN 56258
(507) 537-7005

Melrose, City of
225 East First Street, North
Melrose, MN 56352
(612) 256-4666

Moorhead Public Service Department
500 Center Avenue, Box 770
Moorhead, MN 56561
(218) 299-5400

Moose Lake Water and Light Commission
401 Fourth Street
Moose Lake, MN 55767
(218) 486-4100

Mora Municipal Utilities
117 S.E. Railroad Avenue
Mora, MN 55051
(612) 679-1511

Mountain Iron, City of
City Hall, Box 505
Mountain Iron, MN 55768
(218) 735-8267

Mountain Lake, City of
1015 Second Avenue
Mountain Lake, MN 56159
(507) 427-2999

Nashwauk Public Utilities
301 Central Avenue
Nashwauk, MN 55760
(218) 885-1210

New Prague Municipal Utilities Commission
300 East Main Street
New Prague, MN 56071
(612) 758-4447

New Ulm Public Utilities Commission
310 First North Street
New Ulm, MN 56073
(507) 359-3264

Newfolden, City of
Box 188
Newfolden, MN 56738
(218) 874-3186

Nielsville, City of
Box 68
Nielsville, MN 56568
(218) 946-2881

North Branch, City of
712 Maple Street
North Branch, MN 55056
(612) 674-7100

North Saint Paul, City of
2526 East Seventh Avenue
North Saint Paul, MN 55109
(612) 770-4488

Northern Municipal Power Agency
Box 528
Thief River Falls, MN 56701
(218) 681-8002

Olivia, City of
1009 West Lincoln Avenue
Olivia, MN 56277
(612) 523-2361

Ortonville, City of
315 Madison Avenue
Ortonville, MN 56278
(612) 839-3428

Owatonna Public Utilities
208 South Walnut Avenue, Box 800
Owatonna, MN 55060
(507) 451-2480

Peterson, City of
City Hall, Box 94
Peterson, MN 55962
(507) 875-2510

Pierz Municipal Electric
Box 457
Pierz, MN 56364
(612) 468-6471

Preston Public Utilities Commission
109 St. Paul Two S.W., Box 657
Preston, MN 55965
(507) 765-2153

Princeton Public Utilities Commission
First Street and Tenth Avenue
Princeton, MN 55371
(612) 389-2252

Proctor Public Utilities Commission
200 Second Street
Proctor, MN 55810
(218) 624-4055

Randall, City of
City Hall
Randall, MN 56475
(612) 749-2159

Redwood Falls Public Utilities Commission
333 South Washington Street, Box 48
Redwood Falls, MN 56283
(507) 637-5789

Rochester Public Utilities
4000 East River Road N.E.
Rochester, MN 55906
(507) 280-1540

Roseau, City of
100 Second Avenue, Box 307
Roseau, MN 56751
(218) 463-1542

Round Lake, City of
98 Main Street
Round Lake, MN 56167
(507) 945-8127

Rushford, City of
405 South Elm Street, Box 430
Rushford, MN 55971
(507) 864-2444

Rushmore, City of
Box 227
Rushmore, MN 56168
(507) 478-4338

St. Charles, City of
1242 Whitewater Avenue
St. Charles, MN 55972
(507) 932-3020

St. James, City of
124 Armstrong Blvd. S., Box 70
St. James, MN 56081
(507) 375-3241

St. Peter Municipal Electric Utility
405 West Saint Julien Street
St. Peter, MN 56082
(507) 931-4840

Sauk Centre Water, Light and Power Commission
101 Main Street S., Box 128
Sauk Centre, MN 56378
(612) 352-6538

Sakopee Public Utilities Commission
1030 East Fourth Avenue
Shakopee, MN 55379
(612) 445-1988

Shelly, City of
Box 126
Shelly, MN 56581
(218) 886-8895

Sleepy Eye Public Utility Commission
130 Second Avenue N.W.
Sleepy Eye, MN 56085
(507) 794-4371

Southern Minnesota Municipal Power Agency
500 S.W. First Avenue
Rochester, MN 55902
(507) 285-0478

Spring Grove, City of
118 First Avenue
Spring Grove, MN 55974
(507) 498-5221

Spring Valley Public Utilities Commission
104 South Section Avenue
Spring Valley, MN 55975
(507) 346-7622

Springfield Public Utilities Commission
14 North Marshall Avenue
Springfield, MN 56087
(507) 723-5290

Staples, City of
611 Iowa Avenue, North
Staples, MN 56479
(218) 894-2550

Stephen, City of
Box 630
Stephen, MN 56757
(218) 478-3803

Thief River Falls, City of
803 South Barzen Avenue, Box 528
Thief River Falls, MN 56701
(218) 681-5816

Truman Public Utilities
Box 147
Truman, MN 56088
(507) 776-6501

Two Harbors, City of
522 First Avenue
Two Harbors, MN 55616
(218) 834-5631

Tyler, City of
Box C
Tyler, MN 56178
(507) 247-5556

Virginia, City of
620 Second Street, S., Box 1048
Virginia MN 55792
(218) 741-0740

Wadena, City of
104 North Jefferson
Wadena, MN 56482
(218) 631-1813

Warren, City of
126 West Johnson Avenue
Warren, MN 56762
(218) 745-5343

Warroad, City of
Box 50
Warroad, MN 56763
(218) 386-1873

Waseca, City of
508 South State Street
Waseca, MN 56093
(507) 835-3890

Wells Public Utilities
101 First Street, S.E.
Wells, MN 56097
(507) 553-3119

Westbrook Municipal Light and Power
Box 296
Westbrook, MN 56183
(507) 274-6712

Western Minnesota Municipal Power Agency
212 Second Street, N.W.
Ortonville, MN 56278
(612) 839-2549

Whalan, Town of
Route 1, Box 2
Whalan, MN 55986
(507) 467-3323

Willmar Municipal Utilities Commission
700 Litchfield Avenue, S.W., Box 937
Willmar, MN 56201
(612) 235-4422

Windom, City of
444 Ninth Street
Windom, MN 56101
(507) 831-1539

Winthrop, City of
305 North Main Street, Box Y
Winthrop, MN 55396
(507) 647-5306

Worthington Public Utilities
823 Third Avenue, Box 458
Worthington, MN 56187
(507) 372-8680

MISSISSIPPI

Aberdeen Electric Department
Box 817
Aberdeen, MS 39730
(601) 369-4731

Amory, City of
Box 266
Amory, MS 38821
(601) 256-5633

Canton Municipal Utilities
226 East Peace Street, Box 114
Canton, MS 39046
(601) 859-2921

Clarksdale Public Utilities
Box 70
Clarksdale, MS 38614
(601) 627-8403

Collins, City of
Box 400
Collins, MS 39428
(601) 765-4491

Columbus Light and Water Department
Box 949
Columbus, MS 39701
(601) 328-7192

Durant, City of
106 West Mulberry Street
Durant, MS 39063
(601) 653-3221

Greenwood Utilities Commission
101 Wright Place, Box 866
Greenwood, MS 38930
(601) 453-7234

Holly Springs Electric Department
Highway 4 East, Box 520
Holly Springs, MS 38635
(601) 252-4411

Itta Bena, City of
Box 563
Itta Bena, MS 38941
(601) 254-7231

Kosciusko, City of
Box 486
Kosciusko, MS 39090
(601) 289-1141

Leland, City of
101 Deer Creek Drive
Leland, MS 38756
(601) 686-7623

Louisville Utilities
Box 849
Louisville, MS 39339
(601) 773-7147

Macon Electric Department
105 West Pulaski Street, Box 146
Macon, MS 39341
601) 726-5251

Municipal Energy Agency of Mississippi
600 East Amite Street, Suite 101
Jackson, MS 39201
(601) 353-4763

New Albany Light, Gas and Water Department
100 Cleveland Street, Box 236
New Albany, MS 38652
(406) 534-1041

Okolona, City of
Box 111
Okolona, MS 38860
(601) 447-5482

Oxford Electric Department
107 South Lamar, Box 827
Oxford, MS 38655
(601) 232-2371

Philadelphia Utilities
435 East Myrtle Street, Box 88
Philadelphia, MS 39350
(601) 656-1121

Starkville Electric System
Box 927
Starkville, MS 39759
(601) 323-3272

Tupelo Water and Light Department
Box 588
Tupelo, MS 38802
(601) 842-6460

Water Valley, City of
Box 231
Water Valley, MS 38965
(601) 473-3326

West Point Electric System
331 Washington Street
West Point, MS 39773
(601) 494-2292

Yazoo City Public Serving Commission
125 West Commercial Street, Box 660
Yazoo City, MS 39194
(601) 746-3741

MISSOURI

Albany, City of
106 East Clay Street
Albany, MO 64402
(816) 726-3935

Ava, City of
Box 967
Ava, MO 65608
(417) 683-4122

Bethany, City of
218 West 16th Street, Box 344
Bethany, MO 64424
(816) 425-3511

Butler, City of
101 North Lyons Street
Butler, MO 64730
(816) 679-4182

Cabool, City of
618 Main Street
Cabool, MO 64689
(417) 962-3136

California, City of
Highway 50 West
California, MO 65018
(314) 796-4591

Cameron, City of
205-209 North Main Street
Cameron, MO 64429
(816) 632-2177

Campbell, City of
201 West Grand Street
Campbell, MO 63933
(314) 246-2541

Carrollton Municipal Utilities
707 South Main Street, Box 460
Carrollton, MO 64633
(816) 542-0360

Carthage Water and Electric Plant
149 East Third Street, Drawer 611
Carthage, MO 64836
(417) 358-5904

Centralia, City of
114 South Rollins Street
Centralia, MO 65240
(314) 682-2139

Chillicothe, City of
920 Washington Street, Box 140
Chillicothe, MO 64601
(816) 646-1664

Columbia Water and Light
701 East Broadway, Box N
Columbia, MO 64205
(314) 874-7325

Crane, City of
120 North Commerce Street, Box 17
Crane, MO 65633
(417) 723-5990

Cuba, City of
202 North Smith Street
Cuba, MO 65453
(314) 885-7432

Easton, City of
106 North Woodward, Box 75
Easton, MO 64443
(816) 473-4571

El Dorado Springs, City of
127 West Spring Street
El Dorado Springs, MO 64744
(417) 856-2521

Farmington, City of
110 West Columbia Street
Farmington, MO 63640
(314) 756-2620

Fayette, City of
117 South Main Street
Fayette, MO 65248
(816) 248-2784

Fredericktown City Light and Power
120 West Main Street
Fredericktown, MO 63645
(314) 783-3475

Fulton, City of
Fourth and Market Street
Fulton, MO 65251
(314) 642-6655

Gallatin Municipal Utilities
112 East Grand
Gallatin, MO 64640
(816) 663-3331

Galt, City of
Box 86
Galt, MO 64641
(816) 673-6514

Gilman City, City of
Gilman City, MO 64642
(816) 876-5230

Hannibal, City of
City Hall, 324 Broadway
Hannibal, MO 63401
(314) 221-8050

Harrisonville, City of
300 East Pearl Street, Box 367
Harrisonville, MO 64701
(816) 884-3285

Hermann, City of
207 Schiller Street
Hermann, MO 65041
(314) 486-5400

Higginsville, City of
1922 Main Street
Higginsville, MO 64037
(816) 584-2106

Houston, City of
111 West Main Street
Houston, MO 65483
(417) 967-3187

Hunnewell, City of
108 West Maple, Box 87
Hunnewell, MO 63443
(314) 983-2264

Independence Power and Light
21500 East Truman Road
Independence, MO 64050
(816) 325-7500

Jackson, City of
225 South High Street
Jackson, MO 63755
(314) 243-3536

Kohoka, City of
275 North Washington Street
Kohoka, MO 63445
(816) 727-2512

Kennett, City of
200 Kennett Street
Kennett, MO 63857
(314) 888-2835

Kirkwood, City of
212 South Taylor Avenue
Kirkwood, MO 63122
(314) 822-5842

La Plata, City of
101 South Gex Street
La Plata, MO 63549
(816) 332-7212

Lamar, City of
1104 Broadway Street
Lamar, MO 64759
(417) 682-5554

Lebanon, City of
400 South Madison Street
Lebanon, MO 65536
(417) 532-2156

Liberal, City of
Box 67
Liberal, MO 64762
(417) 843-2135

Linneus, City of
Box 144
Linneus, MO 64653
(816) 895-5583

Lockwood Water and Light Company
107 East Eighth Street, Box O
Lockwood, MO 65682
(417) 232-4221

Macon Municipal Utilities
121-123 West Bourke Street, Box 569
Macon, MO 63552
(816) 385-3173

Malden Board of Public Works
111 East Laclede Street
Malden, MO 63863
(314) 276-2238

Mansfield, City of
City Hall
Jansfield, MO 65704
(417) 924-3719

Marceline Municipal Utilities
116 North Kansas Avenue
Marceline, MO 64658
(816) 376-3528

Marshall Municipal Utilities
75 East Morgan Street
Marshall, MO 65340
(816) 886-6966

Meadville, City of
Box 122
Meadville, MO 64659
(816) 938-4414

Memphis, City of
135 South Main Street
Memphis, MO 63555
(816) 465-2003

Milan, City of
201 North Market Street
Milan, MO 63556
(816) 265-4411

Mindenmines, City of
508 North Main Street, Box 115
Mindenmines, MO 64769
(417) 842-3216

Monett, City of
217 Fifth Street, Box 110
Monett, MO 65708
(417) 235-3300

Monroe City, City of
300 North Main Street, Box 67
Monroe City, MO 63456
(314) 735-4441

Mount Vernon, City of
319 East Dallas, Box 70
Mount Vernon, MO 65712
(417) 466-2122

Mountain View, City of
149 East 2nd Street, Box 115
Mountain View, MO 65548
(417) 934-2601

New Madrid, City of
560 Mott Street, Box 96
New Madrid, MO 63869
(314) 748-2458

Newburg, City of
Second and Main Streets
Newburg, MO 65550
(314) 762-2315

Nixa, City of
Box 395
Nixa, MO 65714
(417) 725-3785

Odessa, City of
Ninth and Dryden Street, Box 128
Odessa, MO 64076
(816) 633-5521

Osceola Municipal Utilities
Second and Walnut Street, Box 321
Osceola, MO 64776
(417) 646-8421

Owensville, City of
109 North Second Street
Owensville, MO 65066
(314) 437-2180

Palmyra, City of
301 South Main Street
Palmyra, MO 63461
(314) 769-3329

Paris, City of
124 West Campbell
Paris, MO 65275
(816) 327-4334

Pattonsburg, City of
Box 206
Pattonsburg, MO 64670
(816) 367-4412

Perry, City of
127 East Main Street, Box 280
Perry, MO 63462
(314) 565-3131

Pleasant Hill Utilities
203 Paul Street
Pleasant Hill, MO 64080
(816) 987-3153

Poplar Bluff, City of
101 Oak Street
Poplar Bluff, MO 63901
(314) 686-8020

Rich Hill, City of
Seventh and Walnut Streets
Rich Hill, MO 64779
(417) 395-4211

Richland, City of
Box 798
Richland, MO 65556
(314) 765-3532

Rock Port, City of
102 West Clay Street
Rock Port, MO 64482
(816) 744-2676

Rolla Municipal Utilities
102 West Ninth Street, Box 767
Rolla, MO 65401
(314) 364-1572

St. James, City of
105 North Bourbeuse Street
St. James, MO 65559
(314) 265-7011

St. Robert, City of
Drawer H
St. Robert, MO 65583
(314) 336-3911

Salem, City of
Third and Grant Streets
Salem, MO 65560
(314) 729-4117

Salisbury, City of
Box 168
Salisbury, MO 65281
(816) 388-6197

Seymour, City of
Box 247
Seymour, MO 65746
(417) 935-4892

Shelbina, City of
127 West Chestnut Street
Shelbina, MO 63468
(314) 588-2150

Sikeston, City of
138 North Prairie
Sikeston, MO 63801
(314) 471-3328

Slater, City of
109 North Main Street
Slater, MO 65349
(816) 529-2271

Springfield, City of
301 East Central Street, Box 551
Springfield, MO 65801
(417) 831-8601

Stanberry, City of
First and Locust Streets
Stanberry, MO 64489
(816) 783-2725

Steelville, City of
103 Brickey, Box M
Steelville, MO 65565
(314) 775-2815

Sullivan, City of
210 West Washington
Sullivan, MO 63080
(314) 468-4612

Thayer, City of
Second and Market Streets, Box 76
Thayer, MO 65791
(417) 264-3291

Trenton Municipal Utilities
115 East Tenth Street
Trenton, MO 64683
(816) 359-2281

Unionville, City of
1611 Grant Street
Unionville, MO 63565
(816) 947-2168

Vandalia, City of
202 East Park Street
Vandalia, MO 63382
(314) 594-3405

Waynesville, City of
201 North Street
Waynesville, MO 65583
(314) 774-6171

West Plains, City of
1910 Holiday Lane
West Plains, MO 65775
(417) 256-7176

Willow Springs, City of
123 East Second Street
Willow Springs, MO 65793
(417) 469-2107

Winona, City of
Box 426
Winona, MO 65588
(314) 325-4443

MONTANA

Troy Power and Light
Box 823
Troy, MT 59935
(406) 295-4540

NEBRASKA

Alliance, City of
324 Laramie Avenue, Box D
Alliance, NE 69301
(308) 762-5400

Ansley, City of
Box 307
Ansley, NE 68814
(308) 935-1400

Arapahoe, City of
Box 235
Arapahoe, NE 68922
(308) 962-7414

Arnold, Village of
209 West First Street, Box 35
Arnold, NE 69120
(308) 848-2228

Auburn Board of Public Works
1600 O Street, Box 288
Auburn, ME 68305
(402) 274-4981

Bartley, Village of
301 West Walnut, Box 205
Bartley, NE 69020
(308) 692-3213

Battle Creek, City of
101 East Main Street
Battle Creek, NE 68715
(402) 675-2165

Bayard, City of
445 Main Street, Box 160
Bayard, NE 69334
(308) 586-1121

Beatrice, City of
205 North Fourth Street, Box 279
Beatrice, NE 68310
(402) 223-5211

Beaver City Light Plant
Box 185
Beaver City, NE 68926
(308) 268-2125

Benkelman, City of
126 Seventh Avenue East, Box 197
Benkelman, NE 69021
(308) 423-2540

Blue Hill, City of
Box 277
Blue Hill, NE 68930
(492) 756-3771

Bradshaw, Village of
430 Lincoln Street
Bradshaw, NE 68319
(402) 736-4634

Brainard, Village of
Box 127
Brainard, NE 68626
(492) 545-2701

Bridgeport, City of
809 Main Street
Bridgeport, NE 69336
(308) 262-0617

Broken Bow, City of
314 South Tenth, Box 567
Broken Bow, NE 68822
(308) 872-6884

Burt County Public Power District
613 North 13th Street, Box 209
Tekamah, NE 68061
(402) 374-2631

Burwell, City of
Box 604
Burwell, NE 68823
(308) 346-4898

Butler County Rural Public Power District
1331 Fourth Street, Box 349
David City, NE 68832
(402) 367-3081

Callaway, Village of
Box 157
Callaway, NE 68825
(308) 836-2262

Cambridge, City of
722 Patterson Street
Cambridge, NE 69022
(308) 697-3713

Campbell, Village of
Box 215
Campbell, NE 68932
(402) 756-8111

Cedar-Knox Public Power District
Box 397
Hartington, NE 68739
(402) 254-6291

Central City, City of
Box 418
Central City, NE 68826
(308) 946-2771

Central Nebraska Public Power
and Irrigation District
415 Lincoln Street, Box 740
Holdrege, NE 68949
(308) 995-8601

Chappell, City of
757 Second Street
Chappell, NE 69129
(308) 874-2401

Chester, Village of
621 Thayer Avenue, Box 335
Chester, NE 68327
(402) 324-5755

Chimney Rock Public Power District
805 West Eighth Street, Box 608
Bayard, NE 69334
(308) 586-1824

Clarkson, City of
Box 18
Clarkson NE 68629
(402) 892-3100

Cornhusker Public Power District
Highway 81 N.W. and 78th Avenue, Box 9
Columbus, NE 68602
(402) 564-2821

Cozad, City of
Box 65
Cozad, NE 69130
(308) 784-3939

Crete, City of
241 East 13th Street, Box 86
Crete, NE 68333
(402) 826-4311

Cuming County Public Power District
500 South Main Street
West Point, NE 68788
(402) 372-2463

Curtis, City of
310 Center Avenue, Box 6
Curtis, NB 69025
(308) 367-4122

Custer Public Power District
625 East South E, Box 10
Broken Bow, NE 68822
(308) 872-2451

Dakota City, City of
Box 482
Dakota City, NE 68731
(492) 987-3448

Davenport, Village of
Second Street, Box 119
Davenport, NE 68335
(402) 364-2296

David City, City of
402 Fifth Street
David City, NE 68632
(402) 367-3135

Dawson County Public Power District
Box 777, 300 South Washington
Lexington, NE 68850
(308) 324-2386

Decatur, Village of
Box 156
Decatur, NE 68020
(402) 349-5360

Deshler, City of
305 Bryson, Box 189
Deshler, NE 68340
(402) 356-4260

De Witt, Village of
Box 208
De Witt, NE 68341
(402) 683-5025

Dorchester, Village of
701 Washington Avenue, Box 287
Dorchester, NE 68343
(402) 946-3201

Edgar Light and Water Department
Box 485
Edgar, NE 68935
(402) 224-5145

Elk Creek, Village of
Box 125
Elk Creek, NE 68348
(402) 874-2430

Elkhorn Rural Public Power District
Box 310
Battle Creek, NE 68715
(402) 675-2185

Emerson, City of
Box 339
Emerson, NE 68733
(402) 695-2554

Endicott, Village of
Endicott, NE 68350
(402) 729-3404

Fairbury, City of
Box 554
Fairbury, NE 67352
(402) 729-3030

Fairmont, Village of
Box 156
Fairmont, NE 68354
(402) 268-2231

Falls City, City of
1820 Towle Street
Falls City, NE 68355
(402) 245-2724

Filley Utilities
Box 85
Filley, NE 68357
(402) 662-3555

Franklin, City of
801 15th Avenue
Franklin, NE 68939
(308) 425-3393

Fremont Department of Utilities
400 East Military, Box 1468
Fremont, NE 68025
(402) 727-2600

Friend, City of
235 Maple Street
Friend, NE 68359
(402) 947-2711

Gering, City of
225 East D Street, Box 687
Gering, NE 69341
(308) 436-5096

Giltner, City of
Box 218
Giltner, NE 68841
(402) 849-2845

Gothenburg, City of
409 Ninth Street
Gothenburg, NE 69138
(308) 532-3668

Grand Island, City of
Box 1968
Grand Island, NE 68802
(308) 381-5487

Grant, City of
346 Central Avenue, Box 614
Grant, NE 69140
(308) 352-2100

Greenwood, Village of
Box 190
Greenwood, NE 68366
(402) 789-2300

Hampton, Village of
Box 277
Hampton, NE 68843
(402) 725-3186

Hastings, City of
1228 North Denver Avenue, Box 289
Hastings, NE 68902
(402) 463-1371

Hebron, City of
216 Lincoln Avenue
Hebron, NE 68370
(402) 768-6322

Hemingford, City of
Box 395
Hemingford, NE 69348
(308) 487-3465

Hickman, City of
115 Locust, Box 127
Hickman, NE 68372
(402) 792-2210

Hildreth, Village of
Box 217
Hildreth, NE 68947
(308) 938-2471

Holbrook Municipal Light Plant
Box 69
Holbrook, NE 68948
(308) 493-5653

Holdrege, City of
502 East Avenue, Box 436
Holdrege, NE 68949
(308) 995-8681

Howard Greeley Rural Public Power District
422 Howard Avenue, Box 105
St. Paul, NE 68873
(308) 754-4457

Hubbell, City of
Box 42
Hubbell, ME 68375
(402) 324-4107

Imperial, City of
South Broadway Street
Imperial, NE 69033
(308) 882-5151

Indianola, City of
Main Street
Indianola, NE 69034
(308) 364-2413

KBR Rural Public Power District
374 North Pine Street, Box 187
Ainsworth, NE 69210
(402) 387-1120

Kimball, City of
223 South Chestnut Street
Kimball, NE 69145
(308) 235-3639

Laurel, City of
101 West Second Street
Laurel, NE 68745
(402) 254-3112

Leigh, Village of
Box 277
Leigh, NE 68643
(402) 487-3303

Lexington, City of
406 East Sixth Street, Box 70
Lexington, NE 68850
(308) 324-2341

Lincoln Electric System
11th and O Streets, Box 80869
Lincoln, NE 68501
(402) 475-4211

Lodgepole, City of
Box 266
Lodgepole, NE 69149
(308) 483-5353

Loup River Public Power District
2404 Fifteen Street
Columbus, NE 68601
(402) 564-3171

Loup Valley Rural Public Power District
312 South 15th Street, Box 166
Ord, NE 68862
(308) 728-3633

Lyman, Village of
414 Jeffers Avenue
Lyman, NE 69352
(308) 787-1444

Madison, City of
210 West Third Street, Box 527
Madison, NE 68748
(402) 454-3412

McCook Public Power District
North US 83 and Q Street, Box 1147
McCook, NE 69001
(308) 345-2500

Minden, City of
325 North Colorado Street
Minden, NE 68959
(308) 832-1820

Mitchell, City of
1444 12th Street
Mitchell, NE 69357
(308) 623-2133

Morrill, Village of
114 South Centre, Box 305
Morrill, NE 69358
(308) 247-2312

Mullen, Village of
Box 187
Mullen, NE 69152
(308) 546-2625

Municipal Energy Agency of Nebraska
521 South 14th Street, Ste. 500, Box 95124
Lincoln, NE 68509
(402) 474-4759

Nebraska City, City of
Central Avenue, Box 670
Nebraska City, NE 68410
(402) 873-3353

Nebraska Public Power District
1414 15th Street, Box 499
Columbus, NE 68601
(402) 564-8561

Neligh Municipal Power
202 M Street, Box 87
Neligh, NE 68756
(402) 887-5042

Nelson, City of
60 East Fourth Street
Nelson, NE 68961
(402) 225-4401

Norris Public Power District
606 Irving Street, Box 399
Beatrice, NE 68310
(402) 223-4038

North Central Public Power District
Box 7
Creighton, NE 68729
(402) 358-5112

North Platte, City of
Third and Vine Streets
North Platte, NE 69101
(308) 532-5320

Northeast Nebraska Rural Public
Power District
511 Main Street, Box 39
Emerson, NE 68733
(402) 695-2642

Northwest Rural Public Power
District
South Highway 87, Box 249
Hay Springs, NE 69347
(308) 638-4445

Omaha Public Power District
444 South 16th Street Mall
Omaha, NE 68102
(402) 636-2000 100

Ord, City of
Box 96
Ord, NE 68862
(308) 728-5937

Oxford, Village of
Box 385
Oxford, NE 68967
(308) 824-3511

Panama, Village of
Box 117
Panama, NE 68419
(402) 788-2733

Pender, City of
Box S Pender,
NE 68047
(402) 385-3121

Pierce, City of
114 South Brown Street
Pierce, NE 68767
(402) 329-4535

Plainview Municipal Utilities
Box 757
Plainview, NE 68769
(402) 582-4928

Polk, Village of
Box 6
Polk, NE 68854
(402) 675-6471

Polk County Rural Public
Power District
120 West Fourth Street
Stromsburg, NE 68666
(402) 764-4381

Prague, Village of
Prague, NE 68050
(402) 663-5235

Randolph, City of
Box 220
Randolph, NE 68771
(402) 337-0553

Red Cloud, City of
540 North Webster Street
Red Cloud, NE 68970
(402) 746-2214

Reynolds, Village of
Main Street, Box 98
Reynolds, NE 68429
(402) 324-3174

Roosevelt Public Power District
1633 13th Street, Box 97
Mitchell, NE 69357
(308) 623-2124

St. Paul, City of
522 Howard Avenue
St. Paul, NE 68873
(308) 754-4483

Sargent, City of
Box 40
Sargent, NE 68874
(308) 527-4200

Schuyler, City of
124 East 11th Street, Box 526
Schuyler, NE 68861
(402) 352-5445

Scribner, City of
Box D
Scribner, NE 68057
(402) 664-3231

Seward, City of
537 Main Street
Seward, NE 68434
(402) 643-2927

Seward County Rural Public
Power District
South Highway 15
Seward, NE 68434
(402) 643-2951

Shickley, Village of
Box 25
Shickley, NE 68436
(402) 627-2055

Sidney, City of
1115 13th Avenue
Sidney, NE 69162
(308) 254-5300

Snyder, City of
125 Ash, Box 247
Snyder, NE 68664
(402) 568-2306

South Central Public
Power District
275 South Main Street
Nelson, NE 68961
(402) 225-2351

South Sioux City, City of
1615 First Avenue
South Sioux City, NE 68776
(402) 494-7520

Southern Nebraska Rural Public
Power District
Box 1687
Grand Island, NE 68802
(308) 384-2350

Southwest Public Power District
221 North Main Street, Box J
Palisade, NE 69040
(308) 285-3295

Spalding, Village of
Box 268
Spalding, NE 68665
(308) 497-2416

Spencer, Village of
Box 15
Spencer, NE 68777
(402) 589-1130

Stanton County Public Power District
807 Douglas Street, Box 319
Stanton, NE 68779
(402) 439-2228

Stratton, City of
Box 116
Stratton, NE 69045
(308) 276-2184

Stromsburg, City of
122 East Third Street
Stromsburg, NE 68666
(402) 764-2561

Stuart, City of
109 West First Street
Stuart, NE 68780
(402) 924-3647

Superior, City of
135 West Fourth Street, Box 160
Superior, NE 68978
(402) 879-4711

Sutton Light and Power
Box 437
Sutton, NE 68979
(402) 773-5501

Syracuse, City of
578 Mohawk Street
Syracuse, NE 68446
(402) 269-2173

Talmage Electric Department
Box 198
Talmage, NE 68448
(402) 264-3825

Tecumseh, City of
112 South Fourth Street
Tecumseh, NE 68450
(402) 335-3025

Thurston, Village of
Box 215
Thurston, NE 68062
(402) 385-2603

Trenton, Village of
Box 68
Trenton, NE 69044
(308) 285-3295

Twin Valleys Public Power District
West Highway 6 and 34, Box 160
Cambridge, NE 69022
(308) 697-3315

University of Nebraska
1700 Y Street
Lincoln, NE 68588
(402) 472-3131

Valentine, City of
323 North Main Street, Box 177
Valentine, NE 69201
(402) 376-2323

Wahoo, City of
605 North Broadway
Wahoo, NE 68066
(402) 443-3222

Wakefield, City of
405 Main Street
Wakefield, NE 68784
(402) 287-2547

Walthill, Village of
224 Main Street, Box 246
Walthill, NE 68067
(402) 846-5921

Wauneta, Village of
45 East Wichita
Wauneta, NE 69045
(308) 394-5390

Wayne Municipal Utilities
208 South Main Street
Wayne, NE 68787
(402) 375-2866

Wayne County Public Power District
303 Logan Street
Wayne, NE 68787
(402) 375-1360

West Point, City of
444 South Main Street
West Point, NE 68788
(402) 372-2468

Weston, Village of
Box 149
Weston, NE 68070
(402) 642-5496

Wheat Belt Public Power District
2104 Illinois Street
Sidney, NE 69162
(308) 254-5871

Wilber, City of
101 West Third Street, Box 486
Wilber, NE 68465
(402) 821-3233

Wilcox, Village of
Box 88
Wilcox, NE 68982
(308) 478-5510

Winside, Village of
Box 206
Winside, NE 68790
(402) 286-4422

Wisner, City of
1115 Avenue E., Box 367
Wisner, NE 68791
(402) 529-6616

Wood River, City of
Box 8
Wood River, NE 68883
(308) 583-2757

Wymore, City of
115 West East Street
Wymore, NE 68466
(402) 645-3377

York County Rural Public
Power District
2122 South Lincoln Avenue, Box 219
York, NE 68467
(402) 645-3377

NEVADA

Alamo Power District No. 3
233 North Main, Box 189
Alamo, NV 89001
(702) 725-3335

Boulder City, City of
401 California Avenue, Box 61350
Boulder City, NV 89006
(702) 293-9200

Caliente, City of
100 Deport Avenue
Caliente, NV 89008
(702) 726-3132

Colorado River Commission of Nevada
1515 East Tropicana, Suite 400
Las Vegas, NV 89119
(702) 486-7060

Fallon, City of
55 West Williams Avenue
Fallon, NV 89406
(702) 423-5107

Lincoln County Power District No. 1
SR 89063, Box 101
Pioche, NV 89043
(702) 962-5122

Overton Power District No. 5
Box 395
Overton, NV 89040
(702) 397-2512

Pioche, City of
ox 35
Pioche, NV 89043
(702) 962-5840

NEW HAMPSHIRE

Ashland Electric Department
2 Collins Street, 385 RR1
Ashland, NH 03217
(603) 968-3083

Littleton, Town of
30 Lafayette Avenue
Littleton, NH 03561
(603) 444-2915

New Hampton Village Precinct
New Hampton, NH 03256
(603) 351-3517

Wolfeboro, Town of
South Main Street, Box 777
Wolfeboro, NH 03894
(603) 569-3900

Woodsville, City of
RR2, Box 66A
Woodsville, NH 03785
(603) 747-2442

NEW JERSEY

Borough of Butler
1 Ace Road
Butler, NJ 07405
(201) 838-7200

LaVallette Electric Department
Washington Avenue
LaVallette, NJ 08735
(201) 793-7477

Madison, Borough of
Hartley Dodge Memorial Building,
Kings Road
Madison, NJ 07940
(201) 593-3043

Milltown, Borough of B
39 Washington Avenue
Milltown, NJ 08850
(201) 828-2100

Park Ridge Electric Department
53 Park Avenue
Park Ridge, NJ 07656
(201) 391-2129

Pemberton, Borough of
50 Egbert Street, Box 261
Pemberton, NJ 08068
(609) 894-8222

Seaside Heights, Borough of
328 Grant Avenue
Seaside Heights, NJ 08751
(908) 793-0359

South River, Borough of
33 Gordon Street
South River, NJ 08882
(908) 257-9051

Vineland, City of
640 East wood Street, City Hall
Vineland, NJ 08360
(609) 794-4166

NEW MEXICO

Aztec, City of
201 West Chaco Street
Aztec, NM 87410
(505) 334-9456

Farmington, City of
800 Municipal Drive
Farmington, NM 87401
(505) 599-1165

Gallup, City of
Box 1270
Gallup, NM 87305
(505) 863-1288

Los Alamos, County of
901 Trinity Drive, Box 1057
Los Alamos, NM 87544
(505) 662-8130

Raton Public Service Company
334 North Second Street
Raton, NM 87740
(505) 445-9861

Springer, Town of
612 Colbert Avenue, Box 488
Springer, NM 87747
(505) 483-2682

Truth or Consequences, City of
505 Sims Street
Truth or Consequences, NM 87901
(505) 894-6671

NEW YORK

Akron, Village of
21 Main Street, Box 180
Akron, NY 14001
(716) 542-9636

Andover, Village of
South Main Street, Box 721
Andover, NY 14806
(607) 478-8455

Angelica, Village of
White Street
Angelica, NY 14709
(716) 466-7431

Arcade, Village of
17 Church Street
Arcade, NY 14009
(716) 492-1111

Bath Electric, Gas and Water Systems
Drawer 310
Bath, NY 14810
(607) 776-3072

Bergen, Village of
11 Buffalo Street
Bergen, NY 14416
(716) 494-1513

Boonville Electric and Water Departments
RR 3, Box 2
Boonville, NY 13309
(315) 942-4461

Brocton, City of
34 West Main Street
Brocton, NY 14716
(716) 792-4160

Castile, Village of
120 North Main Street
Castile, NY 14427
(716) 493-2340

Churchville, Village of
22 South Main Street, Box M
Churchville, NY 14428
(716) 293-3720

Endicott, Village of
1009 East Main Street
Endicott, NY 13760
(607) 757-2450 4

Fairport, Village of
31 South Main Street, Box 500
Fairport, NY 14450
(716) 223-0440

Frankfort Power and Light
126 East Orchard Street, Box 94
Frankfort, NY 13340
(315) 894-8611

Freeport Light and Power
220 West Sunrise Highway
Freeport, NY 11520
(516) 378-4000

Gouverneur, City of
Gouverneur, NY 13642
(315) 287-1100

Green Island, City of
20 Clinton Street
Green Island, NY 12183
(518) 273-2201

Greene, Village of
49 Genesee Street
Greene, NY 13778
(607) 656-8311

Greenport Municipal Utilities
236 3rd Street
Greenport, NY 11944
(516) 477-1748

Groton, Village of
108 Cortland Street
Groton, NY 13073
(607) 898-3001

Hamilton, Village of
3 Broad Street, Box 119
Hamilton, NY 13346
(315) 824-1111

Holley, Village of
72 Public Square
Holley, NY 14470
(716) 638-6587

Ilion, Village of
49 Morgan Street
Ilion, NY 13357
(315) 895-7749

Jamestown Board of Public Utilities
92 Steele Street, Box 700
Jamestown, NY 14702
(716) 661-1670

Lake Placid Village, Inc.
301 Main Street
Lake Placid, NY 12946
(518) 523-2021

Little Valley, Village of
Municipal Building
Little Valley, NY 14755
(716) 938-9151

Marathon, Village of
Box 519
Marathon, NY 13803
(607) 849-6795

Massena Electric Department
71 East Hatfield Street, Box 209
Massena, NY 13662
(315) 764-0253

Mayville, Village of
Box 188
Mayville, NY 14757
(716) 753-2125

Mohawk Municipal Commission
28 Columbia Street
Mohawk, NY 13407
(315) 866-4170

New York Power Authority
123 Main Street
White Plains, NY 10601
(914) 287-3084

Penn Yan, Village of
5 Maiden Lane
Penn Yan, NY 14527
(315) 536-3374

Philadelphia, Village of
Box 70
Philadelphia, NY 13673
(315) 642-3452

Plattsburgh, City of
6 Miller Street
Plattsburgh, NY 12901
(518) 563-2200

Richmondville, Village of
22 East Main Street
Richmondville, NY 12149
(518) 294-7700

Rockville Centre, Village of
Box 950
Rockville Centre, NY 11571
(516) 678-9211

Rouses Point, Village of
139 Lake Street
Rouses Point, NY 12979
(518) 297-5502

Salamanca Board of Public Utilities
225 Wildwood Avenue
Salamanca, NY 14779
(716) 945-3130

Sherburne, Village of
15 West State Street
Sherburne, NY 13460
(607) 674-2300

Sherrill, City of
601 Sherrill Road
Sherrill, NY 13461
(315) 363-6479

Silver Springs, Village of
43 North Main Street
Silver Springs, NY 14550
(716) 493-2500

Skaneateles, Village of
46 East Genesee Street
Skaneateles, NY 13152
(315) 685-5628

Solvay, Village of
507 Charles Avenue
Solvay, NY 13209
(315) 468-6229

Spencerport, Village of
27 West Avenue
Spencerport, NY 14559
(716) 352-4771

Springville, Village of
5 West Main Street
Springville, NY 14141
(716) 592-2310

Theresa Municipal Electric
124 Commercial Street, Box 299
Theresa, NY 13691
(315) 628-4425

Tupper Lake Municipal Electric System
(919) 894-3553
Tupper Lake, NY 12986 (518) 359-3341

Watertown, City of
245 Washington Street, Room 305
Watertown, NY 13601
(315) 785-7740

Watkins Glen Electric Department
303 North Franklin Street
Watkins Glen, NY 14891
(607) 535-2736

Wellsville Electric Department
Box 591
Wellsville, NY 14895
(716) 593-1850

Westfield, Village of
23 Elm Street
Westfield, NY 14787
(716) 326-2145

NORTH CAROLINA

Albemarle, City of
Box 190
Albemarle, NC 28001
(704) 982-0131

Apex, Town of
205 Saunders Street, Box 250
Apex, NC 27502
(919) 362-8166

Ayden, Town of
Box 219
Ayden, NC 28513
(919) 746-7044

Belhaven, Town of
Box 220
Belhaven, NC 27810
(919) 943-3055

Benson, Town of
303 East Church Street, Box 69
Benson, NC 27504 53 Park Street

Black Creek, Town of
Box 8
Black Creek, NY 27813
(919) 243-6439

Bostic, Town of
Main Street, Box 158
Bostic, NC 28018
(704) 245-2187

Cherryville, City of
116 South Mountain Street
Cherryville, NC 28021
(704) 435-4181

Clayton, Town of
231 East Second Street, Box 879
Clayton, NC 27520
(919) 553-5866

Concord, City of
66 Union Street, South, Box 567
Concord, NC 28025
(704) 786-6161

Cornelius, Town of
Box 399
Cornelius, NC 28031
(704) 892-6031

Dallas, Town of
131 North Gaston Street
Dallas, NC 28034
(704) 922-3176

Drexel, Town of
Box 188
Drexel, NC 28619
(704) 437-7421

Edenton, Town of
Box 300
Edenton, NC 27932
(919) 482-4144

Elizabeth City, City of
200 East Colonial Avenue
Elizabeth City, NC 27909
(919) 338-3981

Enfield, Town of
Box 695
Enfield, NC 27823
(919) 445-3146

Farmville, Town of
200 North Main Street
Farmville, NC 27828
(919) 753-3021

Fayetteville Public Works Commission
508 Person Street, Box 1089
Fayetteville, NC 28302
(919) 483-1401

Forest City, Town of
12 North Powell Street, Box 728
Forest City, NC 28043
(704) 245-4747

Fountain, Town of
Box 134
Fountain, NC 27829
(919) 749-3881

Fremont, Town of
Box 818
Fremont, NC 27830
(919) 242-5151

Gastonia, City of
Box 1748
Gastonia, NC 28053
(704) 866-6825

Granite Falls, Town of
30 Park Square
Granite Falls, NC 28630
(704) 396-3131

Greenville Utilities Commission
200 West Fifth Street, Box 1847
Greenville, NC 27835
(919) 752-7166

Hamilton, Town of
Box 249
Hamilton, NC 27840
(919) 798-2001

Hertford, Town of
Box 32
Hertford, NC 27944
(919) 426-5311

High Point, City of
211 South Hamilton Street
High Point, NC 27261
(919) 883-3172

Highlands
Box 460
Highlands, NC 28741
(704) 526-2118

Hobgood, Town of
Box 217
Hobgood, NC 27843
(919) 826-4573

Hookerton, Town of
227 East Main Street, Box 296
Hookerton, NC 28538
(919) 747-3816

Huntersville, Town of
Box 664
Huntersville, NC 28078
(704) 875-6541

Kings Mountain, City of
103 West Gold Street, Box 429
Kings Mountain, NC 28086
(704) 734-0333

Kinston, City of
207 East King Street, Box 339
Kinston, NC 28502
(919) 559-4253

La Grange, Town of
120 East Railroad Street
La Grange, NC 28551
(919) 566-3186

Lake Lure, City of
Box 255
Lake Lure, NC 28746
(704) 625-9396

Landis, Town of
136 North Central Avenue
Landis, NC 28088
(704) 857-2411

Laurinburg, City of
303 West Church Street, Box 249
Laurinburg, NC 28352
(919) 276-8324

Lexington, City of
28 West Center Street
Lexington, NC 27292
(704) 243-2489

Lincolnton, City of
114 West Sycamore Street
Lincolnton, NC 28092
(704) 732-2281

Louisburg, Town of
110 West Nash Street
Louisburg, NC 27549
(919) 496-3406

Lucama, Town of
111 Main Street
Lucama, NC 27851
(919) 239-0560

Macclesfield, Town of
Box 185
Macclesfield, NC 27852
(919) 827-4823

Maiden, Town of
113 West Main Street, Box 125
Maiden, NC 28650
(704) 428-5020

Monroe, City of
300 West Crowell Street, Box 69
Monroe, NC 28111
(704) 282-4501

Morganton, City of
201 West Meeting Street
Morganton, NC 28655
(704) 438-5284

Murphy, City of
301 Peachtree Street, Box 130
Murphy, NC 28906
(704) 837-2211

New Bern, City of
Box 1129
New Bern, NC 28560
(919) 636-4051

New River Light and Power Company
Winkler's Creek Road, Box 1130
Boone, NC 28607
(704) 264-3671

Newton, City of
401 North Main Avenue, Box 550
Newton, NC 28658
(704) 465-7400

North Carolina Municipal
Power Agency No.1
1427 Meadowwood Blvd., Box 29513
Raleigh, NC 27626

(919) 832-9924
North Carolina Eastern Municipal
Power Agency
1427 Meadowwood Blvd., Box 29513
Raleigh, NC 27626
(919) 832-9924

Oak City, Town of
Box 298
Oak City, NC 27857
(919) 798-7721

Pikeville, Town of
Box 9
Pikeville, NC 27863
(919) 243-5126

Pinetops, Town of
Drawer C
Pinetops, NC 27864
(919) 827-4435

Pineville Electric Company
118 College Street, Box 249
Pineville, NC 28134
(704) 889-2291

Red Springs, Town of
217 South Main Street
Red Springs, NC 28377
(919) 843-5241

Robersonville, City of
Box 487
Robersonville, NC 27871
(919) 795-3511

Rocky Mount, City of
1 Government Plaza, Box 1180
Rocky Mount, NC 27802
(919) 972-1325

Scotland Neck, Town of
1310 Main Street, Box 537
Scotland Neck, NC 27874
(919) 826-3152

Selma, Town of
100 North Raiford Street
Selma, NC 27576
(919) 967-9841

Sharpsburg, Town of
Box 1759
Sharpsburg, NC 27878
(919) 446-9441

Shelby, City of
City Hall, Box 207
Shelby, NC 28150
(704) 484-6866

Smithfield, City of
116 South Fourth Street, Box 761
Smithfield, NC 27577
(919) 934-2116

Southport, City of
201 East Moore Street
Southport, NC 28461
(919) 457-6911

Stantonsburg, Town of
108 East Commercial Avenue, Box 10
Stantonsburg, NC 27883
(919) 238-3608

Statesville, City of
915 Winston Avenue, Box 1111
Statesville, NC 28687
(704) 878-3419

Tarboro, Town of
500 Main Street, Box 220
Tarboro, NC 27886
(919) 641-4252

Wake Forest, Town of
401 East Elm Street
Wake Forest, NC 27587
(919) 556-2024

Walstonburg, Town of
East Railroad Street, Box 126
Walstonburg, NC 27888
(919) 753-5667

Washington, City of
East Second Street
Washington, NC 27889
(919) 946-1033

Waynesville, City of
106 South Main Street
Waynesville, NC 28786
(704) 456-3515

Wilson, City of
Herring Avenue, Box 10
Wilson, NC 27893
(919) 399-2424

Windsor, Town of
Box 508
Windsor, NC 27983
(919) 794-2331

Winterville, Town of
Box 1267
Winterville, NC 28590
(919) 756-2221

NORTH DAKOTA

Cavalier, City of
Box B
Cavalier, ND 58220
(701) 265-8668

Grafton, City of
5 East Fourth Street, Box 578
Grafton, ND 58237
(701) 352-2180

Hillsboro, City of
204 Second Avenue, N.W.
Hillsboro, ND 58045
(701) 436-4620

Hope Municipal Utilities
1 Main Street, Box 189
Hope, ND 58046
(701) 945-2772 102

Lakota, City of
Box 505
Lakota, ND 58344
(701) 247-2454

Maddock, City of
Second Street and Dakota Avenue
Maddock, ND 58348
(701) 438-2252 1800

Northwood, City of
Box 397
Northwood, ND 58267
(701) 587-6291

Park River, City of
Box C
Park River, ND 58270
(701) 284-6399

Riverdale, City of
Box 507
Riverdale, ND 58565
(701) 654-7636

Sharon Light and Power Department
Sharon, ND 58277
(701) 524-2377

Stanton, City of
109 Harmon Avenue
Stanton, ND 58571
(701) 745-3395

Valley City Public Works Department
254 Second Avenue, N.E.
Valley City, ND 58072
(701) 845-5149

OHIO

Amherst, City of
647 Park Avenue
Amherst, OH 44001
(216) 984-2146

American Municipal Power-Ohio
601 Dempsey Road, Box 549
Westerville, OH 43081
(614) 890-2805

Arcadia, Village of
104 Gibson Street
Arcadia, OH 44804
(419) 894-6009

Arcanum, City of
104 West South Street
Arcanum, OH 45304
(513) 692-8565

Beach City, City of
301 North Church Avenue
Beach City, OH 44608
(216) 756-2682

Bethel, Village of
120 North Main Street
Bethel, OH 45106
(513) 734-2243

Blanchester Board of Public Affairs
Box 158
Blanchester, OH 45107
(513) 783-2141

Bloomdale, Village of
Box 218
Bloomdale, OH 44817
(419) 454-2941

Bowling Green, City of
Box 218
Bowling Green, OH 43402
(419) 354-6246

Bradner, Village of
Box 599
Bradner, OH 43406
(419) 288-2773

Brewster, City of
910 South Wabash Avenue, Box 86
Brewster, OH 44613
(216) 767-3312

Bryan, City of
841 East Edgerton Street, Box 30
Bryan, OH 43506
(419) 636-4232

Carey, Village of
127 North Vance Street
Carey, OH 43316
(419) 396-7681

Celina, City of
426 West Market Street, Box 297
Celina, OH 45822
(419) 586-6464

Cleveland Public Power
1201 Lakeside Avenue
Cleveland, OH 44114
(216) 664-3922

Clyde Light and Power
222 North Main Street
Clyde, OH 43410
(419) 547-7742

Columbiana, Village of
28 West Friend Street
Columbiana, OH 44408
(216) 482-2173

Custar, City of
9063 High Street
Custar, OH 43511
(419) 669-3537

Cuyahoga Falls, City of
2550 Bailey Road
Cuyahoga Falls, OH 44221
(216) 971-8060

Cygnet, Village of
Box 406
Cygnet, OH 43413
(419) 655-2536

Deshler Municipal Utilities
101 East Main Street
Deshler, OH 43516
(419) 278-1831

Dover, City of
303 East Broadway
Dover, OH 44622
(216) 343-7725

Edgerton, Village of
Box 609
Edgerton, OH 43517
(419) 298-2912

Eldorado, City of
200 North Main Street
Eldorado, OH 45321
(513) 273-3141

Elmore, Village of
340 Clinton Street
Elmore, OH 43416
(419) 862-3454

Galion, City of
700 Primrose Street
Galion, OH 44833
(419) 468-5520

Genoa, Village of
509 Main Street
Genoa, OH 43430
(419) 855-8419

Georgetown, Village of
301 South Main Street
Georgetown, OH 45121
(513) 378-6395

Glouster, Village of
16 Front Street
Glouster, OH 45732
(614) 767-3497

Grafton, Village of
1009 Chestnut Street
Grafton, OH 44044
(216) 926-2401

Greenwich, Village of
47 Main Street
Greenwich, OH 44837
(419) 752-2441

Hamersville, Village of
202 Main Street, Box 146
Hamersville, OH 45130
(513) 379-1745

Hamilton Department of Public Utilities
20 High Street
Hamilton, OH 45011
(513) 868-5908

Haskins, Village of
100 North Church Street, Box 236
Haskins, OH 43525
(419) 823-1911

Hubbard, City of
820 North Main
Hubbard, OH 44425
(216) 534-3054

Hudson Electric Department
27 East Main Street
Hudson, OH 44236
(216) 650-1052

Jackson, City of
Box 664
Jackson, OH 45640
(614) 286-4415

Jackson Center, Village of
Box V, 122 East Pike Street
Jackson Center, OH 45334
(513) 596-5440

Lakeview, Village of
126 North Main Street
Lakeview, OH 43331
(513) 843-2851

Lebanon, City of
50 South Broadway
Lebanon, OH 45036
(513) 932-3060

Lodi Board of Public Affairs
Box 95
Lodi, OH 44254
(216) 948-1099

Lucas, City of
101 First Avenue, Box 213
Lucas, OH 44843
(419) 892-2178

Marshallville, City of
Box 227
Marshallville, OH 44645
(216) 855-5985

Mendon, City of
East Market Street, Box 167
Mendon, OH 45862
(419) 795-7131

Milan, Village of
9 East Church Street, Box 1450
Milan, OH 44846
(419) 499-2133

Minster, Village of
Box 1
Minster, OH 45865
(419) 628-2850

Monroeville, Village of
2 South Main Street
Monroeville, OH 44847
(419) 465-4149

Montpelier, City of
211 North Jonesville Street
Montpelier, OH 43543
(419) 485-8316

Napoleon, City of
255 Riverview Avenue, Box 151
Napoleon, OH 43545
(419) 592-4010

New Bremen, Village of
214 North Washington Street, Box 27
New Bremen, OH 45869
(419) 629-2827

New Knoxville Light Department
Box 246
New Knoxville, OH 45871
(419) 753-2160

Newton Falls, City of
19 North Canal Street
Newton Falls, OH 44444
(216) 872-5990

Niles, City of
34 West State Street
Niles, OH 44446
(216) 652-2622

Oak Harbor Utilities
146 Church Street, Box 232
Oak Harbor, OH 43449
(419) 898-3231

Oberlin, City of
289 South Professor Street
Oberlin, OH 44074
(216) 775-1531

Ohio City, Village of
Box 248
Ohio City, OH 45874
(419) 965-2255

Orrville, City of
207 North Main Street, Box 126
Orrville, OH 44667
(216) 684-5012

Painesville, City of
325 Richmond Street
Painesville, OH 44077
(216) 352-9301

Pemberville, Village of
115 Main Street, Box 109
Pemberville, OH 43450
(419) 287-3832

Pioneer, Village of
205 South State Street, Box 335
Pioneer, OH 43554
(419) 737-2614

Piqua Municipal Power System
123 Bridge Street
Piqua, OH 45356
(513) 778-2077

Plymouth, Village of
49 Sandusky Street
Plymouth, OH 44865
(419) 687-4331

Prospect Corporation
139 North Main Street, Box 186
Prospect, OH 43342
(614) 494-2115

Republic Board of Public Affairs
219 Washington Street, Box 68
Republic, OH 44867
(419) 585-5981

Ripley, City of
14 North Third Street
Ripley, OH 45167
(513) 392-4377

St. Clairsville, City of
100 Market Street
St. Clairsville, OH 43950
(614) 695-1410

St. Marys, City of
101 East Spring Street
St. Marys, OH 45885
(419) 394-3303

Seville Board of Public Affairs
44 West Main Street, Box 46
Seville, OH 44273
(216) 769-2458

Shelby Municipal Light Plant
34 Mansfield Avenue
Shelby, OH 44875
(419) 342-2231

Shiloh, Village of
12 West Main Street
Shiloh, OH 44878
(419) 896-2011

South Vienna Corporation
16 North Urbana
South Vienna, OH 45369
(513) 568-4311

Sycamore, City of
210 South Sycamore Avenue, Box 297
Sycamore, OH 44882
(419) 927-4262

Tipp City, City of
260 South Garber Drive
Tipp City, OH 45371
(513) 667-6305

Tontogany, Village of
Tontogany, OH 43565
(419) 823-4465

Versailles Utilities
177 North Center Street
Versailles, OH 45380
(513) 526-4191

Wadsworth, City of
145 High Street
Wadsworth, OH 45895
(216) 335-1521

Wapakoneta, City of
102 Perry Street
Wapakoneta, OH 45895
(419) 738-7713

Waynesfield, Village of
104 West Perry Street
Waynesfield, OH 45896
(419) 568-1311

Wellington, Village of
115 Public Square
Wellington, OH 44090
(216) 647-3827

Westerville Electric Division
139 East Broadway
Westerville, OH 43081
(614) 890-8540

Wharton, Village of
117 West Sandusky Street, Box 266
Wharton, OH 43359
(419) 458-3431

Woodsfield Board of Public Affairs
203 Roy Street
Woodsfield, OH 43793
(614) 472-0884

Woodville, Village of
219 West Main Street
Woodville, OH 43469
(419) 849-3031

Yellow Springs, Village of
314 Dayton Street
Yellow Springs, OH 45387
(513) 767-7202

OKLAHOMA

Altus Municipal Authority
220 East Commerce
Altus, OK 73521
(405) 477-1950

Anadarko Public Works Authority
Box 647
Anadarko, OK 73005
(405) 247-2481

Blackwell, City of
221 West Blackwell Street, Box 350
Blackwell, OK 74631
(405) 363-5490

Braman, Town of
308 Broadway
Braman, OK 74632
(405) 385-2169

Burlington, City of
Box 216
Burlington, OK 73722
(405) 431-2550

Byng Public Works Authority
Box 331-D
Byng, OK 74820
(405) 436-2545

Claremore, City of
104 South Muskogee, Box 249
Claremore, OK 74018
(913) 341-2895

Collinsville, City of
Box A
Collinsville, OK 74021
(918) 371-2811

Comanche, City of
115 North Second Street
Comanche, OK 73529
(405) 439-8832

Copan, City of
Box 219
Copan, OK 74022
(918) 352-4114

Cordell, City of
101 East Main Street, Box 417
Cordell, OK 73632
(405) 832-3825

Cushing, City of
Box 311, 100 Judy Adams Blvd.
Cushing, OK 74023
(918) 225-2394

Duncan, City of
Eighth and Willow Streets, Box 969
Duncan, OK 73533
(405) 252-0250

Edmond Electric
Box 2970
Edmond, OK 73083
(405) 348-8830

Eldorado, City of
Box 190
Eldorado, OK 75537
(405) 633-2245

Fairview, City of
206 East Broadway, Box 386
Fairview, OK 73737
(405) 227-4416

Fort Supply, Town of
Box 156
Fort Supply, OK 73841
(405) 766-3211

Frederick Public Works Authority
Box 399
Frederick, OK 73542
(405) 335-7551

Geary, City of
515 North Broadway
Geary, OK 73040
(405) 884-5466

Goltry Public Works Authority
Main Street, Box 236
Goltry, OK 73739
(405) 496-2441

Grand River Dam Authority
707 South Wilson Street, Box 409
Vinita, OK 74301
(918) 256-5545

Granite, City of
420 North Main Street, Box 116
Granite, OK 73547
(405) 535-2116

Hominy Public Works Authority
202 West Main Street, Box 219
Hominy, OK 74035
(918) 885-2164

Kaw City, City of
900 Morgan Square, E., Box 26
Kaw City, OK 74641
(405) 269-2525

Kingfisher Public Works Authority
301 North Main Street
Kingfisher, OK 73750
(405) 375-3705

Laverne, Town of
115 North Ohio Street, Box 430
Laverne, OK 73848
(405) 921-3312

Lexington, City of
Box 1180
Lexington, OK 73051
(405) 527-6123

Lindsay, City of
Box 708
Lindsay, OK 73052
(405) 756-2019

Mangum, City of
201 North Oklahoma Street
Mangum, OK 73554
(405) 782-2256

Manitou Light Department
Box 8
Manitou, OK 73555
(405) 397-2241

Mannford, Town of
Box 327
Mannford, OK 74044
(918) 865-4314

Marlow, City of
115 North Second Street, Box 113
Marlow, OK 73055
(405) 658-5401

Miami, City of
129 Fifth Avenue, N.W., Box 1288
Miami, OK 74355
(918) 542-6685

Mooreland, City of
Box 157
Mooreland, OK 73852
(405) 994-5924

Newkirk, City of
106 West Seventh, Box 469
Newkirk, OK 74647
(405) 362-2117

Okeene Light and Water Department
213 North Main Street, Box 800
Okeene, OK 73763
(405) 822-3031

Oklahoma Municipal Power Authority
2300 East 2nd Street, Box 1960
Edmond, OK 73083
(405) 340-5047

Olustee, Town of
Box 330
Olustee, OK 73560
(405) 648-2288

Orlando, Town of
Box 27
Orlando, OK 73073
(405) 455-2523

Pawhuska, City of
Box 539
Pawhuska, OK 74056
(918) 287-3260

Pawnee, City of
513 Illinois Street
Pawnee, OK 74058
(918) 762-2658

Perry, City of
624 Delaware, Drawer 798
Perry, OK 73077
(405) 336-4241

Ponca City Utility Authority
Box 1450
Ponca City, OK 74602
(405) 767-0405

Pond Creek Water and Light Department
Box 45
Pond Creek, OK 73766
(405) 532-6327

Prague Public Works Authority
116 North Broadway
Prague, OK 74864
(405) 576-2279

Pryor, City of
6 North Adair, Box 249
Pryor, OK 74362
(918) 825-2100

Purcell, City of
230 West Main Street
Purcell, OK 73080
(405) 527-6561

Ryan, Town of
Box 489
Ryan, OK 73565
(405) 757-2277

Sallisaw, City of
111 North Elm Street, Box C
Sallisaw, OK 74955
(918) 775-6241

Skiatook, Town of
111 North Broadway
Skiatook, OK 74070
(918) 396-2797

South Coffeyville, City of
207 West Broadway Street, Box 100
South Coffeyville, OK 74072
(918) 255-6045

Spiro, Town of
131 South Main Street
Spiro, OK 74959
(918) 962-2477

Stillwater Utilities Authority
Box 1449
Stillwater, OK 74076
(405) 372-0025

Stilwell Utility Department
9 West Maple Street
Stilwell, OK 74960
(918) 696-3400

Stroud, City of
Drawer K
Stroud, OK 74079
(918) 968-2571

Tahlequah Public Works Authority
101 North College Avenue, Box 29
Tahlequah, OK 74464
(918) 456-2564

Tecumseh Utility Authority
114 North Broadway
Tecumseh, OK 74873
(405) 498-2189

Tonkawa, City of
117 South Seventh Street
Tonkawa, OK 74653
(405) 628-2508

Wagoner Public Work Authority
231 Church Street
Wagoner, OK 74467
(918) 485-0554

Walters, City of
129 East Colorado Street
Walters, OK 73572
(405) 875-3337

Watonga, City of
Wiegel Street, Box 280
Watonga, OK 73772
(405) 623-7354

Waynoka, City of
201 East Cecil Street
Waynoka, OK 73860
(405) 824-2261

Wetumka Municipal Authority
202 North Main Street
Wetumka, OK 74883
(405) 452-3253

Wynnewood City Utilities Authority
Box 219
Wynnewood, OK 73098
(405) 665-4141

Yale, City of
209 North Main
Yale, OK 74085
(918) 387-2406

OREGON

Ashland, City of
20 East Main Street
Ashland, OR 97520
(503) 482-3211

Bandon, City of
555 Highway 101, Box 67
Bandon, OR 97411
(503) 347-2437

Canby Utility Board
154 N.W. First Street, Box 1070
Canby, OR 97013
(503) 266-1156

Cascade Locks, City of
Box 308
Cascade Locks, OR 97014
(503) 374-8484

Central Lincoln People's
Utility District
2129 North Coast Highway, Box 1126
Newport, OR 97365
(503) 265-3211

Clatskanie People's Utility District
469 Nehalem
Clatskanie, OR 97016
(503) 728-2163

Columbia River People's Utility District
64001 Columbia River Highway, Box 1193
St. Helens, OR 97051
(503) 397-1844

Drain, City of
129 West C Avenue
Drain, OR 97435
(503) 836-2417

Emerald People's Utility District
33733 Seavey Loop Road
Eugene, OR 97405
(503) 746-1583

Eugene Water and Electric Board
500 East Fourth Avenue, Box 10148
Eugene, OR 97440
(503) 484-2411

Forest Grove, City of
1818 B Street, Box 326
Forest Grove, OR 97116
(503) 359-3250

McMinnville Water and Light Department
855 Marsh Lane, Box 638
McMinnville, OR 97128
(503) 472-6158

Milton-Freewater, City of
722 South Main Street, Box 6
Milton-Freewater, OR 97862
(503) 938-5531

Monmouth Power and Light
151 West Main Street
Monmouth, OR 97361
(503) 838-0722

Northern Wasco County People's
Utility District
401 Court Street, Box 621
The Dalles, OR 97058
(503) 296-2226

Springfield Utility Board
250 North A Street, Box 300
Springfield, OR 97477
(503) 746-8451

Tillamook People's Utility District
1115 Pacific Avenue
Tillamook, OR 97141
(503) 842-2535

PENNSYLVANIA

Berlin, Borough of
700 North Street, Box 115
Berlin, PA 15530
(814) 267-3837

Blakely, Borough of
1439 Main Street
Peckville, PA 18452
(717) 383-3340

Catawissa, Borough of
118 North Third Street, Box 44
Catawissa, PA 17820
(707) 356-2561

Chambersburg, Borough of
100 South Second Street
Chambersburg, PA 17201
(717) 264-5151

Duncannon, Borough of
428 North High Street, Box 9
Duncannon, PA 17020
(717) 834-4311

East Conemaugh, Borough of
355 First Street
East Conemaugh, PA 15909
(814) 539-0193

Ellwood City, Borough of
525 Lawrence Avenue
Ellwood City, PA 16117
(412) 758-5576

Ephrata, Borough of
114 East Main Street
Ephrata, PA 17522
(717) 733-1277

Girard, Borough of
34 Main Street, West
Girard, PA 16417
(814) 774-3012

Goldsboro, Borough of
53 North York Street, Box 14
Etters, PA 17319
(717) 938-3456

Grove City, Borough of
315 Park Street
Grove City, PA 16127
(412) 457-7070

Hatfield, Borough of
Box 190
Hatfield, PA 19440
(215) 855-0781

Hooversville Boro Electric
Light Company
Pitcairn, PA 15140 Hooversville, PA 15936
(814) 798-8001

Kutztown, Borough of
45 Railroad Street
Kutztown, PA 19530
(215) 683-6131

Lansdale, Borough of
1 Vine Street
Lansdale, PA 19446
(215) 368-1691

Lehighton, Borough of
Box 29
Lehighton, PA 18235
(215) 877-4002

Lewisberry, Borough of
Box 186
Lewisberry, PA 17339
(717) 938-1107

Middletown, Borough of
60 West Emaus Street
Middletown, PA 17057
(717) 948-3038

Mifflinburg, Borough of
333 Chestnut Street
Mifflinburg, PA 17844
(717) 966-1013

New Wilmington, Borough of
140 West Neshannock Avenue
New Wilmington, PA 16142
(412) 946-8167

Olyphant, Borough of
113 Willow Street
Olyphant, PA 18447
(717) 489-2135

Perkasie, Borough of
311 South Ninth Street, Box 275
Perkasie, PA 18944
(215) 258-5065

Pitcairn Municipal Light System
582 Sixth Street Box 176
(412) 372-6500

Quakertown, Borough of
15-35 North Second Street
Quakertown, PA 18951
(215) 536-5001

Royalton, Borough of
Burd and Dock Streets
Royalton, PA 17057
(717) 944-4831

Saint Clair Electric Light
Department
39 North Second Street, Box 25
St. Clair, PA 17970
(717) 429-0640

Schuylkill Haven, Borough of
12 West Main Street
Schuylkill Haven, PA 17972
(717) 385-2841

Smethport, Borough of
412 West Water Street
Smethport, PA 16749
(814) 887-5815

Summerhill, Borough of
Box 289
Summerhill, PA 15958
(814) 495-5610

Wampum, Borough of
Box 65
Wampum, PA 16157
(412) 535-8241

Watsontown, Borough of
4th and Main Streets, Box 273
Watsontown, PA 17777
(717) 538-1000

Weatherly, Borough of
10 Wilbur Street
Weatherly, PA 18255
(717) 427-8640

Zelienople, Borough of
111 West New Castle Street
Zelienople, PA 16063
(412) 452-6610

RHODE ISLAND

Pascoag Fire District
South Main Street, Box 107
Pascoag, RI 02859
(401) 568-6222

SOUTH CAROLINA

Abbeville Water and Electric Plant
Box 639
Abbeville, SC 29620
(803) 459-5058

Bamberg Board of Public Works
619 North Main Street, Box 300
Bamberg, SC 29003
(803) 245-5128

Bennettsville, City of
501 East Main Street, Box 1036
Bennettsville, SC 29512
(803) 469-9001

Camden, City of
Box 7002
Camden, SC 29020
(803) 432-2421

Clinton, City of
404 North Broad Street, Drawer 748
Clinton, SC 29325
(803) 833-7505

Due West, Town of
Box 278
Due West, SC 29639
(803) 379-2385

Easley Combined Utility System
202 North First Street, Box 619
Easley, SC 29641
(803) 859-4013

Gaffney Board of Public Works
210 East Frederick Street, Box 64
Gaffney, SC 29342
(803) 488-8800

Georgetown, City of
Box 1146
Georgetown,, SC 29442
(803) 546-5632 55

Greenwood, City of
Box 549
Greenwood, SC 29648
(803) 942-8100

Greer Commission of Public Works
301 McCall Street, Box 216
Greer, SC 29652
(803) 848-5500

Laurens Commission of Public Works
212 Church Street, Box 349
Laurens, SC 29360
(803) 984-0481

McCormick, Town of
Box 656
McCormick, SC 29835
(803) 465-2224

Newberry, City of
Boyce Street, Drawer 538
Newberry, SC 29108
(803) 321-1018

Orangeburg, City of
195 Russel Street, S.W., Box 1057
Orangeburg, SC 29115
(803) 534-2821

Piedmont Municipal Power Agency
121 Village Drive
Greer, SC 29651
(803) 877-9632

Prosperity, Town of
Box 36
Prosperity, SC 29127
(803) 364-2622

Rock Hill, City of
155 Johnson Street, Box 11706
Rock Hill, SC 29730
(803) 329-5512

Seneca, City of
225 North First Street, Box 4773
Seneca, SC 29679
(803) 885-2723

South Carolina Public Service Authority
One Riverwood Drive
Moncks Corner, SC 29461
(803) 761-8000

Union, City of
Sharp Avenue, Box 987
Union, SC 29379
(803) 429-1717

Westminster, City of
Box 399
Westminster, SC 29693
(803) 647-5071

Winnsboro, Town of
North Congress Street, Box 209
Winnsboro, SC 29180
(803) 635-4041

SOUTH DAKOTA

Arlington, City of
Arlington, SD 57212
(605) 983-5911

Aurora, City of
Box 335
Aurora, SC 57002
(605) 693-3548

Badger, City of
Box 95
Badger, SD 57214
(605) 983-5385

Beresford, City of
101 North Third Street
Beresford, SD 57004
(605) 763-2008

Big Stone, City of
651 Main Street, Box 246
Big Stone, SD 57216
(605) 862-8121

Brookings, City of
525 Western Avenue, Box 588
Brookings, SD 57006
(605) 692-6325

Bryant, City of
Box 145
Bryant, SD 57221
(605) 628-2931

Burke, City of
Box 312
Burke, SD 57523
(605) 775-2692

Colman, City of
Box 54
Colman, SD 57017
(605) 534-3611

Elk Point, City of
Box 280
Elk Point, SD 57025
(605) 356-2141

Estelline, City of
Box 278
Estelline, SD 57234
(605) 873-2388

Faith, City of
Box 368
Faith, SD 57626
(605) 967-2261

Flandreau, City of
136 Second Avenue, East
Flandreau, SD 57028
(605) 997-2492

Fort Pierre, City of
40 East 2nd Street, Box 700
Fort Pierre, SD 57532
(605) 223-2508

Groton, City of
Box 587
Groton, SD 57445
(605) 397-8422

Heartland Consumers Power District
Box 248
Madison, SD 57042
(605) 256-6536

Hecla, City of
Box 188
Hecla, SD 57446
(605) 994-2333

Howard, City of
100 South Main, Box 705
Howard, SD 57349
(605) 772-4391

Langford, Town of
Box 191
Langford, SD 57454
(605) 493-6772

Madison, City of
Box 308
Madison, SD 47042
(605) 256-4586

McLaughlin, City of
Box 169
McLaughlin, SD 57642
(605) 823-4428

Miller, City of
Box 69
Miller, SD 57362
(605) 843-2705

Missouri Basin Municipal Power
Agency
Box 84610
Sioux Falls, SD 57118
(605) 338-4042

Onida, City of
Box 72
Onida, SD 57564
(605) 258-2441

Parker, City of
Box 265
Parker, SD 57053
(605) 297-4453

Pickstown, Town of
Box 107
Pickstown, SD, 57367
(605) 487-7553

Pierre, City of
222 East Dakota Avenue
Pierre, SD 57501
(605) 224-7341

Plankinton, City of
Box 517
Plankinton, SD 57368
(605) 942-7767

Sioux Falls Municipal Light
and Power
2000 North Minnesota Avenue
Sioux Falls, SD 57104
(605) 339-7150

Tyndall, City of
110 East Main Street, Box 29
Tyndall, SD 57066
(605) 589-3481

Vermillion, City of
25 Center Street
Vermillion, SD 57069
(605) 624-5641

Volga, City of
Box 207
Volga, SD 57071
(605) 627-9113

Watertown Municipal Utilities
901 4th Avenue, S.W.
Watertown, SD 57201
(605) 886-5733

Wessington Springs, City of
Box 443
Wessington Springs, SD 57382
(605) 539-1691

White, City of
Box 682
White, SD 57276
(605) 629-8161

Winner, City of
217 East Third Street
Winner, SD 57580
(605) 842-2606

TENNESSEE

Alcoa, City of
264 North Rankin Road
Alcoa, TN 37701
(615) 981-4115

Athens Utilities
100 Englewood Road, Box 689
Athens, TN 37303
(615) 745-4501

Benton County
Box 445
Camden, TN 38320
(901) 584-8251

Bolivar, City of
815 Tennessee Street, Box 188
Bolivar, TN 38008
(901) 658-5257

Bristol Tennessee Electric System
2470 Volunteer Parkway, Box 549
Bristol, TN 37621
(615) 968-1526

Brownsville Utility Department
25 North Lafayette, Box 424
Brownsville, TN 38012
(901) 772-1213

Carroll County
103 West Paris Street, Box 527
Huntingdon, TN 38344
(901) 986-8284

Chattanooga Electric Power Board
537 Cherry Street
Chattanooga, TN 37402
(615) 757-1484

Clarksville Department of Electricity
2021 Guthrie Highway, Box 1007
Clarksville, TN 37040
(615) 648-8151

Cleveland Utilities
2450 Guthrie Drive,N.W., Box 2730
Cleveland, TN 37320
(615) 472-4521

Clinton Utilities Board
1001 Charles G. Seivers Blvd.
Clinton, TN 37716
(615) 457-9332

Columbia Power System
201 Pickens Lane, Box 379
Columbia, TN 38402
(615) 388-4833

Cookeville, City of
45 East Broad Street, Box 998
Cookeville, TN 38501
(615) 526-9591

Covington Electric System
204 East Liberty Street, Box 488
Covington, TN 38019
(901) 476-7104

Dayton, City of
Box 226
Dayton, TN 37321
(615) 775-1817

Dickson, City of
121 South Main Street, Box 627
Dickson, TN 37055
(615) 446-9051

Dyersburg Electric System
211 East Court Street, Box 664
Dyersburg, TN 38024
(901) 287-4600

Elizabethton Electric System
Hatcher Lane, Box 790
Elizabethton, TN 37643
(615) 542-2101

Erwin Utilities Board
244 Love Street, Box 201
Erwin, TN 37650
(615) 743-1820

Etowah Utility Board
110 Ninth Street, Box N
Etowah, TN 37331
(615) 263-9441

Fayetteville Electric System
408 West College Street, Box 120
Fayetteville, TN 37334
(615) 433-1522

Gallatin Department of Electricity
135 Jones Street, Box 1555
Gallatin, TN 37066
(615) 452-5152

Greeneville Light and Power System
Box 1690
Greeneville, TN 37744
(615) 636-6200

Harriman, City of
300 Roane Street, Box 434
Harriman, TN 37748
(615) 882-3242

Humboldt Utilities
207 South 13th Avenue, Box 850
Humboldt, TN 38343
(901) 784-9212

Jackson Utility Division
119 East College Street, Box 68
Jackson, TN 38302
(901) 422-7500

Jellico, City of
400 South Main Street, Box 510
Jellico, TN 37762
(615) 784-8431

Johnson City Power Board
100 North Roan Street, Box 1636
Johnson City, TN 37601
(615) 434-4000

Knoxville, City of
626 South Gay Street, Box 59017
Knoxville, TN 37950
(615) 524-2911

La Follette Utilities
North Tennessee Avenue, Box 1411
La Follette, TN 37766
(615) 562-3316

Lawrenceburg Power System
1607 North Locust Avenue, Box 649
Lawrenceburg, TN 38464
(615) 762-7161

Lebanon, City of
410 Park Drive
Lebanon, TN 37087
(615) 444-0825

Lenoir City Utilities Board
200 Deport Street, Box 449
Lenoir City, TN 37771
(615) 986-6591

Lewisburg Electric System
599 West Ellington Parkway, Box 2727
Lewisburg, TN 37091
(615) 359-2544

Lexington, City of
92 Main Street, Box 200
Lexington, TN 38351
(901) 968-3663

Loudon, City of
Box E
Loudon, TN 37774
(615) 458-2091

Maryville, City of
332 Home Road
Maryville, TN 37801
(615) 981-3300

McMinnville Electric System
200 Morford Street
McMinnville, TN 37110
(615) 473-3144

Memphis Light, Gas and Water Division
220 South Main Street, Box 430
Memphis, TN 38101
(901) 528-4011

Milan Department of Public Utilities
1085 South Second Street, Box 109
Milan, TN 38358
(901) 686-1537

Morristown Power System
441 West Main Street, Box 667
Morristown, TN 37814
(615) 586-4121

Mount Pleasant Power Station
123 North Main Street, Box 186
Mount Pleasant, TN 38474
(615) 379-3233

Murfreesboro Electric Department
205 North Walnut Street, Box 9
Murfreesboro, TN 37133
(615) 893-5514

Nashville Electric Service
1214 Church Street
Nashville, TN 37203
(615) 747-3895

Newbern, City of
East Main Street, Box 460
New Bern, TN 38059
(901) 627-3221

Newport Utilities Board
301-305 East Main Street, Box 519
Newport, TN 37821
(615) 623-3074

Oak Ridge, City of
Box 1
Oak Ridge, TN 37831
(615) 482-8550

Paris Board of Public Utilities
117 East Washington Street
Paris, TN 38242
(901) 642-1322

Pulaski Electric System
203 South First Street, Box 368
Pulaski, TN 38478
(615) 363-2522

Ripley, City of
Box 69
Ripley, TN 38063
(901) 635-2323

Rockwood Electricity Utility
341 West Rockwood Street, Box 108
Rockwood, TN 37854
(615) 354-0514

Sevier County Electric System
315 East Main Street, Box 4870
Sevierville, TN 37864
(615) 453-2887

Shelbyville Power System
308 South Main Street, Box 530
Shelbyville, TN 37160
(615) 684-7171

Smithville, City of
605 East Broad, Box 228
Smithville, TN 37166
(615) 597-4735

Somerville Light Gas and Water
Department
106 East Court Square
Somerville, TN 38068
(901) 465-3676

Sparta Electric System
545 East Bockman Way, Box 468
Sparta, TN 38583
(615) 738-2281

Springfield, City of
718 Central Avenue, Box 788
Springfield, TN 37172
(615) 384-6770

Sweetwater Utilities Board
101 Oak Street, Box 191
Sweetwater, TN 37874
(615) 337-5081

Trenton, City of
109 West Armory, Box 260
Trenton, TN 38382
(901) 855-1561

Tullahoma Utilities Board
901 South Jackson, Box 788
Tullahoma, TN 37388
(615) 455-4515

Union City Electric System
312 North Division Street, Box 369
Union City, TN 38261
(901) 885-9212

Weakley County Municipal Electric
System
501 Lindell Street, Box 170
Martin, TN 38237
(901) 587-9521

Winchester, City of
219 Second Avenue, N.W.
Winchester, TN 37398
(615) 967-2238

TEXAS

Austin, City of
721 Barton Springs Road
Austin, TX 78704
(512) 322-9600

Bartlett, City of
140 West Clark Street, Drawer H
Bartlett, TX 76511
(817) 527-3557

Bastrop, City of
904 Main Street, Box S
Bastrop, TX 78602
(512) 321-3941

Bellville, City of
30 South Holland, Drawer 817
Bellville, TX 77418
(409) 865-3136

Boerne, City of
402 East Blanco Road, Box 1677
Boerne, TX 78006
(210) 249-9511

Bowie, City of
304 Lindsey
Bowie, TX 76230
(817) 872-1114

Brady, City of
101 East Main, Box 351
Brady, TX 76825
(915) 597-2152

Brazos River Authority
Box 7555
Waco, TX 76714
(817) 776-1441

Brenham, City of
210 North Park Street, Box 1059
Brenham, TX 77834
(409) 836-7911

Bridgeport, City of
812 Halsell Street
Bridgeport, TX 76426
(817) 683-5906

Brownfield Municipal Light and Power
201 West Broadway
Brownfield, TX 79316
(806) 637-4547

Brownsville Public Utilities Board
Box 3270
Brownsville, TX 78520
(210) 982-6276

Bryan, City of
205 East 28th Street
Bryan, TX 77801
(409) 361-3750

Burnet, City of
127 East Jackson Street
Burnet, TX 78611
(512) 756-4858

Caldwell, City of
107 South Hill Street
Caldwell, TX 77836
(409) 567-3271

Castroville, City of
1209 North Fiorella Street
Castroville, TX 78009
(512) 538-2224

Coleman, City of
201 North Colorado
Coleman, TX 76834
(915) 625-4116

College Station, City of
1101 Texas Avenue, Box 9960
College Station, TX 77840
(409) 764-3688

Cuero, City of
201 East Main, Box 512
Cuero, TX 77954
(512) 275-6114

Denton, City of
215 East McKinney
Denton, TX 76201
(817) 566-8230

Electra, City of
101 North Main Street
Electra, TX 76360
(817) 495-2432

Farmersville, City of
205 South Main Street
Farmersville, TX 75442
(214) 782-6151

Flatonia, City of
125 East South Main Street, Box 375
Flatonia, TX 78941
(512) 865-3548

Floresville Electric Light and Power
System
1400 Fourth Street, Box 218
Floresville, TX 78114
(512) 393-3131

Floydada, City of
114 West Virginia Street, Box 10
Floydada, TX 79235
(806) 983-2834

Fredericksburg, City of
126 West Main Street, Box 111
Fredericksburg, TX 78624
(512) 997-7521

Garland, City of
200 North Fifth Street, Suite 427
Garland, TX 75040
(214) 205-2650

Garrison, City of
Box 207
Garrison, TX 75946
(409) 347-2201

Georgetown Utilities
Box 409
Georgetown, TX 78627
(512) 869-3636

Giddings, City of
118 East Richmond Street
Giddings, TX 78942
(409) 542-2311

Goldsmith, City of
Box 629
Goldsmith, TX 79741
(915) 827-3404

Goldthwaite, City of
1218 Fisher Street, Box 450
Goldthwaite, TX 76844
(915) 648-3186

Gonzales, City of
820 St. Joseph Street, Drawer 547
Gonzales, TX 78629
(210) 672-2815

Granbury, City of
Box 969
Granbury, TX 76048
(817) 573-1115

Greenville Electric Utility System
6000 Joe Ramsey Blvd.
Greenville, TX 75402
(903) 457-2800

Guadalupe-Blanco River Authority
933 East Court Street, Box 271
Sequin, TX 78155
(512) 379-5822

Hallettsville Municipal Utilities
101 North Main Street, Box 257
Hallettsville, TX 77964
(512) 798-3681

Hearne, City of
210 Cedar Street
Hearne, TX 77859
(409) 279-3461

Hemphill, City of
Drawer L
Hemphill, TX 75948
(409) 787-2251

Hempstead, City of
1125 Austin Street
Hempstead, TX 77445
(409) 826-2486

Hondo, City of
1600 Avenue M
Hondo, TX 78861
(210) 426-3377

Jasper, City of
272 East Lamar Street, Box 610
Jasper, TX 75951
(409) 384-4651

Kerrville Public Utility Board
2250 Memorial Blvd., Box 911
Kerrville, TX 78029
(210) 257-3050

Kirbyville Light and Power Company
107 South Elizabeth Street
Kirbyville, TX 75956
(409) 423-4659

La Grange Utilities
155 East Colorado Street, Box 339
La Grange, TX 78945
(409) 968-3127

Lampasas, City of
302 East Third Street, Box 666
Lampasas, TX 76550
(512) 556-3641

Lexington, City of
Box 56
Lexington, TX 78947
(409) 773-2221

Liberty, City of
1829 Sam Houston Street, City Hall
Liberty, TX 77575
(409) 336-6872

Livingston, City of
200 West Church Street
Livingston, TX 77351
(409) 327-4311

Llano Utilities
301 West Main Street
Llano, TX 78643
(915) 247-4158

Lockhart, City of
308 West San Antonio Street, Box 239
Lockhart, TX 78644
(512) 398-3461

Lower Colorado River Authority
3700 Lake Austin Blvd, Box 220
Austin, TX 78767
(512) 473-3200

Lubbock, City of
916 Texas Avenue, Box 2000
Lubbock, TX 79457
(806) 767-2500

Luling, City of
509 East Crockett Street, Box 630
Luling, TX 78648
(210) 875-2469

Mason, City of
124 Moody Street, Box 68
Mason, TX 76856
(915) 347-6449

Moulton, City of
102 South Main Street, Box 369
Moulton, TX 77975
(512) 596-4621

New Braunfels Utilities
263 Main Plaza East, Box 310289
New Braunfels, TX 78131
(210) 629-8400

Newton, City of
Box 889
Newton, TX 75966
(409) 379-4656

Plains, City of
Box 550
Plains, TX 79355
(806) 456-2288

Robstown, City of
101 East Main Street, Box 71
Robstown, TX 78380
(512) 387-3554

Sam Rayburn Municipal Power Agency
1412 South Houston, Box 1700
Livingston, TX 77351
(409) 327-5303

San Antonio City Public Service Board
145 Navarro, Box 1771
San Antonio, TX 78296
(210) 978-2000

San Augustine, City of
301 South Harrison Street
San Augustine, TX 75972
(409) 275-2121

San Marcos Electric Utility
Box 788
San Marcos, TX 78666
(512) 396-2451

San Saba, City of
303 South Clear Street
San Saba, TX 76877
(915) 372-3131

Sanger, City of
201 Bolivar Street, Box 578
Sanger, TX 76266
(817) 458-7930

Schulenburg, City of
607 Upton Avenue
Schulenburg, TX 78956
(409) 743-4126

Sequin, City of
205 North River Street, Box 591
Sequin, TX 78155
(210) 379-3212

Seymour, City of
301 North Washington Street, Box 31
Seymour, TX 76380
(817) 888-3148

Shiner, City of
Box 308
Shiner, TX 77984
(512) 594-3362

Smithville, City of
317 Main Street, Box 449
Smithville, TX 78957
(512) 237-3267

Texas Municipal Power Agency
Box 7000
Bryan, TX 77805
(409) 873-2013

Timpson, City of
Box 369
Timpson, TX 75975
(409) 254-2421

Toledo Bend Project
Route 1, Box 270
Burkeville, TX 75932
(409) 565-2273

Tulia, City of
201 North Maxwell Street
Tulia, TX 79088
(806) 995-3547

Waelder, City of
Box 427
Waelder, TX 78959
(512) 665-7331

Weathford Municipal Utility System
303 Paio Pinto Street, Box 255
Weatherford, TX 76086
(817) 594-5441

Weimar, City of
106 East Main Street, Box 67
Weimar, TX 78692
(409) 725-8554

Whitesboro, City of
112 West Main Street, Box 340
Whitesboro, TX 76273
(903) 564-3311

Yoakum, City of
900 Irvine Street, Box 738
Yoakum, TX 77995
(512) 293-6321

UTAH

Beaver City Corporation
60 West Center Street
Beaver City, UT 84713
(801) 438-2451

Blanding, City of
50 West 100 South
Blanding, UT 84511
(801) 678-2791

Bountiful City Light and Power
198 South 200 West Street
Bountiful City, UT 84010
(801) 298-6072

Brigham City Corporation
20 North Main Street, Box 1005
Brigham City, UT 84302
(801) 734-2001

Enterprise, City of
15 South 100 East, Box 340
Enterprise, UT 84725
(801) 878-2221

Ephraim, City of
5 South Main Street
Ephraim, UT 84627
(801) 283-4631

Fairview City Corporation
Box 97
Fairview, UT 84629
(801) 427-3858

Fillmore City Corporation
75 West Center, Box 687
Fillmore, UT 84631
(801) 743-5233

Heber Light and Power Company
31 South 100 West
Heber City, UT 84032
(801) 654-1581

Helper, City of
73 South Main Street
Helper, UT 84526
(801) 472-5391

Holden Town Corporation
Box 127
Holden, UT 84636
(801) 795-2672

Hurricane Power Committee
Box 918
Hurricane, UT 84737
(801) 635-2811

Hyrum City Corporation
83 West Main Street
Hyrum, UT 84319
(801) 245-6033

Intermountain Power Agency
480 East 6400 South, Suite 200
Murray, UT 84107
(801) 262-8807

Kanab City Corporation
76 North Main #14
Kanab, UT 84741
(801) 644-2534

Kanosh Corporation, Town of
Box 96
Kanosh, UT 84637
(801) 759-2414

Kaysville, City Corporation
23 East Center
Kaysville, UT 84037
(801) 544-8925

Lehi City
300 North 500 West
Lehi, UT 84043
(801) 768-3030

Levan Town Corporation
20 North Main, Box 40
Levan, UT 84639
(801) 623-1959

City of Logan Light and Power
950 West 600 North
Logan, UT 84321
(801) 750-9940

Manti, City of
50 South Main Street
Manti, UT 84642
(801) 835-2401

Meadow Town Corporation
Box 88
Meadow, UT 84644
(801) 842-7281

Monroe City
10 North Main Street, Box A
Monroe, UT 84754
(801) 842-7281

Morgan City Corporation
48 West Young Street, Box 267
Morgan, UT 84050
(801) 829-3515

Mount Pleasant, City of
115 West Main Street
Mount Pleasant, UT 84647
(801) 462-2456

Murray, City of
153 West 4800 South Street
Murray City, UT 84107
(801) 264-9701

Nephi City Corporation
21 East First North
Nephi, UT 84648
(801) 623-0822

Oak City, Town of
Box 217
Oak City, UT 84649
(801) 846-2018

Paragonah Municipal Light Department
Paragonah, UT 84760
(801) 477-8164

Parowan City Corporation
Box 576
Parowan, UT 84761
(801) 477-3331

Payson City Corporation
439 West Utah Avenue
Payson, UT 84651
(801) 465-5274

Price Municipal Corporation
185 East Main Street, Box 893
Price, UT 84501
(801) 637-5010

Provo City Department of Energy
251 West 800 North, Box 658
Provo, UT 84601
(801) 379-6800

St. George, City of
175 East 200 North
St. George, UT 84770
(801) 674-4212

Salem City Corporation
2721 West Santa Clara Drive, Box 699
Santa Clara, UT 84765
(801) 673-7612

Spanish Fork, City of
40 South Main Street
Spanish Fork City, UT 84660
(801) 798-3568

Spring City Corporation
Box 189
Spring City, UT 84662
(801) 462-2282

Springville, City of
50 Main Street, Box 32
Springville, UT 84663
(801) 489-2752

Strawberry Electric Service District
Box 70
Payson, UT 84651
(801) 465-9273

Utah Associated Municipal Power Systems
8722 South 300 West
Sandy, UT 84070
(801) 566-3938

Utah Municipal Power Agency
40 South Main, Box 818
Spanish Fork, UT 84660
(801) 798-7489

Washington, City of
111 North 100 East, Box 575
Washington, UT 84780
(801) 628-1666

VERMONT

Barton Village, Inc.
Main Street, Box D
Barton VT 02822
(802) 525-4748

Burlington, City of
585 Pine Street
Burlington, VT 05401
(802) 658-0300

Enosburg Water and Electric Department
RR 4, Box 80
Enosburg Falls, VT 05450
(802) 933-5544

Hardwick Electric Department
Box 516
Hardwick, VT 05843
(802) 472-5201

Hyde Park, Village of
Box 190
Hyde Park, VT 05655
(802) 888-2310

Jacksonville, Village of
Jacksonville, VT 05342
(802) 368-2811

Johnson, Village of, Inc.
Box 603
Johnson, VT 05656
(802) 635-2301

Ludlow, Village of
Box 289
Ludlow, VT 05149
(802) 228-7766

Lyndonville, Village of
24 Main Street
Lyndonville, VT 05851
(802) 626-3366

Morrisville Water and Light Department
18 Portland Street, Box 325
Morrisville, VT 05661
(802) 888-4961

Northfield, Village of
26 South Main Street
Northfield, VT 05663
(802) 485-6121

Orleans, Inc., Village of
Memorial Square
Orleans, VT 05860
(802) 754-8584

Readsboro's Electric
Box 247
Readsboro, VT 05350
(802) 423-7010

Stowe, Village of
Main Street, Box 190
Stowe, VT 05672
(802) 253-7215

Swanton, Village of
120 First Street
Swanton, VT 05488
(802) 868-3397

Vermont Public Power Supply
Authority
512 St. George Road, Box 425
Williston, VT 05495

VIRGINIA

Bedford, City of
215 East Main Street
Bedford, VA 24523
(703) 586-7171

Blackstone, Town of
100 West Elm, Box 311
Blackstone, VA 23824
(804) 292-7251

Bristol Virginia Utilities
300 Lee Street
Bristol, VA 24203
(703) 669-4112

Culpeper, Town of
118 West Davis Street
Culpeper, VA 22701
(703) 825-1120

Danville, City of
1040 Monument, Box 3300
Danville, VA 24543
(804) 799-5270

Elkton, Town of
173 West Spotswood Avenue
Elkton, VA 22827
(703) 298-1330

Franklin, City of
Box 179
Franklin, VA 23851
(804) 562-8568

Front Royal Electric Department
520-A East Sixth Street
Front Royal, VA 22630
(703) 635-3027

Harrisonburg, City of
89 West Bruce Street
Harrisonburg, VA 22801
(703) 434-5361

Manassas, City of
8500 Public Works Drive, Box 560
Manassas, VA 22110
(703) 257-8351

Martinsville, City of
55 West Church Street
Martinsville, VA 24114
(703) 638-3971

Radford, City of
17th Street
Radford, VA 24141
(703) 731-3641

Richlands, Town of
217 Railroad Avenue
Richlands, VA 24641
(703) 964-2567

Salem, City of
19 North Broad Street, Box 869
Salem, VA 24153
(703) 375-3030

Virginia Tech Electric Service
1421 North Main Street
Shenandoah Shopping Center
Blacksburg, VA 24060
(703) 231-6437

Wakefield, Town of
Box 550
Wakefield, VA 23888
(804) 899-2361

WASHINGTON

Benton County, Public Utility District
No. 1 of
Box 6270
Kennewick, WA 99336
(509) 582-2175

Blaine, City of
1200 Yew Street
Blaine, WA 98230
(206) 332-8820

Cashmere, City of
101 Woodring Street
Cashmere, WA 98815
(509) 782-3513

Centralia, City of
1100 North Tower Avenue
Centralia, WA 98531
(206) 736-7611

Chelan County, Public Utility District 701
No. 1 of
327 North Wenatchee Avenue, Box 1231
Wenatchee, WA 98807
(509) 663-8121

Cheney, City of
112 Anderson Road
Cheney, WA 99004
(509) 235-7235

Chewelah, City of
East 301 Clay, Box 258
Chewelah, WA 99109
(509) 935-8311

Clallam County, Public Utility District
No. 1 of
2431 East Highway 101, Box 1090
Port Angeles, WA 98362
(206) 452-9771

Clark Public Utilities
Box 8900
Vancouver, WA 98668
(206) 699-3000

Coulee Dam, City of
Box 156
Coulee Dam, WA 99116
(509) 633-1091

Cowlitz County, Public Utility District
No. 1 of
960 Commerce Avenue, Box 3007
Longview, WA 98632
(206) 423-2210

Douglas County, Public Utility District
No. 1 of
1151 Valley Mall Parkway
East Wenatchee, WA 98801
(509) 884-7191

Eatonville, Town of
201 Center Street, West, Box 309
Eatonville, WA 98328
(206) 832-3244

Ellensburg, City of
420 North Pearl Street
Ellensburg, WA 98926
(509) 962-7224

Ferry County, Public Utility District
No. 1 of
686 South Clark Avenue, Box 1039
Republic, WA 99166
(509) 775-3325

Fircrest, Town of
115 Ramsdell Street
Tacoma, WA 98466
(206) 564-8901

Franklin County, Public Utility District
No. 1 of
1411 West Clark Street, Box 2407
Pasco, WA 99302
(509) 547-5591

Grant County, Public Utility District
No. 2 of
30 C. Street, S.W., Box 878
Ephrata, WA 98823
(509) 754-3541

Grays Harbor County, Public Utility District
No. 1 of
2720 Sumner Avenue, Box 480
Aberdeen, WA 98520
(206) 532-4220

Kittitas County, Public Utility District
No. 1 of
1400 East Vantage Highway
Ellensburg, WA 98926
(509) 925-3164

Klickitat County, Public Utility District
No. 1 of
1313 South Columbus Avenue
Goldendale, WA 98620
(509) 773-5891

Lewis County, Public Utility District
No. 1 of
321 Northwest Pacific Avenue, Box 330
Chehalis, WA 98532
(206) 748-9261

Mason County, Public Utility District
No. 1 of
North 21971 Highway 101
Shelton, WA 98584
(206) 426-8255

McCleary, City of
Box 360
McCleary, WA 98557
(206) 495-3667

Milton, City of
1000 Laurell Street
Milton, WA 98354
(206) 922-8738

Okanogan County, Public Utility District
No. 1 of
1331 North Second Avenue, Box 912
Okanogan, WA 98840
(509) 422-3310

Pacific County, Public Utility District
No. 2 of
405 Duryea Street, Box 472
Raymond, WA 98577
(206) 942-2411

Pend Oreille County, Public Utility
District No. 1 of
130 North Washington, Box 190
Newport, WA 99156
(509) 447-3137

Port Angeles, City of
321 East Fifth Street
Port Angeles, WA 98362
(206) 457-0411

Richland, City of
505 Swift Blvd., Box 190
Richland, WA 99352
(509) 943-7403

Ruston, City of
5117 North Winnifred Street
Ruston via Tacoma, WA 98407
(206) 759-3544

Seattle, City of
1015 3rd Avenue
Seattle, WA 98104
(206) 684-3200

Skamania County, Public Utility District
No. 1 of
Box 500
Carson, WA 98610
(509) 427-5126

Snohomish County, Public Utility District
No. 1 of
2320 California Avenue, Box 1107
Everett, WA 98206
(206) 258-8211

Steilacoom, Town of
1030 Roe Street
Steilacoom, WA 98388
(206) 581-1912

Sumas, City of
Box 9
Sumas, WA 98295
(206) 988-5711

Tacoma Public Utilities
3628 South 35th Street, Box 11007
Tacoma, WA 98411
(206) 593-8200

Vera Water and Power North
601 Evergreen Road, Box 630
Veradale, WA 99037
(509) 927-3800

Wahkiakum County, Public Utility
District No. 1 of
45 River Street, Box 248
Cathlamet, WA 98612
(206) 795-3266

Washington Public Power Supply
System
Box 968
Richland, WA 99352
(509) 372-5000

Waterville, Town of
Box 580
Waterville, WA 98858
(509) 745-8871

Whatcom County, Public Utility District
No. 1 of
2011 Young Street
Bellingham, WA 98225
(206) 733-5810

WEST VIRGINIA

New Martinsville, City of
197 Main Street
New Martinsville, WV 26155
(304) 455-9130

Philippi, City of
108 North Main Street
Philippi, WV 26416
(304) 457-3701

WISCONSIN

Algoma Utility Commission
1407 Flora Avenue
Algoma, WI 54201
(414) 487-5556

Arcadia Electric Utility
115 South Jackson Street
Arcadia, WI 54612
(608) 323-7347

Argyle Municipal Electric and
Water Utility
401 Milwaukee Street, Box 246
Argyle, WI 53504
(608) 543-3113

Badger Power Marketing Authority
122 North Sawyer Street
Shawano, WI 54166
(715) 526-2920

Bangor Municipal Utility
106 15th Avenue, North
Bangor, WI 54614
(608) 486-2151

Barron Light and Water Department
1303 East Division Avenue
Barron, WI 54812
(715) 537-3855

Belmont Light and Water Utility
222 Mound Avenue, Box 6
Belmont, WI 53510
(608) 762-5142

Benton, Village of
Main Street, Box 91
Benton, WI 53803
(608) 759-3721

Black Earth Electric Utility
1210 Mills Street, Box 347
Black Earth, WI 53515
(608) 767-2563

Black River Falls, City of
119 North Water Street
Black River Falls, WI 54615
(715) 284-9463

Bloomer Electric and Water
1503 Main Street
Bloomer, WI 54724
(715) 568-3331

Boscobel, City of
1031 Wisconsin Avenue
Boscobel, WI 53805
(608) 375-5002

Brodhead Water and Light Commission
1108 11th Street, Box 227
Brodhead, WI 53520
(608) 897-2505

Cadott, Village of
Box 40
Cadott, WI 54727
(715) 289-4282

Cashton, Village of
709 Main Street
Cashton, WI 54727
(715) 289-4282

Cedarburg Light and Water
Commission
North 30 West, 5926 Lincoln Blvd.
Cedarburg, WI 53012
(414) 375-7650

Centuria Municipal Electric Utility
305 Wisconsin Avenue, Box 280
Centuria, WI 54824
(715) 646-2300

Clintonville, City of
65 East 12th Street, Box 359
Clintonville, WI 54929
(715) 823-2118

Columbus Water and Light Commission
950 Maple Avenue, Box 228
Columbus, WI 53925
(414) 623-5912

Cornell, City of
Box 796
Cornell, WI 54732
(715) 239-3710

Cuba City, City of
108 North Main Street
Cuba City, WI 53807
(608) 744-2152

Cumberland Municipal Utility
1265 Second Avenue, Box 726
Cumberland, WI 54829
(715) 822-2595

Eagle River, City of
Box 218
Eagle River, WI 54521
(715) 479-8121

Elkhorn Light and Water
9 South Broad Street, Box 920
Elkhorn, WI 53121
(414) 723-2910

Elroy, City of
225 Main Street
Elroy, WI 53929
(608) 462-8246

Evansville Municipal Electric Utility
31 South Madison Street
Evansville, WI 53536
(608) 882-2288

Fennimore, City of
860 Lincoln Avenue
Fennimore, WI 53809
(608) 822-6110

Florence Utility Commission
500 Spring Avenue, Box 109
Florence, WI 54121
(715) 528-3330

Gresham, Village of
Main Street, Box 50
Gresham, WI 54128
(715) 787-3244

Hartford, City of
109 North Main Street
Hartford, WI 53027
(414) 673-8236

Hazel Green, Village of
1610 Fairplat Street, Box 367
Hazel Green, WI 53811
(608) 854-2953

Hustisford, Village of
210 South Lake Street
Hustisford, WI 53034
(404) 349-3650

Jefferson Water and Electric
Department
121 West Racine Street, Box 396
Jefferson, WI 53549
(414) 674-7711

Juneau Utility Commission
150 Miller Street, Box 163
Juneau, WI 53039
(414) 386-2521

Kaukauna Electric and Water
Department
777 Island Street, Box 1777
Kaukauna, WI 54130
(414) 766-5721

Kiel Utilities
705 A Washington Street, Box 98
Kiel, WI 53042
(414) 894-2669

La Farge Municipal Electric Company
Main Street
La Farge, WI 54639
(608) 625-2333

Lake Mills, City of
101 Church Street
Lake Mills, WI 53551
(414) 648-2344

Lodi, City of
113 South Main Street
Lodi, WI 53555
(608) 592-3246

Manitowac Public Utilities
1303 South 8th Street, Box 1090
Manitowac, WI 54221
(414) 683-4600

Marshfield Electric and Water
Department
2000 South Roddis Avenue, Box 670
Marshfield, WI 54449
(715) 387-1195

Mazomanie, Village of
133 Crescent Street
Mazomanie, WI 53560
(608) 795-2100

Medford Electric Utility
330 South Whelen Avenue, Box 358
Medford, WI 54451
(715) 748-3211

Menasha Electric and Water Utilities
321 Milwaukee, Box 340
Menasha, WI 54952
(414) 751-5180

Merrillan, City of
101 South Main Street
Merrillan, WI 54754
(715) 333-2322

Mount Horeb, Village of
138 East Main Street
Mount Horeb, WI 53572
(608) 437-3084

Muscoda, City of
206 North Wisconsin Avenue
Muscoda, WI 53573
(608) 739-3390

New Glarus, Village of
313 2nd Street
New Glarus, WI 53574
(608) 527-2913

New Holstein, City of
2110 Washington Street
New Holstein, WI 53061
414) 898-5776

New Lisbon Municipal Light and
Water Department
18 East Bridge Street
New Lisbon, WI 53950
(608) 562-3103

New London Electric and Water Utility
400 East North Water Street, Box 304
New London, WI 54961
(414) 982-8516

New Richmond, City of
156 East 1st Street
New Richmond, WI 54017
(715) 246-4167

Oconomowac, City of
174 East Wisconsin Avenue
Oconomowac, WI 53066
(414) 569-2198

Oconto Falls Water and Light
Commission
104 South Franklin Street
Oconto Falls, WI 54154
(414) 846-4505

Pardeeville, Village of
124 Lake Street
Pardeeville, WI 53954
(608) 429-3054

Plymouth, City of
12 South Milwaukee Street, Box 277
Plymouth, WI 53073
(414) 893-1471

Prairie du Sac, Village of
560 Park Avenue
Prairie du Sac, WI 53578
(608) 643-3133

Princeton, City of
438 West Main Street (
Princeton, WI 54968
(414) 292-6612

Reedsburg Utility Commission 2
344 South Willow Street
Reedsburg, WI 53595
(608) 524-4381

Rice Lake, City of
320 West Coleman Street
Rice Lake, WI 54868
(715) 234-7004

Richland Center, City of
161 North Central Avenue, Box 312
Richland Center, WI 53581
(608) 647-3844

River Falls, City of
125 East Elm Street
River Falls, WI 54022
(715) 425-0900

Sauk City, City of
726 Water Street
Sauk City, WI 53583
(608) 643-8336

Shawano Municipal Utilities
122 North Sayer Street, Box 436
Shawano, WI 54166
(715) 526-3131

Sheboygan Falls Utilities
511 Adams Street
Sheboygan Falls, WI 53085
(414) 467-4906

Shullsburg, City of
112 South Gratiot Street
Shullsburg, WI 53586
(608) 965-4901

Slinger, Village of
220 Slinger Road
Slinger, WI 53086
(414) 644-5265

Spooner, City of
515 Summit Street, Box 200
Spooner, WI 54802
(715) 635-2327

Stoughton, City of
211 Water Street, Box 383
Stoughton, WI 53589
(608) 873-3379

Strafford Electric and Water
212 South 3rd Avenue, Box 12
Stratford, WI 54484
(715) 686-4118

Sturgeon Bay Combined Utilities
230 East Vine Street, Box 259
Sturgeon Bay, WI 54235
(414) 743-5542

Sun Prairie Water and Light
System 125 West Main Street, Box 385
Sun Prairie, WI 53590
(608) 837-5500

Trempealeau, Village of
50 East Third Street
Trempealeau, WI 54661
(608) 534-6434

Two Rivers Water and Light
Department
Two Rivers, WI 54241
(414) 793-5550

Viola Municipal Electric Utility
Main Street, Box 38
Viola, WI 54664
(608) 627-1829

Waterloo Water and Light Commission
122 South Monroe Street
Waterloo, WI 53594
(414) 478-2260

Waunakee, Village of
205 Klein Drive, Box 95
Waunakee, WI 53597
(608) 849-8111

Waupun, City of
220 North Forest Street
Waupun, WI 53963
(414) 324-7920

Westby, City of
104 First Street
Westby, WI 54667
(608) 634-3416

Whitehall, City of
1631 Main Street, Box 155
Whitehall, WI 54773
(715) 538-4253

Wisconsin Dells, City of
300 La Crosse Street
Wisconsin Dells, WI 53965
(608) 253-2542

Wisconsin Public Power, Inc. Commission
1425 Corporate Center Drive
Sun Prairie, WI 53590
(608) 837-2653

Wisconsin Rapids Water Works and
Lighting Commission
221 16th Street South, Box 399
Wisconsin Rapids, WI 54494
(715) 423-6300

Wonewoc, Village of
Box 37
Wonewoc, WI 53968
(608) 464-3114

WYOMING

Basin, Town of
Box 599
Basin, WY 82410
(307) 568-3331

Cody, City of
1338 Rumsey Avenue
Cody, WY 82414
(307) 527-7511

Deaver, City of
180 First Street, Box 207
Deaver, WY 82421
(307) 664-2256

Fort Laramie, Town of
Box 177
Fort Laramie, WY 82212
(307) 838-2711

Gillette, City of Box 3003
Gillette, WY 82717
(307) 686-5262

Guernsey, Town of Box 667
Guernsey, WY 82214
(307) 836-2522

Lingle, Town of
Box 448
Lingle, WY 82223
(307) 837-2422

Lusk, Town of North Main Street, Box 390
Lush, WY 82225
(307) 334-3612

Midvale Irrigation District
Box 128
Pavillion, WY 82523
(307) 856-6359

Pine Bluffs, City of
210 East Fourth
Pine Bluffs, WY 82082
(307) 245-3746

Powell, City of
270 North Clark, Box 1008
Powell, WY 82435
(307) 754-5106

Torrington, City of
2042 East A Street
Torrington, WY 82240
(307) 532-5666

Wheatland, Town of
600 9th Street
Wheatland, WY 82201
(307) 322-2962

Wyoming Municipal Power Agency
Box 900
Lusk, WY 82225
(307) 334-2170

Appendix D

Listing of Rural Electric (Cooperative) System Regulatory Agencies

This listing includes all rural electric (cooperative) system regulatory agencies in the United States. This information, courtesy of the National Rural Electric Cooperative Association, 1800 Massachusetts Avenue, Washington, DC 20036, (301) 984-7333.

Alabama

Alabama Electric Co-op, Inc.
P.O. Box 550
Highway 29, North
Andalusia, AL 36420
(205) 222-2571

Arab Electric Cooperative, Inc.
P.O. Box 426
301 So. Brindlee Mountain Pkwy.
Arab, AL 35016
(205) 586-3196

Baldwin County EMC
P.O. Drawer 220
2610 Robertsdale Foley Highway
Summerdale, AL 36580
(205) 989-6247

Black Warrior EMC
P.O. Box 779
Highway 43, South
Demopolis, AL 36732
(205) 289-0845

Central Alabama Electric Co-op
P.O. Box 370
U.S.Highway 31, North
Prattville, AL 36067
(205) 365-6148

Cherokee Electric Co-op
P.O. Box 0
Clarence Chestnut By-Pass
Centre, AL 35960
(205) 927-5524

Clarke-Washington EMC
P.O. Box 398
1307 College Avenue
Jackson, AL 36545
(205) 246-9081

Coosa Valley Electric Co-op, Inc.
P.O. Box 837
230 East Street, North
Talladega, AL 35160
(205) 362-4180

Covington Electric Co-op
P.O. Box 1357
U.S.Highway 84 East-Sanford
Andalusia, AL 36420
(205) 222-4121

Cullman Electric Cooperative
P.O. Box 1168
501 4th Street, S.W.
Cullman, AL 35056
(205) 734-6511

Dixie Electric Co-op
P.O. Box 30
402 East Blackmon Street
Union Springs, AL 36089
(205) 738-2500

Franklin Electric Co-op, Inc.
P.O. Box 10
225 West Franklin Street
Russellville, AL 35653
(205) 332-2730

Joe Wheeler EMC
P.O. Box 889
500 North Sparkman Street
Hartselle, AL 35640
(205) 773-2515

Marshall DeKalb Electric Co-op
P.O. Box 724
Corner Church Street & Mill Ave.
Boaz, AL 35957
(205) 593-4262

North Alabama Electric Co-op
P.O. Box 628
Highway 72
Stevenson, AL 35772
(205) 437-2281

Pea River Electric Co-op
P.O. Box 969
Roy Parker Road
Ozark, AL 36361
(205) 774-2545

Pioneer Electric Co-op
P.O. Box 468
209 Bolling Street
Greenville, AL 36037
(205) 382-6636

Sand Mountain Electric Co-op
P.O. Box 277
198 Main Street, West
Rainsville, AL 35986
(205) 638-2153

South Alabama Electric Co-op
P.O. Box 449
Highway 231, South
Troy, AL 36081
(205) 566-2060

Southern Pine Electric Co-op
P.O. Box 528
South Boulevard
Brewton, AL 36426
(205) 867-5415

Tallapoosa River Electric Co-op
P.O. Box 675
15163 U.S.Highway 431, South
LaFayette, AL 36862
(205) 864-9331

Tombigbee Electric Co-op, Inc.
P.O. Box 610
1209 11th Street
Guin, AL 35563
(205) 468-3325

Wiregrass Electric Co-op, Inc.
P.O. Box 158
301 East Mill Street
Hartford, AL 36344
(205) 588-2223

ALASKA

Alaska Village Electric Co-op, Inc.
4831 Eagle Street
Anchorage, AK 99503
(907) 561-1818

Barrow Utilities & Electric Co-op
Pouch 449
Barrow, AK 99723
(907) 852-6166

Chugach Electric Assn., Inc.
P.O. Box 196300
5601 Minnesota Drive
Anchorage, AK 99519
(907) 563-7494

Cooper Valley Electric Assn., Inc.
P.O. Box 45
Mile 187 Glenn Highway
Glennallen, AK 99588
(907) 822-3211

Cordova Electric Cooperative
P.O. Box 20
705 Second Street
Cordova, AK 99574
(907) 424-5555

Golden Valley Electric Assn., Inc.
P.O. Box 71249
758 Illinois Street
Fairbanks, AK 99707
(907) 452-1151

Homer Electric Assn., Inc.
3977 Lake Street
Homer, AK 99603
(907) 235-8167

I-N-N Electric Assn., Inc.
P.O. Box 210
1001 Fire Lane
Iliamna, AK 99606
(907) 571-1285

Kodiak Electric Assn., Inc.
P.O. Box 787
515 Marine Way
Kodiak, AK 99615
(907) 486-7700

Kotzebue Electric Assn., Inc.
P.O. Box 44
245A 4th & Lagoon Street
Kotzebue, AK 99752
(907) 442-3491

Matanuska Electric Assn., Inc.
P.O. Box 2929
163 East Industrial Way
Palmer, AK 99645
(907) 745-3231

Metlakatla Power & Light
P.O. Box 359
3Ω Miles on Airport Road
Metlakatla, AK 99926
(907) 886-4451

Naknek Electric Assn., Inc.
P.O. Box 118
Utility Drive
Naknek, AK 99633
(907) 246-4261

Nushagak Electric Co-op, Inc.
P.O. Box 350
1 Powerhouse Road
Dillingham, AK 99576
(907) 842-5251

Tlingit-Haida Electrical Authority
P.O. Box 210149
12480 Mendenhall Loop Road
Auke Bay, AK 99921
(907) 789-3196

Unalakleet Valley Electric Co-op
P.O. Box 186
Main Street
Unalakleet, AK 99684
(907) 624-3474

ARIZONA

Arizona Electric Power Co-op, Inc.
P.O. Box 670
1000 South Highway 80
Benson, AZ 85602
(602) 586-3631

Central Arizona Irrigation District
P.O. Box 605
231 South Sunshine Boulevard
Eloy, Arizona 85231
(602) 466-7336

Duncan Valley Electric Co-op, Inc.
P.O. Box 440
222 North Highway 75
Duncan, AZ 85534
(602) 359-2503

Electrical District #1
P.O. Box 870
41630 West Miller Road
Stanfield, AZ 85272
(602) 424-3344

Electrical District #2
P.O. Box 548
11-Mile Corner Road
Coolidge, AZ 85228
(602) 723-7741

Electrical District #4
P.O. Box 605
231 South Sunshine Boulevard
Eloy, AZ 85231
(602) 466-7336

Electrical District #5
P.O. Box 1008
7Ω Miles S.W. Red Rock
Red Rock, AZ 85245
(602) 682-3442

Gila River Indian Community Utility
P.O. Box 97
Sacaton, AZ 85247
(602) 562-3645

Graham County Electric Co-op, Inc.
P.O. Drawer B
9 West Center
Pima, AZ 85543
(602) 485-2451

Grand Canyon State Electric Co-op
1445 East Thomas Road
Phoenix, AZ 85014
(602) 264-4198

Mohave Electric Co-op, Inc.
P.O. Box 1045
1999 Arena Drive
Bullhead City, AZ 86430
(602) 763-4115

Navajo Tribal Utility Authority
P.O. Box 170
Highway 12 North
Fort Defiance, AZ 86504
(602) 729-5721

Navopache Electric Co-op, Inc.
P.O.Box 308
1878 West White Mountain Blvd.
Lakeside, AZ 85929
(602) 368-5118

Sulphur Springs Valley Electric Co-op
P.O. Box 820
350 North Haskell Avenue
Wilcox, AZ 85643
(602) 384-2221

Tohona O'odham Utility Authority
P.O. Box 816
1-1/2 Miles West Highway 86
Sells, AZ 85634
(602) 383-2236

Trico Electric Co-op, Inc.
P.O. Box 35970
5100 West Ina Road
Tucson, AZ 85740
(602) 744-2944

ARKANSAS

Arkansas Electric Co-op Corp.
P.O. Box 194208
8000 Scott Hamilton Drive
Little Rock, AR 72219
(501) 570-2200

Arkansas Valley Electric Co-op Corp.
P.O. Box 47
1811 West Commercial Street
Ozark, AR 72949
(501) 667-2176

Ashley-Chicot Electric Co-op, Inc.
P.O. Box 431
305 East Jefferson
Hamburg, AR 71646
(501) 853-5212

C&L Electric Co-op Corp.
P.O. Drawer 9
900 Church Street
Star City, AR 71667
(501) 628-4221

Carroll Electric Co-op Corp.
P.O. Box 4000
West Highway 62
Berryville, AR 72616
(501) 423-2161

Clay County Electric Co-op Corp.
P.O. Box 459
Highway 67 North
Corning, AR 722422
(501) 857-3661

Craighead Electric Co-op Corp.
P.O. Box 7503
325 Southwest Drive
Jonesboro, AR 72403
(501) 932-8301

Farmers Electric Co-op Corp.
P.O. Box 400
Highway 67 North
Newport, AR 72112
(501) 523-3691

First Electric Co-op Corp.
P.O. Box 5018
901 North First
Jacksonville, AR 72076
(501) 982-4545

Mississippi County Electric Co-op
P.O. Box 7
510 North Broadway
Blytheville, AR 72316
(501) 763-4563

North Arkansas Electric Co-op, Inc.
P.O. Box 1000
U.S.Highways 62 & 9
Salem, AR 72576
(501) 895-3221

Ouachita Electric Co-op Corp.
P.O. Box 877
700 Bradley Ferry Road
Camden, AR 71701
(501) 836-5791

Ozarks Electric Co-op Corp.
P.O. Box 848
3641 Wedington Drive
Fayetteville, AR 72702
(501) 521-2900

Petit Jean Electric Co-op
P.O. Box 37
Highway 65-B
Clinton, AR 72031
(501) 745-2493

Rich Mountain Electric Co-op, Inc.
P.O. Box 897
1003 Mena Street
Mena, AR 71953
(501) 394-4140

South Central Arkansas Electric Co-op
P.O. Box 476
1140 Main Street
Arkadelphia, AR 71923
(501) 246-6701

Southwest Arkansas Electric Co-op Corp.
P.O. Box 1807
2904 East Ninth Street
Texarkana, AR 75504
(501) 772-2743

Woodruff Electric Co-op Corp.
P.O. Box 1619
3190 North Washington
Forrest City, AR 72335
(501) 633-2262

CALIFORNIA

Anza Electric Co-op, Inc.
P.O. Box 391909
58470 Highway 371
Anza, CA 92539
(714) 763-4333

Plumas-Sierra Rural Electric Co-op
P.O. Box 2000
73233 Highway 70
Portola, CA 96122
(916) 832-4261

Surprise Valley Electrification
P.O. Box 691
Lakeview Highway 299
Alturas, CA 96101
(916) 233-3511

Trinity County PUD
P.O. Box 1216
310 South Miner Street
Weaverville, CA 96093
(916) 623-5536

Truckee-Donner PUD
P.O. Box 309
11570 Donner Pass Road
Truckee, CA 95734
(916) 587-3896

COLORADO

Delta-Montrose Electric Assn.
P.O. Box 59
121 East 12th Street
Delta, CO 81416
(303) 874-8081

Empire Electric Assn., Inc.
P.O. Box K
801 North Broadway
Cortez, CO 81321
(303) 565-4444

Grand Valley Rural Power Lines
P.O. Box 190
2727 Grand Avenue
Grand Junction, CO 81502
(303) 242-0040

Gunnison County Electric Assn.
P.O. Box 180
37250 Highway 50
Gunnison, CO 81230
(303) 641-3520

Highline Electric Association
P.O. Box 57
407 East Denver
Holyoke, CO 80734
(303) 854-2236

Holy Cross Electric Assn., Inc.
P.O. Drawer 2150
3799 Highway 82
Glenwood Springs, CO 81602
(303) 945-5491

Intermountain REA
P.O. Box A
5496 North U.S. Highway 85
Sedalia, CO 80135
(303) 688-3100

K.C. Electric Association
P.O. Box 8
422 Third Street
Hugo, CO 80821
(719) 743-2431

La Plata Electric Assn., Inc.
P.O. Drawer H
45 Steward Drive
Durango, CO 81301
(303) 247-5786

Morgan County REA
P.O. Box 738
20169 Highway 34
Fort Morgan, CO 80701
(303) 867-5688

Mountain Parks Electric, Inc.
P.O. Box 170
81 West Agate
Granby, CO 80446
(303) 887-3378

Mountain View Electric Assn., Inc.
P.O. Box 1600
1655 5th Street
Limon, CO 80828
(719) 775-2861

Poudre Valley REA, Inc.
P.O. Box 1727
4809 South College Avenue
Fort Collins, CO 80522
(303) 226-1234

Rocky Mountain Generation Co-op
3030 South College Avenue, S-202
Ft. Collins, CO 80525
(303) 226-5443

San Isabel Electric Assn.
P.O. Box 892
893 East Enterprise Drive
Pueblo, CO 81002
(719) 547-2160

San Luis Valley REC, Inc.
3625 West U.S. Highway 160
Monte Vista, CO 81144
(719) 852-3538

San Miguel Power Assn., Inc.
P.O. Box 817
1050 Main Street
Nucla, CO 81424
(303) 864-7311

Sangre De Cristo Electric Assn.
P.O. Box 2013
29780 North Highway 24
Buena Vista, CO 81211
(719) 395-2412

Southeast Colorado Power Assn.
P.O. Box 521
901 West 3rd Street
La Junta, CO 81050
(719) 384-2551

Tri-State G&T Assn., Inc.
P.O. Box 33695
12076 Grant Street
Denver, CO 80233
(303) 452-6111

United Power, Inc.
P.O. Box 929
18551 East 160 Avenue
Brighton, CO 80601
(303) 659-0551

White River Electric Assn., Inc.
P.O. Box 958
233 Sixth Street
Meeker, CO 81641
(303) 878-5041

Y.W. Electric Assn., Inc.
P.O. Box Y
250 Main Street
Akron, CO 80720
(303) 345-2291

Yampa Valley Electric Assn., Inc.
P.O. Box 771218
32 Tenth Street
Steamboat Spring, CO 80477
(303) 879-1160

CONNECTICUT

Connecticut Municipal Electric Energy Co-op
30 Stott Avenue
Norwich, CT 06360
(203) 889-4088

DELAWARE

Delaware Electric Co-op, Inc.
P.O. Box 600
U.S. Route 13
Greenwood, DE 19950
(302) 349-4571

FLORIDA

Central Florida Electric Co-op
(813) 995-2121
1424 North Main Street
Chiefland, FL 32626
(904) 493-2511

Choctawhatchee Electric Co-op, Inc.
P.O. Box 512
700 West Baldwin Avenue
DeFuniak Springs, FL 32433
(904) 892-2111

Clay Electric Co-op, Inc.
P.O. Box 308
225 West Walker Drive
Keystone Heights, FL 32656
(904) 473-4911

Escambia River Electric Co-op, Inc.
P.O. Box 428
3425 Highway 4, West
Jay, FL 32565
(904) 675-4521

Florida Keys Electric Co-op Assn.
P.O. Box 377
91605 Overseas Highway
Tavernier, FL 33070
(305) 852-2431

Florida Municipal Power Agency
7201 Lake Ellenor Drive, S-100
Orlando, FL 32809
(407) 859-7310

Glades Electric Co-op, Inc.
P.O. Box 519
U.S. 27 South
Moore Haven, FL 33471
(813) 946-0061

Gulf Coast Electric Co-op, Inc.
P.O. Box 220
Highway 22
Wewahitchka, FL 32465
(904) 639-2216

Lee County Electric Co-op, Inc.
P.O. Box 3455
4980 Bayline Drive
North Ft. Myers, FL 33918 P.O. Box 9

Peace River Electric Co-op, Inc.
P.O. Box 1310
Highway 17, North
Wauchula, FL 33873
(813) 773-4116

Seminole Electric Co-op, Inc.
P.O. Box 272000
16313 North Dale Mabry
Tampa, FL 33688
(813) 963-0994

Sumter Electric Co-op, Inc.
P.O. Box 301
Highways 301 & 471
Sumterville, FL 33585
(904) 793-3801

Suwannee Valley Electric Co-op
P.O. Box 160
1725 South Ohio Avenue
Live Oak, FL 32060
(904) 362-2226

Talquin Electric Co-op, Inc.
P.O. Box 1679
1640 West Jefferson Street
Quincy, FL 32351
(904) 627-7651

Tri-County Electric Co-op, Inc.
P.O. Box 208
U.S. 90 West
Madison, FL 32340
(904) 973-2285

West Florida Electric Co-op Assn.
P.O. Box 127
303 Cottondale Road
Graceville, FL 32440
(904) 263-3231

Withlacoochee River Electric Co-op
P.O. Box 278
601 North 21st Street
Dade City, FL 33526
(904) 567-5133

GEORGIA

Altamaha EMC
P.O. Box 346
Highway 280 West
Lyons, GA 30436
(912) 526-8181

Amicalola EMC
P.O. Box 10
1125 Appalachian Parkway
Jasper, GA 30143
(706) 692-6471

Blue Ridge Mountain EMC
P.O. Box 9
West Main Street
Young Harris, GA 30582
(404) 379-3121

Canoochee EMC
P.O. Box 497
Brazell Street
Reidsville, GA 30453
(912) 557-4391

Carroll EMC
P.O. Box 629
155 Temple Road
Carrollton, GA 30117
(404) 832-3552

Central Georgia EMC
P.O. Box 309
923 South Mulberry Street
Jackson, GA 30233
(404) 775-7857

Coastal EMC
P.O. Box 109
Highway 17, South
Midway, GA 31320
(912) 884-3311

Cobb EMC
P.O. Box 369
1512 Church Street Ext.
Marietta, GA 30061
(404) 424-1504

Colquitt EMC
P.O. Box 400
2912 Rowland Drive
Moultrie, GA 31776
(912) 985-3620

Coweta-Fayette EMC
P.O. Box 488
390 North Highway 29
Newnan, GA 30264
(404) 253-5626

Excelsior EMC
P.O. Box 297
Highway 46, East
Metter, GA 30439
(912) 685-2115

Flint EMC
P.O. Box 308
Marion Street
Reynolds, GA 31076
(912) 847-3415

Grady County EMC
P.O. Box 270
BainBridge Highway 84 West
Cairo, GA 31728
(912) 377-4182

GreyStone Power Corporation
P.O. Box 897
4040 Bankhead Highway
Douglasville, GA 30133
(404) 942-6576

Habersham EMC
P.O. Box 25
Cleveland Highway
Clarksville, GA 30523
(706) 754-2114

Hart EMC
P.O. Box 250
Elberton Highway
Hartwell, GA 30643
(706) 376-4714

Irwin County EMC
P.O. Box 125
915 West 4th Street
Ocilla, GA 31774
(912) 468-7654

Jackson EMC
P.O. Box 38
850 Commerce Road
Jefferson, GA 30549
(404) 367-5281

Jefferson EMC
P.O. Box 312
1001 Peachtree Street
Louisville, GA 30434
(912) 625-7265

Lamar EMC
P.O. Box 40
314 College Drive
Barnesville, GA 30204
(404) 358-1383

Little Ocmulgee EMC
P.O. Box 150
Railroad Avenue
Alamo, GA 30411
(912) 568-7171

Middle Georgia EMC
P.O. Box 157
Tippetville Road
Vienna, GA 31092
(912) 268-2671

Mitchell EMC
P.O. Box 409
Hawthorne Trail
Camilla, GA 31730
(912) 336-5221

North Georgia EMC
P.O. Box 1407
1850 Cleveland Road
Dalton, GA 30720
(404) 259-9441

Ocmulgee EMC
P.O. Box 669
802 Eastman Street
Eastman, GA 31023
(912) 374-7001

Oconee EMC
P.O. Box 37
U.S. Highway 80
Dudley, GA 31022
(912) 676-3191

Oglethorpe Power Corporation
P.O. Box 1349
2100 East Exchange Place
Tucker, GA 30085
(404) 270-7600

Okefenoke REMC
P.O. Box 602
Highway 82 East
Nahunta, GA 31553
(912) 462-5131

Pataula EMC
P.O. Box 289
925 Blakely Street
Cuthbert, GA 31740
(912) 732-3171

Planters EMC
P.O. Box 979
Sylvania Road
Millen, Ga 30442
(912) 982-4722

Rayle EMC
P.O. Box 250
616 Lexington Avenue
Washington, GA 30673
(706) 678-2116

Satilla REMC
P.O. Box 906
101 West 17th Street
Alma, GA 31510
(912) 632-7222

Sawnee EMC
P.O. Box 266
543 Atlanta Road
Cumming, GA 30130
(404) 887-2363

Slash Pine EMC
P.O. Box 356
Highway 84 West
Homerville, GA 31634
(912) 487-5201

Snapping Shoals EMC
P.O. Box 509
14750 Brown Bridge Road
Covington, GA 30209
(404) 786-3484

Sumter EMC
P.O. Box 1048
1120 Felder Street
Americus, GA 31709
(912) 924-8041

Three Notch EMC
P.O. Box 367
116 West 2nd Street
Donalsonville, GA 31745
(912) 524-5377

Tri-County EMC
P.O. Box 487
Highway 129
Gray, GA 31032
(912) 986-3134

Tri-State EMC
P.O. Box 68
Highway #5
McCaysville, GA 30555
(706) 492-3251

Troup Electric Membership Corp.
P.O. Box 160
1336 Greenville Road
LaGrange, GA 30241
(706) 882-2513

Upson County EMC
P.O. Box 31
607 East Main Street
Thomaston, GA 30286
(706) 647-5475

Walton EMC
P.O. Box 260
842 U.S. Highway 78
Monroe, GA 30655
(404) 267-2505

Washington EMC
P.O. Box 598
319 North Smith Street
Sandersville, GA 31082
(912) 552-2577

IDAHO

Clearwater Power Company
P.O. Box 997
4230 Hatwai Road
Lewiston, ID 83501
(208) 743-1501

Fall River REC, Inc.
P.O. Box 830
714 East Main Street
Ashton, ID 83420
(208) 652-7431

Idaho County Light & Power Co-op
P.O. Box 300
Highway 13, East
Grangeville, ID 83530
(208) 983-1610

Kootenai Electric Co-op, Inc.
P.O. Box 278
West 2451 Dakota Avenue
Hayden Lake, ID 83835
(208) 765-1200

Lost River Electric Co-op, Inc.
P.O. Box 420
305 Pine Street
Mackay, ID 83251
(208) 588-3311

Northern Lights, Inc.
P.O. Box 310
1423 Dover Highway
Sandpoint, ID 83864
(208) 263-5141

Raft River REC, Inc.
P.O. Box 617
250 North Main
Malta, ID 83342
(208) 645-2211

Riverside Electric Company
P.O. Box 12
300 South 135 East
Rupert, ID 83350
(208) 436-3855

Rural Electric Company
Route 2, Box 60
Rupert, ID 83350
(208) 436-4781

Salmon River Electric Co-op, Inc.
P.O. Box 384
Main Street
Challis, ID 83226
(208) 879-2283

Snake River Power Assn, Inc.
P.O. Box 608
1734 Overland Avenue
Burley, ID 83318
(208) 678-3027

South Side Electric Lines, Inc.
P.O. Box 69
Highway 77
Declo, ID 83323
(208) 654-2313

ILLINOIS

Adams Electrical Co-operative
P.O. Box 247
U.S. Highway #24 East
Camp Point, IL 62320
(217) 593-7120

Clay Electric Co-op, Inc.
P.O. Box 517
Old Highway 50 West
Flora, IL 62839
(618) 662-2171

Clinton County Electric Co-op, Inc.
P.O. Box 40
475 North Main Street
Breese, IL 62230
(618) 526-7282

Coles-Moultrie Electric Co-op
P.O. Box 709
East Route 316 & Logan Street
Mattoon, IL 61938
(217) 235-1341

Corn Belt Electric Co-op, Inc.
P.O. Box 816
1502 Morrissey Drive
Bloomington, IL 61701
(309) 662-5330

Eastern Illini Electric Co-op
P.O. Box 96
330 West Ottawa Street
Paxton, IL 60957
(217) 379-2131

Edgar Electric Co-op Assn.
P.O. Box 190
Route 6
Paris, IL 61944
(217) 463-1002

Egyptian Electric Co-op Assn.
P.O. Box 38
1005 West Broadway
Steeleville, IL 62288
(618) 965-3434

Farmers Mutual Electric Company
P.O. Box 43
1004 South Chicago Street
Geneseo, IL 61254
(309) 944-4669

Illinois Rural Electric Company
2-12 South Main Street
Winchester, IL 62694
(217) 742-3128

Jo-Carroll Electric Co-op, Inc.
P.O. Box 390
793 U.S. Route 20, West
Elizabeth, IL 61028
(815) 858-2207

M.J.M. Electric Co-op, Inc.
P.O. Box 80
264 North East Street
Carlinville, IL 62626
(217) 854-3137

McDonough Power Co-op
P.O. Box 352
1210 West Jackson
Macomb, IL 61455
(309) 833-2101

Menard Electric Co-op
P.O. Box 200
122 South Sixth Street
Petersburg, IL 62675
(217) 632-7746

Monroe County Electric Co-operative
P.O. Box 128
901 North Market
Waterloo, IL 62298
(618) 939-7171

Norris Electric Co-op
Route 130, South
Newton, IL 62448
(618) 783-8765

Rural Electric Convenience Co-op
P.O. Box 19
Illinois Route 104
Auburn, IL 62615
(217) 438-6197

Shelby Electric Cooperative
P.O. Box 560
Route 128 & North 6th Street
Shelbyville, IL 62565
(217) 774-3986

Southeastern Illinois Electric Co-op
P.O. Box 251
Route 142, South
Eldorado, IL 62930
(618) 273-2611

Southern Illinois Electric Co-op
P.O. Box 100
U.S. Route 51 North
Dongola, IL 62926
(618) 827-3555

Southwestern Electric Co-op, Inc.
P.O. Box 409
South Elm Street & Route 40
Greenville, IL 62246
(618) 664-1025

Soyland Power Cooperative
788 North Sunnyside Road
Decatur, IL 62522
(217) 423-0021

Spoon River Electric Co-op, Inc.
P.O. Box 340
930 South Fifth Avenue
Canton, IL 61520
(309) 647-2700

Tri-County Electric Co-op, Inc.
P.O. Drawer 309
3906 West Broadway
Mount Vernon, IL 62864
(618) 244-5151

Wayne-White Counties Electric Co-op
P.O. Drawer E
Routes 15 & 45 West
Fairfield, IL 62837
(618) 842-2196

Western Illinois Electrical Coop.
P.O. Box 338
524 North Madison
Carthage, IL 62321
(217) 357-3125

INDIANA

Bartholomew County REMC
P.O. Box 467
801 Second Street
Columbus, IN 47202
(812) 372-2546

Boone County REMC
P.O. Box 563
1207 Indianapolis Avenue
Lebanon, IN 46052
(317) 482-2390

Carroll County REMC
P.O. Box 298
119 West Franklin Street
Delphi, Indiana 46923
(317) 564-2057

Central Indiana Power
P.O. Box 188
2243 East U.S. 40
Greenfield, IN 46140
(317) 462-4417

Clark County REMC
P.O. Box L
7810 State Road 60
Sellersburg, IN 47172
(812) 246-3316

Daviess-Martin County REMC
P.O. Box 540
Highway 50, East
Washington, IN 47501
(812) 254-1870

Decatur County REMC
P.O. Box 46
1430 West Main Street
Greensburg, IN 47240
(812) 663-3391

Dubois REC, Inc.
P.O. Box 610
458 Third Avenue
Jasper, IN 47547
(812) 482-5454

Fayette-Union County REMC
P.O. Box 349
101 West Sycamore Street
Liberty, IN 47353
(317) 458-5171

Fulton County REMC
P.O. Box 230
1448 West State Road 14
Rochester, IN 46975
(219) 223-3156

Harrison County REMC
P.O. Box 127
1165 Old Forest Road
Corydon, IN 47112
(813) 738-4115

Hendricks County REMC
P.O. Box 309
10 North Road 500, East
Danville, IN 46122
(317) 745-5473

Henry County REMC
P.O. Box D
201 North 6th Street
New Castle, IN 47362
(317) 529-1212

Hoosier Energy REC., Inc.
P.O. Box 908
7398 North State Road 37
Bloomington, IN 47402
(812) 876-2021

Jackson County REMC
P.O. Box K
274 East Base Road
Brownstown, IN 47220
(812) 358-4458

Jasper County REMC
P.O. Box 129
County Road 400 South
Rensselaer, IN 47978
(219) 866-4601

Jay County REMC
P.O. Box 904
West Water Street
Portland, IN 47371
(219) 726-7121

Johnson County REMC
P.O. Box 309
750 International Drive
Franklin, IN 46131
(317) 736-6174

Kankakee Valley REMC
P.O. Box 157
14 South Main Street
Wanatah, IN 46390
(219) 733-2511

Knox County REMC
P.O. Box 577
Highway 41 South
Vincennes, IN 47591
(812) 882-5140

Kosciusko County REMC
P.O. Box 588
523 South Buffalo Street
Warsaw, IN 46581
(219) 267-6331

LaGrange County REMC
P.O. Box 147
206 South Detroit Street
LaGrange, IN 46761
(219) 463-7165

Marshall County REMC
P.O. Box 250
11299 12th Road
Plymouth, IN 46563
(219) 936-3161

Miami-Cass County REMC
P.O. Box 168
U.S. 31 & County Road 100 North
Peru, IN 46970
(317) 473-6668

Newton County REMC
P.O. Box 125
207 East Goss Street
Kentland, IN 47951
(219) 474-6224

Noble County REMC
P.O. Box 137
Weber Road
Albion, IN 46701
(219) 636-2113

Northeastern REMC
P.O. Box 171
1353 South Governors Drive
Columbia City, IN 46725
(219) 244-6111

Orange County REMC
P.O. Box 208
Highway 337, East
Orleans, IN 47452
(812) 865-2229

Parke County REMC
119 West High Street
Rockville, IN 47872
(317) 569-3133

Rush County REMC
P.O. Box 7
126 South Main Street
Rushville, IN 46173
(317) 932-4121

Shelby County REMC
P.O. Box 100
1504 South Harrison Street
Shelbyville, IN 46176
(317) 398-6621

South Central Indiana REMC
300 Morton Avenue
Martinsville, IN 46151
(317) 342-3344

Southeastern Indiana REMC
South Buckeye Street
Osgood, IN 47037
(812) 689-4111

Southern Indiana REC, Inc.
P.O. Box 219
1776 10th Street
Tell City, IN 47586
(812) 547-2316

Steuben County REMC
P.O. Box 358
1385 South Old 27
Angola, IN 46703
(219) 665-3563

Sullivan County REMC
P.O. Box 450
110 North Main Street
Sullivan, IN 47882
(812) 268-4366

Tipmont REMC
P.O. Box 20
U.S. 231 South
Linden, IN 47955
(317) 339-7211

United REMC
P.O. Box 605
4563 East Markle Road
Markle, IN 46770
(219) 758-3155

Utility District of Western Indiana REMC
P.O. Box 427
Route #2, Highway 54 West
Bloomfield, IN 47424
(812) 384-4446

Wabash County REMC
P.O. Box 598
1101 Manchester Avenue
Wabash, IN 46992
(219) 563-2146

Wabash Valley Power Assn.
P.O. Box 24700
722 North High School Road
Indianapolis, IN 46224
(317) 481-2800 P.O. Box 196

Warren County REMC
P.O. Box 37
14 Midway Street
Williamsport, IN 47993
(317) 762-6114

Wayne County REMC
P.O. Box 638
1450 N.W. 5th Street
Richmond, IN 47374
(317) 962-7521

White County REMC
P.O. Box 599
321 North Main Street
Monticello, IN 47960
(219) 583-7161

IOWA

Adams County Co-op Electric Company
P.O. Box 367
626 Davis Avenue
Corning, IA 50841
(515) 322-3165

Allamakee-Clayton Electric Co-op, Inc.
P.O. Box 715
228 West Greene Street
Postville, IA 52162
(319) 864-7611

Benton County Electric Co-op Assn.
P.O. Box 488
1006 West 4th Street
Vinton, IA 52349
(319) 472-2367

Boone Valley Electric Co-op
Renwick, IA 50577
(515) 824-3565

Buchanan County RECC
P.O. Box 31
1707 First Street East
Independence, IA 50644
(319) 334-2571

Butler County REC
P.O. Box 98
521 North Main Street
Allison, IA 50602
(319) 267-2726

Calhoun County Electric Co-op Assn.
P.O. Box 312
412 5th Street
Rockwell City, IA 50579
(712) 297-7112

Cedar Valley Electric Co-op
P.O. Box 70
605 East Fourth Street
St. Ansgar, IA 50472
(515) 736-4965

Central Iowa Power Co-op
P.O. Box 2517
1400 Highway 13, S.E.
Cedar Rapids, IA 52406
(319) 366-8011

Chariton Valley Electric Co-op
P.O. Box 486
Highway 5 South
Albia, IA 52531
(515) 932-7126

Clarke Electric Co-op, Inc.
P.O. Box 161
Highway 69, North
Osceola, IA 50213
(515) 342-2173

Corn Belt Power Co-op
P.O. Box 508
1300-13th Street, North
Humboldt, IA 50548
(515) 332-2571

Eastern Iowa Light & Power Co-op
East Fifth & Sycamore Street
Wilton, IA 52778
(319) 732-2211

Farmers Electric Co-op, Inc.
P.O. Box 330
102 S.W. 6th
Greenfield, IA 50849
(515) 743-6146

Franklin REC
P.O. Box 437
1 Second Avenue, N.W.
Hampton, IA 50441
(309) 683-2510

Glidden REC
P.O. Box 486
Highway 30
Glidden, IA 51443
(712) 659-3649

315 First Avenue 102 G Avenue, East
Grundy Center, IA 50638
(319) 824-5251

Guthrie County RECA
P.O. Box 7
Highway 44, East
Guthrie Center, IA 50115
(515) 747-2206

Hancock County REC
P.O. Box 149
600 West Third Street
Garner, IA 50438
(515) 923-2654

Harrison County REC
P.O. Box 2
61-65 Fourth Street
Wodbine, IA 51579
(712) 647-2727

Hawkeye Tri-County REC
P.O. Box 90
Highway #9, East
Cresco, IA 52136
(319) 547-3801

Humboldt County REC
1210 13th Street North
Humboldt, IA 50548
(515) 332-1616

Ida County REC
P.O. Box 72
Highways 59 & 175, East
Ida Grove, IA 51445
(712) 364-3341

Iowa Lakes Electric Cooperative
P.O. Box 77
1724 Central Avenue
Estherville, IA 51334
(712) 362-2694

L&O Power Co-op Grundy County REC
Rock Rapids, IA 51246
(712) 472-2531

Linn County REC
P.O. Box 69
999 35th Street
Marion, IA 52302
(309) 377-1587

Lyon REC
P.O. Box 629
116 South Marshall
Rock Rapids, IA 51246
(712) 472-2506

Maquoketa Valley REC
P.O. Box 370
109 North Huber Street
Anamosa, IA 52205
(319) 462-3542

Marshall County REC
P.O. Box 1048
Marshalltown, IA 50158
(515) 752-1593

Midland Power Co-op
1005 East Lincolnway
Jefferson, IA 50129
(515) 386-4111

Monona County REC
P.O. Box 359
Highway 175 East
Onawa, IA 51040
(712) 423-1622

Nishnabotna Valley REC
P.O. Box 714
1317 Chatburn Avenue
Harlan, IA 51537
(712) 755-2166

Northwest Iowa Power Co-op
P.O. Box 240
Highway 75, South
Le Mars, IA 51031
(712) 546-4141

Nyman Electric Co-op, Inc.
P.O. Box J
415 Broad Avenue
Stanton, IA 51573
(712) 829-2211

O'Brien County REC
P.O. Box 458
160 South Hayes
Primghar, IA 51245
(712) 757-0885

Osceola Electric Co-oper, Inc.
P.O. Box 127
204 Eighth Street
Sibley, IA 51249
(712) 754-2519

Pella Co-op Electric Assn.
P.O. Box 106
Highway 163, West
Pella, IA 50219
(515) 628-1040

Plymouth Electric Co-op Assn.
P.O. Box 440
45 First Avenue, S.W.
Le Mars, IA 51031
(712) 546-4149

Rideta Electric Co-op, Inc.
P.O. Box 391
Highway 2 West
Mount Ayr, IA 50854
(515) 464-2244

S.E. Iowa Co-op Electric Assn.
P.O. Box 440
907 East Washington
Mt. Pleasant, IA 52641
(319) 385-1577

Sac County REC
P.O. Box 397
Highway 20 East
Sac City, IA 50583
(712) 662-4275

Sioux Electric Co-op Assn.
415 8th Street, S.E.
Orange City, IA 51041
(712) 737-4935

South Crawford REC
P.O. Box 428
Highway 39, North
Denison, IA 51442
(712) 263-2943

Southern Iowa Electric Co-op, Inc.
P.O. Box 70
Old Highway 2, East
Bloomfield, IA 52537
(515) 664-2277

T.I.P. Rural Electric Co-op
P.O. Box AH
612 West Des Moines Street
Brooklyn, IA 52211
(515) 522-9221

Winnebago RECA
P.O. Box 65
216 Jackson Street
Thompson, IA 50478
(515) 584-2251

Woodbury County RECA
P.O. Box AG
1495 Humboldt Avenue
Moville, IA 51039
(712) 873-3125

Wright County REC
P.O. Drawer 113
Highway 3-West
Clarion, IA 50525
(515) 532-2805

KANSAS

Ark Valley Electric Co-op Assn.
P.O. Box 1246
10 East 10th Street
Hutchinson, KS 67504
(316) 662-6661

Brown-Atchison Electric Co-op Assn.
P.O. Box 230
1712 Central Avenue
Horton, KS 66439
(913) 486-2117

Butler RECA, Inc.
P.O. Box 1242
216-218 South Vine Street
El Dorado, KS 67042
(316) 321-9603

C.& W. Rural Electric Co-op Assn.
P.O. Box 513
524 Dexter Street
Clay Center, KS 67432
(913) 632-3111

C.M.S. Electric Co-op, Inc.
P.O. Box 740
509 East Carthage
Meade, KS 67864
(316) 873-2184

Caney Valley Electric Co-op Assn.
P.O. Box 308
401 Lawrence
Cedar Vale, KS 67024
(316) 758-2262

DS&O Rural Electric Co-op Assn.
P.O. Box 286
129 West Main
Solomon, KS 67480
(913) 655-2011

Doniphan Electric Co-op Assn., Inc.
P.O. Box 588
101 North Main
Troy, KS 66087
(913) 985-3523

Flint Hills RECA, Inc.
P.O. Box B
West Highway 56
Council Grove, KS 66846
(316) 767-5144

Jewell-Mitchell Co-op Electric Company
P.O. Box 307
122 West Main
Mankato, KS 66956
(913) 378-3151

Kansas Electric Power Co-op
P.O. Box 4877
5990 S.W. 28th Street
Topeka, KS 66604
(913) 273-7010

Kaw Valley Electric Co-op, Inc.
P.O. Box 4286
5715 21st Street Southwest
Topeka, KS 66604
(913) 272-4330

Lane-Scott Electric Co-op, Inc.
P.O. Box 758
444 West Long
Dighton, KS 67839
(316) 397-2321

Leavenworth-Jefferson Electric Co-op
P.O. Box 70
507 North Union
McLouth, KS 66054
(913) 796-6111

Lyon-Coffey Electric Co-op
P.O. Box 229
1013 North 4th Street
Burlington, KS 66839
(316) 364-2116

Midwest Energy, Inc.
P.O. Box 898
1330 Canterbury Road
Hays, KS 67601
(913) 625-3437

N.C.K. Electric Co-op, Inc.
P.O. Box 309
2305 East U.S. 81, Frontage Road
Belleville, KS 66935
(913) 527-2251

Nemaha-Marshall Electric Co-op
P.O. Box O
402 Prairie Street
Axtell, KS 66403
(913) 736-2345

Ninnescah RECA, Inc.
P.O. Box 967
West Highway 54
Pratt, KS 67124
(316) 672-5538

Northwest Kansas Electric Co-op Assn.
P.O. Box 168
103 West 4th Street
Bird City, KS 67731
(913) 734-2311

Norton-Decatur Co-op Electric Company
P.O. Box 360
309 East Main
Norton, KS 67654
(913) 877-3323

P.R.& W. Electric Co-op Assn.
P.O. Box 5
Highway 24 East
Wamego, KS 66547
(913) 456-2212

Pioneer Electric Co-op
P.O. Box 368
Highway 160 West
Ulysses, KS 67880
(316) 356-1211

Radiant Electric Co-op, Inc.
P.O. Box 390
102 North 15th
Fredonia, KS 66736
(316) 378-2161

Sedgwick County Electric Co-op
P.O. Box 220
125 North Main
Cheney, KS 67025
(316) 542-3131

Sekan Electric Co-op Assn., Inc.
P.O. Box 40
120 North Ozark
Girard, KS 66743
(316) 724-8251

Smokey Hill Electric Co-op Assn.
P.O. Box 125
208 West First
Ellsworth, KS 67439
(913) 472-4021

Sumner-Cowley Electric Co-op, Inc.
P.O. Box 220
2223 North A Street
Wellington, KS 67152
(316) 326-3356

Sunflower Electric Power Corp.
P.O. Box 980
301 West 13th
Hays, KS 67601
(913) 628-2845

Twin Valley Electric Co-op
P.O. Box 385
501 Houston
Altamont, KS 67330
(316) 784-5500

United Electric Cooperative, Inc.
P.O. Box 326
410 North State Street
Iola, KS 66749
(316) 367-5151

Victory Electric Co-op Assn., Inc.
P.O. Box 1335
North 14th Street
Dodge City, KS 67801
(316) 227-2139

Western Co-op Electric Assn., Inc.
P.O. Box 278
635 South 13th
WaKeeney, KS 67672
(913) 743-5561

Wheatland Electric Co-op, Inc.
P.O. Box 130
101 Main Street
Scott City, KS 67871
(316) 872-5885

KENTUCKY

Big Rivers Electric Corp.
P.O. Box 24
201 Third Street
Henderson, KY 42420
(502) 827-2561

Big Sandy RECC
P.O. Box 1746
504 11th Street
Paintsville, KY 41240
(606) 789-4095

Blue Grass RECC
P.O. Box 990
1201 Lexington Road
Nicholasville, KY 40340
(606) 885-4191

Clark RECC
P.O. Box 478
2640 Iron Works Road
Winchester, KY 40392
(606) 744-4251

Cumberland Valley RECC
P.O. Box 440
Gray, KY 40734
(606) 528-2677

East Kentucky Power Co-op
P.O. Box 707
4758 Lexington Road
Winchester, KY 40392
(606) 744-4812

Farmers RECC
P.O. Box 298
504 South Broadway
Glasgow, KY 42141
(502) 651-2193

Fleming-Mason RECC
P.O. Drawer 328
R.R.#2, Elizaville Road
Flemingsburg, KY 41041
(606) 845-2661

Fox Creek RECC
P.O. Box 150
1200 Versailles Road
Lawrenceburg, KY 40342
(502) 839-3442

Grayson RECC
109 Bagby Park
Grayson, KY 41143
(606) 474-5136

Green River Electric Corp.
P.O. Box 1389
3111 Fairview Drive
Owensboro, KY 42302
(502) 926-4141

Harrison County RECC
P.O. Box 130
Oddville Avenue
Cynthiana, KY 41031
(606) 234-3131

Henderson-Union RECC
P.O. Box 18
64-2 Old Corydon Road
Henderson, KY 42420
(502) 826-3991

Hickman-Fulton Counties RECC
P.O. Box 190
Highway 94-Moscow Avenue
Hickman, KY 42050
(501) 236-2521

Inter-County RECC
P.O. Box 87
1009 Hustonville Road
Danville, KY 40423
(606) 236-4561

Jackson County RECC
P.O. Box 307
127 U.S. Highway 421, South
McKee, KY 40447
(606) 287-7161

Jackson Purchase Electric Co-op Corp.
P.O. Box 3188
2900 Irvin Cobb Drive
Paducah, KY 42002
(502) 442-7321

Licking Valley RECC
P.O. Box 605
271 Main Street
West Liberty, KY 41472
(606) 743-3179

Meade County RECC
P.O. Box 489
1351 Irvington Road
Brandenburg, KY 40108
(502) 422-2162

Nolin RECC 612 East Dixie
Elizabethtown, KY 42701
(502) 765-6153

Owen Electric Cooperative, Inc.
510 South Main Street
Owenton, KY 40359
(502) 484-3471

Pennyrile RECC
P.O. Box 551
2000 Harrison Street
Hopkinsville, KY 42241
(502) 886-2555

Salt River Electric Co-op Corp.
P.O. Box 609
111 West Brashear Avenue
Bardstown, KY 40004
(502) 348-3931

Shelby RECC
P.O. Box 309
Old Finchville Road & U.S.60
Shelbyville, KY 40066
(502) 633-4420

South Kentucky RECC
P.O. Box 910
925-929 North Main Street
Somerset, KY 42502
(606) 678-4121

Taylor County RECC
P.O. Box 100
100 West Main Street
Campbellsville, KY 42719
(502) 465-4101

Warren RECC
P.O. Box 1118
951 Fairview Avenue
Bowling, Green, KY 42102
(502) 842-6541

West Kentucky RECC
P.O. Box 589
1218 West Broadway
Mayfield, KY 42066
(502) 247-1321

LOUISIANA

Beauregard Electric Co-op, Inc.
P.O. Drawer 970
Highway 171, South
DeRidder, LA 70760
(504) 638-3751

South Louisiana Electric Co-op
P.O. Box 4037
2028 Coteau Road
Houma, LA 70361
(504) 876-6880

Southwest Louisiana EMC
P.O. Drawer 90866
3420 Highway 167, North
Lafayette, LA 70509
(318) 896-5384

Teche Electric Co-op, Inc.
P.O. Drawer 472
811 South Canal Road
Jeanerette, LA 70544
(318) 276-6347

Valley EMC
P.O. Box 659
1725 Texas Street
Natchitoches, LA 71457
(318) 352-3601

Washington-St.Tammany Electric Co-op
P.O. Drawer N
950 Pearl Street
Franklinton, LA 70438
(504) 839-3562

MAINE

Eastern Maine Electric Co-op, Inc.
P.O. Box 425
9 Union Street
Calais, ME 04619
(207) 454-7555

Fox Islands Electric Co-op
P.O. Box 527
Main Street
Vinalhaven, ME 04863
(207) 863-4636

Swans Island Electric Co-op
P.O. Box 8
Quarry Wharf Road
Minturn, ME 04659
(207) 526-4336

Union River Electric Co-op, Inc.
HCR 31, Box 240
Aurora, ME 04408
(207) 584-3200

MARYLAND

Choptank Electric Co-op, Inc.
P.O. Box 430
Route 404 Business West
Denton, MD 21629
(410) 479-0380

Southern Maryland Electric Co-op
P.O. Box 1937
Hughesville, MD 20637
(301) 274-3111

MASSACHUSETTS

Massachusetts Municipal Wholesale
Electric Company
P.O. Box 426
Ludlow, MA 01056
(413) 589-0141

MICHIGAN

Alger-Delta Co-op Electric Assn.
426 North 9th Street
Gladstone, MI 49837
(906) 428-4141

Cherryland Electric Cooperative
P.O. Box 298
U.S. 31 South
Grawn, MI 49637
(616) 943-8377

Cloverland Electric Co-op
P.O. Box 97
Highway M-28
Dafter, MI 49724
(906) 635-6800

Fruit Belt Electric Co-op
P.O. Box 127
901 East State Street
Cassopolis, MI 49031
(616) 445-2477

O&A Electric Co-op, Inc.
P.O. Box 800
490 Quarterline Road
Newaygo, MI 49337
(616) 652-1651

Oceana Electric Co-op
P.O. Box 232
1 Water Road
Hart, MI 49420
(616) 873-2155

Ontonagon County REA
P.O. Box 97
500 J.K.Paul Street
Ontonagon, MI 49953
(906) 884-4151

Presque Isle Electric Co-op, Inc.
P.O. Box 308
19831 M-68 Highway
Onaway, MI 49765
(517) 733-8515

Southeastern Michigan REC, Inc.
P.O. Box 869
1610 East Maumee Street
Adrian, MI 49221
(517) 263-1808

Thumb Electric Co-op, Inc.
P.O. Box 157
2231 Main Street
Ubly, MI 48475
(517) 658-8571

Top O'Michigan Rural Electric Company
P.O. Box 70
1123 East Division
Boyne City, MI 49712
(616) 582-6521

Tri-County Electric Co-op
P.O. Box 379
1100 West Grand River Avenue
Portland, MI 48875
(517) 647-7554

Western Michigan Electric Co-op
P.O. Box 248
525 West U.S. 10
Scottville, MI 49454
(616) 757-4724

Wolverine Power Supply Co-op
P.O. Box 229
10125 West Watergate Road
Cadillac, MI 49601
(616) 775-5700

MINNESOTA

Agralite Cooperative
P.O. Box 228
East Highway 12
Benson, MN 56215
(612) 843-4150

Anoka Electric Co-op
2022 North Ferry Street
Anoka, MN 55303
(612) 421-3761

Arrowhead Electric Co-op, Inc.
P.O. Box 39
MM 391-392 Highway 61
Lutsen, MN 55612
(218) 663-7239

Beltrami Electric Co-op, Inc.
P.O. Box 488
2025 Paul Bunyan Drive, N.W.
Bemidji, MN 56601
(218) 751-2540

Brown County REA
P.O. Box 529
Highway 4, North
Sleepy Eye, MN 56085
(507) 794-3331

Carlton County Co-op Power Assn.
P.O. Box 98
Highway 73, South
Kettle River, MN 55757
(218) 273-4111

Clearwater-Polk Electric Co-op
P.O. Box O
315 North Main Street
Bagley, MN 56621
(218) 694-6241

Co-op Light & Power Association
P.O. Box 69
4th Street & 15th Avenue
Two Harbors, MN 55616
(218) 834-2226

Cooperative Power Assn.
14615 Lone Oak Road
Eden Prairie, MN 55344
(612) 937-8599

Crow Wing Co-op Power & Light Company
P.O. Box 507
Highway 371, North
Brainerd, MN 56401
(218) 829-2827

Dairyland Electric Co-op, Inc.
2810 Elida Drive
Grand Rapids, MN 55744
(218) 326-6671

Dakota Electric Association
4300 220th Street, West
Farmington, MN 55024
(612) 463-7134

East Central Electric Assn.
412 North Main Street
Braham, MN 55006
(612) 396-3351

Federated REA
P.O. Box 69
South Highway 71
Jackson, MN 56143
(507) 847-3520

Freeborn-Mower Electric Co-op
P.O. Box 611
City Road 46 East
Albert Lea, MN 46007
(507) 373-6421

Frost-BENCO-Wells Electric Assn.
P.O. Box 8
Highway 169 South
Mankota, MN 56002
(507) 387-7963

Goodhue County Co-op Electric Assn.
P.O. Box 99
224 Main Street
Zumbrota, MN 55992
(507) 732-5117

Itasca-Mantrap Co-op Electric Assn.
P.O. Box 192
South County Road #6
Park Rapids, MN 56470
(218) 732-3377

Kandiyohi Co-op Electric Power Assn.
1311 Highway 71, N.E.
Willmar, MN 56201
(612) 235-4155

Lake Region Co-op Electrical Assn.
P.O. Box W
12 Fifth Avenue, N.E.
Pelican Rapids, MN 56572
(218) 863-1171

Lyon-Lincoln Electric Co-op, Inc.
P.O. Box 639
West Highway 14
Tyler, MN 56178
(507) 247-5505

McLeod Co-op Power Assn.
P.O. Box 70
1231 Ford Avenue, North
Glencoe, MN 55336
(612) 864-3148

Meeker Co-op Light & Power Assn.
P.O. Box 522
503 East Deport
Litchfield, MN 55355
(612) 693-3231

Mille Lacs Electric Co-op
P.O. Box 230
Fleming Route
Aitkin, MN 56431
(218) 927-2191

Minnesota Valley Co-op Light & Power Assn.
P.O. Box 717
501 South First Street
Montevideo, MN 56265
(612) 269-2163

Minnesota Valley Electric Co-op
P.O. Box 125
20425 Johnson Memorial Drive
Jordan, MN 55352
(612) 492-2313

Nobles Cooperative Electric
P.O. Box 788
Highway 59, North
Worthington, MN 56187
(507) 372-7331

North Itasca Electric Co-op
P.O. Box 227
227 South Main Street
Bigfork, MN 56628
(218) 743-3131

North Pine Electric Co-op, Inc.
P.O. Box 8
2200 Finland Avenue
Finlayson, MN 55735
(612) 233-6311

North Star Electric Co-op, Inc.
P.O. Box 719
106 S.E. 8th Avenue
Baudette, MN 56623
(218) 634-2202

Northern Electric Co-op Assn.
P.O. Box 1308
1500 16th Street South
Virginia, MN 55792
(218) 741-8137

P.K.M. Electric Co-op, Inc.
P.O. Box 108
406 North Minnesota
Warren, MN 56762
(218) 745-4711

People's Co-op Power Assn.
P.O. Box 339
3935 Highway 14 East
Rochester, MN 55903
(507) 288-4004

Red Lake Electric Co-op, Inc.
P.O. Box 430
412 8th Street, S.W.
Red Lake Falls, MN 56750
(218) 253-2168

Red River Valley Co-op Power Assn.
P.O. Box 358
109-2nd Avenue East
Halstad, MN 56548
(218) 456-2139

Redwood Electric Co-op
P.O. Box 15
60 Pine Avenue
Clements, MN 56224
(507) 692-2214

Renville-Sibley Co-op Power Assn.
P.O. Box 68
103 Oak Street
Danube, MN 56230
(612) 826-2593

Roseau Electric Co-op, Inc.
P.O. Box 100
903 3rd Street, N.E.
Roseau, MN 56751
(218) 463-1543

Runestone Electric Assn.
P.O. Box 9
7th & Fillmore
Alexandria, MN 56308
(612) 762-1121

South Central Electric Assn.
P.O. Box 150
County Road #57 West
St. James, MN 56081
(507) 375-3164

Southwestern Minnesota Co-op Electric
P.O. Box 336
East Highways 75 & 30
Pipestone, MN 56164
(507) 825-3341

Sterns Co-op Electric Assn.
P.O. Box 40
900 East Kraft Drive
Melrose, MN 56352
(612) 256-4241

Steele Waseca Co-op Electric
P.O. Box 485
115 East Rose Street
Owatonna, MN 55060
(507) 451-7340

Todd-Wadena Electric Co-op
P.O. Box 431
East Highway Ten
Wadena, MN 56482
(218) 631-3120

Traverse Electric Co-op, Inc.
P.O. Box 66
Trunk Highway 27 & 17th Street
Wheaton, MN 56296
(612) 563-8616

Tri-County Electric Co-op
P.O. Box 626
210 West Jessie Street
Rushford, MN 55971
(507) 864-7783

United Power Association
P.O. Box 800
17845 Highway 10
Elk River, MN 55330
(612) 441-3121

Wild Rice Electric Co-op, Inc.
P.O. Box 438
502 North Main
Mahnomen, MN 56557
(218) 935-2517

Wright-Hennepin Co-op Electric Assn.
P.O. Box 330
110 Birch Avenue, South
Maple Lake, MN 55358
(612) 963-3131

MISSISSIPPI

Alcorn County Electric Power Assn.
P.O. Box 1590
403 Waldron Street
Corinth, MS 38834
(601) 287-4402

Central Electric Power Assn.
P.O. Box 477
104 Van Buren Street
Carthage, MS 39051
(601) 267-5671

Coahoma Electric Power Assn.
P.O. Box 188
340 Hopson Street
Lyon, MS 38645
(601) 624-8321

Coast Electric Power Assn.
P.O. Box 2430
302 Highway 90
Bay St. Louis, MS 39521
(601) 467-6535

Delta Electric Power Assn.
P.O. Box 935
1700 Highway 82, West
Greenwood, MS 38930
(601) 453-6352

Dixie Electric Power Assn.
P.O. Box 88
Highway 84 East
Laurel, MS 39441
(601) 425-2535

East Mississippi EPA
P.O. Box 5517
2128 Highway 39, North
Meridian, MS 39302
(601) 483-7361

Four County Electric Power Assn.
P.O. Box 351
5265 South Frontage Road
Columbus, MS 39703
(601) 327-8900

Magnolia Electric Power Assn.
P.O. Box 747
Highway 98 East
McComb, MS 39648
(601) 684-4011

Monroe County Electric Power Assn.
P.O. Box 300
601 North Main Street
Amory, MS 38821
(601) 256-2962

Natchez Trace Electric Power
P.O. Box 609
551 East Madison
Houston, MS 38851
(601) 456-3037

North East Mississippi EPA
P.O. Box 1076
Highway 30/Highway 7 Bypass
Oxford, MS 38655
(601) 234-6331

Northcentral Mississippi EPA
P.O. Box 405
Highway 309, South
Byhalia, MS 38611
(601) 838-2151

Pearl River Valley Electric Power Assn.
P.O. Box 1217
Highway 13, North
Columbia, MS 39429
(601) 736-2666

Pontotoc Electric Power Assn.
P.O. Box 718
12 South Main Street
Pontotoc, MS 38863
(601) 489-3211

Prentiss County Electric Power Assn.
P.O. Box 428
302 West Church Street
Booneville, MS 38829
(601) 728-4433

Singing River Electric Power Assn.
P.O. Box 767
Highway 63, South
Lucedale, MS 39452
(601) 947-4211

South Mississippi Electric Power
P.O. Box 15849
7037 U.S. Highway 49, North
Hattiesburg, MS 39402
(601) 268-2083

Southern Pine Electric Power
P.O. Box 60
110 Risher Street
Taylorsville, MS 39168
(601) 785-6511

Southwest Mississippi EPA
P.O. Box 5
Highway 61
Lorman, MS 39096
(601) 437-3611

Tallahatchie Valley EPA
P.O. Box 513
Highway No. 6 East
Batesville, MS 38606
(601) 563-4742

Tippah Electric Power Assn.
P.O. Box 206
109 East Cooper
Ripley, MS 38663
(601) 837-8139

Tishomingo County EPA
P.O. Box 560
205 Highway 25, North
Iuka, MS 38852
(601) 423-3646

Tombigbee Electric Power Assn.
P.O. Box 1789
1906 South Gloster
Tupelo, MS 38801
(601) 842-7635

Twin County Electric Power Assn.
P.O. Box 158
900 East Avenue North
Hollandale, MS 38748
(601) 827-2262

Yazoo Valley Electric Power Assn.
P.O. Box 8
1408 Grand Avenue
Yazoo City, MS 39194
(601) 746-4251

MISSOURI

Associated Electric Co-op, Inc.
P.O. Box 754
2814 South Golden
Springfield, MO 65801
(417) 881-1204

Atchison-Hold Electric Co-op
P.O. Box 160
East Highway 136
Rock Port, MO 64482
(816) 744-5344

Barry Electric Co-op
P.O. Box 307
100 Main Street
Cassville, MO 65625
(417) 847-2131

Barton County Electric Co-op
P.O. Box 398
91 West 160 Highway
Lamar, MO 64759
(417) 682-5634

Black River Electric Co-op
P.O. Box 31
Highway 72, East
Fredericktown, MO 63645
(314) 783-3381

Boone Electric Co-op
P.O. Box 797
1413 Range Line
Columbia, MO 65205
(314) 449-4181

Callaway Electric Co-op
P.O. Box 250
503 Truman Road
Fulton, MO 65251
(314) 642-3326

Central Electric Power Co-op
P.O. Box 269
2106 Jefferson Street
Jefferson City, MO 65102
(314) 634-2454

Central Missouri Electric Co-op
P.O. Box 939
North Highway 65
Sedalia, MO 65302
(816) 826-2900

Citizens Electric Corp.
P.O. Box 311
150 Merchant Street
Ste. Genevieve, MO 63670
(314) 883-3511

Co-Mo Electric Co-op, Inc.
P.O. Box 220
Highway 5, South
Tipton, MO 65081
(816) 433-5521

Consolidated Electric Co-op
P.O. Box 540
Highway 54, East
Mexico, MO 65265
(314) 581-3630

Crawford Electric Co-op, Inc.
P.O. Box 10
North Service Road I-44
Bourbon, MO 65441
(314) 732-4415

Cuivre River Electric Co-op, Inc.
P.O. Box 160
1112 East Cherry Street
Troy, MO 63379
(314) 528-8261

Farmers' Electric Co-op, Inc.
P.O. Box 680
Highway 36, East
Chillicothe, MO 64601
(816) 646-4281

Gascosage Electric Co-op
P.O. Drawer G
Highway 28, South
Dixon, MO 65459
(314) 759-7146

Grundy Electric Co-op, Inc.
P.O. Box 189
4100 Oklahoma Avenue
Trenton, MO 64683
(816) 359-3941

Howard Electric Co-op
P.O. Box 391
Highway 5 & 240, North
Fayette, MO 65248
(816) 248-3311

Howell-Oregon Electric Co-op, Inc.
P.O. Box 649
North Highway 63
West Plains, MO 65775
(417) 256-2131

Intercounty Electric Co-op Assn.
P.O. Box 209
101 West Maple
Licking, MO 65542
(314) 674-2211

Laclede Electric Co-op
P.O. Drawer M
1000 East Seminole Road
Lebanon, MO 65536
(417) 532-3165

Lewis County RECA
P.O. Box 68
Junction Highways 6 & 16
Lewistown, MO 63452
(314) 497-2281

M&A Electric Power Co-op
P.O. Box 670
Highway PP, West
Poplar Bluff, MO 63901
(314) 785-9651

Macon Electric Go-op
P.O. Box 157
Business Highway 36, East
Macon, MO 63552
(816) 385-3157

Missouri Joint Municipal Electric
2704 West Ash
Columbia, MO 65203
(314) 445-3279

Missouri REC
P.O. Box 111
118 East LaFayette
Palmyra, MO 63461
(314) 769-2104

N.W. Electric Power Co-op, Inc.
P.O. Box 565
1001 West Grand Avenue
Cameron, MO 64429
(816) 632-2121

New-Mac Electric Co-op, Inc.
P.O. Box 310
Highway 86, West
Neosho, MO 64850
(417) 451-1515

Nodaway-Worth Electric Co-op, Inc.
P.O. Box 388
Highway 136, East
Maryville, MO 64468
(816) 582-3186

North Central Missouri Electric Co-op
P.O. Box 220
Highway E, West
Milan, MO 63556
(816) 265-4404

Northeast Missouri Electric Power
P.O. Box 191
Business Route 61, North
Palmyra, MO 63461
(314) 769-2107

Northwest Missouri Electric Co-op
P.O. Box 319
401 North Highway 71
Savannah, MO 64485
(816) 324-3155

Osage Valley Electric Co-op Assn.
P.O. Box 151
Highway 71, North
Butler, MO 64730
(816) 679-3131

Ozark Border Electric Co-op
P.O. Box 400
Highway 67, South
Poplar Bluff, MO 63901
(314) 785-4631

Ozark Electric Co-op
P.O. Box 420
Highway 39, North
Mt. Vernon, MO 65712
(417) 466-2144

Pemiscot-Dunklin Electric Co-op
P.O. Box 657
Highway 84, West
Hayti, MO 63857
(314) 757-6641

Platte-Clay Electric Co-op, Inc.
P.O. Box 1940
425 Main Street
Platte City, MO 64079
(816) 431-2131

Ralls County Electric Co-op
P.O. Box 157
Junction Highways 19 & 61
New London, MO 63459
(314) 985-8711

Sac-Osage Electric Co-op, Inc.
P.O. Box 111
1113 South Main
El Dorado Spring, MO 64744
(417) 876-2721

Scott-New Madrid-Missouri Electric Co-op
P.O. Box 520
Highway 61, South
Sikeston, MO 63801
(314) 471-5821

Se-Ma-No Electric Co-op
P.O. Box 318
North Highway 5
Mansfield, MO 65704
(417) 924-3243

Sho-Me Power Electric Cooperative
P.O. Box D
301 West Jackson
Marshfield, MO 65706
(417) 468-2611

Southwest Electric Co-op
P.O. Box 150
1023 South Springfield Street
Bolivar, MO 65613
(417) 326-5244

Three Rivers Electric Co-op
P.O. Box 918
1324 East Main
Linn, MO 65051
(314) 897-2251

Tri-County Electric Co-op Assn.
P.O. Box 159
Jackson & Green Streets
Lancaster, MO 63548
(816) 457-3733

Webster Electric Co-op
P.O. Box 87
1034 Spur Drive
Marshfield, MO 65706
(417) 468-2216

West Central Electric Co-op, Inc.
P.O. Box 452
Highway 13, South
Higginsville, MO 64037
(816) 584-2131

White River Valley Electric Co-op
P.O. Box 969
East Highway 76
Branson, MO 65616
(417) 335-9335

MONTANA

Beartooth Electric Co-op, Inc.
P.O. Box 1110
North of Red Lodge
Red Lodge, MT 59068
(406) 446-2310

Big Flat Electric Co-op, Inc.
P.O. Box H
333 South 7th Street East
Malta, MT 59538
(406) 654-2040

Big Horn County Electric Co-op
P.O. Box 410
Hardin, MT 59034
(406) 665-2830

Central Montana Electric Power Co-op
P.O. Box 50085
848 East Main Street, Suite 18
Billings, MT 59105
(406) 248-7936

Fergus Electric Co-op, Inc.
HC 85, Box 4040
Highway 87
Lewistown, MT 59457
(406) 538-3465

Flathead Electric Co-op, Inc.
2510 Highway 2 East
Kalispell, MT 59901
(406) 752-4483

Glacier Electric Co-op, Inc.
P.O. Box 2090
410 East Main Street
Cut Bank, MT 59427
(406) 873-5566

Goldenwest Electric Co-op, Inc.
P.O. Box 177
108 West 1 Avenue South
Wibaux, MT 59353
(406) 795-2423

Hill County Electric Co-op, Inc.
P.O. Box 430
2121 Highway #2, Northwest
Havre, MT 59501
(406) 265-7804

Lincoln Electric Co-op, Inc.
P.O. Box 628
Fairgrounds Road
Eureka, MT 59917
(406) 889-3301

Lower Yellowstone REA, Inc.
P.O. Box 1047
Highway 16 North West
Sidney, MT 59270
(406) 482-1602

Marias River Electric Co-op, Inc.
P.O. Box 729
910 Roosevelt Highway
Shelby, MT 59474
(406) 434-5575

McCone Electric Co-op, Inc.
P.O. Box 368
117 East Main
Circle, MT 59215
(406) 485-3430

Mid-Yellowstone Electric Co-op
P.O. Box 386
203 Elliott Avenue
Hysham, MT 59038
(406) 342-5521

Missoula Electric Co-op, Inc.
1700 West Broadway
Missoula, MT 59801
(406) 721-4433

Northern Electric Co-op, Inc.
P.O. Box 287
Main Street
Opheim, Montana 59250
(406) 762-3411

Park Electric Co-op, Inc.
P.O. Box 908
306 South 12th Street
Livingston, MT 59047
(406) 222-3100

Ravalli County Electric Co-op, Inc.
P.O. Box 190
1051 Eastside Highway
Corvallis, MT 59828
(406) 961-3001

Sheridan Electric Co-op, Inc.
P.O. Box 227
Highway 16, North
Medicine Lake, MT 59247
(406) 489-2231

Southeast Electric Co-op, Inc.
P.O. Box 368
Main Street
Ekalaka, MT 59324
(406) 775-8762

Sun River Electric Co-op, Inc.
P.O. Box 217
310 1st Avenue South
Fairfield, MT 59436
(406) 467-2526

Tongue River Electric Co-op, Inc.
P.O. Box 138
Main Street
Ashland, MT 59003
(406) 784-2341

Upper Missouri G&T Electric Co-op
P.O. Box 1069
217 South Central Avenue
Sidney, MT 59270
(406) 482-4100

Valley Electric Co-op, Inc.
P.O. Box 951
1130 Highway 2 West
Glasgow, MT 59230
(406) 367-5315

Vigilante Electric Co-op, Inc.
P.O. Box 71
225 East Bannack Street
Dillon, MT 59725
(406) 683-2327

Western Montana Electric G&T Co-op
1209 Mount Avenue
Missoula, MT 59801
(406) 721-0945

Yellowstone Valley Electric Co-op
P.O. Box 8
113 Northern Avenue
Huntley, MT 59037
(406) 348-3411

NEBRASKA

Burt County PPD
P.O. Box 209
613 North 13th Street
Tekamah, NE 68061
(402) 374-2631

Butler County RPPD
P.O. Box 349
1331 Fourth Street
David City, NE 68632
(402) 367-3081

Cedar-Knox PPD
P.O. Box 397
109 West State Street
Hartington, NE 68739
(402) 254-6291

Central Nebraska PPID
P.O. Box 740
415 Lincoln Street
Holdrege, NE 68949
(308) 995-8601

Chimney Rock PPD
P.O. Box 608
805 West 8th Street
Bayard, NE 69334
(308) 586-1824

Cornhusker PPD
P.O. Box 9
Highway 81 Northwest
Columbus, NE 68602
(402) 564-2821

Cuming County PPD
500 South Main Street
West Point, NE 68788
(402) 372-2463

Custer PPD
P.O. Box 10
625 East South E
Broken Bow, NE 68822
(308) 872-2451

Dawson County PPD
P.O. Drawer 777
300 South Washington Street
Lexington, NE 68850
(308) 324-2386

Elkhorn RPPD
P.O. Box 310
206 North Fourth
Battle Creek, NE 68715
(402) 675-2185

Howard Greeley RPPD
P.O. Box 105
422 Howard Avenue
St. Paul, NE 68873
(308) 754-4457

KBR Rural Public Power District
P.O. Box 187
374 North Pine Street
Ainsworth, NE 69210
(402) 387-1120

Loup River PPD
P.O. Box 988
2404-15th Street
Columbus, NE 68601
(402) 564-3171

Loup Valleys RPPD
P.O. Box 166
312 South 15th Street
Ord, NE 68862
(308) 728-3633

McCook PPD
P.O. Box 1147
North Highway 83 & Q Street
McCook, NE 69001
(308) 345-2500

Midwest EMC
P.O. Box 970
1st Street & Washington Avenue
Grant, NE 69140
(308) 352-4356

Nebraska Electric G&T Co-op, Inc.
P.O. Box 456
3154 18th Avenue
Columbus, NE 68602
(402) 564-8142

Niobrara Valley EMC
P.O. Box 60
427 North Fourth Street
O'Neill, NE 68763
(402) 223-4038

Norris PPD
P.O. Box 399
606 Irving Street
Beatrice, NE 68310
(402) 223-4038

North Central PPD
P.O. Box 90
1409 West Main Street
Creighton, NE 68729
(402) 358-5112

Northeast Nebraska RPPD
P.O. Box 39
511 Main Street
Emerson, NE 68733
(402) 695-2642

Northwest RPPD
P.O. Box 249
South Highway 87
Hay Springs, NE 69347
(308) 638-4445

Panhandle REMA
P.O. Box 677
319 Black Hills Avenue
Alliance, NE 69301
(308) 762-1311

Polk County RPPD
P.O. Box 465
120 West 4th Street
Stromsburg, NE 68666
(402) 764-4381

Roosevelt PPD
P.O. Box 97
1633 13th Street
Mitchell, NE 69357
(308) 623-2124

Seward County RPPD
P.O. Box 69
South Highway 15
Seward, NE 68434
(402) 643-2951

South Central PPD
P.O. Box 406
275 South Main Street
Nelson, NE 68961
(402) 225-2351

Southern Nebraska RPPD
P.O. Box 1687
1306 West 3rd Street
Grand Island, NE 68802
(308) 384-2350

Southwest PPD
P.O. Box J
221 North Main
Palisade, NE 69040
(308) 285-3295

Stanton County PPD
P.O. Box 319
807 Douglas Street
Stanton, NE 68779
(402) 439-2228

Twin Valleys PPD
P.O. Box 160
West Highway 6 & 34
Cambridge, NE 69022
(308) 697-3315

Wayne County PPD
P.O. Box 350
303 Logan
Wayne, NE 68787
(402) 375-1360

Wheat Belt PPD
P.O. Box 177
2104 Illinois Street
Sidney, NE 69162
(308) 254-5871

York County RPPD
P.O. Box 219
2122 South Lincoln Avenue
York, NE 68467
(402) 362-3355

NEVADA

Alamo Power District No.3
P.O. Box 189
233 North Main
Alamo, NV 89001
(702) 725-3335

Lincoln County Power District No.1
SR 89063 Box 101
Pioche, NV 89043
(702) 962-5122

Mt. Wheeler Power, Inc.
P.O. Box 1110
1600 7th Street East
Ely, NV 89301
(702) 289-8981

Overton Power District No.5
P.O. Box 395
601 State Highway 169
Overton, NV 89040
(702) 397-2512

Valley Electric Association
P.O. Box 237
800 East Highway 372
Pahrump, NV 89041
(702) 727-5312

Wells REC
P.O. Box 365
540 Humboldt Avenue
Wells, NV 89835
(702) 752-3328

NEW HAMPSHIRE

New Hampshire Electric Cooperative
RFD 4, Box 2100
Plymouth, NH 03264
(603) 536-1800

NEW JERSEY

Sussex REC
P.O. Box 346
22 East Main Street
Sussex, NJ 07461
(201) 875-5101

NEW MEXICO

Central N.M. Electric Co-op, Inc.
P.O. Box K
Highway 14
Mountainair, NM 87036
(505) 847-2521

Central Valley Electric Co-op, Inc.
P.O. Box 219
13th & Richey Streets
Artesia, NM 88211
(505) 746-3571

Columbus Electric Co-op, Inc.
P.O. Box 631
900 North Gold Avenue
Deming, NM 88031
(505) 456-8838

Continental Divide Electric Co-op
P.O. Box 1087
200 East High Street
Grants, NM 87020
(505) 285-6656

Farmers Electric Co-op, Inc.
P.O. Box 550
3701 Thornton
Clovis, NM 88101
(505) 769-2116

Jemez Mountains Electric Co-op
P.O. Box 128
Chama Highway
Espanola, NM 87532
(505) 753-2105

Kit Carson Electric Co-op, Inc.
P.O. Box 587
118 East Cruz Alta Road
Taos, NM 87571
(505) 758-2258

Lea County Electric Co-op, Inc.
P.O. Drawer 1447
18 West Washington
Lovington, NM 88260
(505) 396-3631

Mora-San Miguel Electric Co-op
P.O. Box 240
Main Street
Mora, NM 87732
(505) 387-2205

Northern Rio Arriba Electric Co-op
P.O. Box 217
1135 Camino Escondido
Chama, NM 87520
(505) 756-2181

Otero County Electric Co-op, Inc.
P.O. Box 227
202 Burro Avenue
Cloudcroft, NM 88317
(505) 682-2521

Plains Electric G&T Co-op, Inc.
P.O. Box 6551
2401 Aztec Road, N.E.
Albuquerque, NM 87197
(505) 884-1881

Roosevelt County Electric Co-op
P.O. Box 389
121 North Main Street
Portales, NM 88130
(505) 356-4491

Sierra Electric Co-op
P.O. Box W
Old Highway 52
Elephant Butte, NM 87935
(505) 744-5231

Socorro Electric Co-op, Inc.
P.O. Box H
215 East Manzanares Avenue
Socorro, NM 87801
(505) 835-0560

Southwestern Electric Co-op, Inc.
P.O. Box 369
220 Main Street
Clayton, NM 88415
(505) 374-2451

Springer Electric Co-op, Inc.
P.O. Box 698
420 Maxwell Avenue
Springer, NM 87747
(505) 483-2421

NEW YORK

Delaware County Electric Co-op
P.O. Box 471
30 Elm Street
Delhi, NY 13753
(607) 746-2341

Oneida-Madison Electric Co-op, Inc.
P.O. Box 27
Route 20
Bouckville, NY 13310
(315) 893-1851

Otsego Electric Co-op, Inc.
P.O. Box 128
East Main Street
Hartwick, NY 13348
(607) 293-6622

Steuben REC, Inc.
P.O. Box 272
9 Wilson Avenue
Bath, NY 14810
(607) 776-4161

NORTH CAROLINA

Albemarle EMC
P.O. Box 69
U.S. 17 Business North
Hertford, NC 27944
(919) 426-5735

Blue Ridge EMC
Caller Service 112
Lenoir, NC 28645
(704) 758-2383

Brunswick EMC
P.O. Box 826
201 Village Road
Shallotte, NC 28459
(919) 754-4391

Cape Hatteras EMC
P.O. Box 9
Light Plant Road
Buxton, NC 27920
(919) 995-5616

Carteret-Craven EMC
Drawer 1499
N.C. Highway 24 West
Morehead City, NC 28557
(919) 247-3107

Central EMC
P.O. Box 1107
304 South Steele Street
Sanford, NC 27330
(919) 774-4900

Crescent EMC
P.O. Box 1831
Highway 64 East
Statesville, NC 28687
(704) 873-5241

Davidson EMC
P.O. Box 948
1900 South Main Street
Lexington, NC 27293
(704) 249-3131

Edgecombe-Martin County EMC
P.O. Drawer 188
201 West Wilson Street
Tarboro, NC 27886
(919) 823-2171

Four County EMC
P.O. Box 667
605 East Fremont Street
Burgaw, NC 28425
(919) 259-2171

French Broad EMC
P.O. Box 9
Highway 213
Marshall, NC 28753
(704) 649-2051

Halifax EMC
P.O. Box 667
208 West Whitfield Street
Enfield, NC 27823
(919) 445-5111

Harkers Island EMC
P.O. Box 190 P.O.
N.C. State Road #1335
Harkers Island, NC 28531
(919) 728-2593

Haywood EMC
1819 Asheville Road
Waynesville, NC 28786
(704) 452-2281

Jones-Onslow EMC
259 Western Boulevard
Jacksonville, NC 28540
(919) 353-1940

Lumbee River EMC
P.O. Box 830
605 East 4th Avenue
Red Springs, NC 28377
(919) 843-4131

Pee Dee EMC
P.O. Box 859
Highway 52, South
Wadesboro, NC 28170
(704) 694-2114

Piedmont EMC
P.O. Box 1179
Highway 86, South
Hillsborough, NC 27278
(919) 732-2123

Pitt & Greene EMC
P.O. Box 249
West Wilson Street
Farmville, NC 27828
(919) 753-3128

Randolph EMC
P.O. Box 40
Highway 42 & Patton Avenue
Asheboro, NC 27204
(919) 625-5177

Roanoke EMC
P.O. Box 440
114 North Main Street
Rich Square, NC 27869
(919) 539-2236

Rutherford EMC
P.O. Box 1569
202 Hudlow Road
Forest City, NC 28043
(704) 245-1621

South River EMC
P.O. Box 305
510 South Main Street
Dobson, NC 27017
(919) 386-8241

Tideland EMC
P.O. Box 159
Highway 264
Pantego, NC 27860
(919) 943-3046

Tri-County EMC
P.O. Box 130
Highway 117, South
Dudley, NC 28333
(919) 735-2611

Union EMC
P.O. Box 5014
1525 Rocky River Road North
Monroe, NC 28111
(704) 289-3145

Wake EMC
P.O. Box 1229
414 East Wait Street
Wake Forest, NC 27588
(919) 556-5211

NORTH DAKOTA

Baker Electric Co-op, Inc.
P.O. Box 608
Cando, ND 58324
(701) 968-3314

Basin Electric Power Co-op, Inc.
1717 East Interstate Avenue
Bismarck, ND 58501
(701) 223-0441

Burke-Divide Electric Co-op, Inc.
Box 6
Columbus, ND 58727
(701) 939-6671

Capital Electric Co-op, Inc.
P.O. Box 730
111 State Street
Bismarck, ND 58502
(701) 223-1513

Cass County Electric Co-op, Inc.
P.O. Box 8
491 Elm Street
Kindred, ND 58051
(701) 428-3292

Cavalier REC, Inc.
P.O. Box 749
1111 Ninth Avenue
Langdon, ND 58249
(701) 256-5511

Central Power Electric Co-op, Inc.
P.O. Box 1576
525 20th Avenue, S.W.
Minot, ND 58701
(701) 852-4407

James Valley Electric Co-op, Inc.
P.O. Box 583
Highways 281 & 13
Edgeley, ND 58433
(701) 493-2281

KEM Electric Co-op, Inc.
P.O. Box 790
107 South Broadway
Linton, ND 58552
(701) 254-4666

McKenzie Electric Co-op, Inc.
P.O. Box 649
Highway 23, East
Watford City, ND 58854
(701) 842-2311

McLean Electric Co-op, Inc.
P.O. Box 399
Highway 37, East
Garrison, ND 58540
(701) 463-2291

Minnkota Power Co-op, Inc.
P.O. Box 1318
1822 Mill Road
Grand Forks, ND 58206
(701) 795-4000

Mor-Gran-Sou Electric Co-op, Inc.
P.O. Box 297
202 6th Avenue, N.W.
Flasher, ND 58535
(701) 597-3301

Mountrail-Williams Electric Co-op
P.O. Box 1346
Highway 2, North
Williston, ND 58802
(701) 572-3765

Nodak Electric Co-op, Inc.
P.O. Box 1478
1405 First Avenue North
Grand Forks, ND 58206
(701) 746-4461

North Central Electric Co-op, Inc.
P.O. Box 9
Highway 5, West
Bottineau, ND 58318
(701) 228-2202

Oliver-Mercer Electric Co-op, Inc.
801 Highway Drive
Hazen, ND 58545
(701) 748-2293

R.S.R. Electric Co-op, Inc.
P.O. Box 159
Highway 13, West
Milnor, ND 58060
(701) 427-5241

Sheyenne Valley Electric Co-op
P.O. Box 217
Highway 200, South
Finley, ND 58230
(701) 524-1110

Slope Electric Co-op, Inc.
P.O. Box 338
116 East 12th Street
New England, ND 58647
(701) 579-4191

Square Butte Electric Cooperative
P.O. Box 1318
1822 Mill Road
Grand Forks, ND 58206
(701) 795-4000

Tri-County Electric Co-op, Inc.
P.O. Box 180
1515 West Main Street
Carrington, ND 58421
(701) 652-3156

Verendrye Electric Co-op, Inc.
RR 1, Box 13
Velva, ND 58790
(701) 338-2855

West Plains Electric Co-op, Inc.
P.O. Box 1038
2156 4th Avenue East
Dickinson, ND 58601
(701) 225-5111

OHIO

Adams REC, Inc.
P.O. Box 247
4800 State Route 136
West Union, OH 45693
(513) 544-2305

Buckeye Power, Inc.
P.O. Box 26036
6677 Busch Boulevard
Columbus, OH 43226
(614) 846-5757

Buckeye REC, Inc.
P.O. Box 279
143 Third Avenue
Gallipolis, OH 45631
(614) 446-1532

Butler REC, Inc.
P.O. Box 13030
1382 Main Street
Hamilton, OH 45013
(513) 867-4400

Carroll Electric Co-op, Inc.
P.O. Box 67
350 Canton Road, N.W.
Carrollton, OH 44615
(216) 627-2116

Darke REC, Inc.
P.O. Box 278
1120 Fort Jefferson Road
Greenville, OH 45331
(513) 548-4114

Delaware REC, Inc.
P.O. Box 630
680 Sunbury Road
Delaware, OH 43015
(614) 363-2641

Firelands Electric Co-op, Inc.
1 Energy Place
New London, OH 44851
(419) 929-1571

Frontier Power Company
P.O. Box 270
770 South Second Street
Coshocton, OH 43812
(614) 622-6755

Guernsey-Muskingum Electric Co-op
17 South Liberty Street
New Concord, OH 43762
(614) 826-7661

Hancock-Wood Electric Co-op, Inc.
P.O. Box 188
2451 Grant Road
North Baltimore, OH 45872
(419) 257-3241

Holmes-Wayne Electric Co-op, Inc.
P.O. Box 112
6060 State Route 83
Millersburg, OH 44654
(216) 674-1055

Licking Rural Electrification, Inc.
P.O. Box 455
State Route 13
Utica, OH 43080
(614) 892-2791

Logan County Co-op Power & Light Assn.
P.O. Box 279
1587 County Road 32, North
Bellefontaine, OH 43311
(513) 592-4781

Lorain-Medina REC, Inc.
P.O. Box 158
22898 West Road
Wellington, OH 44090
(216) 647-2133

Marion REC, Inc.
P.O. Box 501
2859 Marion-Upper Sandusky Road
Marion, OH 43301
(614) 382-1234

Midwest Electric, Inc.
P.O. Box 10
County Road 33-A, East
St. Marys, OH 45885
(419) 394-4110

Morrow Electric Co-op, Inc.
P.O. Box 111
5255 State Route 95
Mount Gilead, OH 43338
(419) 947-3055

North Central Electric Co-op, Inc.
P.O. Box 475
13978 East County Road 65
Attica, OH 44807
(419) 426-3072

North Western Electric Co-op, Inc.
P.O. Box 391
State Route 576 & County Road
Bryan, OH 43506
(419) 636-5051

Paulding-Putnam Electric Co-op
11957 U.S. Highway 127
Paulding, OH 45879
(419) 399-5015

Pioneer REC, Inc.
P.O. Box 604
344 West U.S. Route 36
Piqua, OH 45356
(513) 773-2523

South Central Power Company
P.O. Box 250
2780 Coonpath Road, N.E.
Lancaster, OH 43130
(614) 653-4422

Tricounty REC, Inc.
P.O. Box 100
200 Road K-2
Malinta, OH 43535
(419) 256-7900

Union REC, Inc.
P.O. Box 393
15461 U.S. Route 36
Marysville, OH 43040
(513) 642-1947

United Rural Electric, Inc.
P.O. Box 224
555 West Franklin
Kenton, OH 43326
(419) 673-7289

Washington Electric Co-op, Inc.
P.O. Box 664
406 Colegate Drive
Marietta, OH 45740
(614) 373-2141

OKLAHOMA

Alfalfa Electric Cooperative, Inc.
P.O. Box 39
121 East Main Street
Cherokee, OK 73728
(405) 596-3575

Caddo Electric Co-op
Box 70
Binger, OK 73009
(405) 656-2322

Canadian Valley Electric Co-op
P.O. Box 751
State Highways 99 & I-40
Seminole, OK 74868
(405) 382-3680

Central REC
P.O. Box 1809
3304 South Boomer Road
Stillwater, OK 74076
(405) 372-2884

Choctaw Electric Co-op, Inc.
P.O. Box 758
Highway 93, North
Hugo, OK 74743
(405) 326-6486

Cimarron Electric Co-op
P.O. Box 299
Highway 81, North
Kingfisher, OK 73750
(405) 375-4121

Cookson Hills Electric Co-op, Inc.
P.O. Box 280
1002 East Main Street
Stigler, OK 74462
(918) 967-4614

Cotton Electric Co-op
226 North Broadway
Walters, OK 73572
(405) 875-3351

East Central Oklahoma Electric Co-op
P.O. Drawer 1178
Highway 75, South
Okmulgee, OK 74447
(918) 756-0833

Harmon Electric Assn., Inc.
P.O. Box 393
114 North First Street
Hollis, OK 73550
(405) 688-3342

Indian Electric Co-op, Inc.
P.O. Box 49
U.S. Highway 64
Cleveland, OK 74020
(918) 358-2514

KAMO Electric Co-op, Inc.
P.O. Drawer 577
900 South Wilson Street
Vinita, OK 74301
(918) 256-5551

Kay Electric Cooperative
P.O. Box 607
201 East Blackwell
Blackwell, OK 74631
(405) 363-1260

Kiamichi Electric Co-op, Inc.
P.O. Box 340
Highway 2, South
Wilburton, OK 74578
(918) 465-2338

Kiwash Electric Co-op, Inc.
P.O. Box 100
120 West First Street
Cordell, OK 73632
(405) 832-3361

Lake Region Electric Co-op, Inc.
P.O. Box 127
500 East Fifth Street
Hulbert, OK 74441
(918) 772-2526

Northeast Oklahoma Electric Co-op
P.O. Box 948
Highways 66 & 69
Vinita, OK 74301
(918) 256-6405

Northfork Electric Cooperative
P.O. Box 400
311 East Madden Street
Sayre, OK 73662
(405) 928-3366

Northwestern Electric Co-op, Inc.
P.O. Box 2707
2925 Williams Avenue
Woodward, OK 73802
(405) 256-7425

Oklahoma Electric Co-op
P.O. Box 1208
242 24th Avenue, N.W.
Norman, OK 73070
(405) 321-2024

People's Electric Cooperative
P.O. Box 429
1130 West Main
Ada, OK 74820
(405) 332-3031

Red River Valley REA
P.O. Box 220
1003 Memorial Drive
Marietta, OK 73448
(405) 276-3364

Rural Electric Cooperative, Inc.
P.O. Box 609
Highway 76, North
Lindsay, OK 73052
(405) 756-3104

Southeastern Electric Co-op, Inc.
P.O. Box 1370
Highway 70, East
Durant, OK 74702
(405) 924-2170

Southwest Rural Electric Association
P.O. Box 310
700 North Broadway
Tipton, OK 73570
(405) 667-5281

Tri-County Electric Co-op, Inc.
P.O. Drawer 880
302 East Glaydas
Hooker, OK 73945
(405) 652-2418

Verdigris Valley Electric Co-op
P.O. Box 219
8901 East 146th Street, North
Collinsville, OK 74021
(918) 371-2584

Western Farmers Electric Co-op
P.O. Box 429
701 Northeast 7th Street
Anadarko, OK 73005
(405) 247-3351

OREGON

Blachly-Lane Co. Co-op Electric Assn.
90680 Highway 99
Eugene, OR 97402
(503) 688-8711

Central Electric Co-op, Inc.
P.O. Box 846
2098 North Highway 97
Redmond, OR 97756
(503) 548-2144

Columbia Basin Electric Co-op
P.O. Box 398
171 Linden Way
Heppner, OR 97836
(503) 676-9146

Columbia Power Co-op Association
P.O. Box 97
101 Wilson Street
Monument, OR 97864
(503) 934-2311

Consumers Power, Inc.
P.O. Box 1180
6990 S.W. West Hills Road
Philomath, OR 97370
(503) 929-3124

Coos-Curry Electric Co-op, Inc.
P.O. Box 1268
43050 Highway 101
Port Orford, OR 97465
(503) 332-3931

Douglas Electric Co-op, Inc.
P.O. Box 1327
1981 N.E. Stephens
Roseburg, OR 97470
(503) 673-6616

Emerald People's Utility District
33733 Seavey Loop Road
Eugene, OR 97405
(503) 746-1583

Harney Electric Co-op, Inc.
1326 Hines Boulevard
Burns, OR 97720
(503) 573-2061

Hood River Electric Cooperative
P.O. Box 125
Odell, OR 97044
(503) 354-1233

Lane Electric Co-op
P.O. Box 21410
787 Bailey Hill Road
Eugene, OR 97402
(503) 484-1151

Midstate Electric Co-op, Inc.
P.O. Box 127
51340 North Highway 97
LaPine, OR 97739
(503) 536-2126

Northern Wasco County P.U.D.
P.O. Box 621
401 Court Street
The Dalles, OR 97058
(503) 296-2226

Northwest Irrigation Utilities
825 N.E. Multnomah
Suite 1015
Portland, OR 97232
(503) 233-5823

Oregon Trail Electric Consumers Co-op
P.O. Box 226
3275 Baker Street
Baker City, OR 97814
(503) 523-6671

Pacific Northwest Generating Co-op
711 N.E. Halsey
Suite 200
Portland, OR 97232
(503) 288-1234

Salem Electric
P.O. Box 5588
633 Seventh Street, N.W.
Salem, OR 97304
(503) 362-3601

Tillamook P.U.D.
P.O. Box 433
1115 Pacific Avenue
Tillamook, OR 9714
(503) 842-2535

Umatilla Electric Co-op Assn.
P.O. Box 1148
750 West Elm
Herniston, OR 97838
(503) 567-6414

Wasco Electric Co-op, Inc.
P.O. Box 1110
105 East Fourth Street
The Dalles, OR 97058
(503) 296-2740

West Oregon Electric Co-op, Inc.
P.O. Box 69
715 Maple Street
Vernonia, OR 97064
(503) 429-3021

PENNSYLVANIA

Adams Electric Co-op, Inc.
153 North Stratton Street
Gettysburg, PA 17325
(717) 334-9211

Allegheny Electric Co-op
P.O. Box 1266
212 Locust Street
Harrisburg, PA 17108
(717) 233-5704

Bedford REC, Inc.
P.O. Box 335
R.D. 4, Route 30 East
Bedford, PA 15522
(814) 623-5101

Central Electric Co-op, Inc.
P.O. Box 329
Route 368 East
Parker, PA 16049
(412) 399-2931

Claverack Rural Electric Co-op
Route 2, Box 17
Wysox, PA 18854
(717) 265-2167

New Enterprise REC
P.O. Box 75
Route 869
New Enterprise, PA 16664
(814) 766-3221

Northwestern RECA, Inc.
P.O. Box 207
R.D.#1, Route 86
Cambridge Spring, PA 16403
(814) 398-4651

Somerset REC, Inc.
P.O. Box 270
Industrial Park
Somerset, PA 15501
(814) 455-4106

Southwest Central RECC
P.O. Box 70
75 Airport Road
Indiana, PA 15701
(412) 349-4800

Sullivan County
P.O. Box 65
Route 87
Forksville, PA 18616
(717) 924-3381

Tri-County REC, Inc.
P.O. Box 526
Mansfield, PA 16933
(717) 662-2175

United Electric Cooperative, Inc.
(803) 489-5737
Route 255 North
DuBois, PA 15801
(814) 371-8570

Valley REC, Inc.
(803) 779-4975
Route 26, North
Huntingdon, PA 16652
(814) 643-2650

Warren Electric Co-op, Inc.
320 East Main Street
Youngsville, PA 16371
(814) 563-7548

SOUTH CAROLINA

Aiken Electric Co-op, Inc.
P.O. Box 417
2790 Wagener Road
Aiken, SC 29802
(803) 649-6245

Berkeley Electric Co-op, Inc.
P.O. Box 1234
414 Highway 52, North
Moncks Corner, SC 29461
(803) 761-8200

Black River Electric Co-op, Inc.
P.O. Box 130
1121 North Pike Road, West
Sumter, SC 29151
(803) 469-8060

Blue Ridge Electric Co-op, Inc.
P.O. Box 277
734 West Main Street
Pickens, SC 29671
(803) 878-6326

Broad River Electric Co-op, Inc.
P.O. Box 2269
Spartanburg Highway
Gaffney, SC 29342 P.O. Box 688

Central Electric Power Co-op, Inc.
P.O. Box 1455
121 Greystone Boulevard
Columbia, SC 29202 P.O. Box 477

Coastal Electric Co-op, Inc.
P.O. Box 1457
201 Brown Street
Walterboro, SC 29488
(803) 549-9512

Edisto Electric Co-op, Inc.
P.O. Box 547
Calhoun Street
Bamberg, SC 29003
(803) 245-5141

Fairfield Electric Co-op, Inc.
P.O. Box 150
Highway 321, North
Winnsboro, SC 29180
(803) 635-4621

Horry Electric Co-op, Inc.
P.O. Box 119
1708 Oak Street
Conway, SC 29526
(803) 248-2211

Laurens Electric Co-op, Inc.
P.O. Box 700
Highway 14
Laurens, SC 29360
(803) 68203141

Little River Electric Co-op, Inc.
P.O. Box 220
300 Cambridge Street
Abbeville, SC 29620
(803) 459-2141

Lynches River Electric Co-op, Inc.
P.O. Box 308
1104 West McGregor Street
Pageland, SC 29728
(803) 672-6111

Marlboro Electric Co-op, Inc.
P.O. Box 1057
401 ByPass
Bennettsville, SC 29512
(803) 479-3855

Mid-Carolina Electric Co-op, Inc.
P.O. Drawer 669
I-20 & Road 204
Lexington, SC 29072
(803) 359-5551

Newberry Electric Co-op, Inc.
P.O. Box 477
882 Wilson Road
Newberry, SC 29108
(803) 276-1121

Palmetto Electric Co-op, Inc.
P.O. Box 21239
111 Matthews Drive
Hilton Head, SC 29925
(803) 681-5551

Pee Dee Electric Co-op, Inc.
P.O. Box 491
McIver Road
Darlington, SC 29532
(803) 665-4070

Saluda River Electric Co-op
P.O. Box 929
Highway 14
Laurens, SC 29360
(803) 681-3169

Santee Electric Co-op, Inc.
P.O. Box 548
1500 Longstreet Street
Kingstree, SC 29556
(803) 354-6187

Tri-County Electric Co-op, Inc.
P.O. Box 217
Harry C. Raysor Drive
St. Matthews, SC 29135
(803) 874-1215

York Electric Co-op, Inc.
P.O. Box 150
1630 Old York Road
York, SC 29745
(813) 684-4247

SOUTH DAKOTA

Beadle Electric Co-op, Inc.
P.O. Box 38
East Highway 14
Huron, SD 57350
(605) 352-8591

Black Hills Electric Co-op, Inc.
P.O. Box 112
2 Miles West Highway 16
Custer, SD 57730
(605) 673-4461

Bon Homme Yankton Electric Assn.
P.O. Box 158
134 South Lidice Street
Tabor, SD 57063
(605) 463-2507

Butte Electric Co-op, Inc.
P.O. Box 137
109 South Dartmouth
Newell, SD 57760
(605) 456-2494

Cam-Wal Electric Co-op, Inc.
P.O. Box 135
5061 Scranton
Selby, SD 56472
(605) 649-7676

Charles Mix Electric Assn., Inc.
P.O. Box 10
440 Lake Street
Lake Andes, SD 57356
(605) 487-7321

Cherry-Todd Electric Co-op, Inc.
P.O. Box 169
West Highway #18
Mission, SD 57555
(605) 856-4416

Clay-Union Electric Corp.
P.O. Box 317
1410 East Cherry
Vermillion, SD 57069
(605) 624-2673

Codington-Clark Electric Co-op
P.O. Box 880
3-8th Avenue, S.E.
Watertown, SD 57201
(605) 886-5848

Douglas Electric Co-op, Inc.
P.O. Box 370
400 Main Street
Armour, SD 57313
(605) 724-2972

East River Electric Power Co-op
P.O. Drawer E
121 S.E. 1st Street
Madison, SD 57042
(605) 256-4536

F.E.M. Electric Assn., Inc.
P.O. Box 468
800 5th Avenue
Ipswich, SD 57451
(605) 426-6891

Grand Electric Co-op, Inc.
P.O. Box 39
Main Street North
Bison, SD 57620
(605) 244-5211

H-D Electric Co-op, Inc.
P.O. Box 1007
423 South 3rd Avenue, South
Clear Lake, SD 57226
(605) 874-2171

Heartland Consumers Power District
P.O. Box 248
203 West Center
Madison, SD 57042
(605) 256-6536

Intercounty Electric Assn., Inc.
P.O. Box 850
1420 North Main
Mitchell, SD 57301
(605) 996-7516

Kingsbury Electric Co-op, Inc.
P.O. Box E
551 5th Street, S.W.
DeSmet, SD 57231
(605) 854-3522

Lacreek Electric Assn., Inc.
P.O. Box 220
East Highway 18
Martin, SD 57551
(605) 685-6581

Lake Region Electric Assn., Inc.
P.O. Box 341
1212 North Main Street
Webster, SD 57274
(605) 345-3379

Lincoln-Union Electric Company
P.O. Box 105
Highway 11, North
Alcester, SD 57001
(605) 934-1061

McCook Electric Co-op, Inc.
P.O. Box 250
236 North Main Street
Salem, SD 57058
(605) 425-2661

Moreau Grand Electric Co-op, Inc.
P.O. Box 8
405 9th Street
Timber Lake, SD 57656
(605) 865-3511

Northern Electric Co-op, Inc.
P.O. Box 457
Bath, SD 57427
(605) 225-0310

Oahe Electric Co-op, Inc.
P.O. Box 216
102 South Canford
Blunt, SD 57522
(605) 962-6243

Ree Electric Co-op Assn., Inc.
P.O. Box 227
10th & North Broadway
Miller, SD 57362
(605) 853-2454

Rosebud Electric Co-op, Inc.
P.O. Box 439
114 East 6th
Gregory, SD 57533
(605) 835-9624

Rushmore Electric Power Co-op, Inc.
P.O. Box 2414
1715 Campbell Street
Rapid City, SD 57709
(605) 342-4759

Sioux Valley Empire Electric Assn.
P.O. Box 216
Junction Highways 77 & 34
Colman, SD 57017
(605) 534-3535

Spink Electric Co-op, Inc.
P.O. Box 40
6th East 7th Avenue
Redfield, SD 57469
(605) 472-0380

Tri-County Electric Assn., Inc.
P.O. Box 130
151 South Main
Plankinton, SD 57368
(605) 942-7786

Turner-Hutchinson Electric Co-op
P.O. Box 388
508 South Broadway
Marion, SD 57043
(605) 648-3619

Union County Electric Co-op, Inc.
P.O. Box 459
Main Street
Elk Point, SD 57025
(605) 356-3395

West Central Electric Co-op, Inc.
P.O. Box 17
204 Main Street
Murdo, SD 57559
(605) 669-2472

West River Electric Assn., Inc.
P.O. Box 412
507 Glen Street
Wall, SD 57790
(605) 279-2135

Whetstone Valley Electric Co-op
P.O. Box 512
East Highway 12
Milbank, SD 57252
(605) 432-5331

TENNESSEE

Appalachian Electric Co-op
P.O. Box 710
109 West AJ Highway
Jefferson City, TN 37760
(615) 475-2032

Caney Fork Electric Co-op, Inc.
P.O. Box 272
160 New Smithville Highway
McMinnville, TN 37110
(615) 473-3116

Chickasaw Electric Co-op
P.O. Box 449
17970 Highway 64, East
Somerville, TN 38068
(901) 465-3591

Cumberland EMC
P.O. Box 3300
1940 Madison Street
Clarksville, TN 37043
(615) 645-2481

Duck River EMC
P.O. Box 89
1411 Madison Street
Shelbyville, TN 37160
(615) 684-4621

Fayetteville Electric System
P.O. Box 120
408 West College Street
Fayetteville, TN 37334
(615) 433-1522

Forked Deer Electric Co-op, Inc.
P.O. Box 67
Highway 51-A
Halls, TN 38040
(901) 836-7508

Fort Loudoun Electric Co-op
P.O. Box 307
500 College Street
Madisonville, TN 37354
(615) 442-2487

Gibson EMC
P.O. Box 47
1207 South College
Trenton, TN 38382
(901) 855-4740

Holston Electric Co-op, Inc.
P.O. Box 190
1200 West Main
Rogersville, TN 37857
(615) 272-8821

La Follette Utilities
P.O. Box 1411
301-303 North Tennessee Avenue
La Follette, TN 37766
(615) 562-3316

Lawrenceburg Power System
P.O. Box 649
1607 North Locust Avenue
Lawrenceburg, TN 38464
(615) 762-7161

Meriwether Lewis Electric Co-op
P.O. Box 240
114 North Central Avenue
Centerville, TN 37033
(615) 729-3558

Middle Tennessee EMC
810 Commercial Court
Murfreesboro, TN 37129
(615) 890-9762

Mountain Electric Co-op
P.O. Box 180
604 South Church Street
Mountain City, TN 37683
(615) 727-9111

Pickwick Electric Co-op
P.O. Box 49
530 Mulberry Street
Selmer, TN 38375
(901) 645-3411

Plateau Electric Co-op
P.O. Box 4669
Highway 27, South
Oneida, TN 37841
(615) 569-8591

Sequachee Valley Electric Co-op
P.O. Box 31
512 Cedar Avenue
South Pittsburg, TN 37380
(615) 837-8605

Southwest Tennessee EMC
P.O. Box 959
1009 East Main
Brownsville, TN 38012
(901) 772-1322

Tennessee Valley Electric Co-op
P.O. Box 400
515 Florence Road
Savannah, TN 38372
(901) 925-4916

Tri-County EMC
P.O. Box 40
405 College Street
Lafayette, TN 37083
(615) 666-2111

Upper Cumberland EMC
P.O. Box 159
512 New Highway 53
Carthage, TN 37030
(615) 735-2940

Volunteer Electric Co-op
P.O. Box 277
Highway 58, North
Decatur, TN 37322
(615) 334-5722

TEXAS

B-K Electric Co-op, Inc.
P.O. Box 672
419 North Main Street
Seymour, TX 76380
(817) 888-3441

Bandera Electric Co-op, Inc.
P.O. Box 667
Highway 16, North
Bandera, TX 78003
(210) 796-3741

Bartlett Electric Co-op, Inc.
P.O. Box 200
104 East Pietzsch Street
Bartlett, TX 76511
(817) 527-3551

Belfalls Electric Co-op, Inc.
P.O. Box 598
128 Main Street
Rosebud, TX 76570
(817) 583-7955

Bluebonnet Electric Co-op, Inc.
P.O. Box 240
426 East Austin Street
Giddings, TX 78942
(409) 542-3151

Bowie-Cass Electric Co-op, Inc.
P.O. Box 47
Highway 8, North
Douglassville, TX 75560
(903) 846-2311

Brazos Electric Power Co-op, Inc.
P.O. Box 2585
2404 LaSalle Avenue
Waco, TX 76702
(817) 750-6500

Cap Rock Electric Co-op, Inc.
P.O. Box 700
West Loop 214
Stanton, TX 79782
(915) 756-3381

Central Texas Electric Co-op, Inc.
P.O. Box 553
U.S. 87, South
Fredericksburg, TX 78624
(210) 997-2126

Cherokee County Electric Co-op Assn.
P.O. Box 257
U.S. Highway 69, North
Rusk, TX 75785
(903) 683-2248

Coleman County Electric Co-op, Inc.
P.O. Box 860
200 West Live Oak Street
Coleman, TX 76834
(915) 625-2128

Comanche County Electric Co-op Assn.
P.O. Box 729
210 West Wright
Comanche, TX 76442
(915) 356-2533

Concho Valley Electric Co-op, Inc.
P.O. Box 30130
2530 Pulliam
San Angelo, TX 76903
(915) 655-6957

Cooke County Electric Co-op Assn.
P.O. Drawer 530
U.S. Highway 82, East
Muenster, TX 76252
(817) 759-2211

DeWitt Electric Cooperative Inc.
P.O. Box 231
909 East Broadway
Cuero, TX 77954
(512) 275-2334

Deaf Smith Electric Co-op, Inc.
P.O. Box 753
East Highway 60 & Whittier Street
Hereford, TX 79045
(806) 364-1166

Deep East Texas Electric Co-op, Inc.
P.O. Drawer N
U.S. Highway 21, East
San Augustine, TX 75972
(409) 275-2314

Denton County Electric Co-op, Inc.
3501 FM 2181
Corinth, TX 76205
(817) 497-6525

Dickens Electric Co-op, Inc.
P.O. Box 309
Farm Road 836
Spur, TX 79370
(806) 271-3311

Erath County Electric Co-op Assn.
P.O. Box 290
Junction Highways 67 & 281
Stephenville, TX 76401
(817) 965-3153

Fannin County Electric Co-op, Inc.
P.O. Drawer 250
411 Chestnut Street
Bonham, TX 75418
(903) 583-2118

Farmers Electric Co-op, Inc.
P.O. Box 6037
2000 East I-30
Greenville, TX 75403
(903) 455-1715

Fayette Electric Co-op, Inc.
P.O. Box 490
357 North Washington Street
LaGrange, TX 78945
(409) 968-3181

Fort Belknap Electric Co-op, Inc.
P.O. Box 486
1210 West Main Street
Olney, TX 76374
(817) 564-2343

Gate City Electric Co-op, Inc.
P.O. Box 69
1900 Avenue C, N.W.
Childress, TX 79201
(817) 937-2565

Golden Spread Electric Cooperative
P.O. Box 9898
500 South Taylor Street
Suite 10
Amarillo, TX 79105
(806) 379-7766

Grayson-Collin Electric Co-op, Inc.
P.O. Box 2000
902 North Waco Street
Van Alstyne, TX 75495
(903) 482-5231

Greenbelt Electric Co-op, Inc.
P.O. Box 948
706 10th Street
Wellington, TX 79095
(806) 447-2536

Guadalupe Valley Electric Co-op, Inc.
P.O. Box 118
825 East Sarah DeWitt
Gonzales, TX 78629
(210) 672-2871

Hamilton County Electric Co-op Assn.
P.O. Box 753
420 North Rice Street
Hamilton, TX 76531
(817) 386-3123

Hill County Electric Co-op, Inc.
P.O. Box 127
115 East Main Street
Itasca, TX 76055
(817) 687-2331

Houston County Electric Co-op, Inc.
P.O. Box 52
Loop 304, S.E.
Crockett, TX 75835
(409) 544-5641

J.A.C. Electric Co-op, Inc.
P.O. Box 278
Highway 172
Bluegrove, TX 76352
(817) 895-3311

Jackson Electric Co-op, Inc.
P.O. Drawer C
501 North Wells
Edna, TX 77957
(512) 782-7193

Jasper-Newton Electric Co-op, Inc.
812 South Margaret Avenue
Kirbyville, TX 75956
(409) 423-2241

Johnson County Electric Co-op Assn.
P.O. Box 16
3309 North Main
Cleburne, TX 76033
(817) 556-4000

Karnes Electric Co-op, Inc.
P.O. Box 7
1007 North Highway 123
Karnes City, TX 78118
(210) 780-3952

Kaufman County Electric Co-op, Inc.
P.O. Box 370
1800 Highway 243, East
Kaufman, TX 75142
(214) 932-2214

Kimble Electric Co-op, Inc.
P.O. Box 305
702 Pecan
Junction, TX 76849
(915) 446-2625

Lamar County Electric Co-op Assn.
P.O. Box 580
1485 North Main
Paris, TX 75461
(903) 784-4303

Lamb County Electric Co-op, Inc.
P.O. Box 1071
2415 South Phelps Avenue
Littlefield, TX 79339
(806) 385-5191

Lighthouse Electric Co-op, Inc.
P.O. Box 600
Highway 70, East
Floydada, TX 79235
(806) 983-2813

Lower Colorado River Authority
P.O. Box 220
3700 Lake Austin Boulevard
Austin, TX 78767
(512) 473-3200

Lyntegar Electric Co-op, Inc.
P.O. Box 970
1807 Main
Tahoka, TX 79373
(806) 998-4588

Magic Valley Electric Co-op, Inc.
P.O. Box 267
1-3/4 Mile West Highway 83
Mercedes, TX 78570
(210) 565-2451

McCulloch Electric Co-op, Inc.
P.O. Box 271
Highway 190, East
Brady, TX 76825
(915) 597-2161

McLennan County Electric Co-op
P.O. Box 357
100 North Main
McGregor, TX 76657
(817) 840-2871

Medina Electric Co-op, Inc.
P.O. Box 370
2308 18th Street
Hondo, TX 78861
(210) 426-4384

Mid-South Electric Co-op Assn.
P.O. Box 970
Highway 6 Bypass & FM 3090
Navasota, TX 77868
(409) 825-6436

Midwest Electric Co-op, Inc.
P.O. Drawer 616
Highway 22, West
Corsicana, TX 75151
(903) 874-7411

New Era Electric Co-op, Inc.
P.O. Box 1270
206 Dallas Highway
Athens, TX 75751
(903) 675-5688

North Plains Electric Co-op, Inc.
P.O. Box 1008
Highway 83, North
Perryton, TX 79070
(806) 435-5482

Northeast Texas Electric Co-op
211 East Tyler Street
Suite 507
Longview, TX 75601
(903) 757-3282

Nueces Electric Co-op, Inc.
P.O. Box 1032
709 East Main Street
Robstown, TX 78380
(512) 387-2581

Panola-Harrison Electric Co-op
P.O. Box 1058
410 East Houston Street
Marshall, TX 75671
(903) 935-7936

Pedernales Electric Co-op, Inc.
P.O. Box 467
200 Avenue F
Johnson City, TX 78636
(210) 868-7155

Rayburn Country Electric Co-op
P.O. Box 37
980 Sids Road
Rockwall, TX 75087
(214) 722-1336

Rio Grande Electric Co-op, Inc.
P.O. Box 1509
Highway 90, East
Brackettville, TX 78832
(210) 563-2444

Rita Blanca Electric Co-op, Inc.
P.O. Box 990
Highway 87, North
Dalhart, TX 79022
(806) 249-4506

Rusk County Electric Co-op, Inc.
P.O. Box 1169
506 Highway 79 North
Henderson, TX 75652
(903) 657-4571

Sam Houston Electric Co-op, Inc.
P.O. Box 1121
1501 East Church Street
Livingston, TX 77351
(409) 327-5711

Sam Rayburn G&T, Inc.
P.O. Box 631623
2905 Westward Drive
Nacogdoches, TX 75963
(409) 560-9532

San Bernard Electric Co-op, Inc.
P.O. Box 158
309 West Main
Bellville, Tx 77418
(409) 865-3171

San Miguel Electric Co-op, Inc.
P.O. Drawer 280
Highway 3387
Jourdanton, TX 78026
(210) 784-3411

San Patricio Electric Co-op, Inc.
P.O. Box 400
402 East Sinton Street
Sinton, TX 78387
(512) 364-2220

South Plains Electric Co-op, Inc.
P.O. Drawer 1830
110 North I-27
Lubbock, TX 79408
(806) 741-4200

South Texas Electric Co-op
P.O. Box 119
Farm Road 447
Nursery, TX 77976
(512) 575-6491

Southwest Texas Electric Co-op, Inc.
P.O. Drawer 677
101 East Gillis
Eldorado, TX 76936
(915) 853-2544

Stamford Electric Co-op, Inc.
P.O. Box 1147
225 West McHarg Street
Stamford, TX 79553
(915) 773-3684

Swisher Electric Co-op, Inc.
P.O. Box 67
401 S.W. 2nd
Tulia, TX 79088
(806) 995-3567

Taylor Electric Co-op, Inc.
P.O. Box 250
1610 North 1st Street
Merkel, TX 79536
(915) 928-4715

Tex-La Electric Co-op of Texas
P.O. Box 631623
2905 Westward Drive
Nacogdoches, TX 75963
(409) 560-9532

Tri-County Electric Co-op, Inc.
600 N.W. Parkway
Azle, TX 76020
(817) 444-3201

Upshur RECC
P.O. Box 70
1200 West Tyler
Gilmer, TX 75644
(903) 843-2536

Victoria Electric Co-op, Inc.
P.O. Box 2178
102 South Ben Jordan
Victoria, TX 77902
(512) 573-2428

Wharton County Electric Co-op, Inc.
P.O. Box 31
1701 East Jackson Street
El Campo, TX 77437
(409) 543-6271

Wise Electric Co-op, Inc.
P.O. Box 269
Corner of Hale & Cowan Streets
Decatur, TX 76234
(817) 627-2167

Wood County Electric Co-op, Inc.
P.O. Box 398
501 South Main
Quitman, TX 75783
(903) 763-2203

UTAH

Deseret G&T Cooperative
8722 South 300 West
Sandy, UT 84070
(801) 566-1238

Dixie-Escalante Rural Electric Assn.
Beryl, UT 84714
(801) 439-5311

Flowell Electric Association, Inc.
Star Route, Box 180
Fillmore, UT 84631
(801) 743-6214

GarKane Power Association, Inc.
P.O. Box 790
56 East Center Street
Richfield, UT 87401
(801) 896-5403

Intermountain Consumer Power Assn.
8722 South 300 West
Sandy, UT 84070
(801) 566-3933

Intermountain Power Agency
480 East 6400, South, S-200
Murray, UT 84107
(801) 262-8807

Moon Lake Electric Assn., Inc.
P.O. Box 278
188 West 200 North
Roosevelt, UT 84066
(801) 722-2448

VERMONT

Hardwick Electric Department
P.O. Box 516
25 North Main Street
Hardwick, VT 05843
(802) 472-5201

Vermont Electric Co-op, Inc.
R.D. #2, Box 59
Johnson, VT 05656
(802) 635-2331

Vermont Electric G&T Cooperative
R.D.#2, Box 59
Johnson, VT 05656
(802) 635-2331

Vermont Public Power Supply Authority
P.O. Box 425
512 St. George Road
Williston, VT 05495
(802) 878-5274

Washington Electric Co-op, Inc.
P.O. Box 8
Route 14
East Montpelier, VT 05651
(802) 223-5245

VIRGINIA

A&N Electric Cooperative
P.O. Box 1128
Route 316, South
Parksley, VA 23421
(804) 665-5116

BARC Electric Cooperative
P.O. Box 264
100 Main Street
Millboro, VA 24460
(703) 997-9124

Central Virginia Electric Co-op
P.O. Box 247
Front Street
Lovingston, VA 22949
(804) 263-8336

Community Electric Co-op
P.O. Box 267
52 West Windsor Boulevard
Windsor, VA 23487
(804) 242-6181

Craig-Botetourt Electric Co-op
P.O. Box 265
Route 615
New Castle, VA 24127
(703) 864-5121

Mecklenburg Electric Co-op
P.O. Box 2451
Highway 92 West
Chase City, VA 23924
(804) 372-6100

Northern Neck Electric Co-op
P.O. Box 288
102 St. Johns Street
Warsaw, VA 22572
(804) 333-3621

Northern Virginia Electric Co-op
P.O. Box 2710
10323 Lomond Drive
Manassas, VA 22110
(703) 335-0500

Old Dominion Electric Co-op
P.O. Box 2310
4201 Dominion Blvd., Suite 300
Glen Allen, VA 23060
(804) 747-0592

Powell Valley Electric Co-op
P.O. Box 433
Straight Creek Road
Tazewell, VA 37879
(615) 626-5204

Prince George Electric Co-op
P.O. Box 168
Highway 460 East
Waverly, VA 23890
(804) 834-2424

Rappahannock Electric Co-op
P.O. Box 7388
247 Industrial Court
Fredericksburg, VA 22404
(703) 898-8500

Shenandoah Valley Electric Co-op, Inc.
P.O. Box 236
Route 257
Mt. Crawford, VA 22841
(703) 434-2200

Southside Electric Co-op
P.O. Box 7
Highway 460 West
Crewe, VA 23930
(804) 645-7721

Virginia, Maryland & Delaware
Assn. of Electric Co-op
P.O. Box 2340
4201 Dominion Blvd., Suite 101
Glen Allen, VA 23058
(804) 346-3344

WASHINGTON

Benton REA
P.O. Box 1150
402 7th Street
Prosser, WA 99350
(509) 786-2913

Big Bend Electric Co-op, Inc.
P.O. Box 348
I-90 Ralston Road
Ritzville, WA 99169
(509) 659-1700

Columbia REA, Inc.
P.O. Box 46
115 East Main Street
Dayton, WA 99328
(509) 382-2578

Elmhurst Mutual Power & Light Company
120 132nd Street South
Tacoma, WA 98444
(206) 531-4646

Inland Power & Light Company
P.O. Box 4429
East 320 2nd Avenue
Spokane, WA 99202
(509) 747-7151

Lincoln Electric Co-op, Inc.
P.O. Box 289
1150 Morgan
Davenport, WA 99122
(509) 725-1141

Nespelem Valley Electric Co-op
P.O. Box 31
1009 F Street
Nespelem, WA 99155
(509) 634-4571

OHOP Mutual Light Company
34014 Mountain Highway East
Eatonville, WA 98328
(206) 847-2877

Okanogan County Electric Co-op
P.O. Box 69
265 Riverside
Winthrop, WA 98862
(509) 996-2228

Orcas Power & Light Company
P.O. Box 187
Mt. Baker Road
Eastsound, WA 98245
(206) 376-2252

PUD No. 1 of Douglas County
1151 Valley Mall Parkway
East Wenatchee, WA 98801
(509) 884-7191

PUD No. 1 of Ferry County
P.O. Box 1039
686 South Clark Avenue
Republic, WA 99166
(509) 775-3325

PUD No. 1 of Kittitas County
1400 East Vantage Highway
Ellensburg, WA 98926
(509) 925-3164

PUD No. 1 of Klickitat County
1313 South Columbus
Goldendale, WA 98620
(509) 773-5891

Parkland Light & Water Company
P.O. Box 44426
12918 Park Avenue, South
Tacoma, WA 98444
(206) 531-5666

Peninsula Light Company
P.O. Box 78
13315 Goodnough Drive, N.W.
Gig Harbor, WA 98335
(206) 857-5950

Tanner Electric
P.O. Box 1426
45710 S.E. North Bend Way
North Bend, WA 98045
(206) 888-0623

WEST VIRGINIA

Harrison REA, Inc.
P.O. Box 2464
Route 50, West
Clarksburg, WV 26302
(304) 624-6365

WISCONSIN

Adams-Columbia Electric Co-op
P.O. Box 70
401 East Lake Street
Friendship, WI 53934
(608) 339-3346

Barron Electric Cooperative
P.O. Box 40
1456 East LaSalle Avenue
Barron, WI 54812
(715) 537-3171

Bayfield Electric Co-op, Inc.
P.O. Box 68
Highway 2
Iron River, WI 54847
(715) 372-4287

Buffalo Electric Cooperative
P.O. Box 248
1225 South Main Street
Alma, WI 54610
(608) 685-4440

Central Wisconsin Electric Co-op
P.O. Box 255
150 Depot Street
Iola, WI 54945
(715) 445-2211

Chippewa Valley Electric Co-op
P.O. Box 575
317 South 8th Street
Cornell, WI 54732
(715) 239-6800

Clark Electric Co-op
124 North Main Street
Greenwood, WI 54437
(715) 267-6188

Crawford Electric Co-op
P.O. Box 158
Main Street
Gays Mills, WI 54631
(608) 735-4313

Dairyland Power Co-op
P.O. Box 817
3200 East Avenue, South
LaCrosse, WI 54602
(608) 788-4000

Dunn County Electric Co-op
P.O. Box 220
912 Crescent Street
Menomonie, WI 54751
(715) 232-6240

Eau Claire Electric Co-op
P.O. Box 368
8214 Highway 12
Fall Creek, WI 54742
(715) 832-1603

Grant-Lafayette Electric Co-op
231 North Sheridan Street
Lancaster, WI 53813
(608) 723-2121

Head of the Lakes Electric Co-op
Route 2, Box 563
Superior, WI 54880
(715) 399-2212

Jackson Electric Co-op
P.O. Box 546
119 Harrison Street
Black River Fall, WI 54615
(715) 284-5385

Jump River Electric Co-op
P.O. Box 99
1102 West 9th Street, North
Ladysmith, WI 54848
(715) 532-5524

Oakdale Electric Co-op
P.O. Box 128
Highways 12 & 16
Oakdale, WI 54649
(608) 372-4131

Oconto Electric Co-op
7479 REA Road
Oconto Falls, WI 54154
(414) 846-2816

Pierce-Pepin Electric Co-op
P.O. Box 420
Junction Highways 10 & 63
Ellsworth, WI 54011
(715) 273-4355

Polk-Burnett Electric Co-op
1000 Highway 35
Centuria, WI 54824
(715) 646-2191

Price Electric Co-op, Inc.
P.O. Box 110
508 North Lake Avenue
Phillips, WI 54555
(715) 339-2155

Richland Electric Co-op
P.O. Box 439
1027 North Jefferson Street
Richland Center, WI 53581
(608) 647-3173

Rock County Electric Co-op Assn.
P.O. Box 1758
2815 Kennedy Road
Janesville, WI 53547
(608) 752-4550

St. Croix Electric Co-op
P.O. Box 86
550 Highway 12
Baldwin, WI 54002
(715) 684-3336

Taylor Electric Cooperative
North 1831 Highway 13
Medford, WI 54451
(715) 678-2411

Trempealeau Electric Co-op
P.O. Box 277
625 West Main Street
Arcadia, WI 54612
(608) 323-3381

Vernon Electric Co-op
110 North Main Street
Westby, WI 54667
(608) 634-3121

Washington Island Electric Co-op, Inc.
Route 1, Box 14
Washington Island, WI 54246
(414) 847-2541

WYOMING

Big Horn REC
P.O. Box 270
208 South 5th Street
Basin, WY 82410
(307) 568-2419

Bridger Valley Electric Assn., Inc.
P.O. Box 399
U.S. Highway 30, South
Mountain View, WY 82939
(307) 786-2800

Carbon Power & Light, Inc.
P.O. Box 579
110 East Spring Street
Saratoga, WY 82331
(307) 326-5206

Garland Light & Power Company
755 Highway 14, Route 1
Powell, WY 82435
(307) 754-2881

Hot Springs REA, Inc.
P.O. Box 630
504 Fremont Street
Thermopolis, WY 82443
(307) 864-3157

Lower Valley Power & Light, Inc.
P.O. Box 188
345 North Washington
Afton, WY 83110
(307) 886-3175

Niobrara Electric Assn., Inc.
P.O. Box 697
3951 U.S. Highway 20
Lusk, WY 82225
(307) 334-3221

Riverton Valley Electric Assn.
P.O. Box 713
230 West Main
Riverton, WY 82501
(307) 856-9426

Rural Electric Company, Inc.
P.O. Box 518
6270 County Road 212
Pine Bluffs, WY 82082
(307) 245-3261

Sheridan-Johnson REA
P.O. Box 5087
1095 Brundage Lane
Sheridan, WY 82801
(307) 674-6466

Tri-County Electric Assn., Inc.
P.O. Box 930
221 Main
Sundance, WY 82729
(307) 283-3531

Wheatland REA
P.O. Box 1209
2154 South Road
Wheatland, WY 82201
(307) 322-2125

Wyrulec Company
P.O. Box 359
525 Main Street
Lingle, WY 82223
(307) 837-2225

Appendix E

Miscellaneous Utility Regulation Information

Listed herein is miscellaneous information relating to regulation of electric utilities. This information courtesy of National Association of Regulatory Utility Commissioners, 1102 Interstate Utility Commerce Commission Building, P.O. Box 684, Washington, DC 20044-0684; Phone (202) 898-2200.

Table 1

Agency Authority to Regulate Rates on Retail Sales to End-Users.

AGENCY	ELECTRIC Private	ELECTRIC Public	ELECTRIC Co-op	GAS Private	GAS Public	TELEPHONE	Interstate pipeline companies	Natural gas producers
The Agency has authority to regulate or control rates on retail sales to -	Ultimate Consumers						Industrial Customers of	
FCC						X 10/		
FERC		1/					11/	11/
ALABAMA PSC 6/	X	6/		X	6/	X		
ALASKA PUC	X	X 2/	X 27/	X	X	X		
ARIZONA CC	X		X	X		X		X
ARKANSAS PSC	X		X	X		X		
CALIFORNIA PUC 6/	X	6/		X	6/	X		
COLORADO PUC	X			X		X		
CONNECTICUT DPUC	X			X		X		8/
DELAWARE PSC 6/	X	6/	X	X	6/	X		8/
D.C. PSC	X	X	X	X	X	X		8/
FLORIDA PSC	X	X 17/	X 17/	X		X		8/
GEORGIA PSC	X			X		X		8/
HAWAII PUC 6/	X	6/		X	6/	X		8/
IDAHO PUC 6/	X	6/		X	6/	X 36/		8/
ILLINOIS CC	X			X		X	X	
INDIANA URC	X	X	X	X	X	X		
IOWA UB 32/	X		23/	X		X 14/		
KANSAS SCC	X	X 4/	X 37/	X	X 4/	X		
KENTUCKY PSC 6/	X	6/	X	X	X	X	X 19/	X
LOUISIANA PSC	X		X	X 15/		X		
MAINE PUC	X	X	X	X	X 8/	X		8/
MARYLAND PSC	X	X	X	X	X	X		
MASSACHUSETTS DPU	X	5/		X	5/	X		8/
MICHIGAN PSC	X		X	X		X 35/	X	
MINNESOTA PUC 6/	X	6/	23/	X 28/	6/	X 29/		8/
MISSISSIPPI PSC 38/	X	X 4/		X	X 4/	X		
MISSOURI PSC 38/	X			X		X 40/		
MONTANA PSC 16/	X	X		X	X	X		
NEBRASKA PSC 16/								
NEVADA PSC 6/	X	6/	26/	X	6/	X		
NEW HAMPSHIRE PUC	X	X 3/	X	X		X		8/
NEW JERSEY BPU 41/	X	4/		X		X		
NEW MEXICO PUC	X	22/	X	X				X
NEW MEXICO SCC								
NEW YORK PSC	X 39/	X 7/		X	X 7/	X		
NORTH CAROLINA UC	X			X		X	X	8/
NORTH DAKOTA PSC	X			X		X 31/		
OHIO PUC	X			X		X		
OKLAHOMA CC	X		X	X	8/	X		
OREGON PUC	X			X	4/	X		
PENNSYLVANIA PUC	X	X 4/		X	X 4/	X		8/
RHODE ISLAND PUC	X	X	X	X	X	X		8/
SOUTH CAROLINA PSC	X			X		X		
SOUTH DAKOTA PUC	X			X		X 24/		
TENNESSEE PSC	X			X		X	X	
TEXAS PUC	X	X 18/	X	X		X		
TEXAS RC				X	X 4/			
UTAH PSC 6/	X	6/		X	6/	X 34/		8/
VERMONT PSB 41/	X	X	X	X	X	X		
VIRGINIA SCC 6/	X	6/	X	X	6/	34/ X 30/	X	
WASHINGTON UTC	X			X		X	X	
WEST VIRGINIA PSC	X	X 25/	X	X	LTD	X		8/
WISCONSIN PSC	X	X	9/	X	X	X 33/	8/	8/
WYOMING PSC	X	X 4/	X	X	X 8/	X	X 19/	8/
PUERTO RICO PSC 41/				X		X 13/		8/
VIRGIN ISLANDS PSC 41/		X				X		8/
CANADIAN RTC						X		X 20/
ALBERTA PUB	X	21/		X	22/			
NOVA SCOTIA UARB	X			X	X 8/	X 8/		
ONTARIO EB 41/				X				
ONTARIO TSC						X		
QUEBEC NGB				X				
QUEBEC TB				X				

Table 2

Agency Authority to Regulate Standards for Meter Accuracy, Voltage Levels, Btu Content and Pressure of Natural Gas.

	The Agency has authority to regulate standards by -											
	Testing meters or by setting standards for the accuracy of meters by establishing standards for measuring voltage and/or cubic feet of gas.					Establishing Standards for -						
	ELECTRIC			GAS		Electric Voltage Levels			BTU Content of Gas		Gas Pressure GAS	
AGENCY	Private	Public	Co-op	Private	Public	Private	Public	Co-op	Private	Public	Private	Public
FERC				X					X 9/		X 9/	
ALABAMA PSC	X			X		X			X			
ALASKA PUC	X	X 7/	X 6/	X	X 7/	X	X 7/	X 6/	X	X 7/	X	X 7/
ARIZONA CC	X			X		X		X	X		X	
ARKANSAS PSC	X			X		X		X	X		X	
CALIFORNIA PUC	X		X	X		X		X	X		X	
COLORADO PUC 8/	X		X	X		X		X	X		X	
CONNECTICUT DPUC	X			X		X			X		X	X
DELAWARE PSC	X		X	X		X		X	X		X	
DC PSC	X			X		X			X		X	
FLORIDA PSC	X			X		X			X		X	
GEORGIA PSC	X			X		X			X		X	
HAWAII PUC	X			X		X			X		X	
IDAHO PUC	X			X		X			X		X	
ILLINOIS CC	X			X		X		X	X		X	X 11/
INDIANA URC	X		X	X		X		X	X		X	
IOWA UB	X	X	X	X	X	X	X	X	X	X	X	X
KANSAS SCC	X	X 1/	X	X	X 1/	X	X	X 1/	X	X 1/	X	X 1/
KENTUCKY PSC	X	X 2/	X	X	X 2/	X	X 2/	X	X	X 2/	X	X 2/
LOUISIANA PSC	X		X	X		X		X	X		X	
MAINE PUC	X	X	X	X		X	X	X	X	X	X	X
MARYLAND PSC	X	X	X	X	X	X	X	X	X	X	X	X
MASSACHUSETTS DPU	X	X		X	X	X	X		X	X	X	
MICHIGAN PSC	X		X	X	4/	X		X	X	4/	X	4/
MINNESOTA PUC	X		X	X		X			X		X	
MISSISSIPPI PSC	X		X	X		X		X	X		X	X
MISSOURI PSC	X			X		X			X		X	
MONTANA PSC	X	X		X	X	X	X		X	X	X	X
NEBRASKA PSC												
NEVADA PSC	X		X	X		X		X	X	N/A	X	
NEW HAMPSHIRE PUC	X	X 2/	X	X	12/	X	X 2/	X	X	12/	X	12/
NEW JERSEY BPU 14/	X	X 2/		X	X 4/	X	X 2/		X	X 4/	X	X 4/
NEW MEXICO PUC	X		X	X		X		X	X		X	
NEW MEXICO SCC												
NEW YORK PSC	X	X 3/		X	X	X	X 3/		X	X	X	X
NORTH CAROLINA UC	X			X		X		X	X		X	
NORTH DAKOTA PSC	X	X 13/	X 13/	X	X 13/	X			X		X	
OHIO PUC	X		X	X	X	X			X	X	X	5/
OKLAHOMA CC	X		X	X		X		X	X		X	
OREGON PUC	X			X	4/	X			X	4/	X	4/
PENNSYLVANIA PUC	X			X		X			X		X	
RHODE ISLAND PUC	X	X		X	X	X			X		X	X
SOUTH CAROLINA PSC	X			X		X			X		X	X
SOUTH DAKOTA PUC	X			X		X			X		X	
TENNESSEE PSC	X			X		X			X		X	X
TEXAS PUC	X		X			X		X				
TEXAS RC												
UTAH PSC	X	X	X	X		X	X	X	X		X	
VERMONT PSB 14/	X	X	X	X	X	X	X	X	X	X	X	
VIRGINIA SCC	X		X	X		X		X	X		X	
WASHINGTON UTC	X			X		X			X		X	
WEST VIRGINIA PSC	X	X	X	X	X	X	X	X	X	X	X	X
WISCONSIN PSC	X		X	X	X	X			X	X	X	X
WYOMING PSC	X	X 2/	X	X	4/	X	X 2/	X	X	4/	X	4/
PUERTO RICO PSC 14/				X					X		X	
VIRGIN ISLANDS PSC 14/		X		X					X		X	
CANADIAN RTC												
NATL ENERGY BOARD						X 11/	X 11/				X 11/	X 11/
ALBERTA PUB 10/												
NOVA SCOTIA UARB 10/												
ONTARIO EB 14/												
QUEBEC NGB									X		X	

Table 3

Provisions for Service in Municipally-Annexed Areas.

AGENCY	Are There Provisions for Service in Areas Annexed by Municipality	Who Resolves Service Area Disputes in Annexed Areas?
ALABAMA PSC	Yes 37-14-3 and 37-14-32 basis of "closer to" facilities in place as of 1/1/84	Courts--37-14-9 and 37-14-37
ALASKA PUC	Yes §42.05.221(d) PUC may order exchange of customers and facilities. Also AS 29	PUC--42.05.221(d)
ARIZONA CC	Yes court decision. Municipality may extend service in annexed area, is not required to purchase facilities of utility already serving	CC--40-281[B]
ARKANSAS PSC	Yes 23-18-331, exclusive service areas.	PSC or Circuit Court
CALIFORNIA PUC	Yes Gov. 37350.5 and Pub. U. 6262, city may purchase by exercise of eminent domain	Generally PUC Pub. U. 1001
COLORADO PUC	Yes 31-15-77 or 40-9.5-203 muni has right to "purchase or condemn" IOU or co-op system	Court
CONNECTICUT DPUC	No	Not addressed
DELAWARE PSC	Exclusive service areas assigned by PSC/courts	Generally Delaware Supreme Court
DC PSC	N/A. No municipal utilities.	
FLORIDA PSC	PSC assigns exclusive service areas 366.04[2]	PSC--all service area disputes, 366.04[2e]
GEORGIA PSC	Annexation does not change right to serve for IOUs/co-ops/munis already serving 46-3-7 & 9	PSC--all service area disputes 46-3-13 and 46-3-8[c] and [d]
HAWAII PUC	§§49-1 et seq--muni serves annexed area	Not addressed (one electric utility)
IDAHO PUC	Yes §61-332B & C--muni required to purchase IOU/co-op facilities previously serving area	District Court--61-334B
ILLINOIS CC	Yes 220 ILCS §414 (1993)--previously serving supplier may continue to serve.	CC--220 ILCS §411 (1993) CC approves service territory agreements between muni/co-op
INDIANA URC	Yes 8-1-2.3 assigns exclusive service area. 8-1-2.3-6 governs change in service area. Muni may apply to service annexed area.	URC (appeal to Court of Appeals)
IOWA UB	Annexation does not change right of current utility to serve §476.26. Exclusive service territory under §476.25.	
KANSAS SCC	Yes §66-1, 176--muni may terminate IOU/co-op service 180 days after annexation, ir required to purchase IOU/co-op facilities in order to serve annexed area.	SCC--all service area disputes 66-1, 174
KENTUCKY PSC	Yes §96.538--certified supplier has dominant right to continue service.	PSC--all service area disputes
LOUISIANA PSC	Yes Court decisions--muni may refuse franchise to IOU/co-op, which may not extend service, but may continue service to existing customers	PSC for IOUs/co-ops, not for municipals
MAINE PUC	Yes T. 30, §4251.6--muni has right to purchase or acquire by eminent domain facilities of other suppliers.	PUC--all service area disputes Title 35 §2301
MARYLAND PSC	Does not have exclusive service territories. MAC Article 78 §53--co-ops or IOUs.	Not addressed
MASSACHUSETTS DPU	No.	Not addressed (DPU elsewhere Ch. 164, §47)
MICHIGAN PSC	Yes §117.4f and 213.111--muni has right to purchase other suppliers facilities.	PSC for IOUs/co-ops, Court for municipals
MINNESOTA PUC	Yes §216B.41--Annexation does not affect right of current supplier to serve area.	PUC--all service area disputes 216B.39
MISSISSIPPI PSC	Court can enjoin muni from extending service into newly annexed area already served by a regulated utility.	PSC for IOUs/co-ops, Court for municipals
MISSOURI PSC	Non-exclusive service areas; territorial agreements between power suppliers subject to PSC approval. §394.312	Not specified, probably courts
MONTANA PSC	Yes §69-5-109--current supplier may continue to serve existing customers, but not expand.	District Court (69-5-110) for all service area disputes
NEBRASKA PSC	Power Review Board approves muni application.	Power Review Board--all service area disputes
NEVADA PSC	§§704.330 & 704.340 grant exclusive area.	PSC--all service area disputes 704.330 & .340
NEW HAMPSHIRE PUC	PUC allocates exclusive area §374.22 Ch. 38 governs muni acquisition of utility	PUC--all service area disputes 374:22
NEW JERSEY BPU	Munis may extend without BRC approval 40:62-22	BRC--all service area disputes 48:7-5
NEW MEXICO PUC	Franchises are non-exclusive; if city and annexed area served by 2 different regulated utilities, PUC decides who serves annexed area	PUC--disputes between public utilities; presumably courts for municipals
NEW YORK PSC	Non-exclusive service areas; muni has right, subject to local law and referendum, to construct, purchase or condemn facilities. Gen. Mun. Law Article 14A, §360(6).	Not addressed
NORTH CAROLINA UC	Co-ops/IOUs have exclusive right to serve premises wholly within 300 feet of their lines in existence as of annexation date if premises are wholly more than 300 feet from muni lines.	UC for IOUs/co-ops, courts for municipals

Table 3 (Continued)

AGENCY	Are There Provisions for Service in Areas Annexed by Municipality	Who Resolves Service Area Disputes in Annexed Areas?
NORTH DAKOTA PSC	Yes §40-33-01 for municipalities; utility lawfully serving municipality may expand with certificate §49-03-01	PSC--all service area disputes 49-03-01.4
OHIO PUC	Munis have constitutional authority to appropriate needed facilities, but no obligation.	PUC for IOUs/co-ops, not for municipals
OKLAHOMA CC	IOUs/co-ops serving pre-annexation may continue to serve. 17 OS 1981, §158.21	Not addressed--CC elsewhere 17 OS 1981 158.24
OREGON PUC	City has right to condemn private property for its use in providing power service. 223.005(3)	PUC--758.400 et seq
PENNSYLVANIA PUC	Munis have no right to serve; co-op/IOU which had closest distribution line in 1975 has exclusive right to serve. Tit. 15, §3277 et seq	PUC (appeal to Commonwealth Court) T 15 §3281
RHODE ISLAND PUC	No, other than cities/towns have power to grant franchises; non-exclusive service area.	Not addressed
SOUTH CAROLINA PSC	Muni may serve in adjacent territory if granted certificate §58-27-1230; existing supplier retains all current customers and those within 300 feet of lines §58-27-620.	PSC or courts for all service area disputes §58-27-650[B]
SOUTH DAKOTA PUC	Annexing municipality which owns its system may purchase other suppliers' facilities in area annexed. §49-34A-49	PUC for all service area disputes §49-34A-43
TENNESSEE PSC	Munis have power of eminent domain. §7-34-104[1]. §54-34-105 authorizes munis and co-ops to acquire service areas and equipment of non-consumer owned electric companies.	PSC 65-4-201 et seq; courts for municipals and co-ops (exempt from PSC authority)
TEXAS PUC	Muni has no right to serve or purchase without certificate of convenience and necessity, Tit. 32, Ch. 10, Art. 1446c, §50[2] and 55, unless there is no other service provider.	PUC or courts for all service area disputes Tit. 32, Ch. 10, Art. 1446c, art. VII
UTAH PSC	Munis have primary right to serve area; must pay fair market compensation to co-op/IOU for dedicated facilities. 10-8-14, -20, -21, and 10-2-401[4].	Courts for dispute involving municipality; courts/PSC for dispute between city/co-op/IOU PSC for dispute between co-op/IOU/non-muni.
VERMONT PSB	Munis serve annexed areas. Tit. 30, §2902	PSB--all service area disputes T 30, §249
VIRGINIA SCC	Existing supplier may continue to serve in certified area until municipality exercises purchase option. 56-265.4:2 and court decision	SCC--all service area disputes §56.265.3
WASHINGTON UTC	Exclusive service area franchise not permitted Munis may purchase other suppliers' facilities in certain instances. 35.92.054 and 35.84.020	UTC has authority to authorize service area agreements between public and private utilities.
WEST VIRGINIA PSC	Munis may exercise eminent domain Code 8-19-3	PSC--all service area disputes Code 24-2-1
WISCONSIN PSC	Muni may not extend service area without consent of existing utility or determination by PSC that existing service is inadequate. 196.495 and 196.50. Special rule for co-ops.	PSC--all service area disputes §196.50 and 196.495[1][b]
WYOMING PSC	Municipality may exercise right of condemnation. §1-26-804 and 1-26-808; court decisions	Courts or PSC

Table 4

Number of Electric Utilities Subject to Agency Regulation.

AGENCY	Pri-vate	Citation of Jurisdic-tional Authority	Public	Electric Citation of Jurisdic-tional Authority	Co-op	Citation of Jurisdic-tional Authority
				Power Marketing Agencies		
FERC	179	16 USC 791 et seq 5/	5	16 USC 791 et. seq. 5/	3	16 USC 791 et seq
ALABAMA PSC	1	§37, Code AL 1975	0	No jurisdiction §37-1-34	0	No jurisdiction §37-6-27
ALASKA PUC	22	§6, Ch 113 SLA 1970	2	§6, Ch 113 SLA 1970	11	§6, Ch 113 SLA 1970
ARIZONA CC	5	Art XV, AZ Constitution	0	No jurisdiction	11	Art XV, AZ Constitution
ARKANSAS PSC	4	A.C.A. 23-4-201	15	Safety only	18	A.C.A. 23-18-308
CALIFORNIA PUC	3	CA PU Code §701	0	CA PU Code §8029.5-8057 Limited jurisdiction	4	PU Code 216, 217, 218, 2777
COLORADO PUC	2	§ 40-1-103 CRS 1993	16	§ 40-1-103 CRS 1993	28	§ 40-1-103 CRS 1993 9/
CONNECTICUT DPUC	3	Title 16, CT Gen. Stat.	0	No jurisdiction	0	None in category
DELAWARE PSC	1	Delaware Code, Title 26	0	No jurisdiction	1	DE Code, Title 26
DC PSC	1	DC Code, Title 43 et seq	0	None in category	0	None in category
FLORIDA PSC	5	Ch. 366	33	Ch. 366 (rate structure and territory)	17	Ch. 366 (rate structure and territory)
GEORGIA PSC	2	Title 46	52	Title 46 §3-13 & 3-8[c] & [d] territory only	42	Title 46 Territory and Finance only
HAWAII PUC	5	Ch. 269, HI Rev. Stats.	0	None in category	0	None in category
IDAHO PUC	5	Title 61, Idaho Code	0	No jurisdiction	0	No jurisdiction
ILLINOIS CC	10	220 ILCS 5	0	§11-117-1.1 (1993)--service territory only	0	§11-117-1.1 (1993)--service territory only
INDIANA URC	5	IC 8-1-2-1 et seq.	42	IC 8-1-2-1 et seq. (Rates and territory)	46	IC 8-1-13-18, 8-1-2-1
IOWA UB	2	IA Code Ch 476 & 478	110	IA Code Ch 476 & 478 but not rates	54	IA Code Ch 476 & 478
KANSAS SCC	9	Ch 66, KS Stat. Ann.	14	Ch 66, KS Stat. Ann.	25	Ch 66, KS Stat. Ann. 12/
KENTUCKY PSC	5	Ch 278, KY Rev. Stats.	0	No jurisdiction - rates	24	Ch 278, KY Rev. Stats.
LOUISIANA PSC	4	State Constitution	0	Revised Statutes	15	RS 12:409(g)417.1, Const.
MAINE PUC	6	35-A MRSA	6	35-A MRSA (Rates outside corp. limits, territory)	5	35-A MRSA
MARYLAND PSC	5	Ann. Code MD, Article 78	4	Ann. Code MD, Article 78	4	Ann. Code MD, Article 78
MASSACHUSETTS DPU	8	Chapter 164	40	Chapter 164 (limited) 1/	0	No jurisdiction
MICHIGAN PSC	9	Act 106, PA 1909, Amen.	0	No jurisdiction	14	Act 106, PA 1909, Amended
MINNESOTA PUC	2	Ch. 216B (1974) 6/	126	Ch. 216B (1974) 6/ (Territory/complaints)	54	Ch. 216B (1974) 6/
MISSISSIPPI PSC	2	PU Act 1956 (Amended) PU Act 1983	21	PU Act 1956 (Amended), PU Act 1983	28	PU Act 1956 (Amended), PU Act 1983
MISSOURI PSC	6	§386.250 RSMO supp. 1992	0	No jurisdiction	46	Safety only-394.160 RsMO
MONTANA PSC	5	Title 69, MCA	1	Title 69, Ch. 7, MCA (Certain increases only)	0	No jurisdiction
NEBRASKA PSC	0	None in category	0	No jurisdiction	0	No jurisdiction
NEVADA PSC	3	NRS 704.020	0	No jurisdiction - rates	11	NRS 704.673-704.677
NEW HAMPSHIRE PUC	11	RSA 362:2	3	RSA 362:2 Outside municipal limits only 10/	1	RSA 362:2
NEW JERSEY BPU 13/	4	NJSA 48:2-13, et.seq.	1	Outside corporate limits	1	NJSA 48:2-13, et.seq.
NEW MEXICO PUC	4	NMSA 1978, §62-3-1, 62-31.1	0	NMSA 1978, §62-6-5 (can petition for regulation)	20	NMSA 1978, §62-8-7
NEW YORK PSC	2 4/	Pub. Serv. Law §2(12) (13), 5(1)(b) and Art 4	3 2/	Pub. Service Law, §2 (16), 5(1)(b) and Art 4	5	Rural Elec. Co-op Law §67
NORTH CAROLINA UC	7	NCGS Ch 62, 3(23)a.1	0	No jurisdiction	0	NC GS Ch 62, 110.2 et seq
NORTH DAKOTA PSC	3	49-02-01 NDCC	0	No jurisdiction	0	No jurisdiction
OHIO PUC	9	Title 49, Ohio Rev. Code	0	No jurisdiction	0	No jurisdiction
OKLAHOMA CC	4	Title 17, §151 et seq	0	No jurisdiction	31	Title 17, §158.21 11/
OREGON PUC	6	OR Rev. Stats, Ch 756, 757	0	None, except safety, territory, curtailment	19	Safety, territory, curtailment
PENNSYLVANIA PUC	12	Tit. 15, §3277 et seq	4	Outside corporate limits	0	No jurisdiction
RHODE ISLAND PUC	4	Title 39, Chapter 2	1	Title 39, Chapter 2	0	None in category
SOUTH CAROLINA PSC	4	58-27-140	0	Territory 58-27-610	0	Territory 58-27-610
SOUTH DAKOTA PUC	6	SDCL 49-34A and 49-41B	34	49-34A and 49-41B Territory & siting only	35	49-34A and 49-41B Territory & siting only
TENNESSEE PSC	5	65-4-101	0	No jurisdiction	26	67-901 for Ad Valorem assessment only
TEXAS PUC	10	VTCS, Art 1446c	71	VTCS, Art 1446c 7/ Outside corporate limits	87	VTCS, Art 1446c
UTAH PSC	2	UT Code, §54-2-1(19)	1	UT Code, § 17-6-1.1	10	UT Code, §54-2-1(19)
VERMONT PSB 13/	10	30 VSA	15	30 VSA	2	30 VSA
VIRGINIA SCC	5	VA Code, Title 56	0	No jurisdiction - rates	13	VA Code, Title 56
WASHINGTON UTC	2	Title 80, RCW	0	No jurisdiction	0	No jurisdiction
WEST VIRGINIA PSC	10	WV Code, Ch. 24	2	Limited review authority	3	WV Code, Ch. 24
WISCONSIN PSC	7	Chapter 196	82	Chapter 196	0	No jurisdiction
WYOMING PSC	8	§37-1-101 WY Stats 1977	17	§37-1-101 Outside municipal limits only	1	§37-1-101 WY Stats 1977

AGENCY	Pri-vate	Citation of Jurisdic-tional Authority	Public	Citation of Jurisdic-tional Authority	Co-op	Citation of Jurisdic-tional Authority
				Electric		
PUERTO RICO PSC		None in jurisdiction		No jurisdiction	13/	None in jurisdiction
VIRGIN ISLANDS PSC				Title 30, VIC, §1 Amen,	13/	
CANADIAN AGENCIES						
ALBERTA PUB	3	PUB Act, EEM Act	9 3/	§291 Mun. Govt. Act	165	Hydro & Elec Energy Act
NOVA SCOTIA UARB	1	PU Act RSNS 1989, C.380	7	PU Act RSNS 1989, C.380	0	
ONTARIO EB	0	No jurisdiction	0	No jurisdiction	0	Does not regulate elec.

Footnotes—Table 4

Number of Electric Utilities Subject to Agency Regulation.

1/ One small municipal electric plant on Cuttyhunk Island exempted from Department jurisdiction under 1936 Act of Legislature.

2/ Plus 41 under jurisdiction of NY Power Authority. §1014 of the Public Authorities Law exempts the Power Authority from regulation by the Commission except for siting transmission and generation facilities under Article 7 and 8 and §18(a) of the Public Service Law. Municipalities which buy power from the Power Authority are also exempt from regulation by the PSC under §1005(5)(g) of the Public Authorities Law.

3/ Under partial Board jurisdiction. One municipally owned utility also under Board jurisdiction pursuant to Electric Energy Marketing Act.

4/ Excludes companies regulated from safety standpoint only.

5/ FERC has no jurisdiction over municipal electric utilities; FERC hydro regulation under Part I of FPA includes 82 private utilities and 294 municipals.

6/ Gas and electric regulation established April 12, 1974; rate regulation effective January 1, 1975.

7/ Municipals may elect Commission regulation. Certification required of all retail public utilities, including municipalities and political subdivisions. Four state affiliated river authorities under PUC jurisdiction for rates.

8/ Includes two state owned electric utilities.

9/ The rates of only 1 of the co-ops are under Commission regulation; Colorado still regulates the certificates, service territories, safety and consumer complaints of all cooperatives. Effective 1983, co-ops were permitted to exempt themselves from state agency rate regulation upon a ballot procedure. State commission has jurisdiction over municipal utilities only outside corporate limits and then only if rates charged outside corporate limits differ from rates charged inside corporate limits.

10/ And only if rates charged outside municipal limits are different from those charged within municipal limits.

11/ New law (HB1406), signed in early 1993 allows rural electric co-ops with fewer than 17,000 meters to vote to opt out of state regulation; as of May 1994, two co-ops had done so.

12/ Statute enacted in 1992 allows rural electric co-ops with fewer than 17,000 meters to opt out of state regulation; as of May 1994, 18 co-ops had done so.

13/ Commission did not respond to requests for update information; this data may not be current.

Table 5

Bill Verification - Electric and Gas.

AGENCY	Uniform practices for billing format? Electric	Gas	D15 - Checking the accuracy of billing. What resources are available to customers to check accuracy of their bills? SEE KEY BELOW	Bills must contain - a All back-up data	b Enough data so that a customer can calculate	D 16 Bills are itemized for - a Regular Service Charges	b Other Recurring Charges	c Special Charges	D 17 Agency has analyzed utility billing procedures	Comment
ALABAMA PSC			A, B	YES	NO	YES	NO	---	YES	
ALASKA PUC	NO	NO	A, B	YES	Usually	Some	Some	Varies	NO	
ARIZONA CC			A, B	YES	NO	YES	YES	YES	NO	
ARKANSAS PSC	NO	NO	A, B, D	NO	Usually	YES	YES	varies	NO	
CALIFORNIA PUC			A, B, C, D	YES	YES	YES	YES	YES	YES	
COLORADO PUC			A, B	YES	YES	YES	YES	YES	YES	
CONNECTICUT DPUC 17/	NO	NO	A, B, C, D	YES	YES	YES	YES	YES	YES	
DELAWARE PSC	NO	NO	A, B	YES	NO	YES	YES	YES	YES 12/	
DC PSC	YES	YES	A, B	YES	YES-GAS	YES	YES	YES	YES	
FLORIDA PSC	YES	YES	A, B, C, D	YES	YES	YES	YES	YES	YES	
GEORGIA PSC	NO		A, B	YES	NO	YES	NO 1/	---	YES	
HAWAII PUC	NO	YES	A, B, D	YES	YES	YES	YES	YES	YES 12/	
IDAHO PUC	NO	NO	A, B, C, D	YES	YES	YES	YES	YES	YES	2/
ILLINOIS PSC	YES	YES	A, B, C, D	YES	NO 4/	Varies	Varies	Varies	YES	
INDIANA URC	NO	NO	A, B, D	YES	NO	YES	YES	NO	NO	
IOWA UB	NO	NO	A, B	YES	NO	NO	YES	YES	NO	
KANSAS SCC	NO	NO	A, B	YES	YES	YES	YES	YES	YES	
KENTUCKY PSC	NO	NO	A, B, C, D	NO	Varies	Varies	Varies	Varies	YES	5/
LOUISIANA PSC			A, B, C, D	NO	---	YES	YES	NO	NO	6/
MAINE PUC	NO	NO	A, B, D	YES	YES	Varies	Varies	Varies	YES	
MARYLAND PSC			A, B, C, D 15/	YES	YES	YES	YES	YES	YES 12/	
MASSACHUSETTS DPU	NO	NO	A, B, D	NO	YES	YES	YES	YES	YES	2/
MICHIGAN PSC	NO	NO	A, B, C	YES	YES	YES	YES	YES	YES	7/
MINNESOTA PUC			A, B	YES	YES	YES	YES	YES	YES	
MISSISSIPPI PSC			A, B	YES	NO	YES	YES	YES	YES	8/
MISSOURI PSC	NO	NO	A, B, D	NO	NO 13/	YES	NO	YES	NO	
MONTANA PSC			A, B, C, D	YES	YES	YES	YES	YES	NO	
NEBRASKA PSC	N/A	N/A	Does not regulate electric or gas							
NEVADA PSC 16/	YES	YES	A, B	YES	YES	YES	YES	YES	YES	7/
NEW HAMPSHIRE PUC	NO	NO	A, B	YES	YES	YES	YES	YES	YES	
NEW JERSEY BPU 20/			A, B, D	YES	YES	YES	YES	YES	NO	
NEW MEXICO PUC			A, B, C, D	YES	YES	YES	YES	YES	NO	
NEW YORK PSC			A, B	YES	YES 3/	YES	YES	YES	YES	
NORTH CAROLINA UC	NO	NO	A, B, C, D	YES	NO	YES	NO	10/	YES	
NORTH DAKOTA PSC	NO	NO	A, B, C, D	YES	YES	YES	YES	YES	YES	
OHIO PUC	YES	YES	A, B, C, D	YES	YES	YES	YES	YES	YES	
OKLAHOMA CC			A, B	YES	NO	NO	NO	YES	NO	
OREGON PUC	NO	NO	A, B, C, D	YES	YES	YES	YES	Varies	NO	
PENNSYLVANIA PUC 18/	NO	NO	A, B, C, D	NO	YES	YES	YES	NO	YES	
RHODE ISLAND PUC			A, B, C, D	YES	NO	YES	NO	YES	YES	
SOUTH CAROLINA PSC	NO	NO	A, B, C, D	YES	NO	YES	YES	YES	YES	
SOUTH DAKOTA PUC	NO	NO	A, B, C, D	YES	Varies	YES	YES	NO	NO	
TENNESSEE PSC	YES	NO	A, B, C, D	YES	NO	YES	YES	NO	NO	
TEXAS PUC 19/	NO	N/A	A, B, C, D	YES	YES	YES	YES	Varies	NO	
TEXAS RC	N/A	YES	A, B, C, D	NO	NO	YES	YES	Varies	YES	
UTAH PSC	NO	NO	A, B, C, D	YES	NO	YES	YES	YES	YES	
VERMONT PSB 20/			A, B	YES	NO	YES	YES	YES	YES	
VIRGINIA SCC	NO	NO	A, B, C, D	YES	NO	YES	YES	YES	NO	14/
WASHINGTON UTC	NO	NO	A, B	YES	YES	YES	YES	YES	YES	
WEST VIRGINIA PSC			A, B, C, D	YES	YES	YES	YES	YES	YES	9/
WISCONSIN PSC			A, B, C, D	YES	YES	YES	YES	YES	YES	
WYOMING PSC			A, B, D	YES	YES	YES	YES	YES	NO	
VIRGIN ISLANDS PSC20/	YES	N/A	A, B	YES	YES	YES	YES	YES	NO	
ALBERTA PUB			A, B	YES	NO	YES	YES	YES	NO	
BRITISH COLUMBIA UC	NO	NO	A, B, C, D	YES	NO	YES	YES	YES	YES	
NOVA SCOTIA UARB	NO	N/A	A, B	YES	YES	YES	YES	NO	YES	11/
ONTARIO EB 20/			A, B, C	YES		YES	YES	YES	YES	
QUEBEC NGB	N/A	YES	Rate Structure on invoice	YES	YES	YES	YES	YES	YES	

A = Utility will assist customer
B = Agency will assist customer
C = Utility will provide copy of rate sheet(s) or tariff on request.
D = Utility will test meter on request
E = Other (specify)

Footnotes—Table 5

Bill Verification - Electric and Gas.

1/ For instance, Atlanta Gas Light shows PGA and franchise tax separately on bill, but Georgia Power does not show fuel cost recovery and franchise taxes separately.

2/ Billing procedures reviewed by Consumer Assistance division staff for testimony in general rate cases.

3/ Commission in Fall 1985 directed utilities to provide plain language bills.

4/ Some utilities periodically send rate brochures to customers from which they can calculate bills.

5/ In connection with rate cases or complaints on a case-by-case basis.

6/ Tariffs constantly under review and policies revised as needed.

7/ Audits of utility company practices as they relate to Commission Billing Rules.

8/ Recently revised rules for utility service and maintain ongoing analysis for individuals at their request.

9/ Has expanded number of itemized billing components and provided energy conservation information.

10/ Generally stated separately but not specifically described.

11/ Guidelines for retail credit, collection and cut-off practices of public utility suppliers issued by Ministry of Energy. Compliance is not legally required but used as benchmark for accepted practices.

12/ Commission reviews billing procedures annually.

13/ Commission rules do not require companies to provide rate structures on bills, but some do.

14/ Various studies for billing improvements.

15/ Utilities required to send all customers a reference guide explaining billing methods annually.

16/ Commission adopted Consumer Bill of Rights to standardize billing practices.

17/ Agency has established rules requiring certain information; the format varies from company to company.

18/ 1992 policy statement directed companies to provide plain language bills; regulations outline information to be included on bill but do not prescribe a format.

19/ In 1994, PUC is considering foreign language rules for billing non-English-speaking customers.

20/ Commission did not respond to request for update information; this data may not be current.

Table 6

Approved Rate Design Features for Electric Utility Customers Served With Demand Meters.

AGENCY	Demand Ratchets	Declining-Block Energy Rates	Declining-Block Demand Rates	Flat Energy Rates	Flat Demand Rates	Inverted Energy Rates	Inverted Demand Rates	Seasonal Rates	Power Factor Corrections
ALABAMA PSC	C,I	C,I		C,I	C,I			C,I	C,I
ALASKA PUC	C,I			C,I	C,I			C,I	C,I
ARIZONA CC	I	C,I		C,I	C,I			C,I	C,I
ARKANSAS PSC	C,I	C,I		C,I	C,I			C,I	C,I
CALIFORNIA PUC	I			C,I	C,I			C,I	
COLORADO PUC	C,I			C,I	C,I			C,I	C,I
CONNECTICUT DPUC	C,I	3/			C,I			C,I	C,I
DELAWARE PSC	C,I			C,I	C,I			C	C
DC PSC 1/					C				
FLORIDA PSC				C,I	C,I				C,I
GEORGIA PSC	C,I	C,I						C,I	C,I
HAWAII PUC	C,I	C,I	I	C	C				C,I
IDAHO PUC				C,I	C,I			C	C,I
ILLINOIS CC	C	C,I	C,I	C,I	C,I			C,I	C,I
INDIANA URC	C,I	C,I	C,I	C,I	C,I				C,I
IOWA UB	C,I	C,I	C,I	C,I	C,I			C,I	C,I
KANSAS SCC	C,I	C,I	C,I	C,I	C,I			C,I	C,I
KENTUCKY PSC	C,I	C,I	C,I	C,I	C,I			C,I	C,I
LOUISIANA PSC	C,I	C,I	C,I						I
MAINE PUC	C,I			C,I				C,I	I
MARYLAND PSC	C,I	C,I		C,I	C,I			C,I	C,I
MASSACHUSETTS DPU		C,I		C,I	C,I		C,I	C,I	C,I
MICHIGAN PSC	C,I	C,I		C,I	C,I			C,I	C,I
MINNESOTA PUC	C,I	C,I 2/	I 2/	C,I	C,I			C,I	C,I
MISSISSIPPI PSC	C,I	C,I	C,I	C,I					C,I
MISSOURI PSC	C,I	C,I	C,I	C,I	C,I			C,I	C,I
MONTANA PSC	I	C		C,I	C,I		C,I	C,I	C,I
NEBRASKA PSC								C,I	C,I
NEVADA PSC				C,I	C,I			C,I	C,I
NEW HAMPSHIRE PUC	C,I	C,I	C,I	C,I	C,I				
NEW JERSEY BPU	C,I	C,I	C,I	C,I			C	C,I	
NEW MEXICO PUC	C,I	C,I		C,I	C,I		C,I	C,I	C,I
NEW YORK PSC	C,I	C,I	C,I	C,I	C,I			C,I	I
NORTH CAROLINA UC	C,I	C,I	C,I	C,I	C,I			C,I	C,I
NORTH DAKOTA PSC	C,I	C,I		C,I	C,I			C,I	C,I
OHIO PUC	C,I	C,I	C,I	C,I	C,I	C,I	C,I	C	C,I
OKLAHOMA CC	C,I	C,I		C,I		C,I		C	C,I
OREGON PUC	C,I	C		C,I	C,I		C	C,I	C,I
PENNSYLVANIA PUC	C,I	C,I	I		C,I			C,I	C,I
RHODE ISLAND PUC									
SOUTH CAROLINA PSC	C,I	C,I	C,I	C,I	C,I	C,I		C,I	C,I
SOUTH DAKOTA PUC	C,I	C,I	C,I					C,I	C,I
TENNESSEE PSC	C,I	C		I	C,I				C,I
TEXAS PUC									
UTAH PSC	C,I	C,I		C,I	C,I		C,I		C,I
VERMONT PSB								C,I	C,I
VIRGINIA SCC	C,I	C,I	C,I	C,I	C,I			C,I	
WASHINGTON UTC	C,I			C,I	C,I				C,I
WEST VIRGINIA PSC	C,I	C,I		C,I	C,I				I
WISCONSIN PSC	C,I			C,I	C,I			C,I	C,I
WYOMING PSC	C,I	C,I	C,I	C,I	C,I				I 4/
ALBERTA PUB	C,I	C,I	I		C			C	I
BRITISH COL. UC	I	C		I	I		C		C,I
NOVA SCOTIA UARB	C,I	C,I							

1/   There are no industrial rates offered.
2/   Phasing out declining-block rates.
3/   Energy rates decline as hours of use increase.
4/   As well as certain other large use customers.

Table 7

Costing Methodology for Electric Utilities.

SEE KEYS BELOW AGENCY	Which Principles are Used Most Often in Establishing Rate Designs in General Rate Cases SEE KEY BELOW	Agency Uses or Has Approved a System Expansion Model to Calculate Marginal Costs? Which One; # of Years	To Allocate Costs Among Customer Classes, Agency Uses:	To Allocate Costs to Establish Rates Within Customer Classes, Agency Uses: SEE KEY BELOW	If Marginal Cost Principle is Used, Which Principle is Used to Reconcile w/Revenue Requirement
ALABAMA PSC	Approaching R	No	E	E	
ALASKA PUC	A	No	E	E	
ARIZONA CC	Varies	UPLAN, 10 years	E	Combination	
ARKANSAS PSC	R	No	E	E	
CALIFORNIA PUC	R	No	L	L	Equal %age Adj;
COLORADO PUC	R	Pending IRP rules	E	E	
CONNECTICUT DPUC	R	Done by Utilities	E	E	
DELAWARE PSC	R	No	E	E	
DC PSC	M	PROMOD/Zinder, 20 yrs	L		Inverse Elastic.
FLORIDA PSC	R	Utility model reviewed	E	E	
GEORGIA PSC	A	No	E	E	
HAWAII PUC	R	No	E	E	
IDAHO PUC	R	No	E	E	
ILLINOIS CC	CC seeks class parity in marginal cost recovery.	NERA methodology - 10 years	S	Other	Equal %age Adjustment
INDIANA URC	R	Yes	E	E	
IOWA UB	R	No	E	E--w/some allowance	
KANSAS SCC	R	No	E	E	
KENTUCKY PSC	R	No	E	E	
LOUISIANA PSC	A	No	E	E	
MAINE PUC	M (Some still use R)	UPLAN (energy), 5 yrs	L (Some use E)	L	Equal %age Adj.
MARYLAND PSC	R	Company-specific, 30 Y	E	Combination.	Customer/Demand
MASSACHUSETTS DPU	R	No	E	S-energy; L-demand	Fully Distrib.
MICHIGAN PSC	R	No	E	E	
MINNESOTA PUC	R	No	E	E,L Combined	
MISSISSIPPI PSC	Approaching R	No	E	E	
MISSOURI PSC	R	Production costing	E	Combination	
MONTANA PSC	M	No	L,S Combined	L,S Combined	Equal %age adj.
NEBRASKA PSC					
NEVADA PSC	M	No	L	L	Equal %age Adj.
NEW HAMPSHIRE PUC	M	No	Moving to L,S	L,S Combined	Equal %age Adj.
NEW JERSEY BPU	Full embedded cost	Differential Rev. Req.	E	E	
NEW MEXICO PUC	R	No	E	E	
NEW YORK PSC	R	No	E,L,S Combined	S	Equal %age Adj.
NORTH CAROLINA UC	R	No	E	E	
NORTH DAKOTA PSC	A,E	No	E	E	
OHIO PUC	R	No	E	E	
OKLAHOMA CC	R	No	E	E	
OREGON PUC	M	No	L	L,S Combined	Equal %age adj.
PENNSYLVANIA PUC	R	No	E	E	
RHODE ISLAND PUC					
SOUTH CAROLINA PSC	R	No	E	E	
SOUTH DAKOTA PUC	R	No	Various	Variety of methods	
TENNESSEE PSC	NONE	No	E	E	
TEXAS PUC					
UTAH PSC	R	No	E	E	
VERMONT PSB					
VIRGINIA SCC	R	No	E	E	
WASHINGTON UTC	M,R	No	E	E	
WEST VIRGINIA PSC	R	No	E	L,S	
WISCONSIN PSC	R	No	E	L,S	
WYOMING PSC	R	No	E	E	
ALBERTA PUB	R	Proxy Plant, 35 yrs	E	L	Equal %age adj.
BRITISH COL. UC	A	No	E	L	Equal %age adj.
NOVA SCOTIA UARB	R	No	E	E	
KEYS	M=Rates approach Marginal/Incremental Costs R=Rate of Return for Each Customer Class Approaches Allowed Rate of Return for Co. A=All Customer Classes Are Given Equal Percentage Increases/Decreases		E=Embedded Cost; L=Long-Run Marginal Cost; S=Short-Run Marginal Cost		

Table 8

Seasonal Peaking Electric Utilities, Demand Cost Allocation Methods Used.

AGENCY	Electric Utilities Display Seasonal Peaking	Which Cost Allocation Method Does Agency Use to Allocate Demand Cost Among Customer Classes: A=COINCIDENT PEAK METHOD B=AVERAGE AND EXCESS DEMAND	If Coincident Peak Method Please Describe
ALABAMA PSC	Summer only	Coincident Peak Demands	12-month average.
ALASKA PUC	Summer/Winter	A	3-day coincident peak
ARIZONA CC	Summer/Winter	No firm policy; reviews results of several alternatives, including peak credit
ARKANSAS PSC	Summer only	No firm policy; has recently used Coincident Peak & Average & Peak methods
CALIFORNIA PUC	Summer only	A	4-month coincident peak
COLORADO PUC	Summer/Winter	B	
CONNECTICUT DPUC	Summer only	A (Distribution); B (Transmission & Generation)	12-month average
DELAWARE PSC	Summer only	A and B; Other methods as needed	Four-month
DC PSC	Summer only	B	
FLORIDA PSC	Summer/Winter	A + 1/13th weighted average demand	12-month average + 1/13th weighted average energy
GEORGIA PSC	Summer only	A	Transmission - 4-month; Production - 12-month average
HAWAII PUC	Summer/Winter	B	
IDAHO PUC	Summer/Winter	A, Weighted Coincident Peak, Other	12-month average
ILLINOIS CC	Summer only	A, B	One-month highest
INDIANA URC	Summer/Winter	A (for IOUs); B (for REMCs). Can vary.	12-month average, but depends on demand characteristics of system
IOWA UB	Summer/Winter	A, B	12-month average
KANSAS SCC	Summer only	A, B	12-month average
KENTUCKY PSC	Summer/Winter	No specified method; case by case	
LOUISIANA PSC	Summer/Winter	A, B	4-month
MAINE PUC	Winter only	A	Combination of one-month (highest) and 4-month
MARYLAND PSC	Summer/Winter	A, B	4-month
MASSACHUSETTS DPU	Summer/Winter	Probability of dispatch	
MICHIGAN PSC	Summer/Winter	A--75% coincident peak; 25% energy	12-month average
MINNESOTA PSC	Summer/Winter	A, B & stratification method	One-month highest
MISSISSIPPI PSC	Summer only	A	12-month average
MISSOURI PSC	Summer/Winter	Time of Use (hourly cost allocation)	
MONTANA PSC	Summer/Winter	A (depends on cost function)	Highest winter and summer
NEBRASKA PSC			
NEVADA PSC	Summer	Contribution to loss of load prob.	
NEW HAMPSHIRE PUC	Winter only	A	One-month (highest)
NEW JERSEY BPU	Summer only	System Planning and HCAM	
NEW MEXICO PUC	Summer/Winter	A, B	12-month average
NEW YORK PSC	Summer/Winter	A, Energy demand % relationship, Probability of negative margin	Peak 20 hours
NORTH CAROLINA UC	Summer/Winter	A, Peak and Average	One-month highest
NORTH DAKOTA PSC	Summer/Winter	A, B	12-month average
OHIO PUC	Summer/Winter	A, B, Non-Coincident Peak	Depends on company characteristics 12-mo CP most common
OKLAHOMA CC	Summer only	A, B	Four-month CP method
OREGON PUC	Summer/Winter	A	One-Month highest
PENNSYLVANIA PUC	Summer/Winter	B, Multiple Coincident Peaks	
RHODE ISLAND PUC	Summer/Winter	A (no firm policy)	12-month average
SOUTH CAROLINA PSC	Summer only	A	One-month highest
SOUTH DAKOTA PSC	Summer/Winter	A, B	12-month average
TENNESSEE PSC	Winter only	A	12-month average
TEXAS PUC			
UTAH PSC	Winter only	A	
VERMONT PSB			
VIRGINIA SCC	Summer/Winter	A, B	12-month average
WASHINGTON UTC	Winter only	A	One-month highest
WEST VIRGINIA PSC	Winter only	A	12-month average
WISCONSIN PSC	Summer only	A	12-month average
WYOMING PSC	Summer/Winter	A, B	12-month average
ALBERTA PUB	Summer/Winter	A	12-month aver., weighted
BRITISH COLUMBIA UC	Winter only	1st-ever rate design for BC Hydro scheduled for 1991	
NOVA SCOTIA UARB	Winter only	B	

Table 9

Choice of Electricity Suppliers, Including Retail Wheeling

AGENCY	Are Large Commercial/Industrial Customers Allowed to Choose Retail Electricity Provider From More Than One Utility?
FERC	
ALABAMA PSC	No
ALASKA PUC	No
ARIZONA CC	No
ARKANSAS PSC	No
CALIFORNIA PUC	4/20/94 PUC proposed plan to restructure electric industry. Beginning in 1996, large electricity consumers can choose retail supplier; by 2002, all consumers can do so.
COLORADO PUC	No
CONNECTICUT DPUC	No
DELAWARE PSC	No
DC PSC	N/A. There is only one retail electricity supplier in the jurisdiction.
FLORIDA PSC	No
GEORGIA PSC	Yes, those with a minimum 900 kW load
HAWAII PUC	N/A. There is only one retail electricity supplier in the jurisdiction.
IDAHO PUC	No
ILLINOIS CC	No
INDIANA URC	In July 1994, PSI Energy announced it would seek approval from the URC to offer wheeling to its largest industrial customers.
IOWA UB	No
KANSAS SCC	No
KENTUCKY PSC	No
LOUISIANA PSC	No
MAINE PUC	Not addressed
MARYLAND PSC	No
MASSACHUSETTS DPU	No
MICHIGAN PSC	Yes, if within 300 feet of more than one utility's distribution lines. 4/11/94, PSC approved a 5-year experimental retail wheeling program for end-use customers in service territories of Consumers Power and Detroit Edison.
MINNESOTA PUC	Not generally
MISSISSIPPI PSC	No
MISSOURI PSC	No
MONTANA PSC	Not usually
NEBRASKA PSC	N/A. Any jurisdiction lies with the Power Review Board, not the PSC.
NEVADA PSC	No
NEW HAMPSHIRE PUC	No
NEW JERSEY BPU	No
NEW MEXICO PUC	No
NEW YORK PSC	No
NORTH CAROLINA UC	No
NORTH DAKOTA PSC	Yes, in cities where more than one electric utility has a franchise.
OHIO PUC	Yes, if the alternate supplier is a municipal utility (no authority over munis).
OKLAHOMA CC	Yes, new load.
OREGON PUC	No
PENNSYLVANIA PUC	No
RHODE ISLAND PUC	No
SOUTH CAROLINA PSC	Not generally
SOUTH DAKOTA PUC	Yes, those with a minimum 2,000 kW load
TENNESSEE PSC	No
TEXAS PUC	
UTAH PSC	Yes, on service territory borders.
VERMONT PSB	
VIRGINIA SCC	No
WASHINGTON UTC	No
WEST VIRGINIA PSC	No
WISCONSIN PSC	No
WYOMING PSC	No
NATL ENERGY BOARD	
ALBERTA PUB	No
BRITISH COLUMBIA UC	No
NEWFOUNDLAND BCPU	
NOVA SCOTIA UARB	No
ONTARIO EB	

Table 10

Special Promotional Tariffs
Offered to Customers of Electric Utilities.

AGENCY	Any Promotional Tariffs?	AGENCY HAS SPECIFICALLY APPROVED OR ALLOWED ELECTRIC UTILITIES TO OFFER TARIFFS DESIGNED TO PROMOTE SALES OF ELECTRICITY FOR SPECIFIC END USES - KEY - R=Residential Customers; C=Commercial Customers; I=Industrial Customers						
		Space Heating	Water Heating	Air Conditioning	All-Electric Service	Thermal Energy Storage	Electric Vehicles	Other Tariffs
ALABAMA PSC	YES	R,C,I				X		
ALASKA PUC	NO					X		
ARIZONA CC	YES		R			X		
ARKANSAS PSC	YES	R,C	R	R	R,C			
CALIFORNIA PUC	NO							
COLORADO PUC	NO							
CONNECTICUT DPUC	NO							
DELAWARE PSC	YES	R,C	R,C 1/	R,C,I		X		
DC PSC	YES	C 1/			R 1/			
FLORIDA PSC	YES							
GEORGIA PSC	NO							
HAWAII PUC	NO							
IDAHO PUC	NO							
ILLINOIS CC	YES	R,C,I	R					
INDIANA URC	YES	R,C,I	R,C,I	C,I	R,C	X		YES
IOWA UB	NO							
KANSAS SCC	YES	R,C,I	R,C,I		R,C	X		
KENTUCKY PSC	YES	R,C	R,C		R,C	X		
LOUISIANA PSC	YES	R	R	R				
MAINE PUC	YES	R	R		I	X		YES
MARYLAND PSC	YES	R,C 1/						
MASSACHUSETTS DPU	YES	R,C,I 1/	R		C 1/			
MICHIGAN PSC	NO							
MINNESOTA PUC	YES	R 1/				X		
MISSISSIPPI PSC	YES	C,I	R,C,I		R,C			
MISSOURI PSC	YES	R,C,I	R,C	R	R,C	X		YES
MONTANA PSC	NO							
NEBRASKA PSC 2/								
NEVADA PSC	NO							
NEW HAMPSHIRE PUC	YES	R,C 1/	R,C 1/		R,C 1/	X		
NEW JERSEY BPU	YES	R	R 1/		R			
NEW MEXICO PUC	YES	R,C	R,C			X		
NEW YORK PSC	NO							
NORTH CAROLINA UC	NO							
NORTH DAKOTA PSC	NO							
OHIO PUC	YES	R,C,I	R,C,I		R,C,I	X		YES
OKLAHOMA CC	YES	R,C		R,C,I				
OREGON PUC	NO							
PENNSYLVANIA PUC	YES	R,C,I	R	R,C	R	X		
RHODE ISLAND PUC	NO							
SOUTH CAROLINA PSC	NO							
SOUTH DAKOTA PUC	YES	R				X		
TENNESSEE PSC	YES					X		
TEXAS PUC								
UTAH PSC	NO							
VERMONT PSB								
VIRGINIA SCC	YES	R,C 1/	R,C 1/			X	3/	
WASHINGTON UTC	NO							
WEST VIRGINIA PSC	NO							
WISCONSIN PSC	no							
WYOMING PSC	YES	R,C	C 1/		R	X		
ALBERTA PUB	NO							
BRITISH COL. UC	NO							
NOVA SCOTIA UARB	NO							

1/   But no new customers are being accepted under the tariff.
2/   The Nebraska PSC has no jurisdiction over energy utilities; authority lies with the Power Review Board.
3/   Proposal pending before the Commission.

Table 11

Special Discount Rates Offered to Customers of Electric Utilities.

AGENCY	Special Discount Rates Have Been Approved for Commercial/Industrial Customers C=Commercial Customers			I=Industrial Customers
	Economic Development Rates	Market Retention Rates	Cogeneration Deferral Rates	Other Discount Rates
ALABAMA PSC				
ALASKA PUC		C, I	C, I	
ARIZONA CC	C, I	C, I		
ARKANSAS PSC	I		I	
CALIFORNIA PUC	I	I	I	I
COLORADO PUC				
CONNECTICUT DPUC	C, I	C, I	C, I	C, I
DELAWARE PSC	I	I		
DC PSC				
FLORIDA PSC		I	I	I
GEORGIA PSC				
HAWAII PUC				
IDAHO PUC				
ILLINOIS CC	C, I	I	I	
INDIANA URC	C, I	I	I	
IOWA UB	C, I	C, I	I	
KANSAS SCC	C, I	C, I	I	
KENTUCKY PSC	I	C, I		
LOUISIANA PSC	C, I			
MAINE PUC		I	I	C, I
MARYLAND PSC	C, I			
MASSACHUSETTS DPU	C, I			C, I
MICHIGAN PSC	C, I			
MINNESOTA PUC	I	I	I	
MISSISSIPPI PSC	I	I		
MISSOURI PSC	C, I	I		C, I
MONTANA PSC		I		YES
NEBRASKA PSC				
NEVADA PSC				
NEW HAMPSHIRE PUC	I			
NEW JERSEY BPU	C, I			
NEW MEXICO PUC	C, I	I	C, I	
NEW YORK PSC	C, I	C, I	I	
NORTH CAROLINA UC		I		
NORTH DAKOTA PSC	I			
OHIO PUC	C, I	C, I	C, I	C, I
OKLAHOMA CC	C, I	C, I	I	
OREGON PUC	I	I	I	
PENNSYLVANIA PUC	C, I			
RHODE ISLAND PUC	I			
SOUTH CAROLINA PSC				
SOUTH DAKOTA PUC	C, I	C, I		
TENNESSEE PSC				
TEXAS PUC				
UTAH PSC	I			
VERMONT PSB				
VIRGINIA SCC				
WASHINGTON UTC			I	
WEST VIRGINIA PSC				
WISCONSIN PSC				
WYOMING PSC	C, I	C, I		
GUAM PUC				
PUERTO RICO PSC				
VIRGIN ISLANDS PSC				
NATL ENERGY BOARD				
ALBERTA PUB				
BRITISH COLUMBIA UC	I			
NEWFOUNDLAND BCPU				
NOVA SCOTIA UARB				
ONTARIO EB				

Table 12

Interruptible Sales and Special Contract Service by Electric Utilities.

AGENCY	Are Any Customers Served Under Interruptible Rates? Commercial Customers	Industrial Customers	Do Interruptible Service Tariffs or Contracts Contain a Maximum Number of Interruptions or Hours of Interruption? If so, Please Specify	Were Any Interruptible Customers Interrupted During the Most Recent Power Year?	Are any Commercial or Industrial Customers Served Under Special Contracts Where Exempted From General Rate Increases Are: Demand Charges	Energy Charges	Has Agency Studied Impact of Specific Rate Design on Consumption in the Past 5 Yrs
ALABAMA PSC	NO	YES	YES-600 HOURS/YEAR	NO	NO	NO	NO
ALASKA PUC	NO	YES	ONE TARIFF DOES-12 HOURS	YES	NO	NO	NO
ARIZONA CC	YES	YES	YES-SOME DO	YES	NO	NO	YES-TOU
ARKANSAS PSC	NO	YES	YES-INDIVIDUAL CONTRACTS	YES	YES	NO	NO
CALIFORNIA PUC	YES	YES	YES	NO	YES	YES	NO
COLORADO PUC	YES	YES	NO	YES	NO	NO	NO
CONNECTICUT DPUC	YES	YES	YES-VARIES BY COMPANY	YES	NO	NO	NO
DELAWARE PSC	YES	YES	YES-445 HRS/YEAR	YES	NO	NO	NO
DC PSC	YES	NO	YES	YES	NO	NO	YES
FLORIDA PSC	YES	YES	YES-VARIES BY COMPANY	YES	NO	NO	NO
GEORGIA PSC	YES	YES	YES-240 HRS/YEAR 1/	NO	NO	NO	NO
HAWAII PUC	YES	YES	YES-VARIES	NO	NO	NO	NO
IDAHO PUC	NO	YES	YES-VARIES BY CONTRACT	YES	NO	NO	NO
ILLINOIS CC	YES	YES	YES-VARIES BY UTILITY	YES	YES	YES	NO
INDIANA URC	NO	YES	YES-VARIES BY COMPANY	YES	NO	NO	NO
IOWA UB	YES	YES	YES	YES	YES	YES	NO
KANSAS SCC	YES	YES	YES-VARIES BY COMPANY 2/	YES	YES	YES	NO
KENTUCKY PSC	NO	YES	YES-VARIES BY COMPANY	YES	NO	NO	NO
LOUISIANA PSC	NO	YES	NO	YES	NO	NO	NO
MAINE PUC	YES	YES	YES-VARIES, MAX 200HR/YR	UNKNOWN	NO	NO	NO
MARYLAND PSC	NO	YES		YES	NO	NO	NO
MASSACHUSETTS DPU	YES	YES	YES-VARIES BY COMPANY	N/A	NO	NO	NO
MICHIGAN PSC	YES	YES	YES-VARIES BY UTIL/RATE	YES	NO	NO	NO
MINNESOTA PUC	YES	YES	NSP-150 HRS/MAX OF 80	UNKNOWN	NO	NO	NO
MISSISSIPPI PSC	NO	YES	YES	NO	NO	NO	NO
MISSOURI PSC	YES	YES	YES-INDIVIDUAL CONTRACTS	YES	NO	NO	NO
MONTANA PSC	YES	YES	YES-800 HOURS/YEAR	YES	YES	YES	NO
NEBRASKA PSC							
NEVADA PSC	YES	YES	YES	YES	NO	NO	NO
NEW HAMPSHIRE PUC	YES	YES	YES-45 HOURS/MONTH	YES	NO	NO	NO
NEW JERSEY BPU	YES	YES	YES-15 TO 25 EVENTS/YEAR	YES	NO	NO	NO
NEW MEXICO PUC	YES	YES	YES-VARIES BY CONTRACT	YES	YES	YES	NO
NEW YORK PSC	YES	YES	YES-VARIES, 45-200 HRS	YES	YES	YES	NO
NORTH CAROLINA UC	YES	YES	YES-4 TO 8 HRS/24 HOURS	YES	NO	NO	NO
NORTH DAKOTA PSC	YES	YES	NO	YES	NO	NO	NO
OHIO PUC	YES	YES	YES-VARIES BY COMPANY	YES	YES	YES	NO
OKLAHOMA CC	YES	YES	YES-VARIES BY COMPANY	NO	YES	NO	NO
OREGON PUC	NO	YES	YES-INDIVIDUAL CONTRACTS	YES	YES	YES	NO
PENNSYLVANIA PUC	YES	YES	YES-20 TO 25, 200 HRS	YES	NO	NO	NO
RHODE ISLAND PUC	YES	YES	YES-VARIES BY CONTRACT	UNKNOWN	NO	NO	NO
SOUTH CAROLINA PSC	YES	YES	YES-VARIES BY COMPANY	YES	NO	NO	NO
SOUTH DAKOTA PUC	YES	YES	YES-VARIES BY COMPANY	NO	NO	NO	NO
TENNESSEE PSC	NO	NO			NO	NO	NO
TEXAS PUC							
UTAH PSC	NO	YES	YES	YES	YES	YES	NO
VERMONT PSB							
VIRGINIA SCC	YES	YES	YES-VARIES BY SEASON/CO.	YES	NO	NO	NO
WASHINGTON UTC	YES	YES	NO	NO	YES	YES	NO
WEST VIRGINIA PSC	NO	YES	YES-VARIES BY COMPANY	NO	NO	NO	NO
WISCONSIN PSC	YES	YES	YES-VARIES BY COMPANY	YES	NO	NO	NO
WYOMING PSC	YES	YES	YES	NO	YES	YES	NO
ALBERTA PUB	NO	YES	YES-800 HRS/YEAR	YES	NO	NO	NO
BRITISH COL. UC	NO	NO			NO	NO	NO
NOVA SCOTIA UARB	NO	YES	NO		NO	NO	NO

1/ The Interruptible Service (IS) schedule, approved 5/91, calls for interruptions to last no more than 10 hours/day and no more than 240 hours/year. The Supplemental Energy Rider (curtailable) has no maximum.

2/ KCPL tariff limits interruptions to 25 occurrences per year, 8 hours per day and 120 hours per year. KPL tariff limits interruptions to 150 hours per month and 400 hours per year.

Table 13

Energy Conservation Incentive Programs for Customers of Electric Utilities.

AGENCY	ENERGY CONSERVATION CUSTOMER INCENTIVE PROGRAMS CURRENTLY IN EXISTENCE FOR: Residential Electricity Customers SEE KEY BELOW				Commercial and Industrial Customers SEE KEY BELOW			
	Rebates	Loans	Shared savings	Grants or giveaways	Rebates	Loans	Shared savings	Grants or giveaways
ALABAMA PSC	S,A,W,I 6/	S,A,W,I						H,L
ALASKA PUC		A,W;L 1/	W	1/		H,W,L,M,X1/		W,L 1/
ARIZONA CC	A,W,I,L 7/				L,M 2/			
ARKANSAS PSC	A	S,A						
CALIFORNIA PUC	S,A,W,I,L	X		I,L	H,W,L,C,P,M			
COLORADO PUC	W,L,X,Z				H,W,L,C,P,M			
CONNECTICUT DPUC	A	S,W,I,L,Z		S,W,I,L,Z	H,W,L,C,P,M,Z,E			
DELAWARE PSC					H,L			
DC PSC	S,A,W,I,L,X,Z,E			L	H,W,L,C,X,E			
FLORIDA PSC	S,A,W,I	S,A,W,I			H,W,L,M,Z			
GEORGIA PSC	A,W,I,L,X,Z,E 7/	S,A,W,I		W,L	L,E	L		
HAWAII PUC	L 1/	W 1/			L 1/			E 1/
IDAHO PUC		I,Z		S,W,I,Z	H,L,P,M			
ILLINOIS CC	S,A,W,L 1/				L,M 1/			
INDIANA URC	S,A,W,I,L 2/				H,L,P,M 2/			
IOWA UB	S,A,W,I,L	S,A,W,I		W,I,L	H,W,L,C,P,M			
KANSAS SCC	S,A,W,X	S,A,W,X						
KENTUCKY PSC 8/								
LOUISIANA PSC	A,W							
MAINE PUC		S,W,I,L		W,I,L	H,W,L,C,P,M	H,W,L,C,P,M	H,W,L,C,P,M	W
MARYLAND PSC	S,A,W,I,L,X,Z,E	S,A,W,X		L,Z,E	H,W,L,C,P,M,E	H,L,P,M		E
MASSACHUSETTS DPU	S,WOI,L,X 7/			W,L,E	H,W,L,C,P,M			E
MICHIGAN PSC	A,W,L,X,P	I		W,I,L,E,Z 3/	L,M			E
MINNESOTA PUC	A,W,L	A,L		L	H,L,P,M	H,W,L,P,M		H,L,P,M
MISSISSIPPI PSC		S,A,W,I			H			
MISSOURI PSC 5/								
MONTANA PSC		S,A,W,I		L,Z 3/	L,P,M			H,W,L
NEBRASKA PSC								
NEVADA PSC	A,L	S,I		S,A,W,I	H,L,P,M			
NEW HAMPSHIRE PUC	S,W,I,L	S,I,Z 3/		W,I,L	H,W,L,C,P,M	H,W,L,C,P,M		L
NEW JERSEY BPU	S,A,W,I,L	S,A,W,I		S,A,W,I	H,W,L,P,M			
NEW MEXICO PUC 5/								
NEW YORK PSC	S,A,W,L,X,E	S,W,I,Z		S,W,I,L	H,W,L,I,M,X		L,P,M,E	
NORTH CAROLINA UC		S,A,W,I						
NORTH DAKOTA PSC	S,A,W,X	A,I		E	H,L,C,P,M	H,L,C,P,M		E
OHIO PUC	A,W,I,L,X,Z			W,I,L	H,W,L,M	L,M		
OKLAHOMA CC	S,A,I			S,A,W,I,L	H			
OREGON PUC	W,L,X,Z	Z		W,E	H,W,L,P,M	H,W,L,P,M	H,W,L,P,M	
PENNSYLVANIA PUC	S,A,W,I,L							
RHODE ISLAND PUC	I,L		S,A,W,I,L	S,W,I,L	H,W,L,P,M		H,W,L,P,M	L,M
SOUTH CAROLINA PSC	S,A,X	S,A,I		I,L 1/ 4/	H,P,M			
SOUTH DAKOTA PUC	A,W,X	S,W,I		L	H,W,L,M	H,W,L,M		L
TENNESSEE PSC 5/								
TEXAS PUC								
UTAH PSC				I,X,Z 3/ 4/	H,L,P,M,X,Z			E
VERMONT PSB								
VIRGINIA SCC		S,A,I,X,Z	W					
WASHINGTON UTC		S,A,W,I,L		S,A,W,I,L	H,W,L,C,P,M			H,W,L,C,P,M
WEST VIRGINIA PSC	L			W				L,E
WISCONSIN PSC	S,A,W,I,L,X,Z	W,I,L		I,L,Z 3/	H,W,L,C,P,M,X,E	H,W,L,C,P,M	H,W,L,C,P,M	
WYOMING PSC 5/								
ALBERTA PUB	W,L				M			
BRITISH COL. UC		I		W 4/	W,L,P,M,X	P		
NOVA SCOTIA UARB					M			

KEY - RESIDENTIAL CUSTOMERS: S=Space Heating; A=Air Conditioning; W=Water Heating; I=Insulation; L=Lighting; X=Energy-Efficient Appliances; Z=Weatherization; E=Energy Audits; P=Appliance Pickup/Turn-In

KEY - COMMERCIAL AND INDUSTRIAL CUSTOMERS: H=HVAC; W=Water Heating; L=Lighting; C=Cooking; P=Industrial Process; M=Motors; X=Energy-Efficient Appliances; Z=Weatherization; E=Energy Audits

1/	Pilot program.	5/	No incentive programs.
2/	Under investigation.	6/	Offered mostly through dealers, contractors.
3/	For low-income customers.	7/	Replacement windows.
4/	Water heater insulation.	8/	Incentives for LG&E only.

Table 14

Demand-Side Management Programs for Customers of Electric Utilities.

AGENCY	DEMAND-SIDE MANAGEMENT PROGRAMS CURRENTLY IN EXISTENCE FOR -					
	Residential Electric Customer SEE KEYS BELOW			Commercial and Industrial Customers SEE KEYS BELOW		
	Load Management	Fuel Switching	Other Programs	Load Management	Fuel Switching	Other Programs
ALABAMA PSC				T		
ALASKA PUC	W,O	H		W	H	
ARIZONA CC	W,O		Thermal storage-heating			Thermal storage-cooling
ARKANSAS PSC	W,A,U			W,A,R,T,U		
CALIFORNIA PUC	A	H,A,W,C	TES	A,E,T	A,C,P	Off-peak cooling
COLORADO PUC		A,W,D	Rebates to switch to gas		W,A,P	Rebates to switch to gas
CONNECTICUT DPUC	W,A			W,A,T		Cool storage
DELAWARE PSC	W,A,X			A,L,T		Cool storage
DC PSC	W,A,X,U		Off-peak rates, 2nd fridge removal, eff. heat pumps, eff. A/C, shop doctor	W,A,L, E,T,X,N		Lighting rebates, thermal storage, hi-efficiency A/C, shop doctor
FLORIDA PSC	W,A	C	Swimming pool pump DLC	W,A,T		
GEORGIA PSC	A,X,N		Energy-efficient mortgages Pilot program	T,X,U		
HAWAII PUC				T,U		Tariffed rates
IDAHO PUC	U	H,W	Builder incentives-new construction	T		Pilot programs to help offset cost of energy-efficiency improvements
ILLINOIS CC	A		Pilot programs	T		Group load control cooperative
INDIANA URC	W,A,X, U,N		Promote geothermal	T,X,U,N		
IOWA UB	W,A,O,U		Tree planting	W,A,T, U,X		Low-cost technical assistance, tree planting, cool storage
KANSAS SCC	W,A			A,R,T		
KENTUCKY PSC	W			T,U		
LOUISIANA PSC	A	W		W,T		
MAINE PUC	W,O,U					
MARYLAND PSC	W,A,X, U,N		2nd refrigerator, geothermal	A,T,X, U,N	A	curtailable rates, cool storage shop doctor, custom rebates
MASSACHUSETTS DPU	W,A,N	N	Public housing, neighborhood blitz, pool pump DLC	A,T,N	N	Cool storage, customer-owned generation assistance
MICHIGAN PSC	W,A,O,U		Conservation rates, builder incentives, new construction	T,U		Cool storage
MINNESOTA PUC	W,A,O,U		Residential demand control	T,X,U,R		Cool storage
MISSISSIPPI PSC	A,O	W	Promote weatherization	R,T		
MISSOURI PSC	A,X,U,N		Temp-activated A/C cycling	T,X,U,N		
MONTANA PSC	W,X,N		Space heating	W,T,X,N		Space heating
NEBRASKA PSC						
NEVADA PSC	A		Swimming pool pump trippers	T		Low-pressure irrigation
NEW HAMPSHIRE PUC	W,A,O			W,T		Design assistance
NEW JERSEY BPU	W,A,O			A,T	A	
NEW MEXICO PUC	O			T		
NEW YORK PSC	W,A,O, X,N			W,A,T, L,X,N	W,A	generation assistance
NORTH CAROLINA UC	W,A,X, U,N		TOU Comparative billing, conservation rates, low-income weatherization	W,A,T, X,U		TOU Comparative billing, Thermal storage
NORTH DAKOTA PSC	W,A,O, X,U		Residential demand controller	W,A,T		Encourage standby generators

KEY - LOAD MANAGEMENT:
W=Water Heating Direct Load Control (DLC);
A=Air Conditioning DLC;
O=Off-Peak Heat;
X=Energy Audits;
U=Time of Use Rates;
N=Energy-Efficient New Construction/Design

KEY - FUEL SWITCHING (ELECTRIC TO GAS):
H=Heating; A=Air Conditioning;
W=Water Heating; C=Cooking;
D=Clothes Drying

KEY - LOAD MANAGEMENT:
W=Water Heating DLC; A=Air Conditioning DLC;
R=Irrigation DLC; L=Lighting DLC;
E=EMS DLC; T=Interruptible Rates
X=Energy Audits; U=Time of Use Rates;
N=Energy-Efficient New Construction/Design

KEY - FUEL SWITCHING (ELECTRIC TO GAS):
W=Water Heating; A=Air Conditioning;
C=Cooking; P=Industrial Process;
G=Gas Engines

DEMAND-SIDE MANAGEMENT PROGRAMS CURRENTLY IN EXISTENCE FOR -

AGENCY	Residential Electricity Customers SEE KEYS BELOW			Commercial and Industrial Customers SEE KEYS BELOW		
	Load Manage-ment	Fuel Switch-ing	Other Programs	Load Manage-ment	Fuel Switch-ing	Other Programs
OHIO PUC	W,A,O			T		Cool storage
OKLAHOMA CC	A,X.U,N			T,X,U,N		
OREGON PUC	W,A,U			T,U		Buy back savings from individual customers
PENNSYLVANIA PUC	A,O			A,T		
RHODE ISLAND PUC	W,N	N	Promote energy efficient home construction, appliance rating	W,N	N	Design 2000 promotes design of energy-efficient buildings
SOUTH CAROLINA PSC	W,A,U		Off-peak water heating	W,A,T		
SOUTH DAKOTA PUC	W,A,O,X		Dual fuel heating, blower door testing	W,T,X,U		Dual fuel heating, blower door testing
TENNESSEE PSC	U		TOD rates	U		TOD rates
TEXAS PUC						
UTAH PSC	U			T,U,N		
VERMONT PSB						
VIRGINIA SCC	W,A,X,U		Promote energy efficient homes	T		
WASHINGTON UTC			WAP just starting	T		WAP just starting
WEST VIRGINIA PSC						
WISCONSIN PSC	W,A,O,U,N	H,W,C,D	Appliance turn-in	W,A,R,T	W,A,C,P,G	Statewide motor standards
WYOMING PSC	W,A		Service extenders	W,A,R		
ALBERTA PUB			Promote energy literacy	T,X,U		
BRITISH COL. UC		W	Numerous programs		W	Numerous programs
NOVA SCOTIA UARB						

KEY - LOAD MANAGEMENT:
W=Water Heating Direct Load Control (DLC);
A=Air Conditioning DLC;
O=Off-Peak Heat;
X=Energy Audits;
U=Time of Use Rates;
N=Energy-Efficient New Construction/Design

KEY - LOAD MANAGEMENT:
W=Water Heating DLC; A=Air Conditioning DLC;
R=Irrigation DLC; L=Lighting DLC;
E=EMS DLC; T=Interruptible Rates
X=Energy Audits; U=Time of Use Rates;
N=Energy-Efficient New Construction/Design

KEY - FUEL SWITCHING (ELECTRIC TO GAS):
H=Heating; A=Air Conditioning;
W=Water Heating; C=Cooking;
D=Clothes Drying

KEY - FUEL SWITCHING (ELECTRIC TO GAS):
W=Water Heating; A=Air Conditioning;
C=Cooking; P=Industrial Process;
G=Gas Engines

Table 15

Cost Recovery and Financial Incentive Mechanisms for Demand-Side Activities of Electric Utilities.

Columns under **COST RECOVERY METHODS CURRENTLY IN USE**: (1) Recovered as Operation & Maintenance Expenses; (2) Allowed to Earn Current Return in Rate Base, Capital; (3) True-Up, Balancing Acct, Escrow Acctg to Insure Accurate Cost Recov; (4) Sales Adjustment to Insure Full Recovery of Lost Revenues.

Columns under **FINANCIAL INCENTIVES CURRENTLY IN EFFECT**: (5) No Incentives; Incentives Are Based On: (6) Activity With Customers, (7) Engineering Calculation of Energy Saving, (8) Demand and/or Energy Saving, (9) Net System Benefits 7/; Incentives are Calculated: (10) Net of Free-Riders, (11) On Actual Performance Measure; (12) Designed To Allow Recovery of Lost Revenue.

AGENCY	Op&Maint Exp	Rate Base, Capital	True-Up/Balancing	Sales Adj/Lost Rev	No Incentives	Activity w/ Customers	Engineering Calc	Demand/Energy Saving	Net System Benefits 7/	Net of Free-Riders	On Actual Perf	Design Recov Lost Rev
ALABAMA PSC	X				X							
ALASKA PUC	X	X										
ARIZONA CC	X		1/	1/	X	X 13/						
ARKANSAS PSC	X	X			X							
CALIFORNIA PUC	X		X	X		X	X	X	X	X	20/	
COLORADO PUC	X 2/	X 2/					X 2/	X 2/	X			
CONNECTICUT DPUC	X	X	X			X	X	X			X	X
DELAWARE PSC	X				X							
DC PSC	X	X	X					X		X	X	X
FLORIDA PSC	X	X 3/	X		X 4/							
GEORGIA PSC		X				X			X 6/	X	X	
HAWAII PUC	X 14/		X 15/		X							
IDAHO PUC		X	X									X 18/
ILLINOIS CC	X 2/		X		X 11/							
INDIANA URC	X 1/			X	X 4/							
IOWA UB		X	X			X	X	X		X	X	
KANSAS SCC	X	X			5/							
KENTUCKY PSC	X	X	X 19/	X 19/					X 19/			
LOUISIANA PSC	X				X							
MAINE PUC	X	X	X	X				X	X	X	X	X 10/
MARYLAND PSC	X	X 16/	X	X		X	X	X	X		X 6/	X
MASSACHUSETTS DPU	X	X	X	X			X	X	X	X	X	X 17/
MICHIGAN PSC	X	X	X			X	X	X			X	X
MINNESOTA PUC	X	X	X	X		X	X	X			X	X
MISSISSIPPI PSC	X	X			X							
MISSOURI PSC					X							
MONTANA PSC	X	X			9/							1/
NEBRASKA PSC												
NEVADA PSC	X	X			X							
NEW HAMPSHIRE PUC	X 1/		X	X 11/		X	X	X	X	X		
NEW JERSEY BPU			X		X 4/	X						
NEW MEXICO PUC	X	X			X							
NEW YORK PSC	X	X	X	X			X	X	X	X	X	
NORTH CAROLINA UC	X	X	X									X 4/
NORTH DAKOTA PSC	X	X			X							
OHIO PUC	X	X	X			X	X	X	X			X
OKLAHOMA CC	X	X	X		X							
OREGON PUC	X	X	X	X			X	X	1/	X		X
PENNSYLVANIA PUC	X	X				X					X	
RHODE ISLAND PUC								X	X	X	X	6/
SOUTH CAROLINA PSC	X	X			X							
SOUTH DAKOTA PUC	X	X	X		X							
TENNESSEE PSC		X			X							
TEXAS PUC												
UTAH PSC		X		11/	X 4/							
VERMONT PSB												
VIRGINIA SCC	X	X			X							
WASHINGTON UTC	X	X		X	X	X 1/	X 1/	X 1/				X 8/
WEST VIRGINIA PSC												
WISCONSIN PSC	X	X	X		X							
WYOMING PSC	X	X			X							
ALBERTA PUB	X				X							
BRITISH COL. UC		X			X							
NOVA SCOTIA UARB	X											

Table 16

Cost Allocation and Economic Evaluation of Demand-Side Activities of Electric Utilities.

AGENCY	COST ALLOCATION METHOD USED TO DISTRIBUTE THE COSTS OF ELECTRIC UTILITY DEMAND-SIDE ACTIVITIES TO VARIOUS CUSTOMER CLASSES (See Key Below)	ECONOMIC TESTS USED TO EVALUATE DEMAND-SIDE MANAGEMENT ACTIVITIES OF ELECTRIC UTILITIES (See Key Below)	
		Primary Economic Test(s)	Other Economic Test(s)
ALABAMA PSC		6	4, 5
ALASKA PUC			
ARIZONA CC		3 (considers future costs, not sunk costs)	
ARKANSAS PSC	A, C, D	1, 4, 5, 6	
CALIFORNIA PUC	A	1,4(TRC excludes externalities)	3, 5, 6
COLORADO PUC	D, E	1, 3, 4, 5, 6	
CONNECTICUT DPUC	A, D, E (One company allocates as a peaking plant would be-demand)	4	
DELAWARE PSC	Indirectly assigned via cost of service study in rate case.	Pending before Commission	
DC PSC	Treated like other costs.	1	
FLORIDA PSC	D, E	6	6
GEORGIA PSC	A; F proposed for pilot program 1991	3, 4	1, 5, 6
HAWAII PUC	E proposed for pilot programs	1	4, 5, 6
IDAHO PUC	A, D, E	None specified; use 1, 5	4
ILLINOIS CC	D, then E	1, 3, 4	5, 6
INDIANA URC	A, D, E	None ruled out: use 1, 4	
IOWA UB	Based on benefits/costs or rate design	3	4, 5, 6
KANSAS SCC	A, B	1, 3, 5 (pending)	
KENTUCKY PSC	A	1, 6	
LOUISIANA PSC			
MAINE PUC	F	1	3, DSM programs with rate impact >1% must meet higher standards
MARYLAND PSC	A, E	1, 3, 4, 5, 6	2 - initial screening
MASSACHUSETTS DPU	A, F	3	
MICHIGAN PSC	A, E, Rate Base	1	3, 4, 5, 6
MINNESOTA PUC	F	1, 3	
MISSISSIPPI PSC	B (on a limited basis)	6	1
MISSOURI PSC		1	4
MONTANA PSC	Treated like other costs	Analysis based on avoided costs	3
NEBRASKA PSC			
NEVADA PSC	NONE	1	3, 4, 5, 6
NEW HAMPSHIRE PUC	A, E	1	4, 6
NEW JERSEY BPU	D, E	1, 3, 5, 6 (No formal IRP/LCUP Process)	
NEW MEXICO PUC	A, B, C, D, E		
NEW YORK PSC	A, E	3, 4, 6	
NORTH CAROLINA UC	A, B	4, 5, 6	4, 5, 6
NORTH DAKOTA PSC	A	4	
OHIO PUC	Still under consideration; A likely	1, 6 for relative equity considerations	
OKLAHOMA CC	A	4	
OREGON PUC	D, E	1, 3	
PENNSYLVANIA PUC	Still under consideration	1, 4, 5, 6	
RHODE ISLAND PUC	F	1	
SOUTH CAROLINA PSC	A	1, 6	2, 3, 4, 5
SOUTH DAKOTA PUC	A, D, E	4, 5, Positive Net Benefit	
TENNESSEE PSC	A	NONE	
TEXAS PUC			
UTAH PSC	Still under consideration	None specified, use 1	3, 4, 5, 6
VERMONT PSB			
VIRGINIA SCC	D, E	1, 6	4, 5
WASHINGTON UTC	E, F	4	1, 6
WEST VIRGINIA PSC	A	1	
WISCONSIN PSC	A	2	1, 3, 4, 5
WYOMING PSC	A		
ALBERTA PUB	A	6	
BRITISH COL. UC	E	1, 3	4, 6
NOVA SCOTIA UARB		1, 4, 5	

KEY - COST ALLOCATION	KEY - ECONOMIC EVALUATION METHODS	
A=Direct Assignment/Class;	1=Total Resource Costs;	2=Total Technical Costs;
B=Direct Assignment/Participants;	3=Total Societal Costs;	4=Utility Perspective;
C=Customer Count;	5=Participants Test;	6=Non-Participants Test
D=Demand;		
E=Energy;		
F=Demand/Energy Saved	(See Introduction for Definitions)	

Table 17

State Policies Regarding Integrated Resource Planning for Electric Utilities.

AGENCY	IRP Is Required	Citation and Description of State Policies Governing IRP	Some Policies A Direct Result of the EPAct	IRP Has Been Required Since	Utilities Have Changed Resource Acquisition Decisions as Result of IRP	How Often Utilities File IRPs
ALABAMA PSC						
ALASKA PUC						
ARIZONA CC	X	Order 56313, Docket No. U-0000-88-093		1989	X	3 years
ARKANSAS PSC	X	92-160-U, 92-162-U, 92-165-U, 92-229-U		1992		3 years
CALIFORNIA PUC	1/				X	
COLORADO PUC	X	Dec. C92-1646, Dkt. 91R-642E		1993		3 years
CONNECTICUT DPUC	X	Util. submit plans & forecasts to DPUC		1989	Unknown	2 years
DELAWARE PSC	X	Dkt. 29, Order 3446 has IRP guidelines		9/1992	X	2 years
DC PSC	X	Order 9417, Formal Case 834, Phase II		1988	X	2 years
FLORIDA PSC	X	Order 24989 defines contents of IRPs		1981 2/	X	Annually
GEORGIA PSC	X	O.C.G.A. §46-3A, PSC Rule 515-3-4		1992	X	3 yrs 3/
HAWAII PUC	X	Order 11523, 3/12/92; Order 11630,5/22/92		1992	X	3 years
IDAHO PUC	X	Order 22299, Case U-1500-165, 1/89	4/	1989		2 years
ILLINOIS CC	X	Docket 87-0261, 1/88 and 12/88		1985	X	3 years
INDIANA URC	X	Certificate of need law req. IRP 5/				2 years
IOWA UB	X	Iowa Code Ch. 476A, 476.6(19) & (20); IA Admin. Code 199-35		1990	X	2 years
KANSAS SCC	X	Dkt. 180,056-U; proposed rules currently before the Commission				3 years
KENTUCKY PSC	X	807 KAR 5:058		1991	X	2 years
LOUISIANA PSC						
MAINE PUC	X	PUC Rules Ch. 36,380; Dkts. 88-174, 88-175, 88-176; MRS Ch. 35-A §3191		1985	X	Annually
MARYLAND PSC	X	PSC Law §28(g) and 59A		1986	X	Annually
MASSACHUSETTS DPU	X	DPU 86-36-C, 86-36-D, 86-36-F, 86-36-G; Dkts. 89-239, 91-131, 93-138, 93-157-A. MA Stats §1, Ch. 164 §69I		1988	X	2 years
MICHIGAN PSC	X	U-10292, U-9172		1990	X	2 years
MINNESOTA PUC	X	Dkt. E-999/R-89-201, MN Laws 1993 Ch. 356		9/90	X	2 years
MISSISSIPPI PSC						
MISSOURI PSC	X	Dkt. EX-92-299, Dkt. QX-92-300	6/	1993	Unknown	3 years
MONTANA PSC	X	Admin. Rules 38.5.2001-2012		1993	Unknown	2 years
NEBRASKA PSC						
NEVADA PSC	X	SB 161, 1983, Dkt. 89-752		1984	X	3 years
NEW HAMPSHIRE PUC	X	Order 19052, 19141; RSA 378:37-39[supp.]		1989	X	2 years
NEW JERSEY BPU						
NEW MEXICO PUC		NMPUC Case No. 2383; proposed rules currently before the Commission				
NEW YORK PSC	X	Opinion 88-20, Case 29409		1989	X	7/
NORTH CAROLINA UC	X	Dkt.E-100,Sub58&64;N.C.Gen.Stat.§62-2(3a)		1989	X	3 years
NORTH DAKOTA PSC	X	Case 10,799 8/		1987		2 years
OHIO PUC	X	Order 88-816-EL-OR		1990	X	2 years
OKLAHOMA CC						
OREGON PUC	X	Order 89-507, Dkt.UM 180, Order 93-695		1989	X	2 years
PENNSYLVANIA PUC	X	HB1639,Act 114,1986; Dkt.L-860026,I-90005		1988		Annually
RHODE ISLAND PUC	X	Dkt. 2059, 3/11/93		1988	X	2 years
SOUTH CAROLINA PSC	X	Order 91-885, 10/21/91		1991		3 years
SOUTH DAKOTA PUC						
TENNESSEE PSC	9/					
TEXAS PUC	10/	Tex.Rev.Civ.Stat.Ann.art. 1446c		1984	X	2 years
UTAH PSC	X	Dkt. 90-2035-01, 6/18/92		1992	X	2 years
VERMONT PSB	X	Dkt. 5270, 4/16/90; 30 VSA § 218c(1991)		9/90	X	3 years
VIRGINIA SCC	11/			1987		2 years
WASHINGTON UTC	X	WAC 480-100-251, Dkt. UE-900385, 5/5/90		1988	X	2 years
WEST VIRGINIA PSC						
WISCONSIN PSC	X	Dkt.05-EP-4, 8/86, Dkt.05-EP-6, 9/15/92		1986	X	2 years
WYOMING PSC	X 12/	Dkt. 90000-XO-93-68 (GO 68)	X	13/	X	Varies

Footnotes—Table 17

State Policies Regarding Integrated Resource Planning for Electric Utilities.

1/   All future resource planning exercises have been suspended. The Commission believes that resource planning will change in response to industry restructuring and increasing competition. One part of this change will likely be a considerably smaller role for the Commission in the planning process.

2/   Depends on how IRP is defined; hearings will be held on whether to adopt the definition contained in EPAct.

3/   Also when applying for a Certificate of Public Convenience and Necessity.

4/   Order 25260, Case GNR-E-93-3 considered the IRP requirements of the EPAct. It did not change existing IRP regulations.

5/   Three utilities have been ordered to file IRPs on a regular basis. Generic IRP rulemaking is in progress.

6/   Case EO-93-222 determined that the adopted IRP rules comply with Sec. 111(a) of the EPAct.

7/   IRP filing required in 1992. New filing date has not yet been set.

8/   One utility is required to submit an IRP. There are no formal IRP rules or legislation.

9/   The Tennessee Commission regulates only one small non-generating electric utility.

10/   State law permits, but does not require, comprehensive IRP regulation. These responses are based on the requirements for biennial forecast and resource plans, energy efficiency plans, and standard avoided cost filings (viewed by some in Texas as the functional equivalent of IRP).

11/   Title 56, Code of Virginia requires electric utilities to file plans. It does not specifically mention IRP.

12/   Some utilities are required to file an IRP; it is decided on a case-by-case basis.

13/   IRP has been required for some utilities for three years. The case-by-case policy has been in effect for two months.

Table 18

Required Elements of Electric Utilities Integrated Resource Plans.

AGENCY	State-ment of Plan's Objec-tives	Length of Energy & Demand Forecasts	Evaluation of Resources Existing Capacity	Poten-tial Supply-Side	Poten-tial Demand-Side	Alter-native IRP Plans	The Plan's Rela-tive Sensi-tivity	Impact on Demand	Costs and Bene-fits	Short-Term Action Plan's Length	Exter-nal-ities	Other
ALABAMA PSC												
ALASKA PUC												
ARIZONA CC		10-20 yrs	X	X	X		X	X	X	3 yrs	X	
ARKANSAS PSC	X	20 yrs	X	X	X		X	X	X	3 yrs	X	
CALIFORNIA PUC												
COLORADO PUC	X	20 yrs	X	X	X	X	X	X	X	3 yrs		
CONNECTICUT DPUC	X	20 yrs	X	X	X		X	X	X			
DELAWARE PSC		15 yrs	X	X	X		X	X	X	4 yrs	X	
DC PSC	X	15 yrs	X	X	X	X	X	X	X	4 yrs	X	1/
FLORIDA PSC	X	10 yrs	X	X	X		X	X				
GEORGIA PSC	X	20 yrs	X	X	X	X	X	X	X	4 yrs	X	2/
HAWAII PUC	X	20 yrs	X	X	X	X	X	X		5 yrs	X	
IDAHO PUC		20 yrs		X	X	X	X			x		
ILLINOIS CC	X	20 yrs	X	X	X	X	X		X	3 yrs	X	
INDIANA URC		20 yrs	X	X	X		X	X	X	2 yrs		
IOWA UB		20 yrs	X	X	X		X	X	X	5 yrs	X	
KANSAS SCC		20 yrs	X	X	X		X	X		4 yrs		
KENTUCKY PSC	X	15 yrs	X	X	X		X					
LOUISIANA PSC												
MAINE PUC		30 yrs	X	X	X	X	X	X	X			
MARYLAND PSC	X	15 yrs	X	X	X	X	X	X		2 yrs		3/
MASSACHUSETTS DPU	X	20 yrs	X	X	X	X	X	X	X	4 yrs	X	4/
MICHIGAN PSC	X	15 yrs	X	X	X	X	X	X	X			5/
MINNESOTA PUC	X	15 yrs	X	X	X		X	X	X	5 yrs	X	
MISSISSIPPI PSC												
MISSOURI PSC	X	20 yrs	X	X	X		X	X	X	3 yrs		6/
MONTANA PSC		x	X	X	X	X	X	X	X	x	X	7/
NEBRASKA PSC												
NEVADA PSC		20 yrs	X	X	X	X	X	X	X	3 yrs	X	
NEW HAMPSHIRE PUC	X	15 yrs	X	X	X		X		X	x		T&D plan
NEW JERSEY BPU												
NEW MEXICO PUC												
NEW YORK PSC	X	20 yrs	X	X	X	X	X	X	X	x	X	
NORTH CAROLINA UC	X	15 yrs	X	X	X	X	X	X	X	3 yrs		T&D plan
NORTH DAKOTA PSC		10-20 yrs		X	X	X				2 yrs		
OHIO PUC		20 yrs	X	X	X			X	X	4 yrs		T&D plan
OKLAHOMA CC												
OREGON PUC	X	20 yrs	X	X	X	X	X	X	X	2 yrs	X	
PENNSYLVANIA PUC		20 yrs	X	X	X	X	X	X		2 yrs		
RHODE ISLAND PUC	X	10 yrs	X	X	X		X	X	X			
SOUTH CAROLINA PSC	X	15 yrs	X	X	X	X	X	X	X	1 yr		8/
SOUTH DAKOTA PUC												
TENNESSEE PSC												
TEXAS PUC		15 yrs		X	X				X			9/
UTAH PSC		20 yrs	X	X	X	X	X	X	X	4 yrs	X	
VERMONT PSB		20 yrs	X	X	X	X	X	X	X		X	
VIRGINIA SCC	X	20 yrs	X	X	X			X				
WASHINGTON UTC		20 yrs		X	X					2 yrs		
WEST VIRGINIA PSC												
WISCONSIN PSC		20 yrs	X	X	X	X	X	X	X	5-10yr	X	
WYOMING PSC		Varies	X	X	Some	Some	Some	X	Some	Varies	Some	

1/   Pilot and full-scale DSM programs; process and evaluation programs.

2/   CAA compliance, T&D facilities, purchase and sales options, QF transactions.

3/   Probable environmental costs considered in development of avoided costs used to value benefits of DSM.

4/   RFPs (separate supply- and demand-side or combined) for any capacity need identified within the next 10 years.

5/   Scenarios containing an analysis of renewable resources: the first must contain 50% conservation and renewables, the second must contain 75%.

6/   Environmental factors are considered as "probable environmental costs", i.e., the utilities costs to comply with future regulations that may be imposed, not as external costs.

7/   The only requirement is to file a plan. The contents of the plan is left to the utility's discretion. The commission rules contain guidance for what should be in a plan, these are marked above.

8/   Environmental impacts.

9/   Externalities are considered in power plant licensing proceedings.

Table 19

Public Participation In and Agency Authority Over Integrated Resource Planning for Electric Utilities.

AGENCY	Agency Holds Public Hearings on IRP Plans	Other Ways Public Participates and Comments on Utility IRP Plans	Agency Authority Over IRP Plans	Agency Response in Practice to IRP Plans	How Often Utilities Are Required to File Progress Reports
ALABAMA PSC					
ALASKA PUC					
ARIZONA CC	X	Workshops, collaboratives	R,M	R,M,O 1/	
ARKANSAS PSC	X	Regional focus groups	P,M,Q	2/	Every 6 mths
CALIFORNIA PUC					
COLORADO PUC	X	Prior to plan's submission to PUC	P,J	2/	Annually
CONNECTICUT DPUC	X	Written comments	A,R,P,M,Q	A,R,P,M,Q	
DELAWARE PSC	X		R,Q,K	R,Q,K	
DC PSC	X	Community hearings, filings w/PSC	A,R,P,M,Q,O	A,R,P,Q,O 3/	
FLORIDA PSC	if nec.	Workshops, conservation goals hearings	R,P,M 4/	R,P,M	
GEORGIA PSC	X	Comment on accompanying res. cert. app	A,R,P,M,J	R,M	Quarterly
HAWAII PUC		Advisory groups, hearings by utilities	A,R,P,M,Q	R 2/	Annually
IDAHO PUC	X	Policy advisory group	A,R	A,R	
ILLINOIS CC	X	Circulate notice to interested parties	A,R,P,M,Q	A,R,P,M,Q	
INDIANA URC		Comments made in context of Dkt Case.	A,R,P,Q	R	
IOWA UB	X	Collaboration prior to filing of IRP	A,R,P,M,J	A,R,P,M	3-6 months
KANSAS SCC	X	Collaborative proceedings	A	A	
KENTUCKY PSC		Written comments, informal conferences	5/	5/	
LOUISIANA PSC					
MAINE PUC	X		A,R,Q	A,R,Q	Quarterly
MARYLAND PSC	X	Collaboratives, written comments	A,R,P,Q	A,R,Q 6/	Annually
MASSACHUSETTS DPU	X	Settlement negotiations	R,P,M,Q	R,P,M,Q	7/
MICHIGAN PSC		Public presentations, written comments	A,R	A,R	
MINNESOTA PUC		Written comments, intervene in proc.	A,R,P,M,Q,J	A,R,M,O 6/	6-9 months
MISSISSIPPI PSC	X	Workshops	A,R,P,M,Q		
MISSOURI PSC	X	Written comments	R	2/	
MONTANA PSC	X	Written comments	A,R,Q	R,Q	
NEBRASKA PSC					
NEVADA PSC	X		R,P,Q	R,P,M,Q	w/in 20 mths
NEW HAMPSHIRE PUC	X		R,P,Q	R,P,Q	
NEW JERSEY BPU					
NEW MEXICO PUC					
NEW YORK PSC		Comment period, utility outreach	A,R,P,M,Q	R 8/	
NORTH CAROLINA UC	X	Customer focus/public involv. groups	A,R,P,M,Q	A,R	Annually
NORTH DAKOTA PSC		IRP to be reviewed in another hearing		R	
OHIO PUC	X		A,R,P,M	A,R,P,M	Every 6 mths
OKLAHOMA CC					
OREGON PUC	X	Advisory Groups, written comments	R,M,Q,K	R,M,O 9/	Annually 10/
PENNSYLVANIA PUC			R	R	
RHODE ISLAND PUC	X	Written comments	A,R,P 11/	Q	
SOUTH CAROLINA PSC	X	Comment as programs are instituted	A,R,M,Q,O	A,R,O	Annually
SOUTH DAKOTA PUC					
TENNESSEE PSC					
TEXAS PUC		Written comments, intervene in proceed	A,R	A,R,O 12/	
UTAH PSC	if nec.	Public meetings	Q,K	Q,K	6-12 months
VERMONT PSB	13/	Direct intervention, public advocate	R,P,Q,J	A,R,P,Q	Varies
VIRGINIA SCC		Public can comment on IRPs	A,R,P,M,Q	Staff reviews	
WASHINGTON UTC	X	Tech. advisory comm., written comments	A,R,Q,J	A	
WEST VIRGINIA PSC					
WISCONSIN PSC	X	Public meetings, mailing to ratepayers	A,R,P,M,Q	R,P,M,Q	Varies
WYOMING PSC	X	Public participation & comment meeting	A,R,P,M,Q	A,R,M,Q	Varies

1/ Commission has conducted further studies on key issues.
2/ Currently considering the first plans.
3/ Collaborative working group disbanded, periodic briefing by util.
4/ Comment on plan to other state agencies.
5/ Staff reviews IRP plans and compiles a report with recommendations for the utility's next IRP. Commission does not act on the plan.
6/ Require modifications in the next resource plan.
7/ 120 days after issuance of RFP.
8/ Acknowledge with modifications.
9/ Acknowledge with modifications.
10/ Required for DSM activities only.
11/ Under a recent Memorandum of Understanding, the three investor-owned utilities that are owned by interstate holding companies must modify their IRPs until they obtain a consensus of all states in which they operate.
12/ Modify forecasts and plans as part of the Statewide Electrical Energy Plan.
13/ Evidentiary hearings are held which are open to public attendance.

A=Accept it	R=Review it
P=Approve it	M=Modify it
J=Reject	O=Other
K=Acknowledge it	
Q=Require utility to modify and resubmit it	

Table 20

Open Dockets Regarding Integrated Resource Planning for Electric Utilities.

AGENCY	Agency Has Open Dockets That Affect IRP Process	Citation and Description	Direct Result of the EPAct	Agency Considering Opening a Docket	Some Util. Voluntarily File Plans	Agency Has Decided Not to Require IRP	Citation and Reason
ALABAMA PSC	X	Considering IRP	X		1/		
ALASKA PUC				X			
ARIZONA CC				X			
ARKANSAS PSC							
CALIFORNIA PUC	X	Industry Restructuring					
COLORADO PUC							
CONNECTICUT DPUC							
DELAWARE PSC							
DC PSC							
FLORIDA PSC	X	Dkts. 930548 through 930551	X				
GEORGIA PSC							
HAWAII PUC							
IDAHO PUC							
ILLINOIS CC	X.	Docket 92-0274					
INDIANA URC	2/	Generic IRP Rulemaking					
IOWA UB	X	WOI-93-2	X				
KANSAS SCC	X	Proposed rules					
KENTUCKY PSC							
LOUISIANA PSC	X	Considering IRP					
MAINE PUC	X	Dkt. 93-244	X				
MARYLAND PSC	X	Case 8630	X				
MASSACHUSETTS DPU							
MICHIGAN PSC	X	U-10574					
MINNESOTA PUC							
MISSISSIPPI PSC					X		
MISSOURI PSC							
MONTANA PSC							
NEBRASKA PSC							
NEVADA PSC							
NEW HAMPSHIRE PUC							
NEW JERSEY BPU		Drafting proposed IRP rules		X 3/	X		
NEW MEXICO PUC	X	Considering IRP					
NEW YORK PSC	X	C. 92-E-0886					
NORTH CAROLINA UC	X	Dkt. E-100, sub. 69	X				
NORTH DAKOTA PSC		Considering IRP		X	X		
OHIO PUC							
OKLAHOMA CC	X	Considering IRP					
OREGON PUC	X	UM 573					
PENNSYLVANIA PUC	X	Dkt. L-930079					
RHODE ISLAND PUC							
SOUTH CAROLINA PSC	X	IRP Dockets are on-going					
SOUTH DAKOTA PUC				X			
TENNESSEE PSC							
TEXAS PUC	X	Project 11365, Consid. IRP					
UTAH PSC	X	Dkt. 90-2035-01					
VERMONT PSB	X	Dkt. 5718	X				
VIRGINIA SCC							
WASHINGTON UTC				X			
WEST VIRGINIA PSC	X	Considering IRP		X	X		
WISCONSIN PSC				X			
WYOMING PSC					X		

1/   Some utilities prepare IRP plans but do not file them.
2/   An IRP rulemaking is underway. Technically, this is not an open docket.
3/   Board is in the process of drafting proposed IRP rules.

Table 21

Status of State Policies Regarding Recovery of Electric Utility Investments in Conservation and Demand-Side Management.

AGENCY	State Policy on Investment Recovery Currently In Effect	Citation and Description	Agency Currently Has Open Docket	Citation and Description	Direct Result of the EPAct	Agency Considering Opening a Docket
ALABAMA PSC			X	Docket #22943	X	
ALASKA PUC						
ARIZONA CC	X					X
ARKANSAS PSC	X	A.C.A. §23-2-401 - 405(a)(3)				
CALIFORNIA PUC	X	Expensed, recovered in rates	X	Generic docket opened 1/94 Generic DSM rulemaking	X	
COLORADO PUC	X	Decision No. C93-38				
CONNECTICUT DPUC	X	Dockets 92-07-02, 92-04-01	X	931-199E		
DELAWARE PSC						
DC PSC	X	Order 9868, Formal Case 905				
FLORIDA PSC	X	1/	X	Dkts.93-0444-EI,93-0424-EI		
GEORGIA PSC	X	O.C.G.A. §46-3A-9	X	Dkt. 4229-U lost revenues	X	
HAWAII PUC	X	Order 11523, 3/12/92	X	D.7574,7689,7690,7691,7692		
IDAHO PUC	X	Order 22299, Case U-1500-165				
ILLINOIS CC	X	Dkt. 91-0021, 91-0057 2/				
INDIANA URC	X	Cause 39201, 38986, 39672	X	Cause 39401, 39857		X
IOWA UB	X	Iowa Admin. Code 199-35	X	NOI-93-2	X	
KANSAS SCC	X	KSA 66.117(d), 1980	X	180,056-U		
KENTUCKY PSC			X	Case 341 cost recovery		
LOUISIANA PSC			X	Docket U-20178		
MAINE PUC	X	65-407 CMR 380				
MARYLAND PSC	X	PSC Law §28(g)	X	Case 8630	X	
MASSACHUSETTS DPU	X	DSM costs are expensed-DPU 89-179, 89-175, 89-260, 90-335 and 91-80	X	DPU 91-234-A		
MICHIGAN PSC	X	Base rate surcharges				
MINNESOTA PUC	X	MN Laws 1993, Chp. 49; Dkt. E-002/M-90-1159	X	annual adjustment for conservation		
MISSISSIPPI PSC						
MISSOURI PSC	X	Recover same as O&M expenses				X
MONTANA PSC	X	MCA §69-3-702, -1204, -1206; Order 5360d, Dkt. 88.6.15	X	Dkt. 93.6.24		
NEBRASKA PSC						
NEVADA PSC	X	Dkt. 88-111, 89-651				
NEW HAMPSHIRE PUC	X	Order 19689, 19773				
NEW JERSEY BPU	X	Recover costs &lost revenues				
NEW MEXICO PSC			X	Cases 2383, 2449, 2450		
NEW YORK PSC	X	Case 29409, Opinion 88-20				
NORTH CAROLINA UC	X	Dkt. E-100, Sub. 64				
NORTH DAKOTA PSC	X	PU-400-92-399				X
OHIO PUC	X	Case 90-723-EI-COI mod.10/92				
OKLAHOMA CC	X	Order 240281, 327685	X	Cause No. PUD 001342		
OREGON PUC	X	3/				
PENNSYLVANIA PUC	X	Dkt. I-900005, 11/93				
RHODE ISLAND PUC	X	Dkt. 1939				4/
SOUTH CAROLINA PSC	X	Ord.93-465, Dkt.92-619-E; SB 1273 §58-37-20	X	Dkt. 87-223-E		
SOUTH DAKOTA PUC	X	Recover same as O&M expenses				X
TENNESSEE PSC	X					
TEXAS PUC	X	Subst. Rule 23.22(d), 1984	X	Project 11365		
UTAH PSC	X	Dkt. 92-2035-04	X	Dkt. 92-2035-04		
VERMONT PSB	X	Dkt. 5270, 4/16/90	X	Dkt. 5270-CUC-2		
VIRGINIA SCC	X	Dkt. PUE90070, 3/27/92				
WASHINGTON UTC	X	Rev. Code Wash. 80.28.260				
WEST VIRGINIA PSC	X	Recover same as O&M expenses				
WISCONSIN PSC	X	6680-GR-3, 10/10/77 and 5/				X
WYOMING PSC						

1/   Load management programs are capitalized and amortized; all others are expensed.

2/   Commission authorization in Docket 91-0057 was reversed by State Appellate Court on June 8, 1993. There were also orders issued Feb. 1992, Sept. 1992, Feb. 1993.

3/   Order 89-1700 and DSM cost recovery/incentive mechanisms approved for some utilities.

4/   As a result of the EPAct, the utilities that do not currently receive compensation for lost revenues will request it in their conservation filings next fall.

5/   Wis. Stats. 196.374(3) 1983a27. 6630-UR-100, 12/30/86.

Table 22

Agency Authority Over Rate of Return—Electric Utilities.

AGENCY	Agency determines rate of return under its general authority	Capital structure is adjusted to exclude non-utility financing when it is traceable	No ONE method ALL are considered	Discounted cash flow	Comparable earnings test	Earnings/price ratio	Mid-point approach	Capital asset pricing model	Risk premium	Other	Duration of call protection provision influences judgment in determining rate of return
FERC	X	X	X	X							
ALABAMA PSC	X	X	X								
ALASKA PUC	X	X		X 2/	X						
ARIZONA CC	X	X		X 2/	X 11/						
ARKANSAS PSC	X		X	X 2/	X						
CALIFORNIA PUC	X	X 1/		X 2/	X			X	X	X	Possible.
COLORADO PUC	X	X		X 9/	X						
CONNECTICUT DPUC	X	X		X							
DELAWARE PSC	X	X		X 2/	X					X	
D.C. PSC	X	X		X							
FLORIDA PSC	X	X 1/		X 2/							
GEORGIA PSC	X	X		X 2/	X				X	X 8/	
HAWAII PUC	X	X		X 2/						X	
IDAHO PUC	X	X		X 9/	X	X				X	
ILLINOIS CC	X	X		X 2/			X			X	
INDIANA URC	X		X								
IOWA UB	X	X 1/	X						X	X 6/	
KANSAS SCC	X	X		X							
KENTUCKY PSC	X	X		X 2/	X	X	X			X	
LOUISIANA PSC	X	10/		X							
MAINE PUC	X	10/	X	X 9/							
MARYLAND PSC	X	X		X						X 6/	
MASSACHUSETTS DPU	X	X		X 5/						X 5/	
MICHIGAN PSC	X	X		X 2/	X			X	X	X	
MINNESOTA PUC	X	X		X							
MISSISSIPPI PSC	X	X		X	X						
MISSOURI PSC	X	X		X							
MONTANA PSC	X	X		X	X						
NEBRASKA PSC 4/	X	X		X							
NEVADA PSC	X	X		X	X	X					
NEW HAMPSHIRE PUC	X	X		X							Yes
NEW JERSEY BPU 12/	X	X	X					X	X	X	
NEW MEXICO PUC	X	X		X 2/	X					X	
NEW YORK PSC	X	X	X		X 7/					X	
NORTH CAROLINA UC	X	X		X 2/	X			X	X	X	
NORTH DAKOTA PSC	X		X		X 7/						
OHIO PUC	X	X	X		X 7/			X	X		No decision.
OKLAHOMA CC	X	X			X			X	X		
OREGON PUC	X	X 1/			X					X	Maybe, if soon
PENNSYLVANIA PUC	X	X		X 2/	X	X	X			X 3/	
RHODE ISLAND PUC	X	X	X	X	X						
SOUTH CAROLINA PSC	X	X	X		X			X	X		
SOUTH DAKOTA PUC	X	X			X			X	X		
TENNESSEE PSC	X	X		X 2/	X			X	X		
TEXAS PUC	X			X 2/	X			X	X	X	
UTAH PSC	X	X			X					X	
VERMONT PSB 12/	X	X	X		X					X	
VIRGINIA SCC	X	X		X 2/							
WASHINGTON UTC	X	X			X						
WEST VIRGINIA PSC	X	X		X 2/	X			X	X	X	
WISCONSIN PSC	X	X		X 2/	X			X		X	
WYOMING PSC	X			X 2/	X			X		X	
PUERTO RICO PSC 12/											
VIRGIN ISLANDS PSC	X	10/		X 2/	X	X				X	
ALBERTA PUB	X	X		X 2/	X	X			X	X	
NOVA SCOTIA UARB	X	X		X 2/	X				X	X	
ONTARIO EB 12/	X	X		X 2/	X						

Note: Columns "No ONE method ALL are considered" through "Other" fall under the heading "Method Agency favors in determining rate of return."

Footnotes—Table 22

Agency Authority Over Rate of Return—Electric Utilities.

1/ Non-utility investment dollars are always excluded from rate base. Where non-utility investment is comparatively small, capital ratios are not adjusted. When non-utility investment is large, we usually remove non-utility investment from equity.

2/ Commission favors no single method, but rather that which produces the most reasonable results.

3/ It may use any method it desires especially in the case of a small company.

4/ No Commission regulation of electric or gas utilities.

5/ DCF is preferred, but Department approves other methods which check DCF result; risk spread analysis preferred by a slight margin. Financial condition of utility also given serious consideration.

6/ DCF is preferred; all methods are considered including econometric modeling approach.

7/ No single method, however, discounted cash flow is frequently used.

8/ Discounted cash flow most often used, but risk premium method used also. Determined case by case.

9/ DCF has been the preferred method, but its results should be checked with other methods.

10/ Never an issue before this agency.

11/ Agency favors DCF, but any method presented is considered.

12/ Commission did not respond to request for update information; this data may not be current.

Table 23

Rate of Return on Common Equity Electric Utility Most Recently Approved Rate and Rate Actually Earned by the Same Company

AGENCY	Agency determines rate of return under its general authority	Capital structure is adjusted to exclude non-utility financing when it is traceable	No ONE method ALL are considered	Discounted cash flow	Comparable earnings test	Earnings/price ratio	Mid-point approach	Capital asset pricing model	Risk premium	Other	Duration of call protection provision influences judgment in determining rate of return
FERC	X	X	X	X							
ALABAMA PSC	X	X		X							
ALASKA PUC	X	X			X						Possible.
ARIZONA CC	X	X	X 2/	X							
ARKANSAS PSC	X	X	X	X 11/							
CALIFORNIA PUC	X	X 1/	X 2/	X	X			X	X	X	Possible.
COLORADO PUC	X	X		X 9/	X						
CONNECTICUT DPUC	X	X		X							
DELAWARE PSC	X		X 2/	X	X						X
D.C. PSC	X	X		X							
FLORIDA PSC	X	X 1/	X 2/	X							
GEORGIA PSC	X	X	X 2/	X					X	X 8/	
HAWAII PUC	X	X	X 2/		X					X	
IDAHO PUC	X	X		X 9/	X	X				X	
ILLINOIS CC	X	X	X 2/				X			X	
INDIANA URC	X		X								
IOWA UB	X	X 1/	X						X	X 6/	
KANSAS SCC	X	X	X								
KENTUCKY PSC	X	X	X 2/	X	X	X				X	
LOUISIANA PSC	X		X								
MAINE PUC	X	10/	X 9/	X							
MARYLAND PSC	X	X	X							X 6/	
MASSACHUSETTS DPU	X	X	X 5/							X 5/	
MICHIGAN PSC	X	X	2/	X			X	X	X	X	
MINNESOTA PUC	X	X	X								
MISSISSIPPI PSC	X	X	X	X							
MISSOURI PSC	X	X	X								
MONTANA PSC	X	X	X	X							
NEBRASKA PSC 4/	X	X	X		X						
NEVADA PSC	X	X	X	X							Yes
NEW HAMPSHIRE PUC	X	X	X								
NEW JERSEY BPU 12/	X	X	X	X				X	X	X	
NEW MEXICO PUC	X	X	X	X 7/							
NEW YORK PSC	X	X	X	X				X	X	X	
NORTH CAROLINA UC	X	X	X 2/	X				X	X	X	
NORTH DAKOTA PSC	X			X							
OHIO PUC	X	X	X	X 7/			X	X		X 7/	No decision.
OKLAHOMA CC	X	X 1/	X	X		X	X	X			
OREGON PUC	X	X	X	X						X	Maybe, if soon
PENNSYLVANIA PUC	X	X	X 2/	X	X	X	X			X	X 3/
RHODE ISLAND PUC	X	X	X	X	X			X	X		
SOUTH CAROLINA PSC	X	X	X	X	X						
SOUTH DAKOTA PUC	X	X		X							
TENNESSEE PSC	X	X	X 2/	X	X	X	X	X	X		
TEXAS PUC	X	X	X 2/	X				X	X		
UTAH PSC	X	X		X							
VERMONT PSB 12/	X	X		X	X					X	
VIRGINIA SCC	X	X	X 2/								
WASHINGTON UTC	X	X		X				X	X	X	
WEST VIRGINIA PSC	X	X	X 2/	X				X	X	X	
WISCONSIN PSC	X	X	X 2/	X				X			
WYOMING PSC	X		X 2/	X	X						
PUERTO RICO PSC 12/										X	
VIRGIN ISLANDS PSC	X	10/	X 2/	X	X					X	
ALBERTA PUB	X	X	X 2/	X	X					X	
NOVA SCOTIA UARB	X	X	X 2/	X	X				X	X	
ONTARIO EB 12/	X	X	X 2/	X	X						

Table 24

Summary of Agencies' Jurisdiction Over Utilities and Carriers

AGENCY	Company Name	ELECTRIC UTILITY Rate of Return on Common Equity				Comment
		Approved		Earned		
		Date	% Granted	Date	% Earned	
FERC	Virginia Power	06/22/92	09.78			
ALABAMA PSC	Alabama Power	03/05/90	13.00-14.50	1993	13.14	Under Rate RSE
ALASKA PUC	AK Electric L&P	11/01/90	15.25	1993	15.30	
ARIZONA CC	Tucson Electric Power	01/13/94	11.00			
ARKANSAS PSC	Empire Dist. Electric	06/26/91	12.25			
CALIFORNIA PUC	SoCal Edison Co.	12/03/93	11.00			
COLORADO PUC	Public Service Colo.	10/14/93	11.00	1993	08.56	
CONNECTICUT DPUC	Conn. Light & Power	06/16/93	11.50	04/96	09.62	
DELAWARE PSC	Delmarva Power/Light	10/05/93	11.50	1993	13.20	
DC PSC	PEPCO	03/04/94	11.00	1993	12.35	
FLORIDA PSC	Tampa Electric	12/92	12.00	1992	12.55	
GEORGIA PSC	Georgia Power	10/01/91	12.25			
HAWAII PUC	Citizens Util.-Kauai	11/02/93	11.68	12/31/93	04.15	
IDAHO PUC	Idaho Power Co.	1986	12.25			
ILLINOIS CC	Iowa-Illinois G&E	07/21/93	11.38			
INDIANA URC	IN-MI Power Co.	11/12/93	12.00			
IOWA UB	Iowa-Illinois G&E	02/25/94	11.25			
KANSAS SCC	Empire Dist. Electric	10/23/91	11.00	1992	16.67	
KENTUCKY PSC	Union Light, Heat	05/05/92	11.50			
LOUISIANA PSC	Gulf States Utilities	10/26/90	12.75			
MAINE PUC	Bangor Hydro Electric	03/16/94	10.60			
MARYLAND PSC	Potomac Electric	10/13/93				Settlement-ROE not specified
MASSACHUSETTS DPU	Cambridge Electric	05/28/93	11.00			
MICHIGAN PSC	Detroit Edison Co.	01/21/94	11.00			
MINNESOTA PUC	Northern States Power	09/01/93	11.00			
MISSISSIPPI PSC	MS Power Co.	03/03/93	11.94			
MISSOURI PSC	Show-Me Power Corp.	02/13/92	12.22			
MONTANA PSC	Montana Power Co.	04/28/94	11.00			
NEBRASKA PSC	Does not regulate					
NEVADA PSC	Nevada Power Co.	07/24/92	12.50			
NEW HAMPSHIRE PUC	Granite State Elec.	02/26/93	10.50	1992	09.86	
NEW JERSEY BPU	Jersey Central P&L	06/15/93	12.20			
NEW MEXICO PUC	Public Service NM	04/12/90	12.52			
NEW YORK PSC	Central Hudson G&E	12/16/93	10.60			
NORTH CAROLINA UC	NC Power (VEPCO)	02/26/93	11.80	12/31/93	10.63	
NORTH DAKOTA PSC	Northern States Power	04/07/93	11.50	12/92	06.71	
OHIO PUC	Monongahela Power	07/15/92	11.99			
OKLAHOMA CC	OK Gas & Electric Co.	02/25/94	12.00			
OREGON PUC	Portland Gen. Elec.	02/05/91	12.50			
PENNSYLVANIA PUC	West Penn Power	05/14/93	11.50			
RHODE ISLAND PUC	Newport Electric	09/28/92	11.40			
SOUTH CAROLINA PSC	SCE&G Co.	06/07/93	11.50			
SOUTH DAKOTA PSC	Northern States Power	01/01/91	12.00			
TENNESSEE PSC	Kingsport Power Co.	11/1992	12.00	12/93	13.86	
TEXAS PUC	Texas Utilities Co.	01/28/94	11.35			
UTAH PSC	Utah Power & Light	02/09/90	12.10			
VERMONT PSB	Citizens Utilities	01/26/94	09.89			
VIRGINIA SCC	Virginia Power	02/03/94	10.50-11.50			11.40% used to set rates
WASHINGTON UTC	Puget Sound P&L	10/29/93	10.50			
WEST VIRGINIA PSC	WV Power	02/10/93	10.60			
WISCONSIN PSC	Wisconsin Electric	08/01/93	11.80	12/31/93	12.91	Based on settlement agreement
WYOMING PSC	Montana-Dakota Utils.	12/01/93				Stipulated case, not stated
PUERTO RICO PSC						
VIRGIN ISLANDS PSC						
ALBERTA PUB	TransAlta Utilities	12/10/93	11.88			
NOVA SCOTIA UARB	Nova Scotia Power Inc	03/24/94	11.50-12.00	12/31/93	12.00	1st ROE hearing since privati- zation.
ONTARIO EB						
QUEBEC NGB	Does not regulate electric utilities.					

Table 24 (Continued)

AGENCY	BRIEF SUMMARY OF AGENCY'S REGULATORY JURISDICTION
FCC	Interstate and international communications common carriers.
FERC	Electric Utilities and Licensees (private), Electric (public-Federal Power Marketing agencies, confirmation and approval authority; interstate natural gas (private) and interstate oil pipelines (carriers).
ICC	Interstate motor carriers, railroads, water common carriers, household goods freight forwarders, property brokers, pipeline transportation of commodities other than water, gas, or oil.
ALABAMA PSC	Privately or investor-owned electric, gas, water and steam heating; radio common carriers, COCOTs; resellers; telephone, telegraph; intrastate air carriers; motor vehicle carriers of persons or property for hire; railroads.
ALASKA PUC	Electric (private, public and co-op); gas (private, public and co-op); refuse; steam heating companies; telecommunications (cable TV, cellular, intrastate interexchange telephone, local exchange telephone, radio common carrier); water (investor and municipal); sewer (investor); common carrier gas and petroleum pipelines.
ARIZONA CC	Electric (private, cooperative); gas (private); telephone; cellular; telegraph; water (investor); sewer (investor); railroad safety; gas and hazardous liquid pipelines safety; securities; corporations. RCCs deregulated 1987; motor carriers deregulated 1982.
ARKANSAS HTD	Carriage of persons and property for compensation by air, rail, water, or motor.
ARKANSAS PSC	Electric (private, cooperative); gas (private); telephone; water (investor); sewer (investor); common carrier pipelines (private).
CALIFORNIA PUC	Electric (private); gas (private); telephone; radio common carriers; telegraph; water (investor); sewer (investor); steam heating companies; toll bridge corporation; motor passenger carriers; household goods movers; parcel carriers; motor freight carriers; freight forwarders; motor transportation brokers; railroads; pipelines
COLORADO PUC	Electric (private), electric co-op may elect to be regulated; gas (private, municipal); telephone; telegraph; water (investor); steam heating companies; motor passenger carriers; parcel carriers; baggage carriers (rates); air terminal buses (rates); taxicabs; motor freight carriers; railroads.
CONNECTICUT DPUC	Electric (private); gas (private); telephone; cable television; telegraph; water (investor).
CONNECTICUT DOT	Effective July 1, 1989, all jurisdiction over motor carriers transferred from DPUC to DOT.
DELAWARE PSC	Electric (private, cooperative); gas (private); telephone; cable television; water (investor).
DC PSC	Electric (private); gas (private); telephone; telegraph; securities.
FLORIDA PSC	Electric (private); gas (private, municipal); cooperative and municipal electric (rate structure, territorial and power plant siting); telephone (LEC, IXC, STS, AAV and payphones); water (investor); sewer (investor); securities.
FLORIDA DOT	Motor Carrier and Compliance Office--motor carrier safety inspection and enforcement.
FLORIDA DOT	Rail Office--railroad safety, including rail-highway crossings.
GEORGIA PSC	Electric (private); gas (private); telephone; radio common carriers; telegraph; motor passenger carriers; household goods carriers (rates); parcel carriers (rates); baggage carriers (rates); air terminal buses (rates); motor freight carriers; railroads.
HAWAII PUC	Electric (private); gas (private); telephone; radio common carriers; water (investor); sewer (investor); water carriers; motor passenger carriers; household goods movers (rates); parcel carriers (rates); baggage carriers (rates); air terminal buses (rates); motor freight carriers.
IDAHO PUC	Electric (private); gas (private); telephone; water carriers; motor passenger carriers; parcel carriers; baggage carriers; motor freight carriers; railroads.
ILLINOIS CC	Investor-owned electric, gas, water and sewer utilities; telecommunication carriers; motor carriers of property; motor carriers of passengers; rail carriers; common carriers of oil and gas by pipeline; commercial relocators of trespassing motor vehicles; limited jurisdiction in resolving disputes between electric utilities and electric co-ops.
INDIANA URC	Electric (private, municipal, cooperative); gas (private, municipal); telephone; telegraph; water (investor, municipal, not-for-profit); sewer (investor).
INDIANA DOR	Motor common and contract carriers of passengers (charter and special service, not regular route); air terminal buses (rates, service, safety); motor common and contract carriers of freight (general commodities, bulk commodities, household goods, agricultural goods, parcels, baggage for rates); motor carrier registration.
IOWA UB	Electric (rates for investor-owned with over 10,000 customers); gas (rates for investor-owned with over 2,000 customers); gas & electric (municipal-plant siting, disconnection and safety matters); electric (co-op-service rules, plant siting and safety matters); telephone (rates for over 15,000 customers or access lines); telegraph; water (investor-w/over 2,000 customers)
IOWA DOT	Motor passenger carriers; household goods carriers; parcel carriers; baggage carriers; emergency tow trucks (partial); motor freight carriers; railroads; liquid freight carriers.
KANSAS SCC	Electric (private, municipal, co-op); gas (private, municipal, coop); telephone; radio common carriers; telegraph; water (investor); motor passenger carriers; household goods carriers (rates); parcel carriers (rates); baggage carriers (rates); emergency tow trucks (rates); taxicabs (rates); motor freight carriers; railroads. Oil and natural gas proration and conservation, correlative rights, well classification, prevention of unreasonable discrimination in favor of one common source of supply (oil and natural gas).
KENTUCKY DVR	Driver and vehicle licensing, fuel tax, operating authority, oversize/overweight permits, hazardous materials; intrastate rates & safety of motor carriers; enforcement; solid waste.

Table 24 (Continued)

AGENCY	BRIEF SUMMARY OF AGENCY'S REGULATORY JURISDICTION
KENTUCKY PSC	Electric (private); gas (private); cooperative electric and telephone utilities; telephone (private); radio-common carriers; water (investor); water districts; water associations; sewer (investor).
KENTUCKY RC	Commission has broad powers to regulate intrastate railroad, express and water transportation companies, including rate regulation, issuing certificates, authorizing/directing establishment or curtailment of service, receiving and filing carrier reports and enforcing Kentucky laws applicable to rail, express and water service.
LOUISIANA PSC	Electric; gas (private); telephone; radio common carriers; telegraph; water (investor); sewer (investor); water carriers; railway express agency; motor passenger carriers; household goods carriers (rates); parcel carriers (rates); motor freight carriers; railroads.
MAINE PUC	Electric; gas; telephone; radio common carriers; telegraph; water utilities; water carriers (all utilities subject to MPUC jurisdiction, including investor-owned, municipal, quasi-municipal and cooperative).
MARYLAND PSC	Electric (cooperative, municipal and private); gas (private and municipal); telephone; water (investor and municipal - limited rate jurisdiction); sewer (investor); steam heating companies; motor passenger carriers; air terminal buses (rates); taxicabs (rates and service); flammables carriers; railroads; ferry companies; water taxis; bay pilots-rates only.
MASSACHUSETTS DPU	Electric (private, municipal); gas (private, municipal); energy facility siting; radio common carriers; telegraph; water (investor); street railways; motor passenger carriers; household goods carriers (rates); baggage carriers (rates); tow trucks (rates); motor freight carriers; railroads; parcel carriers (rates).
MICHIGAN DOT	Railroads, air transportation, motor passenger carriers.
MICHIGAN PSC	Electric (private, cooperative); gas (private); telephone; water (investor); steam heating companies; water carriers; household goods carriers; parcel carriers; emergency tow trucks (rates outside the exempt zone); motor freight carriers.
MINNESOTA DOT	Intrastate air transportation -limited; motor carriers of passengers and freight (safety, insurance, leasing, enforcement of rates and service); railroads (limited).
MINNESOTA PUC	Electric (private); gas (private); gas (municipal); electric (municipal, cooperative); telephone; telegraph.
MINNESOTA TRB	Motor passenger carriers, motor freight carriers; railroads (limited).
MISSISSIPPI PSC	Electric (private); gas (private); gas (municipal - safety); telephone; radio common carriers; telegraph; water (investor); sewer (investor); motor passenger carriers; household goods carriers (rates); parcel carriers (rates); baggage carriers (rates); motor freight carriers; railroads (rates only).
MISSISSIPPI DOT	Effective 7/1/92, jurisdiction over railroad safety was transferred to newly created Department of Transportation.
MISSOURI DOT	Motor passenger carriers; household goods carriers (rates); parcel carriers (rates); baggage carriers (rates); motor freight carriers; railroads.
MISSOURI PSC	Electric (investor, cooperative--safety; all--limited jurisdiction over territory); gas (investor; municipal--safety); telecommunications (investor-owned; limited jurisdiction over cooperatives); water (investor); sewer (investor); steam heating (investor).
MONTANA PSC	Electric (private, municipal); gas (private, municipal); telephone; radio common carrier; telegraph; water (private, municipal); street railways; motor passenger carriers; household goods carriers; parcel carriers; baggage carriers; taxicabs; motor carriers engaged in garbage collection (entry only); motor freight carriers; railroads.
NEBRASKA PSC	Telephone; motor passenger carriers; household goods carriers (rates); parcel carriers (rates); taxicabs; limousines; motor freight carriers; grain warehouse licenses; railroads; siting of high-voltage transmission lines; grain dealer licenses; grain moisture testing devices.
NEVADA PSC	Electric (private); gas (private); cooperative electric; telephone; radio-common carriers; telegraph; water (investor); sewer (investor); warehouses; motor passenger carriers, household goods carriers (rates); parcel carriers (rates); baggage carriers (rates); air terminal buses (rates); emergency tow trucks (rates); taxicabs (rates); motor freight carriers; railroads.
NEW HAMPSHIRE PUC	Electric (private, municipal, cooperative); gas (private); gas (municipal); telephone; telegraph; water (investor, municipal); steam heating companies; sewer (private)
NEW HAMPSHIRE DOT	Bureau of Railroads
NEW HAMPSHIRE DOS	Department of Safety, Bureau of Common Carriers: Economic regulation of motor carriers; Division of Enforcement has jurisdiction over safety of motor carriers.
NEW JERSEY BPU	Electric (private); gas (private); gas (municipal - however, there are no municipal gas utilities in the state); electric (municipal); telephone; cable television; telegraph; water (investor, municipal); sewer (investor); solid waste landfills and collectors. As of August 1989 Energy Grants, State Energy Master Plan.
NEW JERSEY DOT	Motor passenger carriers; railroads.
NEW MEXICO PUC	Electric (private); gas (private); gas and electric (municipal - but only if municipality petitions for such regulation); water (investor); water and sanitation districts (rates only); sewer (investor).

Table 24 (Continued)

AGENCY	BRIEF SUMMARY OF AGENCY'S REGULATORY JURISDICTION
NEW MEXICO SCC	Telephone; radio common carriers; telegraph; water carriers; motor passenger carriers; household goods carriers (rates); parcel carriers (rates); baggage carriers (rates); air terminal buses; ambulances; tow trucks; taxicabs; motor freight carriers; freight forwarders; railroads; gas and hazardous liquids pipeline safety.
NEW YORK PSC	Electric (private, municipal - but only if municipality obtains power from a source other than the New York Power Authority); gas (private, municipal); telephone; cellular radio carriers; water (private); steam heating companies.
NEW YORK SDOT	Airfields; motor passenger carriers; household goods carriers (rates); parcel carriers (rates); baggage carriers (rates); air terminal buses over eight passengers (rates); motor freight carriers; railroads.
NORTH CAROLINA UC	Electric (private); gas (private); telephone; radio common carriers; water (investor); sewer (investor); motor passenger carriers; household goods carriers (rates); parcel carriers (rates); baggage carriers (rates); motor freight carriers; railroads; passenger brokers; flume companies exercising right of eminent domain.
NORTH DAKOTA PSC	Electric (private); gas (private); telephone; radio common carriers; weights and measures; warehouse; motor passenger carriers; household goods carriers (rates); parcel carriers (rates); taxicabs (rates); motor freight carriers; railroads; grain elevators; auctioneers and auction clerks; pipelines; mined land reclamation; energy facility & transmission siting.
OHIO PUC	Electric (private); gas (private); telephone; radio common carriers; telegraph; water (investor); sewer (investor); steam heating companies; motor passenger carriers; household goods carriers (rates); parcel carriers (rates); baggage carriers (rates); air terminal buses outside exempt zones; motor freight carriers; railroads; bridge companies; water transportation; oil; natural gas; coal or derivatives pipelines.
OKLAHOMA CC	Electric (private, cooperative); gas (private); telephone; telegraph; street railways; motor passenger carriers; household goods carriers (rates); parcel carriers (rates); baggage carriers (rates); tow trucks (rates); motor freight carriers; railroads (limited); private water carriers; cotton gins. RCCs deregulated 1987.
OREGON PUC	Electric (private); gas (private); telephone; water (investor); Motor passenger carriers; household goods carriers (rates); parcel carriers (rates); motor freight carriers; railroads.
PENNSYLVANIA PUC	Electric (private); gas and electric (municipal - outside corporate limits); telephone; radio common carriers; telegraph; water (investor, municipal); sewer (investor, municipal - rates and services outside corporate limits); steam heating companies; docks and wharves; securities; water carriers; intrastate air transport; motor passenger carriers; household goods carriers (rates); parcel carriers (rates); baggage carriers (rates); buses (rates); taxicabs (rates); motor freight carriers; freight forwarders; railroads; brokers.
RHODE ISLAND PUC	Electric (private, munipal, cooperative); gas (private, municipal); telephone; cable television; telegraph; water (investor, municipal); street railways; water carriers; intrastate air transportation; motor passenger carriers; household goods carriers (rates); parcel carriers (rates); baggage carriers (rates); air terminal buses; emergency tow trucks (rates); taxicabs (rates); motor freight carriers; railroads.
SOUTH CAROLINA PSC	Electric (private); gas (private); telephone; radio common carriers; water (investor); sewer (investor); motor vehicle carriers for hire (territory and rates); motor vehicles (safety); railroads; street railways.
SOUTH DAKOTA PUC	Electric (private); gas (private); telephone; radio common carriers; warehouses; grain dealers; motor passenger carriers; household goods carriers (rates); parcel carriers (rates); baggage carriers (rates); motor freight carriers.
TENNESSEE PSC	Electric (investor); gas (investor); telephone (co-op exempt); radio common carrier (not cellular); water (investor); sewer (investor); motor passenger carriers; household goods carriers (rates); parcel carriers (rates); baggage carriers (rates); air terminal buses (rates); motor freight carriers; railroads (safety); safety of gas distribution systems.
TEXAS PUC	Electric (private, cooperative); electric (municipal - appellate jurisdiction over rates outside city limits); telephone.
TEXAS RC	Gas (private, municipal); motor passenger carriers; household goods carriers (rates); parcel carriers (rates); baggage carriers (rates); Motor freight carriers; railroads (safety); compressed natural gas, liquefied petroleum gas & liquefied natural gas (safety); oil and gas production; surface mining (coal, uranium, iron ore gravel); alternative fuels research and marketing.
TEXAS NRCC	Water and sewer (private-area and rates), (Cooperative-area and appellate rates), (Water districts-appellate rates), (Municipals-appellate rates for out of city), (appellate jurisdiction over wholesale rates for water and sewer).
UTAH PSC	Electric (private, cooperative); gas (private); telephone; radio common carriers; telegraph; water (investor); sewer (investor); railroads; motor carriers (authority, rates and insurance)
UTAH DOT	Safety of motor carriers and railroads.
VERMONT AT	Motor freight carriers
VERMONT PSB	Electric (private, municipal, cooperative); gas (private, municipal); telephone; Cable Television; water (investor).
VERMONT TB	Motor passenger carriers (buses).

Table 24 (Continued)

AGENCY	BRIEF SUMMARY OF AGENCY'S REGULATORY JURISDICTION
VIRGINIA SCC	Electric, intrastate telephone, water and sewer, natural gas utilities (investor-owned); paging and cellular companies; electric cooperatives (member-owned); motor carriers (common carriers of passenger and property, contract carriers, household goods carriers, parcel carriers, petroleum tank trucks, taxi cabs and limousines); rates of harbor pilots; launch services; sightseeing carriers by boat; state-chartered financial institutions; mortgage brokers and lenders; consumer finance companies; money transmitters; money order sellers; debt counseling agencies; financial planners; investment advisors and their representatives; broker-dealers and their agents; franchises; private toll roads; trademarks and service marks; central filing office for limited partnerships/corporations and limited liability companies.
WASHINGTON UTC	Electric (private); gas (private); telecommunications; water (investor); water carriers (private ferries); motor passenger carriers; household goods carriers; parcel carriers; baggage carriers (rates); air terminal buses; motor carriers engaged in solid waste collection; motor freight carriers; private motor carriers having vehicles over 26,000 lbs with truck terminals in Washington; freight forwarders; railroads; petroleum pipelines; low level nuclear waste disposal facilities.
WEST VIRGINIA PSC	Electric (private, municipal, cooperative); gas (private, municipal, cooperative); telephone; radio common carriers; telegraph; water (investor, municipal); sewer (investor, municipal); water carriers; motor passenger carriers; household goods carriers (rates); parcel carriers (rates); baggage carriers (rates); air terminal buses; motor carriers engaged in solid waste collection; motor freight carriers; railroads; pipeline transport of oil, water or gas; commercial solid waste facilities (rates).
WISCONSIN DOT	Vehicle registration, motor carrier licensing and regulation, suspension of vehicle registration, motor carrier insurance, vehicle sales fair trade practices, issuing vehicle trip permits and identification stamps.
WISCONSIN OCT	Created 1977, Ch. 29. Railroad safety, driver license revocation and suspension, driver safety, administrative suspension for OWI, automobile dealers, other highway matters.
WISCONSIN PSC	Electric (private, municipal); gas (private, municipal); telephone; radio common carriers; water (investor, municipal); steam heating companies.
WYOMING PSC	Electric (private, co-op); gas (private, co-op); gas and electric (municipal - outside corporate limits); telephone; radio common carriers; other intrastate telecommunications companies; telegraph; water (investor); steam heating companies; pipelines. Effective 4/1/91, all jurisdiction over transportation matters transferred to Dept. of Transportation.
WYOMING DOT	Effective 4/1/91, newly created Transportation Department, took over transportation matters formerly the jurisdiction of the PSC. These include: intrastate air transport; common, contract and private motor carriers of property and passengers; and railroads.
PUERTO RICO PSC	Gas (private); cable television; water (investor); warehouses; water carriers; motor passenger carriers; ambulances (rates); emergency tow trucks (rates); taxicabs (rates); motor freight carriers.
VIRGIN ISLANDS PSC	Electric (private); telephone; radio common carriers; water (investor); warehouses; docks and wharves; water carriers; motor passenger carriers.
CANADIAN RTC	Supervises all aspects of the Canadian broadcasting system, ie radio, television (cable, pay and educational); as well as federally regulated telecommunications common carriers, ie telephone and telegraph companies.
NATIONAL ENERGY BOARD	Licensing of oil and natural gas imports and exports and permitting of electricity exports; permitting of international power lines and certification of extraprovincial and international pipelines and designated interprovincial and international power lines; setting tolls and tariffs for transportation on extraprovincial or international oil or gas pipelines; and regulating safety of pipelines.
ALBERTA PMC	Gas pipelines; gas.
ALBERTA PUB	Electric (private); gas (private); water (investor).
NOVA SCOTIA URB	Electric; telephone (within the province); water; motor carriers (public passengers); gasoline and fuel oil outlet licensing; automobile insurance; land use planning appeals; property tax assessment appeals; shopping center development approvals; health services tax appeals; gasoline and diesel oil tax appeals; tobacco tax appeals; expropriation compensation appeals; municipal electoral boundaries; school board electoral boundaries; railways (within the province); criminal injury compensation appeals. General supervision of all utilities including capital spending, rates and terms of service provision. Approval of rates, routes and terms of service for all public passenger carriers.
ONTARIO EB	Gas (private).
ONTARIO TSC	Telephone.
QUEBEC NGB	Gas (private)
QUEBEC TB	Telephone; television, cablevision and radio programming (educational for all three).

Table 25

State Agency Authority to Regulate
Rates of Municipal Utilities' Electricity and Gas

** AGENCY	Agency has authority to regulate municipal utility rates? Gas	Electric	Municipal utility regulated inside/outside municipal boundaries?	Municipal Sales Regulated - Retail - Ultimate Consumer	Retail -- Public Authorities	Wholesale
ALABAMA PSC	NO	NO				
ALASKA PUC 10/	YES	YES	INSIDE & OUTSIDE	X	X	X
ARIZONA CC	SAFETY ONLY	NO				
ARKANSAS PSC	SAFETY ONLY	NO				
CALIFORNIA PUC	NO	NO				
COLORADO PUC	LIMITED	LIMITED	OUTSIDE 12/			
CONNECTICUT DPUC	LIMITED 1/	NO				
DELAWARE PSC	NO	NO				
D.C. PSC	NO	NO	No municipal utilities			
FLORIDA PSC	SAFETY ONLY	RATE STRUCTURE	INSIDE & OUTSIDE	X	X	
GEORGIA PSC	NO 11/	TERRITORY	RATES OUTSIDE HOME COUNTY 11/	11/		
HAWAII PUC	NO	NO	No municipal utilities			
IDAHO PUC	NO	NO				
ILLINOIS CC	SAFETY ONLY	NO	INSIDE & OUTSIDE			
INDIANA URC	RATES ONLY	RATES ONLY	INSIDE & OUTSIDE	X	X	X
IOWA UB	NO 2/	NO 2/	INSIDE & OUTSIDE 2/	X 2/	X 2/	
KANSAS SCC	YES	YES	OUTSIDE	X	X	X
KENTUCKY PSC	NO	NO				
LOUISIANA PSC	NO 4/	NO				
MAINE PUC	YES 13/	YES	OUTSIDE	X	X	
MARYLAND PSC	YES	YES	INSIDE & OUTSIDE	X	X	
MASSACHUSETTS DPU	YES	YES	INSIDE & OUTSIDE	X	X	X
MICHIGAN PSC	NO	NO				
MINNESOTA PUC	NO	NO				
MISSISSIPPI PSC	LIMITED	LIMITED	SAFETY INSIDE, FULL OUTSIDE8/	X	X	
MISSOURI PSC	NO-SAFETY ONLY	NO				
MONTANA PSC	YES	YES	INSIDE & OUTSIDE BUT ONLY FOR ANNUAL REVENUE INCREASE >12%			
NEBRASKA PSC	NO	NO	INSIDE & OUTSIDE			
NEVADA PSC	NO	NO				
NEW HAMPSHIRE PUC	YES	YES	OUTSIDE, IF RATES DIFFER	X	X	X
NEW JERSEY BPU 15/	YES	YES	OUTSIDE	X		
NEW MEXICO PUC	NO	NO 4/				
NEW YORK PSC	YES	YES 9/	INSIDE & OUTSIDE	X 9/	X 9/	X 9/
NORTH CAROLINA UC	SAFETY ONLY	NO				
NORTH DAKOTA PSC	SAFETY ONLY	NO				
OHIO PUC	SAFETY ONLY	NO				
OKLAHOMA CC	SAFETY ONLY	NO				
OREGON PUC	NO	NO				
PENNSYLVANIA PUC	YES 5/	YES 5/	OUTSIDE 5/	X		
RHODE ISLAND PUC	YES		INSIDE & OUTSIDE	X	X	
SOUTH CAROLINA PSC	SAFETY ONLY	LIMITED	INSIDE & OUTSIDE			
SOUTH DAKOTA PUC	NO	LIMITED	OUTSIDE			
TENNESSEE PSC	NO	NO	OUTSIDE			
TEXAS PUC	NO	YES 5/	OUTSIDE 5/	X 5/	X 5/	X 5/
TEXAS RC	YES 14/	NO	OUTSIDE 14/	X 14/	X 14/	X 14/
UTAH PSC	NO	NO				
VERMONT PSB 15/	YES	YES	INSIDE & OUTSIDE	X		X 6/
VIRGINIA SCC	NO	NO				
WASHINGTON UTC	SAFETY ONLY	NO	INSIDE & OUTSIDE			
WEST VIRGINIA PSC	LIMITED 7/	LIMITED 7/				
WISCONSIN PSC	YES	YES	INSIDE & OUTSIDE	X	X	
WYOMING PSC	YES 3/	YES 5/	OUTSIDE	X 5/		
CANADIAN AGENCIES						
ALBERTA PUB	LIMITED 4/	LIMITED 4/	INSIDE & OUTSIDE 4/	X 4/	X 4/	X 4/
NOVA SCOTIA UARB	YES 3/	YES	INSIDE & OUTSIDE	X	X	X

Footnotes—Table 25

State Agency Authority to Regulate
Rates of Municipal Utilities' Electricity and Gas

1/   By statute, customers of municipal utilities may appeal disputed bills to the State DPUC only if a termination notice has been issued.

2/   Regulation is limited to disconnection rules, plant siting and safety matters. Municipal utilities are exempt from rate regulation in accordance with Iowa Code Chapter 476.

3/   No municipal gas utilities within the jurisdiction.

4/   Only if municipality petitions for such regulation.

5/   Only over service outside of corporate limits.

6/   Approval of contracts.

7/   Commission has limited review authority over rates and charges; jurisdiction over facilities and service.

8/   Pipeline safety jurisdiction within municipal boundaries; otherwise only with that service which extends one mile beyond the corporate limits.

9/   Not over publicly owned electric utilities served by New York Power Authority.

10/   Municipal utilities are regulated only for service area matters except if competition exists between a municipal and non-municipal utility; however, full economic regulation is imposed on municipal utilities.

11/   When municipally-owned gas systems operate outside county in which municipality is located, Commission has jurisdiction over rates, service and safety for services provided outside home county.

12/   Only if rates charged outside corporate limits differ from those charged within corporate limits.

13/   Small electric utilities may establish rates outside PUC rate process.

14/   Only over service outside of corporate limits and only on appeal by affected persons.

15/   Commission did not respond to request for update information; this information may not be current.

Table 26

Description of State Agency
Regulation of Municipal Utilities' Electricity and Gas

AGENCY	DESCRIPTION OF AGENCY REGULATIONS OVER MUNICIPAL ELECTRIC AND GAS UTILITIES
Alabama PSC	State agency has no jurisdiction over municipal utilities.
Alaska PUC	Municipal utilities subject to total regulation if one utility is in competition with privately owned utility then all utilities owned by that municipality subject to total regulation. Even if no municipal utilities are in competition, they must apply for certificate of public convenience and necessity which prescribes a service area. Also, municipal utility may petition for total, irrevocable regulation, if so desiring.
Arizona CC	Jurisdiction over municipal gas pipeline safety only.
Arkansas PSC	Jurisdiction over municipal gas pipeline safety only.
California PUC	State agency has no jurisdiction over municipal utilities.
Colorado PUC	State commission has jurisdiction only outside corporate limits and then only if rates charged outside corporate limits differ from rates charged inside corporate limits.
Connecticut DPUC	Limited jurisdiction. Municipal utilities required to maintain records in accordance with Uniform System of Accounts and file annual report. Safety of municipal gas operations. May handle disputed bills if customer has received termination notice. Emergency plans.
Delaware PSC	State agency has no jurisdiction over municipal utilities.
DC PSC	Has no municipal utilities.
Florida PSC	Territorial boundaries, rate structures (not rate level), power pooling, interconnection, power plant and transmission needs determination, wheeling of electric utilities, safety, collection of gross receipts taxes. Municipal gas regulated for safety practices, territorial disputes, collection of gross receipts taxes & regulatory assessment fees.
Georgia PSC	When municipally-owned gas systems operate outside county in which municipality is located, Commission has jurisdiction over rates, service and safety for service provided outside home county.
Hawaii PUC	State agency has no jurisdiction over municipal utilities and has no municipal utilities.
Idaho PUC	State agency has no jurisdiction over municipal utilities.
Illinois CC	Gas pipeline safety jurisdiction over municipal gas utilities.
Indiana URC	Jurisdiction over rates, but are prohibited from interfering with their operations, rules or regulations.
Iowa UB	Regulation is limited to disconnection rules, plant siting and safety matters. Municipal utilities are exempt from rate regulation in accordance with Iowa Code Chapter 476.
Kansas SCC	Same regulations for rates and services as any other utility except they are restricted to those customers outside 3 miles from corporate city limits. Also, jurisdiction for gas pipeline safety over all municipal services, regardless of where they are located.
Kentucky PSC	State agency has no jurisdiction over municipal utilities.
Louisiana PSC	1974 constitution exempts city owned or operated utilities from state regulation unless a referendum is held - none to date.
Maine PUC	Jurisdiction over all facilities, service, rates and charges. Expedited procedure for rate increases of not more than 15%.
Maryland PSC	Identical to jurisdiction over private investor and cooperative utilities, involving rates, terms and conditions, standards of service and customer rights.
Massachusetts DPU	Prescribe accounting, review permissible earnings under statute, insure statutes are followed as to street light rates, permit depreciation higher than statutory requirement, regulate as to service, approve issues of revenue bonds, see that rates are not changed more often than once every three months.
Michigan PSC	State has jurisdiction over gas pipeline safety; no jurisdiction over municipal electric.
Minnesota PUC	Municipal utilities under Commission jurisdiction for assigned service areas and some customer complaints.
Mississippi PSC	Gas pipeline safety jurisdiction. Rate and service jurisdiction apply only as to extension of utilities greater than one mile outside corporate boundaries.
Missouri PSC	Municipal gas safety regulation.
Montana PSC	69-7-101 et seq, MCA. If increase is over 12% of total annual revenue and not mandated federal or state improvement.
Nebraska PSC	State has no jurisdiction over any electric or gas utilities.
Nevada PSC	State agency has no jurisdiction over municipal utilities.
New Hampshire PUC	For those customers outside municipal limits, tariffs are required and rates are regulated, ie, that portion of the municipal utility's business is subject to PUC jurisdiction as is the case of any public utility, if rates charged differ from those within municipal limits.
New Jersey BPU	Municipal utilities are subject to Board regulation only for rates on sales outside municipal boundaries. They are required to file annual reports with the Board.
New Mexico PUC	Municipally owned and operated utilities are not subject to PSC regulation, unless the municipality elects to come within the provisions of the Public Utility Act.
New York PSC	Essentially the same as over private utilities except questions of need within municipal boundaries and except electric municipals which take their power from the New York Power Authority (NYPA).
North Carolina UC	Gas Pipeline safety jurisdiction (G.S. 62-50). GS 62-3(23)d specifically exempts municipal electrics from state regulation.
North Dakota PSC	Gas Pipeline safety jurisdiction over municipal gas systems.

Table 26 (Continued)

AGENCY	DESCRIPTION OF AGENCY REGULATIONS OVER MUNICIPAL ELECTRIC AND GAS UTILITIES
Ohio PUC	State agency has no jurisdiction over municipal utilities.
Oklahoma CC	Natural gas pipeline safety.
Oregon PUC	Only safety, curtailment matters during electrical shortages, issuance of certificates of public convenience and necessity for overhead transmission lines less than 230 KV and territorial allocation.
Pennsylvania PUC	When a municipal corporation is deemed to be rendering public utility service beyond its corporate limits, it is then subject to exactly the same regulations as is any other public utility with regard to its extra-territorial service. Its rates must be just and reasonable and its service and facilities must be adequate, efficient, safe and reasonable.
Rhode Island PUC	State agency has authority over municipal gas utilities.
South Carolina PSC	Regulates municipal electric utilities only to the extent of authorizing extensions of service beyond corporate limits by issuing CPCN; full jurisdiction over gas pipeline safety.
South Dakota PUC	Territorial boundaries, complaints and plant siting only.
Tennessee PSC	State agency has no jurisdiction over municipal utilities.
Texas PUC	Certification and appellate rate jurisdiction for areas outside city limits (Electric).
Texas RC	Safety jurisdiction over municipally owned gas utilities and extraordinary appellate rate jurisdiction over those utilities outside the corporate limits of the city.
Utah PSC	State agency has no jurisdiction over municipal utilities.
Vermont PSB	Total regulation: rates, approve sales of wholesale power through contracts, territories, new construction and tariff filings.
Virginia SCC	State agency has no jurisdiction over municipal utilities.
Washington UTC	Gas regulation extends only to granting or transfer of Certificate and protection of public safety in construction and operation of gas pipelines.
West Virginia PSC	Jurisdiction over facilities and services; limited review authority over rates and charges. In early 1979 legislation gave municipalities independent rate setting authority over municipally owned utilities.
Wisconsin PSC	Regulates rates for service, utility plant construction, standards of service, rates for service including billing and customer deposit rules. The jurisdiction is identical to jurisdiction over private utilities, except the Commission does not regulate security issues of municipal utilities.
Wyoming PSC	Regulates electric and gas utilities insofar as they extend outside corporate limits generally to the extent that other utilities are regulated; namely, certification of service area, construction safety, adequacy of service, environment and rates and tariffs, etc. Municipal financing accomplished under laws relating to municipalities - not regulated by PSC. WS 37-1-101(a)(vi)(h) 1977.
Alberta PUB	Municipal utilities subject to total regulation by PUB only if they have passed a by-law, approved by Lieut. Governor in Council. Municipal utilities which have not done so are subject to partial regulation, generally with respect to complaints over rates and approval of supply contracts. The electric utility owned by the City of Edmonton has been brought within Board jurisdiction pursuant to the Electric Energy Marketing Act. The Board has power to fix price at which the City utility sells its electric energy to the Electric Energy Marketing Agency. The purpose of the Agency is to average wholesale electric rates and roll back to the utilities at a uniform rate.
Nova Scotia UARB	Subject to the same degree of regulation as investor-owned utilities (Public Utilities Act)

Table 27

Regulation of Electric Utility Energy Cost Adjustment Clauses

FAC=Fuel Adjustment Clause AGENCY	Has Authority to Establish Energy Cost Adjustment Procedure?	Allows Use of FAC to Recover Cost Changes	Requires FAC Hearing Prior to Cost Recovery? SEE KEY BELOW	Requires Periodic FAC Filing(s)?	Allows Changes in these Cost Components to be Recovered by Way of Fuel Adjustment Clause (FAC)?				Uses a True-up Procedure for Over- or Under- Recoveries
					Fuel Costs	Purchased Power Energy Charge	Purchased Power Demand Charge	Other	
FERC	YES	YES	NO	NO	YES	YES	YES 17/	§35.22(e) R&D	YES
ALABAMA PSC	YES	YES	NO	I	YES	YES	NO	Taxes not assessed uniformly statewide (ie, municipal tax)	YES
ALASKA PUC	YES	YES	NO	Q, O	YES	YES	YES	Interest expense.	YES
ARIZONA CC	NO 7/	NO 1/	Rate Case	M	YES	YES	NO 1/		
ARKANSAS PSC	YES	YES	NO	M	YES	YES	YES	Municipal franchise tax. Co-ops - cost of debt adjustment 9/	YES
CALIFORNIA PUC	YES	YES	YES and Annually	A	YES	YES	YES	Increased franchise fees. Uncollectibles associated with revenue change.	YES
COLORADO PUC	YES	YES	NO,Annual	M, A	YES	YES	YES	Interchange power,	YES
CONNECTICUT DPUC	YES	YES	NO	M, Q	YES	YES	NO	Savings shares to FAC & PGA revenues, generation utilization.	YES
DELAWARE PSC	YES	YES	YES	A	YES	YES	YES		YES
DC PSC	YES	YES	NO	M	YES	YES	YES		YES
FLORIDA PSC	YES	YES	YES & S	M, S	YES	YES	YES		YES
GEORGIA PSC	NO	NO	YES	I	YES	YES	NO	Transportation.	YES
HAWAII PUC	YES	YES	In Rate Case	M	YES	YES	NO	Public service company tax. Public utility fee. Franchise tax on gross revenues.	YES
IDAHO PUC	YES	NO 2/	YES 2/					Power supply cost variation due to changing hydro conditions	
ILLINOIS CC	YES	YES	NO, Annually	M	YES	YES	YES		YES
INDIANA URC	YES	YES	Q	Q	YES		NO	Steam/Hydro generatio	YES
IOWA UB	YES	YES	NO	I	YES	YES	YES		YES
KANSAS SCC 15/	YES	YES	YES for purchased power	M	YES	YES	YES	Costs included in FERC Acct 151, less refunds Acct 555 - co-ops. Acct 555 less demand, capacity & fixed charges for IOUs. Limestone for scrubbers, other. KCC 106.850-U.	YES
KENTUCKY PSC	YES	YES	NO, S & B	M	YES	YES	NO	FERC Acct 151-transp.	YES
LOUISIANA PSC	YES	YES	YES	M	YES	YES	NO	Transportation/taxes	YES
MAINE PUC	YES	YES	NO, Annually	A, M	YES	YES	YES	Conservation cost, indirect fuel cost.	YES
MARYLAND PSC	YES	YES	YES	M	YES	YES	YES	Taxes, transport, DSM	YES
MASSACHUSETTS DPU	NO	YES	YES & Q	Q	YES	YES	YES		YES
MICHIGAN PSC	NO	YES	YES and Annually	A	YES	YES	YES	O&M expenses other than fuel, electric production maintenance costs.	YES
MINNESOTA PUC	YES 3/	YES	NO	M	YES	YES	NO		NO

A=Annually   B=Biennially
Q=Quarterly   M=Monthly
S=Semi-Annually
O=Other Regular Timeframe
I=Irregular Interval or As Necessary

Fuel Adjustment Clause (FAC) is the term used generically to refer to energy cost adjustment procedures for electric utilities.

Table 27 (Continued)

FAC=Fuel Adjustment Clause / AGENCY	Has Authority to Establish Energy Cost Adjustment Procedure?	Allows Use of FAC to Recover Cost Changes	Requires FAC Hearing Prior to Cost Recovery? SEE KEY BELOW	Requires Periodic FAC Filing(s)?	Allows Changes in these Cost Components to be Recovered by Way of Fuel Adjustment Clause (FAC)?				Uses a True-up Procedure for Over- or Under-Recoveries
					Fuel Costs	Purchased Power Energy Charge	Purchased Power Demand Charge	Other	
MISSISSIPPI PSC	YES	YES	YES	NO	YES	YES	NO	Transportation/taxes	YES
MISSOURI PSC	NO 10/	NO							
MONTANA PSC	NO	NO							
NEVADA PSC	YES	YES	YES, A	A	YES	YES	YES	Capacity costs	YES
NEW HAMPSHIRE PUC	YES	YES	YES & M,S	M, S	YES	YES	NO		YES
NEW JERSEY BPU	YES	YES	YES	A	YES	YES	YES	Revenue taxes and energy losses.	
NEW MEXICO PUC	YES	YES	NO	M	YES	YES	YES		YES
NEW YORK PSC	YES 3/	YES 5/	NO, Hearings held min 4 yrs	M	YES	YES	YES	Changes in city/village revenue tax surcharges.	NO
NORTH CAROLINA UC	NO	YES	YES and annually	A	YES	YES	NO	Energy portion of interchanged power.	YES
NORTH DAKOTA PSC	YES	YES	min 4 yrs	M	YES	YES	NO		
OHIO PUC	NO	YES 6/	NO, semi-annually	M, S, A	YES	NO	NO	System loss, Ohio coal R&D costs.	YES
OKLAHOMA CC	YES	YES	NO, A	M	YES	YES	YES	All items charged to fuel in FERC accounts	YES
OREGON PUC	YES	NO							
PENNSYLVANIA PUC	YES	YES	NO	Q, A	YES	YES	NO	Taxes on corp. stock, net income, gross receipts, realty.	YES
RHODE ISLAND PUC	YES	YES	YES	Q, O		YES	NO		YES
SOUTH CAROLINA PSC	YES	YES 8/	NO, S	S	YES	YES	NO	Interchange power.	YES
SOUTH DAKOTA PUC	YES	YES	NO		YES	YES	NO		YES
TENNESSEE PSC	YES	YES	NO	M	YES	YES	YES		
TEXAS PUC	NO	NO							
UTAH PSC	NO	YES	YES, I, S	M	YES	YES	NO	QF energy, geothermal	YES
VERMONT PSB 11/	NO	NO							
VIRGINIA SCC	NO	NO	YES	I	YES	YES	YES	Uses Projected Fuel Factor.	YES YES
WASHINGTON UTC	YES 14/	NO							
WEST VIRGINIA PSC	NO	YES	YES, A, S	A, S	YES	YES	YES	Off system sales.	YES
WISCONSIN PSC	YES	NO 4/	NO, B	B	YES	YES	NO	Transportation.	
WYOMING PSC	YES	NO 16/	12/						
VIRGIN ISLANDS PSC	YES	YES	YES						
ALBERTA PUB	YES	YES	YES	M	YES	YES	YES		
NOVA SCOTIA UARB	YES	NO						Fuel cost built into rates.	

A=Annually B=Biennially
Q=Quarterly M=Monthly
S=Semiannually
O=Other Regular Timeframe
I=Irregular Interval or As Necessary

Fuel Adjustment Clause (FAC) is the term used generically to refer to energy cost adjustment procedures for electric utilities.

Footnotes—Table 27

1/   Automatic fuel adjustment clause was eliminated in November 1978 for investor-owned electric utilities.

2/   Two electric utilities have power cost adjustment clauses (PCA) to reflect changes in hydro-generation due to abnormal stream flows; subject to evidentiary proceeding. In Order No. 24806, Idaho Power was granted a permanent Power Cost Adjustment mechanism to provide for annual adjustments due to changes in streamflows through hydro plants. The PCA for Washington Water Power was approved for a three-year period.

3/   Commission permits utilities to file rate schedules containing provisions for automatic adjustment of charges.

4/   Effective with their first rate case held after July 2, 1983, investor-owned electric utilities which generate more than half of their energy requirements may not have an automatic adjustment clause.

5/   Utilities required to justify continuation of fuel adjustment clauses on an individual basis.

6/   Automatic fuel adjustment clause was eliminated as of 1/01/79 for investor-owned electric utilities. Fuel cost rate changes every 6 months, after hearing and commission order. Company may include demand cost or purchased economic power.

7/   In 1989 Commission eliminated adjustment clause for two large electric utilities.

8/   Adjusted on a semi-annual basis.

9/   "Other" - other areas of automatic adjustment clauses - not included in energy cost adjustment, but as a separate line item. Purchased power for water/sewer utilities.

10/   In Missouri the fuel adjustment was ruled unconstitutional for electric service on October 1, 1979. See: Utility Consumers Council of Missouri v. Public Service Commission, 562S.W.2d688.

11/   Abolished by Vermont Supreme Court Ruling in Docket No. 4496/4504, 1984.

12/   Opportunity for Hearing (Notice).

13/   Commission requires each regulated gas and electric utility to file its cost of fuel adjustment calculations for review and approval prior to implementation. In 1987 changed to annual review and adjustment.

14/   Energy cost adjustment clause previously authorized to one IOU electric was eliminated January 1990 and replaced in April 1991 with a combined decoupling mechanism and comprehensive resource recovery mechanism.

15/   Eliminated April 1992 as a condition of approval of the merger of KPL and KG&E.

16/   No fuel adjustment clause; but a balancing account mechanism for purchased power cost changes.

17/   Yes for certain defined economic purchases.

18/   Commission did not respond to request for update information; this data may not be current.

Table 28

Agency Policy Toward Individual—versus Master— Metering for Electric Service to Multi-Tenant Buildings

AGENCY	AGENCY OR STATE REQUIRES INDIVIDUAL METERING FOR ELECTRIC HOOK-UPS OF NEW BUILDINGS -		AGENCY OR STATE POLICY TOWARD EXISTING MASTER-METERED BUILDINGS AND/OR SUBMETERING
	New Multi-Family Buildings	New Multi-Tenant Buildings (Non-Residential or Mixed Use)	
ALABAMA PSC	YES	YES	Grandfathered if under construction/master-metered before 1/1/81
ALASKA PUC	YES	YES	Grandfathered if under construction/master-metered before 1983. Submetering allowed if cost is rolled into rent.
ARIZONA CC	YES	NO	Grandfathered if constructed/master-metered before 4/83
ARKANSAS PSC	YES	YES	Grandfathered if constructed/master-metered before 7/1/81.
CALIFORNIA PUC	YES	YES	
COLORADO PUC	YES	YES	
CONNECTICUT DPUC	YES-STATUTE	NO	One customer of record-electricity cost in rent. Existing master-metered buildings allowed. Submetering considered case by case.
DELAWARE PSC	YES	NO	Retrofits are not required
DC PSC	NO	NO	Submetering is not allowed except by waiver
FLORIDA PSC	YES	NO	Grandfathered if constructed before 1/1/81. Submetering allowed only to allocate bills.
GEORGIA PSC	NO	NO	
HAWAII PUC	YES	YES	Grandfathered if building permit obtained before 12/19/81.
IDAHO PUC	YES	YES	
ILLINOIS CC	YES	YES	Separate metering required for existing structure for which a building permit is obtained on or after 11/1/81.
INDIANA URC	YES-RULES	YES	Grandfathered if under construction prior to 6/8/80.
IOWA UB	YES	YES	Grandfathered if constructed before 1966. Permitted when electricity used in central heating, cooling, water heating, ventilation; where individual metering impractical; where facility designated for handicapped or elderly and utility costs are part of operating cost and are not apportioned to individual tenants.
KANSAS SCC	YES	YES	Grandfathered until major renovation; then individual meters may be required if cost-effective.
KENTUCKY PSC	YES	YES	
LOUISIANA PSC	YES-RULES		Grandfathered
MAINE PUC	YES	NO	Grandfathered for pre-1983 residential and pre-1986 commercial
MARYLAND PSC	YES-STATUTE	YES	No restrictions
MASSACHUSETTS DPU	YES-STATUTE	YES	Submetering is not allowed
MICHIGAN PSC	YES-RULES	NO	Grandfathered until and unless converted to individual metering
MINNESOTA PUC	YES	YES	Exception is made for nursing homes and similar facilities.
MISSISSIPPI PSC	YES	YES	Submetering is not allowed. No requirement to eliminate existing master-metering, but no line item charge for energy on bill or energy charge part of rent or lease agreement.
MISSOURI PSC	YES	YES	Grandfathered if constructed before 6/1/81, no submetering.
MONTANA PSC	YES-RULES	YES	Grandfathered if in existence before 1984; if master meter is to be replaced, individual meters must be installed.
NEBRASKA PSC			Does not regulate electric utilities
NEVADA PSC	YES	YES	
NEW HAMPSHIRE PUC	YES	YES	If change of use or renovation occurs, structure must be converted to individual meters; no submetering allowed.
NEW JERSEY BPU	NO	NO	
NEW MEXICO PUC	NO	NO	
NEW YORK PSC	YES	NO	Grandfathered in 1976 until renovated with new wiring
NORTH CAROLINA UC	YES-STATUTE	YES	Grandfathered by state law
NORTH DAKOTA PSC	YES	YES	Grandfathered until substantially remodeled
OHIO PUC	NO	NO	Master-metering permitted, but no landlord can charge more for resold electric than the utility would charge and/or cannot charge more than the average cost/kWh the landlord is charged.
OKLAHOMA CC	YES	YES	Grandfathered existing units prior to 1974. Landlords may include price of electricity in rent. Standard is one meter per customer.
OREGON PUC	YES-STATUTE	NO	Grandfathered (statute applies to multi-family built after 1977)
PENNSYLVANIA PUC	NO	NO	Restrictions are by utility tariff rule
RHODE ISLAND PUC	YES	YES	Master metering not permitted
SOUTH CAROLINA PSC	YES-RULES		Grandfathered-1/23/81 for residence; 1/31/80 for commercial. Any exception must be approved by PSC.
SOUTH DAKOTA PUC	YES-RULES	YES	Grandfathered until remodeled
TENNESSEE PSC	YES	YES	Master-metering not permitted
TEXAS PUC			
UTAH PSC	YES	YES	

Table 28 (Continued)

AGENCY	AGENCY OR STATE REQUIRES INDIVIDUAL METERING FOR ELECTRIC HOOK-UPS OF NEW BUILDINGS -		AGENCY OR STATE POLICY TOWARD EXISTING MASTER-METERED BUILDINGS AND/OR SUBMETERING
	New Multi- Family Buildings	New Multi- Tenant Build- ings (Non- Residential or Mixed Use)	
VERMONT PSB			
VIRGINIA SCC	NO	NO	Statutes/rules address submetering and energy allocation devices
WASHINGTON UTC	YES-RULES	YES	
WEST VIRGINIA PSC	YES		
WISCONSIN PSC	YES	YES	Grandfathered
WYOMING PSC	YES	NO	
ALBERTA PUB	YES	NO	Grandfathered
BRITISH COL. UC	NO	NO	
NOVA SCOTIA UARB	NO	NO	

Table 29

Average Voltage Level Requirements

AGENCY	AVERAGE VOLTAGE LEVELS REQUIREMENTS
FERC	Voltages specified in contracts on file are enforceable, if accepted for filing.
ALABAMA PSC	120 ± 6%
ALASKA PUC	ANSI C-84.1, 1990 (AS 18.60.580)
ARIZONA CC	ANSI C-84.1, 1977.
ARKANSAS PSC	The voltage supplied to the customer shall not exceed ± 5% from nominal voltage adopted by utility.
CALIFORNIA PUC	114-122 volts established by Commission policy letter to all electric utilities dated 2/6/77. PUC established voltage levels within range of 114-120 volts in Phase II of its Conservation Voltage Reduction Program for qualifying circuits wherever possible.
COLORADO PUC	Company is to maintain voltage at ± 5% of standard voltage filed in its tariff (normally 120 volts for lighting purposes and ± 10% of filed for industrial purposes.
CONNECTICUT DPUC	3% above and 5% below standard voltages.
DELAWARE PUC	120 ± 10%
DC PSC	120 ± 5%
FLORIDA PSC	120 volts for residential purposes: ± 5%, for industrial power purposes: ± 7.5%
GEORGIA PSC	120.
HAWAII PSC	1. 120/240 Secondary voltages: Retail service except power service, ± 5%; Retail power service ± 7.5%. 2. Primary voltages, ± 5% 3. Transmission voltages, ± 10%
IDAHO PUC	± 10%
ILLINOIS CC	120 ± 7 volts
INDIANA URC	5% ± of residential standard adopted by each utility and filed with URC
IOWA UB	Service voltages to ultimate consumers must be within limits established by ANSI C84.1, 1977 and C84.1a, 1980. Three-phase voltages must be balanced, ratio of maximum voltage not to exceed 0.02. Transmission voltages ± 7.5%
KANSAS SCC	Recommended 120 ± 5%
KENTUCKY PSC	120 ± 5% for lighting and ± 10% for power use.
LOUISIANA PSC	Individual Company service standards (usually nominal voltage ± 5%
MAINE PUC	± 5%
MARYLAND PSC	120 ± 5%, also 12 other standard levels (higher and/or bilevel).
MASSACHUSETTS DPU	Not established.
MICHIGAN PSC	120 ± 5%
MINNESOTA PUC	Not established.
MISSISSIPPI PSC	± 10% nominal voltage adopted.
MISSOURI PSC	4 CSR 240-10.030
MONTANA PSC	ANSI C-84.1, 1989
NEBRASKA PSC	No regulation.
NEVADA PSC	Not established.
NEW HAMPSHIRE PUC	Secondary voltages; min 110, max 125 & multiples thereof; primary voltages: ± 10% nominal
NEW JERSEY BPU	± 4 period of 5 minutes or greater; ± 4% for other periods.
NEW MEXICO PUC	Commission has authority but has not regulated.
NEW YORK PSC	Commission order 12/17/84 established range of 114-123V circuits where such a range can be maintained without requiring major capital investments.
NORTH CAROLINA UC	120-240V required, any other voltage range must be on file. ± 5% variation allowed on residential or specific lighting service; ± 10% variation allowed on any other service. Also 5% voltage reductions are recommended if no additional capital improvements will be required.
NORTH DAKOTA PSC	120-240 ± 7%
OHIO PUC	Allowable optimum voltage 120/240 ± 5%
OKLAHOMA CC	As established by ANSI Standards.
OREGON PUC	120-240 ± 5%
PENNSYLVANIA PUC	± 5% of each utility's standard voltage and a total variation of 8% for primary power service. Standard nominal service voltages specified in utility tariffs have been acceptable.
RHODE ISLAND PUC	113 to 123 with seven other standard levels.
SOUTH CAROLINA PSC	For lighting ± 5% of standard voltage. For power ± 10%
SOUTH DAKOTA PUC	Regulation effective 7/1/75. No voltage level requirements have been set.
TENNESSEE PSC	± 5% of each utility's standard voltage.
TEXAS PUC	± 5% of each utility's standard voltage.
UTAH PSC	ANSI Standards
VERMONT PSB	120 ± 5%
VIRGINIA PSC	± 5% in residential urban areas; ± 7.5% other classes in urban areas and all classes in rural areas.
WASHINGTON UTC	WAC 480-100-191.
WEST VIRGINIA PSC	112-127 v for secondary customers; 10% ± of base voltage for power customers.
WISCONSIN PSC	Basically ± 5% in urban areas; ± 6% in rural areas.
WYOMING PSC	Utility must adopt "standard nominal voltage" for each of its "districts" and maintain within limits specified in ANSI C84.1
PUERTO RICO PSC	
VIRGIN ISLANDS PSC	None established.
ALBERTA PUB	As established by CSA standard C235-69.
NOVA SCOTIA UARB	As established by CSA standard C235-69.

Appendix F

Listing of
Retail Wheeling Information

1. **PUBLISHER**   Edison Electric Institute
                       701 Pennsylvania Avenue, NW
                       Washington, DC 20004
                       202-508-5533
    PUBLICATION   "Retail Wheeling Report"
    COST $210 per year (4 issues per year)

PUBLICATION DESCRIPTION—This publication, as its name indicates, addresses and analyzes retail wheeling of electricity. On a quarterly basis, an update on retail wheeling on a state-by-state basis is provided. For someone who wants to remain current on the status of retail wheeling, this publication will be of benefit.

2. **PUBLISHER**   The National Regulatory Research Institute
                       Ohio State University
                       1080 Carmack Road
                       Columbus, OH 43210 (614) 292-9404
    PUBLICATION   "Overview of Issues Relating to the Retail
                       Wheeling of Electricity"
    COST $30

PUBLICATION DESCRIPTION—This publication provides a good objective analysis of the items that affect retail wheeling of electricity. A good discussion by supporters as well as opponents to retail wheeling is outlined; and, included in this are the legal, technical and economic considerations. For someone that want a good, broad overview of retail electricity wheeling, this publication could be of value.

3. **PUBLISHER**   The EOP Foundation
                       1727 DeSalles, NW

Washington, DC 20004
202-833-3940
PUBLICATION   A report to the U.S. Department of Energy on the "Role of Integrated Resource Plans (IRP) in a Rapidly Changing Industry." (Grant No. DEFG 4493R410608)
COST   Free

PUBLICATION DESCRIPTION—Although the title of this publication does not even have "retail wheeling" of electricity in its title, the subject is addressed in the text. One whole chapter (IV) discusses competition in the electric utility industry. Many aspects of retail wheeling are examined and discussed in this chapter. This publication provides a good overview of many things that are happening in the electric utility industry that will ultimately impact every electricity user.

4.   **PUBLISHER**   Edison Electric Institute
701 Pennsylvania Avenue, NW
Washington, DC 20004
202-508-5533
PUBLICATION   "Issues and Trends-Moving-Forward-18 Key Trends Affecting the Electric Utility Industry." (Report #70)
COST $20

PUBLICATION DESCRIPTION—This publication details 18 different things that are currently taking place that will ultimately affect all electricity users. While retail wheeling of electricity is not directly discussed, many other cost reduction strategies are explored. This publication gives an interesting overview of the many changes that are taking place in the electric utility industry.

5.   **PUBLISHER**   Edison Electric Institute
                               701 Pennsylvania Avenue, NW
                               Washington, DC 20004
                               202-508-5533

     PUBLICATION   Special Report "Innovative Rates"
                               Volume I and II

     COST $25 (both volumes)

PUBLICATION DESCRIPTION—These two volumes provide an insight to 170 different innovative rate structures that have been established by various electric utilities to fight competition. While each of the rates are specific to a particular customer, they do provide a good insight to the types of rates that are being developed to fight competition in the electricity industry.

6.   **PUBLISHER**   Edison Electric Institute
                               701 Pennsylvania Avenue, NW
                               Washington, DC 20004
                               202-508-5533

     PUBLICATION   "The British Model: An Assessment Power Supply
                               Monograph, Issue #2."

     COST $13

PUBLICATION DESCRIPTION—This publication describes the breakup of the British government-owned electric utility industry. The investigation of how this privatization occurred, and what has transpired as a result of it, is detailed in this monograph. This information may be of value to anyone interested in how retail wheeling of electricity may evolve in the United States as well as what may happen to the utilities involved.

7. **PUBLISHER**   Electricity Consumers
                     Resource Council (ELCON) 1333 H Street, NW
                     Washington, DC 20005
                     202-682-1390

    PUBLICATION "Retail Competition in the United States
                     Electricity Industry."

    COST   Free

PUBLICATION DESCRIPTION—This publication lists 8 principles for achieving competitive, efficient and equitable retail electricity markets. Even though this organization is supported by electricity users, these 8 principles are objectively presented and merit investigation by anyone interested in how retail wheeling of electricity should be evaluated by both users as well as producers.

Appendix G

Listing of General Electricity Information Publications

1. **PUBLISHER**   United States Government Printing Office
                                 McPherson Square Bookstore
                                 1510 H Street, NW
                                 Washington, DC 20005
                                 (202) 376-5055

     PUBLICATION   "Electric Power Monthly"
                                 (DOE/EIA 0226, Distribution
                                 Category UC-950)

     COST $87 per year (monthly)

PUBLICATION DESCRIPTION—This publication provides in-depth data on electric utilities operating in the United States on a monthly basis. This publication typically contains at least 250 pages and addresses electric utility as follows:

1. United States electric power at a glance.
2. United States electric utility net generation.
3. United States electric utility consumption of fossil fuels.
4. United States electric utilities sales, revenues and average revenue per kilowatthour.
5. Miscellaneous utility generation, fuel consumption, fuel cost and operational data statistics.

This publication is very comprehensive in its electric utility coverage and can be of value to anyone that is interested in base utility operational characteristics and costs.

2. **PUBLISHER**   Cogen Publications
                                 747 Leigh Mill Road
                                 Great Falls, VA 22066
                                 (703) 759-5060

     PUBLICATION   "Cogen"
     COST $55 per year (monthly)

PUBLICATION DESCRIPTION—This publication discusses electric cogeneration topics and provides good insight into the costs and operational characteristics of cogeneration installations. It generally contains 25-35 pages and as such, can be read and understood rather quickly. This publication could be of benefit to cogeneration operators or to those that are investigating the potential for cogeneration.

3.	PUBLISHER	Flanagan Group, Inc.
		84-54 118th Street
		Kew Gardens, NY 11415
		(218) 723-9477
	PUBLICATION	"World Cogeneration"
	COST	$35 per year (4 issues per year)

PUBLICATION DESCRIPTION—This publication gives a good overview of worldwide cogeneration. It is a relatively small 20-25 page publication and is easily read. It could be of benefit to anyone considering a cogeneration installation.

4.	PUBLISHER	American Public Power Association
		2301 M Street, NW
		Washington, DC 20037-1484
		(202) 467-2900
	PUBLICATION	"Public Power"
	COST	$50 per year (monthly)

PUBLICATION DESCRIPTION—This publication addresses public power, primarily municipal utilities. It is of value to anyone that purchases their electricity from a municipal utility. It covers all aspects of public utilities including the impact of retail wheeling on these entities.

5. **PUBLISHER**   Public Utilities Reports, Inc.
                       2111 Wilson Boulevard
                       Arlington, VA 22201-3008
                       (703) 243-7000
    PUBLICATION   "Public Utilities Fortnightly
    COST $99 per year (22 issues)

PUBLICATION DESCRIPTION—This publication covers all electric utilities especially for-profit entities. This publication has probably the most continuing information on retail electric wheeling across the United States.

6. **PUBLISHER**   Energy Resources
                       P.O. Box 8467
                       Gaithersburg, MD 29898-8476
                       (301) 601-4365
    PUBLICATION   "DSM Quarterly"
    COST $50 per year (4 issues)

PUBLICATION DESCRIPTION—This publication addresses demand-side management processes. It gives a good overview of many energy service companies that are in the business of assisting electricity users in the implementation of demand-side management programs.

7. **PUBLISHER**   The Electricity Journal
                       1932 First Avenue, Suite 809
                       Seattle, WA 98101-1040
                       (206) 448-4078
    PUBLICATION   "The Electricity Journal"
    COST $395 per year (10 issues per year)

PUBLICATION DESCRIPTION—This publication provides varying analysis and commentary on the full range of issues facing the electric utility industry. Areas covered include retail competition, integrated resource planning, transmission policy, industry structure and environmental policy. Generally, both sides of an issue are presented so that the reader can have enough information to draw their own conclusions.

8.	PUBLISHER	United States Government Printing Office
		McPherson Square Bookstore
		1510 H Street, NW
		Washington, DC 20005
		(202) 376-5055
	PUBLICATION	"Energy Policy Act of 1992,
		Report 102-1018, House Rule 776"
	COST	Approximately $20 (443 pages)

PUBLICATION DESCRIPTION—This publication sets forth the Federal Government policies and guidelines relating to energy in the United States. This publication should be of interest to any energy user, electricity or natural gas, since many Federal directives are described in this publication. As Federal publications go, this one is easily understood and in this writer's opinion is a must for any energy user.

9.	PUBLISHER	McGraw Hill, Inc.
		1221 Avenue of the Americas
		New York, NY 10124-0027
		(800) 223-6180
	PUBLICATION	"Industrial Energy Bulletin"
	COST	$635 per year (biweekly)

PUBLICATION DESCRIPTION—This publication covers FERC (Federal Energy Regulatory Commission) actions on a weekly basis. Since

FERC regulates on an interstate basis both electricity and natural gas, their actions are of importance to all electricity and natural gas users. With retail wheeling of electricity becoming a very real possibility, knowing the FERC's regulatory actions concerning this matter is very important. Anyone that wants to remain informed on interstate regulation of both electricity and natural gas might be interested in this publication.

10. PUBLISHER	National Association of Regulatory Utility Commissioners 1102 Interstate Commerce Commission Building P.O. Box 684 Washington, DC 20044-0684 (202) 898-2200
PUBLICATION	"NARUC Bulletin"
COST	$110 per year (monthly)

PUBLICATION DESCRIPTION—This bulletin is distributed by the National Association of Regulatory Utility Commissioners and covers all areas regulated by these Commissioners. Included are electricity, natural gas, energy in general, oil products, railroads, and water and sewer. Since this bulletin is a recap of regulatory actions across the United States, it gives a good overview of what is happening in utility regulation on a national intrastate basis. Since this publication is put out by the various intrastate regulatory commissioners, it tends to be factual and not overly editorialized. Its cost makes it somewhat more affordable than some other publications that are put out by for-profit entities.

11. PUBLISHER	King Publishing Group 627 National Press Building 529 14th Street, NW

Washington, DC 20077-1289
(202) 638-4260

PUBLICATION   "The Energy Daily"
COST $1,260 per year (daily, 250 issues per year)

PUBLICATION DESCRIPTION—As its name implies, it is published every working day of the year. It addresses both electricity as well as natural gas and provides very current information since it is published daily. As with any daily information, if the time to read the material is not taken, the value of the information is diminished. The publication contains about 4 pages and as such can be read in a minimal amount of time. If a need for immediate information concerning both electricity and natural gas is needed, this publication may be of value to you.

12. PUBLISHER   Inside Washington Publishers
                   P.O. Box 7167
                   Ben Franklin Station
                   Washington, DC 20044
                   (703) 892-8500
     PUBLICATION   "Electric Power Alert"
     COST $445 per year (26 issues per year)

PUBLICATION DESCRIPTION—This publication covers electricity generation, transmission and pricing. It also covered the rules, court cases and Congressional actions that affect the electric power industry. Coverage is on a state-by-state basis where applicable. This publication provides a broad range of electricity topics that could be of general interest to any commercial or industrial electricity user.

13. PUBLISHER   United States Government Printing Office
McPherson Square Bookstore
1510 H Street, NW
Washington, DC 20005
(202) 376-5055

PUBLICATION   "Electric Sales and Revenue"
COST $13 per year (1 issue per year)

PUBLICATION DESCRIPTION—The "Electric Sales and Revenue" is prepared by the Survey Management Division, Office of Coal, Nuclear, Electric and Alternate Fuels; Energy Information Administration (EIA); U.S. Department of Energy. This publication provides information about sales of electricity, its associated revenue, and the average revenue per kilowatthour sold to residential, commercial, industrial and other consumers throughout the United States.

The sales, revenue and average revenue per kilowatthour provided in the "Electric Sales and Revenue" are based on annual data reported by electric utilities on a calendar year basis. The electric revenue reported by each electric utility includes the applicable revenue from kilowatthours sold; revenue from income; unemployment and other State and local taxes; energy, demand and consumer service charges; environmental surcharges; franchise fees; fuel adjustments; and miscellaneous charges. The revenue does not include taxes such as sales and excise taxes that are assessed on the consumer and collected through the utility. Average revenue per kilowatthour is defined as the cost per unit of electricity sold and is calculated by dividing retail sales into the associated electric revenue. The sales of electricity, associated revenue, and average revenue per kilowatthour provided in this report are presented at the national, state and electric utility levels.

The data presented in this publication would be of use to any analyst, researcher or statistician engaged in regulatory policy and program areas for electricity customers, or for the electric utilities themselves.

14.	**PUBLISHER**	National Association of Regulatory Utility Commissioners 1102 Interstate Commerce Commission Building P.O. Box 684 Washington, DC 20044-0684 (202) 898-2200
	PUBLICATION	"Utility Regulatory Policy in the United States and Canada"
	COST	$70 per year (1 issue per year)

PUBLICATION DESCRIPTION—This publication is of great value to anyone that wants/needs data on electric and natural gas utility regulation. The book is organized into nine major parts:

1. Part A contains names and addresses of regulatory agencies, names and terms of office of commissioners.
2. Part B displays the general jurisdiction of the agencies: electric, gas, telephone, water and sewer, carriers, as well as other functions performed by the agencies and other types of businesses under the agency's jurisdiction.
3. Part C contains national tables on utility regulation, covering electric, gas and telephone utilities.
4. Part D covers regulation of communications companies.
5. Part E contains information about regulation of energy (electric and gas) utilities.
6. Part F contains information about regulation of electric utilities.
7. Part G covers gas utilities.

8. Part H is about water and sewer utilities.
9. Part I reports on utility rate cases considered by each agency.

15.	PUBLISHER	Public Utilities Reports, Inc.
		Suite 200
		2111 Wilson Boulevard
		Arlington, VA 22201
		(800) 368-5001
	PUBLICATION	"PUR Utility Weekly"
	COST	$459 per year (weekly)

PUBLICATION DESCRIPTION—This weekly publication covers State Commission rulings and Federal Regulatory issues. It may be of value to electricity users as a means of keeping informed on regulatory actions concerning retail wheeling of electricity in a particular state.

16.	PUBLISHER	PennWell Publishing Company
		1421 South Sheridan Road
		Tulsa, OK 74112
		(708) 382-2450
	PUBLICATION	"Electric Light and Power"
	COST	$45 per year (12 issues per year)
		Note: Sometimes this publication is available free to qualified individuals.

PUBLICATION DESCRIPTION—This publication gives a good general overview of the electric utility industry including power generation. It provides a good quick overview of many electric utility related items including retail wheeling when appropriate.

17. **PUBLISHER**   McGraw Hill
11 West 19th Street
New York, NY 10011
(609) 426-5667

    PUBLICATION   "Power"
    COST $55 per year (monthly)
Note: Sometimes this publication is available free to qualified individuals.

PUBLICATION DESCRIPTION—This publication covers power generation technology for electric utilities and independent power and cogeneration plants including boilers and combustion systems, environmental management, hydro, solar and wind instrumentation, controls, computers and software. Natural gas, oil, coal and renewable fuels, nuclear power, pumps, compressors, valves, piping, turbines, engines, generators, and water treatment. This publication provides a good overview of the above topics.

18. **PUBLISHER**   Intertec Publishing Corp.
9800 Metcalf Avenue
Overland Park, KS 66212-2215
(913) 341-1300

    PUBLICATION   "Transmission and Distribution"
    COST $35 per year (monthly)
Note: Sometimes this publication is available free to qualified individuals.

PUBLICATION DESCRIPTION—This publication covers the electric power delivery industry. It contains information that could be beneficial to electricity users interested in transmission by and for electric utilities. Retail wheeling problems/potentials are discussed when appropriate.

19. **PUBLISHER**   McGraw Hill
11 West 19th Street
New York, NY 10011
(609) 426-5667

PUBLICATION   "Electrical World"

COST $55 per year (monthly)
Note: Sometimes this publication is available free to qualified individuals.

PUBLICATION DESCRIPTION—This publication provides a general overall analysis of the electric power industry. It could be of value to anyone wanting to remain current with electric utilities in general. It covers the areas of power marketing, transmission and distribution, and power generation.

20. **PUBLISHER**   National Regulatory Research Institute
1080 Carmack Road
Columbus, OH 43210
(614) 292-9404

PUBLICATION   "The National Regulatory Research Institute Quarterly Bulletin"

COST $120 per year (4 issues per year)

PUBLICATION DESCRIPTION—This publication on a quarterly basis provides updates on regulatory activities in electricity, natural gas, telecommunications, and water/sewer. It provides a good source of information on regulatory activities all over the United States. Retail wheeling regulatory activities are addressed as they occur.

SYNOPSIS OF PUBLICATIONS

Twenty (20) different publications have been presented here and each is of value to the right person. Obviously not all of these publications will apply to all persons but they all have merit. There are many other magazines, periodicals and specialized reports that address various aspects of electricity but space does not allow the inclusion of them in this publication. When trying to decide which, if any, of the listed publications would be of benefit, always request a free sample copy from the publisher. Generally, publishers are willing to do this and this will assist you in making an intelligent decision on the worth of a particular publication to a specific need. The 20 publications listed are not necessarily endorsed or recommended by this writer but rather are presented to provide examples of the types of materials that are available.

Appendix H

Glossary of Electricity Terms

The following director of electricity related terms or glossary is excerpted from information provided by the National Association of Regulatory Utility Commissioners and the Energy Information Administration Agency of the United States Department of Energy. For a complete listing of electricity related terms, the following publications are recommended:

A. *Utility Regulatory Policy in the United States and Canada.* Compilation 1993-1994. (See Item #15 in Appendix G in this publication.)

B. *Energy Information Administration Electric Power Monthly.* (See Item #1 in Appendix G in this publication.)

C. *Energy Information Administration Electric Sales and Revenue 1992.* (See Item #14 in Appendix G in this publication.)

Glossary of Terms

AAV (Alternative Access Vendor): See CAP.

AFUDC (Allowance for Funds Used During Construction): A percentage amount added to Construction Work in Progress (CWIP) account to compensate the utility for funds used to finance new plant under construction prior to its inclusion in rate base.

ALJ: See Administrative Law Judge.

AM/FM: (Automated Mapping/Facilities Management).

ANSI: American National Standards Institute.

APPA (American Public Power Association): Represents the interests of publicly owned electric power utilities.

ASCII (American Standard code of Information Interchange): Computer machine language recognized by many different software packages.

Abandonment: Abandonment of facilities—Retirement of utility plant on the books without its physical removal from its installed location. Abandonment of service—ceasing to provide service.

Above-the-Line: Expenses incurred in operating a utility that are charged to the ratepayer (utility customer), by being allowed in a utility's rate base. The term originated because they are written above a line drawn on the income statement separating them from costs paid by investors (shareholders). See also Below-the-Line.

Accelerated Depreciation: Accounting method allowing company to write off asset more quickly in early years, with progressively smaller increments in later years.

Accrued Depreciation: Monetary difference between the original cost of an article and its remaining value.

Accumulated Deferred Income Taxes: Income taxes collected by utilities through their rates in advance of the time they are actually owed to the government.

Accumulated Deferred Investment Tax Credit: The next unamortized balance of investment tax credits spread over the average useful life of the related property, or some other shorter period. This balance sheet account is built up by charges against income in the years in which such credits are realized and is reduced subsequently through credits to income.

Acquisition Adjustment: The difference between the price paid to acquire an operating unit or system of a utility and the rate base of the acquired property. (See also Plant Acquisition Adjustment).

Administrative Law Judge (ALJ): A Commission staff member who serves as a hearing officer at formal PUC proceedings. He or she may conduct public hearings, issue subpoenas, question witnesses, and prepare draft decisions and orders for the Commission's consideration. See also Hearing Examiner.

Advice Letter: A filing by letter made by a utility to change rate or services. An advice letter filing usually does not require public hearings.

Allocation of Costs: See Cost Allocation.

Allowance for Funds Used During Construction: See AFUDC.

Alternative Regulatory Scheme (or Framework): A means of regulating a utility other than by the traditional rate base, rate of return, method.

American Public Power Association: See APPA.

Amortization: Similar to depreciation. A method by which costs for non-tangible assets, such as a patent, are charged to ratepayers over a number of years until the costs have been recovered by the utility.

Amp (Ampere): Unit of measurement of electric current; proportional to the quantity of electrons flowing through a conductor past a given point in one second.

Appellate Authority: The authority to hear and decide an appeal to a decision. See also Original Authority.

Automated Mapping/Facilities Management (AM/FM): Digitized geographic maps on which is shown the infrastructure of interest (such as location and type of utility poles, transmission lines, substations, generating plant, etc.) See also Geographic Information Systems.

Automatic Adjustment Clause: Allows a utility to increase or decrease its rates to cover costs of specific items without a formal hearing before a Commission. Utility can automatically raise its rates only when the price it pays for those specified items goes up. Changing fuel costs are the primary example of such clauses.

Average Demand: The demand on, or power output of, an electric system over any interval of time, as determined by dividing the total number of kilowatthours by the number of units of time in the interval.

Average Rate Base: Rate base determined on average investment during the test year.

Average Service Life: Used in determining depreciation, the average expected life of all the units in a group of assets.

Avoided Cost: The cost an electric utility would otherwise incur to generate power if it did not purchase electricity from another source. Also the basis of the rate required to be paid to QFs for purchased power under PURPA. See also Negawatt.

BPA (Bonneville Power Administration): One of five Department of Energy power marketing administrations. It operates federal hydroelectric generating facilities in the Pacific Northwest, wholesaling the power to electric distribution companies.

BTU: See British Thermal Unit.

Back-up Power: Electric energy supplied by a utility to replace power and energy lost during an unscheduled equipment outage.

Base Load: The minimum quantity of electric power or gas delivered over a given period of time; minimum demand on the system. Excludes peak usage.

Base Load Capacity: Generating capacity which serves the base load, usually the utility's largest, most efficient facilities with the lowest operating cost.

Base Load Station: A generating station which operates to take all or most of the base load of a system and therefore operates at a nearly constant output. See also Peak Load Station.

Base Rate: Component of utility rates—a fixed amount charged each month for any of the classes of utility service provided to a customer. This rate excludes all special rate components, such as FAC and PGA.

Below-the Line: Expenses incurred in operation of utility that are charged to the investor, not the ratepayer. These expenses are not allowed in rate base. See also Above-the- Line.

Blanket Certificate: Broad approval by the FERC of a particular type of energy transaction, allowing qualifying transactions to take place without case-by-case litigation and approval. Certain contract carriage natural gas arrangements currently hold blanket certificates.

Book Value: The accounting value of an asset. The book value of a capital asset equals its original cost minus accumulated depreciation. The book value of a share of common stock equals the net worth of the company divided by the number of shares of stock outstanding.

British Thermal Unit (BTU): The standard unit for measuring quantity of heat energy. The amount of heat energy needed to raise the temperature of one pound of water one degree Fahrenheit.

Bundled Rate: Several services combined into one tariff offering for single charge. See also Unbundled Rate and Vertical Service.

Buyback Rates: Rates paid to an electric utility's customer who produces his own electricity in excess of his needs.

Bypass: Use of transmission facilities which avoid local utility company network.

CIAC (Contributions In Aid of Construction): Non-refundable donations or contributions in cash or properties from individuals to pay for construction of facilities.

CPCN (Certificate of Public Convenience and Necessity, also know as CCN): License or permit granted to a utility proving that a proposed new facility or service is in the public interest; often required before a utility can start construction or begin doing business.

CWIP (Construction Work in Progress): A subaccount in the utility plant section of the balance sheet representing the costs of utility plant under construction but not yet place in service.

Capacity Costs: Fixed costs of facilities required for the utility to provide service.

Capital Asset Pricing Model: Method of estimating cost of equity in determining rate of return.

Capital Structure: The permanent long-term financing of a firm represented by relative proportions of long-term debt, preferred stock and net worth.

Capitalized Costs: Costs are capitalized when they are expected to provide benefits over a period longer than one year. Capitalized costs are considered investments and are included in rate base to be recovered from customers over a number of years.

Certificate of Public Convenience and Necessity: See CPCN.

Classification of Service: A group of customers with similar characteristics (i.e., residential, commercial, etc.) which are identified for the purpose of setting a rate for utility service.

Cogeneration: Production of electricity from steam, heat, or other forms of energy produced as a by-product of another process.

Cogeneration Deferral Rates: Special discount rates offered to large users who may have the potential capacity to generate their own power via cogeneration.

Coincident Peak: Any demand for electricity that occurs simultaneously with any other demand for electricity on the same system. See also Non-Coincident Peak.

Collocation of Facilities: Generally the requirement that an embedded utility allows access to its network by others on a non-discriminatory basis.

Combined Cycle: The increased thermal efficiency produced by a steam electric generating system when otherwise waste heat is converted into electricity rather than discharged into the atmosphere. One of the technologies of cogeneration in which electricity is sequentially produced from two or more generating technologies. An electricity generating technology in which hot gases turn a turbine and then heat a boiler, which makes team to turn another turbine.

Common Costs: Costs incurred jointly for two or more types of operations that must be allocated among the operations. (See also Cost Allocation).

Construction Work in Progress: See CWIP.

Contributions in Aid of Construction: See CIAC.

Cooperative (Co-op): A group of persons organized in a joint venture to supply services to a specified area.

Cost Allocations: Method of separating and assigning different costs to interstate or intrastate operations. Generally used for costs not readily assignable or for common costs. See also Separations.

Cost of Service Pricing: Method of pricing service strictly in accordance with the costs (expenses and allowable profit) that are attributable to it. Customers of services priced below cost are generally subsidized by customers paying above cost for their services. See also Value of Service Pricing.

Cross-subsidization: Practice of using revenues generated from one (often unregulated) product or service to support another (often regulated) one.

Customer Advances for Construction: A deferred credit account representing cast advances paid to the utility by customers requiring the construction of facilities in their behalf. These advances are refundable—the time or extent of refund depends on revenues from the facilities. This is not the same as Contributions in Aid of Construction (CIAC).

Customer Charge: A component of electric rates designed to cover those costs (such as metering and billing costs) that are related to the existence of the customer rather than to either the size and extent of the facilities needed to serve him or the quantity of electricity the customer uses.

DSM: See Demand-Side Management.

Declining Block Rates: As more energy is consumed the unit price goes down. For example, the first 500 kilowatt hours cost 8 cents each; the next block of 500 kWh is priced at 6 cents each; etc.

Decommissioning: The process of removing a nuclear facility from operation.

Deferred Fuel Costs: Those fuel costs spent in one accounting period which are not reflected in billings to customers until a later billing period.

Deferred Tax Treatment: Actual taxes plus deferred taxes are included in the income statement.

Demand: The maximum rate at which energy is delivered to a specific point at a given moment. Demand is created by a customer's power consuming equipment and differs from load in that load is a measurement of the amount of energy delivered.

Demand/Capacity Cost: The expenses incurred by a utility on behalf of an individual customer in providing sufficient capacity to meet that customer's maximum demand on an as- needed basis.

Demand Change Credit: A credit applied against the buyer's demand charges when the delivery terms of the contract cannot be met by the seller.

Demand Factor: The ration of the maximum demand over a specified time period to the total connected load on any defined system.

Demand Rate: A method of pricing under which prices vary according to differences in usage or costs.

Demand-Side Management (DSM): Generally refers to reducing a consumer's demand for energy through many means, including conservation, more efficient appliances, weatherization, etc. Demand and Supply Side Management are combined in Least Cost Utility Planning (LCUP).

Depreciation: Accounting procedure used to set aside the difference between the first cost of an item of plant (capital) and its estimated net salvage at the end of its expected life. This "amount to be depreciated" is treated as an expense to offset revenues for tax purposes over the years of expected life.

Differential Revenue Requirement: A method of calculating a utility's avoided cost. One calculates the utility's revenue requirement both with and without the costs that would be incurred if the utility were to obtain the power in question from some other source, then one calculates the difference.

Direct Load Control (DLC): When the utility has the ability to directly control a customer's devices and can turn them on or off as necessary to control load.

Discounted Cash Flow: Method of determining the cost of common equity capital where the cost of common equity is equal to the dividends per share divided by the market price per share plus an assumed growth rate.

Distribution Line: For electricity, the line which carries electricity from a substation to the ultimate consumer. See all Transmission Line.

Docket: Formal regulatory proceeding; may also be referred to as a case.

Dual-Fuel Plant: Any plant which can operate on either of two different fuels, such as coal or natural gas.

EEI (Edison Electric Institute): Represents the interests of the investor owned electric utilities.

EIS (Environmental Impact Statement): Required by the National Environmental Policy Act, as EIS must analyze the environmental effects of major actions or projects.

EMF: Electro-Magnetic Field or Electric and Magnetic Field. A common form of radiation generated by appliances, equipment, machinery, transmission lines, distribution lines.

EPAct (Energy Policy Act of 1992)

Earnings/Price Ratio: The annual earnings per share of common stock divided by the market price per share of common stock.

Economic Development Rates: Special discount rates offered to attract new businesses to the area.

Electro-Magnetic Field (EMF) Effect: Effect on health resulting from proximity to energized electric facilities. Whether there are such effects and how significant they may be is still being argued by the experts. Also referred to as Electric and Magnetic Field Effect.

Embedded Costs: Money already spent for investment in plant and in operating expenses.

Emissions Trading: A company that reduces emissions beyond what is required by law at one pollution source can use the excess reduction to permit higher emissions at other sources.

Energy Charge: A component of rates which covers the cost of the energy actually used. See also Commodity Charge and Customer Charge.

Energy Cost Adjustment Clause: The utility may adjust its rates to offset changes in the cost of fuel used to produce electricity. In some states, these adjustments may be made automatically by the utility, subject to Commission review; other States require an Adjustment Clause hearing first. See also Automatic Adjustment Clause.

Equal Life Group Method of Depreciation: Utility plant items with the same life expectancy are depreciated under a common formula.

Equity: The utility investment supplied by the sale of common stock. There is no fixed interest on these common stocks.

Excess Capacity: The amount of energy available over and above the amount of energy needed, plus reasonable reserves, at any given period.

Excess Deferred Taxes: When a utility collects from its ratepayers some portion of the income taxes it will owe in the future, the difference between the amount collected (including future tax obligation) and the amount of its current tax liability. See also Normalization and Flow- Through Tax Treatment.

Externality: Benefit or cost, generated as a by-product of an economic activity, that does not accrue to the parties involved in the activity. Must be considered to determine the true cost or benefit to society.

FAC (Fuel Adjustment Clause): See Automatic Adjustment Clause and Energy Cost Adjustment Clause.

FERC (Federal Energy Regulatory Commission): Federal agency established in 1977, concurrently with the creation of the Department of Energy, charged with regulating sale, transportation and price of natural gas and of wholesale electric power moved in interstate commerce. Successor to the Federal Power Commission (FPC), which was established in 1930.

FPC (Federal Power Commission): Federal agency with authority over interstate energy utilities. It was replaced in 1977 with FERC.

Facilities Charge: Component of rates which reimburses the utility for investment in facilities which benefit the ratepayer.

Fair Rate of Return: The rate of return a utility is entitled to have the opportunity to earn on either its rate base or its common equity. Fair implies balancing keeping rates low for ratepayers, financial integrity of the utility, and investment return for shareholders.

Fair Value Method of Valuation: The value which would be ascertained by a prudent purchaser making thorough inquiry relating to all circumstances affecting value.

Federal Energy Regulatory Commission: See FERC.

Firm Power: Delivery of utility service on a non- interruptible, always-available basis. A utility must supply its firm power customers whenever they demand it, despite conditions. See also Interruptible Rates.

Firm Wheeling: Transmission of electricity for another party that is not subject to interruption except for circumstances beyond the transmitting utility's control.

Fixed Costs: Business costs that remain unchanged regardless of quantity of output or traffic. See also Non- Traffic-Sensitive Plant, Customer Charge, Facilities Charge.

Flat Rate: A rate structure in which everyone within a customer class pays the same price per unit for all energy consumed; method of pricing local telephone service so that customers pay a fixed charge each month for unlimited number of calls. See also Metered Service and Local Measured Service.

Flow-Through Tax Treatment: Only actual taxes to be paid for the period are included in the income statement and collected from ratepayers. See also Excess Deferred Taxes and Normalization.

Forecast Test Year: Use of future 12-month period projected utility financial data to evaluate a proposed tariff revision. See also Test Year.

Fossil Fuel: Any fuel, such as coal, oil and natural gas, derived from the remains of ancient plants or animals.

Franchise: A privilege to do business which may be limited to a specified period of time or geographical area and may or may not be exclusive.

Freedom of Information (Sunshine) Statutes: Any laws designed to guarantee public access to governmental actions.

Fuel Adjustment Clause: See Automatic Adjustment Clause.

Fuel Factor: A component of rates designed to recover changes in the cost of fuel; differs from automatic adjustment in that it requires prior Commission approval.

Fully Distributed Costs (FDC): Regulatory accounting procedure that directly assigns, or arbitrarily allocates, to specific service categories the total costs of providing that service.

G & T: Generation and Transmission. Identifies a utility which both generates and transmits electricity as distinguished from an entity which provides transmission only.

Generating Plant: A facility where electricity is generated.

Geothermal Energy: The natural heat available in the rocks, hot water and steam of the earth's subsurface. Geothermal energy can be used to generate electric power.
Heat Rate: A measure of the efficiency of generating facilities. The number of BTUs

used to produce a kilowatthour of electricity; a low heat rate indicates high efficiency.

Historic Test Year: Use of a past 12-month period (usually the immediately preceding period) utility financial data to evaluate a proposed tariff revision. See also Test Year.

Historical Cost: Original cost minus any expenditures deemed by a Commission to be fraudulent, unwise or extravagant.

Hydroelectric: An electric generating station driven by water power.

IPP (Independent Power Producer): As defined by FERC under PURPA, a generating entity, other than a qualifying facility (QF) and not a utility, that is: (1) unaffiliated with the utility purchaser and (2) lacks significant market power. The facility must not be in the utility's rate base. See also QF.

IRP: See Integrated Resource Planning.

Incremental Costs: The additional amount of money it takes to generate or transmit energy above a previously determined base amount.

Incremental Pricing: A method of charging customers for energy consumption based on the incremental costs involved in energy production.

Independent Power Producer: See IPP.

Informal Complaint: Informal request for assistance from a Commission where resolution is attempted without public hearing or Commission order.

Integrated Resource Planning: Effort to identify all possible options of satisfying end-use energy needs at the lowest possible cost to all ratepayers while minimizing external costs to society. Also called Least-Cost Utility Planning (LCUP).

Interim Rates: Rates that are allowed to go into effect, usually subject to refund and sometimes under bond, until the Commission issues its final order.

Interim Relief Request: An application to a Commission showing that the applicant will suffer irreparable injury, immediate special hardship or inequity if relief from a regulation is denied.

Interruptible Rates: Special rates for energy consumers who are willing to have their energy delivery service interrupted by the utility when necessary. This is a low-priority service with generally lower unit rates. See also Firm Power.

Interstate: From one state to another, or across state lines. Interstate activities generally fall under the jurisdiction of the Federal government. See also Intrastate.

Intervenor: A third party who receives permission from a Commission to participate in a rate case.

Intrastate: Completely within the borders of a single state. Intrastate activities generally fall under the jurisdiction of the State government. See also Interstate.

Inverted Rate Structure: A rate design in which the unit price increases with usage.

Investor-Owned Utility (IOU): A utility owned by and responsible to its shareholders (investors). See also Municipal Utility and Public Power.

Jurisdictional: Within the jurisdiction, or authority, of a particular agency. See also Non-Jurisdictional.

Kilovolt (kV): One thousand volts; measure of electromotive force.

Kilowatt (kW): One thousand watts; measure of electric capacity or load.

Kilowatthour (kWh): 1,000 watts of consumption for one hour. Electric bills are measured in kilowatthours.

LCUP (Least-Cost Utility Planning): See Least Cost Planning.

Least Cost Planning: See Integrated Resource Planning (IRP).

Life Expectancy: Time period during which an article is expected to render efficient service.

"Lifeline" Rates: Special local telephone rates for low- income customers. As approved by the FCC, customers meeting certain eligibility tests may apply to have an amount equal to the Subscriber Line Charge (SLC) deducted from their monthly bills.

Also used generically to designate special rate plans offering very basic utility service at low rates to eligible customers. May also be call "Baseline" rates.

Load: The amount of electric power or gas delivered at any specified point or points on a system. Load originates primarily at the power-consuming equipment of customers.

Load Factor: The ration of the average load supplied during a designated period to the peak load occurring during that period.

Load Management: Techniques designed to reduce the demand for electricity at peak times, such as remote devices to temporarily turn off appliances.

Long-Term Debt: Indebtedness (notes, drafts, bonds, etc.) payable over a period of time longer than one year. See also Short-Term Debt and Capital Structure.

MMBTU: One Million BTU of energy.

MW (Megawatt): One million watts of electric energy. Used to designate the capacity of an electric generating plant and/or measure demand or load.

Maintenance Expenses: Part of operating expenses, including labor, materials, and other expenses, incurred for preserving the operating efficiency and/or physical condition of utility plant.

Management Audit: Analysis of the management practices of a company with an eye toward improving efficiency and effectiveness.

Marginal Cost: The extra cost of producing one more unit at any production level. Marginal Cost of Capital is the cost of an additional dollar of new funds.
Market-Based Prices: Prices fixed in the free market under conditions of pure competition.

Market Retention Rates: Special discount rates offered to large users to keep them from leaving the system.

Market-to-Book Ratio: Comparison of the market and book value of stock. A one-to-one market-to-book ration means the stock is selling on the market at book value.

Master Metering: Installation of one bulk power meter for multiple tenants.

Megawatt: See MW.

Megawatthour (MWh): One megawatt of power for one hour.
Metered Service: Meters record actual energy use in order to accurately bill a customer. See also Flat Rate.

Municipal Utility: Utility (electric, gas, telephone, sewer, water) owned and operated by a city, town or other municipality. Rates charged by a municipal utility within its municipal boundaries are usually exempt from state agency regulatory. See also Public Power.

NARUC (National Association of Regulatory Utility Commissioners): Represents state regulatory agencies in Washington, DC.

NASUCA (National Association of State Utility Consumer Advocates): Members are state officials representing consumer interests in utility matters.

NERC (North American Electric Reliability Council): Established by the industry in the 1970s, it tracks usage and capacity.

NOI (Notice of Intent, also Notice of Inquiry) NOPR (Notice of Proposed Rulemaking): Also know as NPRM.

NRC (Nuclear Regulatory Commission): Established in 1946 to oversee the nuclear industry.

NRECA (National Rural Electric Cooperative Association): Represents the interests of rural electric cooperatives.

NRRI (National Regulatory Research Institute): Established in 1976, the research arm of the NARUC.

Negawatt: A watt of electric energy that is created by conservation rather than generation. See also Avoided Cost.

Net Original Cost: The original cost of utility property minus any accumulated depreciation.

Net Worth: Capital plus capital surplus plus retained earnings.

Non-Coincident Peak: When one customer class reaches maximum energy use. This peak may or may not coincide with the peak for the total system. See also Coincident Peak.

Non-Discrimination: In general usage, reasonably equal treatment for all. See Equal Access and Divestiture.

Non-Firm Power: See Interruptible.

Non-Interruptible Rates: See Firm Power.

Normalization: An accounting method that allows a utility to recover from its customers income taxes that it must pay evenly over its years of operation. See also Flow-Through Tax Treatment.

Notice of Inquiry (NOI): Public notice soliciting information and comments on a specific subject.

Notice of Intent (NOI): A filing of preliminary data which indicates the applicant's intent to pursue a formal proceeding.

Notice of Proposed Rulemaking (NOPR): Notice to the public that an agency is proposing specific new rules.

Off-Peak Period: Period of relatively low system demands.

On-Peak: Period of relatively high system demands.

Operating Costs: Expenses related to maintaining day-to-day utility functions, including operation and maintenance expenses, taxes and depreciation and amortization costs, but not interest payments or dividends. Operating costs are recovered from customers on a current basis, as opposed to capitalized costs.

Operating Ratio: The ratio, generally expressed as a percentage, of operating expenses to operating revenues.

Operating Revenues: Amounts billed by the utility for utility services rendered.

Operating Unit or System: Complete and self-sustaining facility or group of facilities acquired and operated intact.

Original Authority (Or Original Jurisdiction): The jurisdiction or authority conferred on or inherent in an agency in the first instance. See also Appellate Authority.

Original Cost Depreciated: See Net Original Cost.

Original Cost Method of Valuation: The cost of the property to the person first devoting it to public service.

Outage: The period during which a generating unit, transmission line, or other facility, is out of service.

Overall Rate of Return: The monetary allowance for shareholders and bondholders granted by a Commission. It consists of the fixed rate of return in the bondholders' contracts and the Commission's determination of a fair market return to the shareholders' investment.

Overhead Expenses: Expenditures connected with the development and operation of any revenue-producing property.

PUHCA (Public Utilities Holding Company Act): Enacted in 1935, its intent was to prevent electric and gas utilities from using complex corporate structure to evade regulatory oversight.

PURPA (Public Utility Regulatory Policies Act): Part of the National Energy Act of 1978, it requires State regulatory agencies to consider a variety of issues affecting electric and gas utility customers. The intent is to establish standards and policies that promote energy conservation, encourage the efficient use of facilities and resources, and provide equitable rates for consumers. Public Law 95-617, 92 Stat. 3117.

Partial Forecast Test Year: A 12-month period, usually comprised of the immediately preceding 6 months and the immediately following 6 months, utility financial data used to evaluate a proposed tariff revision. See also Test Year.

Party-in-Interest: An individual or group appearing in a formal proceeding.

Peak Demand: The maximum level of operating requirements placed on the system by customer usage during a specified period of time.

Peak Load Pricing: Pricing which reflects different prices for system peak periods or for hours of the day during which loads are normally high.

Peak Load Station: Generating station normally in operation only to provide power during maximum load periods; usually a high operating cost facility or facility which cannot be operated for long periods of time. See also Base Load Station.

Peak Shaving: Means by which an electric utility lowers the peak demand on its system.

Peaking Capacity: See Peak Load Station.

Petitioner: Any party to a proceeding who seeks to appear a Commission Decision, modify a proposed decision, or intervene during a Commission hearing. See also Intervenor.

Photovoltaics (PV): A technology that produces electricity directly from sunlight.

Plant Acquisition Adjustment: The difference between the cost to the utility of acquired plant and the original cost of the plant less the amount credited at the time of acquisition for depreciation and amortization and contributions in aid of construction. See also Acquisition Adjustment.

Plant in Service: The land, facilities and equipment used to generate, transmit and/or distribute utility service. See also Utility Plant.

Pool Capacity: Capacity provided by a power pool member in order for the member to meet installed or reserve capacity obligations.

Pool-to-Pool: An arrangement between power pools to provide electric services to each other.

Pooling: Different utilities share their physical plants or resources to increase their efficiency and conserve energy.

Power Marketing Administration (PMA): Energy Department agencies that sell electricity generated by federally owned power generation projects in five regions of the country. Western Area Power Administration (WAPA), Bonneville Power Administration (BPA), Southeastern Power Administration, Southwestern Power Administration, Alaska Power Administration.

Power Pool: Two or more interconnected electric systems planned and operated to supply power in the most reliable and economical manner for their combined load requirements and maintenance programs.

Preferential Tariffs or Rates: A tariff or rate by which a specified class of customers is given special treatment, for example a "lifeline" rate to provide very basic service to low-income customers.

Price Caps: Relatively recently devised means of regulating utility rates as an alternative to rate of return regulation. The prices the utility charges are capped at a certain level, allowing the utility to earn a larger rate of return if it cuts expenses, increases productivity, etc.

Price/Earnings Ratio (P/E): The market price per share of common stock divided by the annual earnings per share of common stock.

Prudent Investment Method of Valuation: Historical cost less any amounts found to be dishonest or obviously wasteful.

Prudently Incurred: Only investments or expenses that were prudent at the time they were made are includable in Rate Base and Cost of Service.

Public Power: Electric utility owned by a government entity such as a municipality or utility district. See also Municipal Utility.

Public Utilities Holding Company Act: See PUHCA.

Public Utility: A business or service engaged in regulatory supplying the public with some commodity or service. Also, a utility owned and/or operated by a public authority, such as a municipality or district or public housing authority.

Public Utility District: Publicly owned energy producer or distributor. Normally districts incorporate areas larger than a single municipality and operate as special government districts, independent of State regulatory agencies.

QF (Qualifying Facility): Cogenerator who satisfies Section 201 of PURPA (among other things, the owner must not be primarily engaged in generation or sale of electric power, the facility also must meet certain size, fuel use and fuel efficiency requirements).

REA (Rural Electrification Administration): Part of Department of Agriculture established in 1935 and authorized in 1949 to make loans for extending electric and telephone service into rural areas, by making available low cost loans.

ROE: Return on Equity. Rate of return allowed on Common Stock Equity. Also called ROCE.

ROR: Rate of Return. May refer to overall rate of return or rate of return on rate base.

RTG: Regional Transmission Group.

Rate Base: Investment in operating plant, less depreciation, upon which regulated utility is entitled to earn profit.

Rate Base Regulation: Method of regulation in which utility is limited in operations to revenue level which will recover no more than its expenses plus an allowed rate of return on its rate base.

Rate Case: Procedures followed by a regulatory authority so that a utility may present and justify its need for a rate change.

Rate Case Audit: Audit performed in the course of a rate case.

Rate of Return: Percentage allowed by the Commission as a fair and reasonable profit. May refer to rate of return on rate base or overall rate of return.

Rate Structure: The design and organization of billing charges by customer class to distribute the revenue requirement among customer classes and rating periods.

Regulatory Lag: The time elapsed between the filing of an application for a rate change and the issuance of a final decision.

Remaining Life: The expected future service life of an asset at any given age.

Removal Costs: The costs of disposing of plant, whether by demolishing, dismantling, abandoning, sale or other. Removal costs increase the amount to be recovered as depreciation expense.

Renewables: Energy sources that in theory are indefinitely sustainable, such as solar energy, geothermal heat, hydropower and wind.

Reproduction Cost: Estimated cost to reproduce existing properties in their current form and capability at current cost.

Reserve Generating Capacity: A utility's back-up ability to insure sufficient energy supply despite occasional loss of some production capability due to mechanical failures or other problems.

Retained Earnings: Corporate earnings that are not paid out in dividends.

Return on Common Stock Equity: Shareholders' earnings based on Commission's determination of a fair market return on shareholder's investment.

Revenue Requirement: Amount of return (rate base times rate of return) plus operating expenses.

SEC (Securities and Exchange Commission): The federal agency which supervises the operation of securities exchanges and related aspects of the securities business.

Seasonal Rates: Rates designed to encourage conservation during time of the year when energy consumption is high.

Separations: Process by which a utility's expenses and investment in plant are divided between interstate operations and intrastate operations. See also Cost Allocation.

Service Area: Territory in which a utility is required or has the right to supply service to ultimate customers.

Service Life: The period of time from the date a unit of property is place in service until it is taken out of service. Average service life is the weighted average of the lives for all units within a plant account or group.

Service Value: The difference between original cost and net salvage value of utility plant.

Small Power Producer: One that has production capacity of no more than 80 megawatts and uses biomass, waste, or renewable resources (such as wind, water, or solar energy) to produce electric power. Defined under PURPA.

Standby Service: A class of service wherein the utility does not serve the customer on a regular basis, but only when called upon to do so by the customer.

Statutory: Deriving from or ordered by state or federal legislation which has been enacted, thus is a statute (law).

Stipulation: Prior to a rate increase hearing, the different parties may agree on the resolution of one or more issues. The resulting agreement (stipulation) is presented at the hearing.

Straight Line Method of Depreciation: The cost of an asset is spread equally over the number of years the asset is estimated to be useful.

Straight Line Average Service Life: Principal objective is the determination for each year of the expenses of depreciation attributable to that year's operation.

Straight Line Remaining Life: Depreciation reserve is reviewed before applying this method; only the rate is reviewed thereafter.

Substation: An assemblage of equipment for the purpose of switching and/or changing or regulating the voltage of electricity. See also Distribution Line and Transmission Line.

Supply-Side Management: Generally refers to the utility's management of its generating and transmission facilities for maximum efficiency. Demand and Supply Side Management techniques are combined in Integrated Resource Planning (IRP).

TVA (Tennessee Valley Authority): A Federal Government owned corporation established in 1933 to conduct a unified program of resource development in the seven state Tennessee River Valley. Principal efforts are electric power generation, agricultural development and flood control, water supply and river navigation projects.

Tail Block: The last priced block of energy in a stepped rate structure.

Take and Pay: Energy sales contract which requires payment only for energy actually delivered.

Take or Pay (TOP): Energy sales contract which requires payment for a given amount of energy whether the customer takes it or not.

Tariff: A statement that sets forth the services offered and the rates, terms and conditions for the use of those services. Tariffs must often be submitted to, and approved by, the agency with jurisdiction over the utility or carrier.

Tax Treatment: See Flow-Through Tax Treatment and Normalization.

Testimony: A declaration, oral or written, given under oath at a public hearing and subject to cross-examination.

Therm: Heat measurement equal to 100,000 British Thermal Units (BTUs). Equivalent to about 100 cubic feet of natural gas.

Time-of-Day (TOD) Rates: Rate design which prices energy consumption higher during peak usage times of the day. Used to encourage energy conservation. In telecommunications, TOD rates are used to encourage calling during off-peak times.

Time-of-Use Rates: Rate design which prices energy consumption higher during peak usage times. Used to encourage energy conservation.

Total Factor Productivity (TFP): A method of measuring an electric utility's overall productivity.

Transformation: The process by which electricity voltage is increased or decreased. Generally, voltage is increased before electricity enters the Transmission Line, and decreased before it enters the Distribution Line.

Transmission: The movement or transfer of electric energy in bulk. Ordinarily, transmission ends when the energy is transformed for distribution to the ultimate customer.

Transmission Line: For electricity, the line which carries electricity at high voltage from points of supply (generating plant or interconnection with other utilities) to a substation where it is reduced in voltage and handed off to Distribution Lines.

Unbundled Rate: Individual services are listed and priced separately. See also Bundled Rate. Historically, monopoly utilities provided all, or a number of, services for a single rate. With increasing competition, rates for component parts of services are being disaggregated (or unbundled) and offered separately. See also Vertical Service.

Used and Useful Test: Criteria for determining the admissibility of utility plant as a component of rate base. Generally, plant must be in use (not under construction or standing idle awaiting abandonment) and useful (actively helping the utility provide efficient service). See also Imminence Test.

Utility Plant: All equipment used for the generation, transmission and/or distribution of utility service, or an account in which record is kept of this equipment. See also Plant in Service.
Value of Service Pricing: Method of pricing which puts more weight on the perceived value of the service, rather than the cost of the service. See also Cost of Service Pricing.

Variable Costs: Costs which change with the increase or decrease of output or traffic. Also called Traffic-Sensitive Costs.

Vertical Service: The utility company performs all major utility services for its customers, including production, transforming, transmittal and distribution. Monopoly utilities in the past frequently provided vertical service; with increasing competition, rates for component parts of service are being disaggregated (or unbundled) and offered separately. See also Bundled Rates and Unbundled Rates.

Wheeling: Movement of electricity on the transmission system of one utility for someone other than that utility; transmission for others.

Appendix I

Miscellaneous Electricity Conversion Factors

TO CONVERT	INTO	MULTIPLY BY

-A-

amperes/sq cm	amps/sq in.	6.452
amperes/sq cm	amps/sq meter	10^{-4}
amperes/sq in.	amps/sq cm	0.1550
amperes/sq in.	amps/sq meter	1,550.0
amperes/sq meter	amps/sq cm	10^{-4}
amperes/sq meter	amps/sq in.	6.452×10^{-4}
ampere-hours	coulombs	3,600.0
ampere-hours	faradays	0.03731
ampere-turns	gilberts	1.257
ampere-turns/cm	amp-turns/in.	2.540
ampere-turns/cm	amp-turns/meter	100.0
ampere-turns/cm	gilberts/cm	1.257
ampere-turns/in.	amp-turns/cm	0.3937
ampere-turns/in.	amp-turns/meter	39.37
ampere-turns/in.	gilberts/cm	0.4950
ampere-turns/meter	amp/turns/cm	0.01
ampere-turns/meter	amp-turns/in.	0.0254
ampere-turns/meter	gilberts/cm	0.01257

-B-

BTU	Liter-Atmosphere	10.409
Btu	ergs	1.0550×10^{10}
Btu	foot-lbs	778.3
Btu	gram-calories	252.0
Btu	horsepower-hrs	3.931×10^{-4}
Btu	joules	1,054.8
Btu	kilogram-calories	0.2520
Btu	kilogram-meters	107.5
Btu	kilowatt-hrs	2.928×10^{-4}
Btu/hr	foot-pounds/sec	0.2162
Btu/hr	gram-cal/sec	0.0700
Btu/hr	horsepower-hrs	3.929×10^{-4}
Btu/hr	watts	0.2931
Btu/min	foot-lbs/sec	12.96
Btu/min	horsepower	0.02356
Btu/min	kilowatts	0.01757
Btu/min	watts	17.57
Btu/sq ft/min	watts/sq in.	0.1221

TO CONVERT	INTO	MULTIPLY BY

-C-

calories, gram (mean)	B.T.U. (mean)	3.9685×10^{-3}
candle/sq cm	lamberts	3.142
candle/sq inch	lamberts	.4870
circular mils	sq cms	5.067×10^{-6}
circular mils	sq mils	0.7854

-D-

dyne/cm	erg/sq millimeter	.01
dyne/sq cm	atmospheres	9.869×10^{-7}
dyne/sq cm	inch of mercury at 0°C	2.953×10^{-5}
dyne/sq cm	inch of water at 4°C	4.015×10^{-4}
dynes	grams	1.020×10^{-3}
dynes	joules/cm	10^{-7}
dynes	joules/meter (newtons)	10^{-5}
dynes	kilograms	1.020×10^{-6}
dynes	poundals	7.233×10^{-5}
dynes	pounds	2.248×10^{-6}
dynes/sq cm	bars	10^{-6}

-E-

em, pica	inch	.167
em, pica	cm	.4233
erg/sec	dyne - cm/sec	1.000
ergs	Btu	9.480×10^{-11}
ergs	dyne-centimeters	1.0
ergs	foot-pounds	7.367×10^{-8}
ergs	gram-calories	0.2389×10^{-7}
ergs	gram-cms	1.020×10^{-3}
ergs	horsepower-hrs	3.7250×10^{-14}
ergs	joules	10^{-7}
ergs	kg-calories	2.3898×10^{-11}
ergs	kg-meters	1.020×10^{-8}
ergs	kilowatt-hrs	0.2778×10^{-13}
ergs	watt-hours	0.2778×10^{-10}

TO CONVERT	INTO	MULTIPLY BY
ergs/sec	Btu/min	$5,688 \times 10^{-9}$
ergs/sec	ft-lbs/min	4.427×10^{-6}
ergs/sec	ft-lbs/sec	7.3756×10^{-8}
ergs/sec	horsepower	1.341×10^{-10}
ergs/sec	kg-calories/min	1.433×10^{-9}
ergs/sec	kilowatts	10^{-10}

-F-

farads	microfarads	10^6
faraday/sec	ampere (absolute)	9.6500×10^4
faradays	ampere-hours	26.80
faradays	coulombs	9.649×10^4
foot-candle	lumen/sq meter	10.764
foot-pounds	Btu	1.286×10^{-3}
foot-pounds	ergs	1.356×10^7
foot-pounds	gram-calories	0.3238
foot-pounds	hp-hrs	5.050×10^{-7}
foot-pounds	joules	1.356
foot-pounds	kg-calories	3.24×10^{-4}
foot-pounds	kg-meters	0.1383
foot-pounds	kilowatt-hrs	3.766×10^{-7}
foot-pounds/min	Btu/min	1.286×10^{-3}
foot-pounds/min	foot-pounds/sec	0.01667
foot-pounds/min	horsepower	3.030×10^{-5}
foot-pounds/min	kg-calories/min	3.24×10^{-4}
foot-pounds/min	kilowatts	2.260×10^{-5}
foot-pounds/sec	Btu/hr	4.6263
foot-pounds/sec	Btu/min	0.07717
foot-pounds/sec	horsepower	1.818×10^{-3}
foot-pounds/sec	kg-calories/min	0.01945
foot-pounds/sec	kilowatts	1.356×10^{-3}

-G-

gilberts	ampere-turns	0.7958
gilberts/cm	amp-turns/cm	0.7958
gilberts/cm	amp-turns/in	2.021
gilberts/cm	amp-turns/meter	79.58

TO CONVERT	INTO	MULTIPLY BY
gram-calories	Btu	3.9683×10^{-3}
gram-calories	ergs	4.1868×10^{7}
gram-calories	foot-pounds	8.0880
gram-calories	horsepower-hrs	1.5596×10^{-6}
gram-calories	kilowatt-hrs	1.1630×10^{-6}
gram-calories	watt-hrs	1.1630×10^{-3}
gram-calories/sec	Btu/hr	14.286
gram-centimeters	Btu	9.297×10^{-8}
gram-centimeters	ergs	980.7
gram-centimeters	joules	9.807×10^{-5}
gram-centimeters	kg-cal	2.343×10^{-8}
gram-centimeters	kg-meters	10^{-5}

-H-

horsepower	Btu/min	42.44
horsepower	foot-lbs/min	33,000
horsepower	foot-lbs/sec	550.0
horsepower (metric) (542.5 ft lb/sec)	horsepower (550 ft lb/sec)	0.9863
horsepower (550 ft lb/sec)	horsepower (metric) (542.5 ft lb/sec)	1.014
horsepower	kg-calories/min	10.68
horsepower	kilowatts	0.7457
horsepower	watts	745.7
horsepower (boiler)	Btu/hr	33,479
horsepower (boiler)	kilowatts	9.803
horsepower-hrs	Btu	2,547
horsepower-hrs	ergs	2.6845×10^{13}
horsepower-hrs	foot-lbs	1.98×10^{6}
horsepower-hrs	gram-calories	641,190
horsepower-hrs	joules	2.684×10^{6}
horsepower-hrs	kg-calories	641.1
horsepower-hrs	kg-meters	2.737×10^{5}
horsepower-hrs	kilowatt-hrs	0.7457

-I-

international ampere	ampere (absolute)	.9998
international volt	volts (absolute)	1.0003
international volt	joules (absolute)	1.593×10^{-19}
international volt	joules	9.654×10^{4}

TO CONVERT	INTO	MULTIPLY BY

-J-

joules	Btu	9.480×10^{-4}
joules	ergs	10^7
joules	foot-pounds	0.7376
joules	kg-calories	2.389×10^{-4}
joules	kg-meters	0.1020
joules	watt-hrs	2.778×10^{-4}

-K-

kilograms-calories	Btu	3.968
kilograms-calories	foot-pounds	3,088
kilograms-calories	hp-hrs	1.560×10^{-3}
kilograms-calories	joules	4,186
kilograms-calories	kg-meters	426.9
kilograms-calories	kilojoules	4.186
kilograms-calories	kilowatt-hrs	1.163×10^{-3}
kilogram meters	Btu	9.294×10^{-3}
kilogram meters	ergs	9.804×10^7
kilogram meters	foot-pounds	7.233
kilogram meters	joules	9.804
kilogram meters	kg-calories	2.342×10^{-3}
kilogram meters	kilowatt-hrs	2.723×10^{-6}
kilowatts	Btu/min	56.92
kilowatts	foot-pounds/min	$4,426 \times 10^4$
kilowatts	foot-pounds/sec	737.6
kilowatts	horsepower	1,341
kilowatts	kg-calories/min	14.34
kilowatts	watts	1,000.0
kilowatts-hrs	Btu	3,413
kilowatts-hrs	ergs	$3,600 \times 10^{13}$
kilowatts-hrs	foot-pounds	$2,655 \times 10^6$
kilowatts-hrs	gram-calories	859.850
kilowatts-hrs	horsepower-hrs	1,341
kilowatts-hrs	joules	3.6×10^6
kilowatts-hrs	kg-calories	860.5
kilowatts-hrs	kg-meters	$3,671 \times 10^5$
kilowatts-hrs	pounds of water evaporated from and at 212°F.3.53	
kilowatts-hrs	pounds of water raised from 62° to 212°	F. 22.75

TO CONVERT	INTO	MULTIPLY BY

-L-

lumens/sq ft	foot-candles	1.0
lumen	spherical candle power	.07958
lumen	watt	.001496
lumen/sq ft	lumen/sq meter	10.76
lux	foot-candles	0.0929

-M-

megohms	microhms	10^{12}
megohms	ohms	10^6
microfarad	farads	10^{-6}
micrograms	grams	10^{-6}
microhms	megohms	10^{-12}
microhms	ohms	10^{-6}
microliters	liters	10^{-6}

N-

newton	dynes	1×105

-O-

ohm	ohm (absolute)	1.0005
ohms	megohms	10^{-6}
ohms	microhms	10^6

-P/Q/R/S/T/U-

-V-

volt/inch	volt/cm	.39370
volt (absolute)	statvolts	.003336

TO CONVERT	INTO	MULTIPLY BY

-W-

watts	Btu/hr	3.4129
watts	Btu/min	0.05688
watts	ergs/sec	107.
watts	foot-pounds/min	44.27
watts	foot-pounds/sec	0.7378
watts	horsepower	1.341×10^{-3}
watts	horsepower (metric)	1.360×10^{-3}
watts	kg-calories/min	0.01433
watts	kilowatts	0.001
watts (absolute)	B.T.U. (mean)/min	0.056884
watts (absolute)	joules/sec	1
watt-hours	Btu	3.413
watt-hours	ergs	3.60×10^{10}
watt-hours	foot-pounds	2,656
watt-hours	gram-calories	859.85
watt-hours	horsepower-hrs	1.341×10^{-3}
watt-hours	kilogram-calories	0.8605
watt-hours	kilogram-meters	367.2
watt-hours	kilowatt-hrs	0.001
watt (international)	watt (absolute)	1.0002

-X/Y/Z-

Index

-A-

-B-

-C-

-D-

-E-

-F-

-G-

-H-

-I-

-J-

-K-

-L-

-M-

-N-

-O-

-P-

-Q-

-R-

-S-

-T-

-U-

-V-

-W/X/Y/Z-